Rare Birds of North America

STEVE N. G. HOWELL
IAN LEWINGTON
AND WILL RUSSELL

Rare Birds
of North America

PRINCETON UNIVERSITY PRESS   PRINCETON AND OXFORD

Requests for permission to reproduce material from this work should be sent to Permissions, Princeton University Press

Published by Princeton University Press, 41 William Street, Princeton, New Jersey 08540

In the United Kingdom: Princeton University Press, 6 Oxford Street, Woodstock, Oxfordshire OX20 1TW

nathist.press.princeton.edu

Jacket art: Siberian Accentor © Ian Lewington

ISBN 978-0-691-11796-6

Library of Congress Control Number: 2013943112

British Library Cataloging-in-Publication Data is available

This book has been composed in Gill Sans std and ITC Cheltenham std

Printed on acid-free paper. ∞

Printed in China

1 2 3 4 5 6 7 8 9 10

Contents

Preface   vii
Acknowledgments   ix

How to Use This Book   xi
   Abbreviations and Terminology   xv
   Geographic Terms   xvii

INTRODUCTION

WHAT IS A 'RARE BIRD'—AND WHEN
AND WHENCE?   1

MIGRATION AND VAGRANCY
IN BIRDS   4
   MIGRATION   4
   VAGRANCY   6
      Drift   7
      Misorientation   10
      Overshooting   14
      Dispersal   14
      Association   16
      Disorientation   16
      False Vagrancy   16

WHERE DO NORTH AMERICAN
VAGRANTS COME FROM?   16
   OLD WORLD SPECIES   16
      East Asia   19
      Western Eurasia–Africa   22
   NEW WORLD SPECIES   24
      Mainland   24
      Island   29
   PELAGIC SPECIES   30
      Temperate Southern Hemisphere   30
      Subtropical and Equatorial   30

TOPOGRAPHY, MOLT, AND AGING   32
   BIRD TOPOGRAPHY   32
   MOLTS AND PLUMAGES   32
   MOLT AND AGING   35
      Waterfowl   36
      Pelagic Seabirds   38
      Gulls and Terns   39
      Shorebirds   39
      Wading Birds   39
      Raptors and Owls   40
      Larger Landbirds   40
      Aerial Landbirds   40
      Songbirds   41

SPECIES ACCOUNTS

WATERFOWL   44
   OLD WORLD   44
   NEW WORLD   65

SUNGREBES   70
ALCIDS   71

PELAGIC SEABIRDS   74
   PETRELS   74
   ALBATROSSES   92
   STORM-PETRELS   104
   TROPICBIRDS   111
   FRIGATEBIRDS   112
   BOOBIES   117

GULLS AND TERNS   124

SHOREBIRDS   141
   OLD WORLD   141
      Plovers   142
      Oystercatchers   151
      Stilts   152
      Sandpipers   154
      Pratincoles   189
   NEW WORLD   190
      Thick-knees   190
      Plovers   191

WADING BIRDS   194
   OLD WORLD   194
      Herons   194
      Cranes   203
      Rails   206
   NEW WORLD   210
      Herons   210
      Storks   211
      Rails   213
      Jacanas   215

RAPTORS AND OWLS   217
   OLD WORLD   217
   NEW WORLD   230

LARGER LANDBIRDS 237
   OLD WORLD 237
      Nightjars 237
      Pigeons 238
      Cuckoos 240
      Hoopoes 243
      Woodpeckers 244
      Corvids 246
   NEW WORLD 248
      Pigeons 248
      Cuckoos 251
      Trogons 252
      Kingfishers 254

AERIAL LANDBIRDS 255
   OLD WORLD 255
      Swifts 255
      Swallows 259
   NEW WORLD 260
      Hummingbirds 261
      Swifts 272
      Swallows 274

SONGBIRDS 278
   OLD WORLD 278
      Old World Flycatchers 279
      Shrikes 286
      Accentors 288

      Chats and Thrushes 289
      Old World Warblers 303
      Wagtails and Pipits 315
      Larks 322
      Old World Buntings 323
      Finches 334
   NEW WORLD 342
      Tyrant-flycatchers and allies 343
      Mimids 362
      Thrushes 365
      Silkies (Silky-flycatchers) 373
      Wrens 374
      Vireos 375
      Wood-warblers 377
      Grassquits 385
      Tanagers 388
      New World Grosbeaks and Allies 393
      New World Orioles 398

Appendices
**Appendix A. Species New to North America,
   Fall 2011–Summer 2012** 403
**Appendix B: Species of Hypothetical
   Occurrence** 404
**Appendix C: Birds New to North America,
   1950–2011** 408
Literature Cited 411
Index 425

Preface

While several books in Europe have been dedicated to rare and vagrant birds there (e.g., Lewington et al. 1991; Vinicombe & Cottridge 1996; Slack 2009), no comparable synthesis has existed until now for North America (defined here as the United States and Canada, including St. Pierre et Miquelon and excluding Hawaii). State and provincial avifaunal works treat the rarities within their purview, but often (and understandably) in lesser detail than regularly occurring species, and most states and provinces have committees that evaluate records of regional rarities and publish summary reports at varying intervals. Don Roberson's *Rare Birds of the West Coast* (1980) was a pioneering work that encompassed Alaska south to California, and more recently California has been the subject of a book solely dedicated to 'rare birds' (Hamilton et al. 2007). However, many 'rarities' treated in the above works are common elsewhere in North America, and only rare in a given state or province.

Our goal has been to summarize patterns of occurrence for species that are truly rare in North America as a whole (most of which, of course, are common in their normal ranges). Inevitably, defining a 'rare bird' proved to be a challenge—there is an intuitive component that may elude statistical quantification, and what's 'rare' today may be 'common' tomorrow. Thus, no such definition will ever be perfect—nature does not fit into boxes of human construct—but we feel our definition works well for our purposes (see *What Is a Rare Bird—and When and Whence?* p. 1).

We began this project thinking we would learn something about vagrant birds, about their patterns of occurrence and aspects of their identification, and hopefully end up with a book that would be useful and interesting to others curious about bird distribution and identification. The product of our labors is what you hold in your hands.

The authors each made substantial contributions and are listed alphabetically. Will Russell was responsible for the conception of the project, took the lead in writing introductory materials, and drafted accounts for most of the Palearctic species. Ian Lewington was responsible for the illustrations, as well as contributing much knowledge about aspects of identification. Steve Howell was responsible for species with origins in the New World and for pelagic species; he also oversaw comments on age/sex and molt. Each of us reviewed the others' work in an attempt to blend the contents into a single voice.

Acknowledgments

Our primary source for records was the 2008 *ABA Checklist*, and we thank members of the American Birding Association checklist committee for their work in compiling that invaluable reference. We also owe great thanks to the editors and regional editors of the fine journal *North American Birds* (and its predecessors); these are unsung heroes whose work made our job far less challenging than it otherwise would have been. Readers may wish to note that back issues of *North American Birds*, including the insightful *Changing Seasons* overviews, can be accessed online via the Searchable Ornithological Research Archive, SORA (http://sora.unm.edu).

For answering queries, sharing unpublished information, helping with literature and photo research, and thoughtful discussions we thank: Bob Ake, Tom Aversa, Lisa T. Ballance, Pierre Bannon, Matt Bartels, Louis Bevier, Gavin Bieber, David Boertmann, Ryan Brady, Mark Brazil, Edward S. Brinkley, Mark Brogie, Adam Byrne, Colin Campbell, Richard J. Cannings, Steven W. Cardiff, Dan Casey, David Christie, Callan Cohen, Dave Compton, Mark Constantine, Julie Craves, Richard Crossley, Phil Davis, Stephen Dinsmore, Donna L. Dittman, Andrew Dobson, Jon L. Dunn, Wendy Ealding, Cameron Eckert, Martin T. Elliott, Megan Elrod, Richard A. Erickson, Roger Etcheberry, Doug Faulkner, Steven Feldstein, Jim Frank, Steve Ganley, Martin Garner, Kimball L. Garrett, Matt Garvey, Daniel D. Gibson, Robert E. Gill Jr., Greg Gillson, Doug Gochfeld, Carl Goodrich, Michel Gosselin, Joseph A. Grzybowski, Mary Gustafson, Martin Hallam, Bruce Hallett, Greg Hanisek, Jennifer Hansen, Keith Hansen, Floyd Hayes, Steve Heinl, Hendrik Herlyn, Paul Holt, Rich Hoyer, Jocelyn Hudon, Lawrence Igl, Marshall J. Iliff, David Irons, Greg D. Jackson, Brad Jacobs, H. Lee Jones, Ned Keller, Rudolph Koes, Yann Kolbeinsson, Rudolf Koes, Gary Krapu, Andy Kratter, Jim Kushlan, Dan Lane, Paul Leader, Harry LeGrand, Paul E. Lehman, Adrienne Leppold, Nick Lethaby, James Lidster, Paul Linegar, Mark W. Lockwood, Derek Lovitch, Bruce Mactavish, John P. Martin, Guy McCaskie, Ian McLaren, Steve McConnell, Richard Millington, Steve Mirik, Steve Mlodinow, Frank Moore, Nial Moores, Pete Morris, Killian Mullarney, Martin Myers, Harry Nehls, Michael O'Brien, Ryan O'Donnell, Chuck Otte, Brainard Palmer-Ball, Roger Pasquier, J. Brian Patteson, David Pavlik, Gunnlauger Pétursson, Ron Pittaway, Richard Popko, Bill Pranty, Nick Pulcinella, John Puschock, Peter Pyle, Dave Quady, Dan L. Reinking, J. Van Remsen, Robert S. Ridgely, Rob Ripma, Magnus Robb, Stephan Rodebrand, Danny I. Rogers, Gary H. Rosenberg, Bob Sargeant, Bill Schmoker, Scott Schuette, Tom Schultz, Larry Semo, W. Dave Shuford, David A. Sibley, Donna Slyce, Chris Sloan, Alan R. Smith, David W. Sonneborn, Greg Stender, Mark M. Stevenson, Doug Stotz, Diana Stralberg, Brian L. Sullivan, Kasper Thorup, Jim Tietz, Thede Tobish, Rick Toochin, Jeremiah Trimble, Chuck Trost, Peter Vickery, Keith Vinicombe, Andrew Vitz, Brad Waggoner, Nils Warnock, Yoshiki Watabe, Sartor O. Williams III, Doug Wilson, Jean Woods, Alan Wormington, and Roger Wyatt.

Ian McLaren was a frequent source of information and helpful criticism dating back to the very beginnings of the project; Paul Holt gave the taxonomy and identification components of the Old World species his thorough review; Steve Heinl carefully reviewed all of the Alaska species for details of occurrence; Yann Kolbeinsson provided frequent assistance concerning vagrant birds in Iceland; Peter Pyle and Keith Vinicombe reviewed introductory material; and Ned Brinkley and Paul Lehman reviewed the entire manuscript and offered many appreciated comments and corrections. Any errors remaining are obviously our responsibility.

For their assistance and permission to examine specimens in their care we thank: personnel at the California Academy of Sciences (John P. Dumbacher, Maureen Flannery); the Museum of Vertebrate Zoology, University of California, Berkeley (Carla Cicero); the British Museum, Tring (Mark Adams, Robert Prys-Jones); the National Museum of Natural History (Smithsonian Institution), Washington, DC (James Dean, Storrs Olson); the American Museum of Natural History, New York (George F. Barrowclough, Paul Sweet); the University of Alaska, Fairbanks (Daniel D. Gibson, Kevin J. Winker); and the Museum of Comparative Zoology, Harvard University, Cambridge (Jeremiah Trimble). The staff at WINGS helped in numerous ways. Logistical support was also provided to Howell by Point Reyes Bird Observatory (PRBO). Last but far from least, we thank our commissioning editor, Robert Kirk, for his faith and patience in seeing the project to fruition.

How to Use This Book

Our overriding interest when considering vagrant birds in North America has been to look for patterns of occurrence. In order to determine patterns, however, one has to be able to identify a given species, and preferably determine its age, sex, and, if relevant, subspecies. Hence, we also discuss the field identification of all species covered, the majority of which are not treated in most North American field guides. This book thus intertwines occurrence patterns and identification criteria to provide an overview of where and why rare birds occur in North America, and how to identify them.

Rather than trying to keep pace with ever-changing sequences of higher-level taxonomy, we have ordered species in the practical categories suggested by Howell et al. (2009), which is basically waterbirds followed by landbirds (see Contents, pp. v–vi). Orthography, taxonomy, and English names largely follow the International Ornithological Congress (IOC), except for the spelling of gray (vs. grey); for tubenoses we use the names and species sequence of Howell (2012a). In other groups, species sequence within each group largely follows the American Ornithologists' Union (AOU; website accessed 1 May 2012), but undoubtedly in some cases it will have been overtaken by taxonomic shuffling before this book is published. The species accounts contain the following sections.

Species name. Except for some tubenoses (see above), the English names we use are largely those of the IOC (Gill & Wright 2006; and online updates through 1 Jun 2012 at www.worldbird names.org/ioc-lists/master-list/). Measurements for Old World species were taken from the *Handbook of the Birds of the World* (del Hoyo et al. 1992–2011) and the *Birds of Europe* (Svensson et al. 2010), unless otherwise noted; those for seabirds (including gulls and terns) and New World species were taken from museum specimens examined by Howell.

Summary. We summarize the distribution of each species in North America. Terms of abundance, such as 'rare' and 'exceptional' are defined on pp. 3–4. Geographic terms, such as 'Atlantic Canada' or 'Bering Sea islands,' are defined on p. xvii. We tended to use the largest region that we considered made biological sense;

e.g., if there was a cluster of records from Newfoundland to New York falling into a single pattern, we may refer to the records as having occurred in 'the Northeast.' Seasonal terms are defined as spring (Mar—May; but to mid–late Jun when referring to Alaska, and to early Jun for shorebirds in the Lower 48 and southern Canada); summer (Jun—Jul); fall (Aug—Nov, but from mid–late Jun when dealing with shorebirds); and winter (Dec–Feb).

We generally define a 'record' as an arrival event, which can be a single bird on a single day but also may be a small flock that arrived together (or grew in numbers within a few days of 'arrival') and stayed for a week. Birds that reappeared in the same place and at more or less the same time in different years may be considered as a single record.

Taxonomy. We list the total number of subspecies, following the *Handbook of Birds of the World* (del Hoyo et al. 1992–2011) unless otherwise noted. In most cases, only a single subspecies has occurred in North America, and we may dismiss from consideration some or all remaining subspecies if too remote from North America and/or too sedentary to be likely candidates for vagrancy. However, we discuss subspecies that seem potential vagrants to North America, note whether they may be field-identifiable, and summarize their characters. If North American specimens exist, their subspecies identity, if known to us, is noted. Alternate common names may also be noted here.

Distribution and Status. The world distribution given for each species is simply a broad overview of breeding and nonbreeding ranges for context, with more specific information often given for regions closest to North America (such as how far east a species breeds in Asia, or how far north in Mexico). Those wishing more detailed information can consult regional guides. World distribution was derived largely from Cramp (1977–1994), Howell & Webb (1995), Ridgely & Tudor (1989, 1994), Marchant & Higgins (1990), AOU (1998), and in some cases del Hoyo et al. (1992–2011), verified as best we could from our own experience and any recent field guides or regional works. See Figs. 1–3 for geography of adjacent regions; also see geographic terms on p. xvii.

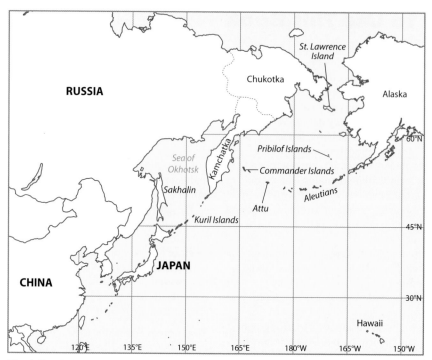

Fig. 1. East Asia, showing political divisions and geographic features mentioned in the text.

Fig. 2. Mexico and adjacent areas, showing political divisions and geographic features mentioned in the text.

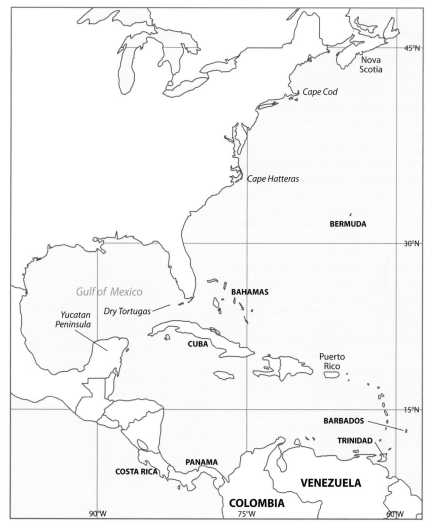

Fig. 3. The Caribbean and adjacent areas, showing political divisions and geographic features mentioned in the text.

Our status comments are general as well. The default assumption is that the species in question is reasonably common within its normal range. Species known to be rare, or in the midst of range expansions or contractions, are so noted.

For North American distribution and status, our primary sources were the *ABA Checklist,* 7th edition (ABA 2008; and in a few cases earlier editions), and the journal *North American Birds* (*NAB*; and its predecessors *Field Notes* and *American Birds*). We attempted to include information published (which does not necessarily include internet websites) through July 2011 (the summer season of *NAB*), but it is inevitable that we overlooked some records. We also included

in the species accounts some records from fall 2011 through October 2012, mainly when these helped fill out patterns for extremely rare species (generally those with fewer than 5 records for North America or from a large region); analyses in the introduction, however, only go through summer 2011. State, provincial, and regional published avifaunas were also reviewed, as well as reports of provincial and state records committees (often available online). We could not independently confirm the validity of each record, and thus may have included records that others believe are incorrect. This doesn't concern us as long as the disputed records fall within the existing pattern of occurrence and, in themselves, are not responsible for that pattern. Records that fell outside of patterns were looked at more carefully, and of course we were interested in every last record for species in which no pattern could be discerned.

If there were 5 or fewer records for a species, we list them chronologically by location (see below) and date, and in some cases provide citations, such as for records subsequent to ABA (2008) and for publications that discuss records in some detail. Specific dates of occurrence are often given, especially for Old World vagrants whose actual arrival dates on well-birded islands may be known with a reasonable degree of accuracy. Records are often grouped by month, in 3 periods: early month (1–10th), midmonth (11–20th), and late month (21–28/31st). If a month is listed without modification, then records span the month; thus, Aug to mid-Oct indicates early August to mid-October, and so forth.

Species with more than 5 records have records broken down by region and by season or date, when relevant. Groups of records that fit within an apparent pattern are lumped; for example, we might say something like: '***Pacific States and Provinces***: About 15 records, Aug–Nov, with a concentration in mid-Sep," reflecting our belief that fall migration records along the Pacific Coast fall within a well-defined pattern and don't need to be broken out further. Records falling outside that pattern, however, such as single winter and spring records, are treated separately. Whenever we list individual records, the number of individuals involved is assumed to be one (1). In cases where multiple individuals are involved in a single record, we list that number after the date— for example, 25 May 2006 (4).

The actual number of records reflects observer effort as much or more than species abundance. When more than 5 records exist, we often use terms such as 'exceptional' or 'very rare' (defined on pp. 3–4), rather than specifying whether there are 7 records or 8 records, and so forth; overall rarity, relative rarity, and patterns are what interest us.

Locations of records within Canada and the Lower 48 are usually treated at the level of county, island, or some other readily identifiable or well-known geographic location (such as Cape Cod, Massachusetts, or Churchill, Manitoba). Alaska lacks counties and we have used the regional subdivisions of Kessel & Gibson (1978), plus islands (simply referred to as Attu, Pribilofs, St. Lawrence, etc., with the suffix of island(s) not

given each time). For the Aleutians we use the divisions of Gibson & Byrd (2007). See p. xvii for a fuller explanation of geographic terms.

In terms of rare birds, simply noting the state or region is usually sufficient to see and interpret vagrancy patterns; specific locations, or even counties, are not overly relevant in most cases. Readers wishing information on specific locations may consult the ABA Checklist (2008) or state and provincial avifaunas.

Comments. Our conclusions on patterns suggested by the statistical record for each species, as well as our ruminations, occur here. If we have anything original to say, it probably appears in this section. In some cases we had pet theories about vagrancy patterns and processes, and attempted to marshal data to support them. If we were successful, citations are provided in support of our theories.

References to records in adjacent countries and regions refer to the following sources unless noted otherwise: Greenland (Boertmann 1994), Iceland (rare birds database at http://www3 .hi.is/~yannk/index-eng.html; last checked 1 Jun 2012, includes records for most species through 2006), Bermuda (Amos 1991), Azores (rare birds database at http://birdingazores.com; last checked 1 Jun 2012 to include most records through 2011), Cape Verde Islands (Hazevoet 1995), Barbados (Buckley et al. 2009), Mexico, northern Central America, and Clipperton Atoll (Howell & Webb 1995), the state of Sonora, northwest Mexico (Russell & Monson 1998), Panama (Ridgely & Gwynne 1989), Hawaii (Pyle & Pyle 2009), Kamchatka (Gerasimov et al. 1999), and Japan (Brazil 1991; OSJ 2000).

Field Identification. We begin typically with a brief overview of the species' field marks. In some cases we may simply say 'unmistakable' without describing a single character. Readers should then simply look at the nearby illustrations; for example, as for Eurasian Hoopoe.

SIMILAR SPECIES. Here we detail characteristics that permit separation of the vagrant from similar North American species, and from other vagrants and potential vagrants. In some cases, there are no similar species.

AGE/SEX/SEASON. This subsection describes any characters that may help refine identification below the level of species. The description may be quite detailed, as patterns of vagrancy may differ by sex and frequently differ by age. In most cases, only characters visible in the field are included, but with the advent of digital photography field characters are increasingly overlapping with in-hand characters, especially with respect to molt contrasts and the shape and relative wear of various feathers. See pp. 32–41 for an overview of bird topography, molt, and aging. Molt information was gleaned mainly from Cramp (1977–1994), Higgins & Davies (1996), and Howell (2012a), unless stated otherwise.

HABITAT AND BEHAVIOR. This subsection details general habitat preferences and typical behaviors (including the most common vocalizations). Usually we emphasize call notes over primary songs, as the former are most likely to be heard from vagrants. Voice descriptions represent our interpretation of vocalizations we have heard in the field, unless otherwise noted. Those based upon recordings from xeno-canto (www.xeno -canto.org) are denoted by catalogue number (e.g., XC79309).

Illustrations. These are provided for all species, usually within each species account, but in some cases a group of similar species (such as snipe) may be placed together on a single page for ease of comparison. Only plumages known or likely to be seen in North America are included; thus, for example, many briefly held juvenile plumages are not shown. In a few cases, similar North American species are shown for comparison.

References. Citations are given for specific information. Typically, we have not included citations for information we consider to be generally known or that we have confirmed personally, even though someone may have published previously on the subject; this policy affects primarily the identification section. Citations for specific records not given herein are often available in ABA (2008).

The following references were used so often that to credit them each time would, we feel, clutter the book needlessly, and to simply list them in the bibliography would be inadequate; we would therefore like to acknowledge them here.

ABA (2008). *ABA Checklist: Birds of the Continental United States and Canada*, 7th edition. This document, prepared by the ABA checklist committee, formed the basic reference for most of the species and records we include. For records not included in, or subsequent to, the ABA checklist we provide citations (often abbreviated to volume and page numbers of the journal *North American Birds*, e.g., *NAB* 65:114).

Gibson, D. D., & G. V. Byrd (2007). *Birds of the Aleutian Islands, Alaska.* The primary source of our data on vagrants in the Aleutians; if we accept records not mentioned by Gibson & Byrd we provide specific references. Steve Heinl also kindly checked our Alaska sections for all species.

Hamilton, R. A., M. A. Patten, & R. A. Erickson (eds.) (2007). *Rare Birds of California.* California records were derived from or checked against the data in this encyclopedic volume; if we discuss records not included therein, we provide specific references. Later information was obtained from http://www.californiabirds.org/cbrcdb .html, and from Guy McCaskie.

Lockwood, M. W., & B. Freeman (2004). *The Texas Ornithological Society Handbook of Texas Birds.* This useful work lists individual records of most rare birds, with additional information for Texas obtained from annual reports available online at http://texasbirds.org/tbrc/annuals.html, and from Mark Lockwood.

Rosenberg, G. H., & J. Witzeman (1998). Arizona Bird Committee report, 1974–1996: part 1 (nonpasserines). *Western Birds* 29:199–224.

Rosenberg, G. H., & J. Witzeman (1999). Arizona Bird Committee report, 1974–1996: part 2 (passerines). *Western Birds* 30:94–120.

Rosenberg, G. H., K. Radamaker, & M. M. Stevenson. 2011. Arizona Bird Committee report: 2005–2009 records. *Western Birds* 42:198–232. This and the preceding two papers provided a foundation for evaluating reports of rare birds in Arizona. Subsequent records from Arizona were obtained mostly from *North American Birds*, and from Gary Rosenberg and Mark Stevenson.

Stevenson, H. M., & B. H. Anderson (1994). *The Birdlife of Florida.* This was our starting point for checking records in Florida, supplemented by communication with Bill Pranty and Jon Greenlaw, and by seasonal reports published in the *Florida Field Naturalist.*

Abbreviations and Terminology

AB. The journal *American Birds* (now *North American Birds* or *NAB*).

Adult. A bird in adult plumage, i.e., a plumage whose appearance does not change appreciably with age, other than perhaps seasonally. Does not necessarily reflect sexual maturity.

AMNH. American Museum of Natural History.

Basic Plumage. The plumage attained by the prebasic molt (which is complete, or nearly so) and presumed homologous among all birds (see p. 32).

BM. British Museum

Culmen. The dorsal ridge of the maxilla, which curves down distally and may project over the tip of the mandible as a hook.

Culmen Bridge. The base of the bill where it meets the forehead.

Culminicorn. The horny plate covering the upper edge of the bill distal to the nostril tubes, contrastingly colored on some albatrosses.

Cycle. A regularly repeated phenomenon, such as a molt cycle. A basic molt cycle extends from the start of one prebasic molt to the start of the next prebasic molt.

Eccentric Molt. An incomplete wing molt in which only the outer primaries and inner secondaries are renewed, with the relatively protected inner primaries and outer secondaries retained. Ostensibly restricted to 1st-cycle (preformative) molts, especially among shorebirds but also occurs in a few passerines.

Flight Feathers. The remiges and rectrices collectively, i.e., the main feathers of the wings and tail; in some literature (as in Britain) used only for the remiges.

Facultative Migrant. A bird that migrates only as needed (as opposed to an obligate migrant), which may range from no migration in one year to moderate distance in another.

FN. The journal *Field Notes* (now *North American Birds* or *NAB*).

Formative Plumage. Any 1st-year plumage (attained by a preformative molt) that lacks a counterpart in the adult plumage cycle (see pp. 34–35).

Humerals. A group of feathers on the inner wing of long-winged birds (such as albatrosses) associated with the humerus, or inner arm bone.

Immature. A general term for any nonadult plumage, including juvenile.

Juv. Juvenile.

Latericorn. The horny plate covering the side of the upper mandible on a tubenose bill.

MCZ. Museum of Comparative Zoology, Harvard University, Cambridge, Massachusetts.

Molt. A period of normal and regular growth of feathers (i.e., molting), by which plumages are attained; feather loss is a passive by-product of molting.

Molt Contrast. A point of contrast between 2 generations of feathers in a nonmolting bird (see pp. 35–36).

Monotypic. Literally, of one type. A monotypic species is one for which no subspecies are recognized, usually indicating that geographic variation is absent or poorly defined.

NAB. The journal *North American Birds*.

Nominate. Refers to a subspecies bearing the same scientific name as the species; e.g., *Charadrius leschenaultii leschenaultii* is the nominate subspecies of Greater Sand Plover, usually written *C. l. leschenaultii*.

Pelagic. Waters beyond the continental shelf.

Preaxilliary notch. A dark mark on the leading edge of the underwing where the wing meets the body.

Preformative. The molt producing formative plumage, which is a plumage unique to a bird's 1st year.

Primaries (p). Primaries are the wing feathers attached to the hand bone, or manus, and their bases are protected by primary coverts. Most birds have ten visible primaries, numbered from p1 (innermost) to p10 (outermost).

Ramicorn. The horny plate covering the side of the lower mandible on tubenoses, sometimes contrastingly colored on albatrosses.

Rectrices (singular: rectrix). The main tail feathers, numbering 12 in most birds (six pairs each side of the central point; r1 is the central rectrix, r6 the outer rectrix).

Remiges (singular: remex). The main flight feathers of the wing, collectively referring to the primaries and secondaries.

Scapulars. A group of feathers that originate from a point at the base of the humerus and fan out to protect the base of the wings at rest; they form a seamless join between the wings and body in flight.

SDNHM. San Diego Natural History Museum.

Secondaries (s). The secondary wing feathers attached to the forearm (ulna) bone (numbering from 6 in hummingbirds to 38 in albatrosses); their bases are protected by secondary coverts (often simply called wing coverts).

Ssp. Subspecies. A taxonomic category below the level of species, referring to populations that can be distinguished by differences in plumage, measurements, etc., but which are not considered distinct enough to be treated as species.

Stepwise Molt. A type of wing molt in which the primaries are renewed by successive waves of molt that overlap in timing, each wave usually starting at p1 and taking 2 or more cycles to complete (see pp. 37–40).

Sulcus. A groove along the side of the ramicorn, contrastingly colored on sooty albatrosses.

Taxon (plural: taxa). A general taxonomic category, helpful when referring to populations whose taxonomic status is unresolved—e.g., taxa can be subspecies or species.

Tertials. Used here for the inner secondaries, which act as coverts on the closed wing.

Ungues (singular: unguis). The plates (maxillary unguis and mandibular unguis) covering the bill tip of tubenoses, sometime contrastingly colored.

USNM. United States National Museum, Smithsonian Institution.

Wear (or plumage wear). The abrasion of feather tips and edgings through day-to-day exposure with the elements and such; compounded by weakening due to bleaching.

Geographic Terms

We consider terms such as Atlantic States and Provinces, or Gulf States, to be self-explanatory; other terms are defined below. States and provinces are indicated by abbreviations (see below). In the species accounts, we use standard abbreviations for compass and other geographic directions, such as n. (north or northern), sw. (southwest or southwestern), s-cen. (south-central), and so forth. Capitals (usually without periods) are used with major (usually continental) landmasses and water bodies, such as SE Asia, NW Pacific, Cen America, S Africa, etc. (the country South Africa is spelled out); lower case abbreviations are used with countries and smaller regions, e.g, n. China, se. Russia, nw. Mexico.

Atlantic Canada. Newfoundland and the Maritime Provinces.

Bering Sea islands. Includes the Pribilofs, St. Matthew, and St. Lawrence islands.

Central Asia (Cen Asia). Asia roughly between the Urals and Lake Baikal, or about 60°–100° E; for songbirds this generally refers to mid-latitude regions (about 30–60° N).

East. Canada and the Lower 48, e. of about the 100°W meridian.

East Asia (E Asia). Asia roughly e. of 100° E, or w. to the vicinity of Lake Baikal, s. to n. China; for songbirds this generally refers to mid-latitude regions (about 30–60° N).

Interior. Canada and the Lower 48 (contiguous) US states exclusive of provinces and states that border the Pacific and Atlantic Oceans.

Kamchatka. Includes the whole Kamchatka Peninsula region, n. to border with Chukotka (see Fig. 1, p. xii); thus includes both Kamchatka and Koryak.

Mid-Atlantic Coast. From Long Island, New York, s. to the Outer Banks, North Carolina.

Middle America. Mexico and Central America.

New England. The 6 ne. states of the US, from Maine sw. to Connecticut.

Northeast. From Atlantic Canada and e. Quebec s. to New York.

Northwest. From British Columbia s. to northernmost California and e. to the Rockies (i.e., e. to w. Alberta and w. Montana and Idaho).

Southeast Asia (SE Asia). Largely warmer and tropical regions from ne. India and s. China through peninsular Malaysia.

Southern Asia (S Asia). Regions s. of around 35° N.

Southwest. The interior region including se. California, s. Nevada, s. Utah, Arizona, New Mexico, and w. Texas.

West. Canada and the Lower 48, w. of about the 100° W meridian.

Western Eurasia (W Eurasia). Eurasia roughly w. of 60° E, or from W Europe e. to the Ural Mountains.

The following Alaska islands are referred to without using the suffix 'island' in each case:

Adak Island, cen. Aleutians
Aggatu Island, w. Aleutians
Amchitka Island, cen. Aleutians
Attu Island, w. Aleutians
Buldir Island, w. Aleutians
Kiska Island, cen. Aleutians
Pribilofs (Pribilof Islands); most records here are from St. Paul Island.
Shemya Island, western Aleutians
St. Lawrence Island, n. Bering Sea; most records here are from around the village of Gambell.
Unalaska Island, e. Aleutians
Unimak Island, e. Aleutians

State and Province Abbreviations:

AB	Alberta
AK	Alaska
AL	Alabama
AR	Arkansas
AZ	Arizona
BC	British Columbia
CA	California

CO	Colorado	NM	New Mexico
CT	Connecticut	NS	Nova Scotia
DE	Delaware	NU	Nunavut
FL	Florida	NV	Nevada
GA	Georgia	NWT	Northwest Territories
IA	Iowa	NY	New York
ID	Idaho	OH	Ohio
IL	Illinois	OK	Oklahoma
IN	Indiana	ON	Ontario
KS	Kansas	OR	Oregon
KY	Kentucky	PA	Pennsylvania
LA	Louisiana	PEI	Prince Edward Island
MA	Massachusetts	QC	Quebec
MB	Manitoba	RI	Rhode Island
MD	Maryland	SC	South Carolina
ME	Maine	SD	South Dakota
MI	Michigan	SK	Saskatchewan
MN	Minnesota	SPM	Saint Pierre et Miquelon
MO	Missouri	TN	Tennessee
MS	Mississippi	TX	Texas
MT	Montana	UT	Utah
NB	New Brunswick	VA	Virginia
NC	North Carolina	VT	Vermont
ND	North Dakota	WA	Washington
NE	Nebraska	WI	Wisconsin
NH	New Hampshire	WV	West Virginia
NJ	New Jersey	WY	Wyoming
NL	Newfoundland (and Labrador)	YT	Yukon Territories

Rare Birds of North America

Introduction

What Is a 'Rare Bird'—and When and Whence?

Every species is rare somewhere, or at some time, but how is 'rare' defined? For our purposes, we include species for which, on average, only 5 or fewer individuals have been found annually in North America since around 1950, when birding and field ornithology started to become popular. We tried to incorporate all species and records through the June–July 2011 summer season, and in some cases noteworthy later records are mentioned, through to the submission of the final manuscript in November 2012 (newly recorded species from fall 2011 through summer 2012 are discussed in Appendix A).

The list of vagrant birds in North America is changing constantly as we learn more about subjects such as migration, taxonomy, and identification. Madness lies down the path of evaluating each and every potential new species for North America, and we extend our gratitude to state and provincial committees whose self-assumed role it is to vet such records.

Inevitably, our analyses are skewed toward the 'modern era'—meaning the period since the late 1970s, when field birding and documentation capability expanded rapidly throughout North America, as measured by the number of reports submitted to the journal *North American Birds* and its predecessors. This bias may have led us to ignore species that have become 'common' beginning at least in the 1990s (and continuing to the present), even though they passed our statistical criteria across the whole period. The shift from 'rare' to 'not rare' may be real, as with Barnacle Goose, Muscovy Duck, Black-capped Gnatcatcher, and Clay-colored Thrush, or it may reflect increased coverage of areas previously not well known (e.g., Murphy's Petrel, White-faced Storm-Petrel, White-tailed Tropicbird).

There are a few species whose periodic irruptions or 'invasions' into North America may have produced an average-per-year total of more than 5 birds, but whose normal annual occurrence rates would qualify them for inclusion. We included such species in our review (e.g., Blue-footed Booby, Northern Lapwing, European Golden Plover).

We have also included a number of species that are regular migrants on the western Aleutians and Bering Sea islands, but that otherwise pass our statistical hurdle if one considers only mainland Alaska and elsewhere in continental North America; examples include Smew and Wood Sandpiper. We have not included birds that breed annually in continental North America, even though some of them are definitely rare away from their breeding ranges and regular migration routes (e.g., Bluethroat, Eastern Yellow Wagtail).

Our emphasis has been on migratory species, and thus we have omitted a few species that today might qualify as rare but which seem to be simply expanding and contracting their 'resident' ranges at the edges of our region (e.g., Buff-collared Nightjar, Tamaulipas Crow, Brown Jay). Conversely, we have included a few species that are borderline statistically, but which present interesting identification or distribution issues (e.g., Garganey, Little Stint, Green Violetear, and Fork-tailed Flycatcher). Other borderline species, such as American Flamingo, Ruddy Ground Dove, Shiny Cowbird, and Brambling, are not included—we had to draw a line somewhere.

We debated whether to include rare subspecies, some of which are well marked and likely represent species in their own right (such as Eurasian taxa of White-winged Scoter, Great Egret, and Herring Gull). However, adequate data were rarely available and we elected not to enter this potential quagmire.

In the course of our review we found records that we did not consider valid, both for regions and for North America as a whole; these may be mentioned in the relevant accounts, if still accepted by official committees. Two questionable identifications we encountered for North America as a whole were Little Shearwater *Puffinus assimilis* in California (Hamilton et al. 2007), and Caribbean Elaenia *Elaenia martinica* in Florida (ABA 2008); both have since been removed from official state lists.

Because we do not constitute a committee that has to either accept or reject records, we treat 11 species that, as yet, are not accepted by ABA or AOU committees as having occurred 'naturally' in North America: West Indian Whistling Duck, White-faced Whistling Duck, Common Shelduck, Ruddy Shelduck, Nazca Booby, Demoiselle Crane, Southern Lapwing, Western Marsh Harrier, Dark-billed Cuckoo, Blue Rock Thrush, and Red-legged Honeycreeper.

Our inclusion of these species does not mean we necessarily accept that North American records pertain to wild birds, only that wild origin is plausible; hence, we felt it worthwhile to include these records with a discussion of their vagrancy pros and cons.

We also include 3 species (Zino's Petrel, Cuban Emerald, Blyth's Reed Warbler) for which records had not been reviewed at the time of going to press, or whose identification has been considered uncertain by North American authorities (2 others, Eurasian Bittern and Common Chiffchaff, are included in Appendix A); and 2 species (Hen Harrier, Kamchatka Leaf Warbler) that have occurred in North America but have not been recognized as full species by the AOU. Moreover, in several cases we include (or sometimes query) regional records of species not accepted (or accepted) by state committees, such as records from California of Stejneger's Petrel, Bulwer's Petrel, and Blue Mockingbird.

Sundry other records that might qualify species for inclusion are not generally accepted on the basis of questions about their origin or identification. These are discussed in Appendix B, and we acknowledge that some may represent potentially wild occurrences in North America. In particular, the burgeoning number of extralimital (or escaped?) Neotropical species is intriguing, especially when the species involved are not known to be kept commonly in captivity. However, until such time as captive birds are effectively monitored and controlled, with public access to the data, our understanding of such vagrancy will be hindered both by the specter of escapes and by bureaucracy.

And lastly, a few rare birds have been recorded in North America based solely on records dating from earlier than our review period. These are mostly detailed by ABA (2008) and are as follows: Slender-billed Curlew (last valid record about 1925), Scaly-naped Pigeon (1929), Bumblebee Hummingbird (1896), Cuban Martin (1895), Gray-breasted Martin (1889), Southern Martin (1890), Black Catbird (1892), Worthen's Sparrow (1884; extirpated breeder?), Tawny-shouldered Blackbird (1936), and Fuertes's (Ochre) Oriole *Icterus [spurius] fuertesi* (1894 in Texas).

Given our criteria, we treat some 262 species of rare birds recorded in North America from 1950 through July 2011; 209 of these were first recorded during the period under review (202 during 1950–2009; Table 1). Thus, 20% of the

rare species we treat were first found in North America prior to 1950. An additional 3 species occurred from fall 2011 through summer 2012 (Appendix A). We consider the origins of North American rare birds in terms of three broad categories: Old World, New World, and pelagic (Table 1, Fig. 4). Viewed by decade, the numbers and percentages of species from these three regions vary somewhat (Fig. 4), although most of the variation reflects the history of birding rather than any geographic or temporal trends.

In the 1950s there was relatively little recreational birding, and most new records were found and collected by field ornithologists, few of whom were active at that time in southern border regions. A marked upswing in the popularity of birding began in the 1960s and 1970s and has continued through the present. The peak of new records in the 1970s largely reflects the 'discovery' in the mid-1970s of the Alaskan islands as spring vagrant traps. Remarkably, the rate of new birds has shown no signs of slowing, and it even increased slightly from the 1980s through the 2000s. In the 1980s and 1990s, although the Aleutian goldmine had been mostly tapped, new records were balanced by increased birding in border regions, mainly Arizona in summer—fall and Texas in winter. The lull in Asian additions in the 1990s largely reflects the period between 'saturated' spring coverage of the Aleutians in the 1980s and 1990s (when few new species were being found) and fall coverage of St. Lawrence Island and the Pribilofs in the 2000s. The increase in pelagic species (especially since about 1990) mostly reflects increased numbers of pelagic trips off both coasts, enhanced by larger numbers of observers carrying digital cameras.

The percentage of species known only from single records is obviously greatest in recent years (Table 1), and the big jump in single records since the 1980s indicates that most of the more regular vagrants had been found in the 1960s and 1970s. Not surprisingly, the highest rate is for pelagic seabirds, 50% of which during 1980–2009 were known from single records. The slight dip in one-time occurrences of New World species in the 1990s may reflect the trend of increasing numbers of Mexican species being found in border states; that is, Mexican species are still being found for the first time but many are also increasing and moving north, and thus are likely to be found again;

1950s xxxxxxxxxxxxxxx (15)
1960s xxxxxxxxxxxxxxxxxxxxxxxxxxxx (28)
1970s xxxxxxxxxxxxxxxxxxxxxxxxxxxxxxxxxxxxxxxxxxxxxxxxx (48)
1980s xxxxxxxxxxxxxxxxxxxxxxxxxxxxxxxxxx (34)
1990s xxxxxxxxxxxxxxxxxxxxxxxxxxxxxxxxxxxxxx (38)
2000s xxxxxxxxxxxxxxxxxxxxxxxxxxxxxxxxxxxxxxx (39)

Fig. 4. Total new species of rare birds in North America by decade, 1950–2009. **x** Old World; x New World; **x** pelagic.

Table 1. Breakdown by region of origin for the 202 rare birds new to North America during 1950–2009. Totals are presented as percentages per 10-year period; actual species totals are given by subregion (East Asia, Western Eurasia, etc.). 'Single records' indicates the percentage of species known (through 2011) from only one record in North America.

	1950–59	1960–69	1970–79	1980–89	1990–99	2000–2009	1950–2009
Old World	80%	43%	60%	47%	44%	43%	51%
E Asia	8	11	26–27	14	8	12	79–80
W Eurasia	4	1	2–3	2	8–9	5	22–24
Single records	0%	0%	10%	13%	44%	53%	21%
New World	13%	39%	27%	41%	38%	31%	33%
Mainland	1	9	11	13	12–13	10	56–57
Caribbean	1	2	2	1	2	2	10
Single records	0%	9%	8%	36%	21%	66%	29%
Pelagic	7%	18%	13%	12%	18%	26%	16%
Pacific	1	3	4	3	4	8	23
Atlantic	0	2	2	1	3	2	10
Single records	100%	20%	0%	0%	43%	70%	36%
Total species	15	28	48	34	38	39	202
Single records	7%	7%	8%	21%	34%	62%	26%

examples include Sinaloa Wren and Blue Mockingbird.

In terms of where rare birds have been first found in North America, of the 202 species initially recorded during 1950–2009, just over a third (35%) were first recorded from AK, 14% from TX, 10% from CA, 9% from FL, 5% from AZ, 4% from NL, and 3% each from MA and NC. The remaining 17% (with 1-3 species per state or province) were from AB, AL, BC, DE, LA, MB, ME, MS, NJ, NM, NS, NU, NY, OK, PA, QC, RI, and WA (see Appendix C).

Abundance Definitions

By necessity, these definitions are relative and can apply to any region and season. Thus, a bird can be exceptional in a state, very rare in a region, and rare on a continent. In cases where status is muddy the terms can be combined—for example, 'rare to very rare in w. Alaska.' If there are only 1-2 records in total we simply say this, and list them in the main status section.

> *Exceptional (accidental)*: Averaging no more than 1-2 records per decade since the 1980s, but with more than 2 records overall.
> *Very rare (casual)*: Not seen most years since the 1980s, but at least a few records per decade.
> *Rare*: One to a few most years since the 1980s or since regular coverage began.
> *Uncommon*: Small numbers annually.
> *Common*: Moderate numbers annually.
> *Irruptive*: In some years, seen in much greater than typical numbers.

Migration and Vagrancy in Birds

Humans have long been fascinated by bird migration, which is usually thought of as the regular comings and goings of birds between their breeding and nonbreeding grounds. But in reality, migration involves many variations on this conventional theme (see Newton 2008 for a readable overview of migration, from which much of the following is synthesized). Vagrancy is one aspect of migration, and at its simplest is usually defined as birds being where they don't normally occur. Given that we don't fully understand how regular migration works, it's unsurprising that we don't understand how vagrancy works, though some theories have been advanced. One fundamental point is that, for a variety of reasons, young birds are inherently more susceptible to vagrancy than adult birds (discussed below).

Migration

Considerable research has gone into how birds can migrate with such precision—in a brain the size of a pea some species have all the facilities (and more?) of modern pilots with a huge control panel of computers at their disposal. Beyond simply navigating by sight—such as following coastlines and other prominent features of the landscape—the 2 primary means of navigation by birds are considered to be celestial (use of the sun, stars, etc.) and geomagnetic (using the Earth's magnetic field). Other factors are likely involved, such as barometric pressure, polarized light, ultrasound, and perhaps even smell, at least in some species; but our understanding of migration is still rather nascent, despite a fairly large body of work published on the subject.

Some aspects of migration are learned, while others are innate. For example, in the many species where adults migrate independently from birds of the year, one popular idea proposes that young birds have a built-in clock and compass that tell them in what direction to fly and for how long. In this way, say, a young Magnolia Warbler with no previous experience of migration can take off from eastern Canada and fly accurately to the species' wintering grounds in southern Mexico or Central America; these compass systems may even have programmed course changes after a certain number of hours flying. With only this system, birds are thought unable to determine their position and thus may not correct their flight direction for displacements such as wind drift. If the inherent clock-and-compass mechanism is faulty in some way, young birds may fly far off course without knowing it or attempting to correct their heading, at least if they are out of sight of land. The potential benefit of this, of course, is that new migration routes and perhaps wintering areas are constantly being pioneered, and some may prove successful, as might be happening with Red-throated Pipits in western North America.

A more refined system of navigation is the bicoordinate system, in which birds sense at least 2 global coordinates, can then determine their geographical position, and thus are able to correct for displacement. This system is apparently used primarily by birds that have successfully completed a migration, and suggests a reason why vagrants usually include relatively few adults.

Some birds, such as geese and cranes, migrate as family units, and the young learn migration routes and stopover sites from their parents. In some cases, social influences can override inherent migratory and directional tendencies. Hence, vagrant geese and cranes, perhaps lost or orphaned individuals, may join and travel with other species. Still other species, such as some pelagic seabirds, appear to have an internal map that enables them to navigate over vast, featureless (to humans) areas, and to find their small and often remote nesting islands—quite how they achieve this we still don't know.

Other questions linked to migration studies relate to which cues are used to initiate migration, and to the basic energetics of migratory flight. For many species in the Northern Hemisphere, waning daylight is the underlying cue to begin a fall migration, but birds still have to await favorable weather conditions and they need to be fueled up. All else being equal, migrant landbirds generally prefer to travel in clear and calm conditions, or with a light tailwind. Precipitation or adverse winds typically suppress migration. Note that the conditions *promoting* migration usually differ from those making migration *visible* to an observer on the ground, when birds are often flying into the wind (Newton 2008:70). Young birds are obviously less experienced in migration and may be more likely to take off in what they perceive as suitable conditions; these may, however, prove to be ultimately contrary winds associated with a storm system that could drift them far off course.

Some species, at least experienced individuals, appear able to detect and interpret changes in barometric pressure and associated wind direction. For example, in early September 2006, a tagged Marbled Godwit flew hundreds of kilometers from Baja California, Mexico, to west Texas for a day, and then back to its original location in Baja California; in the process, it avoided the passage of a hurricane (*NAB* 61:150).

How far can a given species fly on a particular fuel load? Our ideas on such subjects are inevitably constrained by our own terrestrial limitations and by theoretical models—neither of which necessarily constrain birds in the air. Indeed, as noted by Newton (2008:54), 'in their migratory flights, birds are often found to perform better than predicted by simple aerodynamic models.' Put simply, migrating birds are professionals—they do it for a living (i.e., survival)—and we are but curious observers. Thus, while models may predict maximum nonstop flight ranges of around 3000 km for passerines and 4000–7500 km for shorebirds, the trans-Pacific odysseys of 10,000 km and longer made by Bar-tailed Godwits (Gill et al. 2009) suggest that our models are sometimes wanting. In the case of Bar-tailed Godwit, the internal organs of long-distance migrants shrivel up to make room for fat (Piersma & Gill 1998), such that birds might not be able to feed even if they landed along their migration route.

Asian passerine vagrants banded on California's Southeast Farallon Island were sometimes light, but almost all weights were within the normal ranges for the species (Table 2). Most or all of these birds would have been detected shortly after arrival and before making significant weight gains. This suggests they were not outside their normal flight capabilities, whatever their point of last departure and the route they took. We have evidence that some shorebirds can travel farther

Table 2. Comparisons of mass (in grams) of vagrant Asian landbirds on Southeast Farallon Island, California (PRBO unpubl. data) and in their normal range (from Cramp 1988–1992; Cramp & Perrins 1993–1994).

	California	Normal Range
Brown Shrike (2)	27.1–33.4	24–38
Red-flanked Bluetail	12.2	11–18[1]
Dusky Warbler	7.7	7–12
Arctic Warbler (2)[2]	7.8–9	8–15
Lanceolated Warbler	12.3	9–13
Common Rosefinch	24.3	19–27

[1] An exhausted bird weighed 8.7 g.
[2] Taxon uncertain, see account for Kamchatka Leaf Warbler (p.314).

nonstop than was thought previously; perhaps we underestimate the distance and time aloft capacities of many migrant landbirds.

For example, on 28 September 2012 a Common Cuckoo and an Arctic Warbler were found in coastal central California; both species normally would have been fattened up and migrating from Kamchatka south to the Philippines. These birds, likely only a fraction of the Asian vagrants that actually reached California that week, appeared after the passage of a very strong storm system that spanned the North Pacific, with winds blowing at 90–150 kmh (50–80 knots) from Kamchatka to the North American West Coast. Conventional wisdom suggests that landbird migrants could not make a single flight of such magnitude, but what might be possible with such strong wind assistance has yet to be established; the Arctic Warbler (weighing 7.8 g) was at or below the normal weight range for the species (Table 2), suggesting it was near the limit of its flight range. The distance from northern California to Kamchatka (5400 km, or 3360 miles) is comparable to that from Western Europe to an overwater track between northeastern North America and northern South America, and fall Atlantic crossings made by storm-drifted migrants, such as Yellow-billed Cuckoo, Gray-cheeked Thrush, Blackpoll Warbler, and Bobolink, are well documented. Thus, a wind-assisted, North Pacific crossing by some strong-flying East Asian migrants does not seem impossible given the right conditions.

Much more research is needed into the relationships between wind systems, energy use, physiology, and flight range in most migratory birds. That said, a lot of research and predictions on migration have been borne out by observations and can form qualified foundations for theories about vagrancy. In some cases, vagrancy patterns may even provide windows into a better understanding of normal migration. In general, though, it appears that birds are far more capable of achieving 'inhuman' feats than we give them credit for.

Vagrancy

There is no precise definition of a 'vagrant bird.' Many birders might say that a vagrant is a bird that occurs when and/or where it 'should not' occur, but how does one define where a bird 'should' and 'should not' occur? This definition also may confuse frequency of occurrence with a navigational or other error. For example, 1st-year birds may be rare or very rare in a given area, but they are not necessarily vagrants. They may simply be part of an inherent pattern of the much wider dispersal of young relative to adults. Still, vagrancy as defined by birders is statistically based, and presumably could have a statistical definition. For example, one could in theory find the center of a species' range and then map the area around the center until 0.999 of all individuals were included within the mapped range. The 0.001 outside the mapped range could be defined as 'vagrants' for the space and time covered by the data. However, with existing knowledge this sort of precision seems unobtainable for any species, and our definition of a vagrant is likely to remain based on the number of birds we see, not the number of birds actually present.

While population size combined with distance and direction of migration are the ultimate factors that determine vagrancy rates in a species (e.g., DeBenedictus 1971; DeSante 1983b; Veit 2000), the detectability of a species is the proximate factor that perhaps most strongly colors our knowledge of the phenomenon. Detectability may be influenced by weather—in good weather, misoriented species may easily overfly Alaskan islands, whereas storm systems and precipitation force birds to land and reveal them to the terrestrial observer. Detectability is also a function of a bird's appearance and behavior—Jabirus are more easily detected than Lanceolated Warblers, for example. Landbirds migrating over the sea become concentrated on islands, which become well-known migrant hot spots and thus also concentrate observers, compounding the island effect of detectability. It is no coincidence that a large proportion of Asian landbird vagrants recorded in California have been found on small offshore islands with regular observer coverage and relatively little vegetation. The chances of finding a small, secretive landbird such as Red-flanked Bluetail or Lanceolated Warbler on the mainland, even on a coastal headland or peninsula, are far smaller.

In an area as relatively well watched as Britain, it has been calculated that in any heavily birded area, from 11% to 60% of all rare birds go undetected due to factors such as observer coverage, type of species, and habitat (Fraser 1997). Thus, in a vast continental region as relatively under-watched as North America, it seems safe to assume that most vagrants, particularly of smaller and less conspicuous species, are routinely overlooked, and that we treat only a tiny fraction of the rare birds that have occurred in North America. And of course, if we did somehow detect them all, many if not most wouldn't be rare by our current definition.

Inevitably, our data are heavily biased by the whens and wheres of observer coverage. Moreover, once patterns are elucidated, birders often use that knowledge to seek rare birds, and patterns are reinforced. For example, birders learned in the 1970s that the western Aleutian islands were prime vagrant traps, which contributed to relatively intense coverage of some islands, notably Attu in spring migration (mid-May to mid-June). Thus, in the 1970s and 1980s alone, some 30 bird species were added to the North American list from records obtained on the Aleutians (Tobish 2000). As access to the western Aleutians became logistically difficult, attention switched after the 1990s to the fall potential of islands in the Bering Sea, where regular coverage since the late 1990s has produced 10 species (and counting) new to North America (e.g., Lehman 2005). Some of these were far from expected— that is, until the patterns they revealed helped reshape our thinking on vectors of vagrancy in the Bering Sea region.

Vagrancy in birds occurs almost exclusively in species that migrate or are prone to wander in search of more favorable conditions, such as food sources. A popular notion is that vagrant birds are simply wandering randomly and are 'lost' or have been blown off course, and the latter certainly does happen (see 'Drift,' below). But we agree with Vinicombe & Cottridge (1996) that many vagrant birds 'know' what they are doing, and that vagrancy reflects both intrinsic and extrinsic factors. There appear to be a limited number of processes that result in birds occurring where and/or when they are rarely recorded. We have broken these processes into 6 categories discussed below: drift, misorientation, overshooting, dispersal, association, and disorientation. Some of these operate together on occasion. Of these categories, drift (an extrinsic factor) and misorientation (an intrinsic factor) appear to contribute the greatest numbers of vagrant birds. A seventh category is false vagrancy, explained below.

No discussion of vagrancy would be complete without reference to the direct and indirect effects of human activities, which are too numerous and complex to explore here fully. Indirect factors such as bird feeders, which enhance detection and perhaps prolong the survival of individuals, mostly affect the detection of vagrants once they have reached North America. The main direct human factor involved in vagrants reaching North America is undoubtedly the controversial subject of ship assistance. We consider that birds taking advantage of human structures, such as ships or oil platforms, and *which are not restrained or actively assisted*, should be viewed as valid vagrants. Birds that are restrained, or kept alive by directly providing food and water (see Alford 1928 for an example involving European Greenfinch *Chloris chloris*), are not considered as 'wild' vagrants.

Numerous cases of birds resting or riding unrestrained on ships are documented, and include boobies, herons, small falcons, and jackdaws. In other cases, ship assistance is open to speculation, including the degree to which birds might or might not have been consciously assisted. Our treatment of species that have had proven or inferred ship assistance may be viewed as inconsistent, mainly in regard to House Crow (see Appendix B), which is not a migrant in any conventional sense and thus does not fit into our preconceptions of how avian vagrancy is or should be defined.

1. Drift. All else being equal, most species prefer to migrate in clear conditions and with a light tailwind. When birds migrating over land encounter contrary conditions, such as adverse headwinds or rain, they usually simply stop traveling, but landbirds migrating over water normally don't have that option. If it's early

enough in their night's movement, at least some may return to the land from which they departed. In the case of spring flights across the Gulf of Mexico, some birds, depending on where they are, may just press on; this results both in arrival times in the United States that might be delayed 5–10 hours, and sometimes in significant mortality. In some cases, compass errors may combine with drift, such as with fall occurrences of Fork-tailed Flycatchers in the Northeast, or with Asian birds over the North Pacific.

Birds that are drifted offshore may reorient to land if conditions permit or if they can see it. However, from our perspective the most interesting subset of the drift phenomenon involves birds that find themselves over the ocean in conditions that don't permit them to return to land safely.

Migrants, at least adults, with anything less than perfectly aligned winds routinely make heading adjustments to keep to their preferred course. Each of these adjustments requires extra effort and at some point this effort becomes too expensive. At this point, migrants stop trying to keep to a preferred course and either drop to the ground or, if overwater, drift downwind. Such behavior seems obviously adaptive if the choice is between drifting long distances with reduced fuel consumption in the hope of encountering a suitable if unknown landing place, or flying into a strong wind, burning fuel, and gaining little or no ground in the process.

We know nothing of the nature of the tipping point, when a bird decides to give up trying to achieve its normal migratory goal and changes its course or just drifts—but it's clear that something like this happens regularly. For example, a satellite-tagged Bar-tailed Godwit heading from the Korean Peninsula to its Alaskan breeding grounds in late May battled strong headwinds for 48 hours as it flew east over the Pacific beyond Japan. It abandoned its eastward track but continued to fight headwinds as it flew northnortheast toward the Kamchatka Peninsula and Bering Sea. When within 110 km of the nearest land and 450 km of the nearest Alaska breeding area, it abandoned its effort and with tailwinds flew due west back to the coast of Kamchatka. It remained there for 10 days before flying back to Alaska but it did not nest (R. Gill, pers. comm.).

Birds drifting downwind can on occasion cover huge distances, given that the airflows in which they are entrained can be very strong. However, fuel loads ultimately limit how far a downwind drifter can travel, and refueling possibilities limit a drifter's abilities to move on, if it has been fortunate enough to find a place to land.

We believe drift displacement has led to some of the most dramatic examples of vagrancy in North America, such as spring fallouts of Asian birds on the Aleutians and Bering Sea islands. Birds migrating north in spring through the Kuril Island chain and off the East Asian coast are particularly susceptible to being drifted north and east by storms, which on rare occasion carry some birds as far as the Alaska mainland (Fig. 5). The largest spring fallouts of Asian migrant birds on the western Aleutians have been correlated to El Niño-Southern Oscillation climatic events, when storms that originate in central and northern Japan intensify as they track northeast; a strong El Niño signal in fall, indicated by a rise in sea-surface temperature in the eastern equatorial Pacific, typically presages large fallouts of East Asian migrants the following spring on the western Aleutians (Hameed et al. 2009).

Not surprisingly, species that migrate inland (west) of the Sea of Okhotsk, are not as prone to spring drift. For example, Siberian Stonechat remains unrecorded on the Aleutians, but there are several spring records from St. Lawrence Island, in the northern Bering Sea. The offshore versus inland spring routes in Northeast Asia, along with the different compositions of species taking each route, are analogous to circum-Gulf (west of Okhotsk) and trans-Caribbean (up the Kuril Islands) spring migration in North America.

Spring drift also occurs in the Northeast of North America, although it involves far fewer species than in Alaska. When migrants headed to Iceland from Britain are drifted off course by storms and fly downwind, they may continue until they make landfall in Atlantic Canada, especially eastern Newfoundland (Fig. 6). In both the Aleutians and Newfoundland, it appears that many of the drifted spring migrants may rest and reorient; witness the relative paucity of records of Eyebrowed Thrushes away from the western Aleutians, or of European Golden Plovers away from eastern Newfoundland.

Drift displacement is not limited to spring. For example, in mid-September 2004, numbers of Pacific Swifts turned up in the Aleutians on both

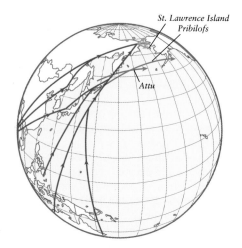

Fig. 5. Both moving north in spring and south in fall, many species with differing wintering grounds and breeding ranges migrate (green lines) offshore or coastally through East Asia (as through the Kuril Islands). Frequent storms move eastward through this region (red lines). In spring, northbound migrants, especially if they have been flying for some time over water, may be tired and are regularly drifted east to the Aleutians and occasionally beyond (as to the Pribilof Islands). In fall, species tend to be well-fueled and perhaps are better able to judge weather conditions before they set off southward; even so, sometimes numerous birds can be drifted back north in fall, as with Pacific Swift and Gray-streaked Flycatcher.

Species migrating inland, west of the Sea of Okhotsk, are not usually exposed to such drift, but in spring some may overshoot the end of their westward migration (orange lines) and reach St. Lawrence Island or the northwest Alaska mainland.

Fig. 6. In spring, some migrants headed north from the British Isles to Iceland or on to Greenland (green line) may intercept storms whose northeast winds drift birds west out over the North Atlantic (red line); the first landfall is often Newfoundland. Examples of such species include European Golden Plover and Black-tailed Godwit. This and the direct crossing shown in **Fig. 7** constitute the 'northern' Atlantic route (cf. **Fig. 8**).

Attu (40+ birds) and Adak (20+ birds). There had been a number of previous records in the western Aleutians, but normally of single birds. It's possible to argue that single vagrants are the result of misorientation, but such an argument cannot be applied reasonably to multiple individuals occurring at once. The most logical explanation is that migrant flocks got caught up in a storm whose prevailing winds and general track drifted them north over a broad front, depositing numbers of birds at points along the Aleutians (the species makes long overwater journeys on its regular migration to and from Australasia). Another example is the late September 2007 arrival of numbers of Eye-browed Thrushes on the western Aleutians and Pribilofs, with one even being found on St. Lawrence. Such occurrences are rare, since adults at least must be very good at avoiding such storms, but obviously they do happen and are likely responsible for numbers of Asian birds in fall on the Aleutians and Pribilofs.

A subset of overwater drift vagrancy may be related to another aspect of North Pacific weather patterns. A few times each fall, on average, an atmospheric pattern known as the Pacific-North American (PNA) teleconnection pattern sets up over the North Pacific. This pattern, which spans most of the Northeast Pacific, significantly alters the path and intensity of North Pacific storm systems. When the PNA is in its so-called negative phase, storm systems originating in far eastern Russia and the Bering Sea often take a trajectory toward the West Coast of North America, sometimes reaching as far south as California (Franzke et al. 2011). Such conditions may contribute to the 'Siberian express' bumper years for Asian vagrants along the West Coast. For example, there is a statistically significant correlation between the negative phase of the PNA teleconnection pattern and the occurrence in California of Dusky Warbler ($p < 0.1$), White Wagtail ($p < 0.1$), and Red-throated Pipit ($p < 0.01$) (S. Feldstein, pers. comm.).

Drift displacement also happens in fall on the East Coast, but as storms there track away from the coast and the birds involved are part of our own avifauna, the effects appear less dramatic. Occasionally, however, they are remarkable, as in October 1998 when a vast number of cuckoos, vireos, warblers, and other passerines showered down on southern Nova Scotia (McLaren et al. 2000). Given the species composition and date, these were almost certainly birds caught up in

strong headwinds and then drifted back northward while migrating to the Caribbean and mainland South America.

Drift vagrants also occur in the Northeast in late fall and winter, usually associated with hard weather that forces birds westward out of the colder interior regions of Europe and to milder coastal regions such as the British Isles. Species prone to late fall and winter drift tend to be ground-feeding birds such as Northern Lapwing, snipe, and thrushes, which are all adversely affected when the ground freezes. Storm tracks and prevailing winds can lead almost directly from Ireland to Newfoundland, as with some large transatlantic flights of Northern Lapwing (Bagg 1967; Fig. 7). In some cases, if birds approach Newfoundland with the winds that circle counter-clockwise around a low, they may even be drifted back into the Atlantic and reach Bermuda rather than the East Coast of the United States.

Farther south in the North Atlantic it appears that a number of species migrating southwest and south through Western Europe and West Africa can be drifted out over the Atlantic and assisted by prevailing easterly trade winds until they either perish or make landfall in the southeast Caribbean (notably Barbados) or northeastern South America (Fig. 8). When these species have an innate urge to migrate in spring they may head north and reach eastern North America, the waterbirds often in company with congeners.

Fig. 7. In cold late fall and mid-winter weather, Northern Lapwings and other ground-feeding species move west (green line) to milder parts of the British Isles, where bad weather and strong winds can drift them across the North Atlantic (red line). In some cases, birds may even be drifted away from land in the Northeast and end up in Bermuda.

 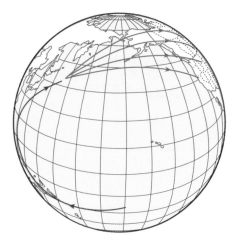

Fig. 8. The 'southern' Atlantic route (cf. Figs. 6–7). Birds migrating in fall between Europe and Africa (green lines) can be drifted offshore and, under certain conditions, may cross the tropical Atlantic (red lines) assisted by the same prevailing easterly Trade Winds that enabled Portuguese sailors to discover the Cape Verde Islands and Brazil. After wintering in northern South America or the Caribbean, some species (such as Little Egret and White-winged Tern) may then move north in spring (red lines) and reach eastern North America.

Fig. 9. Lesser Frigatebirds breeding in the central tropical Pacific have been documented to undergo a gradual counterclockwise drift dispersal pattern (in green) that by mid–late summer takes birds to waters off Japan and even Kamchatka (Sibley & Clapp 1967). From that point, tropical late summer and fall storms tracking east seem likely vectors to convey vagrants to widely scattered points across the North American continent (red lines).

Examples of species that likely took this indirect southern route before reaching eastern North America include Garganey, Little Egret, Western Reef Heron, Whiskered and White-winged terns, Terek Sandpiper, and Spotted Redshank, along with commoner vagrants such as Ruff and Curlew Sandpiper (some of the shorebirds may also reach the East from Alaska and East Asia; see the discussion in Little Stint account).

The phenomenon of seabirds (such as gadfly petrels, frigatebirds, and Sooty Terns) carried well inland in association with tropical storms (mainly in eastern North America) can be viewed as a highly specific subset of drift. Occurrences of Lesser Frigatebird and Streaked Shearwater in North America also may be associated with drift from storms tracking across the North Pacific (see Fig. 9, and the accounts for those species).

2. Misorientation. Many migrants appear to begin their journey with an intrinsic compass telling them in which direction to head, and an intrinsic clock telling them how long to continue flying in that direction (e.g., see review by Newton 2008). In some cases it appears that the compass or clock is faulty, leading birds to travel either in the wrong direction, or in the right direction but for the wrong period of time.

Misorientation ('intentionally' going the wrong way) should not be confused with disorientation (being confused and having no idea of direction; see 6, 'Disorientation,' below).

It has long been noted in both Europe and North America that vagrancy in numerous species shows distinct and even predictable patterns, suggesting that misorientation is not simply random (e.g., Desante 1983a: Vinicombe & Cottridge 1996). A local-scale example of the nonrandomness of misorientation routes can be seen among fall vagrant shorebirds in western Alaska: Wood Sandpiper and Little Stint occur with relative frequency on the western Aleutian and Pribilof islands, but are all but unknown on St. Lawrence Island in the northern Bering Sea; conversely, Lesser Sand Plover and Gray-tailed Tattler occur with about equal frequency in both areas.

Various theories have been proposed to help explain such nonrandom patterns, and teasing apart misorientation from drift and other potential factors can be as problematic as separating nature and nurture in human behavior. In some cases, misoriented birds may head out of Asia on some misprogrammed course over the North Pacific and then be drifted to North America— but to what extent would they have kept to that heading without the assistance of drift?

A well-known form of misorientation is termed 'reverse migration' (Fig. 10), whereby a bird

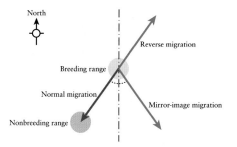

Fig. 10. Schematic diagram of reverse and mirror-image misorientation. Reverse migration basically involves a bird heading in more or less the opposite direction to that in which it should be heading. Mirror-image migration involves what might be thought of as dyslexia, or confusing east and west. In both cases, course changes and distance programmed into the normal heading may or may not be maintained (cf. **Fig. 16**).

migrates roughly in the opposite direction to that in which it would normally migrate (see Vinicombe & Cottridge 1996 for an expanded discussion and examples of this phenomenon). Although some have questioned the reverse migration theory (Gilroy & Lees 2003), it seems to occur more frequently than the 1/360 times that random misorientation would predict, and it fits the data for a number of vagrant species in both North America and Europe. Among vagrants to Western Europe, it has been suggested that reverse migration does not occur as frequently in migrants whose overall heading is mostly north-south as in those with a strong east-west component to their migration (Thorup 2004), although no satisfactory reason has been suggested for this disparity.

Many Asian vagrants recorded in fall on the Bering Sea islands, as well as farther south in western North America, appear to be examples of reverse migration (Figs. 11–12), with routes likely modified on occasion by factors such as drift and association. When considering reverse migration (or any form of long-distance vagrancy) it is helpful to use a globe (or Google Earth), or at least an equal-area map projection, so that distances and routes are not distorted.

Reverse migration occurs most commonly among 1st-year birds in their first fall, but it also appears to occur in spring; instead of returning to the breeding grounds a bird may head off from the wintering grounds in the reverse direction. This has been suggested as the explanation for fall (i.e., austral spring) occurrences of Fork-tailed Flycatcher in the Northeast (McCaskie & Patten 1994), and seems a likely explanation

Fig. 11. Hypothetical reverse fall migration tracks (in red) of a species breeding largely inland in Northeast Asia and wintering in Southeast Asia, and with migration lacking a strong coastal or offshore component. Examples include Siberian Stonechat and Dusky Warbler (**Fig. 12**). In theory, any long-distance migrant with such migration patterns might occur anywhere in North America between the two red lines. Not surprisingly though, most records come from coastal and island migrant traps rather than the vast and under-birded interior regions of the continent. Species with coastal or offshore fall migrations are more prone to drift in the fall and more likely to occur on the Aleutians (cf. **Fig. 5**).

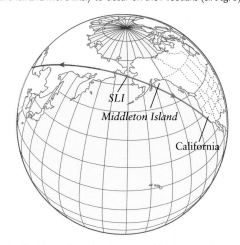

Fig. 12. Dusky Warbler departs its Northeast Asian breeding grounds in Aug–Sep and migrates southwest to wintering grounds in Southeast Asia. Fall records in western North America are concentrated in late Aug–Sep on St. Lawrence Island (SLI), and in late Sep–Oct in California and Baja California, Mexico; between these areas there is a record from Middleton Island, south-coastal Alaska in late Sep. All of these records lie essentially on a reverse track (red line) of the normal migration (green line), with the distance from the breeding grounds to Baja California being about 6500 km, similar to the distance to the normal wintering grounds.

for mid–late spring vagrant records in the southern United States of northern species such as Snow Bunting and Common Redpoll, or for a Blackpoll Warbler in the forests of southern Chile in June (A. W. Johnson 1967). It also may help explain spring occurrences on the Texas coast of species such as Aztec Thrush, Slate-throated Whitestart, Flame-colored Tanager, and Crimson-collared Grosbeak.

In some cases, reverse migration might even help us infer nonbreeding distributions. For example, 4 of the 5 fall records of Piratic Flycatcher from Texas and eastern New Mexico involved juveniles, and the single specimen was a juvenile of the northern-breeding subspecies *variegatus*, whose winter range is essentially unknown. A line projected from eastern New Mexico through the heart of that subspecies' breeding range, in southern Belize, and continued the same distance (about 2500 km, or 1550 miles) to the southeast (i.e., a 'reverse' of the New Mexico track) ends in northern Peru (Fig. 13). Might this region be where some *variegatus* winter? Interestingly, the 3 spring records of Piratic Flycatcher from Texas, as well as the other fall

record from Texas, also lie near this same line, supporting the contention that misorientation by Piratic Flycatchers is not simply random.

Specific examples of birds for which reverse misorientation seem the most likely explanation are the Spotted Flycatcher that occurred at Gambell, on St. Lawrence Island, Alaska, 14 September 2002, and the Greater Sand Plover that wintered at Bolinas Lagoon, central California, in 2001.

The nearest breeding grounds to Alaska for Spotted Flycatcher lie about 4000 km (almost 2500 miles) to the southwest, and the species winters in sub-Saharan Africa. At first glance it might seem an unlikely vagrant to North America. However, Spotted Flycatcher is a long-winged, strong-flying bird that almost certainly fuels up before making long migratory flights to cross large and inhospitable desert areas in Central and Southwest Asia. A line projected backward from the normal migration direction at the eastern edge of its breeding range passes through the western Alaska islands (Fig. 14). How many separate flights were involved and how long the reverse migration took are unknown, but it seems likely that the Gambell bird held to a relatively fixed direction on each of its overnight flights; it's hard to believe that some combination of randomly selected headings could have resulted in it reaching Gambell when it did.

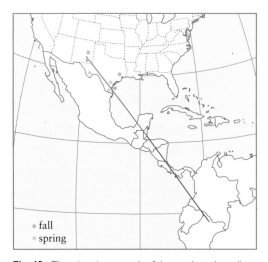

Fig. 13. The wintering grounds of the northern-breeding subspecies of Piratic Flycatcher (*variegatus*) are ostensibly unknown. If we hypothesize that US records reflect reverse-migrants, then a line projected backwards from the heart of that subspecies' breeding range in southern Belize (green line), along the path of northern fall vagrant records in Texas and New Mexico (red line), ends in northern Peru. Might it be that *variegatus* winters in southern Colombia and northern Peru? Interestingly, the 3 spring records in Texas also fall close to this line, even though spring overshoots are generally thought to fly shorter distances than reverse fall migrants (also cf. **Fig. 15**).

Fig. 14. Eastern populations of Spotted Flycatcher (breeding range in yellow) winter in sub-Saharan Africa, but if a bird headed in the reverse direction its path could take it to St. Lawrence Island (SLI) in western Alaska (and beyond, assuming it survived). Fall records of other species in Alaska, such as Lesser Whitethroat and Wood Warbler, also appear to fit this pattern.

Greater Sand Plovers of the nominate subspecies, which the California bird appeared to be, breed in interior East Asia; some of that population migrates southwest for about 10,600 km (or 6500 miles) to winter on the coasts of southern Africa. A Great Circle line drawn from the species' breeding grounds to southern Africa and projected about 180° 'backward' ends some 10,600 km later in central California, having passed through Alaska, where the bird could have staged and refueled (Abbott et al. 2001). Interestingly, the California individual continued to molt its upperwing coverts through the winter, as would a 1st-year bird in the Southern Hemisphere; this suggests its molt clock was also intrinsically programmed but did not respond to being in the wrong hemisphere and a northern winter climate, when locally wintering 1st-year shorebirds do not typically molt their upperwing coverts.

Among other examples of presumed reverse migration are many Fork-tailed Flycatchers appearing in North America (see Fig. 15 and the species account for further discussion). Seabirds may also be prone to this phenomenon: most North American records of White-chinned Petrel are in August–October, when birds should have been heading south to subantarctic latitudes from lower-latitude nonbreeding areas—yet it seems they may have headed north instead.

Another form of misorientation is termed 'mirror-image' (DeSante 1973, 1983a; Fig. 10), whereby birds migrate on what may be thought of as a 'dyslexic' heading, in which east and west are transposed, for example. Thus a bird in fall could head southwest at a 40° angle from due south, rather than normally heading southeast at a 40° angle from due south.

Obviously, when the mirror-image angle approaches 90° it becomes difficult to distinguish mirror-image from reverse migration. However, only the northernmost breeding Asian species might be expected to occur in North America as mirror-image vagrants; such vagrants from southern populations would likely perish out in the vast Pacific before they reached North America. A possible example involving both mirror-image and reverse migration is Eastern Yellow Wagtail, which shows an earlier wave and later wave of vagrants along the West Coast. The August to mid-September records of Eastern Yellow Wagtail (concentrated in California) may represent mirror-image misorientation from Alaskan (and adjacent Asian) breeding grounds, which are vacated in late July—early September. The second wave of birds, in late September—October, is concentrated in southeast Alaska and British Columbia, and may represent birds reverse migrating from farther west in Asia,

(a)   (b)

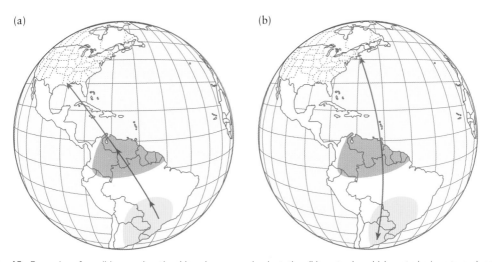

Fig. 15. Examples of possible overshooting (a) and reverse misorientation (b) routes by which austral migrants, such as Fork-tailed Flycatcher, reach North America. In the southern spring (Sep–Nov, or fall in North America), when birds should be migrating back to southern South America, some appear to reverse-migrate north and become entrained in weather systems that drift them to various points in the Northeast (about 3500–4000 km from the north coast of South America). In the southern fall (mainly Feb–Apr), some birds migrating north may overshoot the north coast of South America and, aided by drift, reach the US in the northern spring-summer (about 2500–3000 km from northern South America to the Gulf Coast). Breeding range in yellow, nonbreeding range in blue.

perhaps on headings more likely to take them inland or across the North American continent than down the West Coast.

In some cases, the programmed course changes of a normal migration may not always be replicated by reverse or mirror-image migrants, such that they simply keep to their initial wrong heading, in some instances over-shooting their normal distance of travel. Green-breasted Mango is one such example (Fig. 16). In other cases, subsequent cues may override initial misorientation or displacement, such as associa-tion with congeners (see 4, 'Dispersal,' below). For example, might some juvenile Little Stints reverse-migrating into northwestern North America from East Asia join flocks of Western Sandpipers and move down the West Coast, rather than continue on a misoriented track that would take them east across the continent?

In some cases, a species or individual may reverse-migrate a distance comparable to that of its normal migration (as perhaps with the Greater Sand Plover in California). In other cases it may

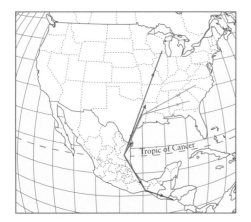

Fig. 16. Northern populations of Green-breasted Mango are migratory and withdraw from east Mexico to winter mainly on the Pacific slope of Middle America (green line). Interestingly, a generalized migration route projected 'backwards' into North America from the northern edge of the breeding range, including a corresponding course change to the east at the same distance as a normal course change, aligns roughly with 2 of the 4 extralimital northern records (in orange). All of the other vagrant records (in red) lie along or near a line projected back from the initial normal migration heading. In the 3 farthest-flung cases, the distance traveled into North America is appreciably greater than that of a normal migration, suggesting that both clock and compass of such birds are faulty. It seems unlikely that such a distribution of vagrant records would result simply from random misorientation.

fly an appreciably shorter or greater distance (as perhaps with Green-breasted Mango; Fig. 16).

3. Overshooting. There are many examples of birds that overshoot their normal 'stopping' area on both spring (especially) and fall migration. It isn't clear to what extent overshoots reflect birds migrating too fast for the right period of time or at the right speed for too long. Whereas most spring vagrants on the western Aleutians are coastal migrants drifted north and east by storms from Asia, a greater proportion of spring vagrants in the northern Bering Sea, such as on St. Lawrence Island, may be overshoots (perhaps often drift assisted) from the nearby Asian mainland (cf. Fig. 5).

For many species, as with Summer Tanager and Orchard Oriole in eastern North America, the spring overshoots are usually 1st-year males, suggesting an innate tendency by age/sex to engage in this sort of behavior. Recent records of Gray-collared Becard and Brown-backed Soli-taire from Arizona both involved 1st-year males, but age data have usually not been considered for most overshooting spring–summer southern vagrants such as Fan-tailed Warbler, Mexican Yel-low Grosbeak, and Flame-colored Tanager. Age/sex data from vagrants in Alaska would also be interesting in this regard, such as for spring Siberian Stonechats on St. Lawrence Island.

There are fewer examples of fall overshoots, perhaps because they occur south of our borders where both knowledge and coverage are limited. However, some spring occurrences of Fork-tailed Flycatchers in the southern United States may be 'fall' overshoots for the species, which breeds in southern South America in the austral summer and migrates north in February–April to its non-breeding grounds in northern South America (Fig. 15a). Overshooting may also be shown by misoriented migrants, if both their compass and clock are faulty. An example may be Green-breasted Mango in eastern North America (Fig. 16).

4. Dispersal. A number of species engage in regular or intermittent dispersal movements, often reflecting food declines, habitat changes, or temperature changes. For whatever reason, some groups of birds are more prone to dispersal than others, such as rails and doves being inherently more dispersive than, say, wood-peckers and crows. In North America, the south-ward winter irruptions of owls and finches are well-known examples of food-related dispersal, and records of Great Spotted Woodpecker (and the recent Asian Rosy Finch) in Alaska likely fall into this category.

Sometimes dispersal movements are so dramatic that a few members of the dispersing group end up in very distant places. Pallas's Sandgrouse *Syrrhaptes paradoxus* from the steppes of Central Asia disperses west periodically—the last big invasion was in 1908 when at least one ended up on the Faeroe Islands, northwest of Scotland. North American records of marsh birds such as Spotted Rail and Paint-billed Crake from the Neotropics, and of Ruddy Shelducks from Central Asia (Fig. 17), might be the end results of dispersal movements as wetlands dried up. To what extent some of the longer-distance dispersals might be compounded by drift is unknown.

Another subset of dispersal may relate to the melting Arctic icecap. Individuals of species that disperse north in late summer from the North Pacific and Bering Sea into the food-rich Arctic Ocean may wander or drift east, in some cases reaching the North Atlantic (as with recent records of Glaucous-winged and Slaty-backed gulls, alcids, and even a Gray Whale). In other cases, individuals are perhaps forced south into the interior East in late fall, as with Long-billed Murrelet, and Ross's and Black-tailed Gulls. In some cases, movement may be from the Atlantic to the Pacific, as likely occurred for a Northern Gannet found in 2012 in California.

Seemingly sporadic, local, and perhaps elevational fall-winter dispersal movements of a few species, notably in northwest Mexico, appear to be multidirectional. Thus, species such as Rufous-backed Thrush, Nutting's Flycatcher, and Streak-backed Oriole disperse in many directions (e.g., Fig. 18). It may be that such scattershot dispersal is more typical of species that do not undergo regular, longer-distance seasonal migrations and thus have not developed a well-programmed and directed migratory instinct. In a sense, these species may be incipient longer-distance migrants, and a study of their vagrancy might even shed light on the evolution of migration. Further understanding of this phenomenon with regard to Mexican border species is hindered by a lack of information from northern Mexico, where birders are few.

In some winters, unusually cold weather in northeast Mexico appears to force some birds out of the highlands, perhaps in combination with cyclic patterns of food abundance. These birds likely head downslope in search of food or warmer areas, regardless of whether these lowland areas are to the north or south; in some

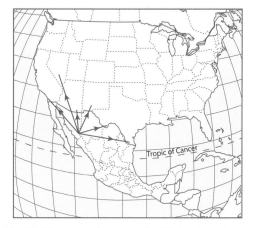

Fig. 18. Vagrant northern records of Rufous-backed Thrush show a seemingly scattershot pattern (end points of the red lines; only farthest spread records are included here, projected from the northern edge of the species' range). This type of dispersal may be typical of species that do not undergo regular, longer-distance seasonal migrations and thus may not have developed a well-programmed and strongly directional migratory instinct. Over time, selection may operate on those birds that overwinter most successfully and a more directed and 'formal' migration route may develop.

Fig. 17. Ruddy Shelducks breed mainly in interior Asia, but when their wetland habitats dry up the birds disperse great distances, often with a northwesterly track and mainly in late summer. This map shows how the seemingly isolated summer record of Ruddy Shelduck from Nunavut fits within the pattern of other extralimital records, scattered from northwest Europe to Iceland and even Greenland.

years the resultant diaspora brings a smorgasbord of rare birds to south Texas.

Post-breeding dispersal can be considered a form of short-distance 'vagrancy,' whereby individuals of ostensibly nonmigratory species can reach the United States, mainly from nearby (and sometimes expanding) Mexican populations. Records of Sinaloa Wren, Rufous-capped Warbler, and some of Blue Mockingbird likely fall into this category; in such cases, the individuals involved often remain for prolonged periods.

5. Association. Some birds have a strong group instinct and, having wandered to point X via some means, may attach themselves to other, usually closely related, species and travel with them on the next migratory movement. Many waterfowl and wading birds, for example, seem likely to have arrived in North America in the company of congeners, such as Little Egret and Western Reef Heron migrating north from the Caribbean into eastern North America, or Common Cranes migrating into Alaska and beyond with flocks of Sandhill Cranes.

6. Disorientation. We suspect there are not many truly disoriented birds except as a short-term phenomenon. If a bird becomes disoriented over water, such as in a storm or even in cloudy or rainy conditions, it may perhaps miscue wind direction and head the wrong way, or perhaps be prone to drift, either error resulting in at least short-distance displacement and vagrancy. Examples may include some short-distance or inter-island migrants in the Caribbean that then turn up in Florida, but this is purely conjectural and the mechanisms of Caribbean vagrancy remain largely unknown.

7. False vagrancy. There will always be birds that occur much more frequently than we know because of their reclusive habits or because they inhabit regions rarely visited by birders. In particular, seabirds remain poorly surveyed in much of North America: Hawaiian Petrel, Bermuda Petrel, and Red-tailed Tropicbird, among others, are surely regular and not truly 'rare' in North American waters, but the number of records we have at present means they have been included in this book. Even some land areas, like the western Aleutians or eastern Newfoundland, are not well understood, although coverage has improved recently. Many Asian shorebirds in the western Aleutians occur every year at about the same time, and are likely to be migrating normally; thus they are not vagrants there, but they may be vagrants on the central Aleutians and Bering Sea islands.

Similarly, southern border regions of the United States may straddle the periphery of the regular range of some species whose low density in North America (compounded by low observer coverage across this vast area) qualifies them as 'rare birds' if not vagrants, even though they are 'supposed' to be there. Examples include Berylline Hummingbird, Aztec Thrush, and the possible molt-migration of Plain-capped Starthroat.

Where Do North American Vagrants Come From?

We consider vagrants to North America as having 3 main points of origin, while recognizing that this is a somewhat simplistic view: Old World (138–139 species in the period, through summer 2011; 53%), New World (86–87 species; 33%), and pelagic (37 species; 14%); the one species of uncertain origin is Gray-hooded Gull, coming from Africa or South America. Within these 3 categories many subgroups can be distinguished, and in examining these lower-level groupings one finds interesting patterns that often link disparate taxa. Here we summarize vagrancy by points of origin and possible vectors of vagrancy.

Old World Species (Tables 3–5)

As a generalization, and as one might expect, species from East Asia occur mainly as vagrants in western North America, whereas those from Western Eurasia occur mainly in eastern North America. But within these broader groupings there are some interesting patterns with respect to the geography (both Old World origin and North American occurrence) and seasonality of vagrants. Given the proximity of East Asia to Alaska, and the prevailing west-to-east flow of weather systems at mid-latitudes, it is unsurprising that 72% of Old World vagrants to North America originate in East Asia, and only 15% in Western Eurasia; the remaining 13% are species of widespread distribution and probably have reached North America from both directions.

One pattern that crops up repeatedly is of species originating in East Asia tending to fan out across North America from west to east, and thus East Coast records of widespread Eurasian species may not necessarily involve birds coming across the Atlantic. While an East Asian origin for records in eastern North America is clearly most likely for species such as Lesser Sand Plover, Great Knot, Red-necked Stint, Long-billed Murrelet, and Brown Shrike, it may not be so obvious for species that are also common in Western Eurasia and could come from either direction, such as Smew, Terek Sandpiper, Spotted Redshank, Little Stint, and Brambling. Plotting records of this last species exemplifies the west-to-east pattern (Fig. 19). As well as being of interest for its own, sake, an appreciation of this pattern may help shed light indirectly on other species. For example, Brambling is more than 3 times as numerous as Common Chaffinch in Iceland but is unrecorded in Greenland or Newfoundland; thus it seems likely that most or all records of Brambling in the East come from East Asia, which would not be a source for records of chaffinch. Such data lends support to the argument that most North American records of chaffinches pertain to escaped cage birds.

Spring records of most East Asian species in Alaska mostly involve drift displacement (mainly of coastal migrants), with smaller numbers of overshoots (mainly interior migrants). Fall records in Alaska mostly involve drift displacement (coastal and overwater migrants) and misorientation (interior species). Fall records of East Asian species in western North America likely result from a combination of drift and misorientation, in some cases compounded by association; spring occurrences in the West mainly or wholly reflect birds that arrived the previous fall and overwintered in the New World.

In eastern North America, most Old World species arrive by the northern Atlantic route (Figs. 6–7, pp. 8–9), via drift displacement from northwestern Europe (such as migrants headed to Iceland in spring). Fewer species come indirectly via the southern route (Fig. 8, p. 10), having been displaced in fall across the tropical Atlantic to the eastern Caribbean and northeastern South America. Few if any species make an unaided crossing of the central North Atlantic.

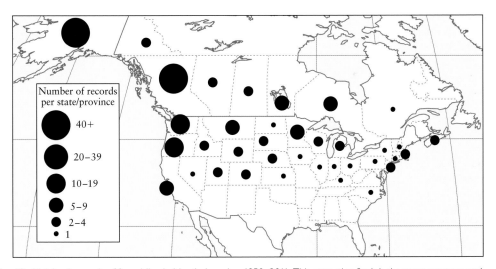

Fig. 19. Mainland records of Brambling in North America, 1950–2011. This attractive finch is the most common and widespread Eurasian vagrant passerine occurring in mainland North America, and is thus not rare enough to earn a place in the main body of this book. It provides some of the best passerine evidence for presumed west-to-east dispersal on the part of vagrants coming from Northeast Asia. Its relative abundance is due in part to its late season distribution, with most records during Nov–Mar. At such times, seed-eating birds are often driven to feeders, where their detection is much more likely than would be the case for a migrant simply passing through some random area, where it might stay only a day or two.

The lack of records from Newfoundland, a likely first landfall for Bramblings coming across the North Atlantic from Western Europe, suggests that even Bramblings in eastern North America (possible escaped cage birds excepted) may have originated in Northeast Asia; we suspect the uptick of records in the Northeast is an artifact of a coastal concentration effect compounded by large numbers of observers. This pattern gives support to the idea that other Asian strays recorded in the East (e.g., Brown Shrike, Siberian Rubythroat, Siberian Stonechat) followed the same route. The concentration of Brambling records in the Pacific Northwest may be partly due to drift of birds across the Northeast Pacific (e.g., as suggested by numerous records from the Queen Charlotte Islands, British Columbia), rather than birds filtering into North America through Alaska, which more likely accounts for most mid-continent and eastern records.

Table 3. East Asian waterfowl and shorebirds recorded as rare birds in North America (through summer 2011), comparing seasonal occurrence in the western Aleutians, Pribilofs, St. Lawrence Island (SLI), mainland Alaska, the Northwest, California, and other regions (MX: Mexico). Parentheses indicate geographic origin uncertain (possibly from Western Eurasia; see Table 5).

Records are summarized by season; when a distinct difference in frequency between seasons is apparent within an area, lower case abbreviations indicate the season(s) with fewer records; for example, Sp, f indicates mainly spring records but one or more fall records. Seasons linked by a dash reflect records that appear to be part of the same pattern; seasons separated by commas (such as Sp-s, F-W) reflect patterns that may have different causes (e.g., spring-summer drift vagrants vs. fall-winter misorientation). Sp: spring (Mar–Jun); S: summer (Jun–Jul); F: fall (Aug–Nov; Jul–Nov for waterbirds); W: winter (Dec–Feb); Sp–W indicates records year-round or in all seasons, with no clear peak season (see species accounts for details).

	W. Al.	Pribs.	SLI	AK	NW	CA	Other/Season
Whooper Swan	F–Sp, s	Sp–S	Sp–S	Sp–S, F	F–Sp	F–Sp	(East/Sp–W)
Tundra B. Goose	Sp	Sp	Sp		F		(QC/F)
Taiga B. Goose	F–W	Sp				W	IA, NE/W–Sp, (QC/F)
Lesser Wh.-fr. Goose	Sp						
Falcated Duck	Sp–s, f	Sp			W	F–Sp	
E. Spot-billed Duck	Sp, F			F-W			
Garganey	Sp–s, F	Sp, F		F	Sp, F	Sp, F–w	MX/W–Sp, (East/Sp, f)
Baikal Teal	F	F		Sp–S	F–Sp	F–Sp	AZ/F–
Com. Pochard	Sp	Sp	Sp	Sp		W	(QC/Sp)
Smew	Sp–s, F–W			s, F–Sp	W–Sp	W–Sp	(East/W–Sp)
N. Lapwing	F						(East/F–W, sp–s)
Euro. Golden Plover				W (S)			(Northeast/Sp, f)
Les. Sand Plover	Sp–s, f	sp–s, F	sp, F	S–F	F	F	East/F
Gr. Sand Plover					W–Sp		(FL/Sp)
Little Ring. Plover	Sp						
Eurasian Dotterel	F		Sp	Sp–S, F	F	F–w	MX/W–Sp
Black-winged Stilt	Sp	Sp					
Jack Snipe		Sp, F	Sp	F	F–W	W	(NL/W)
Solitary Snipe	Sp	F					
Pin-tailed Snipe	Sp						
Common Snipe	Sp–s, f	Sp–s, f	Sp, f			W	(NL/W)
Black-t. Godwit	Sp	Sp–s	Sp–s	S			(East/Sp–s, f–w)
Little Curlew			Sp		Sp	F	
Eastern Curlew	Sp–s	Sp			F		
Spot. Redshank	Sp, F	Sp, F			F, Sp, w	F, Sp	(East/F–w, sp)
	W. Al.	Pribs.	SLI	AK	NW	CA	Other/Season

Table 3. Cont.

	W. Al.	Pribs.	SLI	AK	NW	CA	Other/Season
Marsh Sandpiper	F	F					MX/F
Com. Greenshank	Sp, f	Sp, f	Sp	Sp		F	(Northeast/ Sp, f–w)
Green Sandpiper	Sp, f		Sp				
Wood Sandpiper	Sp, f	Sp, f	Sp, f	Sp–s	F	Sp	MX/F–W, (East/F, sp)
Terek Sandpiper	Sp, f	Sp, f	Sp, f	Sp–S	F	F	(East/S–F)
Com. Sandpiper	Sp, f	Sp, f	Sp	Sp			
Gray-t. Tattler	sp, F	sp, F	sp, F	Sp–S, f	F	Sp, F	
Great Knot	Sp	Sp, f	Sp, f	Sp	F		WV/F
Little Stint	sp, F	sp, F	Sp	Sp-S	sp, F	sp, F	MX/F, (East/F, sp)
Temminck's Stint	Sp, f	sp, F	Sp, f	S	F		
Long-toed Stint	Sp, f	Sp, f	Sp, f		F	F	
Spoon-b. Sandpiper	Sp	F		S	F		
Broad-b. Sandpiper	F	F					Northeast/F
Oriental Pratincole	Sp		Sp				
	W. Al.	Pribs.	SLI	AK	NW	CA	Other/Season

EAST ASIA (Tables 3–4; see Fig. 5 on p. 8 and Figs. 11–12 on p. 11)

We treat 117 species of vagrants (through summer 2011) with origins in East Asia: 51 waterbirds (55% of them shorebirds) and 66 landbirds (74% passerines); 14–17 of the waterbirds and 4 of the landbirds also occur as transatlantic vagrants from populations originating in Western Eurasia. Of the 117 East Asian vagrants, 44% of the waterbirds and 64% of the landbirds have been recorded only in Alaska, which likely reflects the stronger flying capabilities and more conspicuous nature of waterbirds; 51 East Asian vagrants have been found in the West, half of them known from only 1–2 records away from Alaska, and 2 of them unrecorded in Alaska (Greater Sand Plover, Blue Rock Thrush). Some 14–16 species of presumed East Asian origin have also reached eastern North America, including 3 species as yet unrecorded in the West outside of Alaska (Broad-billed Sandpiper, Siberian Rubythroat,

Yellow-browed Warbler) and one species (Citrine Wagtail) unrecorded even in Alaska. (There is, however, a record of Yellow-browed Warbler from northwest Mexico, and, as this book went to press, a Citrine Wagtail was found in British Columbia.)

Commoner in Alaska in Spring. In Alaska overall, 63 species of East Asian vagrants (56% landbirds) have been recorded more frequently in spring than fall (with 24 of them known there only from spring–summer records). These species occur primarily via drift vagrancy to the western islands, especially the Aleutians, with decreasing numbers recorded on the central Aleutians and Bering Sea islands. Only a handful of species occur more frequently in spring on the Bering Sea islands than the Aleutians; these comprise mainly species that migrate inland but which may overshoot or get drifted into the northern Bering Sea (e.g., Great Knot, Siberian Stonechat, Dusky Warbler). In fall, however, at

Table 4. East Asian passerines recorded as rare birds in North America (through summer 2011), comparing seasonal occurrence in the western Aleutians, Pribilofs, St. Lawrence Island (SLI), mainland Alaska, the Northwest, California, and other regions (MX: Mexico). See Table 3 for key.

	W. Al.	Pribs.	SLI	AK	NW	CA	Other/Season
Asian Brown Flycat.	Sp		Sp				
Dark-sided Flycat.	Sp, f	Sp					
Gray-streaked Flycat.	Sp, f	Sp, F					
Spotted Flycat.			F				
Narcissus Flycat.	Sp						
Mugimaki Flycat.	Sp						
Taiga Flycat.	Sp	Sp, F	Sp, F			F	
Brown Shrike	Sp, f	F	sp, F	F	F–W		NS/F
Sibe. Accentor	F		F	W, Sp	F–Sp		
Rufous-t. Robin	Sp	Sp					
Sibe. Rubythroat	Sp, f	Sp	Sp	Sp			ON/W
Sibe. Blue Robin	Sp						YT/Sp
Red-flank. Bluetail	Sp, f	sp, F	F	Sp		F	
Sibe. Stonechat			Sp, f	F		F	NB/F
Blue Rock Thrush					Sp		
Eyebrow. Thrush	Sp, f	Sp, f	Sp, f	Sp		Sp	
Dusky Thrush	Sp, f	Sp	Sp	F	F–Sp, s		
Fieldfare			(Sp)	(Sp)	(W)		(East/F–Sp)
Redwing				F	W		(East/W–Sp, s)
Lanceolated Warbler	Sp–F					F	
Mid. Grassh. Warbler	Sp–s, f	S	s, F				
Sedge Warbler			F				
Blyth's Reed Warb.			F				
Les. Whitethroat			F				
Dusky Warbler	F	sp, F	sp, F	F		F	MX/F
Willow Warbler			F				
Wood Warbler	F	F					
Yellow-brow. Warb.	F	F	F				WI/F, MX/Sp
Pallas' Leaf Warb.			F				
Kamchat. Leaf Warb.	Sp,f						
Citrine Wagtail							MS/W
Gray Wagtail	Sp, f	Sp, f	Sp		F	F	
	W. Al.	**Pribs.**	**SLI**	**AK**	**NW**	**CA**	**Other/Season**

Table 4. Cont.

	W. Al.	Pribs.	SLI	AK	NW	CA	Other/Season
Tree Pipit			Sp, F	Sp			
Olive-back. Pipit	Sp–s, f	Sp, f	Sp, f	S		F	MX/F, NV/Sp,
Pechora Pipit	Sp	F	sp, F				
Eurasian Skylark	Sp–F	Sp–F	Sp, F	Sp	F	F–W	
Pine Bunting	F						
Yellow-browed Bunting			F				
Little Bunting	F	F	sp, F			F	MX/F
Rustic Bunting	Sp, F	Sp, f	Sp, f	F–Sp	F–Sp	F–W	
Yellow-thr. Bunting	Sp						
Yellow-breast. Bunting	Sp		Sp, F				
Gray Bunting	Sp						
Pallas's Bunting	Sp		sp, F	Sp			
Reed Bunting	Sp		F				
Com. Rosefinch	Sp, f	Sp–s	Sp, f	S		F	
Eurasian Siskin	Sp						
Orient. Greenfinch	Sp-s, f	Sp				W–Sp	
Eurasian Bullfinch	Sp, f	f	Sp, f	F–Sp			
Hawfinch	Sp–s	Sp–s	Sp	Sp, W			
	W. Al.	Pribs.	SLI	AK	NW	CA	Other/Season

least 7 of the spring drift species are recorded more frequently on the Bering Sea islands than the Aleutians: Lesser Sand Plover, Taiga Flycatcher, Red-flanked Bluetail, Middendorff's Grasshopper Warbler, Pechora Pipit, Yellow-breasted Bunting, and Reed Bunting. Some 21 of the species commoner in spring than fall in Alaska have been recorded south into the West (57% waterbirds), 6 in fall–winter (e.g., Falcated Duck, Dusky Thrush), 15 in fall (9 shorebirds, 6 passerines), and only 2 in spring (Wood Sandpiper, Little Curlew; both recorded also in fall, when more frequent in the West).

In spring–summer, 23 species of East Asian vagrants (70% waterbirds) have reached the Alaska mainland, mainly the far west (such as the Seward Peninsula) or the north slope. Away from Alaska, spring records of East Asian vagrants in western North America are very rare and presumably reflect birds returning north after overwintering in the New World. Records involve species known or presumed to have overwintered in North America (e.g., Baikal Teal, Eurasian Dotterel, Siberian Accentor, Dusky Thrush, Rustic Bunting), as well as spring migrants presumed to have wintered mainly or wholly south of the United States (e.g., Garganey, Spotted Redshank, Wood Sandpiper, Siberian Blue Robin, Eyebrowed Thrush, Olive-backed Pipit).

Equal Spring and Fall Abundance in Alaska. Of the 20 species (70% waterbirds) recorded with about the same frequency in Alaska in spring–summer and fall–winter, most have been found on the Aleutians and Bering Sea islands about equally in spring and fall, but 4 have been found more often on the Aleutians in spring and more often on the Bering Sea islands in fall (Gray Heron, Solitary Snipe, Oriental

Cuckoo, Brown Shrike). Several of these 20 species have occurred south into the West in fall (or fall–winter, indicated by an asterisk), and include *Garganey, *Smew, White-winged Tern, *Jack Snipe, *Common Crane, Northern Hobby, *Brown Shrike, and *Eurasian Skylark.

Commoner in Alaska in Fall. Of the 26 species (77% landbirds) that are commoner overall in Alaska in fall than spring (19 known only from fall), most have been found more frequently on the Bering Sea islands than on the Aleutians (9 unrecorded in fall on the Aleutians). Some 7 of the 'commoner in fall' species have also been recorded in the West in fall (or fall–winter, indicated by an asterisk): *Baikal Teal, Gray-tailed Tattler, *Little Stint, Eurasian Kestrel, *Siberian Accentor, Dusky Warbler, and Little Bunting; 2 others (Marsh Sandpiper, Yellow-browed Warbler) have occurred just south of the region, in Mexico.

Other. The remaining 8 East Asian vagrants comprise 3 species that often remain for long periods in Alaska, especially the Aleutians, and for which most arrival dates are uncertain (Eastern Spot-billed Duck, White-tailed Eagle, Steller's Sea-Eagle); 2 species known from unda-ted remains (Hen Harrier, Gray Nightjar); and 3 species recorded only outside Alaska, 2 in winter in the United States (Greater Sand Plover, Citrine Wagtail), and 1 in spring in Canada (Blue Rock Thrush).

WESTERN EURASIA-AFRICA (Table 5; see Figs. 6–8 on pp. 8–10)

Through summer 2011, we consider 41–44 species of vagrants to North America as having origins in Western Eurasia: 27–30 waterbirds (52% of them shorebirds) and 14 landbirds (57% nonpasserines). One species recorded in the East (Gray-hooded Gull) may have come from Africa and/or South America; 17 of the waterbirds and 4 of the landbirds also occur as vagrants in western North America, from populations presumably originating in East Asia.

Given adverse, prevailing westerly winds at mid-latitudes over the vast North Atlantic, most Western Eurasian species appear to arrive in North America by one of two routes. The first is via a shorter, high-latitude northern route of 2300–3500 km from northwestern Europe to eastern Canada, with prevailing easterly winds. The second is indirect via a fall crossing of the tropical Atlantic to the eastern Caribbean and northeastern South America, assisted by easterly trade winds (a flight of about 5000 km from southwestern Europe, or 3000 km from West Africa); after wintering successfully, birds then migrate north into the East in spring.

Northern Route. At least 22 species of Old World vagrants presumably reached North America via a northern route; a further 10 species may also have arrived via a northern route but some of these may have originated in East Asia or perhaps crossed the Atlantic via central or southern routes. Of the 22 confirmed northern route species, 65% have occurred mainly or entirely in fall–winter, with mid-winter species often escaping from freezing winter weather in Europe. Another 4–5 species (all shorebirds) are known wholly or mainly in spring, and were likely displaced and drifted off course from their migration to Iceland and Greenland.

A few European species occur as rare fall vagrants to Iceland (e.g., Spotted Flycatcher, Lesser Whitethroat, Barred Warbler *Sylvia nisoria*, Willow Warbler), which might suggest these could occur as vagrants to the East Coast via the northern route. However, given the timing of fall Iceland records, and the normal migration routes of these species, we suspect that Icelandic occurrences represent reverse migration (see pp. 10–14). If this is the case, a continued reverse heading would take these species farther to the northwest, over Greenland, and well away from the East Coast (and cf. the Gray Wagtail record from Arctic Canada). For a bird on such a path to reach the Northeast would require exactly the right (and unlikely) combination of weather conditions, a 'perfect storm' for vagrancy.

Central Route. A few species may cross the North Atlantic at mid-latitudes, including strong-flying birds drifted in spring from West Africa (such as Common Swift and Common House Martin), Yellow-legged Gull in fall from the Mid-Atlantic Azores (2000–2500 km from NL), and some species perhaps or certainly with ship assistance (such as Red-footed Falcon, European Turtle Dove, and Common Cuckoo in spring–summer; Gray Heron and Western Marsh Harrier in late fall). It is also possible that some species reaching Bermuda in fall (about 5000 km from western Europe) may be subsequently drifted north to the Northeast when they attempt to continue south from Bermuda, as with Gray Heron and Corncrake.

Table 5. Seasonal occurrence patterns in the East, and possible transatlantic routes (nothern, central, southern; see Figs. 6–8) for 41–44 North American rare birds presumably or possibly originating in Western Eurasia (through summer 2011). Records are summarized by season; see Table 3 for key. Parentheses indicate geographic origin uncertain with respect to which Atlantic route was taken, or, in some cases, origin possibly from East Asia (see Table 3).

Species known *in the East* only by single records in the period are indicated in italics. Record(s) involving known ship assistance are indicated by #; those likely involving ship assistance are indicated by #?.

	Northern	Central	Southern
Tundra Bean Goose	(F)		
Pink-footed Goose	F–Sp		
Greylag Goose	Sp, F–W		
Common Shelduck	F–W		
Ruddy Shelduck	S		
Garganey			Sp, f
Common Pochard			(Sp)
Smew	(F–W)		
Yellow-legged Gull		F–Sp, s	
White-winged Tern			Sp–S, f
Whiskered Tern			S–F
Northern Lapwing	F–W, sp		
European Golden Plover	Sp, f		
Eurasian Oystercatcher	Sp, f		
Eurasian Woodcock	W		
Jack Snipe	W		
Common Snipe	W		
Black-tailed Godwit	Sp, f		
Eurasian Curlew	F–W, sp		
Spotted Redshank			Sp (f)
Common Redshank	Sp		
Common Greenshank	(Sp, f) w		Sp (f)
Wood Sandpiper			(Sp)
Terek Sandpiper			F
Little Stint			F, sp
Gray Heron	(F)#?	F#	
Little Egret			Sp–F
Western Reef Heron			Sp–F
Corncrake	(F)	(F)	
Eurasian Coot	W		
	Northern	**Central**	**Southern**

Table 5. Cont.

	Northern	Central	Southern
Western Marsh Harrier		(W) #?	(W) #?
Eurasian Kestrel	F–W#? (sp)#?	(sp) #?	
Red-footed Falcon	(F)#?	(F)#?	
Eurasian Hobby	(sp)#?	(sp)#?	
Common Swift	(S)	(S)	(Sp)
Eurasian Jackdaw	F–W#, sp–s#?		
Eurasian Blackbird	F		
Fieldfare	F–W, w–sp		
Redwing	F–Sp, s		
Song Thrush	F		
Common Chaffinch	F–W, Sp		
	Northern	Central	Southern

Southern Route. At least some individuals of 9 species are presumed to have reached eastern North America via a southern route (see Fig. 8 on p. 10), and some or all individuals of at least a further 5 species may have come that way. These species are almost all long-distance migrants that winter in sub-Saharan Africa; they have been detected in the East mainly in spring–summer, largely from the Mid-Atlantic Coast northward. Most fall records presumably reflect birds migrating back south after summering in the New World. The greater number of fall versus spring records in the East of Terek Sandpiper, Little Stint, White-winged Tern, and Whiskered Tern may reflect more coastal shorebirding in fall than spring, in combination with the propensity for fall migrants to linger (and thus be detected). This is in contrast to a typically quicker and shorter spring migration, much of which may occur offshore. In addition, some rare fall shorebirds in the East (such as some Spotted Redshanks and Little Stints) may be coming across the North American continent from East Asia.

New World Species (Tables 6–8)

These 86–87 species (through summer 2011) can be viewed broadly as having 'mainland' origins (in Mexico and the New World tropics; 81%) or 'island' origins (from the Bahamas and the Caribbean; 19%). Unlike Old World vagrants, most New World vagrants are not long-distance migrants, and the potential of escaped cage birds

also plays a greater role than it does for Old World and pelagic species. Moreover, the differing degrees of migration and seasonal movement among species and populations are often poorly known, making it challenging to interpret patterns of occurrence in North America. Patterns can also be difficult to discern if arrival dates are unknown because of a species' retiring nature, because of seasonal or infrequent observer coverage in some regions, or because only a single record exists with little or no context. Examples of records that are difficult to categorize include those of Bare-throated Tiger-Heron, Sungrebe, Double-striped Thick-knee, Collared Plover, Double-toothed Kite, Mottled Owl, Amazon Kingfisher, Bahama Woodstar, and Greenish Elaenia. This being said, several patterns can be discerned and most species can be placed into one or more categories, which may vary within a species by region or by season of occurrence.

MAINLAND (Tables 6–7)

We treat 69–70 species as vagrants from the mainland New World region, 15–16 of them waterbirds and 54 landbirds. Of these totals, at least 47 landbirds and 7 waterbirds originate in Mexico and northern Central America (Table 6), whereas 6–8 landbirds and 7–8 waterbirds originate in S America; 1 species of waterbird (Gray-hooded Gull) may involve a South American or African origin, and 1 passerine (Red-legged Honeycreeper) may involve a Mexican or

Table 6. Seasonal occurrence by region (through summer 2011) for 54 North American rare birds presumed to have come from Mexico. Species known only from single records *originating in Mexico* are indicated in italics. Not surprisingly, most records of Mexican vagrants are from AZ or TX. The elsewhere column summarizes other regions of occurrence in North America; for the 3 species unrecorded in AZ or TX (Sungrebe, Xantus's Hummingbird, Mangrove Swallow), seasons of occurrence are noted in parentheses. Species recorded elsewhere in North America but originating from possibly (or certainly) different regions are not included; for example, FL records of Ruddy Quail-Dove and Yellow-faced Grassquit from the Caribbean, or widespread White-collared Swifts and Piratic Flycatchers of unknown geographic origin.

Records are summarized by season (see Table 3 for key). Sp: spring (Mar–May/early Jun); S: summer (Jun–Jul); F: fall (Aug–Nov); W: winter (Dec–Feb/Mar).

	Arizona	Texas	Elsewhere
Masked Duck		F–Sp, s	LA
Sungrebe			NM (F)
Double-striped Thick-knee		W	
Collared Plover		Sp	
Bare-throated Tiger Heron		W	
Jabiru		S–F	East
Northern Jacana	S–F	F–Sp, s	
Double-toothed Kite		Sp	
Crane Hawk		W	
Roadside Hawk		f–W	
Collared Forest Falcon		W	
Mottled Owl		W, S	
Stygian Owl		W	
Green Violetear		Sp–F	East, West
Green-breasted Mango		s–F–W, sp	East
Xantus's Hummingbird			BC, CA (F–W)
Berylline Hummingbird	Sp–F	F, sp–s	NM
Cinnamon Hummingbird	F		NM
Plain-capped Starthroat	sp–S–F		NM
White-collared Swift		W–Sp	
Mangrove Swallow			FL (F)
Ruddy Quail-Dove		Sp	
Eared Quetzal	Sp–F–w		NM
Amazon Kingfisher		W	
Greenish Elaenia		Sp	
Mexican Tufted Flycatcher	W–Sp, S	F–W, sp	
Nutting's Flycatcher	F–Sp		CA
Piratic Flycatcher		F	
	Arizona	**Texas**	**Elsewhere**

Table 6. Cont.

	Arizona	Texas	Elsewhere
Social Flycatcher		W–Sp	
Gray-collared Becard	S		
Masked Tityra		W	
Yucatan Vireo		Sp	
Sinaloa Wren	F, Sp		
Brown-backed Solitaire	S, F		
Orange-bill. N.-Thrush		Sp	SD
Black-headed N.-Thrush		Sp–F	
White-throated Thrush		W–Sp	
Rufous-backed Thrush	F–W–sp, s	F–W–sp	CA, NM
Aztec Thrush	S–F, w, sp	F–W, sp	NM
Blue Mockingbird	W–Sp	Sp, F	CA, NM
Gray Silky		F–W	
Crescent-chested Warbler	Sp–S, F–W	Sp	
Gray-crowned Yellowthroat		Sp–W	
Fan-tailed Warbler	Sp–s, f	F	NM
Rufous-capped Warbler	Sp–W	Sp–W	NM
Golden-crowned Warbler		F–W, sp	NM
Slate-throated Whitestart	Sp	Sp, s–f	NM
Flame-colored Tanager	Sp–F	Sp–F, w	
Crimson-collared Grosbeak		F–Sp, s	
Mexican Yellow Grosbeak	Sp–S, f		NM
Eastern Blue Bunting		F–Sp	LA
Yellow-faced Grassquit		W–Sp, S, F	
Black-vented Oriole	Sp	Sp–F, w, sp	
Streak-backed Oriole	F–W, sp–s	F	West, East
	Arizona	**Texas**	**Elsewhere**

Caribbean origin. Species with possible shared origins between Mexico and South America are White-collared Swift, Piratic Flycatcher, and Fork-tailed Flycatcher; and 4 species (Masked Duck, Ruddy Quail-Dove, White-collared Swift, Yellow-faced Grassquit) also have known or presumed Caribbean origins.

Of 54 species coming from Mexico, most have been found mainly or wholly in Arizona (21 species) and Texas (44 species), with fewer in other border states, and only 8 known from more distant points in the East and West (Table 6). In Arizona, 62% of species are known mainly or wholly from records in spring–summer, and are typically species from the mountains and foothills of northwest Mexico; only 24% are known mainly or wholly from fall–winter records. Conversely, in Texas only 29% of

Table 7. Seasonal occurrence in North America (through summer 2011) of rare birds originating in South America or southern Central America; species in parentheses may originate in Mexico and northern Central America. Total number of records per species given in parentheses.

	West	East
White-f. Wh. Duck (8)		Mar–Jun, Nov
Large-b. Tern (3)		May–Jul
S Lapwing (2)		Mar–Jun
(White-coll. Swift) (4)	(May)	(May–Jun)
Brown-ch. Martin (8)	Feb	Jun–Jul, Sep–Nov
Dark-b. Cuckoo (1)		Feb
Chilean Elaenia (1)		Feb
(Piratic Flycat.) (6)	(Apr, Sep)	(Mar, Sep–Oct)
Variegated Flycat. (4)	Sep	May, Oct–Nov
Cr. Slaty Flycat. (1)		Jun
Fork-tail. Flycat. (160+)	Jun, Aug–Sep	Apr–Jul, Sep–Nov

species are known mainly or wholly from spring–summer records, with 58% mainly or wholly in fall–winter. This difference largely reflects different climates in adjacent northwest Mexico (mainly dry in winter, lush in summer) and northeast Mexico (relatively wetter but colder in winter), and the shorter distance from Texas to the rich tropical avifauna in northeast Mexico.

Waterbirds. These species often exhibit patterns that reflect nomadic or irruptive dispersal, presumably related to changing water levels and perhaps to crashes in marine food supply. The occurrence patterns of some species appear linked to their routine tracking of seasonal water levels, such as Jabiru in summer-fall, Masked Duck in fall-winter, and Northern Jacana in fall (Arizona) and winter (Texas); these might then be considered overshoots that have gone a bit beyond their normal range. The spring–summer pattern (March–July) in the East shared by White-faced Whistling-Duck, Southern Lapwing, and Large-billed Tern coincides with the end of the dry season in areas of northern South America, suggesting these birds may be forced to disperse as wetlands dry up. The winter pattern (November–February) shared by Paint-billed

Crake, Spotted Rail, and Azure Gallinule also may be linked with seasonal water-level changes in South America. Belcher's Gull feeds in Humboldt Current waters that are prone to cyclic food crashes associated with El Niño events, and thus may be predisposed to occasional long-range vagrancy; this may apply in part to Kelp Gull, but that species has been expanding its range northward worldwide, and its occasional appearances in North America may represent incipient colonization events that have a broader base.

Landbirds. *Post-breeding and post-fledging dispersal.* The appearances in border regions of a few ostensibly resident species that breed not far to the south of the United States likely reflect post-breeding and post-fledging dispersal, mainly in fall. Once they have moved, individuals may remain in the United States for prolonged periods, sometimes staying to breed. Such species include Sinaloa Wren, Blue Mockingbird (Texas), Gray-crowned Yellowthroat, Rufous-capped Warbler, and perhaps Yellow-faced Grassquit (Texas). Other species, not treated in this book, that may fall into this category include Brown Jay, Tamaulipas Crow, and Black-capped Gnatcatcher.

FACULTATIVE MIGRANTS. Some Mexican species not usually viewed as conventional migrants exhibit nomadic and irregular, or irruptive, wandering in the nonbreeding season as facultative migrants, presumably in response to weather conditions and food supply. This phenomenon is more prevalent in east Mexico, where cold fronts can be severe, than in the relatively milder winter climate of west Mexico. Thus, most species associated with these winter wanderings are birds of northeast Mexico, although Blue Mockingbird, Rufous-backed Thrush, and Nutting's Flycatcher are examples from west Mexico. When cold weather forces birds downslope in search of food or warmer conditions, there is no conventional direction to these movements—downslope is the main drive, not necessarily southward, such that individuals may wander north into south Texas. Most of these species are passerines, mainly frugivores and insectivores, although it is possible that occurrences of other species (such as hawks and owls) may reflect the same conditions. Usually these species disappear in late winter or spring, presumably back to Mexico, but individuals of some species (marked with an asterisk) have been recorded in summer. Presumed facultative migrants

Table 8. Seasonal occurrence patterns and presumed origin of 20 Caribbean vagrants recorded as North American rare birds in Florida (through summer 2011). Species known only from single records *originating in the Caribbean* are indicated in italics. Seasonal status (see Table 3 for key) is given for FL; presumed or certain origin indicated by X (lower case x indicates confirmed but less frequent occurrence); and uncertain or possible origin by a question mark. Away from FL, White-faced Whistling-Duck has occurred in VA, and the Cuban subspecies of La Sagra's Flycatcher has been found in AL. Sp: spring (Mar–May/early Jun); S: summer (Jun–Jul); F: fall (Aug–Nov); W: winter (Dec–Feb/Mar).

	Florida	Bahamas	Cuba
White-cheeked Pintail	F–Sp, s	X	?
Masked Duck	F–Sp, s		X
Cuban Emerald	S–F, w, sp	X	?
Bahama Woodstar	Sp–F	X	
White-collared Swift	F		X
Antillean Palm Swift	S–F		X
Bahama Swallow	Sp–S, F	X	
Zenaida Dove	F–Sp, S	?	?
Key West Quail-Dove	Sp–S, F, w	?	?
Ruddy Quail-Dove	W		X
Cuban Pewee	F, w, sp	?	?
La Sagra's Flycatcher	F–Sp	X	?
Loggerhead Kingbird	Sp		X
Thick-billed Vireo	Sp, F	X	
Red-legged Thrush	Sp	X	
Bahama Mockingbird	Sp–s–f	X	
Bananaquit	F–Sp	X	
Western Spindalis	W, Sp, s, f	X	x
Yellow-faced Grassquit	w, Sp, s		X
Black-faced Grassquit	Sp, s, F, w	X	
	Florida	**Bahamas**	**Cuba**

include White-collared Swift, *Mexican Tufted Flycatcher, Social Flycatcher, Masked Tityra, Mangrove Swallow, Gray Silky, White-throated Thrush, *Rufous-backed Thrush, Blue Mockingbird (in the West), *Golden-crowned Warbler, *Crimson-collared Grosbeak, Eastern Blue Bunting, and perhaps Nutting's Flycatcher and Fork-tailed Flycatcher.

POST-BREEDING DISPERSAL OR FALL MISORIENTATION OF MIGRANTS. Individuals of some species apparently occur as misoriented post-breeding or post-fledging dispersers; the age of these birds has been recorded infrequently, but 1st-year birds may be commoner than adults. All of these species except the hummingbirds also occur as spring overshoots (see following), and in some cases (marked with an asterisk) individuals occasionally overwinter or attempt to do so. These species are *Eared Quetzal, Green Violetear, *Green-breasted Mango, *Aztec Thrush, *Crescent-chested Warbler, Fan-tailed Warbler, *Flame-colored Tanager, *Mexican

Yellow Grosbeak, and *Streak-backed Oriole. Plain-capped Starthroat may also fall into this category, although it may be a false vagrant if Arizona lies at the edge of its regular post-breeding molt-migration range. Some Piratic Flycatchers also fall into this category, given that a fall specimen from Texas is a 1st-year of the northern subspecies.

OVERSHOOTING AND MISORIENTED SHORTER-DISTANCE MIGRANTS. Some Mexican species are routinely migratory, at least at the northern edges of their range, and their spring/summer occurrences in the United States likely reflect overshooting spring migrants, perhaps linked in some cases with northward range expansion. Some of these species (marked with an asterisk) have attempted breeding in the border states, and many also occur as post-breeding wanderers (see preceding). These species are *Eared Quetzal, *Berylline Hummingbird, Orange-billed Nightingale-Thrush, Black-headed Nightingale-Thrush, *Crescent-chested Warbler, Slate-throated Whitestart, Fan-tailed Warbler, *Flame-colored Tanager, Mexican Yellow Grosbeak, Black-vented Oriole, and *Streak-backed Oriole. Some Piratic Flycatchers may be spring overshoots from Middle American popu-lations or perhaps reverse-migrating individuals from austral populations.

In some cases, spring vagrants might involve birds that misoriented northward from their wintering areas, perhaps a form of short-distance reverse migration. All examples in this category have occurred during mid-April to mid-May, namely Mexican Tufted Flycatcher in Arizona, Golden-crowned Warbler in Texas and New Mexico, and Aztec Thrush, Flame-colored Tana-ger, and Crimson-collared Grosbeak all from the Texas coast.

AUSTRAL MIGRANTS (Table 7; and see Fig. 15 on p. 13). A number of species (mainly insectivores) breeding in southern South America migrate north in the austral winter, analogous to the southward fall migration of numerous North American species. At least 6 species of austral migrants have on occasion occurred as rare birds in North America, usually in one or both of two periods that correspond to 'fall-winter' overshooting (during February–July, mainly April–June; all 6 species) or to misoriented 'spring' migration, which on occasion is com-pounded by drift (September–November; 3 species). Some North American records of

White-collared Swift and Piratic Flycatcher may pertain to austral migrants, but other records of these species are known to have involved birds with origins in Mexico and Central America. Both adults and 1st-year birds can be involved in North American records, but data are insufficient to discern age-related patterns.

A record that predates our period of coverage involves Lined Seedeater *Sporophila lineola*, an adult male (with tail feathers molting); the bird was collected on the Isle of Shoals, NH, 8 August 1935 (Jackson 1936). Although the record is seemingly dismissed as involving an escaped cage bird, Lined Seedeater is an austral migrant with breeding and nonbreeding distributions similar to those of South American species that have reached North America, and thus may be a plausible vagrant. Unlike other species, however, it does feature in the cage bird trade (although we have no data from the 1930s) and seems less likely to be capable of making long-distance flights.

Austral fall overshoots may be facilitated or enhanced by weather systems that also help drift some North American migrants northward in spring. Most austral vagrant records come from the East, but there are single western records of Brown-chested Martin and Variegated Flycatcher, and 2 records of Fork-tailed Flycatcher from as far west as California.

Fewer species have occurred as misoriented austral spring migrants, although Variegated Flycatcher and Fork-tailed Flycatcher are more numerous in North America at this season than in the austral fall. Relative to austral fall over-shoots, these reverse-migrants often occur farther north in North America, presumably because they are flying a distance commen-surate with their normal southbound migration rather than simply overshooting their non-breeding grounds.

ISLAND (Table 8)
We treat 21 species as vagrants from the Caribbean region, 3 of them waterbirds and 18 landbirds. As with mainland New World species, seasonal movements of Bahamian and Caribbean species (most of which are usually described in the literature as 'permanent resi-dents') are poorly known, making it difficult to infer potential causes of vagrancy; 4 species (Masked Duck, Ruddy Quail-Dove, White-collared Swift, Yellow-faced Grassquit) also

appear to have origins in mainland Mexico and have occurred in Texas. Red-legged Honeycreepers may come from Mexico or Cuba. Most species and individuals occurring in the United States probably originate in the Bahamas, with some also from Cuba and perhaps elsewhere in the Greater Antilles.

Waterbirds. White-cheeked Pintail and Masked Duck have a fall–spring (mainly winter) pattern of occurrence in central and south Florida, whereas the single West Indian Whistling-Duck was observed in spring, in Virginia.

Landbirds. Of 18 species of Caribbean landbirds that occurred in the period as rare birds in North America, 45% certainly or probably originated in the Bahamas, 28% in Cuba, 11% in both, and 16% in one or both (Table 8). All species have been recorded mainly or exclusively in southern Florida (Palm Beach, Broward, and Dade Counties) and the Florida Keys; a few individuals of 2 species (Cuban Emerald, Bananaquit) have been recorded farther north on the east coast of Florida, as is true of the recent record of Red-legged Thrush; a single Bananaquit and Western Spindalis have been found on the west coast of Florida; and a La Sagra's Flycatcher in Alabama (a September specimen, and the first North American record of the species). Species diversity is highest during spring and fall, with fewer records in winter and fewest in mid-summer, although how much this may reflect observer bias is unknown.

   WINTER. Some 5 species, mainly frugivores, have occurred mainly from fall through spring in southeast Florida and the Keys, with most arrivals in September–November and departures in March–May. Occurrences may be linked to post-breeding dispersal and winter wandering in response to fruit abundance and distribution.

   SPRING THROUGH FALL. The other 13 landbirds have occurred mostly from spring through fall (mainly March–October), and in some cases (such as both hummingbirds) records are too few or too scattered in time to allow finer patterns to be discerned. The occurrence in spring of a diverse range of species suggests that local (interisland?) migration may be more frequent than is generally recognized. It would be interesting to know the proportion of 1st-year birds involved in these spring records, but age data are unavailable for most individuals. Occurrences

in late summer and fall may involve post-breeding dispersal (including juveniles of Bahama Swallow and possibly Thick-billed Vireo) and perhaps, in the case of both swifts, hurricane-related displacement.

Pelagic Species (Table 9)

These 37 species (here including Swallow-tailed Gull and Black Noddy) can be viewed as having origins mainly in temperate and subantarctic Southern Hemisphere waters (32%) or in warmer subtropical and equatorial waters (68%). At least 7 species in the latter category, however, probably qualify as false vagrants due simply to limited coverage of North American offshore waters, namely Bermuda Petrel, Hawaiian Petrel, European Storm-Petrel, Red-tailed Tropicbird, Blue-footed Booby, Red-footed Booby, and Black Noddy. The patterns of records for such species indicate that North America is part of their normal range, although in some cases the number of individuals occurring annually may be very small (as with European Storm-Petrel or Black Noddy). Other than the irruptive Blue-footed Booby and perhaps Red-footed Booby, observers could target these species and have a reasonable chance of encountering them in the right season and location.

TEMPERATE SOUTHERN HEMISPHERE

Some 12 species of pelagic seabird vagrants have ranges that ordinarily do not extend into the Northern Hemisphere (Table 9). Most of these species are exceptional in North America, and the vectors of their vagrancy are difficult to divine. Misorientation by 1st-year birds (including perhaps reverse migration) and exploratory wandering by prebreeding immatures, perhaps in some cases with storm-related assistance, may have brought about transfer into the wrong hemisphere of most albatrosses and of White-chinned and Gray-faced petrels. Some individuals have likely remained for years in the 'wrong' hemisphere, where they have recalibrated their migration and molt schedules. Black-bellied Storm-Petrels may on occasion range into the Northern Hemisphere, with western North Atlantic waters being at the very edge of their 'normal' range.

SUBTROPICAL AND EQUATORIAL

Some 18 rare pelagic seabirds in North America breed or range regularly into equatorial and Northern Hemisphere waters (Table 9).

Table 9. Origins and seasonal occurrence patterns of 37 pelagic seabirds recorded as rare birds in North America (through summer 2011); species known only from single records are indicated in italics. Records are summarized by season (see Table 3 for key). Species marked with an asterisk breed only in the N Hemisphere; status marked with # indicates at least some records involve known ship assistance.

	Pacific		Atlantic	
	Temperate/Subantarctic	Subtropical/Equatorial	Temperate/Subantarctic	Subtropical/Equatorial
Wedge-t. Shearwater		F, w, sp		
Streaked Shearwater*		F		
Cape Verde Shearwater*				F
Barolo Shearwater*				F
Newell's Shearwater		F		
Bermuda Petrel*				Sp–F
Zino's Petrel				F
Stejneger's Petrel		F, sp		
Hawaiian Petrel*		Sp–F		
Solander's Petrel		F		
Gray-faced Petrel	S–F			
Parkinson's Petrel		F		
White-chinned Petrel	F		F, sp	
Bulwer's Petrel		F		Sp–F
W Yellow-n. Albatross			Sp–F, w	
Black-browed Albatross			S–F, w–sp	
Tasmanian Shy Albatross	F			
Auckland Shy Albatross	F			
Salvin's Albatross	F			
Chatham Albatross	S			
Antipodes Albatross	F			
Gibson's Albatross	S			
Light-m. Sooty Albatross	S			
Euro. Storm-Petrel*				Sp, f
Wedge-r. Storm-Petrel		F, w		
Tristram's Storm-Petrel*		Sp–S		
Swinhoe's Storm-Petrel*				S–F
Hornby's Storm-Petrel		F		
Black-bell. Storm-Petrel			S–F	
Red-tailed Tropicbird		S–W		
Nazca Booby		Sp#		

Table 9. Cont.

	Pacific		Atlantic	
	Temperate/Subantarctic	Subtropical/Equatorial	Temperate/Subantarctic	Subtropical/Equatorial
Blue-footed Booby		S–F, w–sp		
Red-footed Booby		Sp–F#, w		Sp–F
Great Frigatebird		F, sp		
Lesser Frigatebird		S–F		
Swallow-tailed Gull		Sp–S		
Black Noddy				Sp–F

These species are mainly birds of subtropical waters, and their occasional appearance in North America may be linked to food crashes, misorientation by immature birds, exploratory wandering by prebreeding immatures, and, in the case of frigatebirds and some Wedge-tailed and Streaked shearwaters, to displacement by storm systems (see Fig. 9 on p. 10). Waters associated with the Gulf Stream may be part of the regular range of Barolo Shearwater, Bulwer's Petrel, and Swinhoe's Storm-Petrel, which all may prove to be false vagrants when observer coverage of these areas becomes more frequent. Likewise, with greater coverage, it may be that Stejneger's Petrel, Solander's Petrel, and Streaked Shearwater are found to occur annually, or nearly so, and somewhat predictably in North American waters.

Topography, Molt, and Aging

Bird Topography

To describe birds and their plumages we use standard topography terms, shown in Figs. 20–21 (also see terms on pp. xvi–xvii). We use 'flight feathers' to refer to both the remiges (primaries and secondaries) and rectrices. Primaries are numbered from innermost (p1) to outermost (usually p10); secondaries are numbered from outermost (s1) inward to the tertials, and vary in number from 6 in swifts and hummingbirds to over 30 in albatrosses; rectrices are numbered from central (r1) to outermost (usually r5 or r6, depending on species).

Molts and Plumages

As in all birding, besides simply identifying a bird to species it can be interesting to determine the age and sex of an individual and note any details about its molt. In this way we can learn more about patterns of vagrancy. For example, how many Green Violetears appearing in the United States are 1st-year birds? Is the proportion of adult violetears higher in Texas than in areas farther north? Is the wing-molt timing of a vagrant albatross on a Southern Hemisphere schedule (suggesting it could be newly arrived) or has it switched to a Northern Hemisphere schedule (suggesting it has been here for a while)? How many of the Piratic Flycatchers found in fall are worn adults or fresh juveniles (and thus from northern-breeding populations) versus fresh adults and worn 1st-years (and thus from southern-breeding populations)? A basic understanding of molt and plumage sequence can help in gathering such data, and our species accounts offer some clues on these subjects. There is still much work to be done, however.

To describe molts we use the Humphrey-Parkes (H-P) system, as modified by Howell et al. (2003); also see Howell (2010a) for a fuller overview of molt. The molt and plumage cycles of all but a handful of species in the world are annual; that is, plumages are renewed by molt in a predictable manner on an annual basis. Every bird has a basic plumage, acquired once a year by a complete or near-complete prebasic molt. (Some long-winged birds, such as albatrosses and eagles, don't have time between breeding attempts to replace all of their flight feathers, which can require 2–3 molt cycles to be renewed.) In the modified H-P system, a bird's juvenile plumage (its first coat of 'real' or nondowny feathers) is equivalent to its 1st-basic plumage.

Fig. 20. Topography terms for waterbirds.

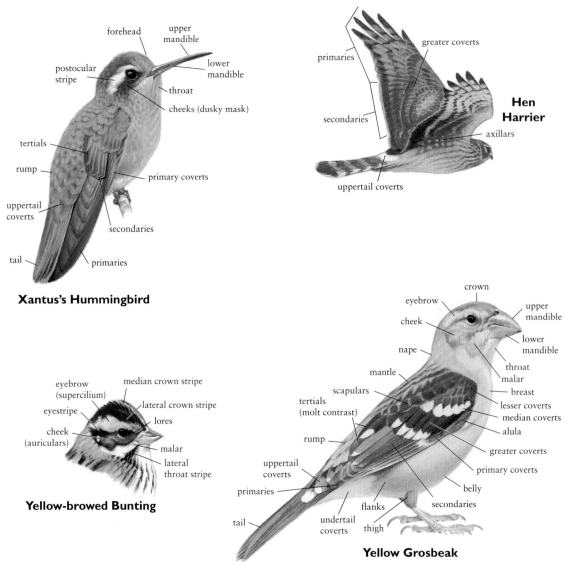

Fig. 21. Topography terms for landbirds.

Some species, including many shorebirds and gulls, and some songbirds, have a second plumage in their annual cycle. This is termed an alternate plumage. It alternates with the basic plumage and is acquired by a prealternate molt; the color and pattern of alternate plumage can be the same as basic plumage (as in some sparrows), duller than basic plumage (as in many ducks), or brighter than basic plumage (as in some passerines). Because of time and energy constraints, prealternate molts usually involve only head and body feathers, wing coverts, and sometimes tertials or rectrices; the main flight feathers and primary coverts are typically renewed only in prebasic molts.

Most small and some large species replace some (rarely all) of their juvenile feathers in their first few months of life (usually just head and body feathers, some to all secondary upperwing coverts, and sometimes one or more tertials and rectrices). This unique post-juvenile molt has no counterpart in subsequent plumage cycles and is termed a preformative molt, producing formative plumage. Formative plumage often looks much like adult plumage, as in most songbirds and shorebirds.

While it is helpful to understand the underlying patterns of molt, it is important to recognize that the processes governing molt and plumage coloration are independent (see Howell 2010a for discussion and examples). Thus, if a bird molts later than usual it may 'miss' the hormonal window in which its usual plumage color and pattern are produced. This phenomenon may occur more frequently in vagrants that are far from home or in the 'wrong' hemisphere. Moreover, if a bird is not healthy or not in breeding condition, its normally bright breeding plumage may not be acquired, and instead it can attain a dull plumage. First-year sandpipers offer a good example of this in their 1st summer; some are as bright as the brightest breeding adults, others look like nonbreeding adults, and others are variably intermediate—yet all are in alternate plumage. Because of the potential disconnect between molts and the appearance of a bird, we have chosen field-friendly terms to describe plumages—such as 1st-year male, or adult, or nonbreeding plumage, rather than trying to determine whether any given feathers are basic, alternate, or even formative.

Molt and Aging

Understanding molt patterns can help in determining a bird's age. For example, because preformative molts are rarely complete, the contrast (known as a molt contrast, or molt limit) between retained juvenile feathers and fresher formative feathers can be helpful in aging many birds in their 1st year of life (Fig. 22). Adults of most smaller species, including all passerines, have complete molts and thus do not show molt contrasts when they have completed molting. Among larger birds, however, such as herons, hawks, and seabirds, the strong juvenile plumage is often worn through the 1st year of life and thus 1st-year birds appear relatively uniform. Conversely, adults of such larger species may not have time to renew all of their flight feathers between breeding seasons; consequently, a bird showing molt contrasts within the primaries or secondaries is older than its 1st year (Fig. 23).

Because of factors such as life history (migration distance, diet, etc.), body size, and even ancestral relationships, the timing, extent, and location of molts within different groups of birds can vary considerably. All species, however, have only one of four fundamental molt strategies (Howell et al. 2003, Howell 2010a), and understanding a little about these can help in determining the age of any rare bird you encounter. However, if in doubt, saying 'age unknown' is the best course rather than overreaching based on partial or ambiguous information. Here we offer some clues to help in determining the age of species among the main groups of rare birds we treat. The four strategies are discussed below.

The *Simple Basic Strategy* (SBS) is the simplest molt strategy, in which a bird simply molts from one basic plumage to another every year and has no alternate or other plumages. The juvenile plumage (equivalent to 1st-basic) is relatively strong and is retained through the 1st year before a bird molts directly into 2nd-basic plumage, and so on. SBS is relatively uncommon and found in species such as petrels, larger hawks, and some swifts.

The *Complex Basic Strategy* (CBS) is the commonest molt strategy among modern birds. As in SBS, adults have only basic plumages, but in the 1st cycle a preformative molt (and formative plumage) are added to get the bird through its 1st year of life before the 2nd-prebasic molt, when it enters into the adult molt cycle at about a year of age. Examples of birds exhibiting CBS include geese, cranes, most herons, owls, pigeons, and all passerines that lack alternate plumages (e.g., swallows, many tyrant-flycatchers, vireos, thrushes, many warblers, and many sparrows).

The *Simple Alternate Strategy* (SAS) includes a prealternate molt (and alternate plumage) in the adult cycle, and in the 1st cycle a single molt is added, which often appears comparable to the adult prealternate molt. SAS is relatively rare, but is shown by large gulls.

The *Complex Alternate Strategy* (CAS) is the most complex molt strategy and features an alternate plumage in all cycles, plus a formative plumage in the 1st cycle. (It is thus like CBS with the addition of an alternate plumage.) Species exhibiting CAS include most ducks, most shorebirds, small gulls, terns, and all songbirds that have alternate plumages.

new 1st-winter (formative)
head, body, scapulars

Little Stint
1st-winter

Black Noddy
1st-cycle

retained juv wing
coverts and tertials

molt contrast

old juv
primaries

faded juv outer primaries
and wing coverts

Brambling

adult ♂
nonbreeding

coverts uniform
and no molt
contrast

1st-year ♀
(fall–winter)

molt contrast,
retained juv
outer coverts

Fig. 22. Incomplete or interrupted molts produce what is known as a molt contrast, which is a point of contrast between 2 generations of feathers in a non-molting bird (obviously, any bird actively molting will have 2 generations of feathers and thus show contrast). In many 1st-winter shorebirds, such as Little Stint, a contrast can often be seen between formative scapulars and retained juvenile upperwing coverts and tertials, or even within tertials and wing coverts. Species with protracted and typically complete preformative molts that are sometimes suspended, such as Black Noddy or Oriental Turtle Dove, can show an obvious contrast between fresh formative inner primaries and retained juvenile outer primaries. In many songbirds, such as Brambling, molt contrasts in 1st-year birds are seen most often within the greater coverts, where fresher inner feathers contrast with retained outer feathers (the outer coverts are relatively protected and thus more often retained). Molt contrasts can also occur quite frequently within the tertials (cf. Mexican Yellow Grosbeak in Fig. 21).

WATERFOWL

Waterfowl molts differ fundamentally between swans and geese on the one hand (with 1–2 molts a year) and typical ducks on the other (with 2–3 molts a year). All species have synchronous molt of their remiges and become flightless for at least 3–4 weeks during molt.

Adult swans and geese have a complete prebasic molt in late summer (wing molt, followed by head and body feathers) and appear to be in fairly uniform plumage through the winter. First-year swans and geese have a partial preformative molt from fall through spring (the timing and extent varies among species and individuals), involving mainly head and body feathers, and sometimes upperwing coverts. Thus, molt contrasts in winter (especially among feathers of the upperparts) indicate a 1st-year

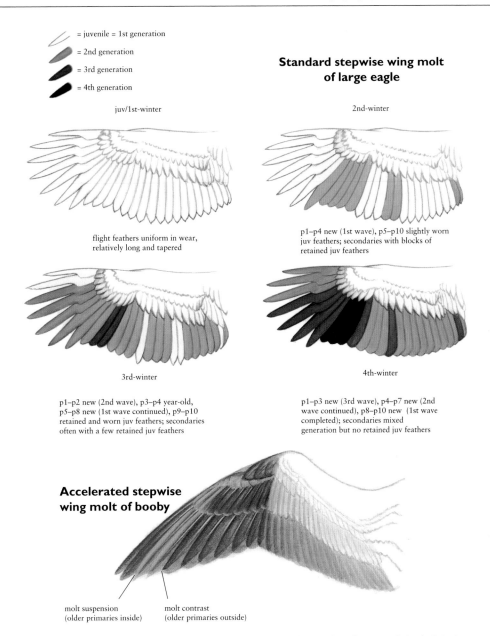

= juvenile = 1st generation

= 2nd generation

= 3rd generation

= 4th generation

Standard stepwise wing molt of large eagle

juv/1st-winter

flight feathers uniform in wear, relatively long and tapered

2nd-winter

p1–p4 new (1st wave), p5–p10 slightly worn juv feathers; secondaries with blocks of retained juv feathers

3rd-winter

p1–p2 new (2nd wave), p3–p4 year-old, p5–p8 new (1st wave continued), p9–p10 retained and worn juv feathers; secondaries often with a few retained juv feathers

4th-winter

p1–p3 new (3rd wave), p4–p7 new (2nd wave continued), p8–p10 new (1st wave completed); secondaries mixed generation but no retained juv feathers

Accelerated stepwise wing molt of booby

molt suspension (older primaries inside)

molt contrast (older primaries outside)

Typical suspended wing molt stage of 2nd-cycle booby. The 1st wave of wing molt (preformative molt) involved p1–p8; after a suspension, p9–p10 were replaced to complete the 1st molt at the same time as p1–p6 were renewed in the start of the 2nd molt wave (2nd-prebasic molt); p7–p8 have been retained from the preformative wing molt and thus are older and slightly faded relative to the adjacent primaries.

Fig. 23. Stepwise wing molt. In large eagles, waves of molt are annual, with the 1st wave starting in 1st summer and completing before 2nd winter. Adults typically show 3–4 waves of primary molt, with no retained juvenile feathers.

In boobies, however, the 1st molt wave is preformative and starts at 6–8 months' of age, often reaching p6–p8 before suspending; the 2nd wave starts at about 14–15 months of age, sometimes before the 1st wave suspends. Thus a 1st-cycle booby can show extensive wing molt, and a 2nd-cycle booby typically has 2 waves of primary molt and sometimes a few retained juvenile feathers; all juvenile secondaries are usually renewed by the 2nd wave. Adult boobies usually show about 3 waves of wing molt, with no retained juvenile feathers.

Assuming that waves of primary molt move outwards, from p1 to p10, then a molt contrast between fresher inner and older outer primaries indicates 2 waves of molt; a contrast between older inner and newer outer primaries indicates that a single wave of molt was suspended (contrasts can be subtle and are exaggerated here in the booby figure).

bird; moreover, juvenile body feathers of geese tend to be smaller and more rounded than on adults. A limited prealternate molt (mainly of head and neck feathers) may occur in some geese but does not substantively change wtheir appearance.

Molts in ducks are more complex and still not fully understood. As in geese, however, adult ducks have a complete prebasic molt in late summer (wing molt, followed by head and body), which in most species produces the bright breeding plumage of males. The early stages of this complete prebasic molt may overlap with the later stages of a variable (and often extensive) molt of head and body feathers in mid-summer, which in males produces the dull eclipse plumage. It also appears that both sexes of many species have a variable molt of head and body feathers in late winter and spring, although in males this may bring about no substantive change in appearance (Garganey being a notable exception). In general, adult ducks tend to have fairly uniform-looking plumage at most times of year.

First-year ducks have a variable, usually extensive, molt of head and body feathers from late summer–fall into early winter (most *Anas* and other dabbling ducks, which then resemble breeding adults), or from fall to mid–late winter (most *Aythya*, which then resemble breeding adults), or from late fall through the winter (most other diving ducks, which often appear patchy through the winter, especially males). The 1st-winter molt can include some to all tail feathers and, in birds with extensive molts (mainly *Anas*), 1st-winter males may be effectively indistinguishable from adults. The best clues for aging often lie with retained, contrasting, and worn juvenile wing and tail feathers, as well as with molt contrasts among larger body feathers and scapulars, as in 1st-year geese. Molts thereafter are like those of adults: partial spring molts probably occur but may bring about no change in appearance (except in males of some species), followed by a partial (eclipse) molt in mid–late summer and a complete 2nd-prebasic molt in fall.

PELAGIC SEABIRDS

Among the tubenoses (petrels, albatrosses, and storm-petrels), juveniles of all species have uniformly fresh plumage for much of their 1st year and relatively tapered flight feathers, often best seen on the outer primaries (especially the

outermost primary of albatrosses). Beware that petrels and storm-petrels recently having completed a prebasic molt can appear uniformly fresh and are often difficult to distinguish from juveniles. The complete 2nd-prebasic wing molt usually occurs earlier than the prebasic molt of breeding adults, and molt timing (best seen in the primaries) is often helpful for inferring age, in combination with the shape and quality of the older or retained wing and tail feathers. In general, the prebasic molts of adult petrels and storm-petrels are complete, but occasionally some secondaries may be retained—a molt contrast among the secondaries indicates a bird not in its 1st year.

Albatrosses rarely renew all of their remiges in a given molt cycle and post-juvenile plumages often show molt contrasts among the primaries and secondaries. Unique wing-molt patterns can enable some species of albatross to be aged up to 5 years or older, especially when used in tandem with bill colors and underwing patterns (mainly in mollymawks). In particular, check whether the outer 3 primaries are slightly fresher or slightly more worn than the adjacent middle primaries (see Howell 2012a and species accounts for details of aging different species).

Molt in tropicbirds, frigatebirds, and boobies is not well known, and populations of some species do not breed on annual cycles or on a typical Northern Hemisphere schedule. Thus, plumages and ages of these groups are best described in reference to plumage cycles rather than calendar years. Juveniles can be identified in all species by a combination of plumage aspect and uniform-generation flight feathers. Tropicbirds and boobies, and perhaps frigatebirds, renew their primaries in waves of accelerated stepwise molt (see below), which can help in aging 1st-cycle and 2nd-cycle individuals. Details of aging criteria are provided in the species accounts.

In stepwise molt, the primaries start molt with the innermost feather and a wave of molt proceeds outward; before this wave completes, a 2nd wave starts with p1 and moves outward, and in some cases a 3rd wave may even start before the 1st has finished (Fig. 23). In standard stepwise molt these waves start each year, such that 3 waves of molt in the wings of a heron or hawk indicate a bird at least 3 years old. In accelerated stepwise molt, however, the 1st wave is part of the preformative molt, such that a bird with 3 generations of primaries may be only 2 years old, as with boobies (Fig. 23; see Howell 2010a for further information).

GULLS AND TERNS

Most gulls and terns exhibit the CAS, although large gulls display the SAS and noddies may have the CBS. Aging is usually straightforward in the 1st year (and often in later years) by plumage aspect. Note that 1st-year (and some 2nd-year) terns generally resemble nonbreeding adults. Terns often have multiples waves of primary molt (thus all ages except fresh juveniles can have obvious molt contrasts in the wings), and wing molt timing can be helpful for aging. Unlike many birds (in which worn feathers are faded and paler than fresh dark feathers), fresh primaries of terns are paler (covered with a silvery bloom that wears off) and worn primaries are darker.

SHOREBIRDS

Most shorebirds exhibit the CAS, but some species may have the SAS and CBS (study is still needed of some species). Adults have complete prebasic molts, whereas the extent of 1st-cycle (preformative) molts is highly variable (see below). Prealternate molts are usually partial (but can include tertials and rectrices) and are often similar in extent between adults and 1st-years. In most species the classic breeding and nonbreeding plumages of adults look distinct, but beware that many 1st-summer birds (and perhaps some sick or hormonally challenged older birds) can look like nonbreeding adults. Thus, a 'nonbreeding' bird in summer is not in basic plumage but is in alternate plumage that did not attain full color.

Among longer-distance migrants, adults usually migrate south in worn breeding plumage and undergo most or all prebasic molt on the nonbreeding grounds; likewise, juveniles usually migrate south and molt mostly or wholly on the nonbreeding grounds. On occasion, some molt of head and body feathers (most visible on the scapulars) occurs before or during migration, and in some cases 1–2 inner primaries may be molted before migration (mainly in failed breeders or nonbreeders, which may feature quite frequently with vagrants); molt is then suspended and interrupted, to complete on the nonbreeding grounds. As a rule, a vagrant sandpiper found undergoing wing molt is likely to be on its nonbreeding grounds. By early winter,

most adults have attained uniform nonbreeding head and body plumage, including the upperwing coverts and tertials. This contrasts with 1st-winter birds, in which worn, retained juvenile feathers (mainly lesser upperwing coverts and tertials) often contrast with fresh nonbreeding (formative) feathers (see Fig. 22).

First-year molts are highly variable in extent among and even within species, which largely reflects migration distance and wintering latitude. In general, individuals (and species) that winter in the Northern Hemisphere replace only head and body feathers in their preformative molt, whereas individuals (and species) that winter in the Southern Hemisphere can replace flight feathers; some even have complete preformative molts, after which they are not safely distinguished from adults. The 1st-cycle wing molts are often incomplete, with only the outer primaries renewed—these are the most exposed feathers and the most important for long-distance flight. Such a wing molt pattern is termed eccentric, as it differs from the standard p1–p10 sequence of prebasic molts. Thus, 1st-summer shorebirds can usually be aged by (1) having uniformly worn and faded (juvenile) primaries relative to fresher adult feathers, or (2) having contrastingly fresh (formative) outer primaries and worn (juvenile) middle and inner primaries.

WADING BIRDS

Most wading birds exhibit the CBS and lack alternate plumages (the fancy plumes of herons and egrets are actually basic feathers that grow slowly in fall–winter), but pond herons (genus *Ardeola*) are an exception and follow the CAS. Some rails and allies may also have alternate plumages but don't change their appearance appreciably. In many species, aging can be achieved simply by observing plumage aspect and sometimes the color of bare parts.

As far as is known, among all wading birds treated here the juvenile flight feathers are retained through the 1st year, and 1st-year birds thus have uniformly fresh (or worn) primaries and secondaries. In contrast, adults of the larger species (herons, storks, some cranes) often have 2 or more generations of remiges, with molt contrasts apparent and molt sometimes proceeding in stepwise patterns. First-year herons typically have a protracted preformative molt over the fall–winter, and by spring can have variable head and back plumes, though not as well developed as the plumes of adults. Rails and allies (and perhaps small bitterns) have synchronous wing molt and thus don't show molt contrasts.

RAPTORS AND OWLS

Among raptors and owls, juveniles have fresh flight feathers of one generation through their 1st year, but adults, especially of larger species, may not renew all of their primaries annually and consequently show molt contrasts. Moreover, in larger hawks (mainly eagles), stepwise patterns of primary molt develop (such that 3–4 waves of primary molt may be apparent; Fig. 23), and whether or not juvenile feathers are retained can inform us about age; this means some species of large eagles can be aged up to 4 or 5 years. Falcons are unusual among birds in that they start molt within the primaries and secondaries in the middle of the tracts (e.g., at p4 or p5); molt waves then move outward in both directions. This means that the middle primaries of adult falcons (which were renewed first) tend to be more worn than the outer and inner primaries, unlike juveniles or 1st-years in which the primaries are uniform in wear or have the exposed outers more strongly worn.

LARGER LANDBIRDS

As a rule, although molts are not well known in a number of species, this diverse group shares the CBS. Pigeons, cuckoos, and woodpeckers usually have complete or near-complete pre-formative molts, but often some juvenile feathers are retained, especially secondaries, outer primaries, and rectrices. Adults of some species, however, especially cuckoos and woodpeckers, can have incomplete prebasic molts (usually retaining some secondaries) or may suspend prebasic molts during migration, such that molt contrasts in fall–winter do not always indicate a 1st-year bird. Whether or not retained feathers are juvenile or post-juvenile is important for determining whether a bird is 1st-year or older.

AERIAL LANDBIRDS

Molt in swifts is poorly known, and our ideas about molt in hummingbirds have recently been revised; thus, much critical study is still needed in these families. Molt in swallows appears to be better known.

Most medium-sized to larger swifts probably retain juvenile plumage through their 1st year,

juvenile   adult

Fig. 24. Comparison of shape differences in r5 of Reed Bunting. The outer rectrices of many species (from hawks and trogons to nightjars and songbirds) show a variably distinct difference in shape between slightly narrower, more tapered juvenile feathers and slightly broader, blunter-tipped adult (or formative) feathers; the difference in Reed Bunting is fairly well-marked.

Using such differences to help with aging requires some comparative experience, because absolute and relative shape differences vary among species. Similar, but generally less easily seen, shape differences also occur in other feather tracts, such as the primary coverts. The outermost rectrix (r6 on most songbirds) can become quite worn, and in such cases the shape difference may be better seen on the adjacent and more protected rectrix, r5 (shown here).

and thus in their 1st summer may appear faded relative to adults. Conversely, adults of larger migratory species molt mainly on the nonbreeding grounds and thus appear relatively fresh in spring but worn in fall, at which season juveniles are in fresh plumage.

The conventional view of hummingbird molt has been that they exhibit CBS with a complete preformative molt over the 1st year (often starting within 1–2 months of fledging and completing within 6–8 months of fledging). After this molt, 1st-years are rarely distinguishable from adults—and this likely still holds true for many species. However, a prealternate molt was documented recently for Ruby-throated Hummingbird

(Dittmann & Cardiff 2009), and may occur at least among other migratory species, which thus would exhibit CAS. Among some larger tropical species, preformative molt may be limited to the head and body feathers, with juvenile wings (or at least some juvenile flight feathers) retained over the 1st year; or there may be an offset in timing between head and body molt (occurring earlier) and wing molt (occurring later in the 1st year of life). Fresh-plumaged juveniles of most species often have buff fringes to their uniformly fresh upperpart feathers, in contrast to duller and more worn feathers on older birds; note that tropical hummingbirds have protracted and poorly known breeding seasons, so juveniles of some species might occur in any month. Best seen when examined in-hand, juveniles show lines of grooves along the sides of the upper mandible, unlike the smooth bill of adults (see Pyle 1997a for details).

Swallows exhibit CBS and are among the few passerines in which juveniles undergo a complete preformative molt in their 1st winter (with wing molt averaging later than the wing molt of adults), such that 1st-summer birds show no molt contrasts and are rarely distinguishable from adults.

SONGBIRDS

All songbirds display either CBS or CAS. Many bird species, including passerines, molt quickly out of juvenile plumage into a stronger formative plumage that often resembles adult basic plumage in color and pattern. The preformative molt in most species is rarely complete; for example, the juvenile flight feathers are usually retained. Consequently, the contrast between retained juvenile feathers and fresher formative feathers (known as a molt contrast, or molt limit) can be helpful in aging many songbirds in their 1st year of life. Because adult songbirds have complete prebasic molts they do not show such contrasts, except in rare cases when the prebasic molt is suspended (as between the breeding and nonbreeding grounds).

Among songbirds, molt contrasts are often present among the greater coverts or tertials, sometimes the rectrices, and even among the primaries in a few species. In particular, look for a contrast within the greater coverts between fresher inner feathers (replaced because these parts of the bird are relatively exposed) and older, more faded outer feathers (most often retained because these feathers are relatively less exposed) (Fig 22). Conversely, the lack of a molt contrast within the greater coverts does not necessarily indicate an adult—it could indicate a 1st-year that replaced all of its juvenile coverts.

Molt contrasts can be useful throughout the 1st year if a species has no prealternate molt, or if its prealternate molt does not include tertials or greater coverts (cf. Fig. 21). However, if the adult prealternate molt can include tertials or wing coverts, then a molt contrast in summer doesn't necessarily help in aging (e.g., wagtails and pipits), unless perhaps 3 generations of feathers (juvenile, formative, and 1st-alternate) can be distinguished, or unless well-founded conclusions (usually based on considerable experience with a given species) can be made based on the quality (and thus relative wear and fading) of retained juvenile feathers.

As in several groups of birds, the shape of feathers (mainly the primaries and rectrices) can offer clues for aging. Perhaps because juvenile feathers all grow at once and there is a need for them to grow quickly for fledging, they do not develop as completely as adult feathers grown sequentially. Thus, juvenile feathers are often slightly narrower and more tapered, less 'filled out' than adult feathers, and they also are of poorer quality. In particular, rectrix shape can often be seen in the field, or in good photos, and can be used to infer age (Fig. 24); this is easier with fresher or moderately worn feathers, usually in fall–spring, than with heavily worn feathers in summer. Beware that shape differences are species specific; some species have relatively tapered feathers as adults (but juvenile feathers of such species are even more tapered), and thus it is important to have a frame of reference for any species being considered.

SPECIES ACCOUNTS

WATERFOWL

We consider 14 waterfowl species of Old World origin and 4 of New World origin to have occurred as rare birds in N America. Our understanding of vagrancy patterns among waterfowl is potentially clouded, however, by the fact that many species are widely held in captivity, both publically and privately, and unknown numbers escape. Generally, it is the more attractively colored species that are most popular, and free-flying Mandarin Ducks or Bar-headed Geese are usually dismissed as escapes from captivity, given the low likelihood that they would occur as natural vagrants. Problems arise when vagrancy and escapes both seem possible, as with whistling-ducks in the Southeast and shelducks in the Northeast. In such cases, we have tried to weigh the odds and present the pros and cons of the arguments. Our inclusion of species here only reflects our opinion that vagrancy is plausible, not that we necessarily accept any records as 'good' or reject others as 'bad.'

Brightly colored male ducks are also more favored in collections than duller females, but within wild populations there is also often a male-biased sex ratio (e.g., Donald 2007), and males also may be more prone to wandering. Hence, we would expect to see more males among wild vagrants. Moreover, brightly patterned males also draw greater attention in the field than females, both among birders and hunters.

Being large, generally conspicuous, and popular, most species of rare waterfowl have now been recorded in N America. Future additions seem most likely to derive from taxonomic splitting. For example, Common Scoter *M. nigra* of W Eurasia (formerly treated as conspecific with Black Scoter) and Velvet Scoter *M. [f.] fusca* also of W Eurasia (split by most European authorities from White-winged Scoter of N America) seem possible vagrants; in the Northeast they should be looked for with wintering scoter flocks. Stejneger's Scoter *M. [fusca] stejnegeri* (also split from White-winged by some Old World authorities) has been found recently in w. Alaska, where it was almost certainly overlooked in past years.

Old World Waterfowl

Among Old World vagrant waterfowl, 5 species originate primarily in E Asia, with records only from AK (Lesser White-fronted Goose, Eastern Spot-billed Duck) or from AK and elsewhere in the West (Whooper Swan, Falcated Duck, Baikal Teal); these occur mainly in spring and fall in AK, and in winter in the West. A further 4 species (Tundra Bean Goose, Taiga Bean Goose, Common Pochard, Smew) largely conform to this same AK/West pattern, but have been recorded in fall and winter as far e. as e. Canada (mainly QC) and the Northeast; it seems likely that most or all of these e. birds (except perhaps Common Pochard) also originated in E Asia and dispersed e. across N America. Of the remaining 5 species, 3 (Pink-footed Goose, Greylag Goose, and Common Shelduck) occur in fall–spring, primarily in the Northeast, and may reflect an overflow of burgeoning European populations, and 1 species (Ruddy Shelduck) has occurred in late summer in Arctic Canada, presumably as part of a dispersal event from interior Asia. The remaining species, Garganey, is also the most widespread vagrant waterfowl in N America, with some birds originating in E Asia and spreading into AK and the West, and others probably crossing the Atlantic in fall from W Europe or Africa to the Caribbean and thence moving n. in spring into the East.

WHOOPER SWAN *Cygnus cygnus*
140–165 cm (55–65")

Summary: *Alaska*: On w. and cen. Aleutians, uncommon in fall–spring (has bred); on Bering Sea islands and n. and w. mainland, very rare (mainly spring); exceptional in s-coastal AK. *West*: Very rare in late fall–spring, s. to n. CA, e. to AB. *East*: Scattered records, but none considered to be from wild populations.
Taxonomy: Monotypic.

Distribution and Status:
World: Breeds from Iceland across N Eurasia to ne. Russia (Kamchatka, e. Chukotka). Winters from W Europe e. locally to E Asia.

North America: *Alaska*: Uncommon in w. and cen. Aleutians in fall–spring (late Sep–May, mainly Nov to mid-Apr); most records are of singles or family groups, max. 31 on Amchitka, 10 Apr 1970; nested on Attu, 1996 and 1997. Very rare in spring–early summer (May–Jun) on Bering Sea islands and w. mainland. Exceptional in

adult with
ochre-stained
head and neck

young birds become
paler through 1st winter

adult

adult

juv
fresh

juv **Trumpeter**

juv **'Bewick's'**

juv
'Whistling'

1st-winter
'Whistling'

Whooper Swan

late fall (late Oct–Nov) in w. and s-coastal AK. **West**: Very rare in winter (Nov to mid-Mar), with about 15 records (exact number confused by presumed returning and wandering birds) from Vancouver Island, BC, s. to cen. CA, and single records (late Nov–early Mar) e. to ID (2008; *NAB* 63:126) and WY (2003). Single summer records from Herschel Island, n. YT, 20 Jun–7 Jul 2006 (1st-year); Vancouver Is., 25–27 Jul 1996 (unknown provenance, rejected on grounds of origin by provincial committee; Davidson 1999). **East**: Scattered records throughout the year, s. to NC and FL, and w. to IA and MN, but none considered to be from wild populations (see McEneaney 2004).

Comments: There has been lengthy debate over the wildness of Whooper Swans in N America (see summary by McEneaney 2004). Birds in the West, particularly ones associated with swans from high-latitude breeding ranges, are now generally considered wild. Whooper Swan populations on the Japanese wintering grounds have increased since the 1980s (Brazil 2003) and records from AK and the West appear to have increased in tandem.

Birds from the Great Plains and eastward are problematic. Whooper Swans have been known

to escape or be released from captivity in MN, NY, MA, and NH, in some cases with small, temporary breeding populations becoming established (McEneaney 2004). On the other hand, the species is a common breeder in Iceland, arriving from its British wintering grounds in early Mar (some overwinter in Iceland) and returning there when its breeding waters freeze. Since 1950, there have been about 15 records from e. Greenland, indicating a degree of wandering. However, as yet there are no records of Whooper Swan from NL or NS, often the first port for many overshoots from Iceland and Greenland.

Field Identification: Very large swan with big, long, wedge-shaped bill; similar in size and shape to Trumpeter Swan, its New World counterpart.

Similar Species: ***Trumpeter Swan*** similar in size and shape but adult has black bill, lacking extensive yellow base to bill. Juv/1st-winter Trumpeter has dark lores and base to bill.

Tundra Swan smaller overall and shorter necked; adult of Eurasian ssp ('Bewick's Swan') has smaller and usually rounded yellow patch at base of bill; juv/1st-winter has smaller, dirty, whitish area at base of bill than Whooper, mirroring adult pattern. Juv/1st-winter of N American ssp ('Whistling Swan') has dark or dusky lores.

Hybrids between Whooper Swan and Tundra Swan may occur in the wild (bonded pairs have been seen in AK and possible hybrids in CA), and Whooper and Trumpeter have been hybridized in captivity in N America, and released (McEneaney 2004); the characters of such birds remain undocumented, but the possibility of a hybrid should be considered for any atypical Whooper Swan.

Age/Sex/Season: Ages differ, with adult appearance attained at about 1 year; sexes similar; no seasonal variation. Complete prebasic molt occurs late summer–fall (wing molt synchronous) but some molting may occur year-round; partial preformative molt occurs fall–spring. ***Adult*** plumage pure white (neck especially can be stained brownish to orange); bill largely yellow with black distal portions. ***1st-year***: Juv (Aug–Oct) dusky overall, becoming paler over 1st winter and spring through fading and protracted preformative molt. Attains white plumage by complete 2nd-prebasic molt at about 1 year of age. Juv bill pattern mirrors adult, but dirty whitish to pink where adult is yellow and black; by 1st summer resembles adult but paler yellow.

Habitat and Behavior: Similar to Trumpeter and Whistling swans, with which, in the Lower 48 states, Whooper is usually found. Adult has rather strident, bugling, or trumpeting calls, lacking the slightly nasal or muffled quality of Trumpeter Swan and distinct from the hollow, hooting quality of Tundra Swan.

TUNDRA BEAN GOOSE *Anser serrirostris*
78–89 cm (30.5–35″)

Summary: Uncertain due to species confusion with Taiga Bean Goose (see Taxonomy, below). *Alaska*: Presumed rare in spring on w. Aleutians, very rare in spring on cen. Aleutians and Bering Sea islands. No certain fall records. ***Elsewhere***: fall records from YT (1999) and QC (1982).
Taxonomy: Monotypic (following Sangster & Oreel 1996), but size increases from w. to e. Smaller w. populations have slightly smaller bill (with less pronounced deep base) and sometimes treated as ssp *rossicus*, with e. populations being nominate *serrirostris*.

Bean Goose was split by AOU in 2007 into Tundra Bean Goose *A. serrirostris* and Taiga Bean Goose *A. fabilis* (*Auk* 124:1109–1115).
Distribution and Status:
World: Breeds tundra zone of Russia, e. to e. Chukotka. Winters locally from W Europe e. to Japan.

North America: *Alaska*: Gibson & Byrd (2007) list all records of bean geese from the Aleutians as being *serrirostris* (i.e., Tundra Bean Goose), but in hindsight many sight records are best considered as 'bean goose sp.' (Gibson et al. 2008). Specimens of Tundra Bean Goose exist from cen. Aleutians, Pribilofs, and St. Lawrence, and the species is presumed rare in spring (May to mid-Jun, exceptionally into Jul) on w. Aleutians, max 14 on Attu, 21 May 1979; and very rare in spring (May–early Jun) on cen. Aleutians and Bering Sea islands (Gibson et al. 2008). ***Elsewhere***: Exceptional in s. YT, 23–24 Oct 1999 (adult; Eckert 2000) and e. QC, 14–21 Oct 1982 (*AB* 37:159).

Comments: Presumed Tundra Bean Geese are drift-overshoots through the w. and cen. Aleutians in spring, and given their northern (tundra) breeding range they are the most likely species to reach St. Lawrence Island in spring. Taiga Bean Goose is thought to be much rarer in spring in the Aleutians, but it has been recorded. Both species have reached the Pribilofs, and 5 of the 7 N American records of bean geese outside of AK (in fall–winter) appear to pertain to Taiga. Both species are unspectacular and thus rare in waterfowl collections (B. Wilson 1985; Mlodinow 2004), suggesting that escapes are likely to be very rare.

Concerning unidentified bean geese, there is a spring record from mainland w. AK (9 Jun 1974), and fall records from Shemya (10 Sep 2002), St. Lawrence (7 Sep 2002) and with migrating geese in YT on 18 Oct 2010 (*NAB* 65:105), and e. cen. AB in 2007 (1st-year; date not given, *NAB* 62:97).

Remarkably, both species have occurred in QC, a Tundra in Oct 1982, and a Taiga in Oct 1987, but whether they came from w. or e. is unclear. While there were only 59 records of bean goose sp. from Iceland through 2006 (mainly Oct–Nov with a smaller peak in Apr–May), the QC specimen was identified as ssp *rossicus*, implying an origin in W Eurasia.
Field Identification: Large 'gray goose' with mostly dark bill that has variable orange subterminal band.

Similar Species: Main concern is separation from ***Taiga Bean Goose***, and many birds may not be safely identified without good views and preferably some experience. Tundra Bean averages smaller and shorter-necked, with shorter legs and a relatively short, deep-based bill that typically has orange restricted to a subterminal band (and thus may recall Pink-footed Goose

short, deep-based bill

both species can have white at base of bill

narrow orange band

Tundra

adult

longer, deep-based bill

Taiga

orange on bill variable

adult

juv

Bean Geese

in several respects). By comparison, Taiga is larger and slightly longer-necked, with a more sloping head shape and a longer bill; and its calls average lower pitched than Tundra. In W Eurasia, Taiga often has more extensive orange on the bill, but in E Asia both species are often similar in this respect. Differences between Tundra and Taiga mirror those between larger Cackling and smaller Canada Geese, and birds with seemingly intermediate features will remain problematic until further study. See Oates (1997) for further information, at least in a European context.

Greater White-fronted Goose rather similar if head/bill pattern or belly barring cannot be seen (as with resting or sleeping birds); note frostier and more contrasting edges to upperparts on Bean (especially tertials). 1st-year White-fronted averages smaller with wholly to mostly pink or orange bill; develops white bill base (Bean can have small white line at bill base) and black belly mottling over 1st winter.

Also cf. Lesser White-fronted, Pink-footed, and Greylag geese.

Age/Sex/Season: Ages differ slightly; sexes similar; no seasonal variation. Complete prebasic

molt occurs late summer–fall (wing molt synchronous) but some molting may occur year-round; partial preformative molt occurs fall–spring. **Adult**: Distinct pale tips to relatively large and square-tipped scapulars and upperwing coverts; distinct neck furrows. **1st-year**: Juv has duller upperparts with smaller and more rounded feathers; less distinct neck furrows. Protracted preformative molt occurs through 1st winter, and usually appears much like adult by spring. Attains adult appearance by complete 2nd-prebasic molt at about 1 year of age.

Habitat and Behavior: Typical upland goose; wintering vagrants likely to associate with other geese. Calls similar to Taiga Bean Goose but averaging higher pitched, and thus also similar to Pink-footed Goose.

TAIGA BEAN GOOSE *Anser fabalis*
90–100 cm (35.5–40.5")

Summary: Uncertain due to species confusion with Tundra Bean Goose (above). **Alaska**: Exceptional in spring and fall–winter on w. Aleutians and Bering Sea islands. **Pacific States**: Single winter records from WA (2003) and CA

(2010/2011). *Elsewhere*: Exceptional in fall–early spring in IA, NE, QC.

Taxonomy: 2 ssp often recognized: nominate *fabalis* of W Eurasia and *middendorfii* of E Asia, but considered monotypic by some authors (e.g., Sangster & Oreel 1996). Size increases from w. to e., and bill averages longer and darker in e. populations (*middendorfii*); some N American records appear consistent with *middendorfii* but variation within and between bean geese species could benefit from elucidation.

Bean Goose was split by AOU in 2007 into Tundra Bean Goose *A. serrirostris*, and Taiga Bean Goose *A. fabilis* (*Auk* 124:1109–1115).

Status and Distribution:

World: Breeds taiga zone from Scandinavia e. across Eurasia to e. Russia (Kamchatka). Winters locally from W Europe e. to Japan.

North America: *Alaska*: Exceptional in spring and fall–winter, at least 2 records in the period; Shemya, 27 Sep 2007–Feb 2008 (3); Adak, 18 May 2009 (*NAB* 63:484); also 1 earlier record, from Pribilofs, 19 Apr 1946. *Pacific States*: 2 winter records (Nov–Jan); Grays Harbor Co, WA, 7–17 Dec 2002, and Imperial Co., CA, 9 Nov 2010–12 Jan 2011 (*NAB* 65:162; identity accepted only as bean goose sp. by state committee). *Elsewhere*: 3 fall–winter records (mid-Oct to early Apr); Harrison Co., IA/Washington Co., NE, 29 Dec 1984–7 Jan 1985 (*AB* 39:172, 182); Phelps Co., NE, 4 Apr 1998 (*FN* 52:350); e. QC, 14–15 Oct 1987 (*AB* 42:46).

Comments: See account for Tundra Bean Goose. Coincidentally, the WA bird occurred in the same season as the first AK fall records of (unidentified) bean geese, on Shemya (10 Sep 2002) and St. Lawrence (7 Sep 2002); and the CA bird occurred in the same season as a fall bean goose in YT (18 Oct 2010).

Migrant bean geese have been seen with Cackling and Canada Geese, although the CA and IA/NE birds associated with White-fronted Geese. Any of these 3 species could serve as a 'carrier species' with which misoriented or orphaned bean geese might travel down the West Coast or into the heartland of N America.

Field Identification: Large 'gray goose' with mostly dark bill that has variable orange subterminal band. See illustration on p. 47.

Similar Species: Main concern is separation from *Tundra Bean Goose* (see above). Also cf. Lesser White-fronted, Pink-footed, and Greylag geese.

Greater White-fronted Goose rather similar if head/bill pattern or belly barring cannot be seen (as with resting or sleeping birds): note frostier and more contrasting edges to upperparts on Bean (especially tertials). 1st-year White-fronted averages smaller, with wholly to mostly pink or orange bill; develops white bill base (Bean can have small white line at bill base) and black belly mottling over 1st winter.

Age/Sex/Season: Ages differ slightly; sexes similar; no seasonal variation. Complete prebasic molt occurs late summer–fall (wing molt synchronous) but some molting may occur year-round; partial preformative molt occurs fall–spring. *Adult*: Distinct pale tips to relatively large and square-tipped scapulars and upperwing coverts; distinct neck furrows. *1st-year*: Juv has duller upperparts with smaller and more rounded feathers; less distinct neck furrows. Protracted preformative molt occurs through 1st winter, and usually much like adult by spring. Attains adult appearance by complete 2nd-prebasic molt at about 1 year of age.

Habitat and Behavior: A typical upland goose; wintering vagrants are likely to associate with other geese. Common calls include a deep, nasal, trumpeting *ung-unk*, difficult to separate from Pink-footed Goose but slightly lower pitched.

PINK-FOOTED GOOSE *Anser brachyrhynchus* 60–75 cm (23.5–29.5")

Summary: *East*: Rare but increasing in the Northeast, fall–spring, almost all records since late 1990s; very rare s. to PA and DE, exceptional w. to NE. *West*: Uncertain, see Comments, below.

Taxonomy: Monotypic.

Status and Distribution:

World: Breeds e. Greenland and Iceland (where increasing), and Spitsbergen. Greenland and Iceland birds winter in British Isles, Spitsbergen birds winter in continental NW Europe.

North America: *East*: Rare (very rare prior to 2000) in the Northeast in fall–spring (Oct–early May, mainly Nov–Mar), mainly from QC and Atlantic Canada, s. to NY, very rarely s. to DE and PA (Dec–Mar); some records presumed to be of birds returning in successive winters; mainly 1s and 2s, max. 3 in Cumberland Co., ME, 14 Oct–6 Dec 2009. Away from this predominantly E Coast cluster, there is 1 record from Clay Co., NE, 30 Jan 2006 (1st-year). *West*: Uncertain, see Comments, below.

Comments: In only 25 years, Pink-footed Goose, like Barnacle Goose (see below), has gone from being treated as a suspected escape to an expected vagrant in the Northeast. The first widely accepted record of wild Pink-footed Goose may be that from NL in early May 1990, but a record from DE, 1 Nov 1953–21 Jan 1954 (considered a possible escape at the time) seems plausible in light of recent events. Through about 2005, most N American records were in Jan–Mar, suggesting that most such birds had arrived undetected in N America, given that early migrants typically return to Iceland or Greenland in late Mar. Records in Oct–Nov have increased since around 2005, perhaps because of increased observer awareness combined with increased numbers of geese; in fact, most recent records have been in Oct–Jan, with few late winter–spring records. At least some Apr–May records from Atlantic Canada likely include displaced spring migrants from Iceland or Greenland, such as the May 1990 record (noted above) and a total of 5 birds in spring 1995 associated with an influx of European Golden Plovers and the first N American records of Common Redshank (Mactavish 1996).

Pink-footed Goose populations wintering in Great Britain have increased more than 10-fold during the last 60 years (Banks et al. 2006), and all of this increase has apparently come from the Iceland/Greenland populations. If this trend continues we can expect N American records to increase, of which the 2006 NE bird may be an example. It is unclear whether Pink-footed Geese reaching (and returning to?) the Northeast represent misoriented (mirror-image?) migrants, birds displaced by storms, or simply random dispersal linked to a greatly increasing population (or a combination of these factors). It seems likely that a small wintering population is establishing itself in N America—time will tell.

There is one anomalous record: Gray's Harbor Co., WA, 5 Nov 2003–10 Apr 2004 (2 apparent adults). Although not accepted by the state committee because of no pattern of vagrancy in w. N America, the species is generally rare in captivity and these birds may have been wild (cf. bean geese occurring in the East).

Like Pink-footed Goose, Barnacle Goose is experiencing a dramatic population increase and its status in N America reflects this. Unlike Pink-footed, however, Barnacle Goose is a popular species in waterfowl collections, which makes it much harder to judge records; ABA (2002) discussed the problems of free-flying feral or escaped Barnacle Geese. Nonetheless, Barnacle Geese banded in Spitsbergen (Montevecchi & Wells 1984) and Scotland (*NAB* 65:223) have been found in the Northeast, and others have been in the company of banded

juv

pink band

adult

gray greater coverts

some have white at base of bill

pale gray upperwing

short neck

broad white tail tip

Pink-foot

Tundra Bean

Taiga Bean

juv **Greater White-front**

Pink-footed Goose

Greenland White-fronted Geese (which also are increasing in the Northeast in winter; *NAB* 62:223) and banded Canada Geese from Greenland (*NAB* 63:43).

Like Pink-footed Goose, most Barnacle Geese occur Nov–Mar in the Northeast, with some suspected of returning in successive years. Since the early 2000s the number of apparently wild Barnacles has easily exceeded our 5 per year threshold and thus we do not treat it as a rare bird. Barnacle Goose also has a wider distribution in N America than Pink-footed, with records of (potentially wild) birds w. to ON and s. to NC, at or beyond which the question of escapes becomes more problematic. Records from CA and NM are presumably escapes, but what of a bird in AR, 27–28 Dec 2010 (*NAB* 65:290), accepted as the first state record … ?

Field Identification: Relatively small and compact 'gray goose' with contrasting dark neck and relatively small, stubby bill; legs pink.

Similar Species: Fairly distinctive if seen well; most likely confusion species in the East is Greater White-fronted Goose. Also cf. bean geese (note dark greater coverts, narrow white tail tip) and Greylag Goose.

Greater White-fronted Goose has orange legs, mostly pink to orange bill, darker leading edge to upperwings, narrow white tail tip; lacks frosty whitish edgings to tertials and greater coverts of adult Pink-footed. Adult White-front has black belly mottling, white band around bill base (Pink-footed can have fine white line around bill base).

Age/Sex/Season: Ages differ slightly; sexes similar; no seasonal variation. Complete prebasic molt occurs late summer–fall (wing molt synchronous) but some molting may occur year-round; partial preformative molt occurs fall–spring. ***Adult***: Distinct pale tips to relatively large and square-tipped scapulars and upperwing coverts; distinct neck furrows. ***1st-year***: Juv has duller upperparts with smaller and more rounded feathers; less distinct neck furrows; averages duller pink band on bill than adult. Protracted, preformative molt through winter, and usually much like adult by spring. Attains adult appearance by complete 2nd-prebasic molt at about 1 year of age.

Habitat and Behavior: Typical upland goose. Flight relatively quick and agile. N American records involve lone birds as well as birds associating with other species, such as Canada Geese. Typical voice a trumpeting *ung-ungk*, lacks laughing quality of higher-pitched White-fronted Goose.

LESSER WHITE-FRONTED GOOSE
Anser erythropus 53–66 cm (21–26")

Summary: *Alaska*: 1 spring record from w. Aleutians (1994).
Taxonomy: Monotypic.
Distribution and Status:

World: Breeds on upland tundra from Scandinavia e. across Eurasia to ne. Russia (e. Chukotka). Winters locally in SE Europe, Cen Asia, and e. China. Uncommon and declining, perhaps especially in the w. parts of its range.

North America: *Alaska*: Attu, 5 Jun 1994 (adult female).

Comments: The combination of high-latitude breeding range, long-distance migration, and a family history of wandering make this species a candidate for vagrancy. The sharp decline in overall numbers worldwide works in a counter direction, however. We do not know whether the AK bird appeared alone or in the company of other geese. In fall, wandering juvs could attach themselves to flocks of Greater White-fronted Geese in Siberia and move into N America; flocks of Siberian White-fronts should be scrutinized with this possibility in mind.

Scattered records from elsewhere in N America, mainly in the East, are not thought to be of wild origin (ABA 2008). There were no records for Iceland through 2005, and the species remains very rare in W Europe.

Field Identification: Small, relatively short-necked, small-billed, and long-winged version of Greater White-fronted Goose.

Similar Species: Main concern is separation from ***Greater White-fronted Goose***, and Lesser very difficult to pick out in an actively feeding flock of white-fronts. Best clues are smaller size, shorter neck, stubbier and often deeper pink bill (differences may suggest those between Ross' Goose and Snow Goose), longer wing-tips (projecting distinctly past tail tip), and (at close range) prominent yellow orbital ring. Adult Lesser has more extensive white forehead blaze that reaches higher on the forehead than Greater, often ending in a point; also averages sparser black belly markings than Greater. Juv Lesser has pink bill with pale nail, unlike black tip typical of juv Greater.

Age/Sex/Season: Ages differ; sexes similar; no seasonal variation. Complete prebasic molt occurs late summer–fall (wing molt synchronous) but some molting may occur year-round; partial preformative molt occurs fall–spring. ***Adult***:

bold yellow
orbital ring

short
bill

juv

**Greater
White-
fronted
Goose**
adult

adult

adult with 5 Greater White-fronts

long wing
projection

adult

Lesser White-fronted Goose

Prominent white forecrown, variable black belly bars; also relatively large and square-tipped scapulars and upperwing coverts; distinct neck furrows. *1st-year*: Juv lacks white forecrown, belly plain; also has duller upperparts with smaller and more rounded feathers, less distinct neck furrows. Protracted preformative molt through winter, by which attains white forecrown and perhaps some blackish belly bars. Attains adult appearance by complete 2nd-prebasic molt at about 1 year of age.

Habitat and Behavior: Typical upland goose. Common flight call a lilting *ay-ya-ya*, higher than White-fronted Goose.

GREYLAG GOOSE *Anser anser* 76–89 cm (30–35")

Summary: *East*: Exceptional or very rare in winter–spring, mainly in Atlantic Canada, also w. to QC, s. to CT. All records recent.

Taxonomy: 2 ssp, intergrading in E Europe and w. Russia: nominate *anser* of Europe averages darker overall with an orange bill; *rubrirostris* of E Asia averages paler overall with a pinkish bill.

Distribution and Status:

World: Breeds from Iceland e. across Eurasia to se. Russia and ne. China, mainly at mid-latitudes in Cen and E Asia. Winters from W and

S Europe, e. locally to n. India and SE Asia. Resident populations introduced locally in W Europe (e.g., Britain).

North America: *East*: In Atlantic Canada, 3 recent records: 310 km (about 185 miles) se. of St John's, NL, on a drill ship, 24 Apr–2 May 2005; cen. NS, 3 Nov–10 Dec 2010 (1st-winter; *NAB* 65:31,190), relocating to sw. NS, 23 Feb 2011 (*NAB* 65:234); at sea 288 km (about 170 miles) e. of Cape Bonavista, NL, 3 Dec 2010 (*NAB* 65:234). Also singles in QC, 14 Nov–8 Dec 2011 (1st-winter; *NAB* 66:34–35) and New Haven Co., CT, 22 Feb–11 Apr 2009 (age uncertain; Kaplan & Hanisek 2012).

Comments: It is perhaps surprising that there haven't been more Greylag records, given the species' increasing abundance in Iceland, although the Icelandic Greylags are relatively short-distance migrants (wintering mainly in Scotland); moreover, an ability to rest on the sea may reduce the odds of becoming a vagrant. The spate of recent records mirrors the changing status of Pink-footed and Barnacle Geese in the Northeast (see account for Pink-footed Goose), and may also reflect changing attitudes among birders about wild versus escaped provenance with respect to waterfowl.

The NL spring record is consistent with a storm-displaced migrant (cf. European Golden Plover, Common Redshank) headed to the

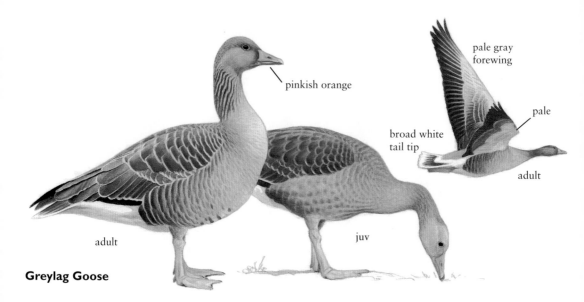

pale gray forewing

pinkish orange

pale

broad white tail tip

adult

adult   juv

Greylag Goose

Iceland breeding grounds, to which birds return from Britain in Mar–Apr, with stragglers into May. Greylags depart Iceland in late Oct, and a misoriented or displaced 1st-year might be expected to arrive in Nov in e. Canada. The second at-sea record is more puzzling, given the relatively late date, but seems more likely to represent a wild bird (attempting to reorient?) than an escape that wandered out into the N Atlantic. The CT bird, which associated with Canada Geese, stayed relatively late compared to the Mar departures associated with Pink-footed Geese, and the possibility it was an escape cannot be ruled out.

Greylag distribution in NE Asia, where it approaches the coast near the se. corner of the Sea of Okhotsk, suggests this species could occur as a vagrant in the w. Aleutians, but it's a vagrant in Japan and unrecorded in Kamchatka.

Field Identification: Large, bulky, and overall fairly plain 'gray goose' with big orange bill, pinkish legs. In flight, note striking silvery-gray forewings, pale underwing coverts. On sleeping birds, note large size, lack of head/body contrast.

Similar species: None if well seen, but cf. 1st-year Greater White-fronted Goose.

Age/Sex/Season: Ages differ slightly; sexes similar; no seasonal variation. Complete prebasic molt occurs late summer–fall (wing molt synchronous) but some molting may occur year-round; partial preformative molt occurs fall–spring.

Adult: Distinct pale tips to relatively large and square-tipped scapulars and upperwing coverts;

distinct neck furrows. **1st-year:** Juv has duller upperparts with smaller and more rounded feathers; less distinct neck furrows. Protracted preformative molt through winter, and usually much like adult by spring. Attains adult appearance by complete 2nd-prebasic molt at about 1 year of age.

Habitat and Behavior: Typical upland goose. Flight relatively slow and ponderous. Common calls much like those of domestic barnyard geese.

COMMON SHELDUCK *Tadorna tadorna*
55–65 cm (21.5–25.5")

Summary: ***Northeast:*** Exceptional in fall–winter (see Comments, below). ***Elsewhere:*** Status confounded by escapes (see Comments).
Taxonomy: Monotypic.
Distribution and Status:
    World: Breeds from NW Europe e. through mid-latitude Asia to around 130°E. Winters from W Europe e. locally to se. China.
    North America: ***Northeast:*** Single recent records from e. NL, 17 Nov 2009 (1st-year female; *NAB* 64:34) and Essex Co., MA, 6–7 Dec 2009 (1st-year; *NAB* 64:229); records not submitted and not accepted, respectively, by regional committees (Pranty & ABA Checklist Committee 2011). ***Elsewhere:*** Status confounded by escapes (see Brinkley 2010a).
Comments: Common Shelduck is popular in captivity and N American records are usually

♀

♂ breeding
(Sep–Jun)

1st-year ♀

♂

Common Shelduck

dismissed as escapes. Indeed, many records surely do refer to escapes or free-flying feral birds. Like Pink-footed, Barnacle, and Greylag Geese, however, shelducks are increasing markedly in Europe and should be considered as plausible vagrants to N America. The species is no longer considered a national rarity in Iceland, where the pattern up to 1997 was mainly of Mar–May arrivals, followed by summering and then disappearance in Jul–Aug (to unknown molting grounds), and with a few winter records in Dec–Feb. Since then, the species has continued to increase in Iceland, with breeding since the early 1990s, and in the order of 50–100 pairs by 2010; the Icelandic population is migratory and present from mid-Mar to about Oct, with the molting grounds unknown and details of fall migration poorly known (Y. Kolbeinsson, pers. comm.).

Brinkley (2010a) tried to reconstruct N American records and occurrence patterns of Common Shelduck, with some interesting findings. Records appear to have increased since the 1980s, with a peak in Aug–Nov and a geographic concentration in the East, especially the Northeast. This may simply reflect observer bias, increased communication, and the geographic center of captive shelducks, but it does give pause for thought. Might the recent early winter records of 1st-years from NL and MA represent European birds displaced across the

Atlantic, as with lapwings and other species, or are they simply wanderers from the Icelandic population? Either scenario seems plausible, but they could also be dispersing escapes. And where does the burgeoning Icelandic population go to molt? Could some be misdirected or displaced into N America? Might a shift in distribution be occurring before our eyes but under our noses? Our concepts of migration may also need to be recalibrated—birds can migrate north (or south) to safe molting grounds in late summer and fall, then south afterward, or north, or east … .

Like Brinkley (2010a) we encourage observers to continue reporting Common Shelduck in N America, so that any patterns of potentially wild occurrence may be elucidated. The first bird that arrives with a European band on its leg will no doubt ignite interest in this under-regarded subject.

Field Identification: Striking and handsome species, appearing intermediate in demeanor between ducks and geese.

Similar Species: None in N America.

Age/Sex/Season: Ages differ, with adult appearance attained at about 1 year; sexes differ slightly; no seasonal variation. Complete prebasic molt occurs in fall, preceded by partial prealternate molt (into eclipse plumage) in mid–late summer. ***Adult:*** Bottle-green secondaries and black primaries lack white trailing edge;

plumage boldly 'pied' with bottle-green head (mottled whitish in eclipse) and neck, broad chestnut breast band (paler and mottled whitish in eclipse). Male bill bright red with large knob on base of culmen, female bill duller without knob. *1st-year*. Aged easily by white trailing edge to secondaries and inner primaries. Juv (Jun–Oct) has mostly dark gray-brown head, hindneck, and upperparts, with white throat and eye-ring, lacks chestnut breast band; bill and legs duskier than adult. Usually attains adult-like plumage by late fall, but messier overall, and protracted molt may continue through winter. Attains adult plumage by complete 2nd-prebasic molt at about 1 year of age.

Habitat and Behavior: Largely coastal in NW Europe, but on inland lakes in Asia. Feeds on mudflats, lake shores, in flooded and arable fields, etc. Mostly feeds while walking, by grazing and sweeping bill in wet mud, also while swimming. Common calls are clucking and slightly purring, gruff grunts, often in fairly rapid series; adult male also gives high, twittering whistles.

RUDDY SHELDUCK *Tadorna ferruginea*
58–70 cm (23–27.5")

Summary: *Nunavut*: 1 mid-summer record (2003). *Elsewhere*: Status confounded by escapes (see Comments, below).
Taxonomy: Monotypic.
Distribution and Status:
World: Breeds from SE Europe e. through mid-latitude Asia to around 130°E; also NW Africa. Asian populations winter from NE Africa locally e. through S Asia to se. China.
North America: *Nunavut*: Southampton Island, 23–24 Jul 2003 (6; Allard et al. 2001); provenance considered uncertain and record not accepted by ABA committee (Robbins & ABA Checklist Committee 2004). *Elsewhere*: See Comments, below.
Comments: Ruddy Shelduck is popular in captivity and N American records are routinely dismissed as escapes, which is almost certainly the case—most of the time. Tracing records of Ruddy Shelduck in N America would be a time-consuming task, but we consider that natural vagrancy is plausible and suggest that observers make an effort to document records of Ruddy Shelduck so that any patterns may be elucidated (cf. Brinkley 2010a and Common Shelduck).

Several records known to us fit the time window of potential vagrants, but patterns shown by free-flying escapes may simply mirror patterns of their wild counterparts. For example, up to 3 returned to a site in s. QC for 3 successive years, most recently 19 Jun–6 Jul 1980, with 1 at the same site 24 Aug–24 Sep 1980 (*AB* 35:161); singles were in coastal VA, 18 Aug 1979 and 10 Jul 1982 (E. S. Brinkley, pers. comm.); and 1 was in NS, 19 Jul 1989 (McLaren 2001).

In Europe, Ruddy Shelduck has a contentious history (e.g., see Vinicombe 2008) but the historical pattern has been of northwestward summer dispersal (linked to droughts) from the Asian breeding grounds, with presumed wild birds exceptionally reaching Iceland and Greenland in mid–late Jul 1892. The mid–late summer peak of records in W Europe corresponds to molt migration, when birds seek safe locations where they can be flightless during molt. When traditional wetland areas in Asia are dry, the resultant diaspora of birds may extend far and wide. And, given that populations in Russia have been increasing, many birds reaching NW Europe in late summer may indeed be wild. A characteristic of these late summer occurrences is for birds to be in small groups, which is typical for irruptive vagrants, whereas one might expect escapes to occur as singles (Vinicombe & Harrop 1999). Thus, while the provenance of the Nunavut birds can never be known, the seasonal timing, remote location, and presence of a small flock, suggest that wild birds were involved in at least that one N American record (see Fig. 17, p. 15).
Field Identification: Striking and handsome species, appearing intermediate in demeanor between ducks and geese.
Similar Species: None in N America, but beware other overall ruddy species of waterfowl often kept in captivity, especially South African (Cape) Shelduck *T. cana*, which resembles Ruddy but has slaty gray head; South African is perhaps seen free-flying in N America as often as is Ruddy (P. Lehman, pers. comm.).
Age/Sex/Season: Ages differ slightly, with adult appearance attained at about 1 year; sexes differ slightly; slight seasonal variation. Complete prebasic molt occurs in fall–winter, preceded by partial prealternate molt (into eclipse plumage) in mid–late summer. *Adult*: Clean white upperwing patch. Male has pale buff head and neck with paler area around eye; distinct black neck-ring in breeding plumage. Female lacks black neck-ring, and in fresh basic plumage has contrasting white area around eye, less distinct

♀

♂ breeding
(Sep–Jun)

1st-year ♀

Ruddy Shelduck

♂

in worn and eclipse plumage. ***1st-year***: White upperwing patch duller, with ash-gray greater coverts, dusky tips to lesser and median coverts (often worn away by spring). Juv (Jun–Oct) resembles female but head and neck duskier, overall buffy gray. Usually attains adult-like plumage by late fall, but may be aged by upperwing panel. Attains adult plumage by complete 2nd-prebasic molt at about 1 year of age.

Habitat and Behavior: Lake shores, grassy steppes, rivers; rarely coastal mudflats. Mostly feeds by grazing while walking, like geese, but also while swimming. Calls include a rather goose-like honking *ahn* and *ahn-ank* in flight, and more varied purring honks in interactions.

FALCATED DUCK *Anas falcata* 46–54 cm (18–21")

Summary: ***Alaska***: On w. and cen. Aleutians, very rare in spring, exceptional in summer, fall, winter; on Pribilofs, exceptional in spring. ***Pacific States and Provinces***: Very rare in late fall–early spring.
Taxonomy: Monotypic.
Distribution and Status:

World: Breeds in E Asia, e. to ne. Russia (Kamchatka); winters mainly from e. China to Japan.

North America: ***Alaska***: On w. and cen. Aleutians, very rare in spring (mid-May to mid-Jun),

exceptional in summer (early–late Jul), fall (late Sep–Nov), and late winter (Feb to mid-Apr); mostly 1s and 2s, max. 6 on Adak, 9 Nov 1970. On Pribilofs, exceptional in spring (early–late Jun). No mainland records. ***Pacific States and Provinces***: Very rare or exceptional in late fall–early spring (mid-Nov to mid-Apr), with about 7 records (all males) from Vancouver Island s. to CA, most from WA to cen. CA, and some involving presumed returning birds in multiple years.

Comments: Spring records in the w. Aleutians and Bering Sea islands are likely drift overshoots from their breeding range in Kamchatka; both spring specimens are first-year males. The 3 fall AK specimens are 1st-year birds, suggesting misorientation. Of fall and winter records from the w. and cen. Aleutians, 9 birds were considered as females and only 5 males, a reversal of the typical sex ratio of ducks for the time and place; the fall specimen record shows 2 males, 1 female.

That all records away from AK were of males suggests the possibility females are being overlooked in the West, but also raises the specter of escapes. The question is especially perplexing in this species, given disconnects in both sex and date of occurrence between presumed wild AK birds and those in Pacific states and provinces. Falcated Ducks commonly consort in Asia with Eurasian Wigeon, and association with migrant flocks of the latter

eclipse ♂
(Jul–Oct)

♀

♂ breeding

juv ♂ (Sep–Oct)

♂ breeding
(Oct–Jul)

Falcated Duck

♀ breeding

species might be a vector for wintering Falcated Ducks in the West. However, we have no data on migration routes, or summering grounds, for the relatively large numbers of Eurasian Wigeon that winter in the Northwest, and thus cannot explore this conjecture further.

Not surprisingly, there are no records from Iceland, the Azores, or Barbados (and very few from W Europe); N American records cannot be expected via those routes. There are a few records of Falcated Duck from elsewhere in N America (e.g., ON, OH, and MD; ABA 2008), but lacking contrary data we treat these as not of wild origin.

Field Identification: Male in breeding plumage distinctive, but other plumages notably nondescript, suggesting something of a cross between a Gadwall and a wigeon.

Similar Species: Breeding male unlikely to be mistaken, but females relatively nondescript. Female and eclipse male **Gadwall** have more rounded head, a white speculum often partially visible at rest, orangy legs and feet, and, in the case of females, an orange-based bill. Female and eclipse male **American Wigeon** have blue bill, ruddier body plumage, contrasting white median underbody; male has white forewings.

Age/Sex/Season: Ages differ, with adult appearance attained in 1st year; sexes differ; marked seasonal variation in males. Complete prebasic molt in late summer–fall into breeding (male) plumage, preceded in mid–late summer by partial presupplemental molt (into eclipse head and body plumage); both sexes likely have partial prealternate molt in spring, although appearance may not change appreciably. Partial to incomplete preformative molt in fall–early winter (includes tail), after which male resembles breeding adult; subsequent molts like adult. See Martin & Garner (2012) for further information.

Breeding (basic) male (Oct–Jul): Striking. Bottle-green head with maroon-chestnut crown and face (bushy, tapered crest often concealed when neck hunched), pearly gray body with long, strongly falcate tertials. *Eclipse (supplemental) male* (Jul–Oct): Overall dull and female-like but with relatively long, black-centered tertials, clearer gray forewing, and gray vermiculations on scapulars (unlike 1st-year male). *Female*: Gray-brown overall with fairly long but straight, gray-based tertials, dusky brownish-gray forewing. *1st-year*: Juv in fall resembles female but body feathers smaller and more rounded; male has paler and clearer gray forewing versus dusky brownish gray on female. Attains adult-like plumage by mid-winter, but elongated tertials on male shorter, less strongly falcate than adult, forewing averages duller; often retains one or more juv rectrices into spring; some may attain fully adult-like tertials in late winter–spring.

Habitat and Behavior: Typical dabbling duck. In Asia, wintering birds frequently associate with Eurasian Wigeon (P. Holt, pers. comm.). Most common call in male a short, low whistle, followed by a wavering *uit-trr*; female gives hoarse, gruff quack (Madge & Burn 1988).

EASTERN SPOT-BILLED DUCK *Anas zonorhyncha* 58–63 cm (23–25")

Summary: *Alaska*: Exceptional year-round on w. and cen. Aleutians.

Taxonomy: Monotypic. Recently split from Indian Spot-billed Duck *A. poecilorhyncha*, which is unrecorded (and unlikely) in N America. Indian distinguished from Eastern by bright red loral spot (brightest on adult males, lacking on juvs), lack of dark cheek bar, paler back and underparts, green not blue speculum (difficult to appreciate), and largely white, versus white-edged, tertials.

Distribution and Status:

World: Breeds E Asia (n. to s. Sakhalin and s. Kuril Islands), n. populations migratory.

North America: *Alaska*: About 6 records from the Aleutians, most involving what were likely long-staying birds: Adak, 10 Apr 1970–18 Apr 1971; Kodiak, 30 Oct–1 Nov 1977; Adak, 29–31 May 1980 and 23 Dec 1980; Adak, 24 Oct 1983 and 25 Mar 1984; Attu, 18–19 May 1993, 23 Sep–5 Oct 1993, and 19 May 1994; and Adak, 28 May–16 Jul 2007 (*NAB* 61:496, 627).

Comments: This conspicuous duck has probably not been overlooked. The closest breeding point to the Aleutians is n. Japan, and even these northernmost birds withdraw in winter only to cen. and s. Japan. It's considered a straggler to Kamchatka. The Alaskan birds follow a pattern common to many long-lived species, with limited normal dispersal; once they arrive they tend to remain. Given limited temporal coverage of the Aleutians it's unclear at what season birds first arrived.

Field Identification: Distinctive, large dark duck, shaped like Mallard, with yellow-tipped black bill and strongly patterned face.

Similar Species: None, if seen well. If details of head and bill are not seen (such as sleeping, or flying away), could be confused with Black Duck.

Age/Sex/Season: Ages/sexes differ slightly; little seasonal variation. Complete prebasic molt occurs late summer–fall; other molts not well known but both sexes may have partial prealternate molt in spring, and partial presupplemental molt in mid–late summer, although appearance may not change appreciably. Plumages not well known. Male averages larger and darker than female with broader and cleaner white tertial edging in breeding plumage (winter–spring, at least); seasonal differences in tertial pattern may exist, as with female Mallard, but study needed.

Habitat and Behavior: A typical dabbling duck of the genus *Anas*. Most common calls much like Mallard (P. Holt, pers. comm.).

GARGANEY *Anas querquedula* 37–41 cm (14.5–16")

Summary: *Alaska*: On w. and cen. Aleutians, rare in spring and fall, exceptional in summer. Exceptional in spring and fall on Pribilofs, and in fall in s-coastal AK. *Pacific States and Provinces*: Very rare, fall and spring; exceptional in winter. *Interior*: Very rare in spring, exceptional in fall.

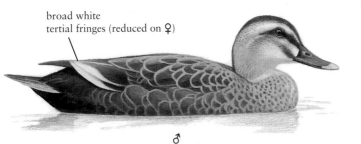
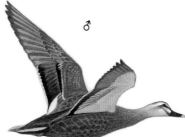

broad white tertial fringes (reduced on ♀)

♂

Eastern Spot-billed Duck   all plumages similar

♂

Atlantic States and Provinces: Very rare in spring, exceptional in fall.

Taxonomy: Monotypic.

Distribution and Status:

World: Breeds across temperate and mid-latitude N Eurasia, e. to e. Russia (Kamchatka). Winters in sub-Saharan Africa, the Indian subcontinent, and SE Asia.

North America: *Alaska*: On w. and cen. Aleutians, rare in spring (May to mid-Jun, exceptionally lingering to Jul), usually pairs or lone males, max. 5 per day; rare in fall (late Aug–early Nov, mainly Sep to mid-Oct), usually 1s and 2s, max. 4 on Attu, 23 Sep 1979 (attempted breeding suspected in 1987). On Pribilofs, exceptional in spring (mid–late May) and fall (late Aug–early Sep). 1 fall record from s-coastal AK, on Middleton Island, 29 Sep 1982. *Pacific States and Provinces*: Very rare in spring (mid-Mar to mid-Jun, mainly late Mar–mid-May) and fall (mid-Sep to early Nov, mainly 1990s), exceptional in winter (Dec–Feb). *Interior*: Very rare in spring (mid-Mar to May; exceptionally into Jun in n., mainly Canada), generally rarer eastward. 3 fall records (Sep–Oct): Davis Co., UT, 27 Oct 1996; Miami Co., KS, 23 Oct 1988 (adult male); Shelby Co., TN, 3 Sep 1994. *Atlantic States and Provinces*: Very rare in spring (mid-Mar to May, very rarely to Jun in Canada). 1 fall record: Accomack Co., VA, 6 Sep 2010.

Comments: Perhaps the most widespread vagrant we treat, having occurred in most states and provinces, with some 175 records overall, about 45% of them from AK, 20% from Pacific states and provinces, 20% from the interior, and 15% from Atlantic states and provinces. Spring records from AK likely reflect drift-overshoots, whereas fall birds are more likely to be misoriented young birds; however, we have no data on the age/sex breakdown of AK fall records. Garganey may even have bred in the w. Aleutians, whence there are a few summer records. Away from AK and the West Coast, virtually all records are of males during Mar–Jun, with relatively fewer records e. of the Mississippi than to the west. Pairs are frequently seen in AK, but the lack of such records from elsewhere in N America suggests that males in the Lower 48 are not arriving from their normal wintering grounds, where pairing would usually occur.

Like Spear et al. (1988), we suggest Garganeys reach our shores from both east and west, via the AK/N Pacific route and the S Atlantic route (see p. 10). Although records from Pacific states and provinces s. of AK are more or less equally split between fall and spring (with a few winter records), the pattern in CA of more fall than spring birds is likely a truer reflection of status. It appears that birds are moving s. in fall, perhaps mostly on or near the coast, but with many passing undetected. Northbound males in conspicuous breeding plumage are more widely distributed and more easily detected—there are spring records of males from most states and provinces w. of the Mississippi.

Records e. of the Mississippi are less frequent, and concentrated along the E Coast from NC northward to e. Canada, with multiple records from MA, ME, NS, SPM, NL, and a remarkable 10+ from QC. This pattern, coupled with 2 spring occurrences on Bermuda (1989, 2010) and 4 fall–winter records from Barbados, suggests that most eastern Garganey may be moving n. with Blue-winged Teal that winter in the se. Caribbean and e. S America, possibly via an overwater route that bypasses the se. US. It is also possible that a few birds may arrive via the N Atlantic route; there were 75 records from Iceland through 2006, almost all in spring and mainly in May, although no birds have been found in Greenland.

The rapid increase in N American records from the 1970s through 1990s is at least in part due to observer awareness, but the lack of records prior to 1957 is puzzling. Spear et al. (1988) suggested that range and population fluctuations of Garganey in Asia, perhaps linked to regional droughts and lowered hunting pressure, may have contributed to a northward breeding expansion and population increase, which was reflected by records in Hawaii and N America. Since the late 1990s, however, records in w. N America have declined markedly, mirroring significant declines recorded in E Asia (Delaney & Scott 2006); records from e. N America appear to be occurring at about the same rate as in recent years.

Field Identification: Small dabbling duck; breeding male unmistakable but female and non-breeding plumages similar to teal. In flight from above, all ages, but especially adults, show rather broad white trailing edge to secondaries, and males in particular have relatively pale 'hand' on upperwing; when the white speculum borders are uneven in width, trailing edge is wider on Garganey, which is the reverse of N American teal.

Similar Species: Female and juv similar to female and juv *Green-winged* and *Blue-winged Teal*, but face and upperwing pattern of

Green-winged Teal

Green-winged Teal ♀

pale orange base

♀

more contrasting head pattern

juv

Blue-winged Teal

1st-year ♀

Garganey

♀ Garganey

narrow eye-ring

pale loral spot

pale hand

adult ♂

broad white speculum borders

Blue-winged Teal juv

striped head

1st-year ♂

juv

♂ breeding (Jan–Jun)

Garganey

Garganey distinctive if seen well. Stripe-faced female Green-winged Teal is a real pitfall, but on Garganey note that pale eyebrow is often contrastingly paler behind eye, and mirrors breeding male pattern; teal typically has white or buffy-white wedge on sides on undertail coverts, which is lacking on Garganey (white edgings to outer rectrices of Garganey can form a similar looking white slash, but on different feathers). Female and juv Garganey have gray bills and legs, further points of separation from Green-winged Teal in the first instance (usually some orange on bill base, but can be gray overall) and Blue-winged Teal in the second (yellowish legs).

Age/Sex/Season: Ages differ, with adult appearance attained in 1st year; sexes differ; marked seasonal variation in males. Complete prebasic molt in summer–fall into nonbreeding plumage, preceded in summer by partial presupplemental molt; partial prealternate molt in winter–spring,

when male attains breeding plumage. Partial to incomplete preformative molt in fall–early winter (usually includes tail); subsequent molts like adult but prealternate molt averages later.

Breeding (alternate) male (Jan–Jun): Striking. Head and chest dark brown with thick white eyebrow, sides pearly gray. **Eclipse (supplemental/basic) male** (Jun–Feb): resembles female but face pattern stronger, forewing silvery blue-gray. **Female**: Gray-brown overall, forewing brownish gray. **1st-year**: Juv in fall resembles female but body feathers smaller and more rounded, face pattern and pale throat average duller and less contrasting; juv male has striking pale forewing similar to adult male; juv female has narrow white speculum borders and speculum lacks distinct green sheen of adult female. Attains adult-like plumage by 1st winter, and male attains breeding plumage late winter–spring, after which rarely separable from adult.

Habitat and Behavior: Much like Blue-winged Teal, with which Garganey often associate. Usually silent, but courting males have a dry rattle on one pitch, females quack.

BAIKAL TEAL *Anas formosa* 38–43 cm (15–17")

Summary: *Alaska*: In fall, very rare on w. Aleutians, exceptional on Pribilofs. Exceptional in spring–summer in n. and w. AK, in winter on e. Aleutians. *West*: Very rare, mainly in winter. *Elsewhere*: Uncertain (see Comments, below).
Taxonomy: Monotypic.
Distribution and Status:
World: Breeds NE Asia (ne. to e. Chukotka), winters e. China, Korea, and Japan.
North America: *Alaska*: On w. Aleutians, very rare in fall (late Aug–early Nov), since the first record in 1983 and mainly since 2001. 1 winter record from e. Aleutians: Unalaska, 20 Dec 2003. Exceptional on cen. Aleutians and Pribilofs in fall (Sep–early Oct) and in w. and n. AK in spring–summer (May–Jul). *West*: Very rare in fall–spring (mid-Oct to mid-Apr, mainly Dec–Jan) in Pacific states and provinces; from s. BC to s. CA, all males and more than half shot by hunters. Also 1 winter record from Maricopa Co., AZ, 2–10 Dec 2010 (*NAB* 65:220, 380), and single spring records from Grant Co., WA, 30 May 2008, and Queen Charlotte Islands, BC, 1 May 1996. *Elsewhere*: Uncertain (see Comments, below).
Comments: Baikal Teal was considered threatened until the discovery in the mid-1980s of large wintering populations in Korea. Perhaps coincidentally, the frequency of N American records increased at about the same time. While there was a pulse of mainland N American records in 2005 and 2006, perhaps matching the increase in records from w. AK, there was a similar peak in 1974 and 1975 with no apparent increase in w. AK. In AK, all fall records, presumably of displaced or misoriented birds, come from the Aleutians and Pribilofs, whereas spring–summer records are presumably overshoots to n. and nw. AK, a pattern recalling that shown by Little Stint.

There are no records of females away from AK. Many small, fast-flying ducks are not specifically identified by hunters, but bright males are preferred targets and curious hunters seek the identity of strange birds in their bag. Male Baikal Teal showing an adult face pattern are more likely to draw comment; females, if present, are more likely to be ignored. Most early fall records from the w. Aleutians were not sexed, but 1 of the 2 late-Aug specimens is a female. Even though males are more likely to occur as vagrants, the absence of females away from the Aleutians suggests they may be overlooked.

The species is a long-distance migrant, and records in s. CA and AZ suggest some birds continue s. into Mexico for the winter. Scattered records of Baikal Teal elsewhere in N America (e.g., CO, OK, LA, ON, OH, PA, NJ, NC) are usually considered of uncertain provenance (ABA 2008), but other than their added distance from natural populations there is little to separate them from accepted records in Pacific states and provinces, and some may be naturally occurring. There are no records from Iceland or the Azores, and the species is an exceptional vagrant in W Europe, suggesting it's unlikely a Baikal Teal would arrive in N America from across the Atlantic.
Field Identification: Small, fast-flying duck, distinctive in male breeding plumage but otherwise should be separated with care from other small dabbling ducks. Note complex face pattern, grayish bill (lacking yellowish base of Green-winged Teal), broad white trailing edge to secondaries (like pintail). Beware hybrid ducks, some of which show face pattern recalling male Baikal Teal. See Garner (2008b) for further information on identification of females.

Similar Species: Female/juv similar to female/juv *Green-winged* and *Blue-winged Teal*, and *Garganey*, but often appears longer tailed, with crown slightly peaked; face and upperwing patterns distinctive. Lacks pale forewing of Blue-winged Teal and male Garganey, and has darker hand on upperwing than female *Garganey*.

Age/Sex/Season: Ages differ, with adult appearance attained in 1st year; sexes differ; marked seasonal variation in males. Complete prebasic molt in late summer–fall into breeding (male) plumage preceded in mid–late summer by partial presupplemental molt (into eclipse head and body plumage); both sexes likely have partial prealternate molt in spring, although appearance may not change appreciably. Partial to incomplete preformative molt in late fall–early winter (usually includes tail); subsequent molts like adult.

Breeding (basic) male (Oct–Jul): Striking, with bright face pattern, long and ornate scapulars.
Eclipse (supplemental) male (Jul–Oct): Resembles female but averages darker with broader and warmer, tawny-brown edgings to upperparts, less well-defined whitish spot at base

pale orange
bill base

mottled dark

Green-winged Teal
♀

broad
speculum

distinctive
pattern

Green-winged Teal

broad
speculum

plain

peaked
rear crown

striking head
pattern

♀ variation

broad white
trailing edge

narrow
speculum

♂ breeding (Oct–Jul)

narrow speculum   ♀

Baikal Teal

of bill. **Female**: Gray-brown overall with well-defined whitish spot at base of bill. **1st-year**: Juv in fall resembles female but body feathers smaller and more rounded. Attains adult-like plumage by 1st winter, and male rarely separable from adult after mid-winter.

Habitat and Behavior: Much as other dabbling ducks. In W Europe, winter Baikal Teal have been noted associating with wigeon rather than teal. Voice not reported in N America, but in normal range said to be a deep, chuckling *wot-wot-wot* (male) and a low *quack* (female) (Madge & Burn 1988).

COMMON POCHARD *Aythya ferina*
42–50 cm (16.5–20")

Summary: *Alaska:* In spring, rare and intermittent on w. and cen. Aleutians, very rare on Pribilofs, exceptional on St. Lawrence and w. mainland. Exceptional in summer–fall on

cen. Aleutians, and in early spring on s-coastal mainland. **California**: 2 winter records (1989–1992, 1994). **Quebec**: 1 spring record (2008).
Taxonomy: Monotypic.
Distribution and Status:
World: Breeds from Iceland e. to cen. Russia, around 120°E, mainly at mid-latitudes. Winters from W Europe and N Africa e. to the Indian subcontinent and Japan.
North America: *Alaska*: On w. and cen. Aleutians, rare and intermittent in spring (late Apr to mid-Jun); max. 9 on Shemya, 17–18 May 1975 (4 male, 5 female), and Attu, 11 May 1998. Single fall and winter records, both on Adak, 16 Oct 1973 (2 female/imms), 1–11 Mar 1994 (3 males). In spring, very rare on the Pribilofs (May–early Jun), and exceptional (mid-May to mid-Jun) on St. Lawrence and w. mainland. One record from s-coastal mainland, 22 Mar 1981 (female). *California*: San Bernardino Co., 11–17 Feb 1989 (male; presumably same bird in Jan–Feb 1991,

Canvasback ♀

peaked crown

very long, dark bill

blocky head

Redhead ♀

distinctive bill pattern

♂ (center right) with 4 ♂ Canvasbacks

♀

rounded crown

pale face

♀ breeding (May–Aug)

bill often lacks pale band

pale band

♀

Common Pochard

♂ breeding (Sep–Jun)

Jan–Feb 1992, Nov 1992), and Orange Co., 26 Dec 1994 (2 males). **Quebec**: 2–11 May 2008 (male; *NAB* 62:375).

Comments: Common Pochard is not mapped as nesting in the Russian Far East (Brazil 2009), although it is considered an uncommon breeder on the Kamchatka Peninsula. Its spring appearances in the w. Aleutians seem correlated with the appearance there of Tufted Ducks, given that high counts of both have been on the same dates. Thus, the pochards may have wintered with Tufted Ducks, perhaps in Japan, and moved n. with them in the spring. Pochards have twice reached the nw. Hawaiian Islands, in Nov and May, the latter a record of 3 males, suggesting significant overwater capacities.

While Common Pochard is regular in spring in the w. Aleutians, there's little evidence that these spring birds make it to mainland N America. We assume that with few exceptions they reorient to the Asian mainland. The AK mainland female was a month before the first w. Aleutian spring arrivals, suggesting it may have wintered locally.

The CA birds may have joined flocks of Greater Scaup in the Aleutians, as those populations winter along the Pacific Coast; but if so they

abandoned them by the time they reached their CA wintering locations. Given the virtual absence of fall pochards in AK, and the species' absence from the vagrant record elsewhere in Pacific states and provinces, additional N American records away from AK will be infrequent, although the CA birds were all adult males and may have been overlooked while in less eye-catching plumage. Perhaps because Common Pochard resembles Canvasback and Redhead, and thus has no special appeal in collections, it is rare in captivity in N America (Patten 1993).

The QC record may represent a bird that arrived either via the southern route and migrated n. undetected through the East, or perhaps directly via the northern route (pp. 8–9); it occurred within a week of a Garganey and a Tufted Duck nearby, and a female Common Pochard was reported from the same site on 3 May 2008 (*NAB* 62:375). There were 227 records of Common Pochard from Iceland through 2006 (mostly Apr–Jun with a peak in May) but none from Greenland. Pochards also occur every few years on the Azores, have twice reached the Cape Verde Islands in winter, and a group of 4 recently reached Barbados following cold conditions in W Europe (*NAB* 65:356, 386).

This all suggests that further records are likely in the East, especially in spring.

Field Identification: Looks intermediate between Canvasback and Redhead, but all ages distinguished by head/bill profile and bill pattern. Beware that hybrid *Aythya* ducks occur, if rarely, and that Canvasback × Redhead hybrids can closely resemble Common Pochard (Haramis 1982).

Similar Species: Adult male **Redhead** and **Canvasback** have different bill patterns: all blue (except nail) in Redhead and all-dark in Canvasback. Redhead also smaller, with shorter, thinner bill, steeper forehead, darker body. Canvasback has a more elongate bill, black (not chestnut) on forehead, paler (often almost silvery whitish) body, and more restricted black on chest.

Female/imm Pochard similar in plumage to Redhead and Canvasback, best distinguished by head/bill profile and bill pattern (beware that bill can be mostly dark on summer birds). Compared to the same age Common Pochard, Canvasback has paler body. In flight, Redhead shows more contrast between dark forewing and gray flight feathers.

Canvasback × Redhead hybrids can closely resemble Common Pochard but are larger, and are not known to exactly match pochard in details of bill shape and pattern.

Age/Sex/Season: Ages differ, with adult appearance attained in 1st year; sexes differ; seasonal variation distinct in males. Complete prebasic molt in late summer–fall into breeding (male) plumage, preceded in summer by partial presupplemental molt (into eclipse head and body plumage); both sexes likely have partial prealternate molt in spring, although appearance may not change appreciably (except perhaps some 1st-year males). Partial to incomplete preformative molt in fall–winter (usually includes tail); subsequent molts like adult.

Breeding (basic) male (Sep–Jun): Bright rufous-chestnut head and black breast contrast with pearly gray body; bill pattern bright. ***Eclipse (supplemental) male*** (Jun–Sep): Pattern resembles breeding male but much duller overall; head, breast, and body variably washed brownish, bill pattern often muted. ***Female***: Head and breast dark brown with variable whitish face pattern; body grayish overall in winter, browner in summer; bill pattern can be muted in summer. ***1st-year***: Juv resembles female but body browner overall, lacks whitish postocular line. Attains adult-like plumage by 1st winter and may not be

separable from adult after mid-winter, although some males have brownish wash to body into spring.

Habitat and Behavior: Typical *Aythya* diving duck. Prefers freshwater and estuaries. Vagrants likely to be found with other *Aythya*. Usually silent, other than when courting.

SMEW *Mergellus albellus* 38–44 cm (15–17.5")

Summary: *Alaska*: On w. and cen. Aleutians, rare in spring and fall–winter; exceptional in summer. On Bering Sea islands, very rare in spring. Exceptional in n. and s-coastal AK. ***Pacific States and Provinces***: Very rare in winter–spring. ***Elsewhere***: Very rare or exceptional in winter–spring, but confounded by possible escapes (see Comments, below).

Taxonomy: Monotypic.

Distribution and Status:

World: Breeds boreal forest zone from Scandinavia e. to ne. Russia (Kamchatka, e. Chukotka). Winters locally from W Europe e. to s. China and Japan.

North America: *Alaska*: On w. and cen. Aleutians, rare in spring (late Apr to mid-Jun) and fall–winter (fall migrants mid-Sep to early Nov; wintering birds Nov–Mar, some lingering to Apr–May), usually singles or small groups, max. 16 on Attu, 15 May 1998; exceptional in summer (late Jun–Jul). On Pribilofs, very rare in spring (May–early Jun). Exceptional on e. Aleutians (9–10 Jun 1989), on St. Lawrence (24 May 2009; pair), and in n. AK (3 Jul 2002; *NAB* 56:472) and s-coastal AK (Nov–Apr). ***Pacific States and Provinces***: Very rare in winter (mid-Nov to early Apr, most in Jan–Mar), all adult males except a female/imm in BC, 28 Feb–21 Mar 1974 (likely a 1st-year male, given an adult male at the same site the following winter). About 11 records, assuming 4 sets of records (1974–1975 in BC, 1981–1984 and 2007–2008 in CA, 1989–1993 in WA) involved returning birds. ***Elsewhere***: Reports from at least AB, MB, MT, ND, MN, WI, MO, ON, NY, and RI, most in winter (Nov–Mar) but with spring (Apr–May) records from MT and AB. Most were adult males, but the Mar 1999 MN bird and both ON birds were said to be females. Birds thought to have returned in successive years were in RI (winter, 1976–1978) and AB (spring, 2007–2008).

Comments: Mainland records of Smew are difficult to evaluate. The geographic and seasonal distribution of records in N America seems reasonable for wild individuals that have moved

1st-spring ♂

♀ (eclipse ♂ and
1st-winter ♂ similar)

Smew

♀

♂

adult ♂ breeding (Oct–Jul)

into N America from E Asia, and is mirrored by numerous Asian species among diverse taxa. Most records come from Pacific states and provinces, but a review of the International Species Information System (ISIS) database (accessed 2011) showed no particular concentration of captive Smew in the Northwest; moreover, more captive females than males were listed, but ISIS only covered larger zoos.

Still, an unknown number of records may involve escapes from captivity, which may live a long time in the wild such that a single individual could account for records in multiple states and provinces. A male in MN, Feb–Mar 2004, was seen to lack a hind toe (a digit often clipped on birds held in captivity) and thus considered a probable escape.

Virtually all N American records of Smew away from the Aleutians are of males. Vagrant waterfowl are generally skewed in favor of males, so these records may reflect nature, but it's interesting to note that of the 16–17 birds in Iceland through 2007 (10–11 in Oct–Feb, 6 in late Apr–early Jul), at least 9 were females and only 5 adult males (Y. Kolbeinsson, pers. comm.), and records from the Aleutians are mostly reported as females (although many fall–winter birds identified as such could have been young males).

In summary, some and perhaps most of the birds in Pacific states and provinces are surely wild. Records elsewhere on the continent may be more suspect, but we feel some (if not most) are likely to be wild, as has been argued for the RI bird (Ryan 1976).

Field Identification: Small, rather compact, and stunning merganser, distinctive in all plumages.

Similar Species: None, if seen well.

Age/Sex/Season: Ages differ, with adult appearance attained in 1st year; sexes differ; marked seasonal variation in males. Molts not well known. Complete prebasic molt in fall–early winter into breeding (male) plumage, preceded in summer by partial presupplemental molt (into eclipse head and body plumage); both sexes may have partial prealternate molt in spring, although appearance may not change appreciably (except perhaps 1st-year male). Partial to incomplete preformative molt in late fall–winter; subsequent molts like adult.

Breeding (basic) male (Oct–Jul): White overall with black back, black lores, black lines on head and sides of body. *Eclipse (supplemental) male* (Jul–Oct): Resembles female but center of back blackish, sides of head may average paler. *Female*: Head chestnut with blackish lores, large white throat patch, back gray. *1st-year*:

Juv/1st-winter resembles female but lores may be dark brown rather than blackish. In mid–late winter, some 1st-year males develop extensive white on cheeks, but others still resemble females; male resembles adult by mid–late spring, but often messier overall.

Habitat and Behavior: A typical merganser, preferring fresh water. Vagrants likely to be mostly silent.

New World Waterfowl

The 4 species of rare waterfowl with New World origins show rather different patterns of occurrence. White-faced Whistling-Duck occurs mainly in spring in Florida (and perhaps elsewhere in the Southeast), corresponding to dispersal from wetlands in n. S America at the end of the dry season; White-cheeked Pintail occurs in fall–spring, mainly in Florida again; and Masked Ducks disperse n. sporadically from Mexico and the Caribbean to Texas and Florida, mainly in fall–spring when water levels in places such as s. Texas are suitable for breeding. The single spring record of West Indian Whistling-Duck is difficult to evaluate without more context.

WHITE-FACED WHISTLING-DUCK
Dendrocygna viduata 43–48 cm (17–19")

Summary: *Florida*: Very rare in spring, exceptional in summer–fall. *Elsewhere*: see Comments, below.
Taxonomy: Monotypic.
Distribution and Status:
World: Breeds and wanders through much of tropical S America, and at least formerly n. to s. Cen America; also tropical Africa and Madagascar.

North America: *Florida*: At least 6 spring records (Mar–May) of singles from the s. third of the peninsula, all since 1998: Polk Co., 19 Mar–4 Apr 1998 (*NAB* 52:321); Orange Co., 7 May 2000 (*NAB* 54:275); Broward Co., 3 Mar 2003 (*NAB* 57:337); Pinellas Co., 23 Mar 2007 (*NAB* 61:434); Polk Co., 29 Apr–May 2007 (*NAB* 61:434); Hendry Co., 14 May 2011 (*NAB* 65:422); also 1 summer record, Manatee Co., 21 Jun 2007 (*NAB* 61:578), 1 late fall record, Hendry Co., 27 Nov 2010 (*NAB* 65:60). *Elsewhere*: See Comments, below.
Comments: Like many wetland birds associated with ephemeral habitats, whistling-ducks are inherently nomadic and dispersive. Perhaps linked to an apparent increase in climatic extremes and frequent droughts, the past 30 or so

years have seen increasing numbers of extralimital whistling-ducks (Black-bellied, Fulvous, and White-faced) throughout the Americas, from Chile to Canada. For example, Black-bellied Whistling-Ducks are spreading n. into Baja California and FL, and are increasing in TX; and the spring of 2003 saw an unprecedented invasion of both Black-bellied and Fulvous Whistling-Ducks into N America, with birds recorded as far north as AB and QC (Brinkley 2003). Something is going on with whistling-ducks, and its magnitude seems to overshadow the possibility that all of it relates to escaped birds. We consider it reasonable to provisionally treat some recent US records of White-faced and West Indian Whistling-Ducks as natural vagrants rather than potentially obscure vagrancy patterns by automatically consigning every record to the 'escape bin.'

White-faced Whistling-Duck is nomadic and dispersive over most of its range, as is true of many neotropical wetland birds, and it has good potential for vagrancy. Vagrants have been recorded in the Caribbean on Cuba, Hispaniola, and Barbados (Rafaelle et al. 1998), and in S America this species has crossed the Andes into Chile on several occasions (Marín 2004), presumably in response to drought conditions in Argentina. It is considered an extirpated breeding resident in Costa Rica and Panama (AOU 1998), but may simply be an irregular and irruptive visitor there, staying to breed after invasions (Ridgely & Gwynne 1989, Wetmore 1981).

The spring pattern of FL records corresponds with the end of the dry season in n. S America, which may force birds to wander at this season, as perhaps occurs also with Southern Lapwing and Large-billed Tern, and as postulated for a recent record of Comb Duck *Sarkidiornis melanotos* from nw. Costa Rica (Dinsmore & Harms 2011). At the same time, White-faced Whistling-Duck is kept in wildfowl collections and some N American records likely pertain to escapes.

Most N American records of this essentially unmistakable species have been fairly recent, but 'presumed escapes' of earlier years may have gone unreported. There have been several records from s. FL since the first in 1991 (Stevenson & Anderson 1994), with a distinct peak in Mar–May. At least the 2003 Florida record, of an unbanded bird whose occurrence coincided with a remarkable whistling-duck invasion in N America, seems a reasonable

White-faced Whistling-Duck

adult

juv

adult

candidate for a wild vagrant, and other records may also be of wild individuals. Records away from FL include singles in Currituck Co., NC, 23 May 1997 (E. S. Brinkley, pers. comm.), and, in company with a Black-bellied Whistling-Duck, in Apr 1998 (Lee 2000). More data are needed to address the issue of vagrancy versus escapes, and we encourage observers to report all sightings so that patterns, if they exist, may be elucidated.

Field Identification: Fairly small, lightly built, and handsomely plumaged whistling-duck.

Similar Species: Nothing really similar although juv White-faced superficially resembles juv of larger and bulkier ***Black-bellied Whistling-Duck***, which has a white eye-ring, dark crown extending forward to bill base, bold white upper-wing panels, and lacks whitish flank barring.

Age/Sex/Season: Ages differ with adult appearance attained in 1st year; sexes similar; no seasonal variation. Presumably has complex basic molt strategy (see p. 35) but timing of molts undescribed, and likely varies with timing of breeding (study needed). ***1st-year***: Juv lacks bold black-and-white head pattern, chest duller and paler than adult; underparts diffusely barred, lacking solidly black belly. Looks much like adult after partial preformative molt within a few months of fledging, and attains fully adult

appearance by complete 2nd-prebasic molt at about 1 year.

Behavior: Wetlands, including fairly open situations such as rice fields, where it could occur with other whistling-ducks. Forages mainly at night. Call a slightly reedy or piping 3–4 syllable whistle, *whih whih whíhiw* or *whi whi whíhiw*; juv, at least, gives a high 2-syllable whistle, *whí híhw*, with adult-like quality, thus unlike more nasal calls of Fulvous Whistling-Duck.

WEST INDIAN WHISTLING-DUCK
Dendrocygna arborea 50–57 cm (19.5–22")

Summary: *Virginia*: 1 spring record (2003). *Elsewhere*: Status uncertain, see Comments, below.

Taxonomy: Monotypic.

Distribution and Status:

World: Breeds and wanders in the Bahamas, Greater Antilles, and n. Lesser Antilles.

North America: *Virginia*: Dismal Swamp, Suffolk, 29 Apr 2003 (Schwab & Suomala 2003). *Elsewhere*: See Comments, below.

Comments: See comments under White-faced Whistling-Duck. Because observers (and committees) tend to write off records of extralimital whistling-ducks as escapes, it is difficult to determine how many reports of West Indian

Whistling-Duck there have been in N America (most are from FL and TX; see Schwab & Suomala 2003 for a summary). Moreover, this species' nocturnal feeding habits make it easy to overlook. Escapes are certainly responsible for some N American records of West Indian Whistling-Duck, such as one in TX in 1992–1995. And about 10 reports of this species in s. FL from the 1960s to 1980s were assumed to have been linked to a nearby waterfowl collection where free-flying birds were kept (Roberstson & Woolfenden 1992).

The status of this species in the West Indies is not well known; some populations are apparently in decline, others are stable or increasing (Schwab & Suomala 2004). On St. Croix, 2 adults in Oct 2002 were the first documented occurrence in the US Virgin Islands since 1941 (McNair et al. 2005), but variable observer coverage and the species' nocturnal habits make it difficult to evaluate such records in the context of inter-island movements, vagrancy, or population trends. A record from Bermuda (in Nov 1907) is usually treated as of wild origin (e.g., AOU 1998), and as noted by W. B. Robertson Jr. & Woolfenden (1992), this species 'is a plausible, even a likely, natural vagrant' to FL. The Virginia state committee accepts this species in its category 3 (identity accepted but provenance unknown, wild occurrence possible), and we treat it provisionally as a wild vagrant. We encourage observers to document all records of this species, so that any patterns may be revealed.

Field Identification: Fairly large and chunky whistling-duck, overall dark brown.

Similar Species: Nothing really similar in N America. ***Fulvous Whistling-Duck*** slightly smaller (48–54cm) with tawny underparts, distinct white flank streaks, and unspotted white tail coverts; in flight, upperwings dark, white upper-tail coverts form contrasting 'U' above black tail.

Spotted Whistling-Duck *D. guttata* of New Guinea region, a possible escape from captivity, is smaller and shorter necked, with grayish face and broad dark eyestripe, pinkish tones to bill and legs, and all-dark upperwings. Post-juvenile plumages have large white spots on flanks; juv duller overall, flanks less strongly patterned.

Age/Sex/Season: Ages differ slightly with adult appearance attained in 1st year; sexes similar; no seasonal variation. Presumably has complex basic molt strategy (see p. 35) but timing of molts undescribed, and likely varies with timing of breeding (study needed). ***1st year***: Juv duller overall than adult, with less distinct flank markings, lacks dark-streaked necklace. Probably looks much like adult after partial preformative molt within a few months of fledging, and attains fully adult appearance by complete 2nd-prebasic molt at about 1 year.

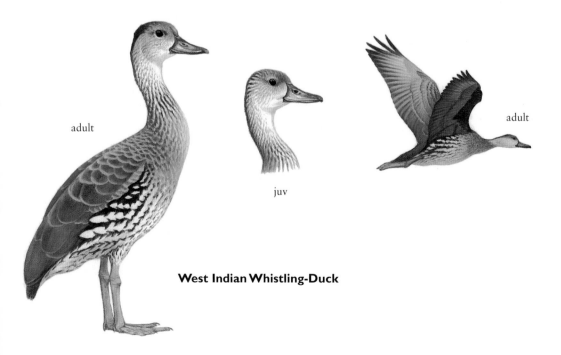

adult

juv

adult

West Indian Whistling-Duck

Habitat and Behavior: Wetlands with surrounding trees, mangroves. A mostly nocturnal forager that roosts readily in trees. Voice a shrill, rather harsh whistled *visisee* (Madge and Burn 1988).

WHITE-CHEEKED PINTAIL
Anas bahamensis 45–50 cm (17.5–19.5")

Summary: *Florida*: Very rare, mainly winter–spring. *Elsewhere*: Status uncertain, see Comments, below.

Taxonomy: 3 ssp, differing in size and overall plumage tones; perhaps separable in the field given good photos and comparison with other species. Specimens from FL have been of n. ssp *bahamensis*, which is widespread in the Caribbean; *rubrirostris* of mainland S America averages larger and darker, and *galapagensis* of Galapagos Islands averages smaller and duller.

Distribution and Status:

World: Breeds and mostly resident locally in the Caribbean n. to Bahamas, locally in tropical and subtropical S America, and on the Galapagos Islands.

North America: *Florida*: Very rare (about 25 records in the period), mainly recorded from the Everglades but also northward through the peninsula. Almost all records in winter–spring (late Nov–early May), with summer records exceptional. *Elsewhere*: Scattered records n. as far as e. Canada and w. to CA are generally considered to be of escapes (ABA 2008), although a bird that wintered in Cameron Co., TX (Nov 1978–Apr 1979) was considered wild by the state committee. 1 in Accomack Co., VA, 4–21 Sep 2010, with huge flocks of ducks driven ashore by Hurricane Earl (*NAB* 65:51), is considered of uncertain provenance by the state committee.

Comments: Populations in the Caribbean fluctuate and move among islands depending on water levels, and the species has occurred as a vagrant on Jamaica, the Cayman Islands, Guadeloupe, and Martinique (Rafaelle et al. 1998). Some of the FL records are surely of wild birds from the Bahamas or elsewhere in the Caribbean, but the specter of escapes clouds the picture of natural occurrence in N America (this handsome species is popular in waterfowl collections, and escapes can wander and occur far from human population centers).

It is unclear whether the dearth of reports from FL since the 1990s reflects a decline in the number of birds occurring or an assumption by birders that individuals of this species are escapes and not worth reporting; for example, a recent record from 29 Dec 2001–5 Feb 2002 was considered an escape without explanation (*NAB* 56:168). Attention to plumage details could help with this question, as with one NJ record that apparently pertained to the ssp *rubrirostris* of S America (*AB* 35:163), an unlikely candidate for vagrancy to the E Coast.

Field Identification: Handsome duck, in size and shape much like Northern Pintail but lacking strongly elongated central rectrices.

Similar Species: Nothing similar likely to occur as a natural vagrant. Similar ***Red-billed Duck*** *Anas eryhrorhyncha* (native to S Africa) could occur as an escape. Differs from White-cheeked Pintail in blacker cap, red bill with black restricted to broad strip on base of culmen, and overall colder plumage tones (but with cinnamon speculum).

Age/Sex/Season: Ages and sexes differ slightly, attaining adult appearance in 1st year; no seasonal variation. Molts undescribed; likely complex alternate strategy (see p. 35) but may

all plumages similar

White-cheeked Pintail   ♂ (averages brighter and longer-tailed than ♀)

lack presupplemental molt (cf. Howell 2010a). *Male* slightly larger, averages brighter and longer tailed than female, with brighter and more extensive red on base of bill. ***1st-year***: Juv duller overall than adult, with a browner cap, duller red to pinkish-red bill sides, and slightly shorter, pale buffy tail. Probably resembles adult by midwinter (study needed).

Habitat and Behavior: Freshwater and saline habitats. FL birds have been found alone or in company with Northern Pintail and Blue-winged Teal. Behavior much like Northern Pintail, feeding in muddy and weedy shallows.

MASKED DUCK *Neomonyx dominicus*
33–38 cm (13–15")

Summary: *East*: Very rare, mainly fall to spring; in TX (where has bred) and FL. Exceptional elsewhere: Single winter–spring records from GA (1962), NC (1982), and PA (1984); see Comments, below.
Taxonomy: Monotypic.
Distribution and Status:
    World: Local and nomadic from Mexico and Greater Antilles to tropical S America.

North America: *East*: Rare but sporadic visitor to Lower Rio Grande Valley and coastal plains of TX (mainly fall–spring, but recorded year-round), exceptionally to w. TX, ne. TX (Jun 2008; *NAB* 62:584), and n. to s. LA (late Dec–early Apr). Very rare and sporadic (mainly Nov–Mar, but records year-round) in s. FL, since the first state record in 1955. Exceptional (Dec–Jun) n. to nw. FL (Dec 1962, Dec 2010), Lowndes Co., GA (11 Apr 1962), Craven Co., NC (20–25 Feb 1982), and Berks Co., PA (12–14 Jun 1984). A report from TN in mid-Apr 1974 (Fintel 1974) was not of a Masked Duck and appears to have been of a hybrid involving Bufflehead.

Comments: As with several denizens of ephemeral wetlands, Masked Duck is prone to wander, and in N America its largely fall and winter occurrences recall those of Northern Jacana and neotropical rails. Masked Ducks are absent most years in TX, with major 'invasions' documented in the late 1880s and early 1890s, 1930s, late 1960s and early 1970s, and early 1990s (Lockwood 1997); at such times the species can be locally common (e.g., a concentration of 37 birds at one site in Feb 1993). There are 2 well-documented US breeding records, both from TX, in Sep–Oct 1967

white upperwing patch and axillars

♀

ragged tips to juv feathers

juv

♂ nonbreeding (can be year-round)'

♀ (variable, some warmer brown)

Masked Duck

♂ breeding (can be year-round)

and Oct–Nov 2007. TX birds likely come mainly from Mexico, whereas records from FL and other e. states are more likely to involve birds from the Greater Antilles.

Masked Ducks do not appear to be a species that is, or has been, kept in captivity (Madge & Burn 1988), which relieves the burden of considering escapes and reveals how widely a conventionally 'resident' neotropical duck can wander. There have been no records since the mid-1980s away from TX and FL, but during 1857–1905 there were single records (all late Aug–Nov) from WI, VT, MA, and MD. Taken together, this may indicate that source populations have been declining over the past 100 or so years.

Field Identification: Easily overlooked denizen of marshy wetlands.

Similar Species: None, if seen well. Confusion perhaps most likely with duckling of ***Black-bellied Whistling-Duck***, which has a short buff eyebrow, dark crown and eyestripe, and buff cheeks with a dark horizontal bar; these ducklings dive when alarmed, may be left unattended by parents, and often occur in similar habitats to Masked Duck. If seen simply in flight at dawn or dusk, fast direct flight in combination with size and shape can suggest ***Hooded Merganser***.

Age/Sex/Season: Ages/sexes differ; seasonal variation pronounced in males. Presumed to have complete prebasic molt after breeding, partial prealternate molt before breeding, but no data exist. ***Breeding male*** (can be seen year-round): Solid black face and crown, upperparts mottled black-and-chestnut; bill bright blue with black tip. Solid white panel on inner secondaries, greater coverts, and median coverts.

Nonbreeding male (year-round): Bill and face resemble female but contrast with chestnut hindneck; upperparts mottled black and chestnut, with scattered buff bars and spots. ***Female***: Face striped buff and blackish brown. Upperparts dark brown with pale buff bars and spots. Some birds more cinnamon-toned (breeding?), others paler and buffier (nonbreeding?). White wing patch may be smaller than on male, with dark bars on inner greater coverts. ***1st-year***: Juv resembles female but head stripes duller and browner; bars and spots on upperparts cinnamon, fading to buff; median coverts dark with white notching, greater coverts of male with dark subterminal marks. Subsequent 1st-year molts and plumages undescribed.

Habitat and Behavior: Freshwater marshes and water bodies with emergent vegetation, from roadside ditches to large lakes. Perhaps mainly a nocturnal feeder, roosting inconspicuously among emergent vegetation and coming out at night on to open water, where dives well. Very unlikely to be seen flying during the day; flies mainly around dawn and dusk (and possibly at night). Takes off directly from water, enabling use of small ponds and ditches where it can be quite confiding during the daytime.

SUNGREBES (FINFOOTS): HELIORNITHIDAE

Small pantropical family of swimming waterbirds that, ironically, most often shun the sun and, unlike grebes, do not dive for food. Three species worldwide, 1 in the Americas, which has occurred as an exceptional vagrant to the sw. US.

SUNGREBE *Heliornis fulica* 26.5–29 cm (10.5–11.5")

Summary: ***New Mexico***: 1 late fall record (2008).
Taxonomy: Monotypic.
Distribution and Status:
   World: E Mexico to Brazil.
   North America: ***New Mexico***: Socorro Co., NM, 13–18 Nov 2008 (female; Williams et al. 2009).
Comments: This ostensibly resident and little-known neotropical species was not on anyone's radar as an addition to the US avifauna.

Sungrebes are not known in captivity, however, and the species apparently has been expanding its range n. in e. Mexico over the past 50 years (Williams et al. 2009). The remarkable NM occurrence may represent a pioneer striking out from the edge of the species' range. Of interest is another recent extralimital occurrence of Sungrebe, the first record from Bonaire, Netherlands Antilles, on 15 Nov 2010 (Rozemeijer 2011), a remarkably similar date to the NM record.

Field Identification: Small swimming bird, unlike any N American species, with a fairly long rounded tail (visible mainly in flight) and stout pointed bill.

rounded wings and
long, broad rear end

♂

♂

♀

Sungrebe

Similar Species: Nothing in N America.

Age/Sex/Season: Ages probably similar following briefly held juv plumage; sexes differ; no seasonal variation. No data on molts. *Male*: Lacks bright tawny cheeks of female, bill may average duller (age-related or possible seasonal changes in bill color in need of study).

Habitat and Behavior: Freshwater habitats with surrounding or overhanging vegetation, from ponds to slow-moving rivers; generally avoids open or fast-moving water. Usually swims close to cover, jerking its neck like a moorhen, and rarely if ever dives. Takes off with brief pattering and flies strongly, usually low over the water. Mostly silent in nonbreeding season, but at times utters a quiet sharp *plik* while foraging, and in territorial interactions or alarm has a barking *wek!* often in series.

ALCIDS (AUKS): ALCIDAE

Small family of marine diving birds that inhabit cold waters of the N Hemisphere, with greatest diversity in the N Pacific; 1 species occurs as a vagrant to N America from E Asia. Long-distance vagrancy is rare among alcids, although Ancient Murrelet has a similar pattern of occurrence to Long-billed Murrelet in interior and e. N America, and both species have even reached W Europe (Haas 2012).

LONG-BILLED MURRELET
Brachyramphus perdix 24–26 cm (9.5–10.2")

Summary: *Alaska*: Exceptional or very rare in late spring on Bering Sea islands; single spring–early fall records from cen. Aleutians, interior, and s. coast. *Pacific States and Provinces*: Very rare to rare, late summer–early winter. *Interior West*: Very rare in late summer–fall, exceptional in early winter. *Interior East*: Very rare, late fall–early winter; 1 spring record. *Atlantic States and Provinces*: Very rare, late fall–early winter, exceptional in spring, summer, and early fall.

Taxonomy: Monotypic.
Distribution and Status:
    World: Breeds NE Asia, from Sea of Okhotsk and Kamchatka Peninsula s. to n. Japan. Winters mainly in Japanese waters, s. to around 25°N.
    North America: *Alaska*: Exceptional or very rare in spring (late May to mid-Jun) on Pribilofs; single records from cen. Aleutians (mid-May), interior (Aug), and s. coast (2 Jun–6 Aug 2011; 3 birds, *NAB* 65:674). *Pacific States and Provinces*: Very rare from s. BC s. to cen. CA, mainly Jul–Aug with a lesser peak in Nov–Dec, and a few Sep–Oct and Feb (*NAB* 65:337) records; mostly

recent and almost half from CA. Mainly singles, but 2 birds on 3 occasions in Jul–Aug. *Interior West*: About 15 records, mostly Jul–Aug from e. WA and e. CA e. and s. to WY and NM; 2 during mid–late Nov from WY and KS. *Interior East*: About 15 records, mostly Nov–Dec (rarely from mid–late Oct), from Great Lakes region and s. QC s. to TN and cen. NC; 1 spring record, Washington Co., WI, 6–7 Mar 2000. *Atlantic States and Provinces*: About 10 records, mainly mid-Nov to mid-Jan from MA s. to FL; 1 earlier fall record, Plymouth Co., MA, 17 Sep 1982; 2 spring records, Cedar Key, FL, 16–28 Mar 1994, and Carteret Co., NC, 29 Apr 2011 (moribund 1st-summer, *NAB* 65:608); and 1 summer record, sw. NL, 15 Jul 1989. Most records coastal, and 5 from FL.

Comments: Long-billed Murrelet is unique among the birds we consider. No other Asian seabird, with the possible exception of Black-tailed Gull, has so many records scattered over the length and breadth of N America. We detect no clear reasons to explain this striking distribution pattern, but some theories are discussed below. Long-billed Murrelet's vagrancy potential is enhanced by being a relatively long-distance migrant; it is around 5000 km (3000 miles) from the northernmost breeding areas to the southernmost wintering areas. Remarkably, there are 3 recent records from Europe, but whether these came from the e. or w. is anyone's guess (Vinicombe 2007).

The species has an interesting distributional history in N America. The first 2 records were 19th-century specimens from coastal AK, identified posthumously. The next record, in mid-Nov 1979, was from QC, and 16 of the next 17 were from interior CA e. to the E Coast. Beginning in 1994, however, records from the W Coast increased sharply, and since then just over half of all N American records have been from the W Coast. We agree with Mlodinow (1997) that this disparity likely can be explained by the relatively easy detection and scrutiny of birds at interior sites, and by the understandable ignorance of W Coast observers, who had no 'need' to distinguish ssp of Marbled Murrelet (Long-billed was not split by the AOU from Marbled until 1997; *Auk* 114:542–552).

Records from AK are few, likely due to relatively low observer coverage in a vast region where small alcids are generally abundant; the spring records may reflect overshoots from Kamchatka, while the summer–fall interior and s. coast records mirror the pattern seen farther

e. and s. on the N American continent. Records from Canada and the Lower 48 fall mostly into 2 groupings: Jul–Aug birds usually in breeding plumage or early stages of prebasic molt, and Nov–Dec birds in nonbreeding plumage or just completing prebasic molt, as detailed by Sealy et al. (1991) and expanded upon by Mlodinow (1997).

The Jul–Aug records may involve mainly 1st-summer birds, perhaps also nonbreeders and failed breeders; young apparently do not fledge until Aug (Konyukhov & Kitaysky 1995), which is presumably when adults would disperse. The Jul–Aug birds may have departed the Asian breeding grounds early to molt, whereas the Nov–Dec records may reflect birds that presumably molted before migrating for the winter. Long-billed Murrelet seems unlikely to migrate any distance when molting, which helps explain the dearth of records during the main molting period in Sep–Oct, when birds are vulnerable and likely to be secretive (the Sep bird in MA was in active wing molt, and was taken by a domestic cat; Sealy et al. 1991).

In the West (both coastal and inland), most records are from Jul–Aug, with a lesser peak in Nov–Dec. Most records in the East are from Nov–Dec; the 3 Mar–Apr records in the East, and perhaps the Jul record from NL, may represent birds that survived the winter somewhere in or s. of N America, and moved n. and w. in spring. The virtual absence of Jan–Jun records from anywhere in Canada and the Lower 48 is notable, but along the W Coast this may be due largely to decreased observer effort (e.g., many records come from Marbled Murrelet surveys, which are mainly in summer–fall); with increased observation, we would expect to see late winter and spring records from the W Coast.

West Coast records may reflect misoriented migrants, perhaps initially storm assisted, that headed south on the 'wrong side' of the Pacific, as occurs with Arctic Loon, small numbers of which winter (perhaps annually) along the W Coast. Interior West records more likely have a greater storm-related component, and have been correlated to late summer and fall storms originating off the coasts of NE Asia and tracking into N America (Sealy et al. 1991, Mlodinow 1997; also see Comments under Lesser Frigatebird account).

Records in the East may have similar causes, as suggested by Sealy et al. (1991) and Mlodinow (1997), although the dearth of Nov–Dec records

Marbled Murrelet
adult breeding

colder brown
than Marbled

adult breeding (Apr–Sep)

less contrastingly
black-and-white
than Marbled

pale nape
patch

adult nonbreeding (Sep–Apr)

juv/1st-winter

Marbled
nonbreeding

adult
nonbreeding

dark spur and
white collar

whitish throat
often contrasts

1st-year

lacks white
back patches

Scripps's Murrelet

broken
white collar

Marbled
nonbreeding

adult nonbreeding

Long-billed Murrelet

from the interior w. two-thirds of the continent is notable. We suspect it is also possible that some murrelets move ne. in late summer–fall into the Bering Sea, where rich feeding grounds could fuel their molt. Some might also continue into the Arctic Ocean, where rapidly receding summer ice in recent years has opened up marine pathways across the north of both Canada and Russia (e.g., Vinicombe 2007). On freeze-up, birds at sea in Arctic Canada could be forced s. and e. (downwind generally) and end up scattered mostly in late fall and early winter across the East (see account for Black-tailed Gull for further discussion of this route).

It has been suggested that the relatively recent appearance of Long-billed Murrelet on the N American scene (inland and eastern records of any small alcid would have drawn historic attention) may be linked to changing atmospheric conditions in the N Pacific; since the

1980s these may have produced an increased frequency of fall and winter storms (Sealy et al. 1991, Mlodinow 1997). The shrinking polar ice cap may also be involved, as noted above.

Field Identification: Small alcid, averaging slightly larger and longer necked than Marbled Murrelet, with a slightly more rounded (less angular) head shape; bill averages longer than Marbled, but difficult to appreciate and not really a field character. See Mlodinow (1997) and Lethaby (2000) for further information.

Similar Species: In breeding plumage, distinguished from **Marbled Murrelet** by colder plumage tones and contrasting whitish throat; molting Marbled can appear whitish throated but with a deeper dark cap and whitish extending back to neck sides (thus shows ghosting of nonbreeding pattern); belly often paler than chest (underparts more uniformly dark on Long-billed). Also cf. Kittlitz's Murrelet.

Juv and nonbreeding Long-billed distinct from **Marbled** in head and neck pattern, and perhaps more likely to be confused with **Scripps's [Xantus's] Murrelet**, from which distinguished by white mottling on scapulars and whitish flanks; at close range, also note pale ovals on nape sides of Long-billed (Scripps's is uniformly dark on hindneck and upperparts). In flight, Scripps's has mostly bright white underwings, versus dark or dusky overall on Long-billed.

Age/Sex/Season: Ages differ, with adult appearance attained in 1st year; sexes similar; marked seasonal variation. **Adult**: Underwings dark overall. Breeding plumage (attained by partial prealternate molt in spring) mottled cold brown overall with contrasting whitish throat (with variable dusky flecking). Nonbreeding plumage attained by complete prebasic molt (mainly Sep–Oct); overall blackish above and white below with white mottling on scapulars. **1st-year**: Usually some whitish to pale gray mottling on greater and median underwing coverts. Juv (Aug–Oct) resembles nonbreeding, but white areas sullied with dusky flecking. Attains adult nonbreeding appearance by partial preformative molt in fall (Konyukhov & Kitaysky 1995). 1st-summer likely variable, as in Marbled Murrelet. Some resemble breeding adult but wings (especially primaries) more heavily worn; others may resemble nonbreeding, and others intermediate, with variable extent of brownish mottling on underparts.

Habitat and Behavior: Favors nearshore waters much like Marbled Murrelet, and thus can be seen from shore; many N American birds have been at inland lakes and reservoirs. A typical murrelet; dives well (at times for prolonged periods) and takes off from the water quickly, rather than running across the surface like heavier-bodied auklets. Most likely to be silent in the region.

PELAGIC SEABIRDS

Some 37 species of pelagic seabirds (including Swallow-tailed Gull and Black Noddy) have occurred as rare birds in N America, with 24 species only in the Pacific region, 10 only in the Atlantic region, and 3 (White-chinned Petrel, Bulwer's Petrel, Red-footed Booby) in both oceans. These 37 species comprise 29 tubenoses (14 petrels, 9 albatrosses, and 6 storm-petrels), 1 tropicbird, 3 boobies, 2 frigatebirds, 1 gull, and 1 tern (see Table 9, pp. 31–32). Because offshore waters are not well known, we suspect that at least 5 species (Bermuda Petrel, Hawaiian Petrel, European Storm-Petrel, Red-tailed Tropicbird, Black Noddy) are regular components of the N American avifauna and not truly vagrants.

Most records of rare seabirds from N American Pacific waters are in late summer–fall, which corresponds to the most intensive period of pelagic birding and may not reflect actual occurrence patterns. Likewise, in the Atlantic region most records are from spring–fall, corresponding to the period of greatest observer coverage.

Two cryptic species that may have occurred in N America are Monteiro's Storm-Petrel *Oceanodroma monteiroi* and Cape Verde Storm-Petrel *O. jabejabe* (see Howell et al. 2010). Beyond those storm-petrels, it's anyone's guess what might be the next new pelagic species documented in N America. While Juan Fernandez Petrel *Pterodroma externa*, Kermadec Petrel *P. neglecta*, Bonin Petrel *P. hypoleuca*, Boyd's Shearwater *Puffinus boydi*, or even White-bellied Storm-Petrel *Fregata grallaria* might seem reasonable candidates, the unpredictable nature of marine systems might just as easily produce something not on the radar, such as another taxon of southern albatross.

WEDGE-TAILED SHEARWATER
Ardenna pacifica L 43–47 cm (17–18.5");
WS 99–109 cm (39–43")

Summary: *Pacific States*: Very rare in fall, exceptional in winter and spring.
Taxonomy: 2 ssp, not distinguishable in the field. For placement in *Ardenna* rather than *Puffinus*, see Nunn &Stanley (1998), Howell (2012a).
Distribution and Status:
   World: Widespread in tropical Pacific and Indian oceans.

North America: *Pacific States*: Very rare in fall (late Aug–Oct; 7 records, 4 light morph, 3 dark morph; Sep 2007 CA record not accepted by state committee). Exceptional in winter, 2 light morphs dead on shore: Monterey Co., CA, 22 Dec 2009; Grays Harbor Co., WA, 18 Jan 2011 (M. Bartels, pers. comm.). Exceptional in spring, 2 dark morphs: Lincoln Co., OR, 26 Mar 1999 (dead on shore); 275 km sw. of Farallon Islands, CA, 29 Apr 2008 (M. Sadowski, photos; not accepted by state committee). 1 record inland: Salton Sea, CA, 31 Jul 1988 (dark morph).

light morph

dark morph

Wedge-tailed Shearwater

Comments: Despite being common in the tropical Pacific and even off the coasts of cen. and s. Mexico, Wedge-tailed Shearwater is decidedly rare in N American waters. It is truly a bird of warmer tropical waters and not at home in the colder waters off the W Coast, as perhaps suggested by 4 recent records involving birds found dead onshore (plus a dark morph dead onshore in CA, Apr 1915, the 1st N American record). It is possible, though, that Wedge-tailed Shearwaters are a little more frequent than accepted records suggest, as they could be missed easily among the thousands of Sooty and Pink-footed Shearwaters off the W Coast in summer–fall.

In general, summer-breeding populations in the N Pacific (in Japan and Hawaii) are almost all light morphs, whereas equatorial populations (breeding mainly Nov–May) are almost all dark morphs (W. B. King 1974). An exception lies with the Mexican breeding population, which is mainly dark morph. That 3 dark-morph birds have been recorded (2 found dead) in Mar–Apr, at a season when few observers are at sea, hints at the possibility of irregular early spring

occurrences. But where do these birds originate? The Oct 1998 dark-morph bird in Monterey Bay was completing primary molt, and was thus on a equatorial rather than Mexican schedule (W. B. King 1974).

Light-morph populations of Wedge-tailed Shearwater fledge mainly in Nov, later than fall records from the W Coast; this indicates that misoriented, recently fledged juvs are not involved except perhaps for 2 recent birds dead onshore in Dec–Jan. Light morphs off the W Coast could come from Hawaii or be swept over from Japan by tropical storms, as with Lesser Frigatebird (see that species account for details of this phenomenon) and perhaps Streaked Shearwater. Wedge-tailed Shearwater has a low wing-loading and is susceptible to storm displacement, as likely occurred with the individual at the Salton Sea. Off w. Mexico, nonbreeding Wedge-tailed Shearwaters, likely mainly from Hawaii, move n. in summer (Apr–Nov) to waters off the tip of the Baja California peninsula(Howell 2012a), whence some could be swept n. by tropical storms into the Gulf of

California and on to the Salton Sea. Some might also wander n. from the tip of Baja to the Pacific coast of CA, but we suspect a route across the N Pacific is at least as probable.

Field Identification: Large, rather lightly built tropical shearwater with broad wings and long, graduated tail; light morph suggests Pink-footed Shearwater in plumage whereas dark morph resembles Flesh-footed Shearwater. Bill varies from grayish to pink with a dark tip. See Howell (2012a) for further information.

Similar Species: Dark Morph. On the water, **Sooty Shearwater** is stockier, shorter necked, and rounder headed, lacking the long tail projection of Wedge-tailed. In flight, Sooty is the opposite of Wedge-tailed—narrow-winged and heavy-bodied with hurried wingbeats and, in windy conditions, steep wheeling. **Flesh-footed Shearwater** is larger, bulkier, and bigger headed, with more evenly broad wings, a shorter, less graduated tail (molting Wedge-tailed's tail can appear similar), and a thicker bill, which is pink with a blackish tip (beware that dark Wedge-tailed can have a dark-tipped pinkish bill).

Light Morph. *Pink-footed Shearwater* similar overall in plumage to light-morph Wedge-tailed but larger, bulkier, and bigger headed with more evenly broad wings, a shorter, less graduated tail (molting Wedge-tailed can appear similar), and a thicker bill, which is pink with a blackish tip. Wedge-tailed has a more buoyant flight with wings pressed slightly forward and crooked, recalling Buller's Shearwater. Wedge-tailed also usually has a more extensively white throat, a more contrastingly dark-capped appearance, and lacks extensive dark smudging on flanks and underwing coverts. On the water, Wedge-tailed is appreciably smaller and slighter in direct comparison, with a thinner neck, smaller head, and typically shows more white on foreneck and sides.

Age/Sex/Season: All plumages similar except for wear and molt. Juv of n. breeding populations fresh in winter, when older birds worn or in wing molt. Wing molt mainly Sep–Apr in n. populations, Apr–Sep in equatorial populations.

Habitat and Behavior: Pelagic, inshore to offshore; associates readily with other shearwaters. Flight in calm to light winds typically unhurried with wings pressed forward slightly and crooked; wingbeats usually shallow and easy, interspersed with buoyant glides. In moderate to strong winds, can glide and wheel for prolonged periods but typically does not bank steeply and wheel high like heavier-bodied species.

STREAKED SHEARWATER *Calonectris leucomelas* L 45–52 cm (17.7–20.5"); WS 103–113 cm (40.5–45")

Summary: *Pacific States*: Very rare in fall. *Wyoming*: 1 fall record (2006).
Taxonomy: Monotypic.
Status and Distribution:
World: Breeds (May–Nov) in NW Pacific, ranging s. (mainly Nov–Feb) to n. Australia and rarely into Indian Ocean.

North America: *Pacific States*: Very rare in fall (mid-Aug to mid-Oct, mainly mid-Sep to mid-Oct,) off CA. Also Lincoln Co., OR, 13 Sep 1996. 1 inland record: Tehama Co., CA, 5 Aug 1993. *Wyoming*: Albany Co., 13 Jun 2006 (desiccated carcass; Faulkner 2007).

Comments: How Streaked Shearwaters reach CA is unclear. Some might simply wander across warmer waters of the cen. N Pacific, perhaps in association with other shearwaters. It also seems plausible that some are swept across the N Pacific by tropical storms such as those associated with the occurrences of Lesser Frigatebird in N America (see that species account for details). In particular, the storm-assisted route seems likely for inland records in n. CA and WY. If other individuals survive this rite of passage they might remain 'trapped' in the E Pacific and be recorded in multiple years, as may be occurring there with Great Shearwaters.

The first N American record of Streaked Shearwater was in 1975 and records off CA seem to have increased in recent years, although some records may involve returning individuals. That over half of the records have come from Monterey Bay reflects a high level of observer coverage there in combination with large fall aggregations of shearwaters in the bay.

Field Identification: Large rangy shearwater with broad wings, fairly long graduated tail, long neck, and small head; note white face (variable in pattern).

Similar Species: Distinctive, but beware of leucistic individuals of other shearwater species that could show a white face.

Age/Sex/Season: All plumages similar except for wear and molt. Juv fresh in late fall and winter, when older birds worn or in wing molt. Wing molt mainly Sep–Mar. Age-related variation may exist in head pattern but has not been studied critically.

Habitat and Behavior: Favors inshore waters, and often found with Pink-footed and Buller's

variable dark
underprimary
coverts

pale head

Streaked Shearwater

Shearwaters. Also associates readily with mixed-species feeding flocks that include gulls, cormorants, and other species. Several individuals have been attracted to flocks of birds following boats that were chumming.

Flight in light to moderate winds is buoyant with easy, fairly loose wingbeats and low wheeling glides on flexed or slightly arched wings, recalling Buller's Shearwater rather than the heavier Pink-footed. Sails higher in stronger winds, more so than Buller's but not as high as Pink-footed.

CAPE VERDE SHEARWATER
Calonectris edwardsii L 42–47 cm (16.5–18.5");
WS 101–112 cm (40–44.5")

Summary: *Atlantic States:* 2 fall records (2004, 2006).
Taxonomy: Monotypic, but has been considered a subspecies of Cory's Shearwater.
Distribution and Status:
    World: Breeds (Jun–Nov) in Cape Verde Islands, ranges to waters off W Africa and s. to Brazil.

    North America: *Atlantic States*: Off Cape Hatteras, NC, 15 Aug 2004; Worcester Co., MD, 21 Oct 2006.
Comments: Further observations in fall are needed to evaluate this species' status in N America. However, cognizant observers have sought this distinctive species for some years, and that only 2 birds have been found suggests that Cape Verde Shearwater is a genuinely rare species in N American waters. The NC bird occurred shortly after the passage of tropical storms that could have displaced it from farther s. in the Atlantic. It is possible, though, that small numbers of (displaced?) nonbreeders occur on occasion with the large number of Cory's Shearwaters that gather in fall off New England and the Mid-Atlantic Coast before migrating s. for the winter; this would parallel fall occurrences in the Pacific of Streaked Shearwaters off cen. CA.
Field Identification: Large white-bodied shearwater, smaller and rangier than Cory's; note dusky pinkish bill.
    Similar Species: Fairly distinctive but poorly known. ***Cory's Shearwater*** larger and bulkier with broader wings, a bigger, more bulbous head,

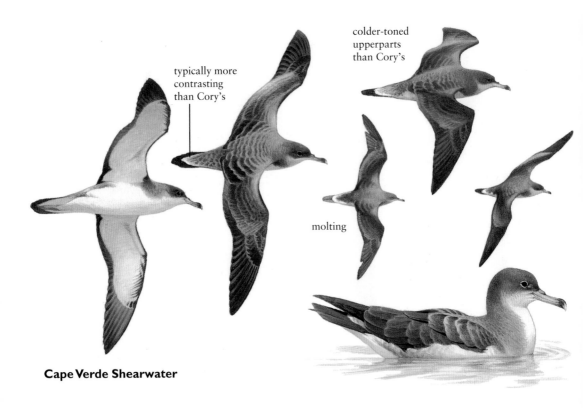

typically more
contrasting
than Cory's

colder-toned
upperparts
than Cory's

molting

Cape Verde Shearwater

and a bigger, bright yellowish bill. Cory's usually has a paler and grayer cast to the head and rarely looks as capped as does Cape Verde.

The chances of a *Wedge-tailed Shearwater* reaching the Atlantic seem slim, but the light morph of this tropical Pacific species shares many similarities in appearance with Cape Verde Shearwater. Wedge-tailed is smaller and lighter in build with slightly longer, slimmer, and more strongly graduated tail, smaller gray to pinkish bill, and dark distal undertail coverts.

Age/Sex/Season: All plumages similar except for wear and molt. Juv fresh in late fall and winter, when older birds worn or in wing molt. Wing molt mainly Aug–Mar.

Habitat and Behavior: Warmer waters, where likely to be found in association with Cory's Shearwaters. Behavior similar to Cory's Shearwater but flight a little lighter, less lumbering, and wings tend to be more notably crooked.

BAROLO SHEARWATER *Puffinus baroli*
L 26–28 cm (10.2–11"); WS 58–61 cm (22.8–24")

Summary: *Northeast*: Very rare in late summer-fall.

Taxonomy: Monotypic, pending review of possible geographic variation (see Howell 2012a). Sometimes known as Macronesian Shearwater (which includes Barolo and Boyd's Shearwaters).

Based on external appearance, Barolo Shearwater was traditionally considered a disjunct ssp of S Hemisphere Little Shearwater *P. assimilis*. Genetic study indicates that it is part of a N Atlantic group of shearwaters, together with Audubon's Shearwater of the Caribbean and Boyd's Shearwater of the Cape Verde Islands (J. J. Austin et al. 2004).

Distribution and Status:

World: Breeds (Jan–May) n. Macronesian islands, from Canaries n. to Azores. Post-breeding dispersal n. (Jun–early Oct) to Bay of Biscay, very rare elsewhere (mainly Apr–Oct) in NW Europe.

North America: *Northeast*: Very rare in late summer–fall (late Jul–Sep), 4 records in the period: 80 km wsw. of Sable Island, NS, 23 Sep 2003; 80 km s. of Sable Island, NS, 24 Sep 2003 (2); 135 km se. of Nantucket, MA, 25 Aug 2007 (*NAB* 62:40, 190); 305 km e. of Nantucket, 29 Jul 2011 (*NAB* 65:596).

Also, in fall 2012, 4 adults (in fresh plumage or completing wing molt) photographed s. of NS in mid-Aug (T. Johnson 2012), and a juv photographed about 200 km se. of Cape Cod, MA, 26 Aug 2012 (N. Bonomo, photos; Howell, pers. obs.).

Comments: The first and only other N American record is a specimen from Sable Island, NS, 1 Sep 1896 (Dwight 1897); a report from SC (probably in Aug 1883; Peters 1924) actually refers to an Audubon's Shearwater (MCZ #220051). Lee (1988) summarized numerous other claims (mainly Aug–Mar) off e. N America, but there have been no adequately documented at-sea N American records until the 2000s.

The Sable Island specimen was molting body and rectrices in early Sep (Dwight 1897), indicating that it was completing prebasic molt, and thus not a misoriented 1st-cycle bird. Photos of the 2007 bird show distinct white tips to the upperwing coverts, also indicating it was not a juv. During fall, the ocean off Atlantic Canada and New England warms up, and at this season hosts White-faced Storm-Petrels and even a few Cape Verde/Desertas (Fea's) Petrels from islands in the e. Atlantic. Unlike storm-petrels and gadfly petrels, small shearwaters tend not be attracted to boats or chum slicks, and thus they are even harder to detect on the open ocean. It seems likely that the waters s. of NS comprise part of the regular pelagic range of Barolo Shearwater, which on occasion ranges w. into waters within reach of New England pelagic trips.

Field Identification: Very small black-and-white shearwater, appreciably smaller than Manx and Audubon's Shearwaters.

Similar Species: Distinctive if seen well, but always beware of molting, bleached, or aberrant Audubon's and Manx Shearwaters. With Barolo, note small size, short bill, medium-length tail (longer than Manx), white face and undertail coverts, whitish-tipped greater and median coverts of adult (obvious at moderate range in good light), and low hurried flight.

Age/Sex/Season: Ages differ slightly; sexes similar; no seasonal variation other than wear. *Adult*: Whitish tips to greater and median upperwing coverts show as distinct lines in fresh plumage (mainly Aug–Feb), weakest and often worn away in Mar–Jul; wing molt mainly May–Aug. *1st-year*: Juv fresh in May–Jul when older birds worn or molting, and lacks white tips to median coverts; pale tips to greater coverts, when present, narrow and dull gray to whitish. 2nd-prebasic molt probably earlier than adult, wing molt perhaps Mar–Jul (study needed).

Habitat and Behavior: Pelagic, favoring warm-temperate waters. Likely to be found singly, or perhaps in association with feeding flocks of other species. Flight similar to Audubon's Shearwater, but quicker-looking under comparable conditions, with hurried, stiffer wingbeats and shorter glides.

white

adult has frosty white tips in fresh plumage

worn plumage (including fall juv) browner above

white face

Barolo Shearwater

NEWELL'S SHEARWATER *Puffinus*
newelli L 35–38 cm (13.8–15"); WS 77–85 cm
(30.5–33.5")

Summary: *California*: 1 fall record (2007).
Taxonomy: Considered monotypic here (see
Howell 2012a); treated by AOU (1998) as conspecific with Townsend's Shearwater *P. auricularis*
of Mexico.
Distribution and Status:
   World: Breeds (Jun–Oct) in Hawaii, ranges at
sea mainly e. and s. of the Hawaiian Islands.
   North America: *California*: San Diego Co.,
1 Aug 2007 (Unitt et al. 2009).
Comments: The San Diego bird occurred in the
middle of the species' breeding season, at a time
when prebreeders would be expected to visit
colonies and perhaps prospect at new sites; that
it chose the mainland coast of s. California rather
than one of the Hawaiian Islands, over 4000 km
(2500 miles) distant, suggests it was severely
compromised in its homing ability, or perhaps it
was simply one of the more adventurous members of its cohort.
   All tubenoses presumably have some inherent
dispersal ability and can appear out of range at
potential breeding sites. Other examples include
Cory's Shearwater at the Coronado Islands, Baja

California, in 2005–2007, a Wedge-rumped
Storm-Petrel at Guadalupe Island, Baja California
(Huey 1952), a Tristram's Storm-Petrel on
Southeast Farallon Island, CA (Warzybok et al.
2009), and Barolo Shearwaters at a colony of
Manx Shearwaters in Wales (P. C. James 1986).
Field Identification: Small black-and-white
shearwater with relatively long tail, black distal
undertail coverts. See Howell et al. (1994) and
Howell (2012a) for further information.
   Similar Species: *Manx Shearwater* slightly
smaller with shorter tail and white undertail
coverts that extend to near tail tip; underside
of Manx's primaries silvery gray rather than
blackish, and black/white division on sides
of head less clean-cut, with dark freckling.
Flight less buoyant, and in windy conditions
often more powerful than Newell's, with
steeper wheeling.
   Townsend's Shearwater (unrecorded in US
waters) slightly smaller than Newell's, with lower
wing-loading, slightly shorter tail, all-black
undertail coverts, and a freckled border between
blackish head sides and white throat.
   Age/Sex/Season: All plumages similar except
for wear and molt. Juv fresh in Oct–Feb when
older birds are worn or in wing molt. Wing molt
mainly Jul–Feb.

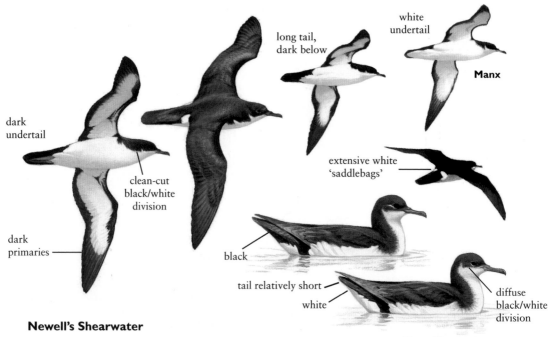

dark
undertail

long tail,
dark below

white
undertail

Manx

clean-cut
black/white
division

extensive white
'saddlebags'

dark
primaries

black

tail relatively short

white

diffuse
black/white
division

Newell's Shearwater

Manx Shearwater

Habitat and Behavior: Pelagic, usually well offshore, but the CA bird was diving at construction workers at night under bright lights (Unitt et al. 2009)! Flight recalls Manx Shearwater, fast and low with quick stiff wingbeats; glides on slightly bowed wings and wheels steeply in windy conditions.

BERMUDA PETREL (Cahow)
Pterodroma cahow
L 35–38 cm (13.8–15"); WS 85–92 cm (33.5–36.2")

Summary: *North Carolina*: Rare offshore, spring–fall. *Massachusetts*: 1 summer record (2009).

Taxonomy: Monotypic.

Distribution and Status:

World: Breeds (Jan–early Jun) on Bermuda, ranges at sea mainly in subtropical N Atlantic.

North America: *North Carolina*: Rare in at least spring–fall (late May–late Sep) over Gulf Stream waters off Cape Hatteras, since the first record in 1993. Records have averaged 1–2 per year since the early 1990s, and have been almost annual since 1998, averaging 2–3 per year during 2000–2009, with 5 individuals in 2009 but then, remarkably, none recorded in 2010–2012 (through Oct). *Massachusetts*: 290 km ese. of Cape Cod, 28 Jun 2009 (juv; Duley 2010).

Comments: Waters off NC (indeed, from NC n. to NL) appear to be part of this species' normal range, and as such it is best considered a 'false vagrant' (see p. 16). This species is simply rare by virtue of its low population, and we suspect that daily offshore coverage from NC n. to Atlantic Canada would produce more than 5 records a year.

Although late May is often considered the peak time for records off NC, this is also when most pelagic trips head offshore. As is so often the case with seabirds, our knowledge of Bermuda Petrel's seasonal occurrence is colored by the times when birders are offshore, and it seems likely that this species occurs year-round in US waters; cf. reports off NC from Apr and Dec (Lee 1984, 1987). Moreover, recent data from tagged breeding adults showed that even in Jan–Mar, some Bermuda Petrels forage w. and n. to cool waters from NC n. to NS and NL (Madeiros 2010).

Field Identification: Lightly built, medium-sized gadfly petrel with long narrow wings,

molting

rarely may show mostly dark uppertail coverts

Bermuda Petrel

long tapered tail, dark cowl, and narrow white rump band. See Howell (2012a) for further information.

Similar Species: Bermuda Petrel is a relatively distinctive species, perhaps as likely to be confused with similarly proportioned Cape Verde/Desertas (Fea's) Petrels as with larger and stockier Black-capped Petrel.

Fea's Petrel and *Zino's Petrel* typically have distinctive dark underwings contrasting with white body, and pale gray uppertail coverts and tail. Some Zino's have extensive white on underwings and fresh-plumage Bermuda can have relatively pale gray cowl; note pattern of uppertail coverts.

Black-capped Petrel larger and stockier with broader wings, broader tail, thicker bill, and much larger white patch on the uppertail coverts. Many Black-cappeds also have bold white hindcollar, but some have dusky hindneck, inviting confusion with Bermuda. Note that more extensive dark head markings of Bermuda typically appear as a cowl, with little contrast between blackish crown and slaty gray hindneck, and no contrast between hindneck and back.

Age/Sex/Season: All plumages similar except for wear and molt. Juv fresh in late May–Aug when older ages normally worn or in wing molt. Fresh plumage can be strikingly gray above, unlike darker brown tones of worn plumage. Wing molt mainly Apr–Sep.

Habitat and Behavior: Pelagic, over warm waters along western edge of Gulf Stream. As likely to be seen alone as in association with Black-capped Petrels, with which it may be found foraging and resting. In calm to light winds, flight buoyant and quick, with easy, slightly clipped wingbeats and low wheeling. In moderate to strong winds wheels higher, although typically lower and less steeply than Black-capped Petrel; but can tower high and loop when maneuvering over food.

ZINO'S PETREL *Pterodroma madeira*
L 34–36 cm (13.3–14.2"); WS 83–88 cm (32.7–34.7")

Summary: *North Carolina*: 1 fall record (1995).
Taxonomy: Monotypic.
Distribution and Status:
    World: Breeds (mid-May to early Oct) on Madeira, E Atlantic; ranges in tropical and subtropical Atlantic. Critically endangered.

North America: *North Carolina*: Off Cape Hatteras, 16 Sep 1995 (Howell 2012a). Record not evaluated by N American committees.

Comments: A poorly known species for which field identification criteria were established only recently (Shirihai et al. 2010). The small and critically endangered world population of Zino's Petrel argues against it being 'common' off NC, and remote tracking of 12 breeding adults shows that they did not reach N American waters, although in fall–winter 1 approached NL (Zino et al. 2011). Thus, prebreeding imms may be the age class most likely to occur off the E Coast, and fall is the most likely period of occurrence.

The species pair of Cape Verde Petrel and Desertas Petrel (collectively Fea's Petrel; Howell 2012a) occurs in N America with greater frequency than our threshold of 5 records per year. Although it is likely that one member of the pair (if not both) qualifies as a rare bird, given that these 2 species are ostensibly indistinguishable at sea (except perhaps by molt timing; Howell 2012a, Shirihai et al. 2010), we have lumped them for the purposes of this book.

Field Identification: Medium-sized, lightly built petrel with fairly narrow wings, fairly long, tapered tail. Notoriously similar to Fea's Petrel. See Shirihai et al. (2010) and Howell (2012a) for further information.

Similar Species: *Fea's Petrel* (see under Comments) notoriously similar to Zino's, and these species often not separable under typical at-sea conditions. Fea's averages larger and more heavily built, and in particular has a stouter bill that is more evenly deep throughout, whereas shallower bill of Zino's is often slightly pinched-in immediately distal to nostril tubes. No plumage features separate these species consistently, but Zino's often has a fairly broad whitish underwing stripe not matched by Fea's. Wing molt timing also likely to be helpful; Cape Verde Petrel molts mainly Mar–Sep and Desertas Petrel mainly Nov–May. Zino's probably molts Sep–Feb. Thus, any bird with molt of inner primaries in fall (as the NC bird showed) should be scrutinized.

Age/Sex/Season: All plumages similar except for wear and molt, but juv fresh in Oct–Feb when older ages normally worn or in wing molt.

Habitat and Behavior: Pelagic, offshore. In calm to light winds, flight buoyant and quick, with easy, slightly clipped to languid deep wingbeats, and low wheeling. In moderate to strong winds wheels higher, and can tower high and loop when maneuvering over food.

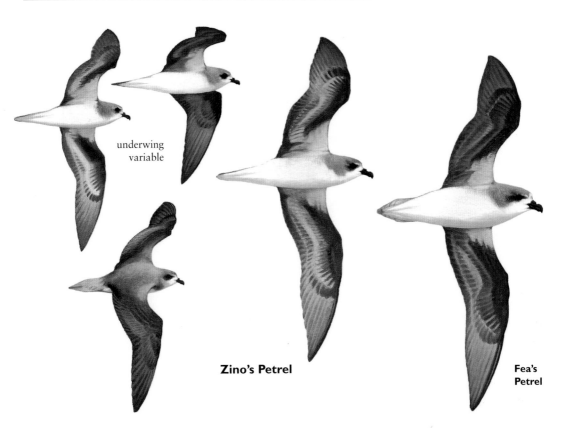

underwing
variable

Zino's Petrel

Fea's Petrel

STEJNEGER'S PETREL *Pterodroma longirostris* L 29–31.5 cm (11.5–12.5"): WS 70–76 cm (27.5–30")

Summary: *California*: Very rare in fall, exceptional in spring. *Texas*: 1 fall record (1995).
Taxonomy: Monotypic.
Distribution and Status:
   World: Breeds (Dec–Apr) on Juan Fernandez Islands, Chile. Nonbreeding range (mainly May–Oct) in NW Pacific.
   North America: *California*: In late fall, very rare offshore in mid-Oct to mid-Nov (5 records). Exceptional in spring, 2 records: Monterey Co., 4 May 2003, and Santa Barbara Co., 14 Apr 2010 (former record not accepted by state committee). Also 3 summer reports (early–late Jul) accepted by state committee but considered uncertain by us. *Texas*: Nueces Co., 15 Sep 1995 (carcass found).
Comments: Stejneger's Petrel may be of annual occurrence in CA waters, especially in Oct–Nov when birds are returning from the NW Pacific to their Chilean breeding grounds; there are mid–late Oct records from waters beyond the 200-mile limit off CA and from waters off Middle America

(Howell, pers. obs.). There are also records of this species during Nov–Jan from New Zealand waters (Marchant & Higgins 1990). Thus, while the main migration route of breeding adults may be direct across the central Pacific, 1st-years and prebreeding imms may wander more widely on their migration, analogous to the fall occurrence of species such as Baird's Sandpiper on the N American continent; adult Baird's migrate south mainly through the middle of the continent, whereas juvs fan out and are regularly seen along both coasts in fall. The paucity of N American records of Stejneger's Petrel may be due largely to difficulties in reaching the waters where it occurs at this season.

Occasional birds, perhaps mainly in their 1st year, may misorient on their northward migration and wander up into the E Pacific in spring, as with the May 2003 bird in Monterey Bay (lack of wing molt suggests it was a 1st-year). Similarly, mid-summer reports may reflect birds 'wintering' on the wrong side of the Pacific, although at this season Cook's Petrels can appear disconcertingly dark capped, and none of the Jul reports of Stejneger's is supported by photos.

all plumages similar

Stejneger's Petrel

The TX record is remarkable and may have been ship-assisted, although it is possible that an errant migrant may have been blown into the Gulf of Mexico from the Pacific by a hurricane.
Field Identification: Small, snappy gadfly petrel with strikingly patterned upperparts and dark slaty cap.

Similar Species: A distinctive species, assuming good views are obtained and size is not misjudged (cf. much larger Buller's Shearwater, which has similar plumage pattern, and also Hawaiian Petrel).

Cook's Petrel slightly larger, with longer and narrower wings, slightly longer bill, and less contrasting upperparts. Under at-sea conditions, however, and without comparative experience, these two species appear basically the same in size and shape. Crown and hindneck of Cook's are typically medium-pale gray, but birds can appear dark capped in some lights, especially when worn in spring–summer.

Age/Sex/Season: All plumages similar except for wear and molt, but juv fresh in Apr–Jul when older ages normally worn or in wing molt. Wing molt mainly Mar–Aug.

Habitat and Behavior: Pelagic, offshore. Likely to be encountered singly, alone or in loose association with Cook's Petrels. In calm to light winds, flight often low to the surface with buoyant glides on bowed wings, interspersed with bursts of quick flicking wingbeats and occasional low wheeling. In moderate to strong winds, flight faster and more erratic, with higher and steeper wheeling, and short bursts of flickering stiff wingbeats; in strong winds at times almost flips back on itself and arcs up and down with a vertical slicing action.

HAWAIIAN PETREL *Pterodroma sandwichensis* L 37.5–40 cm (14.7–15.7"); WS 94.5–104 cm (37.5–41.2")

Summary: *Pacific States*: Rare offshore, spring–fall.
Taxonomy: Monotypic. Formerly considered conspecific with Galapagos Petrel *P. phaeopygia*, and known as Dark-rumped Petrel *P. phaeopygia*.
Distribution and Status:
World: Breeds in Hawaiian Islands (Apr–Oct); ranges in subtropical and tropical E Pacific.

North America: *Pacific States*: Rare offshore in spring–fall (May–Sep; most records Jul–Aug); all records since 1992 and mainly off cen. CA. Also recorded off OR (first in Aug 2002) and WA (first in Sep 2008; *NAB* 63:144, 2009).

Comments: This species is a 'false vagrant' (see p. 16), with waters off the W Coast being part of its regular pelagic range. An awareness of identification criteria, plus increased numbers of pelagic trips directed at seeing this species, may be partly responsible for the apparent trend of increasing occurrence, but the recent spike in records relatively close to shore may also reflect changing oceanic conditions in the E Pacific.

Records from N American waters were considered by ABA (2008) only at the level of Dark-rumped (Galapagos/Hawaiian) Petrel. The normal range of Galapagos Petrel lies over warm tropical waters well to the s., and its occurrence in N American waters, while possible, would be exceptional.

Field Identification: Medium-sized gadfly with long narrow wings and long tapered tail; striking plumage unlike any regularly occurring N American petrel. Note head pattern and striking underwing pattern.

Similar Species: In N America, Hawaiian Petrel is a distinctive species, although observers unfamiliar with gadfly petrels have confused it with much smaller **Stejneger's Petrel**. Also cf. Juan Fernandez and Galapagos petrels, both unrecorded in N America (see Howell 2012a for details).

Age/Sex/Season: All plumages similar except for wear and molt, but juv fresh in Oct–Feb when older ages normally worn or in wing molt. No juvs certainly recorded in N America. Fresh plumage can be strikingly gray above, unlike darker brown tones of worn plumage. Wing molt mainly Oct–Feb.

Habitat and Behavior: Pelagic, offshore. Usually found singly, and in N American waters as likely to be alone as associated loosely with other species. Flight generally easy and buoyant. In calm to light winds, flight leisurely, meandering or weaving low over the water with easy clipped wingbeats, buoyant glides on flexed wings, and

head pattern
varies with
angle of view

worn plumage darker
and browner above

fresh
plumage/juv

Hawaiian Petrel

low wheeling arcs. In moderate to strong winds flight across the wind fast and wheeling, with higher arcs and no flapping or short bursts of a few quick flaps; at other times wheels fairly low, especially when flying into the wind.

SOLANDER'S (Providence)
PETREL *Pterodroma solandri* 43–46 cm (17–18.2"), wingspan 100–107 cm (39–42")

Summary: *Alaska*: 1 fall record (2011). *Washington*: 1 fall record (1983). *Elsewhere*: see Comments, below.
Taxonomy: Monotypic.
Distribution and Status:
   World: Breeds (May–Nov) in subtropical SW Pacific, ranges (mainly Nov–May; but nonbreeders year-round) into NW Pacific.
   North America: *Alaska*: nw. of Attu, 15 Sep 2011 (15+; Cooper & Mackiernan 2011). *Washington*: Grays Harbor Co., 11 Sep 1983 (M. Bartels, pers. comm.). *Elsewhere*: Status uncertain (see Comments, below).
Comments: The trials and tribulations of the 1980s that surrounded the identification and occurrence in N America of Solander's Petrel and the similar Murphy's Petrel remain unresolved (see S. F. Bailey et al. 1989, Howell 2012a).

   Recent fall observations from w. of the Aleutians, however, suggest that Solander's Petrel may be regular in fall, and at times numerous, just within N American waters (Cooper & Mackiernan 2011); thus it may qualify as a 'false vagrant' (see p. 16). Away from the Aleutians there is an accepted record from WA of a bird seen by an experienced observer (photo and description examined by us, May 2012), and several other reports off the W Coast that remain unsubstantiated (summarized by Cooper & Mackiernan 2011). In particular, a bird well photographed 6 Oct 2009 about 50 km w. of Vancouver Island, BC, remains problematic (Howell 2012a).

   Birds in AK have occurred late in the species' breeding season and have been in worn plumage, but not yet in wing molt. Such birds presumably are nonbreeding and prebreeding imms that moved n. in late summer to take advantage of rich feeding grounds. Later in fall–early winter it seems likely they would withdraw back s., mostly

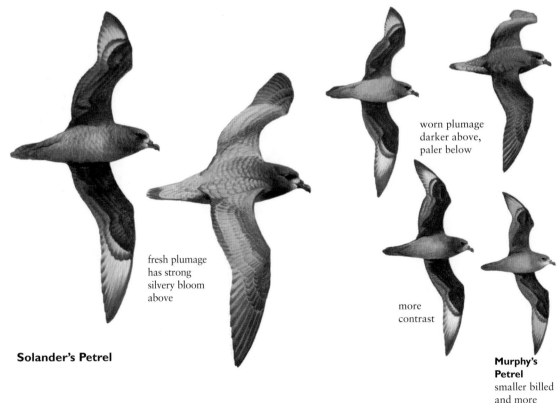

fresh plumage has strong silvery bloom above

worn plumage darker above, paler below

more contrast

Solander's Petrel

Murphy's Petrel smaller billed and more lightly built

into the w. Pacific but with occasional birds perhaps moving into the e. Pacific. Late fall (Sep–Nov?) might thus be the best time to encounter this species off the W Coast, where we believe it will remain very rare.

Field Identification: Large dark gadfly petrel, notoriously similar to slightly smaller and smaller-billed Murphy's Petrel. Note large size, stout bill, double white underwing flashes.

Similar Species: Any suspected Solander's should be distinguished carefully from rather similar **Murphy's Petrel**, which is regular off the W Coast. Solander's is larger overall (a large gadfly petrel vs. the medium-sized Murphy's) with longer wings and, most importantly, a bigger bill. Plumage similar to Murphy's, but Solander's has a darker hood, contrasting noticeably on the underparts, and its underwing has bold, double white flashes (on the primaries and primary coverts), which are usually visible at long range and not reflective as on Murphy's (although variation in underwing pattern of Murphy's remains to be addressed). Whitish around the bill base of Solander's is often as extensive on the forehead as the chin (mainly on the chin in Murphy's). Flight of Solander's typically less bounding than Murphy's, with lower, more measured wheeling in longer wavelength arcs. Also cf. Gray-faced Petrel, and see Howell (2012a) for further information.

Age/Sex/Season: All plumages similar except for wear and molt. Wing molt Oct–Mar in breeding adults, which are in freshest plumage Feb–Jun and most worn in Sep–Jan (when 1st years are in fresh plumage and not molting).

Habitat and Behavior: Pelagic, favoring subtropical waters. Typical large gadfly petrel; at times accompanies ships and attracted to chum slicks. In calm to light winds, flies with easy, powerful wingbeats and buoyant wheeling glides low to the water. In moderate to strong winds, flight strong and fast, often bounding fairly high in wheeling, long-wavelength arcs across the wind.

GRAY-FACED PETREL *Pterodroma [macroptera] gouldi* L 42–45 cm (16.5–17.7"); WS 105–113 cm (41.5–45.5")

Summary: *California*: 1-4 summer–fall records (1996, 1998, 2010, 2011).
Taxonomy: 2 taxa of Great-winged Petrel have been described, their differences greater than those between some species of *Pterodroma*; they

are increasingly treated as 2 species (Onley & Scofield 2007, Howell 2012a). N American records are all of Gray-faced Petrel.

P. [m.] gouldi (Gray-faced Petrel) breeds New Zealand, ranges in SW Pacific w. at least to Australia. Averages larger with very stout bill, moderate to extensive whitish around base of bill, and less prominent dark eye patch.

P. [m.] macroptera (Great-winged Petrel) breeds in S Indian and S Atlantic oceans, ranges from S Atlantic e. to s. Australia. Averages smaller, bill less stout with little to no whitish around base, dark eye patch more prominent.

Distribution and Status:
World: Breeds (May–Nov) subtropical S Atlantic e. to New Zealand (see Taxonomy). Ranges at sea mainly s. of 30°S, although unrecorded in E Pacific.

North America: *California*: Marin Co., 21 Jul and 24 Aug 1996; Monterey Co., 18 Oct 1998; Santa Cruz Co., 18 Sep 2010 (*NAB* 65:157, 197) and 26 Aug 2011 (*NAB* 66:163).

Comments: This species is not a transequatorial migrant, and it wasn't on anyone's list of expected pelagic vagrants. All records have been during this species' austral-winter breeding season, and may have involved only one individual. Wing molt of this species in S Hemisphere is mainly Nov–Apr (Marchant & Higgins 1990). However, primary molt of adult bird(s) photographed in Oct 1998, Sep 2010, and Aug 2011 was completing; this switch in molt timing to a N Hemisphere schedule suggests the bird(s) had been in the N Hemisphere for some time (cf. White-chinned Petrel).

Field Identification: Distinctive, large dark gadfly petrel about the size of Flesh-footed Shearwater. Note large size, long wings, buoyant flight, very stout black bill; lacks distinct white wing flashes.

Similar Species: *Murphy's Petrel* (the 'expected' all-dark *Pterodroma* off the W Coast) is smaller with proportionately shorter wings and longer tail, smaller bill. Higher wing-loading of Murphy's results in a more bounding, impetuous flight. Especially in fresh plumage, Murphy's has glossy gray upperparts with distinct blackish 'M' pattern; whitish on throat can suggest Gray-faced from below, but Murphy's lacks extensive white on forehead.

Solander's Petrel large like Gray-faced and similarly dark overall with whitish around base of bill. Solander's is slightly narrower winged and longer tailed; underwings have bold, double

worn plumage
browner

pale face variable,
some show
little contrast

Gray-faced Petrel

white flashes (on primaries and primary coverts) usually visible at long range. Especially in fresh plumage, Solander's has glossy gray upperparts with distinct blackish 'M' pattern and dark hood, similar to Murphy's Petrel.

Age/Sex/Season: All plumages similar, but juv fresh in Oct–Feb when older ages normally worn or molting (but see Comments, above). Age unknown at which 'adult' attains whitish subterminal band on bill.

Habitat and Behavior: Pelagic, favoring subtropical waters. Typical large gadfly petrel, at times scavenging from fishing boats. In calm to light winds, flight fairly buoyant with prolonged gliding and long-wavelength wheeling arcs interspersed with languid flapping, the flexed wings pressed forward and crooked at the carpals. In moderate to strong winds, flies with high wheeling arcs, at times pausing at the apex of a climb before sweeping down strongly.

PARKINSON'S PETREL *Procellaria parkinsoni* L 41–46 cm (16.2–17.2");WS 112–123 cm (44.5–49")

Summary: *California*: 1 fall record (2005).
Taxonomy: Monotypic.

Distribution and Status:

World: Breeds (Nov–May) n. New Zealand, ranges to E Pacific, from s. Mexico to Peru (mainly 15°N to 5°S).

North America: *California*: Marin Co., 1 Oct 2005 (age unknown).

Comments: Mainly a bird of warmer subtropical and tropical waters, this species is unlikely to be at home in the generally cool waters of the California Current, and occurrences off the W Coast are exceptional. Of note is that the single N American records of Parkinson's Petrel and Hornby's Storm-Petrel occurred in the same fall, which may not be coincidence, but humans still know so little of annual and cyclic variations within marine ecosystems that we can draw no clear link. Other *Procellaria* species of cooler waters may be just as likely to occur as Parkinson's (witness 2-3 recent records of White-chinned Petrel off CA), and an unidentified dark *Procellaria* (Parkinson's or Westland *P. westlandica*) was seen off cen. CA in Jun 1996. A report of Parkinson's Petrel from OR (*NAB* 60:127) does not meet our acceptance criteria.

Field Identification: Large all-dark petrel, about the size of a large shearwater; ivory-colored bill tipped dark. See illustration on p. 90.

Similar Species: Seen well this is a distinctive species, albeit one unfamiliar to many observers. As likely to be passed off as a Flesh-footed Shearwater as it is to be confused with larger *Procellaria* petrels; see Howell (2006b, 2012a) for further information.

Flesh-footed Shearwater more lightly built and longer tailed (toes do not project beyond tail in flight, and wing projection past tail relatively short on swimming birds), with a more slender bill that is pink with a black tip, lacking neat black outlines to the plates; pink feet diagnostic, but in flight these are often tucked in and not visible. Flesh-footed slightly paler and browner overall, less blackish, but this can be difficult to judge.

Westland Petrel of temperate S Pacific essentially identical in plumage and bill pattern but distinctly larger (L 48–53 cm, WS 135–145 cm) with a thicker neck, blockier head, bigger bill, and relatively shorter wing projection past the tail. Non-juvenile Westlands are in wing molt during Oct–Mar (Parkinson's mainly Mar–Aug), but molt timing of vagrants may be atypical.

Age/Sex/Season: All plumages similar except for wear and molt, but juv fresh in May–Aug when older ages normally worn or in wing molt. Wing molt mainly Mar–Aug.

Habitat and Behavior: Pelagic, favoring warmer waters of e. tropical Pacific. Feeds mainly by scavenging and often attracted to fishing boats discarding offal, where it associates readily with other species. In calm to light winds, flies with easy, smooth wingbeats and buoyant glides; often appears a little heavier than large shearwaters such as Flesh-footed; in light to moderate winds, flight languid, with leisurely glides and occasional bouts of loose flapping, wheeling low over the water. In moderate to strong winds holds wings more crooked, and high wheeling flight may recall larger *Pterodroma*.

WHITE-CHINNED PETREL *Procellaria aequinoctialis* L 50–57 cm (19.7–22.5"); WS 132–145 cm (52–57")

Summary: *Atlantic and Gulf States*: Exceptional in spring–fall. *California*: Exceptional in fall.
Taxonomy: Monotypic.
Distribution and Status:
World: Breeds (Nov–Apr) on subantarctic islands; ranges at sea mainly 30–60°S, and in winter (mainly Apr–Oct) n to 6°S in cooler waters off w. S America.

North America: *Atlantic and Gulf States*: Galveston Co., TX, 27 Apr 1986; off NC, 12 and 17 Oct 1996 (not accepted by state committee); Hancock Co., ME, 24 Aug 2010 (*NAB* 65:40, 195). *California*: San Mateo Co., 18 Oct 2009; Santa Barbara Co., 6 Sep 2011 (*NAB* 66:168); Marin Co., 16 Oct 2011 (*NAB* 66:163).

Comments: Of interest is that 5 of the 6 records occurred in the austral spring (Aug–Oct), when most White-chinned Petrels in the S Hemisphere would be heading s. toward the breeding grounds, and at least the Oct 2009 and Aug 2011 CA birds were still on a S Hemisphere molt schedule; this suggests they had not been long in the N Hemisphere. Thus, it seems possible that some White-chinned Petrels may misorient n. from the nonbreeding grounds, as is presumed to occur with a number of landbirds (e.g., Fork-tailed Flycatcher). If the CA records in Oct 2009 (p10 growing) and Aug 2011 (p8–p10 old) were of the same individual, it had retained a S Hemisphere molt schedule. The retarded molt timing of the Oct 2011 bird (with p8–p10 old and worn, projected to complete wing molt in Dec–Jan) suggests it was adjusting to a N Hemisphere schedule, and it may have been the same individual as in Oct 2009.

The TX bird, a weak individual found in the surf, may represent a bird that wandered into the Gulf of Mexico and ended up starving, as cold-water species may do in warm-water environments. There is also a possibility that it fell from a ship or was ship-assisted.

Field Identification: Large all-dark petrel, appreciably larger than large shearwaters; bill ivory colored.

Similar Species: Within N American waters, White-chinned Petrel stands out as something different, being blackish overall, pale-billed, and larger than large shearwaters or Northern Fulmar. Other species of all-dark *Procellaria* petrels should always be considered, namely Spectacled *P. conspicillata*, Westland, and Parkinson's, all of which are unrecorded in the N Atlantic. Attention to overall size, details of bill pattern, and the extent and pattern of any white on the face should enable a bird to be identified, assuming it is seen reasonably well; see Howell (2006b, 2012a) for further information.

Spectacled Petrel of subtropical S Atlantic much like White-chinned in size and shape but has diagnostic (though variably distinct) white ring on head sides, joined across forehead; usually has dark bill tip.

Flesh-footed Shearwater

slender pink bill tipped black

variable dusky tip

longer tail

toes often project

long wing projection

Parkinson's Petrel
all plumages similar

Atlantic birds average larger white chin patch than Pacific birds

pale yellowish tip

small white patch, often hard to see

late fall wing molt might draw attention

White-chinned Petrel
all plumages similar

Westland Petrel of temperate S Pacific much like White-chinned in size and shape but head slightly blockier. Lacks white chin, and bill usually has a distinct blackish tip (rarely almost absent).

Parkinson's Petrel smaller and more lightly built, about the size of a large shearwater. Lacks white chin, and bill usually has a distinct dark tip. On the water, note relatively long wing projection past tail.

Age/Sex/Season: All plumages similar except for wear and molt, but juv fresh in May–Aug when older ages normally worn or in wing molt. Wing molt in S Hemisphere mainly Feb–Aug (but see Comments, above).

Habitat and Behavior: Pelagic, favoring cooler waters. A proficient scavenger, attracted to chum or to fishing boats cleaning their catch, associating readily with large shearwaters, gulls, and albatrosses. Often accompanies ships, following in the wake.

Flight appears heavy relative to large shearwaters, but wheels confidently and easily in moderate to strong winds. In calm to light winds, flies with steady smooth wingbeats and short glides; in light to moderate winds, holds its wings straight out or pressed slightly forward, and slightly bowed, and flies with leisurely glides and occasional bouts of loose flapping, wheeling low over the water; in moderate to strong winds, wings held more crooked, and high wheeling arcs may recall larger *Pterodroma*.

BULWER'S PETREL *Bulweria bulwerii*
L 27–29 cm (10.7–11.5"); WS 63–68 cm (24.8–26.8")

Summary: *Atlantic States*: Exceptional in spring–summer and fall. *California*: 2 fall records (1998, 2003).
Taxonomy: Monotypic.
Distribution and Status:
   World: Breeds (mainly May/Jun–Aug/Sep) and ranges in tropical and subtropical oceans, but absent from E Pacific.
   North America: *Atlantic States*: Off Cape Hatteras, NC, 1 Jul 1992 and 8 Aug 1998; about 160 km (100 miles) off Duval Co., FL, 1 May 1984 (Haney & Wainright 1985); Northampton Co., VA, 2 Sep 2006 (Brinkley 2007). *California*: Monterey Co., 26 Jul 1998; Los Angeles Co., 4 Sep 2003 (not accepted by state committee).

Comments: Bulwer's Petrel may be a very rare visitor (perhaps mainly May–Aug) over warmer offshore Atlantic waters from FL n. to the Carolinas, but relatively few observers are far enough offshore in summer–fall to encounter it. Until recently, the species was considered an exceptional vagrant in the eastern Caribbean, but it is now known to be a scarce visitor there, at least in May–Jun (cf. Brinkley 2007). The Sep record from VA involved a bird seen from shore in Chesapeake Bay following the passage of a tropical storm.

The occurrence of Bulwer's Petrel off the Pacific coast is more likely to be as an exceptional visitor, given the cooler waters prevailing in that region. A 5 Sep 2007 record from s. CA of an unidentified dark petrel may also pertain to Bulwer's Petrel, but photos do not eliminate, and even suggest to some, the possibility of the bird having been Jouanin's Petrel *B. fallax* (Pike & Compton 2010). Jouanin's is an Indian Ocean species that has occurred as a vagrant in the Hawaiian islands, but it is unrecorded in N America.

Field Identification: Small, all-dark petrel with distinctive, low weaving flight, and long tapered tail.

   Similar Species: In life, Bulwer's Petrel really doesn't look much like any other tubenose. Its size (larger than all-dark storm-petrels, smaller than small *Pterodroma* petrels), shape, and buoyant weaving flight are all distinctive. Large ***dark-rumped storm-petrels*** are similar in coloration but all are variably smaller with relatively

tail occasionally spread when banking

prominence of pale upperwing band varies

Bulwer's Petrel

shorter, forked tails (beware the effects of molt or of birds holding their tail closed) and different flight (although they can wheel and bank in windy conditions).

Noddies share similar shape, all-dark plumage, and often fly low over the water. Both species are larger (although Black Noddy is close in size to Bulwer's) with a variable whitish cap, and their flight is tern-like—although in windy conditions they can bank and wheel, suggesting a petrel.

Jouanin's Petrel is appreciably larger (L 32–35.5 cm, WS 76–80 cm) and bulkier, about the size of a small shearwater, such as Black-vented. Plumage and shape much like Bulwer's, but Jouanin's has larger head, broader wings, broader and relatively shorter tail, and its pale upperwing bands are much duller.

Age/Sex/Season: All plumages similar except for wear and molt, but juv fresh in Sep–Dec when older ages normally worn or in wing molt. Wing molt mainly Oct–Apr.

Habitat and Behavior: Pelagic. In many areas this species inhabits oceanic deserts—warm and generally dead tropical waters, where few other birds live. Likely to be encountered singly, often not in association with other species, and typically indifferent to ships. Flight usually low over the water with a buoyant, weaving, switchback progression. In direct flight, fairly quick shallow wingbeats are interspersed with prolonged buoyant glides and sometimes low wheeling, the wings held bowed, pressed slightly forward, and angled back at the carpals. In moderate winds, can wheel higher, recalling a small *Pterodroma*, but generally does not bank steeply and tends to stay low to the water, as fitting its low wing-loading. Foraging birds can fly into the wind with loose, fairly deep, and quick wingbeats, alighting briefly to seize food near the surface.

WESTERN YELLOW-NOSED ALBATROSS *Thalassarche [chlororhynchus] chlororhynchus* L 70–76 cm (27.5–30"); WS 188–215 cm (74–84.5")

Summary: *Atlantic and Gulf States and Provinces*: Very rare; records year-round but mainly spring–fall. *Ontario*: 1 summer record (2010).
Taxonomy: The 2 taxa of Yellow-nosed Albatross are variably treated as ssp or species; they differ slightly in bill structure, face pattern, and adult head color. All N American records, as far as is known, pertain to Western Yellow-nosed Albatross.

T. [c.] chlororhynchus (Western Yellow-nosed Albatross, also known as Atlantic Yellow-nosed) breeds and ranges in S Atlantic. Yellow culminicorn stripe more tapered at forehead and with straighter sides; eye patch larger and triangular. Adult has smoky gray head and neck.

T. [c.] carteri (Eastern Yellow-nosed Albatross, also known as Indian Yellow-nosed) breeds and ranges in s. Indian Ocean. Yellow culminicorn stripe more rounded at forehead and with slightly convex sides; eye patch smaller, less triangular. Adult has gray clouding on head and neck.

Distribution and Status:
World: Breeds (Sep–Apr) and ranges in the S Atlantic, mainly in latitudes 25–50°S.

North America: *Atlantic and Gulf States and Provinces*: Very rare (mainly May–Aug, but records year-round) to inshore waters of e. N America. About 35 records in the period, spread from NL s. to FL and in the Gulf of Mexico from FL w. to TX. Records in the Northeast (s. to New England) are mainly late Mar–Aug; those from the Mid-Atlantic Coast span late Nov to mid-Apr; and those from FL and the Gulf of Mexico, May–Dec. *Ontario*: Lake Ontario shoreline, 4–17 Jul 2010 (*NAB* 64: 584, 666).
Comments: This is the most frequently recorded vagrant albatross in N American waters, in striking contrast to W Europe, where Black-browed Albatross predominates. These vagrant distributions mirror the latitudinal distributions of both species in the S Hemisphere, and also reflect observer concentrations. Thus, Yellow-nosed is a warmer-water species mainly found n. of 45°S (45°N in the ne. Atlantic corresponds to southern France, s. of which there are few seabird observers), whereas Black-browed is a colder-water species, with adults ranging mainly s. of 45°S (45°N in the nw. Atlantic corresponds to Atlantic Canada, n. of which there are few observers); interestingly, though, there are 2 Jul–Aug specimens of Black-browed from w. Greenland. This suggests that once albatrosses cross the equator they seek their preferred habitats; the seasonal southward shift in Atlantic coast records in winter further suggests some birds adopt a N Hemisphere cycle.

Several records refer to adults, but apparent 1st-cycles (e.g., off Maryland, Jan 1975) and 2nd-cycles (e.g., off TX, Sep 2003) have also been recorded. Thus, at least some birds wander n. across the equator in their 1st year or 2 of life, after which they may become 'trapped' in the N Hemisphere and switch to a n. molt cycle (as

adults

adult

1st-year

bill black
overall

bright conditions
can bleach
out gray head

**Western
Yellow-nosed
Albatross**

1st-year with 1st-year
Black-browed Albatross

has happened with adult Black-browed Albatrosses in Europe). The remarkable Lake Ontario bird was an emaciated adult that may have reached the lake via the St. Lawrence River.

Mlodinow (1999b) noted that most N American records of Yellow-nosed Albatross were prior to 1980, with 12 in the 1970s. However, there were at least 18 reports from May 2000 to Jul 2010. Some records surely pertain to wandering individuals and birds returning in subsequent years (such as off the E Coast in the 1970s and in the 2000s), making it difficult to determine how many birds have been seen and whether any trends exist.

Field Identification: Relatively small and lightly built albatross; all ages have white underwings with fairly thick black leading edge. The only other small albatross confirmed to date from the N Atlantic is Black-browed. Other possibilities should always be considered, however, if you are lucky enough to find an albatross in the North Atlantic. See Shirihai (2007) and Howell (2012a) for details of other species.

Similar Species: ***Great Black-backed Gull*** and ***Northern Gannet*** can be mistaken for albatrosses, especially with birds viewed at a distance or in poor conditions.

Black-browed Albatross stockier overall with a relatively shorter and thicker bill and broader wings. All ages have more extensive black on the underwing (although a sunlit adult Black-browed underwing can appear as white as that of a heavily marked imm Yellow-nosed), and adults have a clean white head with a bright orange bill. 1st-cycle Black-browed can have a dusky, black-tipped bill approaching the pattern of juv Western Yellow-nosed, and both species have a variable dusky hindneck shawl; note the all-dark underwings of imm Black-browed. With birds seen only from above, or on the water, note bill color and Black-browed's rounded culmen bridge (squared on Yellow-nosed) and narrow dark browline (vs. the thicker black triangular eye patch of juv Western Yellow-nosed or the smaller beady eye of older imms).

Age/Sex/Season: Ages differ, with adult appearance attained in about 4–5 years; sexes similar but males average larger and longer billed; no seasonal variation other than wear and fading. ***Adult:*** Head and neck smoky gray with whitish crown and triangular black eye patch; gray hood distinct in overcast conditions but paler and less apparent in bright sunlight. Bill black with bright yellow culminicorn stripe leading into orange-red nail. *1st-cycle*: Fledges May with white head, blackish eye patch, and variable dusky gray hindneck shawl; rest of plumage adult-like. Bill dull dark brownish to blackish overall with black tip and dull pale brownish culminicorn stripe visible at closer range; culminicorn stripe pales and becomes dull pale yellowish in 1st year. Primaries uniform and relatively fresh. *Subsequent cycles*: 2nd-prebasic molt (about 8–16 months after fledging) involves head, body, and tail, but no primaries. 2nd cycle overall similar to 1st cycle but eye patch reduced and can appear beady eyed; gray shawl may be smaller; fresh hindneck and back contrast with worn and variably faded upperwings; outer primaries often frayed at tips. Bill blackish (or subtly paler and slaty on the basal half) with pale yellow stripe on basal two-thirds of culminicorn and reddish orange tinge to nail. May attain gray head by 3rd-prebasic molt (at about 2 years of age), and bill pattern then resembles adult but with duller and reduced color; bill probably adult-like by age 4 or 5.

Habitat and Behavior: Favors inshore and shelf waters. Several records are from shore or even slightly inland from the coast, with birds found flying around buildings or resting on beaches and sandy islets in coastal sounds, sometimes in association with other birds, such as Great Black-backed Gulls.

BLACK-BROWED ALBATROSS
Thalassarche [melanophris] melanophris
L 79–86 cm (31–34"); WS 205–230 cm (81–91")

Summary: *Atlantic States and Provinces*: Very rare; records year-round but mainly summer–fall.

Taxonomy: The 2 taxa of Black-browed Albatross are variably treated as ssp or species, and differ primarily in adult eye color and underwing pattern. N American records presumably refer to nominate *melanophris*.

T. *[m.] melanophris* (Black-browed Albatross) breeds and ranges widely in subantarctic latitudes from s. S America e. to New Zealand. Adult eyes blackish brown, underwing averages less extensive black.

T. *[m.] impavida* (Campbell Albatross) breeds Campbell Island, New Zealand, ranges to Australia. Adult eyes pale yellowish, underwing averages more extensive black.

Distribution and Status:

World: Circumpolar in southern oceans, breeding (Sep–Apr) from s. South America e. to New Zealand. Ranges n. (mainly Apr–Nov) in Humboldt Current to Peru, and in Atlantic to s. Brazil.

North America: *Atlantic States and Provinces*: About 10 records (with up to 5 in 2009), mainly adults and subadults from NL s. to MA during Jun–Sep, but also in Feb off VA (imm) and NC (adult in 2012; B. Patteson, pers. comm.), and Mar off MA (subadult). Additional reports from NL s. to FL are not accepted, but some may be correct (most are discussed by Patteson et al. 1999).

Comments: The different N Atlantic distributions of vagrant Black-browed Albatrosses (mainly in the e., off NW Europe) and Yellow-nosed Albatrosses (mainly in the w., off N America) are discussed under Yellow-nosed Albatross. From adjacent waters there is a Nov specimen of Black-browed from Martinique, West Indies, and two Jul–Aug specimens from w. Greenland.

As with Yellow-nosed Albatross, some Black-browed Albatrosses wander n. across the equator in their 1st 1–2 years of life (such as the 1999 VA bird), after which perhaps they may become 'trapped' in the N Hemisphere and switch to a n. molt cycle, as has occurred with adult Black-broweds returning in summer to Northern Gannet colonies off Britain. Several of the recent records have been from observant fishermen equipped with digital cameras, and it remains to be seen whether the upsurge in records suggested in 2009 continues.

Field Identification: Small, fairly stocky albatross; note dark underwing of imm, orange bill of adult.

Similar Species: *Great Black-backed Gull* and *Northern Gannet* can be mistaken for albatrosses, especially with birds viewed at a distance or in poor conditions. Adult Black-browed is distinctive, but imms can be confused with other small albatross species. See under *Yellow-nosed Albatross*, and be aware of species as yet unrecorded in N American waters; see Shirihai (2007) and Howell (2012a) for details of other possibilities.

Age/Sex/Season: Ages differ, with adult appearance attained in about 4–5 years; sexes similar but males average larger and longer billed; no seasonal variation other than wear and fading. *Adult*: White head and neck, with black brow visible at closer range. Underwings with bold black wing-margins, which are thickest along leading edge; at long range, and especially in bright light, underwings can appear white overall with black restricted to a relatively narrow (but still distinct and quite thick) black leading edge. Bill pinkish orange with dark orange tip.

adults

1st-years

dull pale bill,
tipped blackish

2nd-year

Black-browed Albatross

1st-cycle: Fledges Apr/May with variable gray wash to head and hindneck, this soon fading to white with a variable gray hindneck shawl; black brow usually poorly defined. Rest of plumage adult-like except for all-dark underwings, which often show somewhat paler central panel. Bill dark brownish olive to dusky flesh with black tip; often develops variable paler areas and small pale tip toward end of 1st year. Primaries uniform and relatively fresh. ***Subsequent cycles***: Plumage aspect and bill color of imms rather variable within age classes (Prince et al. 1993, Prince & Rodwell 1994, Howell 2010c). 2nd-prebasic molt (about 8–16 months after fledging) involves head, body, and tail, but no primaries. Appearance overall similar to 1st-cycle but gray shawl often reduced; fresh gray hindneck and back contrast with worn and variably faded upperwings; outer primaries often frayed at tips. Bill varies from fairly dark overall to dull pale orange with a blackish tip. 3rd-prebasic molt (Jan–Oct) includes outer primaries, usually molted Jan–Apr (at about 20–23 months of age). Whiter headed with a small black brow, gray shawl reduced or absent; outer primaries (usually p8–p10) blacker and fresher in contrast to faded and often very worn inner and middle primaries (which are still juv feathers); underwings with variable, fairly broad white median panel. Bill typically paler and more orangish overall, usually with extensive

blackish on tip and dusky sides. 4th-prebasic molt (Feb–Oct) includes some middle and inner primaries but not outers, which thus appear slightly faded. Resembles adult overall but underwings average more extensive and messier blackish margins; bill variable, usually pale orange with some blackish on tip and dusky on sides. Following 5th-prebasic molt (which includes outer primaries) much like adult, and some birds perhaps not distinguishable; bill typically duller and paler orange than adult, often with some dark near tip and duskier sides.

Habitat and Behavior: Pelagic, but might be seen from shore. In the southern oceans Black-browed is a professional ship follower that often scavenges from fishing boats where it occurs with other albatrosses, petrels, shearwaters, gulls, etc. Birds in the ne. Atlantic have joined Northern Gannet colonies, built nests, and returned for many years.

TASMANIAN SHY ALBATROSS
Thalassarche [cauta] cauta

AUCKLAND SHY ALBATROSS
Thalassarche [cauta] steadi L 87–100 cm (34.5–39.5"); WS 229–265 cm (90.5–105")

Summary: *Pacific States*: 2–5 fall–winter records (1951, 1996, 1999, 2000, 2001; last 4 may refer to same individual).

Taxonomy: The Shy Albatross complex comprises 4 taxa, all breeding in Australia and New Zealand. These 4 have been united as a single species, Shy Albatross *T. cauta*, but are increasingly treated as 4 species on the basic of morphology, genetics, and breeding chronology (C.J.R. Robertson and Nunn 1998); names used here follow Tickell (2000) and Howell (2012a). The gray-necked Salvin's and Chatham Albatrosses are treated in separate accounts, whereas the white-necked Tasmanian Shy and Auckland Shy are combined here in one account, given that they are rarely distinguishable at sea.

T. [cauta] cauta (Tasmanian Shy Albatross) breeds (Sep–Apr) around Tasmania; ranges w. to S Africa and S Atlantic. Averages smaller (L 87–96 cm, WS 229–251 cm); some adults have distinct yellow base to culminicorn. In Australia known simply as Shy Albatross.

T. [cauta] steadi (Auckland Shy Albatross) breeds (Nov–Jul) in New Zealand; ranges w. to S Africa and S Atlantic. Averages larger (L 90–100 cm, WS 240–265 cm); adults lack distinct yellow base to culminicorn. In New Zealand, known as White-capped Albatross.

Distribution and Status:

World: Breeds around Tasmania and New Zealand (see Taxonomy, above); ranges w. to S Africa and the S Atlantic.

North America: *Pacific States*: At least 2 records, the first of an adult Auckland Shy (see Cole 2000) collected off WA, 1 Sep 1951. Subsequent records may refer to a single individual: Lincoln Co., OR, 5 Oct 1996 (subadult, not identified to taxon), and subsequent records also all involving adult Tasmanian Shy: Mendocino Co./Sonoma Co., CA, 24 Aug and 25 Sep 1999; Gray's Harbor Co., WA, 22 Jan 2000; and Lincoln Co., OR, 7 Oct 2001.

Comments: That N American records of 'Shy Albatrosses' have involved all four taxa is remarkable. Given that the 2 records of Wandering Albatross also appear to represent different taxa, we can only wonder which southern albatross species may appear next!

The relatively narrow window of occurrence for W Coast records of Tasmanian Shy and Chatham albatrosses (1996–2003), with a Light-mantled Sooty Albatross in 1994, may simply reflect increased numbers of pelagic trips in the 1990s relative to the preceding years—but records did not continue into the 2000s. We suspect, instead, that the temporal concentration may also reflect concentrations of albatrosses gathering in those years at drag-netting boats that no longer fish to any extent, at least in CA waters, which is better for the marine environment if not for finding rare albatrosses.

Field Identification: Medium-sized albatross; all ages have mostly white underwing with fine black margins. Note white hindneck and gray face of adult and older imms. As adults, Tasmanian Shy and Auckland Shy are distinctive as a species-pair. Note the white hindneck and crown, smoky gray cheeks, and pale gray-green bill with a yellow tip. Tasmanian averages smaller than Auckland, and as an adult often has yellow on culminicorn base, but all measurements of the 2 taxa overlap and only extremes can be identified, which is aided by knowledge of a bird's sex (Double et al. 2003). See Howell (2006a, 2009, 2012a) and Shirihai (2007) for further information and details of other possibilities. See illustration on page 98.

Similar Species: *Salvin's Albatross* has a gray head and neck, but 1st-cycle Shy can have gray hood similar to Salvin's. Note bill colors and underwing patterns. Imm Salvin's has dusky grayish to dark pinkish-gray bill with less contrasting black tip (vs. paler gray to olive-gray with a contrasting black tip on Shy). Imm Salvin's has more extensive black underwing margins and dusky undersides to the primaries (vs. cleaner and narrower black margins and paler primary bases, which are often whitish on Shy).

Chatham Albatross differs in much the same ways as does imm Salvin's, but imm Chatham has dull yellowish bill (pale grayish on Shy).

Black-browed Albatross smaller and stockier, although size of lone bird hard to judge. Imm Black-browed can have white head and dusky hindneck shawl similar to 1st-cycle Shy, but bill darker, dull brownish, or dusky pinkish, with black tip and narrower, rounded culmen bridge; underwings dark overall.

Yellow-nosed Albatross smaller and slimmer-billed. Imm can have white head and dusky hindneck shawl, but bill dark overall, usually appearing blackish or with narrow paler culminicorn stripe; underwing has broader black leading edge.

Age/Sex/Season: Ages differ, with adult appearance attained in about 4–5 years; sexes similar but males average larger and longer billed; no seasonal variation other than wear and fading.

***Adult*:** Smoky-gray clouding to head sides offsets well-defined white crown and white hindneck. Underwings white with very narrow black wing-margins that pinch out on leading edge near body, accentuating black preaxilliary notch. Bill pale gray-green with a yellow tip, black culmen bridge and nostril strips; many Tasmanian Shy also have a yellow culminicorn base. *1st-cycle*: fledges in Apr/May (Tasmanian) or Jul/Aug (Auckland) with variable gray wash or grayish mottling on head and hindneck (lacks contrast between white hindneck and blackish back), and whitish crown; head often fades to whitish within 1st year except for grayish hindneck shawl; black brow less striking than adult. Rest of plumage adult-like but black underwing margins slightly broader and messier, preaxilliary notch less distinct or lacking. Bill pale to medium grayish with contrasting black tip. Primaries uniform and relatively fresh. *Subsequent cycles*: 2nd-prebasic molt (probably about 8–16 months after fledging) involves head, body, and tail, but no primaries. Plumage adult-like or with variable traces of a gray shawl; underwing margins cleaner but average broader than adult. Fresh hindneck and back contrast with worn and variably faded browner upperwings; outer primaries often frayed at tips. Bill pale grayish with black tip or subterminal band and small pale yellowish tip, sometimes a paler yellowish culminicorn. Subsequent prebasic molts alternate outer and middle primaries. Older imms have adult-like plumage (or head fades to whiter) but bill duller, with variable blackish subterminal band or marks, retained last on lower mandible.

Habitat and Behavior: Mainly pelagic but often forages over shelf waters and thus might be seen from shore. Often follows ships and scavenges from fishing boats along with other albatrosses, petrels, shearwaters, gulls, etc. Birds in the NE Pacific have usually been in areas where other albatrosses congregate, and have associated readily with Black-footed and Laysan Albatrosses.

SALVIN'S ALBATROSS *Thalassarche salvini* L 87–96 cm (34.5–38"); WS 235–255 cm (93–101")

Summary: *Alaska*: 1 fall record (2003).
Taxonomy: Monotypic. See under Shy Albatross.
Distribution and Status:
World: Breeds (Sep–Apr) in New Zealand, ranges at sea to w. S America.
North America: *Alaska*: Near Kasatochi Island, w. Aleutians, 4 Aug 2003.

Comments: The AK bird's dusky-gray hood and dusky olive-gray bill with extensive subterminal black point to it being an imm Salvin's, and not another taxon in the Shy Albatross complex. A published photo (Benter et al. 2005) shows the bird was undergoing wing molt but is not clear enough to determine details. The only other N Hemisphere record of Salvin's Albatross is of a subadult (older than the AK individual) on land in Hawaii, in Apr 2003 (C.J.R. Robertson et al. 2005).

Recent colonization by Salvin's Albatross of the Crozet Islands, in the s. Indian Ocean (Jouventin 1990), might be taken as an indication that the population of Salvin's Albatross is increasing. An alternative explanation is that limited breeding space available on the Bounty Islands is being usurped by a burgeoning fur seal population (Howell, pers. obs.; R. Russ, pers. comm.), forcing albatrosses to seek new nesting sites.

Field Identification: Medium-sized albatross; all ages have mostly white underwing with narrow black margins. Note gray hood of all ages, overall dusky bill coloration. See Howell (2006a, 2009, 2012a) and Shirihai (2007) for further information and details of other possibilities.

Similar Species: *Chatham Albatross* imm typically shows distinct yellowish or orange bill tones lacking in Salvin's. Gray hood of Chatham averages darker, but often bleaches on head and shows whitish crown. By 3rd cycle, yellow bill of Chatham usually obvious. Some adult Salvin's have bill relatively pale and yellowish overall, but this is distinct from adult Chatham, which has bright orange-yellow bill and deeper blue-gray hood without contrasting white crown.

Tasmanian Shy and *Auckland Shy albatrosses* typically have white hindneck after 1st year, but some 1st-cycle birds have extensive gray hood similar to Salvin's. Note bill colors: paler gray to olive-gray with contrasting black tip on Shy, versus dusky grayish to dark pinkish gray with less contrasting black tip on Salvin's. Underwings typically have narrower black margins (lacking Salvin's broad fan of black on primary coverts), and paler primary bases, which are often whitish (dusky on imm Salvin's).

Age/Sex/Season: Ages differ, with adult appearance attained in about 4–5 years; sexes similar but males average larger and longer billed; no seasonal variation other than wear and fading. *Adult*: Head and neck gray with white

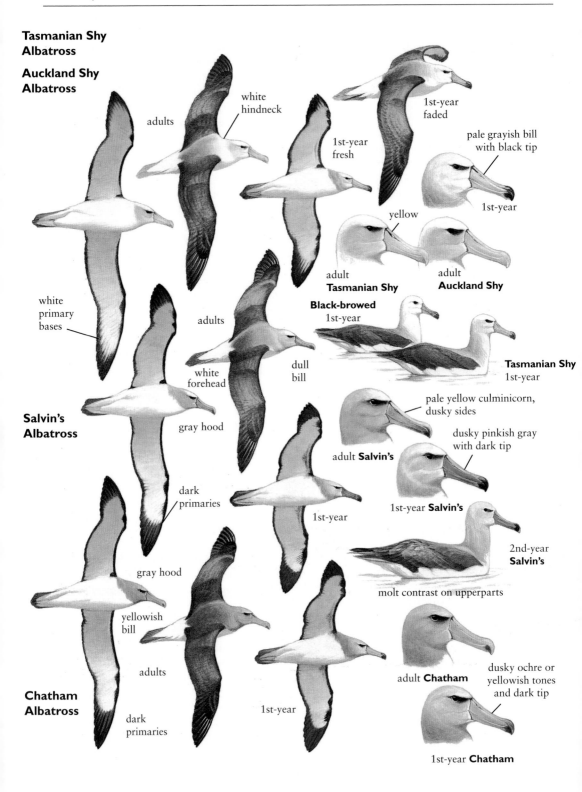

Tasmanian Shy Albatross

Auckland Shy Albatross

adults

white hindneck

1st-year fresh

1st-year faded

pale grayish bill with black tip

1st-year

yellow

adult Tasmanian Shy

adult Auckland Shy

Black-browed 1st-year

white primary bases

adults

white forehead

dull bill

Tasmanian Shy 1st-year

Salvin's Albatross

gray hood

pale yellow culminicorn, dusky sides

adult Salvin's

dark primaries

1st-year

dusky pinkish gray with dark tip

1st-year Salvin's

2nd-year Salvin's

molt contrast on upperparts

gray hood

yellowish bill

adults

Chatham Albatross

dark primaries

1st-year

adult Chatham

dusky ochre or yellowish tones and dark tip

1st-year Chatham

forecrown set off by black brow from eye to culmen base; underwings white with narrow black wing-margins and usually a black preaxilliary notch. Bill pale olive-gray with contrasting pale yellow culminicorn and nail, mostly black mandibular unguis, pale yellow ramicorn stripe, and black culmen bridge and nostril strips. *1st-cycle*: Fledges Apr/May with dusky gray head and neck and dull whitish forecrown; black brow less striking than adult. Rest of plumage adult-like but black underwing margins broader and messier, preaxilliary notch less distinct or lacking. Bill dark grayish to purplish gray with black tip. Primaries uniform and relatively fresh. *Subsequent cycles*: 2nd-prebasic molt (probably about 8–16 months after fledging) involves head, body, and tail, but no primaries. Plumage adult-like but black brow less striking, underwing margins may average broader. Fresh hindneck and back contrast with worn and variably faded browner upperwings; outer primaries often frayed at tips. Bill dusky gray with black tip or subterminal band and pale tip, sometimes a paler culminicorn and hint of orange mandible gape line. Subsequent prebasic molts alternate outer and middle primaries. Older imms have adult-like plumage but bill duller, with more extensive black subterminal band.

Habitat and Behavior: Much like Shy Albatross.

CHATHAM ALBATROSS *Thalassarche eremita* L 86–95 cm (34–37.5");WS 230–250 cm (91–99")

Summary: *California*: 1–2 summer–fall records (2000, 2001).

Taxonomy: Monotypic. See under Shy Albatross.

Distribution and Status:

World: Breeds (Sep–Apr) in New Zealand, ranges at sea to w. S America.

North America: *California*: Marin Co., 29 Jul and 17 Sep 2000 (imm); 27 Jul 2001 (imm).

Comments: The bird in 2000 seems likely to have been the same individual as an older-looking imm in the same area in 2001 (*contra* Garrett & J. C. Wilson 2003). Its dusky-gray hood and relatively small size point to it being a Chatham or Salvin's, as does extensive blackish on the underprimary coverts (evident in photos of the 2000 bird). This bird has been considered as probably a Salvin's Albatross (Hamilton

et al. 2007), but as far as is known the orange-yellow bill tones (especially evident in 2001) are diagnostic of Chatham Albatross and not shown by imm Salvin's (Howell 2012a). This is the only N Hemisphere record for Chatham Albatross.

Field Identification: Medium-sized albatross; all ages have mostly white underwing with narrow black margins. Note gray hood of all ages, yellow bill of adult and older immatures. See illustration on p. 98.

Similar Species: See *Salvin's Albatross*. Note Chatham's gray head and neck, mostly white underwings, and yellow bill tones at all ages. Criteria for separating Chatham from other species of mollymawks are much the same as for Salvin's, with the exception of bill color differences. See Howell (2006a, 2009, 2012a) and Shirihai (2007) for further information and details of other possibilities.

Age/Sex/Season: Ages differ, with adult appearance attained in about 4–5 years; sexes similar but males average larger and longer billed; no seasonal variation other than wear and fading. *Adult*: Head and neck blue-gray with black brow from eye to culmen base. Underwings white with narrow black wing-margins and black preaxilliary notch. Bill bright orange-yellow (slightly duller on sides) with blackish mandibular unguis, culmen bridge, and nostril strips. *1st-cycle*: Fledges Apr/May with dusky gray head and neck, but forecrown often fades to whitish in 1st year; black brow less striking than adult. Rest of plumage adult-like but black underwing margins broader and messier, preaxilliary notch less distinct or lacking. Bill dirty yellowish with a black tip. Primaries uniform and relatively fresh. *Subsequent cycles*: 2nd-prebasic molt (probably about 8–16 months after fledging) involves head, body, and tail, but no primaries. Plumage adult-like but black brow less striking, underwing margins may average broader. Fresh hindneck and back contrast with worn and variably faded browner upperwings; outer primaries often frayed at tips. Bill ochre-yellow to orange-yellow, usually with duskier sides, and with black tip or black subterminal band and small pale tip. Subsequent prebasic molts alternate outer and middle primaries. Older imms have adult-like plumage but bill duller, with more extensive black subterminal band.

Habitat and Behavior: Much like Shy Albatross.

ANTIPODES [Wandering] ALBATROSS *Diomedea [exulans] antipodensis*

GIBSON'S [Wandering] ALBATROSS
Diomedea [exulans] gibsoni L 110–122 cm (43–47.5");WS 280–350 cm (109–127")

Summary: *Pacific States*: 2 summer–fall records (1967, 2008).

Taxonomy: 5 taxa, variably treated as ssp or, perhaps more realistically, as species (C.J.R. Robertson & Warham 1992; C.J.R. Robertson & Nunn 1998; Tickell 2000). Here all are combined in one account because of difficulties in identifying taxa at sea (names follow Tickell 2000; Howell 2012a). Plumage variation within Wandering Albatross taxa is complex, and at-sea identification of different taxa is often provisional (see Field Identification, below). Taxa recorded in N America include presumed *antipodensis* and *gibsoni* (Howell 2012a).

D. [e.] exulans (Snowy Albatross) breeds from S Atlantic e. to SW Pacific; circumpolar at-sea range. Adults average larger, bigger-billed, and whiter than other taxa, but with much variation.

D. [e.] gibsoni (Gibson's Albatross) breeds New Zealand; ranges at sea in SW Pacific. Adults highly variable, some (presumed adult males) extensively white like whitest Snowy Albatross. Averages smaller than Snowy Albatross.

D. [e.] antipodensis (Antipodes Albatross) breeds New Zealand; ranges at sea in S Pacific to w. S America. Adults variable, but rarely very white (upperwings and scapulars mostly to solidly dark), usually with a dark cap. Size similar to Gibson's Albatross.

D. [e.] amsterdamensis (Amsterdam Albatross) breeds Amsterdam Island, subtropical Indian Ocean; at-sea range unknown. A small dark taxon (upperwings, back, and chest typically all-dark), dark cutting edge to greenish-tipped bill also found on some imm female Gough Wanderers.

D. [e.] dabbenena (Gough Albatross) breeds S Atlantic; ranges at sea at least to Australia. Adults variable; males resemble Auckland males, females resemble Antipodes or Auckland females.

Distribution and Status

World: Circumpolar in s. oceans (breeds biennially Dec/Feb–Dec/Feb), ranging n. regularly to around 30°S.

North America: *Pacific States*: Sonoma Co., CA, 11–12 Jul 1967 (on shore), and off s. OR (13

Sep 2008; Anon 2009). Remarkably, what appeared to be the OR individual was seen on 25 Sep 2008, about 510 km (305 miles) off the cen. CA coast (37°N 128°W; Ballance et al. unpubl. data), a testament to how much these birds are attracted to ships.

Comments: Photos of the 1967 bird (Paxton 1968; Hamilton et al. 2007) show that it had small white elbow patches and some white tipping to the humeral coverts, in combination with a well-defined dark cap and extensive dark vermiculations to the uppertail coverts; unfortunately no photos show the scapulars. Antipodes wanderers rarely have white upperwing patches (perhaps only the oldest males), and such birds typically have bright white uppertail coverts. The relatively slender bill may point to a female, but without knowing which taxon is involved this is difficult to judge. The choices appear to lie with an older imm female Gibson's, a younger imm male Gibson's (cf. bottom photo on p. 97 of Shirihai 2007), or perhaps even a younger imm female Snowy.

The 2008 bird showed the classic features of a female Antipodes wanderer in a plumage not shown by Snowy wanderers, and perhaps not by Gibson's, male Antipodes, or male Gough wanderers. Although some Amsterdam and immature female Gough wanderers closely resemble this plumage, these two seem unlikely to reach the e. N Pacific, and both differ in having a greenish bill tip, often with dark cutting edges.

The relatively calm equatorial latitudes of the Pacific and Atlantic oceans constitute a very real barrier to birds whose flight depends on persistent strong winds. Thus, this icon of the windy southern oceans has been recorded only exceptionally in the N Hemisphere, with 5 records from the N Atlantic region off Europe (Lewington et al. 1991), in addition to the two N American Pacific records and a 1st-cycle bird off Panama (Murphy 1938). Smaller and much lighter-bodied albatrosses, in particular Yellow-nosed and Black-browed, range farther n., are able to fly more easily in lighter winds than are Wanderers, and have made the equatorial crossing much more frequently. Albatrosses are well known for accompanying ships, but they do not do so in the absence of wind and they magically disappear as ships start to approach windless regions. No albatrosses have knowingly been found in the N Hemisphere shortly after their transequatorial odyssey, and thus we have

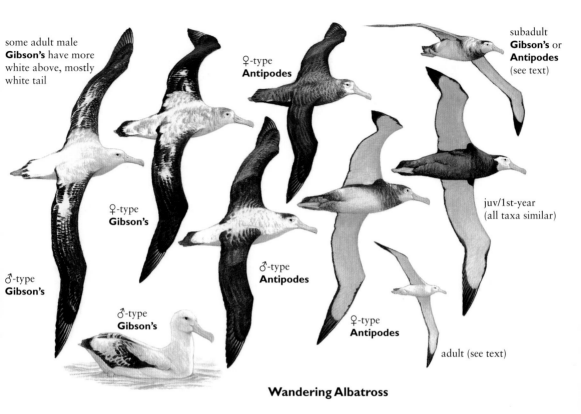

some adult male
Gibson's have more
white above, mostly
white tail

♀-type
Antipodes

subadult
Gibson's or
Antipodes
(see text)

♀-type
Gibson's

juv/1st-year
(all taxa similar)

♂-type
Gibson's

♂-type
Antipodes

♂-type
Gibson's

♀-type
Antipodes

adult (see text)

Wandering Albatross

no information on what weather conditions may promote their vagrancy.

Field Identification: This huge albatross should draw attention if it occurs again in N America; all ages have mostly white underwings.

Similar Species: Huge size, especially the massive body and very long narrow wings, should preclude confusion with all except similarly sized Royal Albatrosses (*D. epomophora* and *D. sanfordi*; unrecorded in N Hemisphere). Beware superficial resemblance of smaller adult **Steller's (Short-tailed) Albatross**, which has bluish bill tip, golden-yellow to brown cap and hindneck, and lacks neat black underwing tip.

Wanderers with extensive brown on their head and body are distinct from Royal Albatrosses. Older adult Wanderers with extensively white upperwings can look similar to Southern Royal Albatross, and some other plumages may suggest Northern Royal Albatross. See Shirihai (2007) and Howell (2012a) for further information.

Age/Sex/Season: Ages/sexes differ; no seasonal variation other than wear and fading. Plumage sequences of all Wandering Albatross taxa remain to be elucidated, and Snowy Wanderers continue to whiten through at least

20 years of age (Prince et al. 1997). Some features or combinations of features appear diagnostic of various taxa, however, such that provisional at-sea identifications can be attempted. See Shirihai (2007) and Howell (2012a) for additional information. Given low vagrancy potential, Amsterdam Albatross is not discussed here.

1st-cycle (similar in all taxa): Fledges Dec to Feb. Dark brown overall with a white face, underwings like adult but with dark patch at base of leading edge; plumage fades within 1st year, especially on hindneck and belly. **Subsequent cycles**: 2nd-prebasic molt of head and body feathers occurs mainly at about 11–22 months of age, when differences between taxa and sexes can become apparent. 3rd-prebasic molt at about 24–34 months of age includes outer 2–3 primaries (so-called phase 1 primary molt), plus head and body. Male Snowy Wanderer at this age mostly white bodied, whereas female Antipodes and Gough wanderers brown-bodied with contrasting white belly. Female Snowy, male Antipodes, and Gough wanderers, and both sexes of Gibson's wanderer fall between these extremes. In general, males become whiter throughout their head and body in 2nd- and

3rd-prebasic molts, whereas females have a mottled to solid brown chest band and mottled to solidly brown upperparts.

Subsequent molts of prebreeding imms alternate the middle and inner primaries (phase 2 primary molt in the 4th, 6th, and 8th cycles) and outer primaries (phase 1 molt in the 5th, 7th, and 9th cycles, etc.). Given good views, or photos, birds can be aged by patterns of wing molt through their 5th or 6th molt cycle (Prince et al. 1997). The following are provisional criteria for distinguishing older imms and adults of different taxa (Howell 2012a). Helpful features to note are any molt contrasts among the primaries, the extent and pattern of white on the body (especially the scapulars), the extent and distribution of any brown mottling (especially on the upperparts), the extent and nature (coarse versus fine) of any dusky vermiculations, and the extent of any white on the upperwings.

Antipodes Wanderer. Male develops mostly white head and body with dark cap and variable brown mottling on upperparts by 5–6 years of age, but scapulars mostly dark overall, and upperwings solidly dark, with no white on elbow; uppertail coverts often whiter than rump and back, the reverse of imm Snowy and Gough wanderers. Female Antipodes retains imm-like plumage, with mostly brown upperparts and brown chest band, solidly dark upperwings. Oldest male Antipodes may lose dark cap and develop some white on elbow, but may be distinguished from Gibson's and imm Snowy by mostly dark longest and 'outer' scapulars.

Gibson's Wanderer. Male develops mostly white head and body (including scapulars) in 5–6 years but often retains a mottled dark cap; upperparts and chest have coarse dark vermiculations; white elbow patch obvious on older imms. Female has brown cowl, brown-mottling and coarse dusky vermiculations on upperparts and chest through at least 7–8 years, by which time some white usually appears at elbow. Relative to Antipodes Wanderer, imm Gibson's distinguished by extensively white scapulars (with coarse vermiculations), and white on elbow. Adult male and female Gibson's distinguished from adult Antipodes by mostly white scapulars and extensive white on upperwing. Many Gibson's Wanderers appear similar to adult Gough Wanderers, and pending critical study these two taxa may be indistinguishable in the field other than on grounds of geographic probability. Oldest and whitest male Gibson's

perhaps not distinguishable from oldest and whitest Snowy.

Snowy Wanderer. Male develops white head and body in 3–4 years, but female can retain brown cap or cowl through breeding age; dusky vermiculations on upperparts and chest usually apparent at close range but finer than typical Gibson's Wanderers; scapulars mostly white, forming broad 'fan' on back; white develops on upperwings of males 4–5 years of age, but females at this age have dark upperwings; tail becomes partly white only after white patches develop on upperwings. Oldest and whitest males perhaps not distinguishable from oldest and whitest Gibson's males, but probably have more white on upperwing than whitest Gough Wanderers.

Gough Wanderer. Male apparently develops mostly white head and body (including scapulars) by 4–5 years but may retain a mottled dark cap, and chest and upperparts vermiculated dusky, often with brownish mottling (similar to imm female Snowy) heaviest on uppertail coverts; dark vermiculations more similar to Snowy Wanderer than to very coarse markings of Gibson's Wanderer. Upperwings may still be solidly dark at 4–5 years (needs study). Older males have clean creamy white head and body but may be slower to develop extensive white on upperwings and tail, and apparently do not become as extensively white as oldest male Snowy and Gibson's Wanderers. Female Gough through at least 3–4 years of age has mostly brown upperparts and brown chest band, and solidly dark upperwings similar to female Antipodes. Subsequent female plumages have whiter head with dusky cap; brownish upperparts (including scapulars) whiten progressively and can have coarse dark vermiculations like Gibson's Wanderer.

Habitat and Behavior: Pelagic, favoring off-shore waters with persistent wind, although the CA vagrant was found on land! Often attracted to ships, and scavenge readily at fishing boats. Flight labored in calm or light winds (when birds usually sit on the water), but sails almost effortlessly in strong winds.

LIGHT-MANTLED SOOTY ALBATROSS *Phoebetria palpebrata* L 89–93 cm (35–36.5"); WS 208–232 cm (81.5–92")

Summary: *California*: 1 summer record (1994).
Taxonomy: Monotypic. Also known as Light-mantled Albatross (AOU 1998).

juv

flying cross

molting
1st-year

dult

adult

adult

**Light-mantled
Sooty Albatross**

adult with Black-footed Albatross

Distribution and Status:

World: Circumpolar in subantarctic southern oceans; breeds Nov–Jun and ranges n. mainly in austral mid-winter (May–Aug) to subtropical latitudes (around 40°S).

North America: *California*: Marin Co., 17 Jul 1994.

Comments: See Comments under Shy Albatross. Given the preference of Light-mantled Sooty Albatross for cold subantarctic waters, and the longevity of albatrosses in general, the 1994 bird may still be roaming the colder northern reaches of the N Pacific. The CA bird constitutes the only N Hemisphere record of this handsome species.

Field Identification: Striking, all-dark albatross; note long angular wings and long tapered tail.

Similar Species: None in N America but cf. congeneric **Sooty Albatross** *P. fusca* of subtropical S Atlantic and s. Indian Ocean (unrecorded in N Hemisphere). See Shirihai (2007) and Howell (2012a) for details.

Age/Sex/Season: Ages differ, with adult appearance attained in about 2 years; sexes similar; no seasonal variation other than wear

and fading. *Adult*: Pale ashy-gray saddle offsets blackish hood (with white postocular crescent) and contrasts along a straight-edged division with dark upperwings. Bill black with pale-blue sulcus stripe, visible at closer range. *1st-cycle*: Fledges May/Jun in plumage similar to adult but dark hood less extensive and less sharply defined, eye crescents duller, and bill appears all-black. Juv head and body plumage often fades to ashy white by Nov–Dec, with black hood reduced to small mask. Molting imms about 6–12 months after fledging have blotched upperparts, with new ashy-gray feathers contrastingly darker than the faded whitish juvenile feathers. Subsequent plumages adult-like and not so prone to fading, with blue bill stripe apparent by 2 years of age; may be aged through 3rd cycle by wing molt patterns (see Howell 2012a).

Habitat and Behavior: Pelagic and unlikely to be seen from shore. Favors cold waters and readily associates with feeding aggregations of other albatrosses (the CA bird was with Black-footed Albatrosses). Flight in moderate to strong winds often spectacular, sailing high and maneuvering easily relative to the lower-flying and heavier-looking Black-footed. Often approaches ships quite closely, although usually makes only one or two circuits before losing interest and flying off.

EUROPEAN (British) STORM-PETREL *Hydrobates pelagicus*
L 15–17 cm (6–6.7"); WS 34.5–37 cm (13.7–14.7")

Summary: *North Carolina*: Rare in late spring. *Nova Scotia*: 1 fall record (1970).

Taxonomy: Some authors consider the species monotypic (Cramp & Simmons 1977) but genetic and vocal work suggests that European Storm-Petrel may best be treated as 2 species: British Storm-Petrel *H. pelagicus* (breeding NW Europe), and Mediterranean Storm-Petrel *H. melitensis* (breeding Mediterranean) (Robb et al. 2008). Mediterranean birds average blacker overall and stouter billed than Atlantic birds, with bill size perhaps an appreciable field character in good photos. NC birds most likely are British Storm-Petrels but at-sea identification is not known to be possible.

Distribution and Status:

World: Breeds (May–Oct) W Europe and Mediterranean, winters (Oct–Apr) off W and S Africa.

North America: *North Carolina*: Small numbers (1-6 birds per year) have been found off Cape Hatteras during mid-May to early June almost annually since 2003 (see Patteson, Sutherland, & Howell 2009). *Nova Scotia*: Sable Island, 10 Aug 1970 (mist-netted).

Comments: Most if not all NC records refer to presumed 1st-year birds in worn plumage, and it seems likely that the species is being overlooked farther n. off the E Coast in summer among the many Wilson's Storm-Petrel (as it may have been in earlier years off NC). The recent spate of records is almost certainly because of increased observer coverage and greater awareness of how to find the species, although 2005 was still an exceptional year in terms of the number of birds seen. It appears that waters off the E Coast are at the edge of this species' regular range and that it is a 'false vagrant' (see p. 16) in N America.

Field Identification: A tiny white-rumped storm-petrel, easily passed over amid large numbers of Wilson's Storm-Petrel.

Similar Species: Relative to ***Wilson's Storm-Petrel***, European is noticeably smaller and blacker with a faster flight, and it often buzzes quickly around groups of rather leisurely looking Wilson's as they flutter and sail with long, stilt-like legs dangling; the tail is rounded and toes do not project past tail tip in flight. European has narrower, blunter-tipped wings with a longer arm and stronger crook at the carpal; it rarely glides in light winds and does not patter and kick off the water as Wilson's often does. Upperwing of European has a narrow, inconspicuous pale line (grayish white in fresh plumage, pale brownish when worn) unlike the broad pale panel on Wilson's, and underwing has a clean-cut white central stripe.

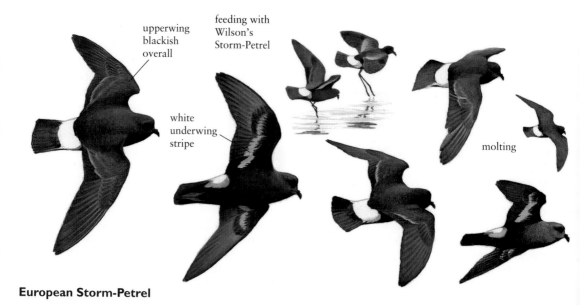

upperwing blackish overall

feeding with Wilson's Storm-Petrel

white underwing stripe

molting

European Storm-Petrel

Age/Sex/Season: All plumages similar except for wear and molt. Juv fresh in fall (Sep–Oct) when older ages worn, and 1st-year birds worn in spring (May–Jun) when older ages in fresh plumage. Wing molt mainly Aug–Apr in adults, probably Jun–Nov in 1st-years (study needed).

Habitat and Behavior: Offshore, although in Europe regularly seen from land. Most likely to be found singly, often in association with Wilson's Storm-Petrels. Flight usually rapid and fluttery, looking small and quick among a mass of Wilson's, with infrequent glides in light winds, more frequent sailing in strong winds.

WEDGE-RUMPED STORM-PETREL

Halocyptena (Oceanodroma) tethys L 14.5–16.5 cm (5.7–6.5");WS 33.5–40 cm (13.2–15.8")

Summary: *California*: Exceptional in fall–winter (see Comments, below).

Taxonomy: 2 ssp, differing distinctly in size and perhaps representing 2 species, although not easily separable at sea without other species for size comparison. For placement in *Halocyptena* see Nunn & Stanley (1998), Howell (2012a).

H. [t.] tethys (Galapagos Storm-Petrel) breeds Galapagos Islands (mainly Apr–Sep), ranges offshore n. to Mexico. Larger overall and longer winged (L 15–16.5 cm, WS 36.5–40 cm) with relatively shallower tail fork (5–9 mm) and shorter tail projection (11–21 mm) beyond white rump patch. Clearly larger than Least Storm-Petrel.

H. [t.] kelsalli (Peruvian Storm-Petrel) breeds Peru (Mar–Aug, at least), ranges inshore s. to Chile, n. to Mexico. Smaller overall (L 14.5–15.5 cm, WS 33.5–36.5 cm) with relatively deeper tail fork (7–10 mm) and longer tail projection (17–24 mm) beyond white rump patch. About same size as Least Storm-Petrel or barely larger.

Distribution and Status:

World: Breeds (mainly Mar–Sep) on Galapagos Islands and off Peru, ranges at sea n. to Mexico, s. to n. Chile.

North America: *California*: Exceptional in fall off s. and cen. coasts (late Jul–early Oct); 1 winter record, Monterey Co., 21 Jan 1969 (on shore); 8 accepted CA records (but see Comments, below).

Comments: Although this species occurs commonly off Mexico (n. to 25°N) it is genuinely rare off CA, where all records have been from the period of warmest ocean temperatures. Most reports involve birds seen far off s. CA, but singles were reported with the fall gatherings of storm-petrels in Monterey Bay in 1977 and 1983, and 1 was with a large raft of Black and Least Storm-Petrels off Los Angeles Co., 2 Oct 2010.

Knowledge of storm-petrel identification has come a long way in recent years, and it is surprising that only 1 Wedge-rumped has been found since the mid-1990s, despite increased pelagic coverage by birders of waters off s. CA. The spate of records during 1976–1996 may reflect different oceanic conditions prevailing at that time versus in more recent years. However, at the time when most sightings of Wedge-rumped were made, the identification pitfall posed by Townsend's Storm-Petrel (see Similar Species, below) was not fully appreciated (interestingly, Townsend's occurs off s. CA primarily in fall). Until the characters of Townsend's are better known, some presently accepted reports of Wedge-rumped Storm-Petrel might best be considered uncertain. Only 2 of the at-sea CA records involve birds photographed, 23 Jul 1989 (*AB* 43:1367, photo published upside down) and 2 Oct 2010 (identification only realized the next day, after review of photos). Some 8 other at-sea reports have been rejected, including a Sep 1997 report supported by photos (Rogers & Jaramillo 2002), which appears comparable to an accepted July 1989 record—in neither case are published photos clear enough to eliminate Townsend's Storm-Petrel. Thus, Wedge-rumped Storm-Petrel may be even rarer in N America than is generally believed.

Both taxa of Wedge-rumped Storm-Petrel may occur off CA, but critical observations are needed to ascertain this. Nominate *tethys* tends to occur farther offshore, whereas the smaller *kelsalli* is commoner inshore (Spear & Ainley 2007). The one CA specimen, and the first N American record, was a bird identified as *kelsalli* found on shore in Monterey Co., 21 Jan 1969. Not far s. of the region, a bird identified as nominate *tethys* was found on shore at Guadalupe Island, Baja California, 31 Jan 1950 (Huey 1952).

Field Identification: Small storm-petrel with notably long white rump patch.

Similar Species: An underappreciated pitfall is provided by white-rumped individuals of ***Townsend's [Leach's] Storm-Petrel*** (*Oceanodroma [leucorhoa] socorroensis*) from Guadalupe Island, Mexico (see Howell 2012a for further information). Townsend's is not well known at sea, but it overlaps in size with nominate Wedge-rumped and is blacker than typical Leach's, with a larger

notched tail

rather even dark/white border

long white rump patch

dark buldges slightly into white patch

Townsend's Storm-Petrel

Wedge-rumped Storm-Petrel

and solidly white rump patch and duller up-perwing band, all features suggestive of Wedge-rumped. Relative to Wedge-rumped, Townsend's has a longer and more deeply forked tail that projects farther beyond the tips of the white uppertail coverts, and blackish from the lower back tends to bulge into the upper edge of the white rump band (vs. a more even cutoff on Wedge-rumped). Good views or clear photos are helpful in assessing these characters, and beware that tail is shorter and less forked in fall molt. Townsend's flies with deeper and more clipped wingbeats than Leach's, which can further sug-gest Wedge-rumped.

Age/Sex/Season: All plumages similar except for wear and molt. Given protracted and poorly known breeding seasons, wing molt may be unhelpful for aging.

Habitat and Behavior: Pelagic. Likely to be encountered singly, at times in association with other storm-petrels, from inshore with rafts of Black and Least Storm-Petrels to offshore in areas with numbers of foraging Leach's Storm-Petrels. Flight generally quick and erratic with deep wing-beats and short glides, recalling Least Storm-Petrel more than Leach's. Glides more frequent and longer in moderate winds, and larger nominate *tethys*, at least, may fly across the wind with steady, fairly deep but not hur-ried wingbeats, and fairly long glides on slightly bowed wings.

TRISTRAM'S STORM-PETREL
Oceanodroma tristrami L 24.5–27 cm (9.7–10.7");
WS 52–57 cm (20.5–22.5")

Summary: *California*: 2 spring–summer re-cords (2006, 2007).
Taxonomy: Monotypic.
Distribution and Status:
    World: Breeds (Dec–May) in nw. Hawaiian Islands and Japan, ranges at sea in subtropical and temperate NW Pacific.
    North America: *California*: Southeast Faral-lon Island, 22 Apr 2006; San Bernardino Co., 21 Jul 2007 (Warzybok et al. 2009; latter record not accepted by state committee).
Comments: This large storm-petrel is normally a bird of the w. subtropical Pacific, with the nearest breeding grounds in the nw. Hawaiian Islands. However, it has occurred as a vagrant s. to Australia (Palliser 2002), and it may be of more frequent occurrence in N American waters than records suggest. Its occurrence on land brings to mind the recent record of Newell's Shearwater on land in s. CA, which also occurred during the species' breeding season.
    The description of a large, dark-rumped storm-petrel off n. CA on 19 Aug 2000 was at odds with it being a Markham's Storm-Petrel (as claimed at the time; the record was not accepted as such) and one observer of that bird, who subsequently saw the Tristram's off s. CA, believes

all plumages similar

Tristram's Storm-Petrel

the earlier bird may also have been a Tristram's (T. McGrath, pers. comm.). Clearly, any aseasonal dark-rumped storm-petrel off the West Coast should be carefully documented; indeed, Tristram's may be more likely than Markham's, which is a bird of warmer southern waters.

Field Identification: Very large, dark-rumped, and fork-tailed storm-petrel. Note size, bold pale upperwing bands, paler rump band. See Howell (2012a) for further information.

Similar Species: Very large size of Tristram's (appreciably larger than Black Storm-Petrel) likely to draw attention, especially if seen with other storm-petrels; also note deeply forked tail, bold pale upperwing bands, paler gray rump patch (variable and often hard to see).

Age/Sex/Season: All plumages similar except for wear and molt. Fresh plumage has strong, steely-gray sheen to head and back, worn plumage browner overall. Juv fresh in May–Aug when older ages worn or in wing molt. Wing molt probably Mar–Nov (study needed).

Habitat and Behavior: Pelagic, although one CA record involved a bird visiting an island at night. Might associate with other storm-petrels, but also occurs alone; does not habitually follow ships. Flight fairly heavy bodied with fairly quick but measured stiff wingbeats, recalling a giant Fork-tailed Storm-Petrel. Across moderate to strong winds, flies with fairly prolonged wheeling or slightly bounding glides on slightly crooked and arched wings, interspersed with bursts of fairly quick wingbeats, at times wheeling fairly high, to 10 m or more above the sea like a miniature gadfly petrel.

SWINHOE'S STORM-PETREL
Oceanodroma monorhis L 18–20 cm (7.2–7.8"); WS 45–50 cm (17.8–19.8")

Summary: *North Carolina*: Very rare or exceptional in summer–fall.
Taxonomy: Monotypic.
Distribution and Status:
World: Breeds (mainly May–Dec) on islands in s. Sea of Japan and Yellow Sea; ranges to N Indian Ocean. Recently found (since 1983) in N Atlantic, where it may breed.

North America: *North Carolina*: Very rare or exceptional off Cape Hatteras in summer–fall (Jun to mid-Aug), 4 records: 20 Aug 1993; 8 Aug 1998; 2 Jun 2008; 6 Jun 2009 (*NAB* 63:408).

Comments: The recent discovery of this species in the N Atlantic has been well chronicled, but it is unknown whether Atlantic birds reflect periodic invasions of misplaced migrants from the Indian Ocean or perhaps a previously overlooked breeding population. Future records of this species in Gulf Stream waters seem likely, perhaps mainly in summer–fall.

Occurrence of this species in the Pacific region also seems possible, and a dark-rumped, fork-tailed storm-petrel considered to be Swinhoe's was videotaped off se. AK in Aug 2003; the video is brief and the record is considered unsubstantiated by the AK Checklist Committee.

Field Identification: Medium-sized, dark-rumped, and fork-tailed storm-petrel. Note plain brown rump and back, white outer primary shafts. See Howell & Patteson (2008) for an identification review.

Similar Species: No particularly similar species are known from the Atlantic, but several dark-rumped storm-petrels occur in the Pacific. Swinhoe's is similar in size to *Leach's Storm-Petrel*, although its shape and flight manner can suggest a larger storm-petrel.

The specter of dark-rumped Leach's has at times been raised as an objection to the presence of Swinhoe's Storm-Petrels in the Atlantic. Although no all-dark Leach's has ever been found in the Atlantic (Flood 2009), some birds have so little whitish on the lateral tail coverts that they can appear wholly dark under at-sea conditions. Leach's typically shows some pale on the uppertail coverts (which contrast with the darker back and black tail) and lacks distinct white bases to the exposed outer primary shafts. It has a bounding erratic flight with slightly quicker wingbeats that rise higher above the body plane, a more double-rounded or lobed tail fork, and a relatively slender bill.

Age/Sex/Season: All plumages similar except for wear and molt. Fresh plumage has gray sheen to head and back, worn plumage browner overall. Juv fresh in fall–winter when older ages worn or in wing molt. Wing molt probably mainly Sep–Apr (study needed).

Habitat and Behavior: Pelagic. Likely to be found singly, and associates readily with other storm-petrels. In light to moderate winds, flight generally unhurried; fairly direct to slightly weaving. Wingbeats loping but not especially deep, interspersed with sailing glides on slightly bowed wings. Flight manner can bring to mind a Black Tern, but Swinhoe's wingbeats are stiffer and

all plumages similar

Swinhoe's Storm-Petrel

shallower than the tern's. Tail often held mostly closed in direct flight but spread in maneuvers and while pattering.

HORNBY'S (Ringed) STORM-PETREL *Oceanodroma hornbyi*

L 20–21.5 cm (7.8–8.5"); WS 48–51 cm (19–20.3")

Summary: *California*: 1 fall record (2005).
Taxonomy: Monotypic.
Distribution and Status:

World: Humboldt Current of w. S America, from Ecuador to cen. Chile (breeding grounds unknown; presumed in Atacama Desert of s. Peru and n. Chile).

North America: *California*: Santa Barbara Co., 2 Aug 2005.

Comments: Although the nesting grounds of this species remain unknown, available evidence suggests a Dec–Jul breeding season (Spear & Ainley 2007). Hornby's Storm-Petrel is not a long-distance migrant, although there appears to be a northward (post-breeding?) shift in abundance in the austral spring, n. to waters at 5–10°S, off s. Ecuador and n. Peru (Spear & Ainley 2007). Being a Humboldt Current species, Hornby's

is likely prone to periodic food crashes and perhaps breeding failures related to the strength of El Niño events, which might cause birds to wander far afield. The CA bird was in mid-primary molt (Pyle et al. 2006), suggesting it may have been an adult rather than a 1st-year bird; it constitutes the only N Hemisphere record. A May 2007 report of this species off OR (*NAB* 61:500) does not meet our acceptance criteria.

Field Identification: Large, handsomely patterned storm-petrel with long, deeply forked tail.

Similar Species: None, if seen well.

Age/Sex/Season: All plumages similar except for wear and molt. Wing molt perhaps mainly Mar–Dec (study needed).

Habitat and Behavior: Pelagic. Might occur in association with other storm-petrels although the CA bird was alone. In light to moderate winds, flight distinct from other storm-petrels and may suggest a hurried Black Tern: mainly steady and fairly direct with fairly deep but quick and fluttery, or slightly floppy, wingbeats and only brief glides (P. Fraser, video); in moderate to strong winds tilts more and flight progression may be less direct, but still only gliding or shearing for brief periods (R. L. Flood, pers. comm.).

molting

all plumages similar

Hornby's Storm-Petrel

BLACK-BELLIED STORM-PETREL

Fregetta tropica L 19.5–21 cm (7.7–8.3"); WS 43–46 cm (17–18.3")

Summary: *North Carolina*: Exceptional or very rare in summer–fall, all records recent.

Taxonomy: Monotypic. *Fregetta* storm-petrels breeding on Gough Island, South Atlantic, sometimes treated as a white-bellied ssp of Black-bellied Storm-Petrel *F. t. melanoleuca* (Marchant & Higgins 1990), but more realistically represent a distinct species of *Fregetta* (Howell 2010b).

Distribution and Status:

World: Largely circumpolar in S Hemisphere, nesting locally (Dec–Apr) on subantarctic islands. Ranges n. to subtropical S Hemisphere waters (mainly May–Sep).

North America: *North Carolina*: Very rare or exceptional off Cape Hatteras in late spring–fall (late May to mid-Aug), 4 records: 31 May 2004, 16 July 2006, 23 Jun 2007 (*NAB* 61:574, 2008), and 14 Aug 2010 (*NAB* 65:57).

Comments: Recent records of Black-bellied Storm-Petrels off NC have been mirrored by 3 recent records from the NE Atlantic—the first confirmed records of this species from the Western Palearctic. These were off Madeira in Aug 2011 (Correia-F. & Romano 2011), off the Canary Islands in Sep 2011 (Lopez-V. & Sagardia 2011), and off the Canary Islands in Aug 2012 (Anon 2012). The apparent spike in records of this species since the mid-2000s may be attributable to increased observer coverage, as with European Storm-Petrel, and not to any change in abundance.

None of the 4 NC individuals was in obvious wing molt, suggesting all were 1st-cycle birds and thus not returning individuals. The first bird was initially thought to be a White-bellied Storm-Petrel, until examination of photos revealed the black belly stripe. The separation of these species is an underappreciated problem, but careful observations or good photos should allow most birds to be identified to Black-bellied or 'White-bellied,' at least in the Atlantic (see Similar Species, below).

Other N Hemisphere records of *Fregetta* include a well-described White-bellied from the Western Palearctic, recently downgraded to *Fregetta* sp. (Crochet & Haas 2008); a possible White-bellied off the UK in Nov 2009 (Martin 2009); and a presumed White-bellied in the N Pacific some 950 km (about 500 miles) off w. Mexico (Pagen et al. 2008). Further records of this genus in N American waters seem quite possible, especially from the Atlantic.

Field Identification: Strikingly patterned large storm-petrel, with white belly and variable black belly stripe.

Similar Species: From below, Black-bellied Storm-Petrel stands out as something different, and its splashing flight style often draws attention. From above, however, and with no size comparison available, it might be passed over

Black-bellied Storm-Petrel

less extensive black hood

White-bellied Storm-Petrel

as **Wilson's Storm-Petrel**. Relative to Wilson's, Black-bellied is larger and broader winged with a narrower and usually duller upperwing band. From below, white belly and underwing coverts are striking (black belly stripe can be surprisingly difficult to see). Vagrants should be distinguished with care from congeneric White-bellied Storm-Petrel complex of subtropical S Atlantic (and S Pacific), which is similar to Black-bellied in size, structure, plumage, and flight manner.

White-bellied Storm-Petrel realistically comprises at least 4–5 species, 3 in the Pacific, and 1–2 in the Atlantic (Howell 2010b). All populations differ from Black-bellied in their less extensive black hood. Black-bellied Storm-Petrels lacking a black belly stripe (not known in Atlantic but rare in Pacific; Marchant & Higgins 1990; Howell 2010b) tend to have a forward-pointing (vs. straighter-cut) division between white belly and black undertail coverts, but good views are needed to evaluate this feature. Toe projection beyond tail tip of Atlantic White-bellieds not significantly different from Black-bellied (Howell 2010b), although this difference may be valid for Pacific populations. Further study of this complex is needed.

Habitat and Behavior: Pelagic; most likely to be found in association with Wilson's Storm-Petrels. Direct flight across wind often low and direct, with fairly quick, stiff, and fluttery wingbeats interspersed with short glides, recalling Wilson's Storm-Petrel but wingbeats a little looser. At other times flies into or across the wind with eye-catching 'kick-sail' progression, alternating bursts of flapping with one-footed kicks off the sea surface and veering glides, at times skipping low over the waves on stiff flattish wings, breaking into bursts of jerky scything motions, and splashing belly down into waves.

RED-TAILED TROPICBIRD *Phaethon rubricauda* L 43–48 cm + 28–38 cm streamers (L 17–19" + 11–15" streamers); WS 99–116 cm (39–45")

Summary: *California*: Very rare, mainly late summer to mid-winter; 1 spring record (2012). *British Columbia*: 1 record (1992).
Taxonomy: 4 ssp, not known to be distinguishable in the field; species considered monotypic by some authors (Marchant & Higgins 1990).
Distribution and Status:
    World: Breeds and ranges in tropical Indian and Pacific oceans.

North America: *California*: Very rare in late summer to mid-winter (Jul–Jan) off s. and cen. CA, all records since 1979; 1 recent spring record, 30 Apr 2012 at Año Nuevo Island, San Mateo Co. Most records are from more than 100 km (60 miles) offshore, but 3 individuals have been over land at Southeast Farallon Island (Jul–Sep), 1 over Año Nuevo Island (above), and 1 on the coast in Orange Co., 10 Jul 1999. *British Columbia*: Vancouver Island, Jun 1992 (carcass inland, presumably storm blown).
Comments: This species breeds in the Cen and W Pacific and perhaps in the E Pacific on Mexico's Revillagigedo Islands. It is a wide-ranging pelagic species and probably occurs as a regular, low-density visitor to waters far off CA, mainly during Jul–Jan but potentially year-round. Elsewhere in the E Pacific this species has been recorded at sea during Jun–Nov and Jan–Mar, with highest number in Aug–Nov and Mar (Gould et al. 1974).
Field Identification: Large, broad-winged tropicbird; usually appears wholly white in the field.
    Similar Species: Distinctive if seen well, but can be confused (particularly by eager observers) with Red-billed Tropicbird, at long range with Cattle Egret, and at very long range with White Tern; this last species is unrecorded in N America and not discussed further here.

Red-billed Tropicbird smaller and more slightly built with narrower, more pointed wings and a more hurried flight. All ages of Red-billed have mostly black primary coverts and outer primaries forming bold black leading wedge on upperwing, and most ages have ribbonlike white tail streamers conspicuous on birds at rest and in flight (some subadults may have narrower streamers that could suggest Red-tailed, especially if only one streamer is fully grown). Red-tailed has white primary coverts, and black shaft streaks on outer primaries inconspicuous other than at close range. 1st-cycle Red-tailed has grayish bill, unlike yellowish bill of 1st-cycle Red-billed.

White-tailed Tropicbird (Pacific ssp *dorotheae*) much smaller and more lightly built, but juv has dense blackish barring on back and dense blackish crown spotting rather similar to juv Red-tailed, which might cause confusion with birds on water (and is very unlike juv of Atlantic ssp *catesbyi*). Red-tailed juv has stouter, blackish to grayish bill versus pale greenish bill on juv White-tailed; in flight, outer 3 primaries of juv *dorotheae* have fairly thick black stripes versus fine

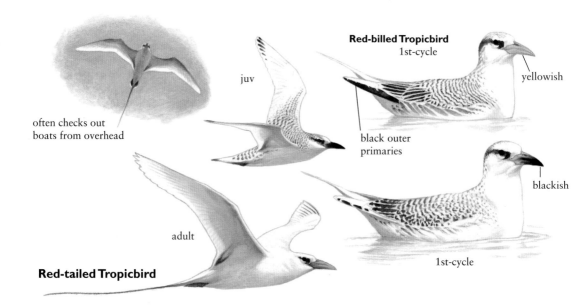

often checks out
boats from overhead

Red-billed Tropicbird
1st-cycle

juv

yellowish

black outer
primaries

blackish

adult

1st-cycle

Red-tailed Tropicbird

black shaft streaks and black subterminal spots on
juv Red-tailed.

Translucent white appearance of Red-tailed
Tropicbird, in combination with relatively
rounded wings and steady flight, can lead to
confusion with *Cattle Egret* far out at sea, but
egrets are broader winged and have steadier
flight; this underappreciated pitfall should only
apply to distant birds.

Age/Sex/Season: Ages differ, with adult
appearance probably attained in about 3 years;
sexes similar; no seasonal variation. Molts poorly
known but wing molt follows accelerated stepwise pattern (see pp. 37–38). *Adult*: Lacks barring
on upperparts; primaries white with fine black
shaft streaks rarely visible; red tail streamers long
and wire-like, one often shorter than the other;
bill bright red. *Juv/1st-cycle*: Upperparts barred
black, crown densely spotted black, primaries
with black shaft streaks expanding into small
black subterminal spots, lost by wear; tail, including slightly elongated central rectrices, tipped
black; belly with dusky barring. 1st wave of wing
molt (preformative) probably begins about 6–10
months after fledging: new primaries lack black
tips, new central rectrices appreciably longer
than juv feathers but not as wirelike as adult
feathers, whitish or tinged pink. Bill blackish with
gray base, becoming yellow-orange when 1st
wave of wing molt has reached middle or outer
primaries. *2nd-cycle*: New primaries lack black
tips of juv plumage; often has 2 waves of primary

molt, the old juv outer primaries with obvious
black tips or heavily worn. Crown and upperparts
with variable, usually sparse, black spots and
bars, belly variably mottled dusky; medium-
length tail streamers white or pink, wirelike; bill
mostly orange. *Subsequent cycles*: May attain
adult plumage in 3rd cycle (needs study), but
streamers at this age may be shorter and paler
than adult, bill may average paler, orange-red.

Habitat and Behavior: Favors deep pelagic
waters, where usually encountered in ones and
twos, separate from feeding flocks. Like other
tropicbirds, often rests on the sea. Foraging
birds fly high and steadily, often coming in to
check out boats briefly, occasionally giving gruff
barking clucks when two or more birds circle
a boat; flight usually appears less hurried than
Red-billed Tropicbird due to larger surface area
of Red-tailed's more rounded wings. Feeds by
near-vertical plunge dives that produce a vertical
plume of water suggesting a whale blow.

FRIGATEBIRDS: GENUS *FREGATA*
Frigatebirds as a group are unmistakable, with
their large size, long angular wings, deeply forked
tails, long hooked bills, and predominantly black
plumage. Specific identification, however, can be
problematic, with a succession of variable
immature plumages before adult plumage is
attained at about age 10, and adults themselves
can also be difficult to identify to species.
Females average appreciably larger and longer

billed than males. More detailed identification treatment is available elsewhere for Great and Magnificent Frigatebirds (Howell 1994), for Great, Lesser, and Christmas Island (*F. andrewsi*) Frigatebirds (D. J. James 2004), and for Ascension Frigatebird *F. aquila* (Walbridge et al. 2003).

Age determination is an important starting point for species identification. In each species, 5 presumed ages (and 8 plumage stages) can be recognized: Juv/1st-cycle (sexes similar), 2nd-cycle (sexes similar), 3rd-cycle male and female, 4th-cycle male and female, and adult male and female. The duration of these plumage cycles is unknown, but frigatebirds may have 2-year cycles (Howell 2010a). Juvs have a broad black chest band, clean white belly, and, in Great and Lesser, a tawny head that fades to whitish (Magnificent has a white head). 2nd-cycle birds lose the chest band from the center outward and have a pale head. In 3rd cycle, males and females start to show traces of the adult pattern, with white areas on head and underparts becoming increasingly marked with black (females remain clean white on the chest, which can be flecked black on males). 4th-cycle birds look enough like adults that they can usually be identified to species, but they retain some whitish mottling on head and underparts.

GREAT FRIGATEBIRD *Fregata minor*
L 82–99 cm (32–39"); WS 180–220 cm (70–86")

Summary: *California*: Single fall and spring records (1979, 1992). *Oklahoma*: 1 winter record (1975).

Taxonomy: 5 ssp have been recognized, differing slightly in size, but samples are small, variation in size and bare-part colors is complex, and a thorough revision of geographic variation in this species is desirable. Orbital ring of females in most populations is red (including those in the E Pacific), but lilac or blue-gray in SW Pacific.

Distribution and Status:

World: Breeds and ranges from tropical Indian Ocean through tropical Pacific, e. to Revillagigedo Islands, Mexico; also breeds in tropical S Atlantic off Brazil.

North America: *California*: Monterey Co., 13 Oct 1979 (adult male); San Francisco Co., 14 Mar 1992 (adult female). *Oklahoma*: Noble Co., 3 Nov 1975 (adult male).

Comments: Given breeding populations of Great Frigatebird in Mexico and Hawaii, it is unsurprising that 2 of the 3 N American records

come from CA. Both, however, were outside the Jul–Sep period when Magnificent Frigatebirds are most frequent on the W Coast, and it is possible that Great Frigatebirds have been overlooked in CA during summer–early fall. The remarkable OK specimen was found exhausted after a period of sw. winds, suggesting a Pacific origin (Heller & Barclay 1977), perhaps from across the Isthmus of Tehuantepec and n. through the Gulf of Mexico.

Field Identification: Relatively stocky, full-chested frigatebird; all ages/sexes have pale pinkish feet. See illustration on p. 114.

Similar Species: The first step is to determine a bird's age (see genus introduction, above). Separation from Magnificent and Lesser are dealt with here. See D. J. James (2004) and Walbridge et al. (2003) for details of Christmas Island and Ascension frigatebirds (both unrecorded in N America).

Magnificent Frigatebird averages larger and tends to look longer, less thickset than Great. *Adult male Magnificent* lacks distinct pale axillar scallops and pale alar bars, feet grayish. *Adult female Magnificent* has solid black hood, pale bluish orbital ring, and narrower, pointed black belly patch projecting into white chest. *Juv Magnificent* has white head, smaller and diamond-shaped white belly patch enclosed by pointed black chest patches, and pale bluish gray feet. *2nd-cycle Magnificent* has white belly patch narrower and more tapered at rear, with steeper-angled black sides, some (females?) may develop a broken black neck-ring, or collar, not shown by Great. *3rd- and 4th-cycle male Magnificent* variably mottled black on underparts and do not develop solid, female-like black belly patch of subadult Great. *3rd- and 4th-cycle female Magnificent* develop black collar and pointed border to black belly patch, suggesting pattern of adult Magnificent and distinct from patterns of adult female Great.

Lesser Frigatebird averages smaller and shorter billed, and is less stocky. *Adult male Lesser* has prominent, diagonal white axillar tabs. *Adult female Lesser* has solid black hood, and narrower, pointed black belly patch projecting into white chest. *Juv Lesser* shares tawny head with juv Great but white belly patch smaller and triangular, with rectangular white tabs projecting from front corners into axillars. *2nd-cycle Lesser* has white belly patch more tapered at rear, variable white axillar tabs, and often a broken black neck-ring, or collar, not shown by Great. *3rd- and 4th-cycle male Lesser* develop black hood and belly patch much like

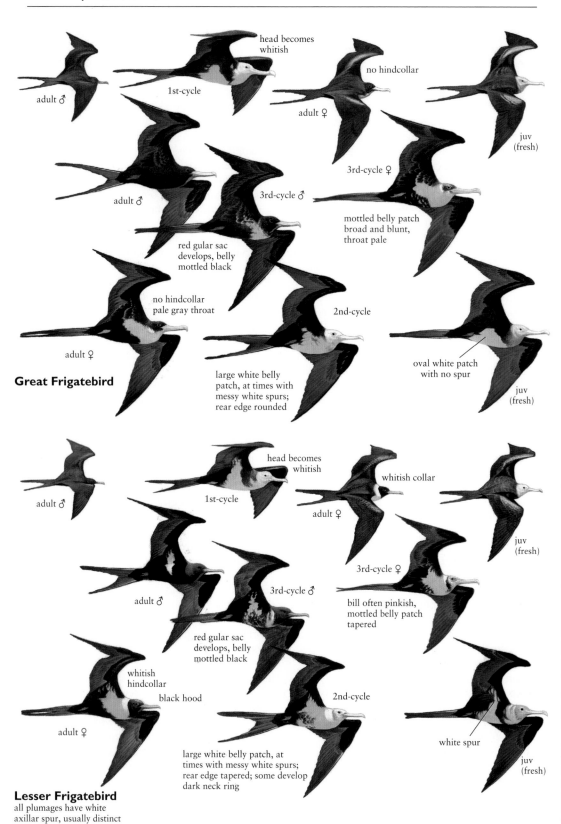

head becomes whitish

adult ♂

1st-cycle

no hindcollar

adult ♀

juv (fresh)

adult ♂

3rd-cycle ♂

3rd-cycle ♀

mottled belly patch broad and blunt, throat pale

red gular sac develops, belly mottled black

no hindcollar pale gray throat

2nd-cycle

adult ♀

oval white patch with no spur

Great Frigatebird

large white belly patch, at times with messy white spurs; rear edge rounded

juv (fresh)

head becomes whitish

whitish collar

adult ♂

1st-cycle

adult ♀

juv (fresh)

adult ♂

3rd-cycle ♂

3rd-cycle ♀

bill often pinkish, mottled belly patch tapered

red gular sac develops, belly mottled black

whitish hindcollar

black hood

2nd-cycle

adult ♀

white spur

Lesser Frigatebird
all plumages have white axillar spur, usually distinct

large white belly patch, at times with messy white spurs; rear edge tapered; some develop dark neck ring

juv (fresh)

adult
♂

1st-cycle

adult ♀

juv
(fresh)

adult ♂

3rd-cycle ♀

mottled belly
patch tapered

3rd-cycle ♂

blue
orbital ring

2nd-cycle

adult ♀

white
head

no white hindcollar,
pointed black bib

black belly
extension
beginning
to appear

small, diamond-
shaped white
belly patch

juv
(fresh)

Magnificent Frigatebird

adult female Lesser (and unlike Great), and usually have distinct white axillar tabs. **3rd- and 4th-cycle female Lesser** develop black collar and bluntly pointed border to the black belly patch, suggesting pattern of adult female Magnificent and distinct from patterns of adult female Great.

Age/Sex/Season: Ages/sexes differ strikingly in plumage, and females average larger and longer-billed than males; no seasonal variation beyond wear and fading. Adult appearance probably attained in about 10 years (Howell 2010a). See genus introduction, above, for discussion of age/sex classes. **Adult male**: Black overall with pale gray axillar scallops, pale alar bar, and glossy green to purple sheen on upperparts; bill steely dark gray with darker tip. **Adult female**: Black hood set off by pale grayish throat and also often a partial pale grayish or brownish hindcollar; bill pale pinkish and orbital ring red (at least in E Pacific). **Juv/1st-cycle**: Tawny head of fresh plumage fades to whitish; broad and blunt black chest patches help enclose large, egg-shaped white belly patch. **2nd-cycle**: Head whitish or with some tawny smudging, chest patches mottled white or absent, belly patch broad and white, often with some black markings that form the outline of a female-like pattern and sometimes with distinct white axillar tabs. **3rd-cycle male**: Head (including throat) and belly mottled black, broad saddle-shaped chest band white or with few black flecks; traces of reddish gular sac may be apparent. **3rd-cycle female**: Head (but not throat) and belly mottled black, broad saddle-shaped chest band white, without black flecks; bill and orbital ring may show pinkish traces.

4th-cycle male: Head, throat, and belly black, saddle-shaped chest band mottled black-and-white; bill grayish; gular sac red. *4th-cycle female*: Head and belly black with some white mottling, throat grayish; bill usually pale pinkish, orbital ring pinkish to red.

Habitat and Behavior: Highly aerial, usually over the ocean or along coasts, but storm-blown birds could occur anywhere. Perches readily on boat rigging, in trees, and even on phone wires, but does not alight on water because plumage not strongly water repellant.

LESSER (Least) FRIGATEBIRD
Fregata ariel L 66–79 cm (26–31"); WS 155–190 cm (61–75")

Summary: *North America*: 4 late summer–fall records, widely scattered.

Taxonomy: 3 ssp have been recognized, differing slightly in size, but samples are small and a thorough revision of geographic variation in this species is desirable.

Distribution and Status:

World: Breeds and ranges from tropical Indian Ocean through tropical W and Cen Pacific, e. to Tuamotu Archipelago; also breeds in tropical S Atlantic off Brazil.

North America: 4 records in late summer–fall (Jul to mid-Sep): Hancock Co., ME, 3 Jul 1960 (adult male); Big Horn Co., WY, 11 Jul 2003 (adult female, moribund); Wayne Co., MI, 18 Sep 2005 (adult male); Humboldt Co., CA, 15 Jul 2007 (imm female).

Comments: Snyder (1961) presumed a S Atlantic origin for the ME individual, and the MI record followed the passage of Hurricane Katrina, which swept n. from the Caribbean—although one would not expect that it intercepted the normal Atlantic range of Lesser Frigatebird. The small S Atlantic population of Lesser Frigatebird is considered endangered, declining, and mostly sedentary (Murphy 1936; Antas 1991), and we believe a Pacific origin most likely for all N American records of this species. A partial counterclockwise dispersal pattern has been documented for Lesser Frigatebirds breeding in the tropical Cen Pacific; these move as far n. and w. as Japan and Russia (to near 49°N), where records are mainly late May–late Jul, with birds having traveled up to 10,000 km (6000 miles) from where they hatched (Sibley & Clapp 1967). It is not inconceivable that summer and fall storms could displace

frigatebirds from the NW Pacific and carry them rapidly across n. latitudes to deposit them in places such as the Great Lakes and the Northeast in late summer and fall (Fig. 9, p. 10). The WY bird was emaciated and appeared there in association with a low-pressure system that originated in the N Pacific (Faulkner 2006), and the CA bird also appeared in conjunction with the passage of a similar system (Sullivan et al. 2008).

Of interest are 5 records of unidentified frigatebirds from AK (all in late Jun to mid-Sep; Mlodinow 1998; *NAB* 63:139), some of which, given the above conjecture, might as likely have involved Lesser Frigatebird as the conventionally 'expected' Magnificent Frigatebird, whose main window of West Coast occurrence has also been in fall.

This is a species that could occur anywhere in N America, but perhaps most likely in late summer–fall, in contrast to the winter 'pattern' shown by Great Frigatebird. The seeming spate of records since 2000 may simply reflect increased observer awareness, although it would be interesting to know whether tropical storms in the N Pacific have been changing in their frequency and course in recent years; cf. Long-billed Murrelet.

Field Identification: Relatively small and lightly built frigatebird, which would appear appreciably smaller than Magnificent Frigatebird in direct comparison. See illustration on p. 114.

Similar Species: The first step is to determine a bird's age (see genus introduction, above). Separation from Magnificent is dealt with here; differences from Great Frigatebird are given under that species. See D. J. James (2004) and Walbridge et al. (2003) for details of Christmas Island and Ascension frigatebirds (as yet unrecorded in N America).

Magnificent Frigatebird appreciably larger (L 89–107 cm, WS 210–240 cm), although size can be difficult to judge on a lone bird. *Adult male Magnificent* lacks white axillar tabs and pale alar bars. *Adult female Magnificent* can have whitish axillar scallops but lacks large white tabs of Lesser; also note pale bluish orbital ring, bluish-gray bill, lack of distinct white hindcollar. *Juv Magnificent* has white head, diamond-shaped white belly patch enclosed by pointed black chest patches. *2nd-cycle Magnificent* lacks such distinct white axillar tabs but some very similar to Lesser, and perhaps not always safely distinguished by plumage pattern at this age. **3rd- and 4th-cycle male Magnificent** lack white axillar tabs and often more evenly mottled black on underparts, not developing the solid, female-like black belly patch of subadult Lesser. **3rd- and 4th-cycle female Magnificent** lack distinct white axillar tabs and white hindcollar, and have gray to pale bluish (not pink to red) orbital ring and grayish bill (often with pinkish tones on Lesser).

Age/Sex/Season: Ages/sexes differ strikingly in plumage, and females average larger and longer-billed than males; no seasonal variation beyond wear and fading. Adult appearance probably attained in about 10 years (Howell 2010a). See genus introduction for discussion of age/sex classes. **Adult male**: Black overall with prominent diagonal white axillar tabs, pale alar bar, and glossy green to purple sheen on upperparts; bill steely dark gray with darker tip. **Adult female**: Black hood set off by distinct white hindcollar; chest and axillar tabs white, often with dirty tawny smudging on chest; bill pale pinkish or bluish gray; orbital ring red. **Juv/1st-cycle**: Tawny head of fresh plumage fades to whitish; broad black chest patches help enclose small triangular white belly patch with forward-pointing white axillar tabs. **2nd-cycle**: Head whitish or with some tawny smudging; chest patches mottled white or absent; belly patch broad and white, often with some black belly markings and a broken blackish neck-ring. **3rd-cycle male**: Head and belly mottled black; chest band and flanks white or with black flecks; axillar tabs usually distinct; traces of reddish gular sac may be apparent. **3rd-cycle female**: Head and belly mottled black, chest band and axillar tabs white without black flecks; bill and orbital ring often pinkish. **4th-cycle male**: Head and underparts black with white axillar tabs, variable white mottling on chest and flanks; bill grayish; gular sac red. **4th-cycle female**: Head and belly black with some white mottling; orbital ring pinkish to red.

Habitat and Behavior: Much like Great Frigatebird.

NAZCA BOOBY *Sula granti* L 73–81 cm (29–32");WS 152–173 cm (60–68")

Summary: *California*: At least 1 spring record (2001). See Comments, below.
Taxonomy: Monotypic; formerly considered a ssp of Masked Booby (see Pitman & Jehl 1998).

Distribution and Status:
World: Breeds Galapagos Islands, and locally n. to w. Mexico; ranges mainly over shelf and shelf-break waters from Ecuador n. to Mexico.
North America: *California*: San Diego Co., 27 May 2001 (1st-cycle).
Comments: The one confirmed N American record of this species involves a bird that rode into US waters from adjacent Mexico on a fishing boat; identification was confirmed by genetic analysis (Garrett & J. C. Wilson 2003). Despite allusions to the contrary, there is no evidence that any attempt was made to feed the bird (G. McCaskie, pers. comm.). Thus, we view this record as no different from records of Red-footed Booby that routinely rest on ships, or indeed from records of any other species that benefits from human assistance.

In addition to the May 2001 record, there are 7 CA records (mid-Feb to Jul) of specifically unidentified imm Masked/Nazca Boobies, mainly of 1st-cycle birds (the terms HY/SY for hatching-year/2nd-year used in Hamilton et al. 2007 are meaningless for birds that breed year-round). Claims by Roberson (1998) that some of these birds can be identified as Nazca Booby (based largely on chronology) are unfounded, given potential breeding in any month by both species in the E Pacific (cf. Pitman & Ballance 2002). That said, however, some of these records may refer to Nazca Boobies–but which ones? Until variation and characters of 1st-cycle Masked and Nazca Boobies are critically studied, the jury will remain out on this question.

Field Identification: Any booby in the West is a good find and should be identified carefully. Separation from Masked Booby is the main concern, and study is still needed of this problem. Imm Nazca also can be confused with Brown and Blue-footed Boobies, and adult with white-morph Red-footed Booby.

Similar Species: **Masked Booby** similar in all ages, and no features known to reliably distinguish 1st-cycle birds until orange or pinkish tones appear on bill of Nazca. 2nd-cycle and older Nazca have diagnostic orange to pinkish-orange bill. 1st-cycle Nazca usually lacks white hindcollar, but some Masked similar, and juv Nazca rarely if ever shows very broad white hindcollar typical of many juv Masked.

Brown Booby slightly smaller, more lightly built, narrower-winged, and proportionately longer-tailed, with uniform dark brown

juv with white collar (rare)

typical juv

Masked Booby
juv (some lack white collar)

juv

note bill/face patterns

juv
white lower chest

Brown Booby juv

late 1st-cycle

adult

2nd-cycle

Nazca Booby

orange

adult

yellow

adult Masked

upperparts (except whitish-headed adult male). Underparts of Brown show variable contrast between dark brown chest and white to brownish underbody; contrast on 1st-cycle Nazca is between brown neck and white chest; underwings of 1st-cycle Nazca extensively white, with narrow dark trailing edge, versus extensively dark on Brown.

Blue-footed Booby has slightly slimmer bill, proportionately longer tail; grayish bill and face lack contrasting black 'mask' and feet gray to bluish. All plumages have white uppertail coverts and white central rectrices (unlike blackish tail of Nazca), and overall dusky underwings, with white limited mainly to axillars. 1st-cycle Blue-footed has dark brown head and neck messily demarcated from white underparts, and white 'hindcollar' reduced to nape patch.

Adult white-morph **Red-footed Booby** smaller and more lightly built with narrow, crooked wings, proportionately longer tail (black or white), slender bluish bill, pink face, and eponymous red feet. Red-footed has white humerals,

thus on flying birds black trailing wing edge does not meet body, and resting birds show much more white than Nazca; from below, Red-footed has large, white-bordered black patch on primary coverts.

Age/Sex/Season: Ages differ, with adult appearance attained in 3–4 years. Sexes similar in plumage, but adult male gives high-pitched whistles whereas female brays. No seasonal variation. Breeding can vary in timing between years, and juvs can fledge year-round; thus plumages are described here in terms of cycles based on waves of primary molt. Wing molt follows accelerated stepwise pattern (see pp. 37–38).

Adult: Head, body, and lesser and median wing coverts clean snowy white. Eyes yellow; facial and gular skin blackish; bill orange to pinkish orange (brighter in breeding condition). *1st-cycle*: Juv has head and neck dark gray-brown; back and upperwings dark gray-brown overall, occasionally with variable (usually narrow) white hindcollar and often with whitish patch in middle of back; primaries uniform in wear. Underwing coverts white with narrow dark bar on lesser coverts, large blackish patch on outer median primary coverts. Head, neck, and lesser upperwing coverts start to show white spotting and blotching within 6 months of fledging. By the time preformative primary molt has reached p4–p5 (usually about 10–12 months after fledging), much of head, hindneck, scapulars, lesser upperwing coverts, and lateral uppertail coverts tend to be white, although usually with some dusky clouding on hindneck. Eyes dark brown on fledging, becoming pale yellowish or greenish white within a few months; facial and gular skin dark slaty to blackish; bill pale greenish gray to greenish yellow; age unknown at which pinkish or orange tones appear on bill base, but probably late in 1st cycle (study needed). **2nd-cycle**: By start of 2nd-prebasic primary molt (about 14–15 months after fledging), head, neck, back, and lesser upperwing coverts extensively clean white with scattered dark marks (mainly on back), but humerals and rump still mostly dark, becoming mostly to wholly white over 2nd cycle; underwing coverts white with variable dark on primary coverts. Bare parts resemble adult but bill duller. **3rd-cycle**: Mostly resembles adult, but some may show scattered dark marks on rump and underprimary coverts. Presumably like adult by 4th cycle.

Habitat and Behavior: Favors shelf and shelf-break waters. Roosts on inshore rocks and islands, and at times will land on ships (especially curious 1st-cycle birds). Tends to feed by fairly steep dives from high above the ocean.

BLUE-FOOTED BOOBY *Sula nebouxii*
L 71–79 cm (28–31"); WS 148–166 cm (58.5–65.5")

Summary: *Southwest and Pacific States*: Rare and irruptive disperser (mainly late summer–fall, with birds lingering) from Gulf of California to interior Southwest, exceptionally n. as far as UT, e. as far as TX. Very rare on Pacific coast of s. CA (mainly fall), exceptionally n. to WA.

Taxonomy: 2 ssp, not known to be distinguishable in the field. Nominate *nebouxii* breeds locally from Mexico to Peru and presumably occurs in N America.

Distribution and Status:
World: Breeds locally, and ranges mainly over inshore waters, from Gulf of California, Mexico, to n. Peru (nominate *nebouxii*), and in Galapagos Islands (*excisa*).

North America: ***Southwest and Pacific States***: Irruptive in the Southwest, absent most years and with the last major invasion in 1972 (when 40+ birds occurred) and recent minor influxes in 2006 (at least 7 birds) and 2009 (about 15 birds). From the head of the Gulf of California, records fan out mainly to the n. and nw., with most from the Salton Sea but a few w. to the coast in s. CA, n. to s. NV (Aug 1971–Jan 1972), several e. to s. AZ, exceptionally to NM (Aug–Sep 2009; *NAB* 64:120) and cen. TX. Pronounced arrival window in late Jul–Sep, with birds often lingering into Oct–Nov, and sometimes staying months at suitable lakes and reservoirs. The TX bird was found in Jun 1993 and lingered in the state for almost 2 years; it likely arrived somewhere in the Southwest the previous fall. West Coast records show a related pattern, with about 15 records from s. CA n. to OR and WA, mainly Aug–Sep, but also from CA in Nov, Jan, Mar (2), and Jun.

Comments: Seabirds breeding in the Gulf of California are prone to periodic food crashes (often related to El Niño events), which can cause partial or wholesale breeding failure and lead birds to disperse farther afield in search of food. Inexperienced 1st-cycle birds seem more prone to long-distance dispersal, which probably occurs mainly when food crashes occur around or shortly after fledging in about Aug. In years when food shortages preclude breeding, few or no young are produced and consequently few or no birds may reach the US, despite well-publicized El Niño events. US records are mainly of 1st-cycle birds, but older imms and adults also occur (McCaskie 1970).

The 'offshore' Pacific Ocean birds, and an aggregation of 37 Blue-footed Boobies on the Coronado Islands, n. Baja California, in late Nov 1971, may be birds that continued to wander after dispersal from the Gulf of California, either reaching the Pacific overland in s. CA or by wandering out of the Gulf around the tip of the Baja California peninsula.

Field Identification: Larger and bulkier than Brown Booby; all ages have white hindneck patch, white base to tail, and mostly white central rectrices.

Similar Species: Fairly distinctive, but might be confused with imm Masked, Nazca, and Brown boobies. All ages have an extensively white tail base and mostly white central rectrices. Only adults have bright blue feet; imms have uneventfully grayish feet.

juvs

late 1st-cycle

juv

juv

adult

adults

Blue-footed Booby

Brown Booby slightly smaller and more lightly built with solidly dark brown upperparts at all ages. Adult and older imm Brown have more cleanly demarcated border between dark brown neck and white or whitish underparts, whiter underwing coverts, and pale yellowish bill and feet.

Masked Booby and Nazca Booby average larger and stockier with stouter bill. 1st-cycles have dark brown head and neck sock more cleanly demarcated from white underparts and, on Masked, usually a white hindcollar; also note dark brown tail, more extensively white under-wing coverts (greater and primary coverts mostly white, versus dark on Blue-footed), and paler grayish to yellowish bill that contrasts more strongly with dark bluish face.

Age/Sex/Season: Ages differ, with adult appearance attained in 3–4 years. Sexes similar in appearance, but adult male gives high-pitched whistles whereas female brays. No seasonal variation. Breeding can vary in timing between years; plumages are described here in terms of

cycles based on waves of primary molt. Wing molt follows accelerated stepwise pattern (see pp. 37–38).

Adult: Head and upper neck sharply streaked white and dark brown (often looks white overall with 'furrowed' lines of fine brown streaking), scapulars boldly tipped white, lower back with bold white band, base of tail and central rectrices mostly white; wings with at least 3 waves of primary molt. Eyes staring pale yellow to whitish, bill grayish and face gray-blue, legs and feet bright turquoise-blue to greenish blue.

1st-cycle: Juv (mainly Jul–Jan) head, neck, chest, and upperparts dark brownish (slightly paler scapular tips may bleach dull whitish by spring) with white hindneck patch, small white back patch, uniform generation primaries; chest smudgily demarcated from whitish belly; distal uppertail coverts and shafts of central rectrices white (white tail base can be exposed through wear by mid-winter). Eyes dark to dusky pale grayish, face and bill dark gray or with face slightly bluer, legs and feet dusky pinkish (rarely?) to blue-gray. Over 1st winter, head and neck fade to show fine whitish spotting and streaking, lower neck and chest fade to paler brown or even whitish, eye becomes paler, and face and legs can become bluer. 1st wave of primary molt (preformative) starts Dec–Feb, and head, body, and tail molt often start around this time, with new scapulars tipped pale gray to whitish. *2nd-cycle*: By 2nd fall and winter, plumage suggests adult but averages less contrastingly marked, and has only 2 waves of primary molt. Head and neck dusky brownish with heavy but diffuse whitish streaking, or whitish overall with dark brown streaking; scapulars tipped whitish; tail base and central rectrices more extensively white than juv. Eyes dirty pale grayish to staring whitish, face and bill blue-gray with a duskier bill tip and bluer face, legs and feet blue-gray to dull chalky bluish. *3rd-cycle*: By 3rd winter much like adult (some perhaps not distinguishable from adult?), but averages duller overall, head and neck not so snowy white; legs and feet duller turquoise-blue to gray-blue. Presumably like adult by 4th cycle.

Habitat and Behavior: Favors inshore waters. Roosts readily on inshore rocks or jetties, alone or with other waterbirds; imms in particular can be absurdly unconcerned by humans. Healthy birds tend to feed by steep dives from high above the ocean.

RED-FOOTED BOOBY *Sula sula* L 66–74 cm (26–29"); WS 134–150 cm (52.5–59")

Summary: *Atlantic and Gulf States*: Rare in s. FL, mainly spring–fall on Keys, exceptional n. to SC and in Gulf of Mexico w. to TX. *California*: Very rare, mainly in fall.

Taxonomy: 3 ssp usually recognized, differing slightly in size and relative distribution of adult color morphs; not separable in the field other than by presumption of origin for certain morphs. Nominate *sula* breeds in the Caribbean and tropical Atlantic, *websteri* in the E Pacific, and *rubripes* from Indian Ocean to tropical Cen Pacific (e. to Hawaii).

Caribbean and Atlantic adults comprise white morphs and white-tailed brown morphs, with brown morphs absent or very rare; Pacific adults are both brown morph (white-tailed brown morphs uncommon) and white morph (white-tailed in Hawaii, dark-tailed in the Galapagos, and mixed off Mexico, where 85% dark-tailed).

Distribution and Status:
   World: Pantropical, the nearest Pacific colony being on Mexico's Revillagigedo Islands. In the Caribbean, breeds on Half Moon Cay off Belize, on the Swan Islands, Cayman Islands, and locally from Puerto Rico through the Lesser Antilles, with occasional pairs nesting on Alacran Reef, Mexico, and in e. Bahamas.

   North America: *Atlantic and Gulf States*: Rare in s. FL, spring–fall (mid-Mar to Oct), with 1st N American record there in 1963. Most FL records are from the Dry Tortugas during Apr–Jul, with a few elsewhere in the state during spring–summer (mainly off the Atlantic coast, where increasing in recent years), and a few storm-blown birds onshore in Sep–Oct. Exceptional n. to SC (late Jul) and very rare (Mar–Apr, Jun, Oct–Nov) in Gulf of Mexico w. to TX. *California*: Very rare in late spring–late fall (late May to mid-Nov, mainly mid-Aug to mid-Oct; once in Feb) off the s. and cen. coast, with 1st record in 1975.

Comments: Records from both Pacific and Atlantic regions show a well-defined and unsurprising pattern. The Red-footed Booby favors warm tropical waters, and N America lies at the edge of its normal range; most US records refer to 1st-cycle birds from spring through fall. Winter records are exceptional but this may reflect, at least in part, that fewer observers are offshore at this time.

   In the Atlantic region, most individuals have been brown-plumaged, 1st-cycle birds, although 2 white-tailed brown adults have been reported, and white morph imms have occurred in the Gulf of Mexico (Apr–Jun 2008) and off the Atlantic coast of FL (May 2011; *NAB* 65:423). Similarly, off CA most have been brown-plumaged 1st-cycle and 2nd-cycle birds, but there have been 3 adult white morphs (2 white-tailed, 1 dark-tailed). Dark-tailed white-morph adults originate in the E Pacific, whereas white-tailed birds are perhaps more likely to originate in Hawaii (only 15% of Mexican white morphs are white-tailed).

Field Identification: Small lightly built pelagic booby, rangier in build than Brown Booby with wings often held more crooked; plumage highly variable and adults polymorphic.

   Similar Species: Note rangy build, bare-part colors. Beware juv Brown Booby also has pink feet.

   Brown Booby averages larger and stockier with overall darker brown plumage, lacks white tail tip (white tail tip can be absent on worn

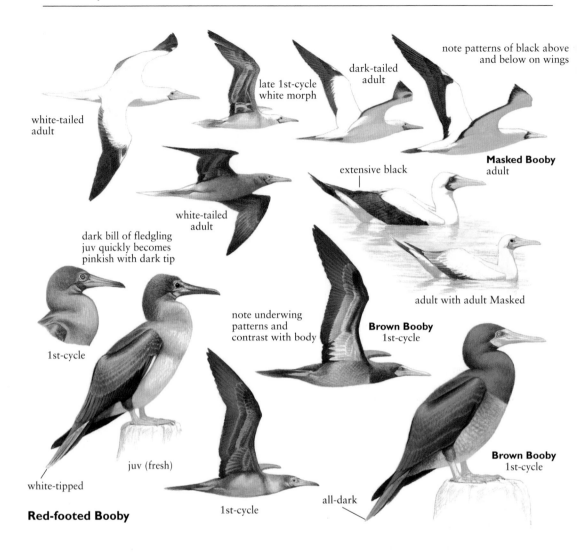

white-tailed adult

late 1st-cycle white morph

dark-tailed adult

note patterns of black above and below on wings

Masked Booby adult

extensive black

white-tailed adult

dark bill of fledgling juv quickly becomes pinkish with dark tip

adult with adult Masked

note underwing patterns and contrast with body

Brown Booby 1st-cycle

1st-cycle

juv (fresh)

white-tipped

1st-cycle

all-dark

Brown Booby 1st-cycle

Red-footed Booby

1st-cycle Red-footed, and on any age when central rectrices are shed). *1st-cycle Brown* has variable contrast between darker head and neck and paler underbody, with body darker than underwings, which have extensively pale coverts; bill gray and feet pink to yellowish pink. *2nd-cycle and older Brown* have stronger contrast of dark brown head and neck with pale to white underbody; feet pale yellowish.

Masked Booby appreciably larger and bulkier with broader and straighter-held wings, stouter bill. *Adult Masked* could be confused with white-morph Red-footed Booby (as yet only recorded in N America off CA) but has stout pale yellow bill, dark face, and yellowish to grayish legs and feet. Masked has black tail and black humerals (hence, on flying birds the black trailing wing edge meets the body, and

swimming or sitting birds show much more black than white-morph Red-footed).

Age/Sex/Season: Plumage highly variable. Ages differ, with adult appearance attained in 3rd–4th cycle. Sexes similar (including voice), no seasonal variation. Breeding can vary in timing between years, and juvs can fledge year-round; thus plumages are described here in terms of cycles based on waves of primary molt. Wing molt follows accelerated stepwise pattern (see pp. 37–38).

White Morph. Adult: Head, body, underwing secondary coverts, upperwing lesser, median, and tertial coverts clean white; head and neck with variable yellow wash; tail white (Pacific and Atlantic) or black (E Pacific only). Eyes dark with turquoise-blue orbital ring, pink base to culmen and lower mandible; bill pale turquoise-blue to greenish; feet bright red to orange-red. Bare-part colors brightest on breeding birds. *1st-cycle*: Juv gray-brown overall with white-tipped central rectrices, pale distal uppertail coverts; head, neck, and underparts slightly to distinctly paler with narrow dark chest band. Plumage often fades within a few months such that head, neck, and underparts appear dingy pale buffy gray (with narrow dark chest band) by around 6 months after fledging; whitish tips to central rectrices often wear away. By the time 1st wave of primary molt has reached mid-primaries (probably around 12 months after fledging), head, neck, and underparts become mostly dirty whitish with variable dusky clouding and mottling, and dusky chest band can be lost; back, scapulars, and lesser upperwing coverts gray-brown and variably tipped whitish. New tail feathers typically dark brown overall, tipped whitish on central pair. Juv eyes gray-brown to medium-pale gray, often becoming staring pale gray later in 1st cycle. Juv face and bill dark gray to blackish on fledging, or with bluish orbital ring; face becomes bluish and bill mostly dull dusky pinkish with dark tip before 1st wave of primary molt starts, at about 6–8 months after fledging; on some birds late in 1st cycle, base of bill may become pinkish and bill pale bluish overall with a dark tip; legs and feet pinkish (rarely dull yellow, at least on sick birds), on some birds becoming bright pinkish red by late in 1st cycle. *2nd-cycle*: Head, neck, and underparts mostly white, often with variable dusky chest band; upperparts and wing coverts brown, variably mottled and flecked white; underwings dark overall with variable white mottling on secondary coverts; tail becomes wholly (to mostly?) white on white-tailed morphs. Bare-part colors change to resemble adult (eye becomes darker again) but face and bill duller overall. *3rd-cycle*: Resembles adult but in early stages of 3rd-prebasic primary molt often has variable (at times fairly heavy and extensive) dark brown mottling on back, rump, scapulars, inner lesser coverts, axillars, and underwing secondary coverts. These areas become whiter through 3rd cycle, and presumably like adult by 4th cycle. Bare parts in 3rd cycle like adult but averaging duller; bill rarely still with dark tip.

Brown Morph. **Adult**: Brown overall, often slightly paler and warmer-toned on head, neck, and underparts, which contrast with dark under-wings; tail coverts can be paler, even whitish, and

some birds (mainly Galapagos) have contrastingly pale distal scapulars. Flight feathers blackish overall with at least 3 waves of primary molt; central rectrices tipped whitish. Bare parts as white-morph adult, and thus distinct from brown imm plumages. *1st-cycle*: Juv like juv white morph but slightly darker and more uniformly brown overall; head, neck, and underparts often slightly paler and grayer, but not fading to strikingly pale bodied in 1st cycle. By the time 1st wave of primary molt has reached mid-primaries (probably around 12 months after fledging), head, neck, and body brown overall, the belly sometimes still mottled with paler (faded) juv feathers; dusky chest band can be lost. Bare parts like white morph. *2nd-cycle*: Plumage brown overall (including tail coverts), with only 2 waves of primary molt. Bare-part colors change to resemble adult (eye becomes darker again) but face and bill duller overall. Apparently resembles adult by 3rd cycle, although bill colors may average duller.

White-tailed Brown Morph. **Adult**: Head, neck, and underparts milky brown to sandy brown or (mainly Cen and W Pacific) dirty buffy whitish overall, becoming whitish on undertail coverts, contrasting with dark brown underwings; often shows indistinct, narrow brownish chest band. Back and upper-wings dark brown overall, with contrasting creamy whitish rump and white tail; humerals often darker brown, contrasting variably with paler scapulars (distal scapulars silvery gray on some birds) and outer lesser and median coverts. *1st-cycle*: Probably similar to brown morph, and not safely distinguishable until 2nd cycle except for some birds that attain one or more white central rectrices late in 1st cycle. *2nd-cycle*: Head, neck, underparts, and rump change from plain gray-brown to adult-like, and tail becomes wholly (or mostly?) white. Bare-part colors change to resemble adult (eye becomes darker again) but face and bill duller overall. Apparently resembles adult by 3rd cycle, although bill colors may average duller.

Habitat and Behavior: Pelagic, but readily alights on ships and lands more easily on masts, radar scanners, and other potential perches than do other boobies. Relatively agile, snatching prey at (or above, in the case of flyingfish) the sea surface. Wings typically crooked in flight and wingbeats easy, not as strong and measured as in larger boobies.

GULLS AND TERNS

These familiar, strong-flying birds are well known around the world, and in general have high vagrancy potential. In N America we consider 6 gulls and 4 terns as rare birds, 2 of which (Swallow-tailed Gull, Black Noddy) are best viewed as pelagic seabirds. Of the gulls, 1 originates in NE Asia (Black-tailed), 1 in W Europe (Yellow-legged), 1 in w. S America (Belcher's), and 1 in the tropical E Pacific (Swallow-tailed); the remaining 2 species (Kelp and Gray-hooded) may originate in S America and/or Africa. Of the terns, 2 species originate in Eurasia (White-winged and Whiskered), 1 in S America (Large-billed), and 1 in the tropical Atlantic (Black Noddy).

None of the rare gull species are highly migratory in the conventional sense, and their occurrences in N America presumably reflect post-breeding and other dispersal related to food distribution. The occurrences of Kelp Gull may be further linked to the species' ongoing global range expansion, the causes of which are not fully understood. The 2 Eurasian terns likely reached e. N America by the southern route (see pp. 9–10). West Coast records of White-winged Tern presumably reflect drift and perhaps misorientation from NE Asia, followed by wandering. Large-billed Tern records may reflect misoriented dispersal following the drying up of wetlands, or perhaps overshooting austral migrants. Because both gulls and terns are long-lived and wander widely, determining how many records there are for a given species is often difficult if not impossible.

The species of gulls and terns recorded to date as rare birds in N America have diverse origins, making it difficult to suggest which species might be next to occur, and from where. Candidates from the Old World include Heuglin's Gull *Larus [fuscus] heuglini* (which may already have occurred in Alaska, but identification and taxonomic issues are unresolved), Mediterranean Gull *Icythyaetus melanocephalus*, and Little Tern *Sternula albifrons* (see Appendix B). Other species, seemingly less likely yet recorded from neighboring regions include Gray Gull *Leucophaeus modestus* in Mexico (from w. S America; MacKinnon et al. 2012) and White Tern *Gygis alba* in Bermuda (presumably hurricane driven) and Mexico.

SWALLOW-TAILED GULL *Creagrus furcatus* 56–61 cm (22–24")

Summary: *California*: 2 spring–early summer records (1985, 1996).
Taxonomy: Monotypic.
Distribution and Status:
    World: Breeds year-round Galapagos Islands, also on Isla Malpelo, Columbia. Ranges at sea s. to cen. Chile (around 33°S), n. to s. Cen America (around 11°N).
    North America: *California*: Monterey Co., 6–8 Jun 1985 (onshore; breeding adult); Marin Co., 3 Mar 1996 (offshore; breeding adult).

Comments: This pelagic species is known mainly from the Humboldt Current region, an area prone to food-web crashes that can cause seabirds to disperse both n. and s.; thus, vagrant occurrences can be 'expected.' All northerly records of Swallow-tailed Gull, n. to waters off s. Cen America (n. to Nicaragua; *NAB* 62:489), as well as those off CA, have been in Mar–Jul (Howell & Dunn 2007; *NAB* 60:452). Given the relative intensity of fall pelagic trips off the West Coast (but no records of Swallow-tailed Gull at that season), it may be that spring–summer is the best times to hope for this species again off CA.

Field Identification: Large, spectacular pelagic gull with long broad wings, forked tail, and long, pointed, slightly droop-tipped black bill, tipped pale gray on adult. All plumages have bold white upperwing panel suggesting much smaller Sabine's Gull.
    Similar Species: None, if seen well.
    Age/Sex/Season: Ages differ with adult appearance probably attained in 2nd cycle (breeds on less than annual cycle, thus not aged in years); sexes similar; seasonal variation in head pattern. Complete prebasic molt follows breeding, overlapping with partial prealternate molt before breeding.
    Adult nonbreeding (year-round): Head white with black 'mascara' eye patch and dusky ear-spot; upperparts gray with white tips to outer primaries, white tail; bill black with pale-gray tip, legs and feet pinkish. *Adult breeding* (year-round): Attains blackish-slate hood with white lore spot and small white spot below gape; legs and feet brighter pink, pale-gray bill tip bolder.
    1st-cycle: Juv upperparts dark sooty brown with pale scaly edgings (soon attains plain gray

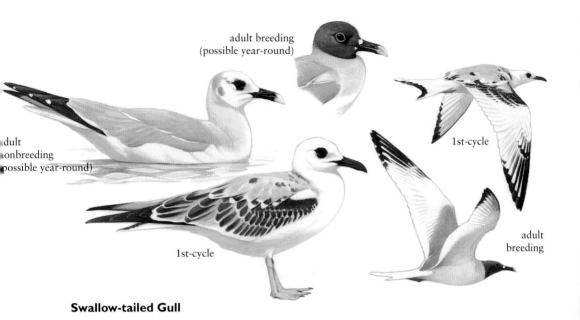

adult breeding
(possible year-round)

adult
nonbreeding
(possible year-round)

1st-cycle

adult
breeding

1st-cycle

Swallow-tailed Gull

upperparts); outer primaries lack white tips, tail has black distal band. Upperwing pattern similar to adult but with a dark ulnar bar, more extensive dark markings on primary coverts and outer primaries; bill black; legs dusky dull pinkish. Subsequent 1st- and 2nd-cycle molts and plumages undescribed.

Habitat and Behavior: Pelagic. A nocturnal feeder, sometimes attracted to lights on ships. Spends much of the day resting, but also may fly around a vessel and check it out briefly. On land favors rocky coasts, where often very confiding.

GRAY-HOODED GULL *Chroicocephalus cirrocephalus* 39–45 cm (15.3–17.7")

Summary: *Florida*: 1 winter record (1998). *New York*: 1 late summer record (2011).
Taxonomy: 2 ssp, probably not distinguishable in the field. Relative to African ssp *poiocephalus*, nominate New World ssp averages slightly larger, paler above, and with fainter dusky head markings in nonbreeding plumage. Has been treated in the genus *Larus*, and also known in the Old World as Grey-headed Gull.
Distribution and Status:
World: Breeds locally in tropical and subtropical S America (n. to Ecuador and n. Argentina) and sub-Saharan Africa.
North America: *Florida*: Franklin Co., nw. Gulf Coast, 26 Dec 1998 (adult in breeding

plumage). *New York*: Brooklyn, 24 Jul–4 Aug 2011 (adult in worn breeding plumage; *NAB* 65:602).
Comments: Not a particularly well-known species in the Americas, where other extralimital northerly reports are from Panama (Pacific coast), mainly in Aug–Sep and Mar (*NAB* 55:113, *NAB* 58:156, *NAB* 59:163, *NAB* 64:508–509), the Galapagos in Aug (Jones 2000), and recently Barbados (31 May–5 Jun 2009; *NAB* 63:664). Panama birds presumably originate from w. S America, with most records in the post-breeding period; the Barbados bird might as easily have come from W Africa, whence it might have been assisted by trade winds. The FL bird had a heavily worn tail, which is often a sign of captive origin, perhaps as a bird held on a ship, and the NY bird was also in heavily worn plumage and starting prebasic wing molt; however, Gray-hooded Gull is not known to be kept in aviaries (McNair 1999), although the NY bird was found near a major port and may have been ship-assisted, at least in part.

The nearest part of this species' regular range to FL is Ecuador, and the Pacific coast of S America is presumably the source for Gulf of Mexico records of Belcher's Gull, Gray Gull (in Yucatán, Mexico; MacKinnon et al. 2012), and perhaps Kelp Gull—the Isthmus of Panama is not an obstacle to most gulls. However, breeding of Gray-headed Gulls on the Pacific coast of S America occurs mainly during Apr–Sep, and adults from this population would not normally

1st-year

adult
breeding

1st-year

adult nonbreeding
(possible year-round)

adult breeding
(possible year-round)

2nd-year
nonbreeding

Gray-hooded Gull

be in breeding plumage during Dec. The claim by McNair (1999) that 'adults in breeding plumage were captured along the coast of Peru in December and January' is based on a misreading of Murphy (1936), who instead stated that Gray-hooded Gulls 'collected [in Peru] in December and January, refer … to captures during the height of the breeding season.' No indication was given by Murphy of what plumage these birds were in, and he assumed (wrongly, as it turns out) that this would be the breeding season in Peru (no nests had been found there at that time). The breeding season in Argentina, however, is mainly Sep–Apr, and an austral summer breeding season also pertains in S Africa, but with a northern summer breeding season in W Africa (Cramp 1983).

That the FL bird was in breeding plumage in late Dec suggests that either it had not been in the N Hemisphere long enough to switch its molt to a northern cycle (and thus originated from the Atlantic region, either S Africa or S America) or perhaps it had been around long enough to adjust its molt cycle to 'winter' breeding (and thus would have come from w. S America). Worn breeding plumage in late summer suggests the NY bird, if newly arrived, originated in w. S America or W Africa, although it has been suggested in could have moved n. with Laughing Gulls from ne. Brazil (*NAB* 65:602). Hopefully, further records will help elucidate vagrancy

patterns in this handsome gull and give more clues to origin.

Field Identification: Medium-sized, 2-year gull, similar in size to Laughing Gull but with a slimmer bill, broader wings, pale gray upperparts. Diagnostic upperwing pattern has a white leading wedge inside a large black tip.

Similar Species: A generally distinctive species, but nonbreeding plumages should be distinguished with care from Black-headed Gull. For separation from similar S American species (unrecorded in N America) see Howell & Dunn (2007).

Black-headed Gull averages smaller and narrower winged with a slightly smaller bill. Black-headed also has dark eyes (pale on adult Gray-hooded), whitish underwing coverts (pale gray to smoky gray on Gray-hooded), slightly paler gray upperparts, and a darker ear-spot in nonbreeding plumages. Black-headed upperwing has longer white leading wedge, lacking the large black wing-tip area of Gray-hooded, and underwings have a white stripe on the leading edge of the primaries.

Age/Sex/Season: Ages differ with adult appearance attained in 2nd year; sexes similar; seasonal variation in head pattern. Complete prebasic molt mostly after breeding, partial prealternate molt before breeding.

Adult: Wing-tip extensively black with a small white mirror-band, eyes pale lemon, bill and legs red (brightest on breeding birds). Nonbreeding has white head with diffuse dusky smudging strongest as a dusky ear-spot; breeding plumage (mainly Mar–Sep in w. S America, Jul–Mar in e. S America) has pearl-gray hood with white eye-arcs. *1st-year*: Juv (unlikely in N America) has brown mottling on upperparts soon replaced by gray in preformative molt. Upperwings have dark secondary bar, no white mirror-band; tail has narrow black distal band (sometimes absent in 1st-alternate); attains variable gray on hood in 1st alternate plumage; bill and legs pinkish to orange-red, bill tipped black. *2nd-year*: Resembles adult but some birds distinguishable by dark bases to tertials and secondaries; wing-tip may average more black and less white; eyes can be dark; and bill averages duller reddish to pinkish red, tipped black.

Habitat and Behavior: Coastal and inland, at lagoons, lakes, beaches, river mouths, harbors, and even dumps. Associates readily with small and medium-sized gulls, less often with larger gulls.

BELCHER'S GULL *Larus belcheri* 45–54 cm (17.7–21.2")

Summary: *Florida*: 2–3 fall–spring records (1968, 1974/1975, 1976). *California*: 1 fall–winter record (1997/1998).

Taxonomy: Monotypic. Has been considered conspecific with Olrog's Gull *L. atlanticus* of Atlantic coast of S America, with the combined species then known as Band-tailed Gull *L. belcheri.*

Distribution and Status:

World: Breeds (mainly Oct–Mar) and ranges along coasts of Peru and n. Chile.

North America: *Florida*: 2–3 records: Escambia Co., nw. Gulf coast, early Sep 1968 (adult; kept captive till its death in 1983); Collier Co., on s. Gulf coast, 11 Nov 1974–29 Jan 1975 (adult or near-adult) and 5 Jan–early Mar 1976 (adult or near-adult). *California*: San Diego Co., 3 Aug 1997–2 Jan 1998 (3rd-year or adult).

Comments: Although often treated as a Belcher's Gull (e.g., Howell & Dunn 2007, ABA 2008), an adult 'Band-tailed Gull' in Jun 1970 from Collier Co., on s. Gulf coast of FL, was not considered specifically identifiable at the level of Belcher's versus Olrog's (Olson 1976). Given the longevity of gulls, it's possible the 1974–1976 (and 1970?) FL records involved a wandering and returning individual.

Seabirds nesting on the w. coast of S America are prone to food crashes and breeding failures related to El Niño events, after which they might be expected to disperse and wander in search of food. The main breeding season for this species is Oct–Mar, but some birds may nest year-round. Vagrants could thus occur northward in any season, depending on the timing and strength of El Niño events and on how quickly birds travel. Once birds cross into the Gulf of Mexico (perhaps via the Panama Canal), they might wander around for years, as has happened with Kelp Gulls, and it might be years before they reach, or are detected in, the US. Vagrants also occurred (May, Aug, Dec) n. to cen. Panama during 1962–1967 (Ridgely & Gwynne 1989).

The coincidence of records from Panama in 1962–1967 and FL in 1968–1976 suggests that some event may have pushed numbers of birds n. in this period, but no such dispersal has occurred since, or been detected. This recalls the push of Kelp Gulls into the Gulf of Mexico in the late 1980s and 1990s, and more data are needed to evaluate what prompts such events.

Interestingly, the recent surge in gull watching in N America has not brought more records of this distinctive species. While the FL records involved white-headed birds in 'winter,' the CA bird was dark-hooded when found, at a time of year when breeding adults typically are white-headed. By Jan the CA bird was attaining white (presumably alternate) head feathering, whereas most S American adults undergo prealternate molt in Jun–Aug. Whether reversed molt timing indicates the CA bird had been in the N Hemisphere for some time is unclear, as is the mechanism by which vagrants switch their molt schedules when they switch hemispheres.

Field Identification: A striking, medium-large, rather lanky 3-year gull with a relatively long, fairly stout bill and relatively long yellowish legs. All ages have pinkish to yellow bill with black-and-red tip. Dark hood in nonbreeding plumages distinctive.

Similar Species: Distinctive, and likely to stand out in N America as something different. Note long stout bill with black-and-red tip, solid dark hood of nonbreeding and imm plumages, and broad black tail band of all plumages. Especially on the Atlantic and Gulf coasts, beware the possibility of a vagrant Olrog's Gull, breeding in Argentina and formerly considered conspecific with Belcher's Gull; see Howell & Dunn (2007) for details.

broad black
tail band

2nd-year
breeding

1st-year

adult
breeding
(possible year-round)

dark
hood variable

adult
nonbreeding
(possible year-round)

adult
nonbreeding

2nd-year
nonbreeding

all-black
wing-tips

Belcher's Gull

1st-year

Age/Sex/Season: Ages differ with adult appearance attained in 3rd year; sexes similar but male averages larger and bigger-billed; seasonal variation in head pattern. Molt timing varies; apparently follows simple alternate strategy (see p. 35).

Adult has slaty-black upperparts with a broad white trailing edge to the wings, a broad black subterminal tail band boldly tipped white, and reduced black on bill. **1st-year** has dark brown head and neck, variegated upperparts, pinkish to yellowish legs. **2nd-year** has head and neck ranging from dark slaty brown to mostly clean white, upperwings mixed with brownish and with narrower white trailing edge than adult, and bill pink to yellow with broad black subterminal band and red tip.

Habitat and Behavior: Coastal, including rocky coasts, stony to sandy intertidal areas, fishing harbors, and sewage outfalls. Associates readily with other gulls, terns, and waterbirds; feeds by foraging in the intertidal and scavenging.

BLACK-TAILED GULL *Larus crassirostris*
43–51 cm (17–20")

Summary: *North America*: Status complex (see below). About 70 records in the period, about a third each from AK (spring–fall) and E Coast (year-round), fewer from the interior (mainly fall–early winter) and West Coast (mainly fall–winter).
Taxonomy: Monotypic.
Distribution and Status:

World: Breeds on coasts of E Asia from Sakhalin s. to n. Yellow Sea, winters mainly from Japan to s. China.

North America: Although the first N American record was in 1954, in s. CA, most records have been since 1990. The species is most

adult with American Herring Gull

adult nonbreeding

1st-year

2nd-year

adult
breeding
(Mar–Sep)

3rd-year

adult
nonbreeding
(Sep–Mar)

2nd-year

1st-year

Black-tailed Gull

frequent in AK, where very rare in spring–fall (late Apr–Sep) in the sw. (mainly w. Aleutians) and on Bering Sea islands, and in summer–fall (Jun–Oct) on the s. coast and in the se. On the W Coast, very rare from BC s. to CA, with records year-round (mainly fall–winter). In the Interior, very rare in summer–early winter (Jun–Dec) from NWT and MN se. to Great Lakes region, exceptionally s. to NM (*NAB* 63:128-129). Very rare on Atlantic coast (records year-round) from NL s. to VA, exceptionally in late winter (Feb–Mar) to Gulf Coast of TX.

Comments: The increasing number of records of Black-tailed Gull in N America is no doubt due partly to an increase in observer awareness, and the relatively large number of records in e. N America recalls the pattern shown by Slaty-backed Gull. That Slaty-backed Gulls have been found only recently in well-watched locales such

as St. John's, NL, where they would not all have escaped detection in past years, argues that Asian gulls are genuinely increasing in e. N America. The seeming imbalance of W Coast records (of both Black-tailed and Slaty-backed gulls) relative to E Coast records can be at least partly explained by the large numbers of dark-backed gulls on the Pacific Coast, among which vagrants of other dark-backed species are easily overlooked.

The e. bias in records of Black-tailed Gull may also reflect changing dispersal patterns, perhaps linked to global warming. Thus, if more Asian gulls are moving n. in summer, and if those that do move n. encounter relatively unimpeded access into the Beaufort Sea, they can continue e. but may be forced s. in fall by the onset of cold weather. This would send them into cen. and e. N America. A similar phenomenon may help explain the mid-continent and e. bias in N American records of Ross's Gull, which is similarly rare on the W Coast; after molting in the Beaufort Sea, some adult Ross's may wander e. and be forced s. by winter weather rather than be able to return w. out into the Bering Sea (also cf. Long-billed Murrelet). Sooner or later, interior Black-tailed Gulls may reach the coast. East Coast records exist for all months, with a general trend of summer records northward, and fall–winter records southward. Some records probably involve wandering individuals, including birds that returned to sites over a period of years in the mid–late 1990s. It is also possible that some initial fall displacements are storm related (see Comments under accounts for Lesser Frigatebird and Long-billed Murrelet). Two other New World records pad out the N American pattern: Belize (mid-Mar 1988) and nw. Mexico (early Jun 1997; Garrett & Molina 1998).

Most N American records of Black-tailed Gull refer to adult or near-adult individuals, with exceptional 2nd-year birds in MN and TX; in AK, a few 1st-summers and 2nd-summers have been found. The absence of 1st-year birds in fall–winter in N America (as also seen with Slaty-backed Gull) lends support to the idea of a vagrancy pattern that originates with northward dispersal of nonbreeding birds in spring–summer from NE Asia into AK waters, rather than with fall dispersal from breeding areas, which would likely involve at least some 1st-winter birds.

Field Identification: Medium-sized, 4-year gull similar in size to Ring-billed Gull but with long wing projection more like California Gull. Bill relatively long and even in depth. Plumage progression much like California Gull; note clean-cut black tail band and pale eye on adult and older imms.

Similar Species: Fairly distinctive, but could be overlooked among large numbers of California Gulls. Relative to **California Gull**, Black-tailed averages smaller and lighter in build but with a proportionately longer bill and shorter legs. 1st-year Black-tailed Gull distinguished from California Gull by longer bill, white eye-arcs, and contrasting white uppertail coverts without extensive dark barring; greater coverts often plainer brown overall. 2nd-year from California by darker upperwings, distinct white eye-arcs, and solidly black tail; often has pale eyes. 3rd-year Black-tailed has pale eyes, clean-cut black tail band, lacks white mirrors in wing-tips.

Age/Sex/Season: Ages differ with adult appearance attained in 4th year; sexes similar; seasonal variation in 2nd-year and older. Complete prebasic molts in fall–early winter, partial prealternate molts in fall–spring.

Adult: Upperparts slaty-gray with black wing-tips lacking white mirrors on outer primaries; tail has clean-cut broad black subterminal band; long bill has black-and-red tip; eyes pale yellow; legs yellow. Nonbreeding plumage has dark-streaked cowl; breeding has clean white head. *1st-year* dark overall with whitish face and white eye-arcs; black-tipped pink bill; pinkish legs; black tail contrasts with mostly white uppertail coverts. *2nd-year* develops adult-like gray on back in 2nd summer; legs become greenish; eyes often become pale. *3rd-year* overall like adult but legs duller and greener; white tips on outer primaries smaller.

Habitat and Behavior: Mainly coastal but has also been found inland. Habits much like other medium-sized gulls, with which it is likely to be found (several N American records have been with Mew, Ring-billed, and California gulls); scavenges readily at dumps and fishing harbors.

YELLOW-LEGGED GULL *Larus michahellis*
53–67 cm (21–26.5")

Summary: *Newfoundland*: Rare (formerly very rare) in fall–spring. *Elsewhere*: exceptional in the East, but records clouded by identification issues (see below).

Taxonomy: 2 ssp widely recognized; the larger, bulkier, and longer-legged nominate *michahellis* breeding in the Mediterranean region has paler upperparts in adult plumage (Kodak Scale 6–7); the smaller, shorter-legged *atlantis* of the Azores archipelago has slightly darker upperparts (Kodak Scale 7–8.5). Other populations in W Europe show subtle differences, and Yellow-legged has been considered conspecific with Caspian Gull *L. cachinnans* of SE Europe. N American records involve *atlantis* and perhaps *michahellis*.

Distribution and Status:

World: Breeds S Europe and islands off NW Africa; post-breeding dispersal from Mediterranean to NW Europe.

North America: *Newfoundland*: Very rare to rare in e. NL since 1985, almost annual since 1995; most or all believed to be *atlantis*. Records span Oct–May, with most in Nov–Mar. Almost all records involve adults, and recent winter records are often presumed to involve returning

individuals; a 3rd-cycle bird in May 2006 consti-
tuted the latest record by 6 weeks. ***Elsewhere***:
Exceptional. 2 summer records (Aug 1973, Jun
2003) of *atlantis* from the Madeleine Islands, QC,
in Gulf of St. Lawrence. An adult gull thought
to be nominate *michahellis* was found in 4 of
5 winters in the DC area, from Feb 1990 to Feb
1995 (Wilds & Czaplak 1994). A putative adult
Yellow-legged Gull from Cape Cod, MA, 6 Oct
2002 (Rines 2005) looks to us more like a hybrid
Lesser Black-backed × Herring Gull; the record
is likely to be re-reviewed (M. Iliff, pers. comm;
and see Comments, below). 1st-year and 2nd-year
gulls identified as Yellow-legged have been found
in winter (Dec–Apr) in VA, FL, and coastal TX.

Comments: Identification difficulties no doubt
cloud the true status of this enigmatic species
in N America. In particular, the appearance of
hybrid Lesser Black-backed Gull × Herring Gull
(at all ages) remains to be elucidated. Presumed
hybrids can very closely resemble Yellow-legged
Gull and are much more numerous in the East,
yet such hybrids are infrequently reported or
may be misidentified as Yellow-legged Gulls. For
example, an apparently classic, white-headed
Yellow-legged Gull (which everyone was happy
with) was present 9–17 Apr 2011 in MA (*NAB*
65:413), but when what was almost certainly the
same individual returned in Nov its dusky head
and chest streaking and pinkish-yellow legs indicated it was a hybrid (M. Iliff, pers. comm.)!

The Canadian birds likely originated from the
Azores, which lie in the middle of the N Atlantic;
they may have been birds that wandered out
to sea, their vagrancy perhaps enhanced by
weather systems that drifted birds toward
N America. Whether the vagrants arrived as
adults, or as imms, remains unknown. Given that
imm gulls typically winter to the south of adults,
the Canadian adults may have first arrived farther
s. in the New World where they were overlooked.

The trend of wintering birds in NL and
summering birds in QC suggests that when
vagrants reach Atlantic Canada they can remain
for years, and a very small (nonbreeding?)
population may even exist in e. Canada. Yellow-
legged Gulls have hybridized with other large
gulls, so breeding by this species in N America
seems possible. However, given how long it has
taken to find evidence of N American breeding
by the much commoner Lesser Black-backed
Gull (Ellis et al. 2007), we may wait some time for
evidence of Yellow-legged Gulls breeding in
N America.

In Britain, populations of nominate *michahellis*
Yellow-legged Gulls have increased dramatically
since the 1980s, and the species is now a locally
common visitor, mainly from fall to early winter,
with small numbers breeding there since 1995
(Holling & Rare Breeding Birds Panel 2011). This
increase has not been reflected in
N America, suggesting that an Atlantic crossing
at these latitudes in fall is inhibited by the
dominant weather systems, which track west-
to-east; there were only 2 records (Apr and Aug)
from Iceland through 2006.

Field Identification: Large, 4-year, white-
headed gull. Adult intermediate in appearance
between Herring Gull and Lesser Black-backed
Gull, and the first N American record of Yellow-
legged Gull, a specimen from QC, was first reported as a hybrid between these 2 species (Gosselin et al. 1986). Imm plumages much like Lesser
Black-backed Gull, and some 1st-year birds may
not be identifiable to species. See Howell & Dunn
(2007) for further details of identification, including for imms and hybrids.

Similar Species: Should be identified with
great care. As with many large gulls, once you
are very familiar with the common species then
vagrants such as Yellow-legged are easier to find.
Note that adult Yellow-legged typically has a
fairly early prebasic molt (something that could
change with vagrants) and has dusky head markings mainly in fall (Aug–Sep); by early winter
most Yellow-legged Gulls are white-headed and
often stand out on this feature alone.

Main confusion species in N America are
Herring Gull and ***Lesser Black-backed Gull***
(both of which as adults have distinct dark head
streaking in winter), plus hybrids of these two
species. Relative to Yellow-legged, adult hybrids
have heavy dusky head and neck streaking in
winter, and often have pinker legs (at least in
winter, but these may brighten to yellow in spring;
study needed). The appearance of imm hybrids
has not been elucidated.

Adult: Yellow-legged paler above than palest
Lesser Black-backed Gull, but in some lights
can appear relatively dark (especially *atlantis*).
Black wing-tip on underwing more sharply
defined on Yellow-legged than on Lesser, and
Yellow-legged tends to be bulkier and
broader-winged.

Relative to Herring Gull, Yellow-legged has
slightly to distinctly darker upperparts, yellow
legs, reddish orbital ring. However, Herring Gulls
with yellow legs are not infrequent, at least in

hybrid **Lesser Black-backed ×
American Herring Gull**
possibly not separable in
summer from Yellow-legged

adult
atlantis

adult with American
Herring Gull (Dec–Feb)

2nd-year *atlantis*
(Sep–Oct)

adult
nonbreeding
(Oct–Feb)

2nd-winter
michahellis

adult *atlantis*
nonbreeding
(Sep–Nov)

adult breeding
(Dec–Mar, after which
white primary tips abrade)

2nd-winter
michahellis

1st-winter
atlantis

2nd-year *atlantis*
(Sep–Oct)

1st-winter *michahellis* with
1st-winter Lesser Black-backed Gull (left)

1st-winter
atlantis

Yellow-legged Gull

spring; such birds have pale gray upperparts and
yellowish orbital ring typical of Herring; wing-tip
pattern variable in all gulls but Herring (especially in Atlantic Canada) tends to have less black
and more white than Yellow-legged.

Vocalizations likely to be distinct from Herring
Gull but not studied.

1st-year and 2nd-year Yellow-legged looks
much like Lesser Black-backed Gull but by 2nd
summer tends to have some medium-gray on

upperparts. Yellow-legged is a little bulkier and broader winged than Lesser, and bill often appears slightly stouter and more bluntly tipped. White bases to outer rectrices of 1st-year Yellow-legged typically have few or no dark bars, whereas Lesser usually has distinct dark barring. Legs of Yellow-legged are pinkish in 1st year (often with dusky 'shin-pads' into winter), usually becoming yellow by 2nd summer.

3rd-year: Differs from other species in structure and tone of upperparts, as does adult, but head and neck have more extensive dusky streaking which, on *atlantis*, often forms a dark-streaked hood retained into winter.

Age/Sex/Season: Ages differ with adult appearance attained in 4th or 5th year; sexes similar but male averages larger and bigger billed; seasonal variation in 2nd-year and older. Complete prebasic molt occurs in summer–fall, partial prealternate molts in fall–winter.

Adult has medium gray to pale slaty-gray upperparts; white mirrors on p10 or p9–p10; pale yellowish eyes with a reddish orbital ring; a yellow bill with a long red gonys spot and few or no dark subterminal markings; and yellow legs (often fairly rich yellow). Nonbreeding has fine dusky streaking on crown and cheeks; breeding plumage cleanly white-headed. *Imm* plumage progression much like Lesser Black-backed Gull, but upperparts show paler gray from 2nd-year onward (see Similar Species, above).

Habitat and Behavior: Mainly coastal but does wander inland, mainly along rivers. Behavior typical of other large gulls, with which it readily associates.

KELP GULL *Larus dominicanus* 53–63 cm (21–25")

Summary: *Gulf States*: Very rare year-round, and has bred. *Elsewhere*: Single records from IN (1996), MD (1998–2005), CO (2003), and ON (2012).

Taxonomy: 5 ssp, differing slightly in bill size, darkness of upperparts, and wing-tip pattern, but rarely likely to be separable in the field (see Howell & Dunn 2007). N American vagrants are likely nominate *dominicanus*, of S American origin.

Distribution and Status:

World: Circumpolar in the S Hemisphere and expanding its range; in the Americas breeds n. to Ecuador and s. Brazil.

North America: *Gulf States*: Status unclear due to hybridization with Herring Gull; most records from LA. At least 7–8 apparently pure Kelp Gulls were reported from the Chandeleur Islands, LA, during 1989–2000 (Dittman & Cardiff 2005). Specific records include: 1 apparently mated pair in summers of at least 1989–1994; 1 adult female paired with a Herring Gull in 1990–1998, 1 adult female paired with a Kelp × Herring hybrid in 1994–1998, and 1 adult male paired with a Kelp × Herring hybrid in 1999; a nonpaired adult male Kelp was collected in 1998. No pure Kelp Gulls and only 1 Herring Gull were seen on the Chandeleurs in summer 2004, when there were at least 18 pairs of hybrids breeding there (Dittman & Cardiff 2005). In coastal TX, 3–4 winter-spring records of adults, 2–3 during 1996–1997, 1 in 2008 (*NAB* 63:118–119, 2009), including 1 bird probably returning in 2 successive winters. In Pasco Co., FL, an apparently pure near-adult Kelp Gull was on the cen. Gulf Coast, 28 Dec 2010–8 Jan 2011 (*NAB* 65:260). *Elsewhere*: Lake Co., IN, 19–26 Oct 1996 (near-adult); long-staying in St Mary's Co., MD, Jan 1998–Apr 2005 (adult); Jackson Co./Larimer Co., CO, 17 Sep–2 Nov 2003 (adult); Point Pelee, ON, 7–9 Sep 2012 (adult; A. Wormington, photos).

Comments: Small numbers of Kelp Gulls were found in the Gulf of Mexico in the late 1980s and 1990s. These birds may have originated from w. S America (as with Belcher's Gull), although some may be transatlantic vagrants from s. Africa; genetic analysis of the 1998 LA specimen might address this question. Breeding was reported in LA and also may have occurred in Yucatán, Mexico, in the early 1990s (Howell et al. 1993), and wintering birds were seen in the 1990s in coastal TX, adjacent Tamaulipas, Mexico, and along the n. coast of the Yucatan Peninsula, Mexico. Records have been few since 2000. The hybridization event with Herring Gulls in LA has added another dimension that will complicate field identification for years to come, and critical study of the hybrids and their appearance is still needed. In AL, hybrids were first found in 2009, and a pair was nesting there in 2010 (*NAB* 64:441).

The MD and IN birds may have been linked to the 'mini-invasion' of the late 1980s, or it may be that odd individuals are wandering n. from time to time as part of the global northward spread of Kelp Gulls, which has been ongoing for the past 50 or so years. This species is mainly coastal throughout its range but birds occur well inland in S America, so records from the Great Lakes and CO are plausible. The first European record of Kelp Gull was also well inland, in Paris, France

adult

3rd-year

late
2nd-year

1st-year

3rd-year

adult

early 2nd-year

late
2nd-year

Kelp Gull

1st-year

(Jiguet & Defos du Rau 2004), so perhaps pioneering birds are more prone to wander inland. Reminiscent of the LA scenario, the first Kelp Gull for the Western Palearctic, in Mauritania, stayed many years (1997–2003, at least) and bred with a Yellow-legged Gull (Pineau et al. 2001).

Other recent extralimital reports of Kelp Gull in the Americas include Trinidad (Jul 2000–Feb 2001) and Barbados (Dec 2000) (Hayes et al. 2002), Panama (Nov–Dec 2001, Apr–May 2009, Feb–Apr 2010; *NAB* 64:509), and El Salvador (Feb 2009; *NAB* 63:335), perhaps indicating further waves of immigrants. It has been suggested that some of these birds originated in Africa (Hayes et al. 2002), which is certainly possible (as with Gray-hooded Gull), although that idea was based on a misunderstanding of field characters of Kelp Gulls from S Africa relative to S American birds (see Howell & Dunn 2007).

A 1st-year gull in Brazoria Co., TX, 19 Dec 2008, was accepted as Kelp Gull by the state

committee. Given the specter of potential hybrids in the Gulf of Mexico, and how little is known of their field characters, we consider uncertain the identification of putative 1st-year Kelp Gulls in this region. An adult gull photographed in AL, 14 Mar 2009 and identified as Kelp (*NAB* 63/3:446) was not accepted by the state committee (S. McConnell, pers. comm.) and is likely a darker example of a hybrid.

Field Identification: Large, black-backed, yellow-legged 4-year gull. Most plumages very similar to Lesser Black-backed Gull, but note Kelp's greater bulk, broader wings (with shorter wing projection at rest), and, especially, its bigger bill with a variably bulbous tip. See Howell & Dunn (2007) for further details of identification, including imms and hybrids.

Similar Species: Should be identified with great care, especially given the number of Kelp Gull × Herring Gull hybrids that reportedly exist, and because the appearance of hybrids is not well known (Dittman & Cardiff 2005).

Main confusion risks in N America are **Lesser Black-backed Gull** (averages smaller and more lightly built than Kelp, with longer and narrower wings) and **hybrid Kelp Gull × Herring Gull**, which are far commoner in the Gulf of Mexico than pure Kelp Gulls. Relative to Kelp Gull, many adult hybrids are paler above and thus closely resemble Lesser Black-backed Gull; hybrids differ from Lesser in often being bulkier and in having a heavier, slightly swollen-tipped bill more like Kelp. Some backcross hybrids may be almost as black-backed as Kelp Gull, however, and identification criteria remain to be elucidated. The appearance of hybrid imms remains poorly known.

Adult Kelp is blacker above than darkest Lesser Black-backed Gulls known from N America; it is a bulkier bird with broader wings, a shorter wing projection, and a slightly swollen-tipped bill. Even in fresh basic plumage, adult Kelp has very little dusky head streaking and it looks white-headed year-round, not showing the distinct dusky head and neck streaking typical of Lesser in winter.

1st-year and 2nd-year Kelp look much like same-age Lesser Black-backed Gull in plumage and are best separated by bulkier structure, broad wings (with a shorter wing projection at rest), and slightly swollen-tipped bill.

3rd-year Differs from same-age Lesser Black-backed in structure and blacker upperparts, as in adult; head and neck have more extensive dusky streaking than adult Kelp, but still much less than typical of Lesser.

Age/Sex/Season: Ages differ with adult appearance attained in 4th year; sexes similar but male averages larger and bigger-billed; seasonal variation in 2nd year and older. Molt timing varies with breeding season, and new arrivals may be on a S Hemisphere molt schedule; apparently follows simple alternate strategy (see p. 35).

Adult has slaty-blackish upperparts; white mirror on p10, rarely also p9; pale yellowish to dusky eyes with a yellow-orange to reddish orbital ring; yellow bill with red gonys spot and few or no dark subterminal markings; and yellow to greenish-yellow legs. Imms much like Lesser Black-backed Gull in plumage but with darker gray upperparts from 2nd year onward (see Similar Species, above). Some 3rd-year birds relatively 'advanced' and adult-like.

Habitat and Behavior: Mainly coastal but does wander inland along rivers and to large lakes. Behavior typical of other large gulls, with which it readily associates.

BLACK NODDY *Anous minutus* 31–34 cm (12.2–13.5")

Summary: *Gulf States*: Very rare in FL, spring–fall; 2 spring–summer records from TX (1975, 1998).

Taxonomy: In need of critical review. Up to 7 ssp recognized, some poorly defined and others perhaps representing cryptic species (unlike Atlantic populations, Pacific birds typically have contrastingly paler tail). US records presumed to involve Caribbean ssp *americanus*.

Distribution and Status:

World: Breeds locally and ranges in tropical Pacific and tropical Atlantic oceans. In Caribbean region, breeds mainly on islands off n. Venezuela, formerly Belize.

North America: *Gulf States*: At or near Dry Tortugas, s. FL, very rare (Apr–early Sep, most records late Apr–Jul), where first found in 1960; recorded on average in 2–3 of every 4 years. Usually singles occur, occasionally 2 birds, and an exceptional max. of 5 in spring 1997; most records involve 1st-summer birds but adults have occurred. Exceptional away from Dry Tortugas, with singles in Pinellas Co., cen-w. FL, 12 June 2003 (Anon 2004); Nueces Co., TX, 22 Jun 1975; and Galveston Co./Aransas Co., TX, 15 Apr–27 Jul 1998.

Comments: N American records of Black Noddy fit within a pattern of spring–summer wandering by nonbreeders in the n. Caribbean region, along with single Jul–Aug records from the Yucatan Peninsula and Honduras Bay Islands. The preponderance of records from late Apr–Jul may reflect observer coverage as much as actual occurrence patterns. The FL Keys lie at the edge of this species' normal range and it probably qualifies as a 'false vagrant' in N America (see p. 16).

Field Identification: Small dark tern, similar to larger and much commoner Brown Noddy but with very slender bill, darker plumage.

Similar Species: Should be distinguished with care from **Brown Noddy**. Black Noddy is appreciably smaller in direct comparison, with a proportionately longer and more slender bill (absolute bill length similar to Brown Noddy, but bill depth half that of Brown). Black is darker in all plumages, with no distinct contrast between black wing-tips and tertials at rest. Adult Black

well-defined white cap

1st-year

long
slender
bill

faded juv primaries

1st-summer

adult

adult

Black Noddy

adult

**Brown
Noddy**
adult

adult with Brown Noddy

has white cap contrasting more strongly with slaty nape; 1st-year Black also has extensive and strongly contrasting white cap, unlike diffuse and restricted whitish frontal area of 1st-year Brown.

Age/Sex/Season: Ages differ, with adult appearance probably attained in 2nd year; sexes similar; no seasonal variation. Molts not well known; may follow complex basic strategy (see p. 35), with complete preformative molt.

Adult slaty brownish black with white cap blending fairly abruptly into slaty-gray nape; upperparts uniform overall. *1st-year* has white cap sharply contrasting with blackish nape, the cap's hind edge sometimes messy and mottled blackish; upperparts typically not uniform, often with contrasting and faded upperwing coverts. Active wing molt often apparent in 1st summer, with faded juv outer primaries.

Habitat and Behavior: Tropical marine waters and adjacent coasts, usually in association with Brown Noddy. Perches readily on trees, bushes, breakwaters, and other places where Brown Noddies roost or nest. Flight quicker and often more erratic than Brown Noddy, with floppy wingbeats and frequent swooping to pick prey from near the sea surface. Readily rests on the sea, less often on driftwood and flotsam than does Brown Noddy. Gutteral growls and chatters higher and sharper than Brown Noddy, which might draw attention.

LARGE-BILLED TERN *Phaetusa simplex*
38–42 cm (15–16.5")

Summary: *East*: 3 spring–summer records (1949, 1954, 1988).

Taxonomy: 2 ssp sometimes recognized, not known to be separable in the field; molt timings may differ (study needed). Equatorial breeders average slightly darker upperparts than s. breeders (Kodak Score 10–11 vs. 9–10: AMNH and BM specimens), *contra* Blake 1977, who suggested the opposite; but beware imms are appreciably paler above than adults.

Distribution and Status:
World: Breeds and ranges from tropical S America s. to cen. Argentina.

North America: *East*: 3 records, none very recent: Cook Co., IL, 15 Jul 1949; Mahoning Co., OH, 29 May 1954; and Hudson Co., NJ, 30 May 1988.

Comments: This species' spring–summer pattern of occurrence in e. N America is shared by White-faced Whistling-Duck and Southern Lapwing. This coincidence of records corresponds with the end of the dry season in n. S America, which may force waterbirds to wander before the summer rains arrive.

Large-billed Tern is a very rare visitor n. to Panama (mainly late Mar–Jul), and the 1st reports from Costa Rica (mid-Mar) and Honduras (late Apr) were both in 2003 and from the Caribbean

adult breeding

1st-year

molting adult

white

dark

adult nonbreeding
(possible year-round)

Large-billed Tern

adult breeding
(possible year-round)

coast (*NAB* 57:415); another recent record comes from Grenada, Lesser Antilles, 31 May–1 Jun 2010 (*NAB* 64:512). Farther n., vagrants in Cuba (late May) and Bermuda (mid-Jun) support a pattern of extralimital n. records during spring–summer, and further N American records seem quite possible. Whether n. records reflect post-breeding wanderers or overshooting austral migrants is unclear (data on molt stage and plumage state could address this question); age data would also be of interest. Descriptions of the N American birds do not specifically mention molt, but observers have not always paid attention to this subject.

Field Identification: Fairly large and essentially unmistakable tern; overall size similar to Elegant Tern but disproportionately large bill more like Royal Tern's in size. All ages have big yellow bill, greenish-yellow legs, slaty-gray upperparts, boldly tricolored upperwing pattern suggesting Sabine's Gull, and moderately forked tail.

   Similar Species: Unlikely to be confused with any N American species.

   Age/Sex/Season: Ages differ with adult appearance probably attained in 2nd year; sexes similar; limited seasonal variation mainly in adults. Molts and plumages need study.

   Adult breeding has solid black crown separated from bill base by white lores and narrow white forehead band; upperparts slaty gray with white median primary coverts; alula

bicolored with dark inner and paler outer web. *Adult nonbreeding* has smoky-gray forecrown with a broad black auricular mask joined across hindneck. *1st-year*: Juv recalls adult nonbreeding but crown, hindneck, and upperparts average paler overall with dark brown scalloping and mottling (fresh pale cinnamon wash to upperparts fades quickly after fledging), rectrices with whitish tips and indistinct dark subterminal marks, secondaries dusky gray with whitish tips; bill diffusely tipped dusky into 1st-year. May have protracted complete preformative molt over 1st year, after which resembles adult nonbreeding, but black eyestripe-mask shorter, median primary coverts mottled dark overall, alula usually all-dark; some birds develop black crown mottled with smoky gray, perhaps a 1st-alternate plumage. May attain adult plumage by 2nd prebasic molt.

   Habitat and Behavior: Freshwater lakes and rivers, estuaries, coastal lagoons. N American birds have been alone or in loose association with other terns. Feeds mainly by plunge-diving for fish, also by snatching prey from near the surface.

WHITE-WINGED TERN *Chlidonias leucopterus* 23.5–24.5 cm (9.2–9.7")

Summary: *Alaska*: Exceptional in spring–fall on Aleutians, Bering Sea islands, and mainland.

California: Exceptional in summer–fall. *Interior*: Exceptional in spring–summer from Great Lakes region to n. MB. *Atlantic States and Provinces*: Very rare, spring–fall.

Taxonomy: Monotypic. Often known as White-winged Black Tern.

Distribution and Status:

World: Breeds mid-latitude Eurasia, from E Europe e. to ne. China; winters sub-Saharan Africa and from SE Asia to n. Australia.

North America: *Alaska*: Exceptional in spring–fall (mid-May to early Sep): 3 records from w. and cen. Aleutians (mid-May to mid-Jul), singles from Pribilofs (Jun 2004), and cen. (Jul 2003) and s-coastal (Aug–Sep 1992) mainland. *California*: 2 records: Humboldt Co., 20 Jun–30 Aug 1996 (absent about 2 months but assumed the same bird), and Monterey Co., 4 Sep–16 Oct 1999. *Interior*: 3–4 records: Lake Co., IN, 17 Jul 1979; sw. ON, 8 May–2 Jun 1991 and 8 May 1992 (perhaps the same bird), and Churchill, MB, 24 Jun–14 Jul 1995. *Atlantic States and Provinces*: Very rare with about 20–30 records (see Comments, below), mostly mid-May to mid-Sep (peaking Jul–Aug on the Mid-Atlantic Coast), from e. QC and NB s. to GA; 1 in Jasper Co., SC, 15 Nov 2000, is the latest. Occurrences in N America through the late 1990s were discussed by C. Campbell (2000).

Comments: Virtually all N American records are of birds identified as adults (mainly in, or molting out of, breeding plumage), but a 1st-summer occurred in NJ (Jun–Aug 1989), a 2nd-fall bird in CA (Sep–Oct 1999), and a presumed 2nd- or 3rd-year bird in nonbreeding plumage in VA (Sep 2002; Brinkley 2010b). The distribution and timing of occurrences in e. N America suggest that wandering White-winged Terns are joining American Black Terns or perhaps Common Terns wintering near the coast of ne. S America, and moving n. with them to N America in their 2nd (rarely 1st) and subsequent summers; most individuals of these species spend their 1st summer on the wintering grounds. 4 recent Oct–Nov records (all of juvs) from Barbados support this theory, as does the relative lack of records from the se. US, suggesting, as in Little Egret and others, the possibility of an overwater spring flight and arrival on the Mid-Atlantic Coast and points n. There are also 2 May–Jun records from the Bahamas (White 2004), presumably northbound spring migrants.

There's no indication that eastern N American birds crossed the N Atlantic, although a recent juv from Bermuda (29 Sep–4 Oct 2010; *NAB* 65:201) suggests that some could reach the se. US directly from Europe. There were only 11 records from Iceland through 2006 (mainly since 1990 and during Jun–Aug), and 5 from the Azores (3 in fall); given that most White-winged Terns migrate through E Europe, this paucity of records is unsurprising.

Because White-winged Terns are long-lived, and, as breeding-plumaged adults, are wildly conspicuous, the relatively large number of e. N American records may have involved only a few birds. The 3 records in the mid-1960s from VA seem likely to have involved a single bird, but it's even possible that the 1987–1997 records from VT, NY, NJ, DE, and NC stemmed from only 1, or at most 2, birds (e.g., the 1997 NY record was from exactly the same site as the 1991 record; *NAB* 51:978). We suspect that a relatively leisurely fall migration, versus a short and direct spring migration, helps explain the preponderance of fall records in the East, perhaps in combination with larger numbers of coastal observers in fall (e.g., looking for shorebirds).

The W Coast records probably involve birds that overshot their NE Asian breeding range and ended up in AK; some of these then moved s. on the N American side of the Pacific.

Field Identification: Small attractive marsh tern, likely to be found with Black Terns from which distinguished by a number of features.

Similar Species: Only real confusion species is *Black Tern*, but cf. Whiskered Tern. Also, as there are at least two N American records of mixed pairs of Black Tern and White-winged Tern (in QC and NY), hybrids are a possibility, although none have been detected or suspected in N America.

White-winged Tern has almost squared tail, and slightly shorter bill but longer legs than Black Tern. Breeding plumage ostensibly unmistakable, but beware that Black Tern can show strikingly silvery upperwings in some light. Nonbreeding similar to Black Tern but upperparts appreciably paler, fairly pale gray with whitish rump and pale gray tail; lacks distinct black cap; and lacks dark patch at breast sides. Juv differs from Black Tern by dark back contrasting with pale upperwings, pale rump; lacks dark breast patch.

Age/Sex/Season: Ages differ, with adult appearance attained in 2nd or 3rd year; sexes similar; marked seasonal variation. Complete prebasic molt in fall–spring, incomplete prealternate

American Black Tern
adult breeding (Apr–Jul)

juv
(Aug–Oct)

adult
nonbreeding
(Aug–Mar)

adult nonbreeding
(1st-summer similar)

adult breeding
(Apr–Jul)

2nd-summer
(May–Jul)

juv

White-winged Tern

molt in late winter–spring (often includes inner primaries); complete preformative molt in late fall–summer. ***Adult***: Nonbreeding has upperparts pale gray, head and underparts white with black cheek spot and dusky cap; underwing coverts can have some black patches in winter. Prebasic wing molt protracted from late summer or fall to spring, usually suspended over fall migration with dark and worn outer primaries; prealternate wing molt of inner to mid-primaries (often out to p7–p8) mainly in mid-winter to spring, and sometimes a presupplemental molt of inner primaries in late winter–spring. Breeding plumage has solidly black head, body, and underwing coverts contrasting with white upperwing coverts and whitish underside to remiges. ***1st-year***: Juv has back mottled dark brown, often retained through fall migration into early winter. 1st-winter/1st-summer resembles adult nonbreeding but outer primaries relatively fresh in fall–winter but worn and blackish in spring–summer; often retains some juv tertials into mid-winter. 1st wing molt

starts early to mid-winter, usually completing by late 1st summer, with 2nd wave of inner primary molt starting in 1st summer. ***2nd-year***: 2nd-winter resembles adult nonbreeding but may differ in molt timing and relative freshness of primaries and in always having white underwing coverts, without black (needs study); 2nd-summer like adult breeding but averages duller, with dark alula (whitish on adult), often some dark marks on upper primary coverts, and white feathers scattered in underwing coverts.

Habitat and Behavior: Freshwater marshes, reservoirs, estuaries, rarely coastal beaches; several summer records have been of individuals visiting tern colonies, from those of Arctic and Aleutian Terns in the Aleutians to those of Common and Black Terns in e. Canada. Not habitually pelagic like nonbreeding Black Tern. Most common flight call reminiscent of Black Tern, but most notes longer, lower, and harsher, including a cracked *grrrrk*, often doubled or in series (P. Holt, pers. comm.).

WHISKERED TERN *Chlidonias hybridus*
26–27.5 cm (10.2–11")

Summary: *New Jersey and Delaware*: 1–2 mid–late summer records (1993, 1998).

Taxonomy: 3 ssp, differing slightly in size and plumage tones. Nominate *hybridus*, breeding across Eurasia, is the only ssp likely to occur in N America; *delalandii* of E and S Africa averages darker below in breeding plumage, *javanicus* of India to Australia averages paler overall in all plumages.

Distribution and Status:

World: Breeds locally across mid-latitude Eurasia from SW Europe e. to China; also in E and S Africa, Australia. N populations winter in sub-Saharan Africa and from SE Asia to n. Australasia.

North America: *New Jersey and Delaware*: Single adults in Cape May Co., NJ, 12–15 Jul 1993 (presumably moving across Delaware Bay to Kent Co., DE, 19 Jul–24 Aug 1993), and again in Cape May Co., NJ, 8–12 Aug 1998.

Comments: Given that terns are long-lived, it's possible that both N American records refer to one bird, which likely drifted s. and w. across the Atlantic in fall to end up in ne. S America or the E Caribbean. 2 recent fall (1st-year) and spring (breeding adult) records from Barbados and a spring 2003 record (breeding adult) from Great Inagua, Bahamas (White 2004) support this conjecture (and see Comments under White-winged Tern).

Chlidonias terns are gregarious and migrate and wander in flocks, and it seems likely that a vagrant wintering in the e. Caribbean or ne. S America could attach itself to a flock of Black Terns or Common Terns heading to N America. As with White-winged Tern, we suspect that northbound birds might be missed on their relatively direct (and perhaps more offshore?) spring migration, versus a more leisurely fall migration when marsh terns often stage or linger at coastal sites frequented by observers.

There were only 2 records from Iceland (Apr–May and Jul) through 2003, suggesting records via the northern route are unlikely. However, there have been 6 records from the Azores since 2002 (3 in Oct, including 1 of multiple birds), suggesting significant overwater capabilities and the possibility of direct movement to the se. US.

Whiskered Tern has an E Asian range and migration similar to White-winged Black Tern, and seems a possible vagrant to the Pacific coast of N America.

Field Identification: Relatively large and broad-winged marsh tern, more likely to be mistaken for a *Sterna* tern than for Black Tern.

Similar Species: Breeding adult and juv Whiskered Tern unmistakable if seen well (but cf. breeding Common and Arctic Terns). Imm and nonbreeding Whiskered can be confusing.

Sterna terns have longer, more slender wings and more deeply forked tails, and most have white rumps. *Sterna* tend to be more purposeful in flight and typically plunge-dive.

Black and *White-winged terns* smaller, finer-billed, and more agile; both have somewhat different face patterns from Whiskered, with a black cheek patch offsetting a white eye-ring. Black Tern appreciably darker gray above.

Age/Sex/Season: Ages differ, with adult appearance probably attained in 2nd year; sexes similar; marked seasonal variation. Complete prebasic molt in fall–winter, incomplete prealternate molt in winter–spring (often include inner primaries); complete preformative molt in fall–summer. *Adult*: Nonbreeding has upperparts pale gray, head and underparts white with solid black eye mask running into black-steaked hindcrown. Prebasic wing molt late summer to spring, usually suspended over fall migration with dark and worn outer primaries; prealternate wing molt of inner to mid-primaries mainly in mid–late winter, and sometimes a presupplemental molt of inner primaries in late winter–early spring. Breeding plumage has duskier gray upperparts, solid black cap, and white cheeks contrasting with dark gray underbody and whitish undertail coverts. *1st-year*: Juv has back mottled dark brown and cinnamon, but usually molted within 1–2 months of fledging and unlikely to be seen in N America. 1st-winter/1st-summer resembles adult nonbreeding but outer primaries relatively fresh in fall–winter, often retains some juv tertials into mid-winter. 1st wing molt starts early to mid-winter, completing or suspending by spring, with 2nd wave of inner primary molt starting late winter. *2nd-year*: 2nd-winter resembles adult nonbreeding but may differ in molt timing and relative freshness of primaries (needs study); 2nd-summer probably like adult breeding but some may have variable nonbreeding aspect.

Habitat and Behavior: Fresh and brackish marshes, rivers, and lakes, rarely over marine waters except during migration. Typically picks food off the water surface but occasionally

adult
nonbreeding
(1st-summer similar)

juv
(Jul–Aug)

1st-winter

adult
breeding
(Apr–Aug)

Whiskered Tern

plunge dives. Most common vocalization a harsh, scratchy, fairly abrupt *kerrr*, often in series and given in flight.

SHOREBIRDS

A diverse array of species comprises the world-wide group of birds known collectively in N America as shorebirds (and in the Old World as waders). Sandpipers and plovers are the two largest shorebird families, and include many long-distance migrant species; not surprisingly, these families are the best represented among rare shorebirds in N America. We consider 36 shore-birds as rare birds in N America: 24 sandpipers, 8 plovers, 1 thick-knee, 1 pratincole, 1 oyster-catcher, and 1 stilt. All but 3 species originate in the Old World.

Old World Shorebirds

Of the Old World shorebird vagrants, most come from E Asia, with fewer from Europe. The Asian species, known mainly from AK, show the common pattern of drift migrants/vagrants and overshoots in spring, and misoriented migrants (mainly juvs) in fall. Species breeding farther west and not migrating offshore in spring are, not surprisingly, less common in AK than overwater migrants that breed in far NE Asia, and 3 species (Northern Lapwing, Marsh Sandpiper, Broad-billed Sandpiper) are known in AK only from fall records.

Records of Asian species elsewhere in N America are mostly from fall–winter, and mainly in the West, where species recorded to date are Lesser and Greater Sand Plovers, Eurasian Dotterel, Spotted Redshank, Common Greenshank, Wood and Terek Sandpipers, Gray-tailed Tattler, Little and Eastern Curlews, Great Knot, Little, Temminck's, and Long-toed Stints, and Jack and Common Snipe. Away from Alaska, spring records of Asian shorebirds tend to be much less frequent than fall records, and likely reflect birds that overwintered in the New World and were detected migrating n. in spring. Rare shorebirds with spring records in the West include only Eurasian Dotterel, Spotted Redshank, Wood Sandpiper, Gray-tailed Tattler, and Little Stint.

The European shorebird species appear to arrive via both northern and southern routes (see pp. 8–10). Via the northern route, spring displacement of migrants headed to Iceland and Greenland has produced records in the Northeast of Eurasian Oystercatcher, European Golden Plover, Black-tailed Godwit, and Common Redshank; fall displacement may produce Eurasian Curlew; and hard-weather winter movements have produced Eurasian Woodcock, Jack and Common Snipe, and Northern Lapwing. Via the southern route, other species in the East may have first crossed the Atlantic in fall to winter in e. S America or the se. Caribbean, and then been detected moving n. in spring (and subsequently in fall). Such species likely include

Spotted Redshank, Common Greenshank, Terek Sandpiper, Little Stint, and perhaps Black-tailed Godwit and Eurasian Curlew. Several fall records of Asian shorebirds in the East likely involve birds that came from the w., across N America, such as Lesser Sand Plover, Spotted Redshank, Wood Sandpiper, Gray-tailed Tattler, Great Knot, Little Stint, and Broad-billed Sandpiper.

It appears that most potential vagrants within this globetrotting group have been recorded in N America, although possible future additions include Latham's Snipe *Gallinago hardwickii*, Swinhoe's Snipe *Gallinago megala*, Collared Pratincole *Glareola pratincola*, and perhaps the recently split Kentish Plover *Charadrius alexandrinus* (cf. Appendix B).

NORTHERN LAPWING *Vanellus vanellus*
28–31 cm (11–12.2")

Summary: *Newfoundland*: Almost annual in late fall–winter, with major influxes in some years; 1 spring record (2010). *Elsewhere in East*: Very rare or exceptional in late fall–winter, w. to OH and s. to FL; exceptional in summer. *Alaska*: 1 fall record from w. Aleutians (2006).

Taxonomy: Monotypic.

Distribution and Status:

World: Breeds across temperate Eurasia from Britain to ne. China and se. Russia (around 135°E); winters from W Europe and N Africa e. locally to s. China.

North America: *Newfoundland*: Almost annual during the late Oct–Mar period (mainly late Nov–Jan), with occasional major influxes as in 1966 (when hundreds occurred) and a recent small influx in 2010/2011. 1 spring record: 25 Apr 2010 (*NAB* 64:388). *Elsewhere in East*: Very rare or exceptional in winter (late Oct–Mar, mainly late Nov–Jan), with about 15 records from NS and scattered records in other coastal provinces and states s. to the Mid-Atlantic region, exceptionally s. to Highlands Co., FL (7 Dec 1997–4 Jan 1998; Pranty & Woolfenden 2000), and as far w. as Adams Co., OH (29–30 Dec 1994). 3 summer records: NB 5 May–22 Aug 1991; PEI, 13 Jul 1994; Kent Co., DE, 6–7 Jul 1996. *Alaska*: Shemya, 12 Oct 2006.

Comments: During harsh weather there can be very substantial westward winter movements of lapwings from their wintering areas in continental Europe to the frost- and snow-free regions of Britain and Ireland. Some birds, and occasionally

large numbers, overshoot, and if there are strong easterly winds across the N Atlantic then a few birds to hundreds may reach N America, as they did famously in 1927 and again in 1966 (Bagg 1967). It's interesting to note that these New World incursions follow a narrow corridor apparently defined by the width of 'suitable' winds, and as such may completely bypass Iceland. There were, for example, no unusual numbers of lapwings recorded in Iceland during the 1966 influx to NL. If lapwings arriving overwater encounter low-pressure systems on approaching the Northeast, then the prevailing winds may displace birds se. and back offshore, which may account for records from Bermuda and the relative paucity, in major flight years, of continental records s. of NL (Bagg 1967; Fig. 7, p. 9). Northern Lapwings in the e. Caribbean, however, may have arrived by a more easterly route via the trade winds, given that the species is a regular wanderer to the Azores.

The single spring record from NL coincided with e. winds and a flight of European Golden Plovers; thus it may have come from Iceland rather than from wintering grounds in the New World. The 3 summer records did not follow invasion years and may simply have been overlooked somewhere in the East in the preceding winters.

We would expect a few more records from extreme w. Alaska, but lapwings are relatively short-distance migrants in early spring and late fall, at which time there are few observers in the field. The single record may represent a misoriented (reverse?) migrant, or perhaps a migrant displaced by weather systems.

♂ breeding
(Mar–Aug)

adult ♂

narrower
hand

broad
hand

♀/1st-year

adult ♂
nonbreeding
(Aug–Mar)

Northern Lapwing

1st-year ♀
(Aug–Mar)

Field Identification: Large striking plover with long wispy crest; at a distance appears dark above and white below, and at close range shows green and purple sheens above.

Similar Species: None.

Age/Sex/Season: Ages and sexes differ slightly; slight seasonal variation. Complete pre-basic and partial preformative molts occur late summer–early winter, before winter dispersal; partial prealternate molt in late winter. **Adult male**: Broad rounded wings with 'swollen' hand apparent in flight; throat and chest shield solidly black in spring–summer; throat white in winter. **Adult female**: Broad rounded wings lack 'swollen' hand; throat and chest shield mottled whitish in spring–summer; throat white in winter. **1st-year**: Juv (unrecorded N America) has shorter crest than adult, scaly upperparts (beware, adult also has pale tips to upperparts in fresh basic plumage), buff notches on tertial fringes. By early winter resembles nonbreeding adult and difficult to age; 1st-winter averages narrower and browner breast shield, broader buff tips to scapulars and upperwing coverts. 1st-summer resembles breeding adult of respective sex. Male attains 'swollen' wing-tip by complete 2nd-prebasic molt.

Habitat and Behavior: Favors grassy and plowed fields, often far from water; also ranges to coastal mud flats and estuaries. Flight usually fairly high, with fairly deep, slightly clipped wingbeats. Common flight call a penetrating and distinctive *pway-eech*; hence a common local English name, Peewit.

EUROPEAN GOLDEN PLOVER *Pluvialis apricaria* 26–29 cm (10.2–11.5")

Summary: *Atlantic Canada and Quebec*: Almost annual but intermittent in spring to e. NL; very rare or exceptional elsewhere (mainly spring). *East Coast*: Single fall records from ME (2008), DE (2009). *Alaska*: Single records in summer (1980) and winter (2001).

Taxonomy: Northern breeders (sometimes separated as ssp *altifrons*) average more extensive black on face and underparts than s. breeders, but much variation and usually considered monotypic.

Status and Distribution:

World: Breeds from Iceland (and locally in e. Greenland) across N Europe to tundra of cen. Russia (around 100°E). Winters from W Europe s. to N Africa and e. to SW Asia.

North America: *Atlantic Canada and Quebec*: In NL, almost annual in spring in recent years, with major flights in 1961, 1978, 1988, 1992, 1994, 1995, and 2002; usually small flocks or even singles, but with max. 350 in spring 1988, 205 in

American Golden Plover

juv

juv

white wing-linings

dusky wing-linings

juv (Aug–Nov)

longer primary projection

finely patterned

some juvs washed gold above, especially rump

coarsely patterned

European
♂ breeding (Mar–Aug)

American
♂ breeding (Apr–Aug)

long tertials

1st-summer (Mar–Aug)

shorter primary projection

relatively short legs

juv (Aug–Oct)

European Golden Plover

spring 1994. Most birds occurred from mid–late Apr to mid-May, with a few lingering into Jun. Elsewhere, very rare in same spring period on SPM (max. 7 on 5 May 1994), exceptional in NS (mid–late May) and QC (2 late Jun–Jul records in 1988, following a large spring flight). Single fall records from NL (adult, Funk Island, 12 Aug 1988) and s-cen. NS (adult, 15–21 Oct 1988), both following a large spring flight. *East Coast*: Cumberland Co., ME, 9–11 Oct 2008 (adult; *NAB* 63:44); Kent Co., DE, 14–15 Sep 2009 (adult; *NAB* 64:46). *Alaska*: Barrow, 13 Jun 1980 (Gibson et al. 2003); Ketchikan, 13–14 Jan 2001 (1st-winter). **Comments:** There's little question that birds reaching e. N America are displaced en route to Iceland and/or Greenland, and they typically arrive with ne. winds. Most of these birds apparently relocate successfully, as there are practically no records away from NL, even though the biggest spring influxes may total in the thousands (Mactavish 1988), and spring golden plovers in

the Northeast draw attention. In s. Greenland, the pattern of occurrence is similar to that in NL, with adults being spring–summer vagrants, mainly late Apr–Jun, but also with a few 1st-years recorded in Sep–Oct.

In N America there are only 4 fall records from the Northeast (all of adults, or perhaps 1st-summers), which is surprising given the tendency of juv shorebirds to wander, although a juv European Golden Plover would be far less obvious in the autumn avifaunal landscape. The main fall departure from Iceland is in Sep–Oct, after adults have molted, yet the adults in ME and DE both retained blackish feathering on the belly. The NL and NS fall adults, both in 1988, followed a major spring flight and may have summered in N America, although the offshore island location of the NL bird suggests the possibility of a fall wanderer from Iceland or Greenland. Neither the ME or DE birds occurred after an exceptional spring flight.

The AK summer record, from the n. slope, may represent a drift-overshoot from Greenland or Iceland, given prevailing easterly winds at these high latitudes. The AK winter record, a 1st-year male (specimen), is anomalous and may represent a bird coming from the w., perhaps as a reverse-migrant; given the date, it was likely attempting to winter locally.

Field Identification: Old World counterpart to American Golden Plover but stockier and shorter winged (suggesting a small Black-bellied Plover), befitting its status as a shorter-distance migrant; note flashing white underwings. Although underwing, if well seen, clearly distinguishes European Golden Plover, apparent tone can vary strikingly depending on light intensity and angle.

Similar Species: Main concern is separation from American Golden and Pacific Golden Plovers; also cf. bright juv Black-bellied Plover in fall. *American Golden Plover* slightly smaller with more attenuated shape, longer primary projection, longer legs, dusky underwings. Breeding birds blacker below, often showing white only at neck sides, but females can show white on flanks and undertail coverts. Nonbreeding and juv grayer overall, with more distinct white eyebrow, less golden spangling on back. Voice usually a disyllabic whistled *pee-ee* with the 2nd syllable lower and sometimes inaudible. *Pacific Golden Plover* overall much more similar to European in plumage than is American, but also smaller and more delicate in proportions, with relatively longer legs and bill, dusky underwings. Breeding birds show more white on forehead, less white along flanks (often heavily flecked with black), and variably black-and-white to occasionally all-black undertail coverts. Nonbreeding and juv can be very similar to European. Voice distinct, a whistled *chu-wik* like hard Semipalmated Plover.

Age/Sex/Season: Ages/sexes differ slightly; seasonal variation pronounced in most birds. Complete prebasic and partial preformative molts of Icelandic birds usually occur late summer–fall, before migration, but W European birds often interrupt wing molt during migration; preformative molt can include some upperwing coverts, tertials, and rectrices. Partial prealternate molt in early spring, before migration. *Adult*: All rectrices with distinct pale barring; primaries relatively fresh in spring–summer; upperwings and tertials uniform in fall/winter. Breeding male averages more extensive black on face and underparts than female. *1st-year*: Juv tail darker

than adult with variable pale notching on feathers (often mixed with new, adult-like feathers in spring); primaries relatively worn and brownish in spring–summer; upperwings and tertials often with molt contrasts in fall/winter. By 1st summer resembles breeding adult but note retained juv remiges and usually some rectrices.

Habitat and Behavior: Meadows, agricultural fields, roosts in shallow water. Habits much like other golden plovers, and readily associates with other large plovers. Common call a plaintive, flat whistle, *peuu*.

LESSER SAND PLOVER *Charadrius mongolus* 18–20 cm (7.2–8")

Summary: *Alaska*: On w. and cen. Aleutians, uncommon in spring, rare in fall. On Bering Sea islands, very rare in spring, uncommon in fall. Very rare on n. and w. mainland; exceptional in s-coastal AK. *West*: Very rare in fall; 1 spring record from AB (1984). *East*: Exceptional in spring and fall, mostly on Atlantic and Gulf coasts, but once in ON.

Taxonomy: 5 ssp in 2 groups, the groups often separable in breeding plumage and perhaps representing separate species. N American specimens are referred to ssp *stegmanni* in *mongolus* group. See Garner et al. (2003) for more information.

C. [m.] atrifrons group of 3 ssp (Lesser Sand Plover; unrecorded N America) breeds interior S Cen Asia, winters from E Africa to SE Asia. Averages longer bill and legs than *mongolus* group but smaller in bulk overall. All plumages average paler upperparts than *mongolus* group, with clean white flanks, uppertail fairly concolorous with back, and extensive white on sides of tail coverts. Breeding male has forehead black (or virtually so) and lacks narrow black border separating white throat from rufous breast; breeding female relatively pale overall, without strongly contrasting face and chest pattern.

C. [m.] mongolus group of 2 ssp (Mongolian Sand Plover) breeds NE Asia, winters mainly from Philippines s. to Australia. Averages shorter bill and legs than *atrifrons* group but larger in bulk overall. All plumages average darker above than *atrifrons*, typically with dusky smudging on flanks, uppertail darker than back, and reduced white on sides of tail coverts. Breeding male has extensively white forehead and narrow black border separating white throat from rufous breast; breeding female relatively dark overall, typically with contrasting dark cheeks and breast band, some almost as bright as male.

Distribution and Status:

World: Breeds Cen and NE Asia (e. to Chukotka), winters E Africa to SE Asia and Australia (see Taxonomy, above).

North America: *Alaska*: On w. Aleutians, uncommon in spring (mid-May to Jun, exceptionally displaying birds to early Jul), mainly singles and small groups, max. 20 on Shemya, 31 May 1983; rare in fall (mid-Jul to mid-Sep). On cen. Aleutians, very rare in spring (mid-May to early Jun), exceptional in summer–fall (early Jul, mid–late Sep). On Bering Sea islands, very rare in spring (mid-May to early Jun; and bred in 2006 on St. Lawrence, *NAB* 60:565, 594), uncommon in fall (mid-Aug to Sep, all or almost all juvs), and exceptional in summer–early fall on Pribilofs (mid–late Jul). Very rare on n. and w. mainland (Jun to mid-Sep; has bred). 1 record from s-coastal AK, 10 Jun 1959. *West*: In Pacific states and provinces, very rare in fall (late Jun–Oct); about half of the 20 or so records involve breeding plumage adults in late Jun–Aug, the other half comprises juvs in Sep–Oct. 1 spring record; ne. AB, 18 Jun 1984. *East*: In fall, 2 adults from Atlantic Coast (mid–late Jul) in RI and NJ; a 1st-summer in VA (early Sep; *NAB* 64:51, 188); and 2 juvs from Gulf Coast (mid-Sep to mid-Oct) in LA and nw. FL. In spring (late Apr–early May), 2 adults from LA and ON.

Comments: Records from AK fit the common pattern of spring drift vagrants being commoner in the w. Aleutians, and fall misoriented (reverse-migrating?) juvs being commoner in the Bering Sea. West Coast fall records show the classic pattern of adults earlier and juvs later. It appears that some birds overwinter successfully in the New World, given spring records from LA and ON; the AB bird also may be part of this pattern. Northward migration of such birds appears not to include the West Coast.

As there are no records of Lesser Sand Plover from Iceland, the Azores, or the Caribbean, N American records in the East seem unlikely to involve birds that crossed the Atlantic, but *atrifrons* should always be considered for e. individuals. Despite the small sample size, records from the East show a dichotomy between earlier fall adults on the Atlantic coast and later juvs on the Gulf Coast.

A 1st-summer sand plover in VA, 6–8 Sep 2009 (*NAB* 64:51, 188) was accepted by the state committee only to the level of sand plover sp. (W. Ealding, pers. comm.), but we consider it

identifiable as a Lesser. Images we have seen, however, are of insufficient quality for us to determine which ssp group of Lesser was involved, although *mongolus* is more likely (individuals in 1st-summer plumage may not be easily identified to ssp group, even with good images).

Field Identification: All comments below refer to *mongolus* group, which is slightly larger, longer-legged, and often more upright in stance than Semipalmated Plover.

Similar Species: Generally distinctive in N American context, but cf. Snowy Plover, Greater Sand Plover. Differs from all small N American *Charadrius* plovers in lack of white hindcollar, dark legs, voice; rufous chest band distinctive in breeding plumage, but cf. Greater Sand Plover.

Age/Sex/Season: Ages differ, with adult appearance attained in 1st year; sexes differ in breeding plumage. Complete prebasic molt in fall–winter, wing molt mostly or wholly on nonbreeding grounds, and fall migrants often mostly or wholly in breeding plumage. Partial to incomplete preformative molts in fall–winter, mainly on nonbreeding grounds (incomplete primary molts follow eccentric pattern), with perhaps complete wing molt of some individuals through 1st summer. 2nd-prebasic molt averages earlier than on adult. Partial prealternate molt in late winter-spring, before migration. *Adult*: Primaries relatively fresh in spring–summer; upperwings and tertials uniform in fall/winter; primary molt mainly Sep–Feb. Breeding plumage has bright rufous chest band; male has black cheeks, female has dark brown cheeks, and often duller face and breast pattern overall. *1st-year*: Juv resembles nonbreeding plumage but in fall has neat, scaly buff fringes (quickly lost by wear and molt) on upperparts, fresh primaries; upperwings and tertials often show molt contrasts in 1st winter. In spring–summer, primaries relatively worn and brownish (some may have incomplete preformative molt, with fresher outer primaries); any primary molt mainly Feb–Jul. By 1st summer, some resemble breeding adult but average duller overall, with paler and less extensive rufous below; others retain nonbreeding aspect. Most can be aged by relatively worn juv remiges or eccentric primary molt pattern (see p. 39).

Habitat and Behavior: Coastal mud and sand flats, estuaries, beaches, lake shores; nests on tundra. Typical small plover, with walk-stop-peck feeding action. Common call a slightly trilled or

shorter, blunt-tipped bill

♀ breeding
(Apr–Sep)

nonbreeding

nonbreeding
(Sep–Apr)

darker, gray-green legs

♂ breeding
(Apr–Sep)

smudgy markings

juv
(Aug–Oct)

fine black border to
broad chest band

can look
long-legged
when feeding

Lesser Sand Plover

nonbreeding

longer, pointed bill

toes often
project
noticeably

nonbreeding
(Aug–Mar)

restricted
breast band

♂ breeding
(Mar–Aug)

clean sides
and flanks

juv
(Aug–Oct)

paler, yellow-green legs

♀ breeding
(Mar–Aug)

Greater Sand Plover

rattled *chi-tik* or *chi-ti-tit*, which may suggest Ruddy Turnstone.

GREATER SAND PLOVER *Charadrius leschenaultii* 20–23 cm (7.8–9")

Summary: *California*: 1 winter record (2001). *Florida*: 1 spring record (2009).

Taxonomy: 3 ssp, differing slightly in average bill size and breeding plumage, with extremes perhaps separable in the field. CA record thought to refer to nominate *leschenaultii* and FL record may also be this ssp.

Relatively slender-billed *columbinus* breeds Turkey and Middle East. Shorter-distance migrant, wintering mainly in Red Sea region and ne. Africa, and molting 1–2 months earlier than e. ssp. In breeding plumage, averages paler face and more extensive rufous on underparts than e. ssp.

Stouter-billed *leschenaultii* and *crassirostris* breed in Cen Asia. Longer-distance migrants, wintering to South Africa and Australia. Average later molt and, in breeding plumage, darker face and less extensive rufous on underparts than *columbinus*.

Status and Distribution:

World: Breeds from Turkey e. to Cen Asia (around 110°E). Winters mainly on coasts, from S and E Africa e. across S Asia to Australia.

North America: *California*: Marin Co., 29 Jan–8 Apr 2001. *Florida*: Duval Co., 14–26 May 2009 (*NAB* 63:414, 532).

Comments: It's not surprising that a species that doesn't breed or winter within many thousands of km of N America has only occurred twice, but those 2 occurrences reinforce the idea that any long-distance migrant, no matter what its normal range, is a possible vagrant to N America. Note too that there is a Jul 2002 record from Iceland.

Although found in late Jan, it is likely the CA bird arrived the preceding fall but was overlooked. It has been suggested that the CA bird was a misoriented reverse-migrant that headed to CA rather than South Africa; interestingly, it continued to molt through the winter, as it would have in a S Hemisphere environment but unlike shorebirds in the N Hemisphere temperate environment where it wintered (Abbott et al. 2001).

The FL bird showed characters of a breeding male *leschenaultii* and could have come from either direction, perhaps after wintering in the New World.

Field Identification: Medium-sized 'ringed' plover that recalls Wilson's Plover in size and shape. See illustration on p. 147.

Similar species: Only real concern is separation from Lesser Sand Plover (formerly Mongolian Plover), but also cf. nonbreeding plumages of Wilson's Plover and Mountain Plover.

Relative to **Lesser Sand Plover**, Greater is slightly larger and bulkier with its relaxed posture more horizontal overall, which may suggest Black-bellied Plover (Lesser is more upright and recalls Semipalmated Plover); bill of Greater is slightly longer and heavier with a slightly more pointed (less blunt) tip; legs (especially tibia) slightly longer and typically paler, yellow-olive to pinkish green (vs. darker, olive-gray on Lesser); white wingstripe of Greater tends to be narrow and less distinct on inner wing and contrastingly wide on inner primaries, versus more evenly broad throughout on Lesser. In breeding plumage, adult Greater has narrower rufous breast band without fine black upper border typical of *mongolus* group Lesser; however, females have less rufous than males, and 1st-summers notably variable. Also beware geographic variation. See Taylor (1982), Shirihai et al. (1996), Hirshfeld et al. (2000), and Abbott et al. (2001) for further information on identification and geographic variation.

Age/Sex/Season: Ages differ, with adult appearance attained in 1st year; sexes differ slightly in breeding plumage. Complete prebasic molt in late summer to mid-winter, wing molt often interrupted for fall migration, and head and body molt often extensive by fall migration. Partial to incomplete preformative molts in fall–winter, mainly on nonbreeding grounds (incomplete primary molts follow eccentric pattern), with perhaps complete wing molt of some individuals through 1st summer. 2nd-prebasic molt averages earlier than adult. Partial prealternate molt in late winter–early spring, before migration. **Adult**: Primaries relatively fresh in spring–summer; upperwings and tertials uniform in fall/winter; primary molt mainly Aug–Jan. Breeding plumage has bright rufous chest band; male has black cheeks, female has dark brown cheeks, and often duller face and breast pattern overall. **1st-year**: Juv resembles nonbreeding plumage but in fall has neat, scaly buff fringes (quickly lost by wear and molt) on upperparts, fresh primaries; upperwings and tertials often show molt contrasts in 1st winter. In spring–summer, primaries relatively worn and brownish (some have fresher outer primaries);

any primary molt mainly Feb–Jul. By 1st summer, some resemble breeding adult but average duller overall, others retain nonbreeding aspect. Most can be aged by relatively worn juv remiges or eccentric primary molt pattern (see p. 39).

Habitat and Behavior: Coastal mud and sand flats, beaches. Typical plover with walk-stop-peck feeding action. Common call a musical, slightly trilled *chi-it* or *tri-it-it*, may suggest Ruddy Turnstone and perhaps not safely told from Lesser Sand Plover, pending critical study (Hirschfeld et al. 2000).

LITTLE RINGED PLOVER *Charadrius dubius* 15–17 cm (5.8–6.7")

Summary: *Alaska*: Exceptional in late spring on w. Aleutians.

Taxonomy: 3 ssp, not known to be separable in the field; only the wide-ranging Eurasian ssp *curonicus*, to which the N American specimen is referred, is considered here.

Distribution and Status:

World: Breeds from W Europe and N Africa e. across Eurasia to se. Russia (to Sakhalin and w. side of Sea of Okhotsk) and Japan, mainly at mid-latitudes; also resident from Indian subcontinent and SE Asia locally to New Guinea. Northern populations winter mainly in sub-Saharan Africa and from SE Asia to Indonesia.

North America: *Alaska*: Buldir, 15–16 Jun 1974 (male); Attu, 18–30 May 1986; Shemya, 18–19 May 1988.

Comments: Little Ringed Plover breeds well s. and w. of w. AK, and is unreported from Kamchatka or the Commander Islands. The few Alaskan records are consistent with drift-overshoots, given the species' range, migration behavior, and abundance. Fall records also seen possible.

It is perhaps surprising there are no records of Little Ringed Plover from Iceland or Greenland, especially given this species' steady expansion in Britain; it is the only relatively common and widespread W European shorebird still undetected there. Little Ringed Plover is also scarce in the Azores, with 4 or fewer records in the last 20 years. There is a single recent record for the Caribbean, an adult female on Martinique, 17 Apr 2005 (Lemoine 2005), so records in e. N America are not entirely out of the question. Perhaps the greatest reason for the lack of vagrancy in the species is that its normal migration movements are largely north-south across continental land masses, with no major coastal staging areas or long overwater flights.

Field Identification: Small 'ringed' plover, appearing small-headed and slender overall; note bright yellow orbital ring (adult), pale pinkish legs.

Similar Species: All small 'ringed' plovers are somewhat similar, but Little Ringed is rather

♀ breeding (Mar–Aug)

attenuated rear end

wing-bar faint or absent

white across crown

♂ breeding (Mar–Aug)

juv (Aug–Oct)

adult nonbreeding (Aug–Mar)

Little Ringed Plover

distinctive. Note its yellowish-pink legs, slender dark bill (pink base to lower mandible in some breeding birds), prominent yellowish orbital ring, and indistinct wingstripe. Long tertials largely cover the primaries, thus has less primary projection than other ringed plovers; tail tip projects slightly past wing-tips. Nonbreeding plumages lack pronounced white eyebrow, so head appears dark overall.

Age/Sex/Season: Ages differ; sexes differ in breeding plumage. Complete prebasic and partial to incomplete preformative molts in fall to midwinter, interrupted for migration, and finished on staging or nonbreeding grounds; preformative molt rarely may be complete; many birds in Europe migrate in juv plumage. Partial prealternate molt in late winter–spring, before migration. *Adult*: Primaries relatively fresh in spring–summer; upperwings and tertials uniform in fall/winter. Breeding male averages more extensive black on face than female. *1st-year*: Primaries relatively worn and brownish in spring–summer (some may have complete preformative molt and be indistinguishable from adult); upperwings and tertials often with molt contrasts in fall/winter. By 1st summer resembles breeding adult but most can be told by relatively worn juv remiges, sometimes also worn and faded juv rump feathers and lesser upperwing coverts, and brown patches in black chest band.

Habitat and Behavior: Typical 'ringed' plover but often rather solitary and not joining flocks of other small shorebirds. Prefers freshwater margins and estuaries, rather than coastal mudflats. Flight call a whistled, downslurred *pew*.

EURASIAN DOTTEREL *Charadrius morinellus* 20–23 cm (7.8–9")

Summary: *Alaska*: On w. Aleutians, very rare in fall but unrecorded in spring. On Bering Sea islands and n. mainland, very rare in late spring but unrecorded in fall. 1 fall record from s-coastal mainland. *Pacific States and Provinces*: Very rare in fall; 1 winter record from CA (2001), 1 spring record from BC (2008).

Taxonomy: Monotypic.

Status and Distribution:

World: Breeds locally across N Eurasia (e. to Chukotka), probably also in w. AK. Winters from N Africa e. to the Middle East.

North America: *Alaska*: Probably breeds (or bred?) sparingly and irregularly on mountains adjoining the Bering Strait and on Seward

Peninsula, based on presence of pairs and collection of females with internally well-formed eggs; no nests or young found. Formerly almost annual in early Jun on St. Lawrence (once 4 birds together), but none since 2002. On w. Aleutians, 6 fall records (late Aug to mid-Sep), 2 involving 2 birds. In n. AK, exceptional in late spring (early–late Jun, at least 5 records). 1 fall record from s-coastal mainland, 27 Aug 1981. *Pacific States and Provinces*: Very rare in fall (late Aug to mid-Oct; remaining till late Nov), with over half of the birds first found in early to mid-Sep, including 2 together in Del Norte Co., CA, 9–12 Sep 1992. 1 winter record: Imperial Co., CA, 22–23 Jan 2001. 1 spring record: Queen Charlotte Is., BC, 23 Apr 2008 (*NAB* 62:466). All fall–winter records of known-age birds from AK and the West Coast in the period have involved 1st-years, but a 1934 specimen from WA is reportedly an adult (Wahl et al. 2005).

Comments: Who knows how many dotterels breed on the remote mountaintops of nw. AK? Adults may fly direct to the breeding areas unless knocked down by contrary weather, a pattern known from Europe. Interestingly, there are no spring records from the Aleutians and no fall records from St. Lawrence Island, suggesting birds arrive in n. AK from the w. and that fall migrants overfly the Bering Sea on their initial flight. There are no records from the Pribilofs in either season. The relatively early spring date of the BC bird suggests it wintered somewhere in the Americas; in addition to the mid-winter record from s. CA, a dotterel wintered in Baja California, Mexico, Jan–Mar 1998.

There were 3 records (May, Sep–Oct) from Iceland through 2007. There are no records from the se. Caribbean but a mid-Sep 1958 specimen from Bermuda and 12 records (mainly Sep–Oct) from the Azores since 2003, suggesting that records in e. N America are possible.

Field Identification: Striking and attractive, medium-sized plover of tundra and grassy habitats. Note bold whitish eyebrow, narrow white breast band, plain wings.

Similar Species: None in N America, but cf. juv Pacific Golden Plover, juv and nonbreeding Mountain Plover.

Age/Sex/Season: Ages differ, with adult appearance attained in 2nd year; sexes differ slightly in breeding plumage. Complete prebasic molt in fall–winter, wing molt on nonbreeding grounds, but head and body molt can start late summer–fall; fall migrants often mostly in

♀ breeding

plain
wings

juv

♀ breeding
(Apr–Aug; ♂ duller)

juv
(Aug–Oct)

adult
nonbreeding
(Aug–Apr)

Eurasian Dotterel

breeding plumage. Partial to incomplete preformative molt in fall--winter, sometimes starting on
breeding grounds or migration; some birds molt
outer primaries in 1st winter. Partial prealternate
molt in late winter–spring, before migration.
Adult: Primaries uniformly relatively fresh in
spring–summer; upperwings and tertials uniform
in fall/winter. Breeding plumage has chestnut
breast and blackish belly; male averages duller
than female, with less solidly black crown.
Nonbreeding plumage has whitish underparts,
cinnamon edgings to upperparts. *1st-year*: Juv
resembles nonbreeding plumage but buffier
overall with pale cinnamon wash to underparts,
scapulars have spangled buff fringes, primaries
fresh; upperwings and tertials often show molt
contrasts in 1st winter. In 1st summer, overall
resembles nonbreeding but with some rufous
mottling on breast; also note relatively worn juv
remiges or eccentric primary molt pattern
(see p. 39).

Habitat and Behavior: Rocky tundra and
mountaintops, grasslands and plains, often far
from water. Typical plover feeding action. Flight

calls include a low, burry *ehrr* and a fairly quiet,
slightly plaintive *teup*.

EURASIAN OYSTERCATCHER
Haematopus ostralegus 40–47.5 cm (15.5–18.5")

Summary: *Newfoundland*: Exceptional in
spring and fall. *Alaska*: 1 spring record from
w. Aleutians (2012).
Taxonomy: 3 ssp recognized, differing primarily in bill length but not certainly separable in
the field (bill averages longest in E Asia, short-
est in Europe). N American records in the East
presumably nominate *ostralegus* of W Eurasia,
whereas AK record presumably involved E Asian
ssp *osculans*.
Status and Distribution:
World: Breeds from Iceland and NW Europe
e. into Cen Asia, disjunctly in coastal E Asia, n. to
Kamchatka; winters coastally from W Europe to
N Africa and the Middle East, and from Korea
to s. China.
North America: *Newfoundland*: 3 records
(ages unknown) from e. NL: 22–25 May 1994,

American
Oystercatcher
adult (year-round)

white rump and back

Eurasian

all birds have
white collar in
nonbreeding plumage

American

longer white stripe

Eurasian
adult breeding
(Feb–Aug)

note back, leg, and eye
color, also bill shape

1st-year
(Sep–Mar)

**Eurasian
Oystercatcher**

Eurasian (left) with American

3 Apr–2 May 1999, 5 Aug 2006. *Alaska*: Buldir, 26 May–13 Jun 2012 (adult).

Comments: Eurasian Oystercatcher is a common summer resident in Iceland and, while considered a rare vagrant in Greenland (with 25 records in the w. of the country, Apr–Oct), it's one of the most frequently recorded nonbreeding shorebirds there. It is also a regular vagrant to the Azores, averaging slightly less than 1 bird every other year. It's perhaps surprising there haven't been more records in NL, where every oystercatcher is scrutinized, but should one reach MA or points s., where oystercatchers are routine, it might be overlooked in spite of major differences in appearance.

In E Asia, Eurasian Oystercatcher breeds in Kamchatka and has been collected in the Commander Islands, albeit in 1893, and an AK record in spring was almost expected.

Field Identification: Old World counterpart of American Oystercatcher.

Similar Species: Relative to American Oystercatcher, Eurasian has blackish (vs. brownish) upperparts, red eyes, and deeper pink legs; adult has less swollen bill; nonbreeding birds have white foreneck collar. Eurasian is obvious in flight, with white back stripe, longer white wingstripe, and extensive white at base of tail.

Age/Sex/Season: Ages differ, with adult appearance attained in 2nd year; sexes similar; seasonal variation in adults. Adult has complete prebasic molt late summer–winter, often interrupted for migration, rarely arrested in midwinter with outer primaries retained; partial prealternate molt in late winter–spring. 1st-year has partial preformative molt in fall–winter, possibly a second partial molt in late winter–spring (needs study). *Adult*: Bill lacks dark tip, eyes and legs bright; upperparts blacker overall. *1st-year*: Bill tipped dusky, eyes dull, legs paler than adult; upperparts browner overall and retains white foreneck collar through 1st summer. *2nd-year*: Resembles adult but may retain traces of dark bill through 2nd winter.

Habitat and Behavior: Like American Oystercatcher, but in parts of its range has spread inland, sometimes far from saltwater coastline. Calls similar to American Oystercatcher, including a loud, far-carrying, shrill *peep*, often repeated rapidly.

BLACK-WINGED STILT *Himantopus himantopus* 35–40 cm (13.5–15.5")

Summary: *Alaska*: Exceptional in spring on w. Aleutians and Bering Sea islands.

...ways has white upper back
(black on Black-necked)

♂ (right) with Black-necked Stilt

dult ♂ variation

white upper back not
apparent when hunched

white
eye patch

♀ has dark
brownish back

adult ♂

adult ♀

retained juv
coverts

Black-winged
tilt

1st-year ♀
(Aug–Feb)

Taxonomy: Taxonomy uncertain, sometimes considered conspecific with Black-necked Stilt of New World. Old World Black-winged Stilt either monotypic or with 2 ssp: nominate *himantopus* breeds widely across warmer regions of Eurasia and Africa; *leucocephalus* breeds from Philippines to New Zealand, has wandered exceptionally n. to Japan (Brazil 2009). Nominate adult typically has variable dark smudging on head and hindneck (rarely all-white), versus solidly black hindneck of *leucocephalus*; 1st-years probably not safely identifiable to ssp in field. N American records are considered to be of nominate *himantopus*.

Distribution and Status:

World: Widespread in Old World (breeding e. to sw. corner of Sea of Okhotsk); n. populations migratory, wintering mainly in sub-Saharan Africa and SE Asia.

North America: *Alaska*: Nizki, 24 May–3 Jun 1983; Pribilofs, 15 May 2003; Shemya, 1–9 Jun 2003 (2).

Comments: In E Asia, Black-winged Stilts occur regularly as spring overshoots to n. Japan and

Sakhalin, rarely to s. Kamchatka, and the AK records are consistent with spring drift-overshoots. We have no data on age or sex of the AK birds.

Field Identification: Old World counterpart to Black-necked Stilt.

Similar Species: Very similar in structure and plumage to Black-necked Stilt but distinguishable in all plumages by restricted black or dusky on head and neck (white upper back not always obvious), and lack of discrete white area over eye. Nonbreeding adult can appear white headed, as new dusky head feathers have white tips.

Age/Sex/Season: Ages differ, with adult appearance attained in 2nd fall/winter; sexes differ; slight seasonal variation. Adult has complete prebasic molt late summer–winter, often interrupted for migration; partial prealternate molt in late winter–spring. 1st-year has partial to incomplete preformative molt in fall–winter (often including some to all rectrices), possibly a second partial molt in late winter–spring (needs study). *Male*: Upperparts glossy black. *Female*: Back dark brownish, contrasting with black wings. ***1st-year***: Upperparts sooty brownish gray with buff fringes (soon fading and abrading), secondaries and inner primaries tipped white; legs paler pink than adult; eye dull (red by mid–late winter). By 1st winter resembles adult of respective sex but usually retains some juv wing coverts, which are molted by spring; note white-tipped secondaries through 1st summer. Attains adult appearance by 2nd-prebasic molt in 2nd fall–winter.

Habitat and Behavior: Much as Black-necked Stilt, including similar voice.

EURASIAN WOODCOCK *Scolopax rusticola* 33–36 cm (13–14.2")

Summary: *New Jersey:* 1 winter record (1956).
Taxonomy: Monotypic.
Distribution and Status:

World: Breeds in boreal and temperate forest zones from W Europe e. across Eurasia to e. Russia (Sakhalin and w. side of Sea of Okhotsk) and n. Japan; winters primarily in W and S Europe, n. India, s. Japan, and SE Asia.

North America: *New Jersey*: Cape May Co., 2–9 Jan 1956.
Comments: Eurasian Woodcock was a very rare visitor to e. N America in the late 1800s. It's not clear why there have been so few records in more recent times, given that there have been

3 from Greenland during the 1900s and over 500 records from Iceland (where there has been no visible decline in frequency, and where the species now breeds, at least on occasion). There are 4 recent records of American Woodcock from Bermuda, so it seems plausible that the larger Eurasian Woodcock could make it to N America given a strong wind assist. Perhaps it's simply that woodcock hunting, like rail hunting (see Corncrake) is not as popular in the Northeast as it once was, and those few birds that do arrive now pass undetected; most ne. N America arrivals would be in late Oct–early Nov (the fall push of birds into Iceland begins in mid-Oct) when conditions can be harsh and field activities are at a diminished level.

Given the E Asian breeding range, a vagrant to AK in late fall does not seem out of the question.
Field Identification: Old World counterpart to American Woodcock, which is appreciably smaller.

Similar Species: More than 20% larger than American Woodcock; otherwise separated by barred underparts, barred flight feathers and coverts, and normal outer primaries (vs. narrow and modified for sound production on American). At rest, primaries of Eurasian project well beyond tertials (no projection on American).

Age/Sex/Season: Ages/sexes similar; no seasonal variation. Complete prebasic molt and

Eurasian

barred

American
Woodcock

Eurasian
Woodcock

plain

partial to incomplete preformative molt (can include tail) occur in fall, mostly before migration; partial prealternate molt reported in late winter–spring. *1st-year*: Some may be distinguishable in winter by molt contrasts in upperwing coverts, and 1st-summer has outer primaries browner and more faded than adult. Pale tips to primary coverts average wider but duller than adult.

Habitat and Behavior: Similar to American Woodcock. Unlike American Woodcock, Eurasian's wings don't 'twitter' in flight, but flushed birds may give a harsh *shaap* call, similar to snipe.

JACK SNIPE *Lymnocryptes minimus* 17–19 cm (6.7–7.5")

Summary: *Alaska*: Exceptional in spring and fall on Bering Sea islands; 1 fall record from s-coastal AK (2010). *Pacific States and Provinces*: Exceptional in fall–winter. *Newfoundland*: 1 winter record (2011).

Taxonomy: Monotypic.

Status and Distribution:

World: Breeds in taiga zone from Scandinavia e. across Russia to around 160°E; winters locally from W Europe s. to sub-Saharan Africa and e. to Indian subcontinent.

North America: *Alaska*: In spring, single records from Pribilofs, 16–17 Jun 2004, and St. Lawrence, 4–7 Jun 2008 (*NAB* 62:602). In fall, singles on Pribilofs, 11–19 Sep 2010, 11 Sep 2012 (St. Paul Island Tour), and in s-coastal AK, 16 Oct 2010 (NAB 65:142). *Pacific States and Provinces*: 4 winter records, 3 shot by hunters: Colusa Co., CA, 2 Dec 1990; Lane Co., OR, 20 Oct 2004 and 16 Nov 2007; and Clatsop Co., OR, 4 Jan 2009 (D. Irons, pers. comm.). *Newfoundland*: In the se., 14 Feb 2011 (*NAB* 65:234-235).

Comments: Jack Snipe are amazing. They get everywhere, it seems, but are virtually undetectable given their marshy preferences and cryptic ways. They are long-distance migrants breeding at high latitudes, yet there are only a few recent spring and fall records from AK. Remarkably, 2 of the 3 OR records involve birds shot by Greg Stender, an avid snipe hunter, in a 3-year span. Mr. Stender (pers. comm.) noted that he wasn't aware what he was shooting in the first instance but had an inkling in the second. Still, snipe hunting in the wind and rain is largely reflexive and comes close to random sampling. Imagine how many Jack Snipe must occur undetected. There are also earlier records from AK in spring (1919) and CA in winter, again collected (1938).

There were 179 records from Iceland through 2006, mainly in recent years, where the species is found by looking in ditches carrying heated geothermal water, especially when the rest of the ground is covered with snow (Y. Kolbeinsson, pers. comm.). It is thus unsurprising that the occasional bird reaches ne. N America.

all plumages similar

Jack Snipe

short bill

dark central crown

In addition to the recent NL record there is a Dec 1927 specimen from NL, in the year of a great Northern Lapwing flight (O. L. Austin 1929).

There have been more than 25 Jack Snipe records from the Azores since 2000, and a there is a single mid-Nov 1960 specimen from Barbados (1st-year), suggesting substantial overwater capacity. Jack Snipe are notably solitary, however, and what few might winter in the se. Caribbean or ne. S America seem unlikely to join Wilson's Snipe or other shorebirds on their migration to N America.

Field Identification: Small, notably short-billed snipe with bold golden-buff back stripes.

Similar Species: ***Wilson's and Common Snipe*** are appreciably larger with long bills (beware, recently fledged juvs can have relatively short bills, mainly in Jun–Jul), pale median crown stripes, and barred flanks; both lack distinctive bouncing gait when feeding (but Wilson's, at least, can bob quite strongly at times), typically call when flushed, and often fly farther and more strongly.

Age/Sex/Season: Ages/sexes similar; no seasonal variation. Prebasic and presumed partial preformative molts occur before fall migration; prealternate molt in spring includes tail. *1st-year*: Not known to be distinguishable from adult.

Habitat and Behavior: Wet meadows and pool margins, much as Wilson's Snipe. Typically flushes from underfoot, silently and without towering; usually flies only a short distance before dropping back to cover, where can be very difficult to find or flush again. Has a distinctive bouncing action when feeding.

SOLITARY SNIPE *Gallinago solitaria*
29–31 cm (11.5–12.3")

Summary: *Alaska*: 1 fall record from Bering Sea islands (2008); 1 spring record from w. Aleutians (2010).

Taxonomy: 2 ssp usually recognized, not separable in the field. N American specimen is consistent with e. ssp *japonica*.

Status and Distribution:

World: Disjunct range in Cen and E Asia, from n. India n. and e. to ne. Russia (Kamchatka). Winters mostly in or adjacent to breeding range but some birds (presumably from ne. parts of breeding range) winter s. to Japan and Korea.

North America: *Alaska*: Pribilofs, 10 Sep 2008 (Bieber & Schuette 2009); Attu, 24 May 2010 (Withrow & Sonneborn 2011).

Comments: As with many shorebird records in AK, the N American records likely represent a drift vagrant in spring and a misoriented or displaced migrant in fall.

Field Identification: Large, rather pot-bellied, and very long-billed dark snipe. Besides size and shape, note heavy dark barring on breast and flanks, long and continuous dark eyeline from bill to nape, relatively narrow whitish mantle and scapular braces, and mostly plain grayish uppertail overts.

Similar Species: None in N America, although all snipe and woodcock are somewhat similar,

all plumages similar

heavy barring

gray

Solitary Snipe

especially given typical (flushed) views. **Common**, **Wilson's**, and **Pin-tailed Snipe** all appreciably smaller with less extensive dark barring below and overall buffier, less dark and reddish. **Eurasian Woodcock** (unknown in AK) is fatterbodied and shorter billed, with less patterned face, banded nape, broad black distal tail band, and primaries projecting beyond tertials at rest.

See Bieber & Schuette (2009) for further information on identification, including discussion of other Asian species.

Age/Sex/Season: Ages may differ slightly as in other snipe (not well known); sexes similar; no seasonal variation.

Habitat and Behavior: In normal range, prefers damp valleys, wooded watercourses, and bogs. Most common vocalization when flushed is a harsh *pench*, somewhat similar to Common Snipe (Brazil 2009).

PIN-TAILED SNIPE *Gallinago stenura*
25–27 cm (9.8–10.7")

Summary: *Alaska*: Exceptional in spring on w. Aleutians; 1 fall record from Bering Sea islands (2012).

Taxonomy: Monotypic. Often known in Old World as Pintail Snipe.

Distribution and Status:

World: Breeds s. of tundra zone in cen. and ne. Russia (e. to e. Chukotka); winters mainly in Indian subcontinent and SE Asia.

North America: *Alaska*: At least 3 spring records, all on Attu: 25 May 1991, 19 May 1998, 17 May 2010 (Withrow & Sonneborn 2011). 1 fall record: Pribilofs, 28 Jul–26 Aug 2012 (St. Paul Island Tour).

Comments: The 3 spring records are all specimens and presumably involve drift vagrants, although, at the latitude of the Aleutians, Pin-tailed Snipe nests no closer than the w. side of the Sea of Okhotsk (Brazil 2009) and is only a straggler to Kamchatka. A record from Attu on 30 May 1998 (*FN* 53:374) also likely involved Pin-tailed Snipe but was not collected.

The recent Pribilofs bird was photographed and recorded in flight; although the diagnostic outer rectrices could not be seen, the bird showed characters of Pin-tailed Snipe (and was obviously not Common or Wilson's), including long toe projection and call (both of which argue against Swinhoe's Snipe, see below). Despite the early date it may have been a misoriented juv,

given fresh-looking plumage and apparently narrow pale edgings to the scapulars.

As noted for Common Snipe, digital cameras are becoming the new shotguns for identifying cryptic and challenging species, and the observers of the Pribilofs bird deserve a lot of credit for their careful documentation.

Field Identification: Very similar to Wilson's and Common Snipe but with 24–28 rectrices, the outer 7–9 pairs extremely narrow and 'pin-like'. See Carey & Olsson (1995), and Leader &Carey (2003) for further information. See illustration on p. 158.

Similar Species: Distinguished from **Wilson's** and **Common Snipe** with great care. Diagnostic outer tail feathers extremely difficult to see in the field but critical for certain identification (see Swinhoe's Snipe, below). All of the following differences are subtle but collectively may be helpful in picking out a Pin-tailed candidate. Relative to Wilson's and Common, Pin-tailed averages slightly larger bodied and plumper, but with a shorter tail (toes often project more noticeably in flight) and shorter bill, and often has a slightly 'bug-eyed' or surprised expression caused by large eyes and relatively narrow and more even-width dark loral stripe. Juv also has narrower fringes to outer webs of lower scapulars than Common or Wilson's. Differs from Common Snipe also by narrow, diffuse pale trailing edge to secondaries, and darker, fully barred underwing much like Wilson's. Averages warmer brown overall than Wilson's, similar to Common; in flight, upperside of remiges may average paler and grayer than Common (study needed).

Swinhoe's Snipe unrecorded in N America but a possible (if unlikely?) vagrant; breeds taiga and forest-steppe zones of cen. and e. Russia, winters SE Asia. No confirmed characters for field separation from Pin-tailed (Leader & Carey 2003) unless diagnostic outer rectrices can be seen, likely only discernible in-hand: usually 20–22 rectrices with outer 5–7 pairs progressively narrower outward, but not pin-like. However, longer tail of Swinhoe's means that toes often project less than on Pin-tailed, and differences in call between Swinhoe's (lower, gruffer) and Pin-tailed (higher, more nasal) seem useful but require further study (Leader & Carey 2003).

Age/Sex/Season: Ages differ slightly; sexes similar; no seasonal variation. Complete prebasic molt in fall–early winter, often interrupted for migration. Partial to incomplete preformative molt occurs fall–winter, with tail molted on wintering

Common Snipe
all ages similar; averages warmer and buffier overall than Wilson's, but both species variable; no reliable plumage features known for standing birds

broad white trailing edge

Common   Wilson's

diagnostic outermost rectrix narrow and parallel-sided with broader dark bars in Wilson's; broader and rounded with wider-spaced, narrow bars in Common

Common

note secondary tip pattern

whiter underwing (much variation)

outer tail feathers visible when stretching

narrow white trailing edge

Wilson's Snipe
all ages similar

narrow white tips hook around

darker underwing (much variation)

faint trailing edge

note facial expression

narrower outer rectrices with bolder dark bars

relatively short bill

Pin-tailed Snipe
all ages similar

pin-like outer tail feathers

grounds. Extent and timing of any prealternate molt unknown. **Adult**: In fall, wings relatively worn or molt interrupted with fresher inner primaries; scapulars with broad buff fringes to outer webs. **1st-year**: In fall, wings uniformly fresh and juv scapulars with narrow whitish fringes to outer webs; molts scapulars and upperwing coverts in fall–winter, after which some may be aged in 1st winter by molt contrasts in greater coverts and perhaps tertials. Aging criteria in spring unknown, but juv primaries likely relatively worn and faded relative to fresher and darker adult feathers.

Habitat and Behavior: Similar to Wilson's and Common Snipe but more often in drier habitats. Calls on being flushed include a short *etch* and *chet* (P. Holt, pers. comm.), often slightly drier, more nasal, and squeakier than Wilson's Snipe. In flight display (unknown in N America) gives intensifying 'whisking' calls, which suggest a fast-cutting scythe, before diving to produce a slightly metallic, vibrating rush that ends with a whooshing crescendo (M. Robb, recording).

COMMON SNIPE *Gallinago gallinago*
25–27 cm (9.8–10.7")

Summary: *Alaska*: On w. Aleutians, fairly common to rare in spring, rare in summer–fall, exceptional in winter. On cen. Aleutians, very rare in spring. On Bering Sea islands occurs spring and fall, but much rarer on St. Lawrence than Pribilofs. *Newfoundland*: 1 winter record (2011). *California*: 1 winter record (2011)

Taxonomy: 2 ssp, not separable in the field, but Iceland birds (*faeroeensis*) average more rufescent overall than *gallinago* of Eurasia. AK specimens are referred to nominate *gallinago*.

Distribution and Status:

World: Breeds in Iceland and across N and mid-latitude Eurasia from W Europe to ne. Russia (Kamchatka, Chukotka). Winters from W Europe s. to Cen Africa and e. to Indian subcontinent, SE Asia, and s. Japan.

North America: *Alaska*: On w. Aleutians, fairly common to rare in spring (late Apr–early Jun), with daily counts up to 20 birds not unusual, max. 50 on Attu, 16–19 May 1998; rare to uncommon in fall (Aug to mid-Oct); very rare into summer and has bred, exceptional in winter. On cen. Aleutians, very rare in spring (mid-May to early Jun). On Pribilofs, uncommon to rare in spring (mid-May to mid-Jun, very rarely displaying birds into late Jul) and rare in fall (mid-Aug to early Oct). On St. Lawrence, very rare in spring (mainly late May–early Jun) and very rare or exceptional in fall (late Aug–Sep). *Newfoundland*: In the se., 19 Feb 2011 and 22 Feb 2011 (2) (*NAB* 65:235, 379). *California*: Riverside Co., 11 Dec 2011 (shot by hunter).

Comments: The first recent N American winter record came from NL (whence there is also a winter specimen from Dec 1927; O. L. Austin 1929), and, as with Wilson's Snipe in Europe,

digital photos may start to replace the hunter's bag as a means of documenting rare snipe. Common Snipe is a common breeder in Iceland and apparently a regular vagrant to Greenland, but even though Icelandic Common Snipe average warmer-toned than nominate *gallinago* (and thus would be the most different in the context of Wilson's Snipe), detection of a vagrant requires good views and preferably the opportunity to study a bird and recheck features—difficult, at best, when the typical view of a snipe is a surprise encounter as a bird flies quickly away from underfoot.

The recent CA winter record may represent the tip of the iceberg for records of Common Snipe in w. N America away from the AK islands, but detection is extremely difficult. Greg Stender, the Oregon snipe hunter who shot both Jack Snipe (see p. 155), has for years been looking unsuccessfully for both Common Snipe and Pin-tailed Snipe in his take. However, with greater awareness of field characters and widespread use of digital cameras, we suspect further records of Common Snipe will start to trickle in from locations other than the AK islands (and cf. Jack Snipe).

Field Identification: Old World counterpart to Wilson's Snipe, which is extremely similar in appearance. See Carey and Olsson (1995), Bland (1998), and Leader (1999) for further notes on identification. See illustration on p. 158.

Similar Species: Common and *Wilson's Snipe* are so similar (and variable) that certain field recognition may not be possible unless the outer rectrices and tips to the secondaries are closely observed (and photographed) or the characteristic flight 'drum' is heard (and preferably recorded). Common typically has 14 rectrices (typically 16 on Wilson's) with the outer 2 broader than Wilson's and often with sparser and less distinct dark bars. White tips to secondaries on Common broader and more even in width across both webs, versus narrower and curling around tip of inner web on Wilson's (beware that width of white trailing edge to wings can be exaggerated markedly in blurred photos). Supportive characters include the following: (1) Common averages more white on underwing coverts and axillars, which are less heavily barred (e.g., white bars on axillars typically wider than black bars on Common, vs. narrower than or equal in width on Wilson's; again, blurred images can exaggerate the apparent white on underwings); (2) Common averages bolder tertial barring, with cinnamon and blackish contrast to base (contrast on Wilson's often fades out basally); and (3) Common averages warmer brown overall versus colder brown on Wilson's (e.g., warm brown flanks often contrast with black-and-white barring on axillars, vs. being similar in tone on Wilson's).

Also cf. Pin-tailed Snipe.

Age/Sex/Season: Ages/sexes similar; no seasonal variation. Complete prebasic molt and partial to incomplete preformative molt (tail molted on wintering grounds) in fall–early winter; adult wing molt often interrupted for migration. Partial prealternate molt late winter–spring on wintering grounds, may include some rectrices. *Adult*: In fall, wings relatively worn or molt interrupted with fresher inner primaries; median and lesser upperwing coverts with pale buff tips and variable dark shaft streak often splitting pale tip. *1st-year*: In fall, wings uniformly fresh; white tips to secondaries average narrower than adult; median and lesser upperwing coverts with broad pale buff tips and fine dark subterminal line, fine dark shaft streak typically does not split pale tip. Some may be aged in 1st winter by molt contrasts in greater coverts and tertials (see p. 36). In spring, juv primaries relatively worn and faded relative to fresher and darker adult feathers.

Habitat and Behavior: As in Wilson's Snipe, but 'drum' produced in dive of flight display is audibly lower pitched and faster-paced, with a vibrating, slightly buzzy quality. By contrast, the 'drum' of Wilson's is slower-paced and higher-pitched, with an almost hooting cadence recalling Boreal Owl song. Flight calls do not appear separable to our ears.

BLACK-TAILED GODWIT *Limosa limosa*
36–44 cm (14–17")

Summary: *Alaska*: Spring–summer only. Rare and irregular on w. Aleutians; very rare on cen. Aleutians and Bering Sea islands; exceptional on n., w., and s-coastal mainland. *Atlantic Canada and Quebec*: Very rare in spring, exceptional in fall–winter. *Elsewhere in East*: Very rare in spring–fall, exceptional in winter.

Taxonomy: 3 ssp, not certainly separable in the field but average differences may allow separation given good photos or comparative experience. AK specimens are referred to *melanuroides*. Eastern birds are thought to be *islandica*, but certain separation from *limosa* is difficult.

Of 2 ssp in W Europe, nominate *limosa* (breeding W Eurasia) averages longer bill and

legs than *islandica* (breeding Iceland); juv and breeding plumages of *islandica* average brighter rusty on underparts and on edgings to upperparts, but 1st-year female *islandica* may overlap in appearance with adult male *limosa*.

E Asian *melanuroides* (considered specifically distinct by Brazil 2009) averages smaller, with shorter bill and legs, more prominent whitish eyebrow, darker upperparts, and narrower white wingstripe (Brazil 2009); breeding plumage has narrower dark barring on underparts.

Distribution and Status:

World: Breeds from Iceland e. to cen. Russia, disjunctly in NE Asia (Kamchatka and e. Chukotka). W. populations winter primarily in W Europe (*islandica*) and sub-Saharan Africa (*limosa*). E. populations winter mainly Indonesia to Australia.

North America: *Alaska*: On w. Aleutians, rare and intermittent in spring (May–early Jun, mainly late May), very rarely e. to cen. Aleutians in late May; usually singles or pairs, but with exceptional max. 35 on Attu, 22 May 1998. On Bering Sea islands, very rare in spring–early summer (May–early Jul). Exceptional (late Jun–Jul) in n. AK, sw. AK, and s-coastal AK. *Atlantic Canada and Quebec*: Very rare in spring (May to mid-Jun, mainly mid–late May), most records from e. NL but also from NS, SPM, QC. In e. NL, exceptional in fall (early–late Oct, juv *islandica*). 1 winter record: PEI, 19 Dec 1998–6 Mar 1999 (adult). *Elsewhere in East*: Very rare in spring–fall, mainly in coastal states but also ON (Sep–Dec), and VT (late Apr). Spring records mainly Apr to mid-May (from LA and FL n. to New England). Some birds have lingered and wandered in spring–fall on Mid-Atlantic and ne. coasts, and one was in Brazoria Co., TX, 4 Jun–10 Aug 2012 (M. Lockwood, pers. comm.). Fall records mainly mid-Jul to Oct (from MA s. to NC); all of known age were considered adults. At least 1 winter record: Dare Co., NC, 27 Dec 1979–12 Jan 1980, but also may have wintered in 1970s in SC and GA (*AB* 34:264).

Comments: Records from AK are typical of drift migrants, and on occasion birds (sometimes displaying) remain into summer. The lack of fall records in AK is somewhat surprising and not easily explained; at the least, an occasional misoriented 1st-year might be expected. The lack of records elsewhere in w. N America is also noteworthy.

In e. N America, critical attention to ssp and age could help address several questions about occurrence patterns. Black-tailed Godwit is a

white
underwing

W European
limosa averages
rangier than
islandica

islandica
juv

adult ♂ breeding

islandica nonbreeding
(Sep–Mar)

dark
culmen

long primary
projection

finer barring

**Hudsonian
Godwit**
juv (Aug–Oct)

E Asian
melanuroides
adult ♂
breeding (Apr–Aug)

coarser
barring

melanuroides
juv (Aug–Oct)

Icelandic
islandica
adult ♂
breeding (Apr–Sep)

averages brightest of ssp

islandica
juv (Aug–Oct)

islandica
1st-summer ♀ (Apr–Sep)

not readily separable from *limosa*

Black-tailed Godwit

large and striking species that can be long-lived, and a single bird could account for multiple records at distant points in space and time. There are several between- and within-year sets of records in e. N America that might each involve a single bird: for example, the 1993–1994 MA, DE, and NC birds; the 2001 CT and NY birds; and the 2006–2007 MA, VT, and perhaps even QC birds. If these or other records involve single birds seen in multiple years, it's unclear whether the birds involved stayed in N America or returned to

Iceland or some other part of the species' normal range.

Black-tailed Godwit is a common breeding bird in Iceland, where it arrives from its W European wintering grounds in mid-Apr to mid-May, peaking in late Apr. The preponderance of spring records in Atlantic Canada and QC is consistent with birds displaced en route to Iceland (and perhaps mainly less experienced and prebreeding individuals, given the relatively late timing); that most have occurred at the same time as influxes of European Golden Plover is supportive. Usually, it appears that most golden plovers relocate back to Iceland, and spring-overshoot godwits may also relocate. Some, however, may wander sw. into N America and be detected at points south.

Black-tailed Godwit is a scarce but regular visitor to the Azores and there are 4 fall–winter records from the Cape Verde Islands. Perhaps surprisingly, there are no records from Barbados or the se. Caribbean, but there is a recent Sep–Jan record from Trinidad (Hayes & Kenefick 2002) and it seems possible that birds may reach N America from that quarter.

Of note is that spring records s. of Canada are mainly earlier than presumed displacements of Icelandic migrants into e. Canada (Apr to mid-May vs. mid–late May), and thus may involve birds that wintered in the New World and were detected moving n. Fall–winter records may involve a mix of newly misoriented individuals from the Icelandic population and birds returning s. from undetected summering grounds, having successfully overwintered in the New World in previous years. One might expect more 1st-years in the former category, whereas the latter would comprise adults. Given the normal wintering latitudes of different populations, birds wintering in ne. N America may be mainly *islandica*, whereas birds wintering in the Southeast, along with some spring migrants on the E Coast and Gulf Coast, might include nominate *limosa*, a longer-distance migrant.

While it's possible that some records in the East involved birds with origins in NE Asia (cf. Lesser Sand Plover, Broad-billed Sandpiper), the lack of W Coast records s. of AK, and the lack of fall records from AK, would argue against Black-tailed Godwits coming from that direction; again, critical attention to ssp could address this question.

Field Identification: Fairly large, lanky godwit with striking wing and tail patterns.

Similar Species: *Hudsonian Godwit* similar, especially in juv and nonbreeding plumages, but Black-tailed averages longer-legged and has shorter primary projection; bill has pink base to upper mandible in all ages (dark above in juv and nonbreeding Hudsonian); white wingstripe more extensive, and underwings flashingly white. Breeding males brighter than females, but both sexes of Black-tailed have orange to rufous neck and upper breast, these areas grayish on breeding Hudsonian. Juv *islandica* much brighter

than juv Hudsonian, with cinnamon neck and breast.

Age/Sex/Season: Ages differ; sexes differ slightly in breeding plumage and females of all ssp average larger and longer-billed than males; pronounced seasonal variation. Complete prebasic molt and partial to incomplete preformative molt (can include some primaries, at least in *melanuroides*) in fall–winter; wholly or mostly on nonbreeding grounds but can start head and body molt on migration. Partial prealternate molt late winter–spring on wintering grounds. *Adult*: In fall migration has worn breeding plumage or head and body variably mixed with nonbreeding feathers, relatively worn primaries; in spring has bright breeding plumage (averaging brighter and more extensively rufous on males), uniformly relatively fresh primaries. *1st-year*: In fall, juv plumage (with fresh scaly edgings) worn through migration, or with a mix of nonbreeding feathers on head and body. In 1st winter, usually aged by molt contrasts in upperwing coverts and tertials. In spring–summer, juv primaries relatively worn and faded, extent of bright breeding plumage highly variable.

Habitat and Behavior: Mudflats, marshes, flooded fields and ponds. Probes deeply. Calls of W Eurasian birds include a hoarse *sheh* and chippering *sh-shehk* and *sh-sh-shehk*.

LITTLE CURLEW *Numenius minutus*
29–34 cm (11.5–13.5")

Summary: *California*: Exceptional in fall. *Elsewhere*: Single spring records from AK (1989) and WA (2001).

Taxonomy: Monotypic.

Status and Distribution:

World: Breeds montane taiga zone of ne. Russia, e. to w. Chukotka; winters s. New Guinea and Australia.

North America: *California*: 1–4 records, 3 in fall from Santa Barbara Co., 16 Sep–14 Oct 1984, 23–24 Sep 1988, and 4–20 Aug 1993; and 1 from Monterey Co., 6–28 Sep 1994. *Elsewhere*: Pacific Co., WA, 6 May 2001, and St. Lawrence, AK, 7–8 Jun 1989.

Comments: Little Curlew is a medium-sized shorebird with a very long migration that includes a large overwater component. Misoriented or drifted stragglers can be expected almost anywhere in the world, and, with following winds, a west-east Pacific crossing s. of the Aleutians seems possible. The WA bird may have wintered in the Americas.

Whimbrel

plain primaries
and secondaries

significantly
smaller than
Whimbrel

juv (Aug–Oct)

Little Curlew

adult with Whimbrel

The 3 Santa Barbara Co. records and the Monterey Co. record (and perhaps even the WA record?) may have involved the same individual; the first record was of a juv, with subsequent records considered adult or age unknown. There is no demographic data for Little Curlew, but others in the genus live 10–30 years or longer (Gill et al. 1998).

Field Identification: Very small, overall buffy curlew with slender, slightly decurved bill, pale lores; legs often pinkish.

Similar Species: None in N America, but cf. Upland Sandpiper and presumed extinct Eskimo Curlew. Optimistic observers may be fooled by appreciably larger Whimbrel.

Age/Sex/Season: Ages differ slightly; sexes similar; no appreciable seasonal variation. Complete prebasic molt and partial to complete preformative molt in fall–winter; wing molts occur on nonbreeding grounds, but on adult often some head and body molt before or during migration. Partial prealternate molt in spring. **Adult:** Dark streaking on neck and chest relatively distinct; upperparts with relatively large buff notches and paler, more patterned feather centers (appearing relatively spangled overall). **1st-year:** Juv plumage usually worn through fall migration. Dark streaking on neck and chest finer and less distinct than adult; upperparts with relatively small, pale buff notches and darker, less patterned feather centers (appearing darker overall, with fine pale spotting). In 1st winter, some may

be aged by molt contrasts in upperwing coverts and tertials. In spring–summer, some may be indistinguishable from adult, but birds with partial molts can be aged by retained, relatively worn and faded juv primaries.

Habitat and Behavior: An upland curlew, but frequents beaches and mudflats as well as grassland and fields. Call a hurried *pipipipi*; suggests Whimbrel but more excited and higher pitched (P. Holt, pers. comm.).

EURASIAN CURLEW *Numenius arquata*
50–60 cm (20–24")

Summary: *The Northeast*: Exceptional in fall, winter, and spring. *Florida*: 1 fall record (1982).

Taxonomy: 2 ssp, not certainly separable in the field and intergrading over a broad area in Cen Eurasia: e. breeding *orientalis* averages longer billed, longer legged, and paler, with finer streaking overall, than w. breeding *arquata*. N American records presumably are of nominate *arquata*.

Status and Distribution:

World: Breeds from NW Europe e. across temperate Eurasia to around 120°E; nominate *arquata* winters mainly in W Europe and N Africa; *orientalis* is a longer-distance migrant, wintering s. to S Africa, India, and from SE Asia n. to s. Japan.

North America: *The Northeast*: 3–5 records: Barnstable Co., MA, 19 Sep–12 Oct 1976 (age unknown, possibly juv), and 5 Sep–23 Nov 1984 (adult); Martha's Vineyard, MA, 18 Feb–18 Mar

1978 (possibly present since Oct; *AB* 32:322); NS, 6 May 1978; e. NL 7–8 Jan 1991. **Florida**: Brevard Co., 5 Sep 1982.

Comments: Eurasian Curlew is a regular wintering bird in Iceland, where there has been an increase in recent decades and where breeding was first recorded in the late 1980s. Perhaps surprisingly there has been no parallel increase in e. N America. The main winter arrival into Iceland is in late Dec, with a smaller arrival peak in Sep–Oct.

N American records presumably represent overshoots from Iceland. The 1984 adult in MA has been considered possibly the same individual as involved in the fall–winter 1976 and 1978 MA records (*AB* 39:27), but the May 1978 bird in NS appeared following ne. winds that brought European Golden Plovers and Black-tailed Godwits to NL. The FL bird may have come via Iceland, or perhaps crossed via the Mid-Atlantic or was swept south by weather systems (cf. Fig. 7, p. 9), as with a Nov–Dec record from Bermuda in the early 1960s.

Although all records to date are from e. N America, Eurasian Curlew should be considered when looking at a large curlew in AK or the Pacific Northwest, especially in fall when reverse-migrants are most likely to occur. A report from Nunavut, 21 Jun 1977, is considered hypothetical by Godfrey (1986) and Richards et al. (2002).

Field Identification: Large, overall gray-brown, long-billed curlew; European counterpart to Long-billed Curlew. Note white wedge on rump and uppertail coverts, much like European ssp of Whimbrel.

Similar species: ***Long-billed Curlew*** buffier overall and lightly streaked below; in flight shows bright cinnamon on upperwings and underwings.

Eastern Curlew averages richer brown above, especially compared to E Asian populations of Eurasian Curlew, and lacks white above or below (best seen in flight); however, identifying resting birds of these 2 species at anything other than close range can be surprisingly difficult.

Age/Sex/Season: Ages differ slightly; sexes similar but females average longer-billed; no appreciable seasonal variation. Complete prebasic molt in fall–winter, wing molt wholly or mostly on nonbreeding grounds; partial preformative molt occurs late summer–fall in short-distance migrants, but in fall–winter after migration in longer-distance migrants. Partial prealternate molt late winter–spring. ***Adult***: Neck and chest heavily and coarsely streaked blackish brown; tertials grayish with dark bars and variable buff margins. ***1st-year***: Juv plumage (with fresh edgings to upperparts) may be worn through migration, or with a variable extent of nonbreeding feathers on head and body. Neck and chest with finer dark streaking than adult; tertials with dark

juv ♂

white rump and tail
(like European Whimbrel)

whitish

adult ♀

variable white
wing-linings

♀ longer
billed than ♂

**Eurasian
Curlew**

centers and notched buff margins; bill appreciably shorter in fall, especially male. In 1st winter,
may be aged by molt contrasts in upperwing
coverts and tertials. In spring–summer, juv primaries relatively worn and faded.

Habitat and Behavior: Much as Long-billed
Curlew, with which vagrants in the Lower 48
might occur. Most common call a rising minor-
key whistle *courr-lee*.

EASTERN (Far Eastern) CURLEW
Numenius madagascariensis 53–66 cm (21–26")

Summary: *Alaska*: Very rare in spring–summer
on w. and cen. Aleutians; exceptional in spring
on Bering Sea islands. *British Columbia*: 1 fall
record (1984).
Taxonomy: Monotypic.
Distribution and Status:
World: Breeds E Asia (e. to Kamchatka); winters mainly in Australia.
North America: *Alaska*: On w. (mostly) and
cen. Aleutians, very rare in spring–early summer
(mid-May to mid-Jul, mainly late May–early Jun),
usually singles but up to 3 on 2 occasions. On
Pribilofs, 4 records in spring (late May to mid-
Jun). *British Columbia*: Westminster Co., 24 Sep
1984 (juv).

Comments: It's surprising that Far Eastern
Curlew hasn't been recorded more often on the
w. Aleutians. Attu birding groups recorded the
species on fewer than half of their spring trips
(Osgood 2003) even though it's considered a
common nesting bird in the Kamchatka Peninsula. Perhaps its large size and strong flight make
it less susceptible to east-west displacement, and
populations may also be declining through habitat loss, as with many Asian shorebirds.

The absence of fall records from AK suggests
that the inevitable misoriented birds overfly the
w. Aleutians. Species that migrate from
Kamchatka through Japan and e. Russia have a
major overwater leg early in their migration
and likely carry increased fuel loads. A early
Sep report from the nw. Hawaiian Islands
supports this theory, and strong storms may
drift some across the N Pacific, as with the
BC bird.

Field Identification: Very large curlew with
very long bill; shows no white above in flight.
Variably streaked below, with ground color
of lower belly and undertail coverts buff to
pale brownish.

Similar species: *Long-billed Curlew* has buffy-
cinnamon tones above and especially below,
with cinnamon underwing coverts.

juv ♂

cinnamon inner
primaries

unbarred
cinnamon
wing-linings

Long-billed Curlew

buff
ground color

adult ♀

barred
underwing

Eastern Curlew

Eurasian Curlew has extensively white back and rump and white underwing coverts; tends to show a more pronounced eyebrow (but there is overlap); tends to be less streaked below, but even in more heavily streaked individuals, ground color of lower belly and undertail coverts is white; primary projection averages shorter than Eastern. In spite of these differences, separation of standing Eastern and Eurasian can be very difficult when birds are not close.

Age/Sex/Season: Ages differ slightly; sexes similar but females average longer-billed; no appreciable seasonal variation. Molts not well known. Complete prebasic molt in fall–winter, wholly or mostly on nonbreeding grounds but may start head and body molt on migration. Partial prealternate molt presumed in late winter–spring. Extent and timing of preformative molt unknown. *Adult*: Neck and chest heavily and coarsely streaked blackish brown; scapulars and upperwing coverts with variable dark shaft streaks and some notching on pale fringes. In fall migration has worn breeding plumage, relatively worn primaries; in spring has fresh breeding plumage, uniformly relatively fresh primaries. *1st-year*: Juv plumage (with fresh edgings to upperparts) may be worn through migration, or with a mix of nonbreeding feathers on head and body. Neck and chest with fine dark streaking, appearing paler overall than adult and slightly paler than upperparts; scapulars and upperwing coverts with neat cinnamon-buff edging, dark centers. Into early winter, bill often appreciably shorter than adult. In 1st winter, may be aged by molt contrasts in upperwing coverts and tertials. In spring–summer, juv primaries relatively worn and faded.

Habitat and Behavior: Away from breeding areas, likely to be found on beaches and estuaries. Common call *curr-lee*, very similar to Eurasian Curlew.

SPOTTED REDSHANK *Tringa erythropus*
29–32 cm (11.4–12.6")

Summary: *Alaska*: In fall and spring, very rare on w. Aleutians, exceptional on cen. Aleutians and Bering Sea islands. *West*: Exceptional in fall and spring, mainly Pacific provinces and states; 1 winter record. *East*: Very rare in fall, exceptional in spring, mainly Atlantic provinces and states; 1 winter record. Few records recently.
Taxonomy: Monotypic.

Status and Distribution:
World: Breeds mainly in wooded tundra from Scandinavia e. to ne. Russia (e. to cen. Chukotka); winters from S Europe s. to equatorial Africa and e. to SE Asia.

North America: *Alaska*: On w. Aleutians, very rare in fall (late Aug to mid-Oct) and spring (mid–late May). On cen. Aleutians and Pribilofs, exceptional in spring (late May) and fall (late Aug–early Oct). Unrecorded on AK mainland. *West*: In Pacific provinces and states, exceptional in fall (early Jul, Oct–Nov) and spring (Mar–early Apr, late Apr–May); 1 winter record, Clatsop Co, OR, 21 Feb–15 Mar 1981, but 1 in s. BC, 1 Mar–1 Apr 1981, also may have been wintering. At least 2 interior fall reports (mid-Aug to early Sep): s-cen. SK, 2–6 Sep 1994 (age unknown), Clark Co., NV, 16–20 Aug 1975 (age unknown). *East*: In Atlantic provinces and states, very rare in fall (Jul–Oct; mainly in the Northeast, a few s. to Mid-Atlantic Coast) and exceptional in spring (mid–late May; NC n. to NL); some within- and between-year duplication probably involved in record totals; at least 1 winter record (late Nov to mid-Mar), NY in 1992/1993, returning 1993/1994; but status unknown of 1 collected 15 Nov 1969 in CT and of 1 seen 21 Feb–26 Apr 1981 in SC. Exceptional in e. interior in fall (mid-Jul to Sep) and spring (early May) n. to ON, s. and w. to KS and cen. TX. See Mlodinow (1999a) for a summary and discussion of records through the late 1990s.

Comments: There were clusters of records in the 1980s (West) and 1990s (East), some of which probably involved multiple sightings of the same birds. Records everywhere in N America have declined since the 1990s, and in Japan numbers have declined significantly in recent years (Shimba 2007). Even before the decline, Spotted Redshank was a surprisingly rare vagrant to the w. Aleutians and Bering Sea islands. No other species with a similar distribution and migration pattern was recorded so infrequently. Perhaps the species is much less common than we think in the remote ne. portions of its breeding range or, like so many shorebirds, its global population is declining.

Eastern records seem complex. There were only 10 records of Spotted Redshank from Iceland through 2006 (5 in late Apr–early Jun, 5 in Aug–Sep), none from Greenland, and only 11 from the Azores (mostly mostly late Oct–Nov and before 1980). This all suggests that most birds reaching ne. N America are not coming directly from NW Europe.

There seem to be 3 other possibilities: in fall, some birds (likely juvs) may be coming from the nw. and traveling e. and s. across N America (as suggested by Mlodinow 1999a); some of these may winter. Unfortunately, age data are rarely noted, or available. Several other shorebirds seem to take such a route, at least in part (e.g., Sharp-tailed Sandpiper, Red-necked Stint, and cf. Lesser Sand Plover, Broad-billed Sandpiper), and multiple species in several families also follow this pattern.

Spring records may have two origins. The first is birds that came from the nw. and wintered in N or S America. These birds return n. and are sighted along the way, with Feb–Mar records likely reflecting birds that wintered undetected in N America. The second is birds that cross in fall from Africa to ne. S America and the se. Caribbean (e.g., Barbados has 6 Oct–Mar records) and move n. in spring with related species. The N American spring records in late Apr–May likely represent birds in this second category.

Field Identification: Elegant shorebird with long red to orange legs (often dark in breeding plumage) and slender, red-orange based bill with subtle but distinctive drooped tip. In flight shows white wedge up back.

Similar Species: None, if well seen, but beware yellowlegs with abnormal or discolored legs. Also cf. Common Redshank.

Age/Sex/Season: Ages differ; sexes differ slightly in breeding plumage; pronounced seasonal variation. Complete prebasic molt and partial preformative molt in fall–winter; adult wing molt mainly on nonbreeding grounds but can be interrupted for migration, head and body molt often on migration. Partial prealternate molt spring on wintering grounds. *Adult*: in May–Jul usually in black-bodied breeding plumage, but by Jul–Aug head and body usually a mix of worn breeding and fresh, plain, nonbreeding feathers.

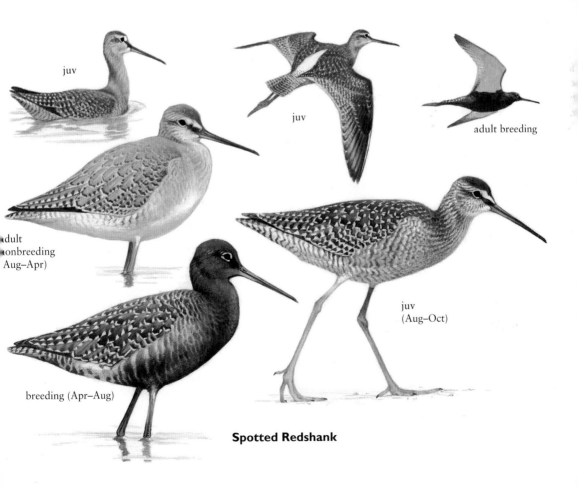

juv

juv

adult breeding

adult nonbreeding (Aug–Apr)

breeding (Apr–Aug)

juv (Aug–Oct)

Spotted Redshank

In fall, outer primaries relatively worn; in spring has uniformly quite fresh primaries, extensively black breeding plumage (more solidly and extensively black on male, without extensive whitish tipping to belly and undertail coverts). *1st-year*: In fall, juv plumage (with fresh notched edgings) worn through migration and appreciably darker than adult nonbreeding; often with mix of nonbreeding feathers on head and body in late fall. In 1st winter, usually aged by molt contrasts in upperwing coverts and tertials. In spring–summer, juv primaries relatively worn and faded; extent of black plumage variable, averaging less than adult and upperparts often mostly plain.

Habitat and Behavior: In migration favors marshes and lagoons, typically avoids open coast. Most common call an emphatic *chu-ick*, similar to Semipalmated Plover or, especially, Pacific Golden Plover. In N America, s. of Alaska, most often found with Greater Yellowlegs or dowitchers.

COMMON REDSHANK *Tringa totanus*
27–29 cm (10.7–11.4")

Summary: *Newfoundland*: Exceptional in late winter–spring.

Taxonomy: 6 ssp, none certainly separable in the field. NL birds presumed to be *robustus*, from Icelandic breeding population, which averages larger than nominate *totanus* of W Europe.

Status and Distribution:

World: Breeds from Iceland and NW Europe across mid-latitude Eurasia to se. Russia (n. only to about 45°N); winters from W Europe (some in s. Iceland) and N Africa e. to SE Asia.

North America: *Newfoundland*: 6 late winter–spring records from e. NL: 6 birds (1 record of 2 birds) during 28 Apr–14 May 1995 (details in Mactavish 1996), the other at Terra Nova National Park, 6 Mar–22 Apr 1999.

Comments: Most of Iceland's breeding Common Redshank winter in Britain and return to Iceland in Mar–Apr. The relatively late dates of most NL redshank records mirror the late-end dates for Black-tailed Godwits relative to their main spring arrival in Iceland. This suggests that N American records of both species may involve younger individuals (perhaps 1st- and 2nd-year birds?), which typically migrate later than adults, are less experienced in migration, and are more likely to be displaced by weather systems. The 1995 records were associated with an atypically large storm system bringing rain, snow, and

sustained ne. winds to NL along with 90+ European Golden Plovers, 5 Pink-footed Geese, and Eurasian Whimbrel, Teal, and Wigeon (Mactavish 1996). The 1999 bird may have wintered locally or could represent an early Iceland spring migrant blown off course.

There are at least 16 records of Common Redshank from Greenland, including 4 in Apr–Jun from sw. Greenland, suggesting that NL is likely to see more records. A report from n. AK, at Barrow, 6 Jun 2009 (*NAB* 63:639) is not accepted by the state committee; photos suggest an aberrant *Tringa* or perhaps a hybrid *Tringa* × Ruff.

Field Identification: Somewhat chunky, medium-sized, brownish *Tringa* with red base to rather stout bill, orange legs, white wedge on lower back, and strikingly broad white trailing edge to upperwing.

Similar Species: None in N America, but beware yellowlegs that very rarely show orangy legs. Another pitfall is adult ***Ruff***, which can have orange legs and bill base but has shorter and slightly decurved bill, upperparts more scalloped, face often pale, and in flight, lacks striking wing pattern and white back 'wedge' of redshank.

Spotted Redshank in juv and nonbreeding plumages shares orange leg color and bill base (lower mandible only) but has conspicuous white supraloral line, longer legs, a longer, finer, droop-tipped bill, and lacks striking upperwing pattern. Juv Spotted uniformly barred below, nonbreeding paler gray above, whiter below.

Age/Sex/Season: Ages differ; sexes similar; distinct seasonal variation. Complete prebasic molt and partial preformative molt in late summer–winter; wing molt can be interrupted for migration, head and body molt often during migration. Partial prealternate molt late winter–spring. ***Adult***: In fall, head and body usually a mix of worn breeding and fresh, plainer, nonbreeding feathers, with outer primaries relatively worn. In winter, upperparts uniformly fairly plain gray-brown; in spring has extensive dark spotting and streaking on upperparts and underparts, uniformly relatively fresh primaries. *1st-year*: In fall, juv plumage (with fresh notched edgings) often mixed with plainer nonbreeding feathers on head and body. In 1st winter, usually aged by molt contrasts in upperwing coverts and tertials. In spring–summer, averages less extensive dark markings than adult, juv primaries relatively worn and faded.

nonbreeding with
Greater Yellowlegs
(behind)

adult
nonbreeding
(Aug–Mar)

adult breeding

breeding (Mar–Aug)

juv (Aug–Oct)

Common Redshank

Habitat and Behavior: Near coasts as a nonbreeder, preferring salt marshes, flooded fields, protected mud flats. Common calls are a whistled minor-key *teu* and longer *teu-hu* or *teu-huhu*.

MARSH SANDPIPER *Tringa stagnatilis*
22–25 cm (8.7–9.8")

Summary: *Alaska*: Exceptional or very rare in fall on w. and cen. Aleutians and Bering Sea islands.
Taxonomy: Monotypic.
Distribution and Status:
   World: Breeds n. mid-latitude Eurasia, between about 30°E and 120°E. Winters from sub-Saharan Africa e. through India and SE Asia to Australia.
   North America: *Alaska:* 8 fall records (late Aug–early Oct) from w. and cen. Aleutians and Pribilofs; all records of known-age birds involve juvs/1st-years.
Comments: Marsh Sandpiper distribution is too westerly and its migration is too much overland to contribute birds to the spring drift pattern of vagrant shorebirds in the Aleutians and Bering Sea islands. The few fall records, all 1st-years, are likely misoriented (reverse?) migrants.

The species has substantial overwater capabilities, as evidenced by at least 2 fall records from Hawaii, and there is a recent fall record from Baja California, Mexico, 12–16 Oct 2011 (*NAB* 66:173–174), which suggests that W Coast fall records are possible, as might be spring records of birds that wintered in the New World.
   There are no records from Iceland, just 5 from the Azores, and none from the se. Caribbean. These data, coupled with those from AK, suggests an occurrence in e. N America would be unexpected, but cf. Broad-billed Sandpiper.
Field Identification: Fairly small but tall-standing, generally pale *Tringa* with thin bill, very long and spindly greenish legs.
   Similar Species: None if seen well, but cf. Common Greenshank and nonbreeding Wilson's Phalarope.
   Age/Sex/Season: Ages differ; sexes similar; distinct seasonal variation. Complete prebasic molt and partial to incomplete preformative molt (can include some outer primaries in late winter) in fall–winter; adult wing molt interrupted for migration, head and body molt often during migration. Partial prealternate molt late winter–spring on wintering grounds. *Adult*: In fall migration, head and body usually with a mix of worn breeding and fresh, plain, nonbreeding feathers,

breeding
(Mar–Aug)

molting to
1st-winter
(Sep–Nov)

nonbreeding
(Aug–Apr)

juv (Aug–Oct)

Marsh Sandpiper

relatively worn outer primaries; in spring has extensively patterned breeding plumage, uniformly rather fresh primaries; legs often brighter, more yellowish than in fall–winter. *1st-year*: In fall, juv plumage (with fresh scaly edgings) worn through migration, or with a mix of nonbreeding feathers on head and body; legs greenish. In 1st winter, usually aged by molt contrasts in upperwing coverts and tertials. In spring–summer, juv primaries relatively worn and faded or outers contrastingly fresh; extent of patterned plumage variable, upperparts often mostly plain on birds remaining on nonbreeding grounds.

Habitat and Behavior: Similar to Lesser Yellowlegs. Common flight call a ringing *kyew*, similar to Lesser Yellowlegs and perhaps easily passed over amid a flock of *Tringa* sandpipers.

COMMON GREENSHANK *Tringa*
nebularia 30–34 cm (11.8–13.4")

Summary: *Alaska*: On w. Aleutians , uncommon in spring, very rare in fall; on cen. Aleutians and Bering Sea islands, very rare in spring,

exceptional in fall; exceptional in spring on w. and s-coastal mainland. *California*: 1–2 fall records (2001, 2002). *Eastern Canada*: Exceptional in spring and fall, 1 winter record (long-staying); mainly in Atlantic provinces.

Taxonomy: Monotypic.

Status and Distribution:

World: Breeds mainly in taiga zone across N Eurasia (e. to Kamchatka and w. Chukotka); winters primarily in sub-Saharan Africa, tropical Asia, and Australasia.

North America: *Alaska*: On w. Aleutians, uncommon in spring (mid-May to mid-Jun), usually 1s and 2s, max. 11 on Shemya, 25–26 May 1976; very rare in fall (mid-Jul to Sep). On cen. Aleutians and Pribilofs, very rare in spring (mid-May to mid-Jun, exceptionally to early Jul), exceptional in fall (mid-Aug to early Sep). On St. Lawrence, very rare in spring (late May to mid-Jun). Exceptional on w. mainland (5–6 Jun 2000) and in s-coastal AK (13–19 Jun 2008; *NAB* 62:602). *California*: 1–2 fall records from Humboldt Co., 27 Aug–17 Sep 2001, 18–25 Oct 2002 (judged same bird by state committee). *Eastern Canada*: Exceptional in spring (early–late May, 4 records)

nonbreeding
(Aug–Mar) with
Greater Yellowlegs
(behind)

juv

breeding
(Mar–Aug)

juv (Aug–Oct)

**Common
Greenshank**

and fall (Sep–early Oct, 2 records); 1 long-staying bird in se. NL, 3 Dec 1983–2 Feb 1985. All records from Atlantic Provinces except an early May record from QC. See Mlodinow (1999a) for a summary and discussion of records through the late 1990s.

Comments: It's notable that a species as regular on the w. AK islands should be so rare on mainland w. N America, but this pattern seems typical of shorebirds with breeding ranges mainly on the taiga. Vagrant records of such species in N America are typically of spring drift migrants, which presumably reorient. Vagrants from among the tundra breeders occur more frequently as misoriented fall juvs, and as a group are more numerous as vagrants than taiga breeders. For example, while there have been fewer than 10 records in N America away from AK for Common Greenshank and Wood Sandpiper, the less numerous but tundra-breeding Spotted Redshank has occurred over 30 times.

The origin of Common Greenshanks in the Northeast is not settled. The species is a distinctly uncommon vagrant to Iceland (only 18 records

through 2003, 6 in May, 12 in Aug–Oct) and there is one late May record from w. Greenland. On the other hand, there are up to 100 migration and winter records per year on the Azores, 7 Oct–Apr records from Barbados, and a single Oct–Dec record from Bermuda. Like Little Egret and others, Common Greenshank that reach the se. Caribbean and n. S America may on occasion join flocks of congeners and move n. with them in spring, perhaps via long overwater legs that bypass the Southeast and even the Mid-Atlantic Coast.

Field Identification: Old World counterpart to Greater Yellowlegs, with stout, slightly upturned and two-toned bill, gray-green legs (sometimes dull yellow-green), and white wedge on back.

Similar species: Most similar in N America to Greater Yellowlegs, from which told readily; also cf. Marsh Sandpiper.

Greater Yellowlegs has dark rump and back, longer and bright yellow legs (legs of juv Greenshank rarely dull yellowish). In all plumages, Greater Yellowlegs darker than corresponding plumage of greenshank, and on average longer winged, with primary tips extending beyond tail at rest; in greenshank, primary tips usually fall short of tail tip. These are small points but might be useful on a sleeping bird.

Nordmann's (Spotted) Greenshank Tringa guttifer (unrecorded in N America) very similar to Common Greenshank, especially in juv and nonbreeding plumages but slightly smaller with shorter and thicker neck, shorter and more yellowish legs, and, on average, a proportionately thicker-based, straighter, and more sharply two-toned bill. Breeding adult heavily spotted with black on upperparts, lower neck, breast, and flanks. Underwing coverts flashingly white (barred dusky on Common).

Age/Sex/Season: Ages differ; sexes similar; distinct seasonal variation. Complete prebasic molt and partial to incomplete preformative molt (can include some outer primaries in late winter) in fall–winter; adult wing molt mainly on nonbreeding grounds but can be interrupted for migration, head and body molt often on migration. Partial prealternate molt in late winter–spring on wintering grounds. *Adult*: In fall migration, head and body usually with a mix of worn breeding and fresh, plain, nonbreeding feathers, relatively worn outer primaries; in spring has extensively patterned breeding plumage, uniformly quite fresh primaries. *1st-year*: In fall, juv plumage (with fresh scaly edgings) worn through migration, or with a mix of nonbreeding feathers on head and body. In 1st winter, usually aged by molt contrasts in upperwing coverts and tertials. In spring–summer, juv primaries relatively worn and faded or outers contrastingly fresh; extent of patterned plumage variable, upperparts often mostly plain on birds remaining on nonbreeding grounds.

Habitat and Behavior: Very similar to Greater Yellowlegs. Usually found singly or in small groups. Typical calls two or three ringing notes, *tew-tew-tew*, similar to Greater Yellowleg but subtly different in tone and more likely to be on one pitch.

GREEN SANDPIPER *Tringa ochropus*
21–24 cm (8.3–9.5")

Summary: *Alaska*: On w. Aleutians, very rare in spring, exceptional in fall; 2 spring records from Bering Sea islands (1982, 2009).
Taxonomy: Monotypic.
Status and Distribution:
World: Breeds boreal forest zone from N Europe e. across Eurasia to around 160°E; winters mainly sub-Saharan Africa and S Asia, locally n. to W Europe and s. Japan.

white rump

blackish underwing

breeding (Mar–Sep)

Solitary Sandpiper

breeding (Mar–Aug)

juv (Aug–Sep)

Green Sandpiper

North America: *Alaska*: On w. Aleutians, very rare in spring (mid-May to mid-Jun), with 8 records since the first in 1978; 1 fall record, on Attu, 16–19 Aug 1983 (juv). 2 spring records from St. Lawrence, 5–7 Jun 1982, 22–23 May 2009.

Comments: Green Sandpiper is not a breeder or migrant in extreme NE Asia, and is considered a straggler to Kamchatka. The number of AK records and May–Jun dates are consistent with drift-overshoots. Except for the 1998 and 2009 individuals, AK records are clustered in two 2-year intervals, 1978–1979 and 1982–1983, for no reasons that we have determined.

The lack of records from e. N America is unsurprising given that Green Sandpiper is an extremely rare vagrant to Iceland (only 4 records through 2006, all mid-Apr to Jul) and is rare on the Azores (9 records, none since 1978).

Field Identification: Old World counterpart to Solitary Sandpiper, and similar in all plumages—until seen in flight, or heard.

Similar Species: **Solitary Sandpiper** slightly less thickset, slightly longer legged, and longer winged (primary projection clearly longer), averaging paler overall than Green. Bright white rump of Green striking in flight, contrasting with blackish wings. Also cf. Wood Sandpiper.

Age/Sex/Season: Ages differ slightly; sexes similar; slight seasonal variation. Complete pre-basic molt and partial to incomplete preformative molt (rarely includes outer primaries in mid–late winter) in fall–winter, mostly on nonbreeding grounds or interrupted for migration. Partial prealternate molt in late winter-spring. *Adult*: In fall migration, head and body often a mix of worn breeding (tertial edges with worn, pale notches) and fresh, plainer, nonbreeding feathers, relatively worn outer primaries; in spring has darker upperparts with sparse whitish spotting, uniformly rather fresh primaries. *1st-year*: In fall, juv plumage (with fresh, finely buff-spotted upperparts) sometimes mixed with a few plainer feathers on upperparts; tertial edges with fine buff spots. In 1st winter, usually aged by molt contrasts in upperwing coverts and tertials. In spring–summer, resembles adult but juv primaries relatively worn and faded or outers contrastingly fresh; many upperwing coverts faded juv feathers, lacking distinct dots of fresher adult coverts.

Habitat and Behavior: Much like Solitary Sandpiper, including 'flitting' flight when flushed. Common flight calls are a clear, ringing, whistled *tlú-eet-weet* and *tlúeet-weet-weet*; unlike the more plaintive whistled calls of Solitary, these are quite distinct from calls of Spotted Sandpiper.

WOOD SANDPIPER *Tringa glareola*
19–21 cm (7.5–8.3")

Summary: *Alaska*: On w. and cen. Aleutians a regular migrant, uncommon to common in spring, rare in fall (has bred). On Bering Sea islands, rare in spring, very rare in fall; exceptional in spring on e. Aleutians. Very rare on w. and n. mainland. *Pacific States and Provinces*: Exceptional in fall and spring. *Yukon*: 1 fall record (1996). *Atlantic States and Provinces*: Exceptional in fall and spring.

Taxonomy: Monotypic.

Distribution and Status:

World: Breeds in taiga and boreal forest zones of N Eurasia (e. to Kamchatka and Chukotka). Winters mainly in sub-Saharan Africa and from S Asia to Australia.

North America: *Alaska*: On w. and cen. Aleutians, regular in spring (May–Jun), sometimes common and in flocks up to 20–40 birds, exceptional max. 700+ on Attu, 18 May 1998, and 430+ birds in mid-May 1976 from Shemya e. to Adak; rare in fall (Aug–Sep), usually 1s and 2s. Has bred several times in w. (and probably cen.) Aleutians. In e. Aleutians, very rare in late spring (late May–Jun). On Bering Sea islands in spring, uncommon or rare on Pribilofs (mid-May to Jun, exceptionally lingering into Jul; max. 53 on St. Paul, 21 May 2006), very rare on St. Lawrence (late May–early Jun); in fall, rare on Pribilofs (Aug–early Oct; usually 1s and 2s) but only 3 records from St. Lawrence (all juvs in late Aug). Very rare on w. and n. AK mainland (late May to mid-Jul). *Pacific States and Provinces*: Exceptional in fall (late Sep–early Nov), 4 records of juvs: Queen Charlotte Is., BC, 3–9 Nov 1994; Lane Co., OR, 26 Sep–5 Oct 2008; Westminster Co., BC, 12–16 Oct 2010; San Diego Co., CA, 24–29 Sep 2012; and 1 adult, Skagit Co., WA, 5–6 Aug 2011 (*NAB* 66:158). 1 spring record: Kern Co., CA, 22–23 May 2007. *Yukon*: Herschel Island, 9 Aug 1996. *Atlantic States and Provinces*: Westchester Co., NY, 31 Oct–5 Nov 1990 (juv); se. NL, 11–14 Nov 1998 (juv); Sussex Co., DE, 5–12 May 2008; Newport Co., RI, 14–22 Oct 2012 (juv).

Comments: In continental N America, Wood Sandpipers probably go undetected among the large numbers of Lesser Yellowlegs that pour through the West, and their tolerance, perhaps even preference, for small grass-margined pools

breeding with Lesser Yellowlegs (left)

juv

breeding (Mar–Aug)

juv (Aug–Oct)

Wood Sandpiper

makes detection even less likely. There's no intrinsic reason to think their occurrence should be any less likely than Spotted Redshank, for example. That 4 of the 5 W Coast records occurred in the last 5 years may reflect increased observer awareness rather than a true change in abundance. Just s. of our region, a Wood Sandpiper wintered in Baja California Sur, Mexico, Aug 2010/Feb 2011 and late Jul 2011/Feb 2012 (*NAB* 66:173; Howell, pers. obs.), perhaps having migrated (at least) twice through the West.

The relative fall abundance of Wood Sandpipers on the Pribilofs versus St. Lawrence is notable and recalls the fall pattern shown by Little Stint; in contrast, both Lesser Sand Plover and Gray-tailed Tattler are as common in fall on St. Lawrence as on the Pribilofs.

The 4 records from e. N America may have different origins. The May bird in DE seems likely to have drifted off Europe or Africa and found its way to the se. Caribbean or ne. S America; about 20 records from the Azores since 2000 indicate substantial overwater capabilities, and 5 Oct–Apr records from Barbados, including a bird that overwintered, support such a routing. In spring, it then moved n., perhaps in association with Lesser Yellowlegs, a species that shares the same

habitat preference; 2 spring records from Bermuda support this theory.

The late fall birds in NL, NY, and RI (all juvs) might have crossed the N Atlantic on favorable winds, and there is an Oct 1981 record from Bermuda. However, this last seems unlikely to have come by the N Atlantic route; there were 31 records from Iceland through 2003, but mostly Apr–Jun, only 5 in Aug–Oct. As with a number of Asian shorebirds (e.g., Lesser Sand Plover, Little Stint, Broad-billed Sandpiper), it seems more likely that juv Wood Sandpipers in the Northeast crossed the N American continent from the west.

Field Identification: Between Solitary Sandpiper and Lesser Yellowlegs in appearance, but much more likely to be mistaken for the latter.

Similar Species: ***Lesser Yellowlegs*** slightly larger, longer legged (legs bright yellow rather than dull greenish yellow), longer-winged (wings extending well beyond tail at rest), and less heavily spotted white of buff above. Also cf. Green Sandpiper.

Age/Sex/Season: Ages differ; sexes similar; distinct seasonal variation. Complete prebasic molt and partial to incomplete preformative molt (can include outer primaries in mid–late winter) in fall–winter, mostly or wholly on nonbreeding grounds. Partial prealternate molt late winter–spring on wintering grounds. *Adult*: In fall migration, head and body often a mix of worn breeding and fresh, duller, nonbreeding feathers, relatively worn outer primaries; in spring has extensively patterned breeding plumage, uniformly relatively fresh primaries. *1st-year*: In fall, juv plumage (with fresh, notched and spotted upperparts) usually worn through migration. In 1st winter, usually aged by molt contrasts in upperwing coverts and tertials. In spring–summer, resembles adult but juv primaries relatively worn and faded or outers contrastingly fresh; upperparts average less extensively patterned than adult.

Habitat and Behavior: Prefers grassy pools and margins. Teeters like most *Tringas*. Flight call a rapid monotonic *chif-chif* and *chif-chif-chif*, may vaguely suggest flight call of American Goldfinch.

GRAY-TAILED TATTLER *Tringa brevipes*
25–28 cm (9.8–11")

Summary: *Alaska*: On w. Aleutians, rare and irregular spring migrant, uncommon in fall; very rare in cen. Aleutians and exceptional in e. Aleutians. On Bering Sea islands, very rare in spring, uncommon in fall. Exceptional in late spring–summer on mainland; 1 fall record from s-coastal AK (1982). *Pacific States and Provinces*: Exceptional in spring and fall. *Massachusetts*: 1 fall record (2012).

Taxonomy: Monotypic.

Status and Distribution:

World: Breeds mainly in taiga zone of ne. Russia, e. to Kamchatka and s. Chukotka. Winters from SE Asia to SW Pacific islands and Australia.

North America: *Alaska*: On w. Aleutians, rare and irregular in spring (mid-May to mid-Jun), mainly singles and small groups, exceptional max. 77 on Attu, 30 May 1983; uncommon in fall (Jul to mid-Oct). On cen. Aleutians, very rare in spring (late May–early Jun) and fall (Aug–early Oct); on e. Aleutians, exceptional in fall (late Sep). On Bering Sea islands, very rare in spring (mid-May to mid-Jun) and uncommon in fall (Jul–early Oct). Exceptional in late spring–summer (Jun–early Jul) on n., w., and s-coastal mainland; 1 fall record from s-coastal AK, on Middleton Island, 24 Sep 1982. *Pacific States and Provinces*: Pacific Co., WA, 8 Sep 1975 (juv); Los Angeles Co, CA, 23 Jul 1981 (adult); Marin Co., CA, 24–26 May 1998 (adult); last record not accepted

by state committee. *Massachusetts*: Nantucket Island, 18–20 Oct 2012 (juv; J. Trimble, pers. comm., photos).

Comments: In AK, Gray-tailed Tattler is among a minority of shorebird vagrants that are more common in fall than spring. Spring records on the w. Aleutians presumably reflect drift migrants, but on the Bering Sea islands and nw. mainland more may be drift-assisted overshoots. Fall records involve a few adults in Jul–Aug and many more juvs (presumably misoriented) in late Aug–Oct.

Despite being perhaps the second most frequently seen Asian shorebird in fall on the Bering Sea islands (after Sharp-tailed Sandpiper), this abundance hasn't been mirrored by records in the Pacific states and provinces, where but a single fall juv Gray-tailed Tattler has been found. There are disproportionately more records of Sharp-tailed Sandpiper in w. N America, even though it shares similar breeding and wintering ranges with Gray-tailed Tattler. The tattlers, however, winter on islands in the Pacific, a strategy that requires navigational accuracy, but even so it seems likely they are being overlooked in the West. Any tattler away from the immediate West Coast should be looked at carefully, as should any tattler on a mudflat or beach. The spring 1998 CA record coincided with an unprecedented fallout on the W Coast of storm-drifted migrant Bristle-thighed Curlews; this same storm may have been responsible for the tattler record, or the bird may simply have been moving n. after wintering in the New World (cf. the CA fall adult).

The recent MA record fits within the pattern shown by a number of E Asian shorebirds (e.g., see discussion in Wood Sandpiper and Little Stint accounts) and we suspect it traversed N America from the w. rather than coming from across the Atlantic.

Field Identification: Asian counterpart to Wandering Tattler, and the two species similar in all plumages; often best identified by call. See Paulson (1993, 2005), and O'Brien et al. (2006) for more information.

Similar Species: All plumages of Gray-tailed average paler than very similar *Wandering Tattler* and differ in nasal groove extending to around half of bill length, versus clearly more than half on Wandering; judging this requires excellent views but is quite possible in the field. Breeding Gray-tailed has finer, often lacy-looking, dark barring below, and extensively white belly. *Juv* Gray-tailed has whiter flanks, a more distinct

Gray-tailed

broader white
supraloral

Wandering

dark forehead
to bill

nonbreeding

nasal groove about
two-thirds of bill length

nasal groove about
half bill length

pale fringes

darker

adult
breeding
(Apr–Sep)

sparser, finer
dark barring

adult
breeding

heavily barred

**Wandering
Tattler**

whitish

juv (Aug–Oct)

**Gray-tailed
Tattler**

gray flanks

juv

whitish eyebrow, and averages bolder whitish tips and dots on upperparts (can be matched by strongly marked Wandering). Nonbreeding plumage not certainly separable from Wandering Tattler other than by voice and extent of nasal groove.

Age/Sex/Season: Ages differ slightly; sexes similar; pronounced seasonal variation. Complete prebasic molt and partial to incomplete preformative molt (can include outer primaries in late winter–spring) in fall–winter, wholly or mostly on nonbreeding grounds. Partial prealternate molt in spring. ***Adult***: Breeding plumage has fine dark barring on whitish neck and chest; nonbreeding has plain gray neck and chest. In fall migration, head and body usually worn breeding plumage, with relatively worn outer primaries; in spring has extensively patterned breeding plumage, uniformly rather fresh primaries. ***1st-year***: Juv plumage (with fresh, finely spotted

upperparts) usually worn through migration. In 1st winter, usually aged by molt contrasts in upperwing coverts and tertials. In spring–summer, resembles adult but juv primaries relatively worn and faded or outers contrastingly fresh; underparts average less extensively patterned than adult, and birds remaining on nonbreeding grounds can appear like nonbreeding adult.

Habitat and Behavior: Similar to Wandering Tattler but more likely to be found on sand or mud and, at least in normal range, also more likely to be in small flocks. Migrants on Pacific islands associate readily with Wandering (Howell, pers. obs.), although favor slightly different habitats when feeding. Primary vocalization distinct: a plover-like, upslurred whistle, *tu-ee* or *tuee-ti-ti*, very different from Wandering Tattler's trilled, piping whistle. In flight, also gives a fairly soft, whistled *t-tu-tu-tu* that might recall Lesser Yellowlegs.

TEREK SANDPIPER *Xenus cinereus*
22–25 cm (8.7–9.8")

Summary: *Alaska*: On w. Aleutians, rare and irregular in spring, very rare in fall. On cen. Aleutians and Bering Sea islands, very rare in spring, exceptional in fall. Exceptional on AK mainland. *Pacific States and Provinces*: 1–2 fall records (1987, 1988). *East*: Exceptional in summer–fall.

Taxonomy: Monotypic.

Distribution and Status:

World: Breeds mainly in taiga zone from NE Europe e. to ne. Russia (to n. Kamchatka and w. Chukotka). Winters coastally from W Africa e. through tropical Asia to Australia.

North America: *Alaska*: On w. Aleutians, rare and intermittent in spring (late May to mid-Jun), usually singles or small groups, max. 21 on Attu, 25 May 1980; very rare in fall (Aug–early Sep). On cen. Aleutians and Bering Sea islands, very rare in spring (late May–early Jun) and exceptional in fall (Jul–early Sep); exceptional in spring (late May–Jun) on e. Aleutians and w. mainland, and in summer–fall (mid-Jun to mid-Aug) on s-coastal mainland, where no fewer than 7 records from Anchorage area (1977, 1979, 1982, 1984, 1987, 1988, and 1998). *Pacific States and Provinces*: Vancouver Island, BC, 21 Jul–6 Aug 1987 (adult);

and Monterey Co., CA, 28 Aug–23 Sep 1988 (adult). *East*: Churchill, MB, 13 Jul 1972; Essex Co., MA, 23 Jun 1990; Portsmouth, VA, 9 Aug 2008 (*NAB* 63:56, 189).

Comments: AK records conform largely to the pattern of spring drift-overshoots vagrants and misoriented fall migrants (perhaps mainly juvs, although age often unreported). The remarkable series of summer records from the Anchorage area in 1977–1988 might involve a single bird that had wintered in the Americas (as may be true for the 1998 record there), and it is even possible that the BC and CA records refer to the same individual. Both West Coast records were considered to involve adults (unusual among fall vagrants) and the species has wintered in Mexico, presumably having passed through w. N America between years; a Terek Sandpiper spent late Apr–May 2002 and (presumably the same bird) 22 Aug 2002–at least 10 Feb 2003 just s. of our area, in Baja California Sur, Mexico (Galindo et al. 2004).

There are no records of Terek Sandpiper from Greenland, Iceland, or the Azores. However, a single spring 2000 record from Barbados, a late Jun 1999 record from Trinidad and Tobago, and at least 3 Dec–Mar records (1987–1997) from the e. coast of S America (summarized by Galindo et al. 2004), suggest the species is prone to arrive

variable dark braces

dark shoulder

breeding (Mar–Aug)

juv (Aug–Oct)

energetic feeder

Terek Sandpiper

in the New World via a southern Atlantic crossing (see p. 10). It seems possible that the birds in MA and VA reached the Americas via this route, and the same may be true for the MB individual.

Field Identification: Distinctive medium-sized sandpiper with long upturned bill, short yellow to bright orange legs, and conspicuous white trailing edge to upperwings.

Similar Species: None, if well seen.

Age/Sex/Season: Ages differ slightly; sexes similar; distinct seasonal variation. Complete prebasic molt and partial to incomplete preformative molt (can include outer primaries in mid–late winter) in fall–winter, mostly on nonbreeding grounds, but adult often starts head and body molt in fall. Partial prealternate molt in late winter–spring. *Adult*: Breeding plumage has contrasting blackish braces; nonbreeding plumage relatively plain grayish above, with black braces reduced or lacking. In fall migration, head and body often a mix of worn breeding and fresh nonbreeding feathers; outer primaries relatively worn. *1st-year*: Juv plumage usually worn through migration, slightly browner than adult, with subtle pattern of paler fringes and dark subterminal marks on upperwing coverts, fine dark braces, fresh outer primaries. In 1st winter, usually aged by molt contrasts in upperwing coverts and tertials. In spring–summer, resembles adult but juv primaries relatively worn and faded or outers contrastingly fresh.

Habitat and Behavior: Often picks food from the surface with dashing moves, but also probes in mud, like a godwit. At times teeters like a front-heavy Spotted Sandpiper. Call typically 2–5 mellow, monotonic, whistled notes *tu tu tu.*

COMMON SANDPIPER *Actitis hypoleucos*
19–21 cm (7.5–8.3")

Summary: *Alaska*: Rare spring and very rare fall migrant on w. Aleutians (has bred). Very rare in spring and fall on cen. Aleutians and Bering Sea islands. 1 spring record on w. mainland (1989).

Taxonomy: Monotypic.

Status and Distribution:

World: Breeds N Eurasia (e. to Kamchatka and s. Chukotka); winters sub-Saharan Africa and S Asia to Australia.

North America: *Alaska*: On w. Aleutians, rare in spring (mid-May to mid-Jun) and very rare in fall (late Jul to mid-Sep); usually singles or small numbers, max. 34 on Shemya, 29 May 1983; has bred on Attu (1983). On cen. Aleutians and

Bering Sea islands, very rare in spring (late May to mid-Jun), exceptional in fall (late Jun–early Sep). 1 spring record from w. mainland: 30 May 1989 (*AB* 43:525).

Comments: Although much rarer in fall than spring on the AK islands, it seems likely that Common Sandpiper has escaped detection in w. N America, given its similarity to Spotted Sandpiper. Both species are long-distance migrants that have found their way to many remote islands.

Common Sandpiper is scarce as a vagrant in Iceland (10 records through 2006; 5 Spotted Sandpipers in the same period) and unrecorded in Greenland. N American records from that source seem unlikely. There are no confirmed records from the e. Caribbean (Buckley et al. 2009), which likely reflects Common's similarity to the widespread Spotted Sandpiper. Common occurs regularly on the Azores, suggesting it could occur as a vagrant in the se. Caribbean and ne. S America, whence birds could move n. into e. N America.

Field Identification: Similar to Spotted Sandpiper, its New World counterpart.

Similar Species: *Spotted Sandpiper* similar in all plumages other than breeding. In general, bill and legs duller on Common (legs olive to grayish yellow rather than yellow, but some overlap); gray breast smudges show fine dark streaking (plain in Spotted); tail projects farther beyond wing-tip; white wingstripe broader and more extensive on inner wing. Juv Common has tertial fringes finely notched pale (plain on Spotted). Breeding adult Common lacks ventral spotting; bill dark.

Age/Sex/Season: Ages differ; sexes similar; distinct seasonal variation. Complete prebasic molt and incomplete to complete preformative molt in fall–winter, wholly or mostly on nonbreeding grounds. Partial prealternate molt in spring. *Adult*: Breeding plumage with blackish anchor marks on upperparts, dark tertial bars; variably worn in fall or mixed with plainer, nonbreeding feathers; nonbreeding plainer and paler above, tertials with poorly contrasting darker marks. *1st-year*: In fall, juv plumage fresh, with dark subterminal feather fringes on upperparts, notched tertial fringes. In 1st winter, usually aged by molt contrasts in upperwing coverts and tertials. In spring–summer, resembles adult but some may be aged by retained and worn juv inner primaries.

Habitat and Behavior: Similar to Spotted Sandpiper but wingbeats a little more fluid, less

breeding
(Mar–Aug)

Common

more extensive
white wing stripe

Spotted

notched
edge

longer tail

plain breast
sides

juv (Aug–Oct)

Spotted Sandpiper

Common Sandpiper

juv

legs average
brighter

stiff and fluttery. Flight call a slightly descending, high-pitched, piping *swee-swee-swee*, or *sii-sii sii-sii*, often 4 notes; suggests Spotted but more plaintive and, unlike Spotted, not easily confused with calls of Solitary Sandpiper.

GREAT KNOT *Calidris tenuirostris* 26–28 cm (10.2–11")

Summary: *Alaska*: In spring, very rare on St. Lawrence Island and Seward Peninsula, exceptional on w. and cen. Aleutians and Pribilofs. In fall, exceptional on Bering Sea islands. *Oregon*: 1 fall record (1990). *West Virginia*: 1 fall record (2007).
Taxonomy: Monotypic.
Status and Distribution:
   World: Breeds on montane tundra in ne. Russia, e. to Chukotka. Winters mainly in Australia; in smaller numbers along s. coasts of Asia w. to Persian Gulf.
   North America: *Alaska*: On St. Lawrence and w. Seward Peninsula, very rare in spring (late May to mid-Jun), mainly singles or small groups, max. 19 on St. Lawrence, 30 May 1994; few records in

recent years. On w. and cen. Aleutians and Pribilofs, exceptional in spring (late May–early Jun). 2 recent fall records of juvs: St. Lawrence, 22 Aug 1997; Pribilofs, 13 Aug 2010 (*NAB* 65:142). *Oregon*: Coos Co., 1–19 Sep 1990 (juv). *West Virginia*: Putnam Co., 13 Aug 2007 (adult).
Comments: Spring records from the Bering Sea islands and Seward Peninsula are consistent with spring overshoots from the easternmost parts of the species' breeding range. The relative lack of Great Knots in the w. Aleutians in spring appears to be a function of the spring migration route: most birds make their northward migration in 2 huge hops; from Australia nonstop to the Yellow Sea region in China and Korea, and then direct to their breeding grounds; the latter hop is over the Sea of Okhotsk rather than offshore or along the Kuril Islands, and hence they are not overly prone to spring drift.
   The virtual absence of fall records in the West is not easily explained, but as in spring, a relatively 'inland' southward migration means the species is not predisposed to drift from the N Pacific and the few fall records, all juvs, may be

nonbreeding with Red Knot (right)

juv

adult
breeding

adult breeding
(Apr–Sep)

Great Knot

juv (Aug–Oct)

misoriented (reverse?) migrants. The marked decline in N American records since around 2000 mirrors the global decline of this species, linked to loss of habitat at stopover sites in E Asia; for example, some 30–50% of the former tidal flat area of the Yellow Sea has been destroyed in the last 3 decades (Rogers et al. 2009).

There are 3 other reports from the West Coast: Clallam Co., WA, on 6 Sep 1979 (adult in breeding plumage; placed on the state's supplementary list), and singles from Vancouver, BC, 13 May 1987 (oddly in nonbreeding plumage as the species does not usually migrate n. in its 1st summer, cf. Paulson 1993) and 12 Jan 1998. Given the recent misidentification as an adult Great Knot of a hybrid sandpiper (presumed Surfbird × knot sp.) in s. CA, records of Great Knot in N America away from AK should be carefully documented.

The WV bird likely traversed N America from the w., an idea supported by the absence of Great Knot records from Iceland and only a handful from W Europe. It fits into a pattern of adult Siberian shorebirds (such as Lesser Sand Plover and Sharp-tailed Sandpiper) reaching the East in Jul–Aug, and suggests some adults are prone to (reverse?) migration, perhaps after their first

summer spent on the breeding grounds. Most 1st-summer Great Knots and an unknown proportion of 2nd-summers (and even a few 3rd-summers) remain on the nonbreeding grounds or migrate only partially n. (Rogers et al. unpublished ms.; D. I. Rogers, pers. comm.).

Field Identification: Largest *Calidris*, similar in overall structure to Red Knot but somewhat larger, rangier, and averages proportionately longer-billed.

Similar Species: Breeding and juv plumages distinctive, but beware the possibility of hybrid sandpipers that might resemble Great Knot, such as a Surfbird × knot sp. in San Diego Co, CA, in Aug 2009 and Jul 2012 (Lehman 2012). Nonbreeding plumage (unlikely in N America?) resembles slightly smaller Red Knot, which is portrayed poorly in most N American field guides. In flight, tail of Great Knot contrastingly darker than whiter uppertail coverts, and whitish wingstripe narrower and less distinct than Red Knot; dark flank markings consist of smudgy spots and short streaks versus short bars or chevrons typical of Red Knot (which can, however, have smudgy flank spots).

Age/Sex/Season: Ages differ; sexes similar; pronounced seasonal variation. Complete prebasic molt and partial to incomplete preformative molt (sometimes includes outer primaries) in fall–winter; wholly or mostly on nonbreeding grounds. Partial prealternate molt occurs late winter–spring on wintering grounds, with presupplemental molt at spring staging grounds (Battley et al. 2006). *Adult*: In fall migration has worn breeding plumage, relatively worn primaries; in spring has bright breeding plumage, uniformly relatively fresh primaries. *1st-year*: Juv plumage worn through migration, with fresh scaly edgings. In spring–summer, juv primaries relatively worn and faded, or with outer few primaries contrastingly fresh; most if not all 1st-summers attain less extensive breeding plumage than adults and some have a drab nonbreeding plumage. *2nd-year*: Some 2nd-years remain on nonbreeding grounds and average a duller breeding plumage than full adults (3–4 years and older).

Habitat and Behavior: Coastal mudflats, estuaries, and marshes. Behavior much as Red Knot, with which vagrants might occur. Most calls coarser and huskier than those of Red Knot (P. Holt, pers. comm.).

LITTLE STINT *Calidris minuta* 13–15 cm (5.2–5.8")

Summary: *Alaska*: On w. and cen. Aleutians and Bering Sea islands, rare or very rare in fall, exceptional in spring. Very rare in early summer on n. mainland. *West*: In Pacific states and provinces, very rare in fall, exceptional in winter and spring. In the interior, exceptional in spring. *East*: In Atlantic states and provinces, very rare in fall from DE n. In the interior, exceptional in early fall.

Taxonomy: Monotypic.

Status and Distribution:

World: Breeds on Arctic tundra from Scandinavia e. across Eurasia to ne. Russia (Chukotka); winters mainly in sub-Saharan Africa, also e. through tropical India to SE Asia.

North America: *Alaska*: On w. Aleutians, very rare in fall (Aug–early Sep, all juvs), exceptional in spring (late May–early Jun). On cen. Aleutians, exceptional in fall (mid-Aug to mid-Sep; all juvs). On Pribilofs, very rare in fall (late Jul to mid-Sep; about 20 records, 2 adults in late Jul–early Aug, juvs in Aug –Sep), exceptional in spring (mid-May to early Jun). On St Matthew, 1 fall record: 16–21 Aug 1986 (1–2 juvs). On St. Lawrence, exceptional in spring (late May–early Jun); no fall records.

Exceptional in n. AK in early summer (early–late Jun). *West*: In Pacific states and provinces, very rare in fall (Jul to mid-Oct, including 18 adults Jul–early Sep, 10 juvs late Aug to mid-Oct). 2 spring records (mid-May to early Jun): Salton Sea, CA, 18 May 1991; Westminster Co., BC, 2–4 Jun 1992. 2 early winter records (late Nov to mid-Dec): San Bernardino Co., 21 Nov 1988 (1st-year, collected); Marin Co., CA, 16–17 Dec 2010 (1st-year). In the interior, 2 spring records (mid–late May): Judas Creek, YT, 19 May 1997; Chaves Co., NM, 31 May 2005. *East*: In Atlantic states and provinces, very rare in fall (late Jun–Oct, including 17 adults late Jun to mid-Aug, 3 juvs Sep–Oct) all from NB to DE. 2 spring records (late May–early Jun): Kent Co., DE, 23 May 1979; Queens Co., NY, 5 Jun 1984. In the interior, exceptional in fall (Jul–Aug, all adults), with records from ND, s. ON (2), and KY. Iliff & Sullivan (2004) summarized N American records and occurrence patterns through the early 2000s.

Comments: This species has a complex pattern of occurrence. As far as is known, Little Stint doesn't breed commonly e. of around 150°E, about 1600 km (1000 miles) from the nearest parts of w. N America, although the species has been found breeding e. to the Chukotsk Peninsula (see Gibson & Kessel 1992). It is a rare migrant in E Asia, although detection there among huge numbers of Red-necked Stints is clearly a problem. Likewise, a true picture of this species' occurrence patterns in N America is clouded by identification issues, and we suspect that most Little Stints in N America go undetected among the large numbers of Semipalmated and Western Sandpipers.

Spring records from AK may represent overshoots from Asia and perhaps even some birds that have translocated to the Americas. Juvs in w. N America are almost certain to be misoriented individuals from their E Asian breeding range, and likely entered N America across some part of the Bering Sea. The ratio of juvs in fall in N America changes from 90% in AK, to 40% in the West, to 15% in the East. Of note is the absence of juvs from well-watched St. Lawrence in the n. Bering Sea, which strongly indicates that fall misorientation is not randomly directed.

The preponderance of records along the Pacific Coast may be as much the result of the paucity of Semipalmated Sandpipers as anything else. Spring records in the West may involve wayward 1st-years heading n. Some of these vagrants may live out their lives in the Americas, which may account for many fall records of adults in the

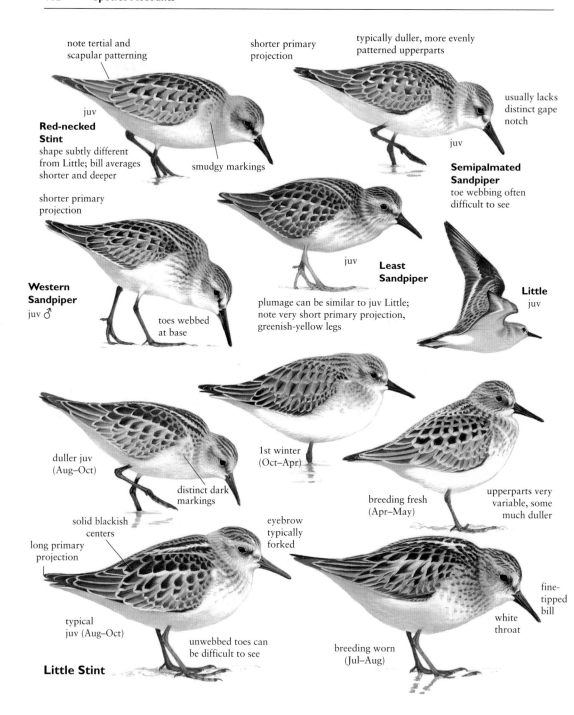

note tertial and scapular patterning

shorter primary projection

typically duller, more evenly patterned upperparts

juv

Red-necked Stint
shape subtly different from Little; bill averages shorter and deeper

smudgy markings

usually lacks distinct gape notch

juv

Semipalmated Sandpiper
toe webbing often difficult to see

shorter primary projection

Western Sandpiper
juv ♂

toes webbed at base

juv

Least Sandpiper

plumage can be similar to juv Little; note very short primary projection, greenish-yellow legs

Little
juv

duller juv (Aug–Oct)

distinct dark markings

1st winter (Oct–Apr)

breeding fresh (Apr–May)

upperparts very variable, some much duller

solid blackish centers

long primary projection

eyebrow typically forked

fine-tipped bill

typical juv (Aug–Oct)

unwebbed toes can be difficult to see

breeding worn (Jul–Aug)

white throat

Little Stint

West and perhaps some of the summer records from n. AK. Occasional individuals may attempt to winter in the US, as with 1 collected in late Nov in San Bernardino Co., CA, and a mid-Dec 1st-year in Marin Co., CA, which easily could have been overlooked before and after the dates it was seen.

Eastern records seem more complicated. Some of the birds, notably the juvs, likely came from the nw. and traversed the continent, a pattern seen in a number of other species across several families. Among other widespread Eurasian vagrant shorebirds recorded in the East, juvs represent fewer than 10% of fall records for Curlew Sandpiper and Ruff, versus much higher percentages in the West (such as 50% of CA records of Curlew Sandpiper); juvs of these species could easily all have come from E Asia, as presumably occurs with juv Sharp-tailed Sandpipers in the East.

The origin of adults is more problematic. That most records of Little Stint from the East involve adults might argue that E Asian origin isn't often the case, but most fall adult Lesser Sand Plovers and Red-necked Stints in the East presumably originated in E Asia, suggesting this route is possible for adult Little Stint. Moreover, separation of juv Little Stint from the vast numbers of Semipalmated and Least Sandpipers that flood the East in fall makes detection difficult, so the true ratio of adults to juveniles is not known.

It seems possible that some or most Little Stints found in the East (along with Curlew Sandpipers and Ruffs) originally crossed the tropical Atlantic to winter in ne. S America, and moved n. into N America. We favor this explanation for most records in the East, as it helps explain the concentration of records along the E Coast; e. breeding Semipalmated Sandpipers have more e. wintering ranges, and vagrant Little Stints wintering in ne. S America would be most likely to join those populations and migrate with them. That Little Stint is regular in the Azores on fall migration supports this theory; all long-distance migrants recorded frequently in the Azores have also been recorded in ne. S America and/or the se. Caribbean; there are also 4 Apr–May records from Barbados since 1998 and 1 record from Bermuda, 8–11 Jun 1975.

It is also possible that some records of Little Stint in the East (along with Curlew Sandpipers and Ruffs) involve birds that traveled s. down the W Coast and wintered in S America before returning n. in spring (cf. spring records of Lesser Sand Plover in LA and ON).

We suspect the virtual lack of spring records of Little Stint in the East reflects a relatively rapid (and perhaps largely offshore?) northward migration, versus a more leisurely southbound migration that coincides with greater observer coverage; a similar spring versus fall imbalance is also shown in records of White-winged Tern, likely for the same reasons. It is unclear to what extent the lack of Little Stint records s. of DE indicates that birds migrate offshore between the E Coast and S America versus being perhaps overlooked in the Southeast and Gulf States.

There seems little likelihood that Little Stints cross the n. N Atlantic other than perhaps exceptionally. The species is rare in Iceland, with only 19 records through 2006 (all in fall), and unrecorded in Greenland. For Bar-tailed Godwit,

while at least 90% of records in the East refer to the W European ssp *lapponica*, we know of no confirmed record of a juv of this ssp, supporting the contention that a direct fall crossing of the n. N Atlantic by European shorebirds happens only very rarely, even for High Arctic breeders. By contrast, about 70% of CA fall records of Bar-tailed Godwit involve juvs, a more typical ratio for direct shorebird vagrancy.

Field Identification: Very similar, especially in nonbreeding plumage, to other small, dark-legged *Calidris* (see below). Note pot-bellied shape, thicker and more prominent gape mark (relative to Semipalmated and Western), and unwebbed toes (often difficult to see). For further information see Viet & Jonsson (1984), Paulson (1993, 2005), O'Brien et al. (2006).

Similar Species: ***Semipalmated Sandpiper*** similar in all nonbreeding plumages. Shape typically stockier, due in part to shorter primary projection; bill often thicker with blunter tip and lacks distinct gape notch typical of Little Stint. Juv Semipalmated colder-toned, lacking rusty edges to the upperwing coverts and typically the scapulars, although some show narrow rusty edges to upper scapulars and crown; the longest scapulars have less solidly black centers (usually having a blacker shaft streak or anchor); and typically, they also lack the pronounced split eyebrow and well-defined white 'braces' of Little Stint. Finally and definitively, the feet are partially webbed between the front toes, but this can be very difficult to see in the field. Winter birds are even more similar and possibly not safely identifiable in the field unless toe webbing is seen. Typical calls include a rough *cherk* and a clipped *kip*.

Red-necked Stint: Subtly shorter legged, longer bodied, and deeper billed than Little Stint. Breeding birds always show rufous somewhere on the throat (bordered below with dark streaks), an area that is white on Little Stint. Wing coverts and tertials dark-centered and fringed buff to pale grayish, lacking the rusty fringe coloration of breeding Little. Juv Red-necked has bright rusty-edged scapulars contrasting with grayish-edged upperwing coverts; whitish 'braces' typically less pronounced; and head and chest typically more diffusely patterned, with dusky streaking at sides of breast averaging blurrier. Nonbreeding Red-necked averages plainer and paler above, lacking the slightly mottled look of Little; scapulars and upperwing coverts pale gray with narrow dark shaft streaks. Typical call a short *stit*, similar to Little Stint.

Western Sandpiper averages larger, with a larger head, longer and heavier bill (very rarely with distinct gape notch), and partially webbed toes. However, bright fall juv male Western (which is shorter-billed than female) can be rather similar in plumage to juv Little Stint (with reddish upperparts, white braces, split eyebrow, etc.). Little tends to have darker and rustier, more contrasting sides of breast, and has longer primary projection. Typical calls of Western are a slightly Dunlin-like, downslurred *dzew* and high, slightly reedy *chiit*. Juv Little and Red-necked Stints, like Semipalmated Sandpiper, delay most or all preformative molt until reaching the wintering grounds. Thus, a small 1st-year *Calidris* in active body molt in N America is probably a Western Sandpiper, but 1st-year Little Stints attempting to winter in N America may exhibit the same pattern.

Least Sandpiper overlaps in size with Little Stint and upperparts of brightly patterned juv can strongly suggest juv Little. Note Least's short primary projection, yellowish legs (can be stained dark by mud), more extensive brownish wash across breast, and voice.

Age/Sex/Season: Ages differ; sexes similar; pronounced seasonal variation. Complete prebasic molt and incomplete to complete preformative molt in fall–early winter, mostly on nonbreeding grounds, but adult can have variable molt of head and body before and during migration. Partial prealternate molt in late winter–spring on wintering grounds. ***Adult***: In fall, wings relatively worn or molt interrupted with fresher inner primaries; head and upperparts in worn breeding or with a mix of nonbreeding feathers; in spring, not distinguishable from 1st-years that have a complete preformative molt. ***1st-year***: In fall, wings uniformly fresh; upperparts wholly or mostly juv, with fresh scaly edgings; winter wing molt averages later than adult wing molt (mainly Dec–Apr vs. Sep–Jan). In spring, some 1st-years may be aged by any retained juv primaries being relatively worn and faded, or with the outer primaries contrastingly fresh.

Habitat and Behavior: Typical small *Calidris*, associating readily with other small sandpipers. Most common call a short, high-pitched *stit* or *tiit*, at times in rapid short series, as when flushed.

TEMMINCK'S STINT *Calidris temminckii*
13–15 cm (5.2–5.8')

Summary: *Alaska*: On w. Aleutians, uncommon but intermittent in spring, exceptional in fall.

On cen. Aleutians and Bering Sea islands, very rare or exceptional in spring and fall. Exceptional in n. AK. ***Pacific States and Provinces***: Single fall records from BC (1982) and WA (2005).

Taxonomy: Monotypic.

Distribution and Status:

World: Breeds on tundra across N Eurasia, e. to Chukotka. Winters in equatorial Africa, India, and SE Asia.

North America: ***Alaska***: In spring, uncommon and intermittent on w. Aleutians (mid-May to early Jun), mainly singles and small groups, exceptionally max. 43 on Attu, 23 May 1991; very rare on cen. Aleutians and Bering Sea islands (mid-May to mid-Jun). In fall, exceptional (records Aug and later being juvs) on w. and cen. Aleutians (mid-Jul to mid-Sep), very rare on Pribilofs (Jul–early Sep); 1 record from St. Lawrence, 28 Aug 1999. Exceptional in n. AK (mid–late Jun; *FN* 48:977, *FN* 52:491). ***Pacific States and Provinces***: Westminster Co., BC, 1–4 Sep 1982 (juv); Grays Harbor Co., WA, 9–13 Nov 2005 (worn juv).

Comments: There are unexpectedly few records of this species on mainland N America. We suspect this is in part a detection issue, given this species' penchant for freshwater marshes. In e. N America, the likelihood of occurrence is further diminished by the species' scarcity in areas that mirror vagrant occurrences in e. N America; for example, there were only 2 records from Iceland through 2012 (Jun and Oct), 2 mid-Jul records from ne. Greenland, only 3 from the Azores since 1978, and none from Barbados.

Field Identification: A small, relatively long-tailed stint with a slender bill, greenish-yellow legs, and bright white outer rectrices.

Similar Species: Fairly distinctive but could be passed off as Least Sandpiper, especially in nonbreeding plumage. Note long, white-sided tail of Temminck's, distinctive juv and breeding plumages, and call.

Age/Sex/Season: Ages differ; sexes similar; distinct seasonal variation. Complete prebasic molt and partial to incomplete preformative molt (sometimes outer primaries molted on wintering grounds) in fall–winter; adult wing molt mostly or wholly on nonbreeding grounds, but some head and body molt before migration. Partial prealternate molt late winter–spring on wintering grounds. ***Adult***: In fall, wings relatively worn or molt interrupted with fresher inner primaries; head and upperparts often mostly nonbreeding and gray overall, or mixed with worn breeding feathers; in spring, primaries uniformly relatively

adult
breeding

white sides

adult breeding
(Apr–Aug)

long tail

adult
nonbreeding
(Aug–Apr)

juv (Aug–Nov)

Temminck's Stint

fresh. *1st-year*: In fall, wings uniformly fresh; upperparts mostly or wholly juv, with fresh scaly edgings. Some may be aged in 1st winter by molt contrasts in greater coverts and tertials (see pp. 35–36). In spring, juv primaries relatively worn and faded, or with outer few primaries contrastingly fresh.

   Habitat and Behavior: Prefers pools, marshes, pond and stream edges; typically avoids open mudflats. Can be inconspicuous, creeping slowly, hunched on flexed legs. When flushed tends to rise quickly, and quick deep wingbeats can suggest a swallow or Solitary Sandpiper. Common flight call a dry trilled *tirrrrr*, often repeated and suggesting trilled flight call of Snow Bunting.

LONG-TOED STINT *Calidris subminuta*
13–14.5 cm (5.2–5.7")

Summary: *Alaska*: On w. Aleutians, uncommon but irregular in spring, rare in fall. Very rare in spring on cen. Aleutians and Bering Sea islands; exceptional in fall on Bering Sea islands. *Pacific States and Provinces*: Single fall records from OR (1981) and CA (1988).

Taxonomy: Monotypic.
Distribution and Status:
   World: Breeding range not well known, but mainly in taiga zone of ne. Russia, e. to Chukotka. Winters from tropical India e. through SE Asia to Australia.
   North America: *Alaska*: On w. Aleutians, uncommon but irregular migrant in spring (May–Jun, mainly mid-May to early Jun), usually singles and small groups, exceptional max. 110 on Attu, 9 May 1998; rare in fall (mid-Jul to Sep, mainly Aug–early Sep). Very rare in spring on cen. Aleutians (mid–late May) and Bering Sea islands (mid-May to early Jun). Exceptional in fall (late Jul to mid-Sep) on Bering Sea islands. No acceptable records from mainland. *Pacific States and Provinces*: single juvs in Clatsop Co., OR, 2–6 Sep 1981, and Monterey Co., CA, 29 Aug–2 Sep 1988.
Comments: The spring distribution of Long-toed Stint in w. AK is typical of a drift migrant/vagrant, and the species breeds nearby on the Commander Islands. The relative scarcity of fall records is not easily explained.
   Away from the Aleutians and Bering Sea islands, and like Temminck's Stint, Long-toed

Least Sandpiper

forehead usually pale

1st-winter (Sep–Apr)

broad dark shafts

wing coverts edged rusty

black lower mandible

juv

nonbreeding

toes project noticeably

dark centers

juv worn (Sep–Oct)

usually pale base to lower mandible

nonbreeding (Aug–Apr)

wing coverts edged whitish

dark forehead joins lores

juv fresh (Aug–Sep)

breeding (Apr–Aug)

stance often upright

Long-toed Stint

Stint is probably overlooked given that acceptable habitat is widely distributed and the species is not identifiable at a glance by most observers. Several other fall reports from the West Coast, some accepted by state committees, lack photo documentation or diagnostic photos; for example, numerous unsubstantiated reports from BC (see R. W. Campbell et al. 1990). Given the challenges inherent in separating Long-toed Stint from Least Sandpiper, we consider such records uncertain (also see Paulson 1993; Hamilton et al. 2007).

Field Identification: Very similar to Least Sandpiper but toes project noticeably beyond tail in flight, and call often distinct. Plumage pattern can suggest much larger Pectoral and Sharp-tailed sandpipers. For further information see

Viet & Jonsson (1984), Alström & Olsson (1989), Paulson (1993, 2005), O'Brien et al. (2006).

Similar Species: Similar to *Least Sandpiper* in all plumages but less compact in build, with slightly longer legs and toes (beware, Least Sandpiper has relatively long toes); in flight, toes project noticeably beyond tail tip (and may even suggest Wood Sandpiper!), whereas toe tips do not or only barely project on Least; bill of Long-toed has pale base to lower mandible (sometimes restricted). A number of plumage features are also helpful, but most can be matched by Least Sandpiper. On Long-toed, dark forehead typically reaches bill and joins with dark lores (most pronounced on juv, occasionally absent on nonbreeding). Juv Long-toed has whitish-edged wing coverts that contrast with rusty-edged scapulars (wing coverts and scapulars both edged rusty on Least); Long-toed breeding plumage has scapulars and tertials broadly edged rusty; on nonbreeding, longest scapulars have large, clearly defined dark centers (vs. narrower centers on Least).

Age/Sex/Season: Ages differ slightly; sexes similar; distinct seasonal variation. Complete prebasic molt and partial to incomplete preformative molt (sometimes outer primaries molted on wintering grounds) in fall–early winter; adult wing molt wholly or mostly on nonbreeding grounds, but some head and body molt before migration. Partial prealternate molt late winter–spring on wintering grounds. *Adult*: In fall, wings relatively worn or molt interrupted with fresher inner primaries; head and upperparts can have mix of fresh nonbreeding and worn breeding feathers; in spring, primaries uniformly relatively fresh. *1st-year*: In fall, wings uniformly fresh; upperparts wholly or mostly juv, with fresh scaly edgings. Some may be aged in 1st winter by molt contrasts in greater coverts and tertials (see pp. 35–36). In spring, juv primaries relatively worn and faded, or with outer few primaries contrastingly fresh.

Habitat and Behavior: Much like Least Sandpiper, but longer legs and neck cause foraging birds to bend over more; when alert, stretched upright stance is characteristic. Common flight call distinct, a trilled *churrt*, often repeated, and lower than Least Sandpiper's typical, reedier flight call (beware that call of Least notoriously variable, and has lower-pitched variations).

SPOON-BILLED SANDPIPER
Calidris pygmaea 14–16 cm (5.5–6.3")

Summary: *Alaska*: Exceptional in spring and fall. *British Columbia*: 1 fall record (1978).
Taxonomy: Monotypic.
Distribution and Status:

World: Breeds on coastal tundra in extreme ne. Russia (e. to Chukotka); winters in SE Asia. Population declining, and species widely considered in danger of extinction.

North America: *Alaska*: 4 records, at least 3 of adults: Buldir, 2 Jun 1977 (female); Attu, 30 May–3 Jun 1986 (2–3); Pribilofs, 20 Aug 1989 (age unknown); and n. AK, 27 Jun 1993. *British Columbia*: Westminster Co., 30 Jul–3 Aug 1978 (adult).

We have not accepted 2 records from s. AB (19 May 1984 (2) and 9 May 1992); these were included by ABA (2008) but reclassified by the provincial committee as 'identification not established' (Hudon et al. 2011).

juv

bill shape not obvious in profile

nonbreeding
(Sep–Apr)

juv (Aug–Oct)

**Spoon-billed
Sandpiper**

breeding
(Apr–Sep)

Comments: Most if not all records involve adults in breeding plumage, including an earlier record of 2 collected at Wainwright, nw. AK, 15 Aug 1914. The far ne. breeding range of this species and its lengthy E Asian migration routes make it a likely candidate for drift-overshoot or misorientation occurrences in w. Alaska and elsewhere in w. N America. However, its tiny and declining world population and the surprising difficulty of picking one out from large flocks of small sandpipers, especially in fall, sadly makes further detection in N America an unlikely event.

Field Identification: Very similar to Red-necked Stint but with less attenuated rear end and distinctive bill, with heavy base and unique spatulate tip (latter not always obvious in profile).

Similar Species: Unique bill diagnostic, but can be difficult to see clearly amid a feeding flock, and of course hidden when roosting. Breeding plumage much like **Red-necked Stint** but dark streaking extends down flanks, rear end less attenuated. Juv and nonbreeding plumages similar to Red-necked Stint, but with whiter face and pale eyebrow setting off dark cheek patch.

Age/Sex/Season: Ages differ; sexes similar; pronounced seasonal variation. Molt and aging probably like other small, long-distance migrant *Calidris*, but unknown whether has preformative wing molt of outer primaries. Prebasic and preformative molts occur in fall–winter, wholly or mostly on nonbreeding grounds; partial prealternate molt occurs late winter–spring. *Adult*: In fall, wings relatively worn (or molt interrupted with fresher inner primaries?); head and upperparts mainly worn breeding plumage, possibly with a mix of fresh nonbreeding feathers. In spring, primaries uniformly rather fresh, head and breast bright rufous. *1st-year*: In fall, wings uniformly fresh; upperparts wholly or mostly juv, with fresh scaly edgings. Some probably can be aged in 1st winter by molt contrasts in greater coverts and tertials (see pp. 35–36). In spring, juv primaries relatively worn and faded (or outer few primaries contrastingly fresh?); head and breast may average duller and paler than adult, with extensive whitish throat area (N. Moores and D. Rogers, pers. comm.)

Habitat and Behavior: Coastal. Prefers shallow tidal pools and sandy substrate, though also mudflats, pool and pond edges. Watch for characteristic, Avocet-like side-to-side bill action while wading in shallow water. Usually silent, migrants occasionally give a shrill, piping whistle, *peet* (P. Holt, pers. comm.).

BROAD-BILLED SANDPIPER *Calidris falcinellus* 16–18 cm (6.3–7")

Summary: *Alaska*: Very rare in fall on w. and cen. Aleutians and Bering Sea islands. *The Northeast*: Single fall records from NY (1998) and MA (2002).

Taxonomy: 2 ssp recognized, not certainly separable in the field except perhaps extremes in breeding plumage: relative to nominate *falcinellus* of Scandinavia and w. Russia, e. Russian ssp *sibirica* averages brighter, with more rufous on upperparts and often a rufous wash to breast. AK specimens are referred to *sibirica*.

Distribution and Status:

World: Breeds locally in taiga zone of Scandinavia and n. Russia, e. to around 165°E; winters in tropics from E Africa e. through coastal SE Asia to Australia.

North America: *Alaska*: Very rare in fall (mid-Aug to early Sep; all specifically aged birds being juvs) on w. and cen. Aleutians, max. 5 on Shemya, 30 Aug–6 Sep 1978; also 1 on Pribilofs, 29–31 Aug 2009 (*NAB* 64:133). *Northeast*: Single juvs at Queens Co., NY, 27 Aug–4 Sep 1998, and Essex Co., MA, 10 Sep 2002. 2 fall reports from NS (Sep 1990, Sep 2008; McLaren 2012) appear not to be widely accepted.

Comments: All records are from fall, as with Marsh Sandpiper, and these are the only 2 vagrant shorebirds with this seasonal distribution. Records of both may reflect reverse migration, mostly or wholly of 1st-year birds. Spring migration of Broad-billed Sandpiper in E Asia is not well known but appears to be mainly coastal, with most birds perhaps turning inland from the coast of China (Higgins & Davies 1996); thus, spring drift vagrants to AK are unlikely.

There were just 5 records from Iceland through 2002 (4 in May–Jun, 1 in Aug) and no records from the Azores or the se. Caribbean, suggesting that E Coast records are likely of birds that traveled from the w.

Field Identification: Distinctive small sandpiper, in size between Dunlin and peeps. Relatively long, deep-based bill straight throughout most of its length but with distinctive kink at tip; legs relatively short and dark olive. Forked eyebrow usually distinct (but matched by many peeps, especially in juv plumage).

Similar Species: None in N America.

adult nonbreeding
(Aug–Apr)

paler
juv

juv

breeding (Apr–Aug)
becomes darker with wear

**Broad-billed
Sandpiper**

juv (Aug–Oct)

brighter
individual

Age/Sex/Season: Ages differ; sexes similar; pronounced seasonal variation. Fresh breeding (Mar–Apr) frosty, becoming appreciably darker through wear by mid–late spring (May–Jun). Complete prebasic molt and partial to incomplete preformative molt (tail and sometimes outer primaries molted on wintering grounds) in fall–early winter; adult wing molt wholly or mostly on nonbreeding grounds, but often much head and body molt before migration. Partial prealternate molt late winter–spring on wintering grounds. **Adult**: In fall, wings relatively worn or molt interrupted with fresher inner primaries; head and upperparts often mostly nonbreeding and gray overall, or mixed with worn breeding feathers; in spring, primaries uniformly quite fresh. **1st-year**: In fall, wings uniformly fresh; upperparts mostly or wholly juv, with fresh scaly edgings. Some may be aged in 1st winter by molt contrasts in greater coverts and tertials (see pp. 35–36). In spring, juv primaries relatively worn and faded, or with outer few primaries contrastingly fresh.

Habitat and Behavior: Mudflats, marshes, salt ponds, coastal lagoons, etc. Associates readily with other small sandpipers. Feeds on mud or in shallow water, by probing. Call a rather Dunlin-like, buzzy *dzeerrt* with an upward inflection.

ORIENTAL PRATINCOLE *Glareola maldivarum* 23–25 cm (9–9.5")

Summary: *Alaska*: Single spring records from w. Aleutians (1985) and Bering Sea islands (1986).
Taxonomy: Monotypic.
Distribution and Status:
   World: Breeds from n. India e. to se. Russia (to around 130°E); winters SE Asia to Australia.
   North America: *Alaska*: Attu, 19–20 May 1985; St. Lawrence, 5 Jun 1986.
Comments: The paucity of Oriental Pratincole records in N America isn't surprising given that the nearest point of the species' breeding range is about 3500 km (over 2000 miles) from AK. The AK records are consistent with drift-overshoot vagrancy. Arguing in favor of future records (which also seem possible in fall) are the species' large population size and long-distance migration with substantial overwater segments, although this last point may be mitigated by the species being largely a diurnal migrant, at least in E Asia.
Field Identification: Distinctive, aerial-feeding shorebird unlike any bird species in N America.
   Similar Species: None in N America, but similar to **Collared Pratincole** and **Black-winged Pratincole** *G. nordmanni* of W Eurasia, neither

adult breeding
(Feb-Aug)

adult
nonbreeding
(Aug-Mar)

adult
breeding
(Feb-Aug)

juv
(Aug-Sep)

**Oriental
Pratincole**

of which has been recorded in N America (but Collared has reached Barbados, and both have reached Iceland). Oriental differs primarily by its much shorter tail, falling short of the wing-tip at rest. In flight shows rufous underwing coverts like Collared (can be hard to see), and lacks white trailing edge to secondaries like Black-winged (but lacks that species' uniform upper-wing surface). Note too that white trailing edge of Collared can become worn and is occasionally difficult to see. See Driessens & Svensson (2005) for further identification criteria.

Age/Sex/Season: Ages differ, with adult appearance attained in 1st winter–spring; sexes similar; seasonal variation pronounced in adults. Complete prebasic and (usually) complete preformative molts in fall–winter usually interrupted (somewhere in middle primaries) for migration; 1st-year averages later molt than adult. Partial prealternate molt in winter–spring before migration. *Adult*: in fall lacks scaly buff tips to upperparts, outer primaries worn and faded. *1st-year*: In fall has variable extent of buff-tipped juv feathers above, fresh outer primaries; bill base duller pinkish than adult, at least through 1st winter (P. Holt, pers. comm.). Resembles adult by spring but some birds can retain some worn juv inner-middle secondaries, and occasionally outer primaries.

Habitat and Behavior: Open ground, including cultivated fields, mud flats, rice paddies and the like. Feeds mainly by hawking insects in flight,

like a giant swallow or marsh tern; flight buoyant with fluid, easy wingbeats and only brief glides, usually 3–30 m above a marsh, field, or beach. Largely a diurnal migrant. Most common calls, given in flight and at rest, are a loud, staccato *krer-dik* or *cheer-it*, recalling Least Tern (P. Holt, pers. comm.).

New World Shorebirds

The 3 species of New World vagrant shorebirds show different 'patterns' of occurrence; the single records of Double-striped Thick-knee (in early winter; arrival date unknown) and Collared Plover (spring) are both from Texas and likely represent wandering individuals from nearby populations in Mexico. The record(s) of Southern Lapwing in spring–summer may reflect misoriented dispersal after the drying up of wetlands in n. S America, but also may be linked to the species' steady northward range expansion through Middle America.

DOUBLE-STRIPED THICK-KNEE
Burhinus bistriatus 45.5–50.5 cm (18–20")

Summary: *Texas*: 1 winter record (1961).
Taxonomy: 4 ssp, not known to be distinguishable in the field. TX specimen presumably of Middle American ssp *bistriatus*.
Distribution and Status:
    World: Resident locally from e. Mexico to n.S America; also Hispaniola.

juv

adult

adult

Double-striped Thick-knee

North America: **Texas**: Kleberg Co., 5 Dec 1961 (female, probably imm, collected; MacInnes & Chamberlain 1963).

Comments: In Mexico at least, Double-striped Thick-knees adapt to farmland that retains at least a semblance of the aspect of native grassland and savanna. However, the species has not shown any appreciable, or at least rapid, range expansion that would seem possible given the extensive deforestation that has created much apparently suitable thick-knee habitat in e. Mexico (Howell, pers. obs.).

In parts of Latin America this species may be kept as a 'watch-dog,' and a tame bird found in s. AZ in Nov 1989 was apparently transplanted from Guatemala (Rosenberg 1991). The TX record has long stood alone as a unique vagrant occurrence, but the discovery in 2003 of a pair of nesting Double-striped Thick-knees on Great Inagua, in the Bahamas (*NAB* 57:418, 432), suggests the species wanders on occasion.

Field Identification: Large nocturnal shorebird, with long yellow legs, staring yellow eyes.

Similar Species: Nothing similar in N America; the possibility of other thick-knees (known as stone-curlews in Europe) should be considered from the viewpoint of potential escapes.

Age/Sex/Season: Ages differ, with adult appearance presumably attained in 1 year; sexes

similar; no seasonal variation. Molts not well known. **1st-year**: Relative to adult, juv has shorter and broader black-and-white head stripes that do not extend much forward of eye, and an additional short blackish stripe under rear end of white eyebrow; neck and chest more finely streaked than adult; eyes duller and bill base grayer. Resembles adult after preformative molt, which probably occurs within a few months of fledging.

Habitat and Behavior: Grassland and farmland, often with scattered bushes and trees. A nocturnal feeder, spending the day sleeping on the ground or in the shade of bushes, when can be overlooked easily. Runs strongly, and in the daytime often reluctant to fly. Sharp barking and clucking calls given mainly at night, at times in steady series when agitated; at a distance may suggest a chorus of frogs.

SOUTHERN LAPWING *Vanellus [chilensis] cayennensis* 34–36 cm (13.5–14.2")

Summary: *East*: 1–2 spring–early summer records from FL (2006) and MD (2006).

Taxonomy: 4 ssp in 2 groups, probably representing separate species (Fjeldsa & Krabbe 1990): *chilensis* group (ssp *chilensis* and *fretensis*) of Chile and adjacent s. Argentina differs

striking and
unmistakable

adult

adult

Southern Lapwing

appreciably from smaller, proportionately longer-legged, and vocally distinct *cayennensis* group (ssp *cayennensis* and *lampronotus*) that occurs to the e. and n.

N American records involve ssp *cayennensis*, distinguished from other taxa by solidly sandy gray-brown foreneck, lacking a black median stripe that connects the black chest patch to the relatively small black throat patch. On *lampronotus*, black throat stripe usually extends noticeably down into the foreneck; in *chilensis* group, black throat and chest patches are connected. Head sides and neck bluish gray on *chilensis* group, distinct from sandy gray-brown of *cayennensis*.

Distribution and Status:
   World: S America n. to s. Cen America, where expanding range northward.

   North America: *East*: Single *cayennensis* in Wakulla Co., nw. FL, 6 May–11 Jun 2006 (*NAB* 60:520) and Worcester Co., MD, 17 Jun 2006 (*NAB* 60:514, 596); conceivably the same bird involved in both records. Considered of uncertain provenance by state committees and not accepted by ABA (2008) as occurring in N America.

Comments: Populations of *cayennensis* in n. S America fluctuate seasonally and have been expanding for an undetermined period, perhaps in association with forest clearing. The rate of spreading may have increased since about 1980, as noted in Panama and Ecuador (Ridgely

& Gwynne 1989; Ridgely & Greenfield 2001). The first records for Costa Rica were in 1995 (with breeding recorded in 2005; *NAB* 59:338), Mexico in 1996 (Martin 1997), and Belize in 2004 (*NAB* 59:163). The 2 recent US records fit this pattern and it seems reasonable to consider them as being of wild vagrants. Assuming the range expansion continues in Latin America, we would expect more records to follow in N America.

   5 records from FL in 1959–1962 predate the recent range expansion and have been treated as escapes, and 2 individuals in FL (2002–2003) included an escaped non-*cayennensis* individual with a color band (Pranty 2004).

Field Identification: Large handsome plover; boldly patterned wings and tail striking in flight.

   Similar Species: None in N America, but beware escapes involving other taxa of Southern Lapwing (see Taxonomy, above).

   Age/Sex/Season: Ages differ slightly, with adult appearance attained in 1 year; sexes similar; no seasonal variation. Molts not well known. *1st-year*: Juv duller overall than adult, with shorter crest, white-freckled forehead and throat, and buff-spotted crown and upperparts; looks much like adult following partial preformative molt in first few months of life.

   Habitat and Behavior: Open country in general, from farmland to beaches and lake shore, but usually avoids tidal mud flats. Conspicuous and, at least in S America, often noisy, giving a variety of strident shrieking cries and barks.

COLLARED PLOVER *Charadrius collaris*
14–15 cm (5.5–6")

Summary: *Texas*: 1 spring record (1992).
Taxonomy: Monotypic.
Distribution and Status:
    World: Local resident from tropical Mexico s. to cen. Chile and cen. Argentina, mainly in coastal lowlands.
    North America: *Texas*: Uvalde Co., 9–12 May 1992 (1st-year).
Comments: Although many observers might have predicted this species would instead be first found at a coastal location in TX, it does occur regularly up to elevations of 1500 m (5000 feet) in the interior of Mexico (mainly Oct–May; Howell and Webb 1994). Elsewhere it undergoes poorly known local migrations and seasonal movements, and has been reported as a vagrant in the s. Caribbean (Raffaelle et al. 1998). It thus seems a candidate for future vagrancy. At least in w. Mexico, however, coastal breeding populations appear to have declined in the past 25 years, presumably due to increased human (and associated canine) disturbance and habitat alteration (Howell, pers. obs.).
Field Identification: Slightly smaller and more lightly built than Semipalmated Plover with slender black bill and fairly long, pale pinkish legs.
    Similar Species: Superficially suggests other small plovers, especially **Wilson's Plover** (which shares black-and-rufous head markings, pale pinkish legs, and has somewhat similar call), but note Collared's small size, light build, slender black bill, and (ironically) lack of a whitish hindcollar (except when faded, on some 1st-years).
    Age/Sex/Season: Ages differ, with adult appearance attained in 1 year; sexes similar, although males average brighter and blacker head markings, as in other small plovers; no distinct seasonal variation, but head pattern can be veiled in fresh plumage. Molts not well known.
1st-year: Juv has chest 'band' restricted to dark patches at sides of chest, lacks strong head patterning (black frontal band absent); resembles adult after preformative molt within 1–2 months of fledging. 1st-year birds average duller than adults, and can show molt contrasts on upperparts, especially faded upperwing coverts (see pp. 35–36).

collar varies with posture

adult fresh (colors subdued)

♂ breeding (♀ averages duller)

juv

Collared Plover

faded and molting 1st-year can show paler hindcollar

Habitat and Behavior: Coastal and inland, from sandy beaches, coastal lagoons, and aquaculture ponds to lakes, reservoirs, and stony river banks. Associates at least loosely with other small plovers, especially when roosting. At other times tends to feed on its own with typical stop-start plover action. Flight call a sharp *pik!* or *peek*, which may suggest Wilson's Plover.

WADING BIRDS

Wading birds as defined here include a variety of species typically associated with marshes, namely herons, storks, cranes, rails, and jacanas. Migratory herons are prone to vagrancy via drift and overshooting, and birds of tropical marshes have demonstrated often spectacular dispersal abilities, presumably linked to the potentially ephemeral nature of their wetland habitats. In N America we consider 18 species of wading birds as rare birds. Of these, the Old World contributes 12 species (7 herons, 2 cranes, 3 rails) and the New World 6 (1 heron, 1 stork, 3 rails, and 1 jacana).

Identification of herons and egrets often requires attention to structure (especially bill size and leg length), as well as to coloration of bare parts. Calls of various egrets (most often given in flight on being flushed, or while migrating at night) may be diagnostic, but we have insufficient experience to make useful comparisons for most species treated here.

Old World Wading Birds

Vagrant herons in the US have occurred in both w. AK and the Northeast. From the AK islands there are records, mainly in spring, of Yellow Bittern, Eurasian Bittern (see Appendix A), Gray Heron, Chinese Pond Heron, and Intermediate, Little, and Chinese Egrets. Of heron species recorded in the East, Gray Herons have arrived by the northern route in fall, whereas Little Egret and Western Reef Heron have arrived in spring–summer, presumably via the southern route (see p. 10). Common Crane and Demoiselle Crane have both been recorded in the West and interior West, and presumably arrived via AK, often in association with Sandhill Cranes. Eurasian Coot has one late fall record from the Bering Sea and a winter record from e. Canada (whence there are also a few pre-1950 winter records); Common Moorhen has one recent fall record from AK; and Corncrake is a very rare late fall vagrant to the Northeast.

Other Old World wading birds that have reached the Lesser Antilles and ne. S America, but to date have not been detected in N America, include Little Bittern *Ixobrychus minutus*, Purple Heron *Ardea purpurea*, Squacco Heron *Ardeola ralloides*, White Stork *Ciconia ciconia*, European Spoonbill *Platalea leucorodia*, and Spotted Crake *Porzana porzana* (Ebels 2002; Buckley et al. 2009). Possibilities from E Asia include Striated Heron *Butorides striata*, Baillon's Crake (see Appendix B), and Brown-cheeked (Eastern Water) Rail *Rallus indicus*.

YELLOW BITTERN *Ixobrychus sinensis*
30–40 cm (12.8–15.8")

Summary: *Alaska*: 1 spring record from w. Aleutians (1989).
Taxonomy: Monotypic.
Distribution and Status:
    World: India e. to Japan and se. Russia (n. to about 45°N), s. locally to New Guinea and Micronesia; ne. populations migratory, wintering to and perhaps beyond s. edge of breeding range.
    North America: *Alaska*: 1 record: Attu, 17–22 May 1989 (female; Gibson & Kessel 1992).
Comments: Presumably a drift vagrant, as with other Asian herons found in the Aleutians.
Field Identification: E Asian counterpart to Least Bittern.
    Similar Species: None in AK. All plumages of *Least Bittern* darker overall, with rufous to chestnut greater upperwing coverts, cinnamon to rufous tips to alula and primary coverts (all-blackish on Yellow Bittern); post-juvenile plumages of Least have back black (male) to dark brown (female).
    Age/Sex/Season: Ages differ, with adult appearance attained in 2nd year; sexes differ; no seasonal variation. Molts not well known. *Adult* has uniform generation plumage and relatively fresh remiges in spring–summer, lacks dusky streaking on upperwing coverts. *Male* has blackish median crown with little or no brown streaking, relatively indistinct dark streaking on foreneck, more uniform back. *Female* has browner median crown, often suffused rufous at sides, stronger dark streaking on foreneck, and more distinct pale striping on back. *1st-year*: Juv has distinct streaking on neck and upperparts, dusky centers to upperwing coverts; remiges relatively worn in spring–summer. Overall resembles adult of respective sex following partial

adult ♀

adult ♂

♂

juv

Yellow Bittern

preformative molt, probably in fall–winter, but may retain some tertials and upperwing coverts (study needed).

Habitat and Behavior: Similar to Least Bittern. Common call a sharp, staccato *kik-kik-kik*, often given in flight (P. Holt, pers. comm.).

CHINESE POND HERON *Ardeola bacchus* 42–46 cm (16.5–18")

Summary: *Alaska:* Exceptional in spring–fall on w. Aleutians and Bering Sea islands.
Taxonomy: Monotypic.
Distribution and Status:

World: Breeds E Asia, e. to s. Japan and on the mainland n. to around 45°N in se. Russia; winters from s. parts of breeding range s. and e. to Borneo.

North America: *Alaska:* Single breeding plumage adults on Pribilofs, 4–9 Aug 1996 (Hoyer & Smith 1997), Attu, 20 May 2010 (*NAB* 64:480), and St. Lawrence, 14–15 Jul 2011 (*NAB* 65:672,713).

Comments: Chinese Pond Heron has increased in recent years in Japan (and now breeds there) and E Asia, with birds appearing with increasing frequency in spring–summer and on offshore islands. The spring AK bird was likely a drift vagrant, and the late summer birds also may have been assisted by tropical storms moving ne. off the Asian coast, as was thought for the Pribilofs bird (Hoyer & Smith 1997).

Field Identification: Distinctive heron, especially in breeding plumage, and unlike any N American species.

Similar Species: None in N America, but non-breeding and 1st-year plumages very similar to other pond heron species (genus *Ardeola*) of Asia and Africa, which are unlikely as vagrants to AK. However, Squacco Heron of W Eurasia and Africa is similar in 1st-year/nonbreeding plumage, and is a possible vagrant to e. N America (with several records from ne. S America).

Age/Sex/Season: Ages differ, with adult appearance attained in 2nd year; sexes similar; marked seasonal variation in adults. Molts poorly known, but presumed complex alternate strategy (see p. 35). *Adult*: Tail clean white, without dusky mottling; outer primaries white or with some dusky tipping. Breeding plumage (attained in spring by partial prealternate molt) has maroon head and neck, turning darker on upper breast; dark slaty back. Nonbreeding (attained in fall by complete prebasic molt, before migration) has head and neck heavily streaked brown and whitish. *1st-year*: Tail mottled dusky, mainly toward tip; outer primaries with extensive dusky tipping. Juv/1st-winter resembles nonbreeding adult but note dusky on tail and wing-tip; 1st-summer resembles breeding adult (or perhaps averaging duller overall, with some streaking on head and neck; needs study) but juv flight feathers retained. Probably resembles adult following 2nd-prebasic molt.

adult breeding

adult breeding

adult nonbreeding
(1st-year similar)

Chinese Pond Heron

Habitat and Behavior: Favors marshes, flooded fields, and ditches, where can be skulking in tall grassy vegetation; also found on lake shores and tidal flats. A wait-and-watch feeder. Flushed birds can give a harsh, scolding croak much like other pond herons (P. Holt, pers. comm.).

GRAY HERON *Ardea cinerea* 90–98 cm (35.5–38.5")

Summary: *Alaska*: Exceptional on w. Aleutians in spring, on Pribilofs in fall. *Newfoundland*: 2 fall records (1996, 2002).

Taxonomy: 4 ssp, the 2 N Hemisphere migratory ssp not certainly separable in the field, although *jouyi* of E Asia averages paler above than widespread nominate *cinerea* found in most of Eurasia and Africa. 2 sedentary African ssp not considered here.

Distribution and Status:

World: Breeds across mid-latitude Eurasia from W Europe e. to Russia (Sakhalin and w. side of Sea of Okhotsk) and Japan; also in Africa and SE Asia. Winters from W Europe and S Asia s. through remainder of breeding range.

North America: *Alaska:* Pribilofs, 1–2 Aug 1999, 1–2 Oct 2007; Shemya, 29 Apr–2 May 2010 (*NAB* 64:480). *Newfoundland*: 11 Oct 1996; 28 Sept–2 Oct 2002.

Comments: The first NL record was of a juv/ 1st-winter found moribund along the coast and misidentified as Great Blue Heron, only to be

'discovered' (and correctly identified) years later in a university collection. The second involved 1 of 3 birds (ages unknown) that landed on a ship nw. of the Azores on 26 Sep 2002 about 1750 km (1050 miles) e. of NL and was carried to Conception Bay, NL, where the ship docked on 3 Oct; it died shortly thereafter (Renner & Linegar 2007).

Gray Heron is a scarce but regular migrant and winter visitor (mainly Sep–Apr, some lingering into summer) to Iceland, with recoveries of birds banded in Norway (Y. Kolbeinsson, pers. comm.), and there are about 15 records (mainly Sep–Nov) from Greenland. There are 2 records from Bermuda, and Gray Heron is a regular visitor to the Azores (mainly in winter), where 150–300 birds (mainly 1st-years) are estimated to occur each year. There have been sporadic records in the se. Caribbean (including birds banded in France; Buckley et al. 2009), notably Trinidad and Tobago (6 records, mainly imms; Kenefick & Hayes 2006) and the species is considered a rare resident on Barbados, with new individuals (1st-years) arriving most years. Of the 2 Bermuda birds, the 7 Oct 2005 bird was found dead and may have arrived direct from Europe; the bird that arrived 22 Apr 2006 and remained into 2007 fits the pattern of birds that initially drifted to the se. Caribbean and moved n. in spring. Given this pattern of occurrence in the N Atlantic, it seems likely there will be additional records in e. N America. Away from

Great Blue Heron

adult

juv

Great Blue Heron
adult

duskier, tinged pinkish

cinnamon shoulder and thighs

juv

cinnamon can fade to whitish

paler gray

shorter projection

adult

juv

more contrasting black stripe

whitish shoulder and thighs

adult

white

juv

Gray Heron

areas such as NL, where Great Blue Heron is uncommon, picking one out will be a challenge.

The AK birds presumably represent drift vagrants.

Field Identification: Old World counterpart to Great Blue Heron, from which it should be separated with care.

Similar Species: In all plumages recalls *Great Blue Heron* but smaller and shorter-necked,

with slightly shorter bill, less massive head, and appreciably shorter legs. In flight, legs and feet of Gray project less beyond tail tip (foot projection often greater than leg projection, vs. appreciably less on Great Blue), and shape overall more compact, lacking exaggerated deep neck bulge of Great Blue; Gray tends to curl its toes more, reminiscent of American Bittern, which often contributes to a shorter foot projection.

All plumages of Gray Heron tend to be paler and purer gray (less suffused with dusky pinkish) overall than Great Blue, and lack distinct cinnamon coloration on the shoulders and thighs (beware that thighs can be difficult to see on relaxed birds, when covered by flanks, and some juv/1st-winter Gray can have buff tones to the thighs). Adult and 2nd-year Gray often have a whiter face and foreneck, and a more contrasting black stripe along sides (can be striking from below in flight). See Lethaby & McLaren (2002) for a fuller discussion of various characters; however, reported differences in coloration of lores and legs between 1st-year Gray and Great Blue Herons appear not to be consistent and at best should be considered as only suggestive in identification (Howell, pers. obs.).

Age/Sex/Season: Ages differ, with adult appearance attained in 3rd year; sexes similar. Molts follow complex basic strategy (see p. 35), with seasonal variation in adults via protracted prebasic molt of ornamental plumes over fall and winter; wing molt can show stepwise patterns (see p. 37).

Adult: Forehead and median crown white, often mixed with some gray; neck gray or with variable dull pinkish blush; neck and scapular plumes well developed; bill yellow-orange overall, sometimes variably dark above (especially at base), at least in fall; primaries can show up to 3 generations and waves of molt. **Juv/1st-winter:** Forehead and median crown dark gray, sometimes whole cap; upper mandible dark; plumage evenly fresh with uniform generation wings, no ornamental plumes in fall–early winter; variable molt of head, neck, back, and sometimes upperwing coverts in 1st winter/spring, when short ornamental plumes may be attained. **2nd-year:** Attained by complete molt in summer and fall, although as in Great Blue, some birds may retain 1–2 juv outer primaries (study needed). Resembles adult but forecrown more extensively gray, bill averages darker on upper mandible, and ornamental plumes average shorter; at most has 2 generations of primaries.

Habitat and Behavior: As Great Blue Heron. Typical call a grating *raah*, higher than throatier call typical of Great Blue.

INTERMEDIATE EGRET *Mesophoyx intermedia* 56–72 cm (23–29.5″)

Summary: *Alaska*: Single spring and fall records from w. Aleutians (2006, 2010).
Taxonomy: 3 ssp, but largely resident ssp in Africa (*brachyrhyncha*) and Australasia (*plumifera*)

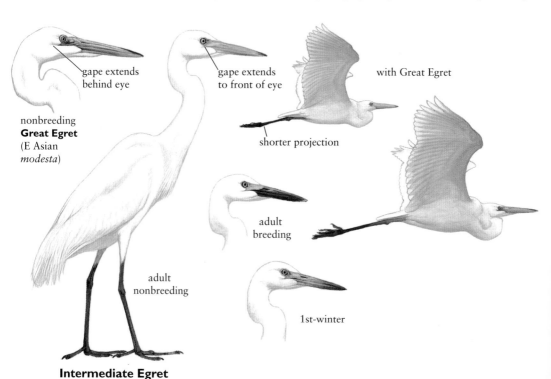

gape extends behind eye

gape extends to front of eye

with Great Egret

nonbreeding
Great Egret
(E Asian *modesta*)

shorter projection

adult breeding

adult nonbreeding

1st-winter

Intermediate Egret

likely represent distinct species and not considered here. N American specimens are of nominate *intermedia*. Often placed in the genus *Egretta*.

Distribution and Status:

World: Sub-Saharan Africa, and India e. to Japan and s. to Australia; ne. populations migratory, wintering s. to SE Asia.

North America: *Alaska*: Buldir, 30 May 2006 (corpse, believed to have arrived mid-May; Lorenz & Gibson 2007); Shemya, 28 Sep 2010 (1st-year, collected; *NAB* 65:142).

Comments: The NE Asian populations of Intermediate Egret undertake lengthy overwater migrations, and the spring bird, which may have arrived with other heron species (Great Egret and Black-crowned Night-Heron; Lorenz & Gibson 2007) was presumably a drift vagrant. The fall bird may represent a misoriented migrant, likely weather assisted.

Field Identification: Similar in overall appearance to Great Egret but smaller in all measurements, with shorter neck and stubbier bill that suggest Cattle Egret.

Similar Species: Any white heron in w. AK will draw attention, and should be identified with care. Also cf. Chinese Egret.

East Asian ssp of Great Egret *Ardea alba modesta* is appreciably smaller than nominate *alba* of N Eurasia and *egretta* of the Americas, and has also occurred as a spring and fall vagrant on Aleutians. *Modesta* still somewhat larger, longer-necked, and longer-billed than Intermediate, with gape line extending distinctly behind eye (ending under eye on Intermediate); nonbreeding and 1st-year *modesta* may have an all-yellow bill (but N American Great Egret often has small black bill tip, much like Intermediate); adult *modesta* also often has dull pinkish tibia. In flight, legs of Great Egret project farther beyond tail tip (projecting length of leg often greater than feet, vs. slightly less than feet on Intermediate) and neck bulge deeper and more exaggerated.

If size is misjudged, confusion quite possible with 1st-year/nonbreeding Eastern Cattle Egret *Bubulcus [ibis] coromandus*, which is larger and longer-necked than Western Cattle Egret found in mainland N America. Cattle Egret is smaller, shorter-legged, and shorter-necked than Intermediate, with a uniformly yellow bill; Cattle has slightly more extensive gular feathering extending forward under lower mandible (but Intermediate has rather similar 'jowls' to Cattle Egret).

Age/Sex/Season: Ages differ, with adult appearance attained in 2nd year; sexes similar.

Molts poorly known, presumed complex basic strategy (see p. 35), with seasonal variation in adults via protracted prebasic molt of ornamental plumes over fall and winter. *Adult*: Develops neck plumes and long scapular plumes via protracted prebasic molt; nonbreeding bill yellow with black tip, becoming wholly black in breeding condition, with yellow lores. *1st-year*: Juv lacks ornamental plumes, but short plumes may be attained by 1st summer via protracted prefomative molt of head and body feathers (study needed); bill yellow with black tip. Probably resembles adult following 2nd-prebasic molt.

Habitat and Behavior: Much as Great Egret.

CHINESE EGRET *Egretta eulophotes*
65–68 cm (25.5–27")

Summary: *Alaska*: 1 late spring record from w. Aleutians (1974).

Taxonomy: Monotypic. Also known as Swinhoe's Egret.

Distribution and Status:

World: Breeds e. China and Korea, winters mainly in Philippines and Borneo; rare and perhaps declining.

North America: *Alaska*: Aggatu, 16 Jun 1974 (adult female with heavy fat; Byrd et al. 1978).

Comments: The Alaskan record represents a significant extralimital occurrence for this rare and poorly known species, and future N American records seem unlikely. Given the species' northward overwater migration, the AK bird was likely swept n. and e. by weather systems, as with other Asian herons found on Alaskan islands.

Field Identification: Medium-sized white egret, adult with loose, shaggy-plumed crest and lengthy breast plumes.

Similar Species: Any white heron in w. AK will draw attention, and should be identified with care. Also cf. Great and Intermediate Egrets.

Nonbreeding ***Snowy Egret*** and ***Little Egret*** slightly smaller with relatively longer legs and more slender, dark bills with little or no pale yellowish below; adult Little has only two long head plumes.

Age/Sex/Season: Ages differ, with adult appearance probably attained in 2nd year; sexes similar. Molts poorly known, presumed complex basic strategy (see p. 35), with seasonal variation in adults via protracted prebasic molt of ornamental plumes over fall and winter. *Adult*: Develops long nape and scapular plumes via protracted prebasic molt; bill yellowish

adult
breeding

1st-winter

adult
nonbreeding

Chinese Egret

overall. *1st-year*: Juv lacks ornamental plumes, but short plumes may be attained by 1st summer via protracted prefomative molt of head and body feathers (study needed); bill dark overall with yellowish base below. Probably resembles adult following 2nd-prebasic molt.

Habitat and Behavior: Similar to Snowy Egret but largely restricted to salt water environments. Habits like Reddish Egret (Poole et al. 1999) but vagrants may not exhibit normal behavior.

LITTLE EGRET *Egretta garzetta* 55–65 cm (21.5–25.5")

Summary: *Alaska*: 1 spring record from w. Aleutians (2000). *Atlantic States and Provinces*: Very rare, spring–fall (mostly spring in the Northeast).

Taxonomy: 2 ssp. Nominate *garzetta*, breeding Eurasia and Africa, has yellow feet; *nigripes* of SE Asia to Australia has black feet. N American records refer to nominate *garzetta*.

Distribution and Status:

World: W Eurasia, Africa, and from S Asia and Japan s. to Australia. Northern populations migratory, wintering mainly in Africa and SE Asia. Since mid-1990s has bred se. Caribbean.

North America: *Alaska*: Buldir, 27 May 2000 (age unknown). *Atlantic States and Provinces*: About 30–40 records since the first in e. NL, 8 May 1954, mainly mid-Apr to Jul in the Northeast, with fewer records late Apr–Sep on Mid-Atlantic Coast; about 10 records may involve returning individuals in multiple years. All records except a mid-Sep 1998 'immature' in RI (P. Buckley, pers. comm.) are of adults.

Comments: It isn't clear how Little Egret reached e. N America. While there are no records from Greenland and there were only 14 from Iceland through 2006 (the 1st in Apr 1985), the species has increased notably in W Europe in recent years, and the timing of Iceland and NL records, at least in spring, is similar. An equally possible route, in spite of the huge distances,

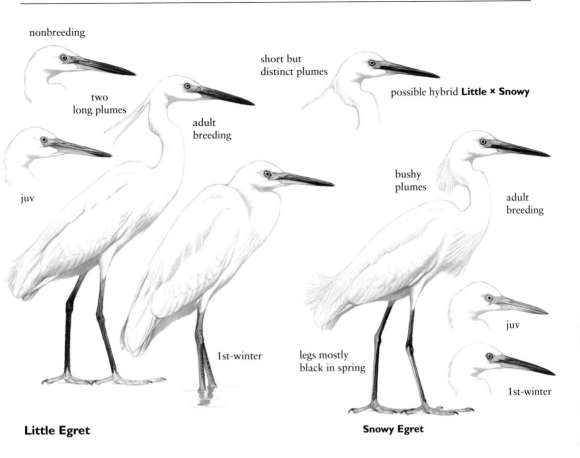

nonbreeding

short but
distinct plumes

possible hybrid **Little × Snowy**

two
long plumes

adult
breeding

bushy
plumes

adult
breeding

juv

1st-winter

legs mostly
black in spring

juv

1st-winter

Little Egret

Snowy Egret

involves migrants from Europe overshooting their wintering areas in sub-Saharan Africa and, helped by the ne. trade winds, making landfall in ne. S America and on nearby islands such as Trinidad and Barbados. Recoveries of Spanish-banded Little Egrets in Trinidad, Suriname, and Martinique (Haverschmidt 1983) support this theory, as does the fact that both Trinidad and N America recorded their first Little Egrets in spring 1954. The New World's first Cattle Egrets were thought to have arrived via a similar route. These Little Egrets could reach N America by mi-grating n., perhaps in association with returning migrant Snowy Egrets and Little Blue and Tricol-ored Herons. Little Egrets have bred in Barbados since the mid-1980s (15–25 pairs now breed there annually, with 3–4 young fledged per nest) and in 2008 were found breeding on Antigua (Kushlan & Prosper 2009). We thus expect an increasing number of Little Egret records in e. N America, although at least some of the new Caribbean populations appear to be resident.

The virtual lack of N American records s. of MA may indicate that Little Egrets arrive in the

Northeast by an overwater route from the Caribbean (and some probably have) but the extreme difficulty in detecting one among the mass of Snowy Egrets at more southerly lati-tudes seems an equally reasonable explanation. The concentration of records from mid-Apr to early Jun correlates with the concentration of birdwatcher activity in the same period, and also comes before the annual northward post-breeding dispersal of egrets, which would make Little Egret less detectable farther n.

The single AK record probably represents a drift-overshoot vagrant from the migrant popula-tion inhabiting E Asia (Japan is the nearest breeding area). Given the propensity of egrets to overshoot in spring, it's perhaps surprising there aren't more records from the w. Aleutians.

Field Identification: Old World counterpart to Snowy Egret, and overall very similar to that spe-cies. Presumed hybrid Little × Snowy Egrets may become an increasing identification concern in the Northeast, where at least one has been docu-mented (*FN* 49:227); on Barbados, where both Little and Snowy breed, mixed pairs do occur but are rare (Buckley et al. 2009). See Massiah (1997) for further information.

Similar Species: In all ages, very similar to **Snowy Egret**, and beware the possibility of hybrids. Possible or presumed hybrids can resemble Snowy overall, with yellow lores and yellowish or greenish hind tarsi, but have 2 distinct, lanceolate head plumes (often shorter than on Little, at least in fall) or mixed head plumes, with 2 long plumes projecting beyond a bushy crest of filamentous plumes. More study is needed of this problem, preferably involving known hybrids.

Little Egret averages larger, longer-necked, and longer-legged than Snowy Egret, with a slightly longer, thicker bill and thicker legs. Facial feathering of Little often appears to project farther at base of bill, accentuated by lower, more sloping forehead, versus shorter facial feathering, yellow bill 'saddle' across forehead, and slightly higher, more rounded forehead of Snowy. **Adult** Little has two long, lanceolate head plumes (absent only for a short period in fall molt) unlike the bushy, filamentous head plumes of Snowy. For most of the year, Little Egret has duller, grayish to greenish-yellow lores (bright yellow on Snowy). At the height of courtship, the lores of both species brighten greatly, sometimes to brilliant red (and in Little, at least occasionally to bright yellow) but such birds should be distinguishable on the basis of head plumes. Breeding adults of both species have black legs, those of Little Egret contrasting with yellow-green feet, the green extending only on rare occasions a short distance up the hind tarsi. On Snowy Egret, the feet are bright yellow, the yellow normally extending well up the hind tarsi in fall–winter.

Nestling and recently fledged juv Snowy Egrets are dimorphic with respect to lore color (yellow or dark gray), bill (yellowish or dark), and orbital ring (yellow or dark) (McVaugh 1975) but should be identifiable as juvs based on retained down. Most of these individuals acquire typical Snowy Egret characters (yellow lores, pale-based dark bill, and darkening legs) within a month of fledging, and often by fledging. Juvs of both species fledge with greenish or yellowish legs, which darken within a month or so after fledging. Most nonbreeding Little Egrets have completely dark legs. Most nonbreeding adult Snowy Egrets have yellow-green hind legs, this color most extensive on 1st-years.

Age/Sex/Season: Ages differ, with adult appearance attained in 2nd year; sexes similar. Molts presumed to follow complex basic strategy

(see p. 35), with seasonal variation in adults via protracted prebasic molt of ornamental plumes (timing varies with breeding season). **Adult:** Develops long scapular plumes and 2 long head plumes via protracted prebasic molt (can lack plumes in fall). **1st-year:** Juv lacks ornamental plumes, but short plumes may be attained by 1st summer via protracted prefromative molt of head and body feathers (study needed). Probably resembles adult following 2nd-prebasic molt.

Habitat and Behavior: Much as Snowy Egret.

WESTERN REEF HERON *Egretta gularis*
55–65 cm (21.5–25.5")

Summary: *Northeast*: 2–4 records, spring–fall.
Taxonomy: 2 ssp, not known to be separable as white morphs, although e. ssp *schistacea* averages larger than w. ssp *gularis*, the latter ssp presumably recorded in N America. Dark morph *schistacea* averages paler than dark morph *gularis*.

Distribution and Status:
World: Resident and dispersive in W Africa, and disjunctly from E Africa to w. India.

North America: *Northeast*: 2–4 records, all dark morphs: Nantucket Island, MA, 26 Apr–13 Sep 1983; sw. NL, 14 Jun–6 Sep 2005; Cape Breton Island, NS, 26 Jun–2 Aug 2006, probably relocating to Piscatagua River (York Co., ME/Rockingham Co., NH), 9 Aug–20 Sep 2006; New York area (Middlesex Co., NJ/Brooklyn Co., NY), 30 Jun–8 Aug 2007. The 2005–2007 records may all refer to a single individual.

Comments: There are no records of Western Reef Heron from Britain, Ireland, Iceland, or Greenland, and only 1 recent fall record (Oct) from the Azores (T. Clark 1999), but there are now 9 records from Barbados (mainly mid-winter to summer, only 1 in late fall), 2 from Trinidad and Tobago, and others in the Lesser Antilles from St. Lucia, St. Vincent, and the Grenadines (Kenefick & Hayes 2006). This suggests that N American birds came via the se. Caribbean, perhaps moving n. in spring with other heron species. As in Little Egret, all N American records are from the Mid-Atlantic Coast and northward; thus, they may have arrived via a long overwater route, or the species has been overlooked in the se. US, where Little Blue Herons are common. See Little Egret for a fuller discussion of this migration route.

Field Identification: Overall resembles Snowy Egret in size and shape but bill slightly thicker

molting 1st-year
white morph
Western Reef Heron

breeding

nonbreeding

white morph
nonbreeding

molting 1st-year
Little Blue Heron

Western Reef Heron

and longer, with more strongly decurved culmen. Dimorphic, with only dark morph found in N America.

Similar Species: Dark morph could be overlooked as *Little Blue Heron*, whereas white morph could be overlooked as *Snowy (or Little) Egret*. Note that bill of 1st-year and nonbreeding reef heron is mostly dull yellowish (becoming mostly black with orange tip and orange-yellow lores in adult breeding condition); bill slightly longer and bigger than Snowy or Little Blue, and at times appears slightly decurved overall. Breeding plumage has 2 head plumes, like Little Egret.

White morph further differs from *Snowy Egret* by dark olive legs with paler yellowish feet; some birds have scattered dark feathers that suggest molting 1st-year Little Blue Heron; note differences in bill shape and color. *Dark morph* distinctive if seen well; dark slaty gray overall with contrasting white throat, and yellow feet contrast strongly with dark legs.

Age/Sex/Season: Ages differ, with adult appearance probably attained in 2nd year; sexes similar. Molts poorly known, presumed complex basic strategy (see p. 35), with seasonal variation in adults via protracted prebasic molt of ornamental plumes (timing varies with breeding season). *Adult*: Develops long scapular plumes and 2 long head plumes via protracted

prebasic molt. Dark morph dark slaty gray overall. *1st-year*: Juv lacks ornamental plumes, but short plumes may be attained by 1st summer via protracted prefomative molt of head and body feathers (study needed). Dark morph duskier and browner overall than adult, underparts often mottled white. Probably resembles adult following 2nd-prebasic molt.

Habitat and Behavior: Favors rocky shorelines and mudflats, occasionally in freshwater. Associates readily with Snowy Egrets while feeding and roosting; varied feeding methods at times very dashing and animated, even more so than Snowy (Cardillo et al. 1983).

DEMOISELLE CRANE *Anthropoides virgo*
90–100 cm (35.5–39.5")

Summary: *California*: 1 winter record (2001/2002). *British Columbia/Alaska*: 1 spring record (2002).

Taxonomy: Monotypic.

Distribution and Status:

World: Breeds mid-latitude Eurasia between about 30°E and 125°E. Winters mainly in sub-Saharan Africa and the Indian subcontinent.

North America: *California*: San Joaquin Co., 30 Sep 2001–18 Feb 2002. *British Columbia/Alaska*: Smithers, Prince Rupert Co., BC, 2 May

late 1st-winter

adult

adult

Demoiselle Crane

2002 (Bain 2002) and Gustavus, se. AK, 13–18 May 2002 (N. Drumheller, pers. comm. and photos), presumed same as CA individual.

Comments: Demoiselle Crane is a long-distance migrant, and has been reported as a straggler to Kamchatka. It is not inconceivable that having misoriented to the ne. in Asia one might join with Sandhill Cranes, as is presumed to happen with Common Cranes occurring in N America (although Commons breed considerably closer to Sandhills). Hence we consider a wild vagrant Demoiselle Crane plausible in N America, and provisionally include the record here. The species is, however, relatively popular in captivity, although no specific escape could be traced that might be linked to the CA record (placed on the state's supplemental list, given uncertainty about origin). That presumably the same bird was seen migrating with Sandhill Cranes in BC and se. AK might be viewed as evidence pointing to a wild bird. It is even possible the bird was overlooked in N America in previous (and subsequent?) years, which would be quite easy to do (cf. no mid-winter US records of Common Crane), particularly in its 1st winter before attaining the striking adult appearance.

Field Identification: Relatively small and delicately built crane with handsome adult plumage.

Similar Species: None, if seen well. Juv/1st-winter paler and grayer than juv/1st-winter **Sandhill Crane**, with pale head and dark throat; in flight note more extensive, and more contrasting blackish on upperwings; diagnostic face marking appear by late winter.

Age/Sex/Season: Ages differ, with adult appearance perhaps attained in 2 years; sexes similar but males average larger; no seasonal variation. Molts not well known but presumed to follow Complex Basic Strategy (see p. 35). **Adult:** Well-defined black-and-white head and neck pattern with long black foreneck feathers; long and drooping gray 'bustle' (modified tertials) tipped blackish. **1st-year:** Juv (fall–early winter) has head and upper neck pale ashy gray with darker throat and foreneck; shorter 'bustle' lacks blackish tips. Protracted preformative molt over 1st winter–spring produces dull version of adult face and neck pattern by spring. May attain adult appearance by (complete?) 2nd-prebasic molt in summer–fall (study needed).

Habitat and Behavior: Similar to Sandhill Crane, with which the N American bird was found. Adult call higher pitched than adult Sandhill, with faster-paced, slightly trilling quality (vs. more measured rolling of Sandhill); 1st-winter has a high, piping, slightly trilled *treeet* (Van den Berg et al. 2003).

COMMON CRANE *Grus grus* 95–120 cm (37.5–47.5")

Summary: *Alaska and Interior West*: Very rare, fall–spring. *Pacific States and Provinces*: Single spring–summer records from CA and BC (2011). *East*: Exceptional fall records from IN (1999) and QC (1999–2001).

Taxonomy: Monotypic; E Asian populations average paler than those of W Eurasia and sometimes separated as ssp *lilfordi*.

Distribution and Status:

World: Breeds from N Europe e. through N Eurasia to around 150°E in Russia (w. of Sea of Okhotsk). Winters from S Eurasia s. to sub-Saharan E Africa, in the Indian subcontinent, and in SE Asia.

North America: *Alaska and Interior West*: Possibly only 4 records (see Comments, below) scattered from cen. AK s. through AB to KS (23 Mar 2008; *NAB* 62:438) and NM. Most records are during spring migration (Mar–Apr) on Great Plains, especially NE, and once in cen. AK (24 Apr–10 May 1958); also 2 fall records (mid–late Sep) in cen. AK and cen. AB, and 2 winter records (mid-Dec to early Jan) in se. AB and sw. SK (Wrishko 2004). *Pacific States and Provinces*: Del Norte Co., CA, 5–8 May 2011 (adult), and Queen Charlotte Islands, BC, 3 Jul 2011 (possibly same bird as CA; *NAB* 65:513, 569). *East*: Fall records from Pulaski Co., IN, 30 Oct–13 Nov 1999 and Abitibi Co., QC, 1–7 Oct 1999, 30 Sep–7 Oct 2000, and 26 Sep–8 Oct 2001, all probably involving a single bird of unknown provenance.

Comments: Records from w. and interior N America are presumed to be of birds that joined western populations of (Lesser) Sandhill Cranes (*G. c. canadensis*) in NE Asia and accompanied them to and from their wintering areas on the Great Plains (although to date there are only 2 winter records in N America). That most records are from staging grounds is no doubt because Sandhills from many regions are concentrated for extended periods in such locations, and the spectacle draws the attention of many observers. Records of Common Crane from w. N America fall into 3 periods: 1957–1961 (AK, AB, NM), 1971–1974 (NE in spring), and

1st-year

adult

late 1st-winter

juv

Sandhill Crane adult

adult

with Sandhills

Common Crane

1998–2012 (fall in AK, winter in SK, spring on Great Plains). Given the longevity of cranes, most of these records might conceivably involve only 4 individuals (the 2003/2004 SK bird was found dead on 8 Jan 2004; Wrishko 2004). The recent CA and BC spring–summer records may involve a 'new' individual that was overlooked in the West in the previous winter(s); it was alone in CA and when first seen in BC, but later joined by Sandhill Cranes (British Columbia Rare Bird Alert, July 2011). A Mar 1979 report from w. TX was not accepted by the state committee and is not included here.

The 1999–2001 records from QC and IN are thought to refer to a single bird, of unknown provenance. In each year this Common Crane appeared to be paired with a Sandhill Crane and accompanied by up to 2 juvs that were considered hybrids; moreover, on 20–22 Sep 1999, 2 presumed hybrid Common × Sandhill Cranes (at least 1 year old) were also seen in QC (*NAB* 54:24). It remains unknown whether the QC/IN bird was an escape, an Asian bird that wandered farther e. than usual and joined local Sandhill Cranes, or perhaps a vagrant from Europe. There were 39 records of Common Crane from Iceland through 2006, mostly in the last 25 years (but mainly late Apr–May, vs. the fall records in e. N America), and an Aug 1988 record from ne. Greenland.

A Common Crane with a damaged foot in NY, Apr 1991, and in VT, 9–10 Jun 1991, was determined to have escaped from captivity in the Catskills, and perhaps the same bird (with a damaged foot) was seen in NJ, Jan 1993 (*NAB* 45:1094; *NAB* 54:24). In 1995–1996, what was likely the same Common Crane bred successfully in NJ with a Sandhill Crane (Walsh et al. 1999), and hybrids have been reported periodically in NJ through at least the early 2000s.

Field Identification: Large handsomely patterned crane widespread in Eurasia. Some long-staying birds have hybridized with Sandhill Cranes, offering novel identification challenges; detailed descriptions of hybrids appear to be unpublished.

Similar Species: None if seen well, but possibility of hybrids should be considered (such birds may show head and neck patterns suggesting Common but "not quite right"; cf. *NAB* 54:24). *Sandhill Crane* similar in shape, but while there is marked regional size variation in Sandhills and sexual dimorphism in both species, Common averages more than 15% larger with a proportionately shorter, stouter bill. In flight, large size

should be obvious among Lesser Sandhills. Also note more extensive and more contrasting black on remiges of Common. Adult Common identified readily by striking head and neck pattern. Juv similar to Sandhill but larger and grayer (any rusty staining faint and usually restricted to head); diagnostic face markings appear by late winter.

Age/Sex/Season: Ages differ, with adult appearance attained by 3rd year; sexes similar but males average larger; no seasonal variation. Molts not well known, presumed complex basic strategy (see p. 35), with primaries molted every other year. *Adult*: Well-defined black-and-white head and neck pattern with red crown patch (crown naked with sparse bristles); prominent black-tipped 'bustle' (modified tertials); flight feathers uniform with relatively broad primaries (either fresh or worn, as molted every 2 years). *1st-year*: Juv (fall–early winter) has feathered head and upper neck dingy buff to pale cinnamon; upperparts with variable brown cast; much shorter 'bustle' lacks black tips; flight feathers uniform and relatively tapered. Protracted preformative molt over 1st winter–spring produces dull version of adult face pattern by spring, with dingy whitish cheek patch, variable dark gray on crown, throat, and neck. *2nd-year*: Attains adult-like head and body plumage by 2nd prebasic molt of head and body in 1st summer–fall but crown not as bare, may retain some faded and brownish juv tertials and upperwing coverts; retained primaries worn and tapered.

Habitat and Behavior: Similar to Sandhill Crane, with which typically found. Flight call similar to Sandhill but lower pitched.

CORNCRAKE *Crex crex* 27–30 cm (10.5–11.8")

Summary: *Northeast*: Exceptional in late fall.
Taxonomy: Monotypic.
Distribution and Status:
World: Breeds from NW Europe e. through mid-latitude Eurasia to around 115°E; winters mainly in sub-Saharan E Africa. Declining in much of range, dramatically so in W Europe.

North America: *Northeast*: In our time frame, 4 late fall records: Suffolk Co., NY, 2 Nov 1963; SPM, 22 Oct 1989; Shelburne Co., NS, 28–30 Nov 1997; Ferryland Co., NL, 2 Nov 2002. Formerly more frequent (or at least more often detected), and occurred regularly in late 19th century, with records in the East from mid-Aug to early Nov.
Comments: Corncrake is one of the few Palearctic vagrants whose frequency of occurrence in

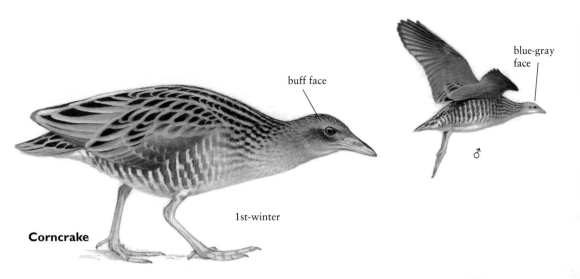

buff face

blue-gray face

1st-winter

♂

Corncrake

N America declined during the 20th century. Many bird species suffered population reductions during this period, and Corncrake was no exception, but in all except this species and Eurasian Woodcock, the huge increase in the number of people looking for vagrants tended to offset the natural declines. Confounding any review of the status of these two species is the fact that the human behavior most associated with early records (bird hunting in wet grasslands, woods, and meadows, often with dogs) has also declined.

Since 1950, Iceland had 32 records through 2006, about two-thirds in fall with a peak in late Sep–Oct; many birds were found dead or dying by farmers around their fields. The Azores has about 10 modern records, and, not surprisingly for a species with Corncrake's migration route and length, there's a late Sep 2003 record from Guadeloupe, in the se. Caribbean. Perhaps even more interesting, Bermuda has had no fewer than 5 modern records in late Sep–early Oct (1978-1991), all of them picked up dead on the highway or removed from the claws of cats.

With this evidence in-hand, it seems likely that Corncrake is making regular landfall in e. N America but going undetected. The 2002 bird was flushed at Cape Race, NL, a likely first point of land for birds coming across the N Atlantic (and also the location for the first 2 NL records), and the 1997 bird, seen through a kitchen window 'bopping' around a backyard garden, was at Little Harbor, NS, another possible first point of land.

We can offer no data to explain why records from the Northeast are a month or more later than those from Bermuda and the se. Caribbean; we have no data on the age of birds involved.

Field Identification: Medium-sized, short-billed rail of damp grassy areas.

Similar Species: None really, but flushed rails usually show themselves for very short periods. Perhaps could be confused with a young pheasant that might fly weakly.

Age/Sex/Season: Ages and sexes differ slightly, with adult appearance attained in 1st year; no seasonal variation. Complete prebasic and partial preformative molts occur before fall migration; partial prealternate molt reported on winter grounds. **Adult**: Face and chest blue-gray, brighter on male, but overall duller and veiled brownish in fall. **Juv**: Face and chest buff, reportedly molting into adult-like plumage in fall (Cramp 1977–94, vol. 2).

Habitat and Behavior: Normally wet meadows and hayfields, where typically secretive. Flushed birds rarely fly for long distances, typically with legs dangling. Unlikely to be heard away from breeding grounds.

COMMON MOORHEN *Gallinula chloropus*
32–35 cm (13.5–14.7")

Summary: *Alaska*: 1 fall record from w. Aleutians (2010).
Taxonomy: 5 ssp, differing slightly in size and plumage tones, with shield averaging larger in tropical populations. Widespread nominate *chloropus* of temperate Eurasia is the only ssp considered here (e. populations of *chloropus* average smaller and sometimes separated as ssp

smaller, rounded
shield

larger, flat-
topped shield

browner
upperparts

longer neck
and legs

Common Gallinule
adult

**Common
Gallinule**

adult

adult

compact
proportions

Common Moorhen

juv/1st-winter

indica). Split by AOU in 2011 from New World moorhens, which have been named Common Gallinule *G. galeata* (*Auk* 128:600–613).

Distribution and Status:

World: Breeds from NW Europe and N Africa e. across Eurasia to Japan and s. Sakhalin; n. and interior populations withdraw w. and s. in winter to W Europe and SE Asia. Also mostly resident in sub-Saharan Africa and S Asia, e. to the Philippines.

North America: *Alaska*: Shemya, 14 Oct 2010 (1st-year; *NAB* 65:142; Pranty & ABA Checklist Committee. 2011).

Comments: Away from outposts such as the AK islands and NL, it is likely that Common Moorhen would go overlooked in N America; cf. the relatively distinctive Eurasian Coot. Iceland had 94 accepted records of moorhen through 2006, mainly Oct–May with peaks in Nov and Apr–May; given the propensity of rallids to wander, an E Coast record seems just a matter of time. There are 6 records (4 specimens) of Common Gallinule/Common Moorhen from w. Greenland (Sep–Nov and May), although all specimens are of the N American taxon.

Any species of *Gallinula* is very rare at any season in NL and likely to be scrutinized carefully, although 1st-years may not be identifiable in the field. A recent NL bird, 25 Jan–5 Feb

2011, was unidentified to species but occurred, intriguingly, at the same time as both Common Snipe and Jack Snipe (*NAB* 65:236).

Field Identification: Old World counterpart to Common Gallinule, and much like it in overall appearance and habits but with distinct voice. See Constantine & The Sound Approach (2006) and Garner (2008a) for further information.

Similar Species: Very similar to ***Common Gallinule*** but Common Moorhen averages smaller (more compact bulk might be appreciable in direct comparison) and shorter billed, with shorter legs and toes (thus less 'leggy' than gallinule). Importantly, adult moorhen has smaller frontal shield with narrower, more rounded upper edge, versus broader and more squared upper edge on gallinule (but beware sex and possible seasonal differences, with shield being smaller on female and nonbreeding gallinules). Yellow bill tip of adult moorhen often more 'blob-shaped' and extends back farther along bottom of lower mandible, versus strongly V-shaped border typical of gallinule (but patterns of both species variable and in need of study). Unclear when differences in shield shape and bill pattern are developed by 1st-years, but fall–winter birds perhaps not separable in the field (study needed). Upperparts of adult moorhen typically olive-toned, not the deeper, more reddish-brown typical of gallinule.

Age/Sex/Season: Ages differ, with adult appearance attained in 1st year; sexes similar; no seasonal variation. Complete prebasic molt occurs before fall migration; partial preformative molt occurs from late fall–spring; partial prealternate molt reported in spring. **Adult**: Head, neck, and underparts slaty blackish to slaty blue-gray overall (female averages broader whitish fringes to belly and vent feathers); bill and frontal shield bright red (shield averages larger on adult male than female), bill tipped bright yellow (bill duller overall in winter); legs and feet yellow-green with upper tibia orange-red; eyes deep red. **1st-year**: Juv sooty brownish overall, paler below, with whitish throat; attains adult appearance via protracted preformative molt over 1st winter/spring. Bill dark grayish with yellow-green tip, becoming like adult in fall–winter; shield develops by late winter–spring; legs and feet duller greenish than adult, little or no orange on tibia before spring; eyes duller and paler in fall–winter, becoming red by spring.

Habitat and Behavior: Like Common Gallinule, and often relatively skulking. Calls varied, and study of context and differences between the 2 species still needed. Presumed territorial call of moorhen a fairly abrupt, purring bleat *prrreh!* very different from shrill laughing or cackling series typical of Common Gallinule; the latter, however, also gives sharp single clucks in other contexts. Moorhen also emits a 2–3 syllable, sharp clucking *k'dek!* or *k'd'dek!* distinct from gallinule, and varied grunts and clucks, often with less of a barking quality than most clucks of gallinule. Occasional longer series given by moorhen have a rhythmic, slower, chippering cadence unlike laughing series of gallinule (Constantine & The Sound Approach 2006).

EURASIAN COOT *Fulica atra* 36–42 cm (14.2–16.5")

Summary: *Alaska*: 1 fall record from Bering Sea islands (1962). **_Quebec_:** 1 winter record (1995).
Taxonomy: 4 ssp, differing mainly in size, but nominate *atra* is the only N Hemisphere ssp and the only one considered here.
Distribution and Status:
World: Breeds from NW Europe and N Africa e. across mid-latitude Eurasia to Japan and e. Russia (Sakhalin and sw. side of Sea of Okhotsk); n. and interior populations withdraw w. and s. in winter to W Europe and SE Asia. Also mostly resident from SE Asia to Australasia.
North America: **_Alaska_:** Pribilofs, 31 Oct–5 Nov 1962. **_Quebec_:** Duplessis Co., 14 Dec 1995.
Comments: It's remarkable that there aren't more e. N American records for Eurasian Coot. Through 2006, there were 271 records for Iceland (where it's an occasional breeder) scattered throughout the year but with Apr–May and Nov–Dec peaks; there are 10 records for

adult

some young birds show dusky marks

1st-winter

white undertail coverts

American Coot

Eurasian

Eurasian Coot

w. Greenland; and it's a regular if uncommon vagrant to the Azores. If American Coots are any indication, Eurasian Coots could have a long flight range and, of course, can alight on water. It's hard to explain their absence other than by arguing that no one looks at American Coots where they're common.

American Coot, however, is not common in the Maritime Provinces, especially NL, and any coot there is certainly scrutinized. During the conspicuous Dec 1927 influx of Northern Lapwings into Atlantic Canada, there were also specimen records from Labrador of Eurasian Coot, Common Snipe, and Jack Snipe (O. L. Austin 1929). These occurrences were judged to have been the result of the same forces that propelled the lapwings. These species should all be kept in mind in the event of another lapwing incursion.

The Pribilofs record is interesting. Eurasian Coot is considered as only a straggler to Kamchatka, but like other early or late migrants, its possible occurrence in w. Alaska comes at a time when few ornithologists are in the field.

Field Identification: Old World counterpart to American Coot, and much like it in overall appearance and habits.

Similar Species: Very similar to **American Coot** but slightly larger with a more extensive and all-white frontal shield (somewhat reduced in 1st-winter birds); a pointed wedge of dark feathers indenting the frontal shield; and dark undertail coverts. Eurasian Coot bill and shield usually white or dirty pinkish white (bill with dusky distal marks on some 1st-years), lacking the dark reddish shield patch of American Coot.

Age/Sex/Season: Ages differ, with adult appearance attained in 1st year; sexes similar; no seasonal variation. Complete prebasic and partial preformative molts occur before fall migration; limited prealternate molt reported in winter–spring. **Adult**: Blackish overall with large and clean white bill shield, white or pink-tinged bill, deep red eyes. **1st-year**: Resembles adult but upperparts tinged brown, face and throat may be grizzled with whitish (at least into winter); shield smaller (at least into winter); bill sometimes with dusky distal marks; eyes average duller red. Juv (unlikely in N America unless breeding occurs) sooty blackish with white lower face and foreneck; bill pinkish to dull pale grayish white with small shield; eyes reddish brown.

Habitat and Behavior: Like American Coot. Has a wide vocabulary, most commonly a loud *cowk* and a high, shrill, clipped *kiit!*

New World Wading Birds

None of the New World species is considered a traditional migrant, but some are known to engage in post-breeding dispersal and others have patterns of dispersal linked to seasonal changes in water levels. Thus, the late summer–fall occurrences of Jabiru in the s. US fit into a wider pattern of post-breeding dispersal; likewise, fall records of Northern Jacana in AZ and winter occurrences in TX fit with known patterns, and the same could even be said for Azure Gallinule in NY. Records of Bare-throated Tiger-Heron in s. TX and of Paint-billed Crake and Spotted Rail in the East as yet do not conform to known dispersal patterns.

BARE-THROATED TIGER-HERON
Tigrisoma mexicanum 71–81 cm (28–32")

Summary: *Texas*: 1 winter record from Lower Rio Grande Valley (2009/2010).

Taxonomy: No ssp, although w. Mexican birds average paler than those elsewhere in the range.

Distribution and Status:

World: Mexico (n. to s. Sonora and s. Tamaulipas) s. to nw. S America.

North America: *Texas:* Hidalgo Co., 21 Dec 2009–20 Jan 2010 (2nd-year; Nirschl & Snider 2010).

Comments: This tropical species, along with many others still unrecorded in the US, is a resident of the tropical lowlands in e. Mexico only about 300 km (180 miles) s. of s. TX, seemingly well within striking range for a large waterbird. As with so many neotropical birds, we have no data on possible seasonal movements of Bare-throated Tiger-Heron in Mexico or elsewhere, or any supportive data on extralimital occurrences in e. Mexico that might be linked to the TX record. Like many tropical waterbirds, the species may be prone to nomadic movements linked to water levels in the marshes it inhabits; the TX bird was in its 2nd year of life and might have been wandering for a year or so.

Field Identification: Large and striking heron of tropical marshes.

Similar Species: None in N America. Distinguished in flight from **Great Blue Heron** by more thickset and massive, almost 'prehistoric' shape, with short legs not projecting far beyond tail.

Age/Sex/Season: Ages differ, with adult appearance probably attained in 3rd year; sexes similar; no seasonal variation. Molts undescribed; probably follows complex basic strategy (see p. 35).

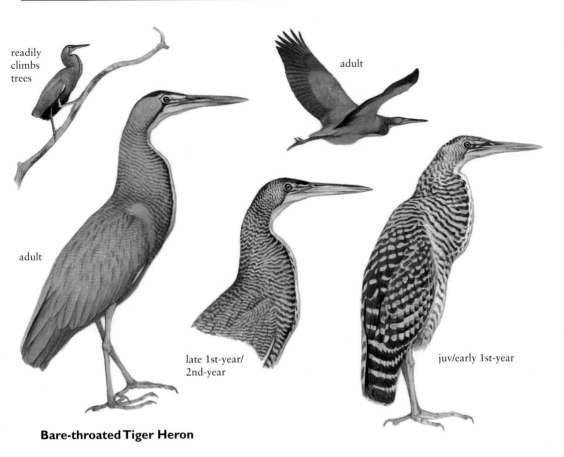

readily climbs trees

adult

adult

late 1st-year/ 2nd-year

juv/early 1st-year

Bare-throated Tiger Heron

Adult: Sides of head unbarred blue-gray, offset by black cap and black stripe bordering sides of naked orange-yellow throat; upperparts with fine dark vermiculations, appearing relatively plain at a distance. Flight feathers unbarred dark slaty with narrow white tips to primaries. ***1st-year***: Flight feathers blackish brown with sparse but striking buff to whitish barring. Juv overall boldly and coarsely barred with blackish brown and cinnamon (fading to buff). Protracted preformative molt over 1st year produces variable appearance: some birds suggest juv but have narrower barring overall and less rufescent tones, others grayer overall with variable blackish barring and more adult-like in general appearance. ***2nd-year***: Incoming remiges (inner primaries) plain dark slaty with white tips like adult; remainder of plumage suggests adult but with coarser neck barring, sides of head duller, brownish gray with variable dark barring. Probably attains adult appearance in 3rd year but study needed of known-age birds.

Habitat and Behavior: Freshwater and brackish marshes and ponds, including mangroves.

Often skulks in tall vegetation (usually avoids open situations) and readily perches in trees. Hunts by patient waiting and slow stalking, standing still for long periods. Flight heavy but strong, with slightly stiff wingbeats and emphasis on the upstroke; flights usually short, at or below treetop height. Flushed birds often give a deep throaty *woh*, often in short series. 'Song' given mainly at dusk and at night is a deep, far-carrying roar, *rrohr* … , repeated every 1–2 secs.

JABIRU *Jabiru mycteria* 130–155 cm (51–61")

Summary: ***Texas***: Very rare in summer–fall. ***Elsewhere***: 3 late summer–fall records from OK (1973), LA (2007), and MS (2008).
Taxonomy: Monotypic.
Distribution and Status:

World: Breeds and ranges locally from se. Mexico to tropical S America.

North America: ***Texas***: 10 summer–fall records, all since 1971: 9 records of single birds during Jun to mid-Sep, and an outlying record of 2 birds in late Oct. ***Elsewhere***: 3 singles (late

adult with throat inflated

1st-year

adult

with Wood Storks and Great Egrets

Jabiru

Jul–Aug) from Tulsa Co., OK, 28 Jul–9 Aug 1973 (1st-year); Sunflower Co., MS, 24–25 Aug 2007 (age unknown); and St Mary/Iberville Parish, LA, 27–31 Jul 2008 (adult; *NAB* 62:574).

Comments: Like many tropical wetland birds, Jabirus time their breeding according to the rainy season. Thus, young in s. Mexico and Belize fledge in about May, around the start of the rainy season. Many Jabirus then disperse w. in Jul–Nov to the Usumacinta marshes, in the sw. of the Yucatan Peninsula, whence some may wander on to the US. Perhaps not surprisingly, most US records have been of 1st-year birds but all-white 'adults' have also occurred.

The dearth of records in the 1990s and early 2000s seems surprising, particularly given several years of dry conditions in se. Mexico in the late 1980s and 1990s. One might expect such conditions to cause wetland birds to wander more widely (e.g., as with the colonization in the 1990s of w. Mexico by Limpkins and Snail Kites, corresponding to the drought in e. Mexico; Howell, pers. obs.); conversely, a drought might preclude breeding for several years such that no potentially wandering young were produced. There are no data that indicate a decline in the small population of Jabirus breeding in Mexico

and Belize, but whether US records originate from this population or from farther afield is unknown.

Field Identification: Huge, tall-standing white bird with long black legs, massive black bill, and naked black head and neck with broad red band at the base of neck.

Similar Species: None.

Age/Sex/Season: Ages differ, with adult appearance probably attained in 1–2 years; sexes similar; no seasonal variation. Molts undescribed; presumed complex basic strategy (see p. 35). *Adult* has all-white plumage, including a patch of down-like feathers on nape. *1st-year*: Juv has pale gray upperparts with silvery gray-brown feather edgings, the white primaries washed pale brown on the inner webs. Plumage whitens quickly via fading and a partial preformative molt, such that birds in their 1st winter appear white overall with dusky feathers scattered on the upperparts, especially upperwing coverts. *2nd-year* probably resembles adult but may retain some brownish feathers, and also perhaps some juv primaries (study needed).

Habitat and Behavior: Open marshes and wetlands, flooded fields. Likely to be found in areas with concentrations of other wading birds such as egrets and Wood Storks. Flies with stiff, strong wingbeats mostly above the body plane, and glides and soars with wings in a slight dihedral.

PAINT-BILLED CRAKE *Neocrex erythrops*
18–19 cm (7–7.5")

Summary: *East*: Single winter records from TX (1972) and VA (1978).

Taxonomy: 2 ssp, not known to be distinguishable in the field. N American records appear to be of widespread ssp *olivascens* (Blem 1980).

Distribution and Status:

World: Local in tropical S America, n. on occasion to s. Cen America.

North America: *East*: Brazos Co., TX, 17 Feb 1972; Henrico Co., VA, 15 Dec 1978.

Comments: Like many reclusive aquatic species of the Neotropics, Paint-billed Crake is poorly known in terms of its distribution and seasonal movements. In s. Cen America the few records are during Aug–Feb, which might reflect a northward dispersal in the boreal winter, a pattern into which the N American records could fit; with so little data, however, this is simply conjecture. That all records of this species and Spotted Rail occurred in the 1970s is an interesting coincidence.

Field Identification: Sora-sized crake, dark overall with a brightly colored bill.

Similar Species: Distinct in appearance from other N American birds. Rather similar ***Columbian Crake*** *Neocrex columbianus* largely replaces Paint-billed Crake in nw. S America, and should be considered in any identification. Columbian is darker overall than Paint-billed, has rufous-toned upperparts, lacks black-and-white barring below (hind flanks rufous-brown, undertail coverts cinnamon), and has yellow bill with smaller and duller orange basal area.

Age/Sex/Season: Ages differ slightly, with adult appearance attained in 1st year; sexes similar; no seasonal variation. Molts undescribed. ***1st-year***: Juv (unlikely in N America?) apparently duller than adult, with fainter barring below, duller and darker bill with no red at base (Taylor 1998).

Habitat and Behavior: Freshwater marshes, from overgrown ditches and flooded fields to reedbeds around larger lakes. Retiring and

juv

Paint-billed Crake

adult

Spotted Rail

adult

usually seen only when flushed, but sometimes comes out at edges near cover, mainly early and late in the day. Vagrants likely to be silent.

SPOTTED RAIL *Pardirallus maculatus*
25.5–28 cm (10–11")

Summary: *East*: Single fall–early winter records from PA (1976) and TX (1977).
Taxonomy: 2 ssp, probably not distinguishable in the field. N American records are of n. ssp *insolitus* (Parkes et al. 1978).
Distribution and Status:
    World: Locally from tropical Mexico to tropical S America; also Greater Antilles.
    North America: *East*: Beaver Co., PA, 12 Nov 1976; Brown Co., e. TX, 9 Aug 1977.
Comments: In Mexico this species is poorly known. It can be locally and seasonally fairly common in some areas when conditions are suitable, but then seemingly absent from the same areas for several years. That all records of this species and Paint-billed Crake occurred in the 1970s is an interesting coincidence.
Field Identification: Strikingly patterned, medium-sized rail with bright yellow-green bill and pinkish-red legs; remiges wholly dark.
    Similar Species: Intermediate in size between Virginia and Clapper rails, the Spotted Rail is a striking species, not likely to be confused with any other N American bird. Juvs seem unlikely to occur in N America before attaining some diagnostic white-spotted plumage.
    Age/Sex/Season: Ages differ, with adult appearance attained in 1st year; sexes similar; no seasonal variation. Molts not well known. *Adult*: Head, neck, and upperparts with bold white spotting, underparts barred and mottled blackish-and-white; bill bright yellow-green with red spot at base, legs pinkish red. *1st-year*: Juv reportedly variable (Dickerman & Haverschmidt 1971), with some birds dark brown overall, sootier below, with sparse white flecks on back and underparts, sparse white barring below; others (perhaps actually in formative plumage?) resemble adult in pattern but browner overall with duller whitish markings. Probably resembles adult after partial preformative molt within 1–2 months of fledging.
    Habitat and Behavior: Freshwater marshes, from overgrown ditches to reedbeds around large lakes. Mostly retiring, but sometimes walks boldly in the open, even at midday. Vagrants likely to be silent.

AZURE GALLINULE *Porphyrula flavirostris*
22–23 cm (8.7–9")

Summary: *New York*: 1 winter record (1986).
Taxonomy: Monotypic.
Distribution and Status:
    World: Local and somewhat nomadic in tropical S America.
    North America: *New York*: Suffolk Co., Long Island, 14 Dec 1986 (adult killed by a cat; Spencer & Kolodnicki 1988).
Comments: Azure Gallinules move seasonally in S America, and the Dec record from NY fits in with S American records of vagrants and migrants found during late Oct–Jan, the presumed nonbreeding season (Remsen & Parker 1990). There is no evidence for this species ever having been kept in captivity (Spencer & Kolodnicki 1998), and gallinules are well-known for wandering, as exemplified by Purple Gallinules, and by Allen's Gallinule *P. alleni* of the Old World. However, an anonymous 2nd-hand report claimed that the NY bird escaped from captivity, where it was held illegally (Dunn 1999). Consequently, this record is accepted by the AOU and by the state records committee, but not by the ABA, and the truth may never be known. The NY record plausibly represents a wild bird, and we treat it provisionally as such.
Field Identification: This petite gallinule is appreciably smaller than Purple Gallinule, and all ages have a largely yellowish bill.
    Similar Species: In head and body size, Azure Gallinule is not much larger than Sora (!) but it stands much taller with its long legs and big feet. Adult distinct in appearance from other N American birds, although its blue tones can appear pale gray at a distance or in poor light. Juv plumage similar to much larger and bulkier *Purple Gallinule*, but back browner with dark feather centers and contrasting black rump, bill and shield yellowish overall.
    Age/Sex/Season: Ages differ, with adult appearance attained in 1st year; sexes similar; no seasonal variation. Molts not well known. *Adult*: Face, neck, and chest milky turquoise, with contrasting white belly; eyes amber. *1st-year*: Juv has face, neck, and chest buff; eyes paler brownish; resembles adult after partial preformative molt, presumably within a few months of fledging.
    Habitat and Behavior: Much like Purple Gallinule but more skulking. Vagrants could appear in atypical and even open habitats, as do wandering Purple Gallinules.

pale
underwing

black rump

dark-centered
scapulars

adult

juv

Azure Gallinule

NORTHERN JACANA *Jacana spinosa*
21.5–24 cm (8.5–9.5")

Summary: *Texas*: Very rare, mainly in winter; has bred. *Arizona*: Exceptional or very rare since 1985, mainly in summer–fall.

Taxonomy: 3 ssp, not known to be distinguishable in the field. N American records presumed to be n. ssp *gymnostoma*.

Distribution and Status:

World: Resident from Mexico (n. to s. Sonora and cen. Tamaulipas) s. to w. Panama; also on Cuba, Jamaica, and Hispaniola.

North America: *Texas*: Very rare and sporadic visitor (mainly Nov–Apr, but recorded in all months) to lower Rio Grande Valley, occasionally n. to coastal prairies, and exceptionally once to Brewster Co., w. Texas, 7–11 Oct 1982. A resident population of over 40 birds was established during 1967–1978 in Brazoria Co., but breeding has not occurred since. *Arizona*: 5 records through 2008, all since 1985 in the s. Several birds stayed for months but all were first found in Jun–Nov.

Comments: Northern Jacana appears to have been a rare resident of the lower Rio Grande Valley prior to 1910, and may again establish

breeding populations in TX. Like many birds of aquatic habitats, jacanas are prone to wander as wetlands flood and dry up. Although vagrants could (and do) occur at any season, breeding in Mexico commonly occurs during fall and winter (Howell, pers. obs.), in and following the rainy season, at which time birds may be most prone to disperse in search of suitable breeding conditions—and wander n. into TX. The individual in w. TX occurred following the passage of a tropical storm that originated in w. Mexico, and thus may not have come from e. Mexico (Williams 1987). Since the mid-1990s, jacanas have been all but absent in TX, although 3 occurred in fall 2006 and 1 in late fall 2009 (*NAB* 64:112).

The recent AZ records (2 in the 1980s, 1 in the 1990s, 2–3 in the 2000s) mirror a range expansion by jacanas in nw. Mexico. Prior to the 1990s the species was only known n. to cen. Sinaloa (around 24°N), but since at least the mid-1990s there have been increased sightings from s. Sonora (to around 27°N), where jacanas may now be nesting (S. Ganley, pers. comm.).

Reports for FL (mainly in Mar–Apr) are considered unsubstantiated (Stevenson & Anderson 1994), although the species seems a

1st-year

adult

1st-year

adult

juv

Northern Jacana

plausible vagrant from populations in the Greater Antilles.

Field Identification: Striking species, with long legs, very long toes, bright yellow remiges, shrieky calls.

    Similar Species: Looks unlike any other N American bird, but beware the possibility of other jacana species occurring as escapes. Northern ssp of Wattled Jacana *J. jacana*, which replaces Northern Jacana from Panama s., is wholly black as an adult, with a red bill shield and wattle; however, some S American ssp of Wattled have a chestnut body much like Northern but differ in having a red shield and wattles. Imm Wattled very similar to Northern, but bill has rudimentary pinkish shield and wattles.

    Age/Sex/Season: Ages differ, with adult appearance attained in 1 year; sexes similar but female averages larger; no seasonal variation. Molts need study; probably has complex basic strategy (see p. 35). **Adult:** Chestnut bodied with green-glossed black head, neck, and chest, and bright yellow shield and bill divided by pale blue saddle below small crimson band;

legs olive-gray to blue-gray. *1st year*: Juv has face, foreneck, and underparts whitish, with dark eyestripe, crown, and hindneck; brownish upperparts with broad cinnamon tipping; bill yellow with dark culmen and rudimentary shield. Attains similar-looking formative plumage within 1–2 months of fledging, but rump and uppertail coverts solidly chestnut, hindneck blacker, and often some chestnut on upperwing coverts; legs average yellower than adult, often olive to olive-gray. Attains adult plumage by complete 2nd-prebasic molt at about 1 year of age; olive patches on adult-plumaged birds may occur at any age and do not necessarily indicate immaturity (study needed).

    Habitat and Behavior: Aquatic freshwater habitats with emergent and often floating vegetation, over which birds walk by spreading their very long toes. Walks with a fairly high-stepping gait, picking at food like a moorhen. Flies with stiff wingbeats and glides, the long legs and toes trailing. In breeding, 1 female mates with up to 4 males and defends a territory. Loud shrieky clicks and chatters can draw attention.

RAPTORS AND OWLS

These popular families of birds occur worldwide in a variety of habitats. A number of species are long-distance migrants, with others being somewhat dispersive. We treat 7 hawks, 4 falcons, and 4 owls as rare birds in N America. Of these, the Old World contributes 4 hawks, 3 falcons, and 2 owls; the New World contributes 3 hawks, 1 falcon, and 2 owls.

Old World Raptors and Owls

Of the 9 species we treat, White-tailed Eagle and Steller's Sea Eagle likely occur from time to time in sw. and w. AK; and White-tailed has occurred exceptionally in the Northeast. The 2 harriers, 3 falcons, and 2 owls are all long-distance migrants with variable, often lengthy, overwater compo-nents to their migrations. Away from AK, the occurrences of Old World falcons are less readily explained. However, falcons in particular have a distinct advantage as vagrants in that they can rest readily on ships, whence they can forage over the ocean for phalaropes and storm-petrels,

as well as for migrant landbirds. There are numerous cases of Eurasian Hobby and Eurasian Kestrel associating with ships (e.g., see Pranty et al. 2004) and some, perhaps most, vagrant falcons from the Old World may at some point have used these convenient and mobile perches.

Other migratory Old World raptors reported in the New World, mainly in fall from the Caribbean and Bermuda, include Black Kite *Milvus migrans* and Booted Eagle *Hieraaetus pennatus* (Ebels 2002; Buckley et al. 2009). Also of interest in the realm of vagrant raptors in the Pacific region are records (mainly in fall–winter) from the Hawaiian islands of White-tailed Eagle, Steller's Sea Eagle, Black-eared [Black] Kite *Milvus [migrans] lineatus*, and Chinese Sparrow hawk *Accipiter soloensis* (Pyle & Pyle 2009; also see Appendix B). In addition to the preceding species, European Honey Buzzard *Pernis apivorus* and Amur Falcon *Falco amurensis* are both highly migratory species that seem candi-dates for N American vagrancy; indeed, there is a sight record of the former from DE (see Appendix B).

WHITE-TAILED EAGLE *Haliaeetus albicilla*
76–92 cm (30–36"); WS 180–245 cm (71–97")

Summary: *Alaska*: Very rare on w. Aleutians (records year-round; has bred); exceptional on cen. Aleutians (fall), Bering Sea islands (spring-fall), and in sw. AK (winter).
Taxonomy: Monotypic.
Distribution and Status:
    World: W. Greenland and Iceland e. across N Eurasia to ne. Russia (Kamchatka, Chukotka). N Eurasian populations largely migratory, winter-ing s. to Arabia, Japan, and se. China.
    North America: *Alaska*: About 10 records from w. Aleutians, scattered throughout the year. A pair nested on Attu in the early 1980s (Tobish & Balch 1987) and one adult (presumed of the pair) was seen there intermittently from 1984 through 1996. Elsewhere in w. Aleutians (Shemya and Ag-attu), and subsequently on Attu, single imms and subadults have been seen on at least 8 occasions (in all seasons), with 2 imms together on Shemya, Mar–Apr 2002. Elsewhere in AK, exceptional on St. Lawrence (late May–early Jun, at least 3 records in the period) and single records from the Pribilofs (subadult), 16 May–Sep 2012 or later (St. Paul Island Tour); Kiska, 9 Aug 2005 (sub-adult); and Kodiak Island, 28 Jan 2009 (adult;

NAB 63:210). We assume records of 'imms' refer to birds up to 3 years of age, and 'subadults' to be bird 3–4 years of age.
Comments: White-tailed Eagles are summer residents in small numbers right up to the Asian side of the Bering Straits; the paucity of vagrant records may be in part because the prime periods of such vagrancy are before and after the time when most observers are afield in the region. And of course, most large raptors are well known for their aversion to cross large bodies of water, although *Haliaeetus* eagles will do so more readily than most. Infrequent visits by observers, combined with potentially long periods of resi-dence by wide-ranging eagles, makes it impos-sible to identify any seasonal patterns of when eagles have first appeared in the w. Aleutians. The 2012 spring season was remarkable, with dif-ferent subadults found on Shemya, St. Lawrence, and the Pribilofs; birds were first found late Apr–late May, but again, this may simply reflect observer coverage versus actual arrival dates.

Of interest are 3 old late fall–winter records of White-tailed Eagle from the Northeast (all from MA, and 2 of adults), the most recent in 1944 (Veit & Petersen 1993). These records of adults seem counterintuitive, given that imms tend to be the age class that wanders. This suggests the

pale brownish upperparts

adult

long 4th primary

3rd-year

juv/1st-year

note tail pattern

3rd-year

dark tail coverts (white on Bald)

adult

adult

7 'fingers'

broader dark band

juv/1st-year

Bald Eagle

6 'fingers'

juv/1st-year

dark anchors on pale ground

dark streaking

more extensive white

typically plainer upperparts

shorter tail usually pale

juv

White-tailed Eagle

more evenly buff, contrasting with dark trousers

longer tail dark overall

juv

Bald Eagle

juv/1st-year

possibility that imm White-tailed Eagles from Greenland or Iceland have been overlooked in the Northeast; indeed, it would take an acute observer to detect a perched imm White-tailed Eagle, and even flying birds would need to be closely observed. A subadult eagle, believed to have been White-tailed, was seen in Oswego Co., NY, on 24 Apr 1993 (*AB* 47:398). The record was not accepted by the state committee, but subsequent research supports the identification,

and the record may be re-evaluated (E. S. Brinkley, pers. comm.).

Field Identification: Old World counterpart to Bald Eagle. Adult lacks white head; on imms note tail pattern (with narrow dark feather tips) and number of emarginated outer primaries. See Forsman (1999) for further information.

Similar Species: The only real concern is separation from ***Bald Eagle***. All ages of

White-tailed have 7 emarginated outer primaries (Bald has 6). Adult White-tailed unmistakable if seen well: huge and broad-winged with large yellow bill, creamy head and neck blending into brown body, short white tail (with dark tail coverts). *Juv/1st-year* similar to, and equally variable as, same age Bald Eagle but rectrices more tapered and pale, with dark fringes creating a serrated pattern to the tail tip (Bald has broad dark distal tail band). Typical White-tailed has less extensive white on underwing (mainly on axillars and lesser coverts) and dark-streaked belly contrasting less with paler leggings. Perched juv typically has extensive pale bases to upperparts creating a more variegated pattern, with dark subterminal anchor marks on median and greater coverts. *2nd-year* differences similar to 1st-year: White-tailed typically has less extensive white on underwings, narrow dark edging to rectrices, and does not develop bold white back 'saddle' often shown by 2nd-year Bald. *3rd-year*: Bald has broad dark tail tip; head can be whitish overall with broad dark mask; both species can show white 'saddle' but often more solid on Bald. *4th-year*: Bald often has extensively whitish head, often with dark mask, rectrices with broad dark tips. *5th-year and older* appear enough like adult that identification should be relatively straightforward, given a reasonable view.

Age/Sex/Season: Ages differ, with adult appearance attained in about 5 years; sexes similar but females average larger; no seasonal variation. *Adult*: Tail white (rarely with dark-tipped feathers); underwings uniform; head and neck coarsely streaked pale creamy brown. *1st-year*: Flight feathers uniform in generation, with evenly serrated trailing edge to wings; rectrices tapered, with narrow dark edging; underbody brownish overall with coarse paler streaking; upperparts neatly mottled paler brown. *2nd-year*: 1st molt May–Oct usually involves 3–4 inner primaries and some secondaries, but whole tail. Plumage resembles 1st-year but note molt contrasts in wings; central rectrices often darker than juv; underbody extensively mottled white, with contrasting dark head and leggings; upperparts variably mottled whitish. *3rd-year*: Wing molt Mar–Oct, involves middle primaries and most remaining juv secondaries (but usually at least juv s4 and s7–s9 remain); 2nd wave of inner primary molt can include at least p1-p2. Appearance highly variable, some resemble 2nd-year, others more adult-like; head usually concolor with rest of plumage; bill still with extensive dark tip; best aged by molt contrasts in wings. *4th-year*:

Remaining juv outer primaries molted (rarely, juv p10 still retained) and 2nd molt wave continues with inner to middle primaries. Overall resembles adult but has darker head and body, usually a few scattered whitish feathers on upperparts and underbody; yellow bill often has dusky tip; tail usually has 1 or more dark or dark-tipped feathers (rarely dark overall, like some 3rd-years). Attains adult appearance in 5th year but some birds in 5th and 6th years may still show a few subadult characters.

Habitat and Behavior: Like Bald Eagle. Usually silent when not breeding. Calls suggest Bald Eagle but have a slightly more yelping quality.

STELLER'S SEA EAGLE *Haliaetus pelagicus* 85–94 cm (33.5–37"); WS 210–250 cm (83–99")

Summary: *Alaska*: Very rare on Aleutians, exceptional in w. and se. AK.

Taxonomy: Monotypic.

Distribution and Status:

World: Breeds Russian Far East (Kamchatka and around Sea of Okhotsk), winters s. to Japan and Korea.

North America: *Alaska*: 7 records: Unimak, adjacent sw. mainland, and Shumagin Islands, 20 Oct 1977–Mar 1981 (all considered same adult); Attu, 9 May 1980 (imm); se. AK, 25 Sep 1989–21 Sep 2002 (winter whereabouts unknown; not sighted 1999–2000) and possibly paired with a Bald Eagle in some years (W. S. Clark 2008); Attu, 26 May–2 Jun 1994 (subadult); Amchitka, 4 Sep 1998 (adult); Shemya, Mar 2002 (adult); and sw. AK, 27 Aug 2001 (adult), apparently returning for 3 consecutive summers to Nushagak River, whence last reported 12 Sep 2004 (*NAB* 59:129-132).

Comments: It seems likely the few N American records were of, or derived from, young birds that dispersed from their home range (as near as Kamchatka) to and along the Aleutian chain to the mainland. 3 of the 7 birds apparently remained for years, sometimes disappearing in a certain season or for a year or two within their overall residency.

Field Identification: Huge, striking, and massive-billed eagle; adults unmistakable and young also difficult to misidentify.

Similar Species: None if well seen due to massive size, wedge-shaped tail, paddle-shaped wings, and huge, bright orange-yellow bill. But beware possible hybrids; a 3rd-year eagle seen

adult

adult

adult

dark
juv

some juvs
very dark

3rd-year

juv

juv

juv

Steller's Sea Eagle

8–21 Dec 2004 on Vancouver Island, BC, was never definitively identified. Some thought it to be the offspring of a Bald Eagle × Steller's Sea Eagle pairing (W. S. Clark 2008).

Age/Sex/Season: Molts and succession of imm plumages not well known; wing molts likely similar to those of White-tailed and Bald Eagles. Ages differ, with adult appearance probably attained in about 5 years; sexes similar but females average larger; no seasonal variation. ***Adult:*** Clean white tail, tail coverts, thighs, and lesser wing coverts contrast with blackish plumage. ***1st-year:*** Flight feathers uniform in generation, with evenly serrated trailing edge to wings; whitish rectrices tapered, with narrow dark tips; axillars and underwing coverts mottled white. ***2nd-year:*** 1st molt in summer–fall probably involves inner primaries and some secondaries. Plumage overall resembles 1st-year but note molt contrasts

in wings. ***3rd-year:*** Wing molt in spring–fall probably involves middle primaries; possibly a 2nd molt wave starts in inner primaries. Appearance likely variable, cf. White-tailed Eagle; some start to show white on lesser coverts, above and below. ***4th-year:*** Remaining juv outer primaries probably molted, and a successive molt wave starts with inner primaries. Probably resembles adult but may have a few scattered dark feathers in white areas, and tail may have 1 or more dark or dark-tipped feathers. Probably attains adult appearance in 5th year, but some birds in 5th and 6th years may still show a few subadult characters (study needed).

Habitat and Behavior: Similar overall to Bald Eagle but soars with wings in strong dihedral (Wheeler & W. S. Clark 1995). Calls lower pitched than Bald Eagle and with quality than may suggest a braying gull or goose (XC 40205).

WESTERN MARSH HARRIER
Circus aeruginosus L 43–55 cm (17–21.7");
WS 115–140 cm (45–59")

Summary: *Virginia*: 1 early winter
record (1994).
Taxonomy: 2 ssp; NW African ssp *harterti* has
paler head and underparts than widespread
nominate *aeruginosus*. Formerly considered conspecific with Eastern Marsh Harrier *C. spilonotus*
and Swamp Harrier *C. approximans*; often known
in Europe simply as Marsh Harrier.
Distribution and Status:
  World: Breeds from W Europe and NW Africa
e. across mid-latitude Eurasia to around 95°E;
winters from S Europe e. to Indian subcontinent,
s. to sub-Saharan Africa.
  North America: *Virginia*: Accomack Co.,
4 Dec 1994 (Anon 1998, Rottenborn &
Brinkley 2007).

Comments: Western Marsh Harrier is a long-
distance migrant from W Europe to Africa. On
occasion, migrants appear to be drifted offshore
and carried by prevailing ne. trade winds across
the Atlantic. There have been 10 records from
the Azores since 1998, mainly 1st-year birds in
fall–winter but also a spring record from mid-
Apr, along with 3 recent fall–winter records in
the Caribbean: Guadeloupe, 11 Nov 2002–14 Apr
2003 (1st-year; Levesque & Malgalaive 2004); and
Puerto Rico, 14 Jan–30 Mar 2004 (female/1st-
year) and 11 Jan–11 Feb 2006 (1st-year male)
(Merkord et al. 2006). Birds wintering in the Caribbean may move n. in spring into e. N America,
as with Little Egret, White-winged Tern, and
several other species.
  Whether the VA bird first arrived on the
E Coast in fall or reached there via the Caribbean
is unknown, and certainty about its age could
help address this question; the bird has been

buff on head variable,
sometimes absent

darker juv/
1st-year

adult ♂

adult ♀

adult ♀

2nd-year ♂

typical juv/
1st-year

adult ♀

paler adult ♂

adult ♀

adult ♂

Western Marsh Harrier

reported variously as an adult female (Rotten-born & Brinkley 2007) or as a juv (Levesque & Malgalaive 2004). In our view, the original descriptions and field sketches (examined Sep 2012) do not allow certain aging.

Only 9 records of Marsh Harrier from Iceland through 2006 (mainly Apr–May and Sep–Nov) suggest this species is unlikely to reach N America via the northern route (see p. 8).

Field Identification: Distinctive, and unlike any regularly occurring N American raptor; broader-winged than Northern Harrier.

Similar Species: None in N America, but cf. dark buteos. Also beware other possible Old World vagrants, notably Booted Eagle and Black Kite. See Forsman (1999) for further information.

Age/Sex/Season: Ages differ, with adult appearance attained in about 2 years; sexes differ, with female larger and broader-winged than male; no seasonal variation. Very rare dark morph (all ages) has head, body, and wing coverts solidly dark brown; flight feathers as in normal age/sex. *Adult male*: Overall fairly pale underwings (variable brownish markings on coverts) and large pale gray upperwing panels, with contrasting black wing-tips; tail plain gray. *Adult female*: Dark brown overall with tail tinged rufous; crown, throat, and shoulders buff; under-wing often with pale buff mottling on coverts, remiges often with contrasting broad dark tips; eyes pale. *1st-year (both sexes)*: Juv resembles adult female and often not easy to distinguish, especially at moderate range, but fresh in fall (adult in wing molt in fall–early winter), with richer-toned crown (faded, paler buff on adult). Tail dark brown, and greater coverts finely tipped buff. Flight feathers uniform in generation, with outer primaries relatively worn in winter–spring. *2nd-year*: 1st wing and tail molt starts in summer, typically interrupted for fall migration to com-plete in early winter. *Male*: New inner primaries gray with broad dark tips, outer primaries black-ish; tail gray with broad dark tip. Body plumage resembles female but chest and underwing co-verts coarsely streaked buff. *Female*: Resembles adult but underwings average more uniformly dark; eye usually dark. Attains adult plumage by 3rd prebasic molt, with wing molt often inter-rupted for fall migration.

Habitat and Behavior: Open country, espe-cially marshes. Habits similar to Northern Harrier, flying with loose, relaxed wingbeats, and gliding and soaring with wings held in a shallow V. Mostly silent in nonbreeding season.

HEN HARRIER *Circus cyaneus* L 42–50 cm (16.6–19.8"); WS 100–121 cm (39–47")

Summary: *Alaska*: 1 certain record (1999), but see Comments, below.
Taxonomy: Monotypic. Considered specifically distinct from Northern Harrier *Circus [cyaneus] hudsonius*, following most recent authors.
Distribution and Status:
   World: Breeds from W Europe e. across N Eurasia to ne. Russia (sw. Chukotka, and possibly Kamchatka; Brazil 2009); winters from W Europe and N Africa e. across S Asia, and n. to Japan.
   North America: *Alaska*: At least one record from the w. Aleutians, a salvaged wing in Jun 1999 (1st-year male; no phenology inferred). See Comments, below.
Comments: Hen Harrier is a fairly long-distance migrant from NE Asia to SE Asia, and is considered a rare transient in Kamchatka. It is unsurprising that on occasion birds may drift to the w. Aleutians, but the species' status there is clouded by identification issues with respect to Northern Harrier. On the w. Aleutians, Hen/Northern Harrier is very rare in fall (mid-Sep to early Oct) and exceptional in winter (Jan 1991) and spring (mid-May to early Jun; 2 records); these records are tentatively referred to Hen Har-rier by Gibson & Byrd (2007). Records of harriers from the cen. Aleutians, where very rare in fall–winter, are considered of uncertain identity, while records from the e. Aleutians are inferred to be Northern Harriers.

A juvenile harrier banded 8 Nov 2010 at Cape May, NJ, was considered as a probable Hen Harrier (Duffy et al. 2012), highlighting the difficulties in identifying atypical birds out of range.

Field Identification: Old World counterpart to Northern Harrier, from which should be sepa-rated with care; adult male relatively distinctive. See Forsman (1999) and Duffy et al. (2012) for further information, and Martin (2008) for identi-fication of 1st-year birds.

Similar Species: *Northern Harrier* similar in all plumages. Adult male Hen is much cleaner gray-and-white than Northern, without extensive brownish mottling on upperparts, and also lacks variable rusty brown spotting on underparts and underwing coverts of Northern; Hen has broad

juv averages fewer dark bars on outer primaries

juv

adult ♀

adult ♂

black on 6 primaries

adult ♂

Northern Harrier

adult ♂

buff, coarsely streaked

dark trailing edge weaker than secondaries (all plumages)

cinnamon, finely streaked

adult ♂

clean white below

hooded

Northern Harrier juv

black on 5 primaries

2nd-year ♂

juv

2nd-year ♂

variable brownish above in fresh plumage

Hen Harrier

black tips to 6 outer primaries (vs. 5 on Northern) and evenly dusky gray trailing edge to secondaries and inner primaries (vs. broader and bolder black trailing edge to secondaries on Northern). Females and juveniles can be very similar, but Hen has evenly dark trailing edge to secondaries and inner primaries (vs. contrastingly darker trailing edge to secondaries on Northern) and averages fewer and broader dark bars on remiges, best seen from below; thus, juv Northern has 5–6 dark bars on longest primaries (3–5 on p10) whereas juv Hen has 3–4, rarely 5, dark bars on longest primaries (3 on p10). Juv Hen further differs from juv Northern in having extensively dark-streaked underparts (like adult female Northern but unlike relatively plain underparts of juv Northern), and is rarely such a bright cinnamon below in fresh plumage (body plumage variable in both species and coloration may not be diagnostic).

Age/Sex/Season: Ages differ, with adult appearance attained in about 1 year; sexes differ, with female larger and broader-winged than

male; no seasonal variation. **Adult male**: Head, chest, and upperparts plain gray, with black wing-tips, clean white underparts and underwing coverts. **Adult female**: Brownish overall with whitish underparts streaked dark brown; upperside of remiges gray-brown, without contrastingly dark secondaries. **1st-year (both sexes)**: Juv resembles adult female but has buff to pale cinnamon underparts (fading to whitish), contrasting dark secondaries, and contrasting pale tips to greater upperwing coverts. Male has paler iris than female, apparent by mid-winter but often difficult to see. Flight feathers uniform in generation, with outer primaries relatively worn in winter–spring, but can replace 1–2 tail feathers in 1st winter. 1st complete molt starts in spring–summer, typically completed before fall migration. **2nd-year** like adult but male often has mottled brownish wash to head and back, at least into mid-winter; occasionally retains 1 or more juv secondaries.

Habitat and Behavior: Open country, especially rough grassland and marshes. Habits similar to Northern Harrier. Mostly silent in non-breeding season.

EURASIAN KESTREL *Falco tinnunculus*
31–37 cm (12.2–14.5"); WS 68–78 cm (27–31")

Summary: *Alaska*: Exceptional in spring and fall on w. Aleutians; exceptional in fall in se. Bering Sea. *Pacific States*: Single fall records from WA (1999) and CA (2007). *Atlantic States and Provinces*: Exceptional in fall, winter, and spring. **Taxonomy:** 11 ssp, but non-migratory ssp and mostly African and island ssp not considered here; 2 n. breeding migratory ssp (nominate *tinnunculus* of W and Cen Eurasia, *interstinctus* in E Asia) not certainly separable in the field. An AK specimen has been identified as *interstinctus* (Gibson & Kessel 1992). Also known as Common Kestrel.

Distribution and Status:

World: Breeds throughout temperate and mid-latitude Eurasia, from W Europe e. to ne. Russia (around 165°E); n. and interior populations migratory, wintering s. to sub-Saharan Africa, the Indian subcontinent, and se Asia. Also resident locally in sw. India and Africa.

North America: *Alaska*: On w. Aleutians, exceptional in spring (May–early Jun; 5 birds, including 2 male, 2 female) and fall (Sep to mid-Oct; 5 birds, all female/imm). In se. Bering Sea, single female/imm birds on a ship, 4–7 Oct 1991, and an oil platform, 12–14 Sep 1983 (Gibson & Kessel 1992). *Pacific States*: Skagit Co., WA, 31 Oct–11 Nov 1999 (imm); Marin Co., CA, 23 Oct 2007 (juv female). *Atlantic States and Provinces*: Cape May Co., NJ, 23 Sep 1972 (juv female); Westmorland Co., NB/Cumberland Co., NS, 18 Jan to mid-Mar 1988 (female/imm); Cape Cod, MA, 14 Apr–5 May 2002 (adult male); Orange Co., FL, 26 Feb–22 Mar 2003 (female/imm). Pranty et al. (2004) summarize and discuss records through 2003.

Comments: There were 86 records for Iceland through 2006 with a distinct peak in Sep–Oct,

adult ♂

adult ♂

adult ♂
(flight)

American
Kestrel ♀

adult ♀

broad dark
band on
duller tail

Eurasian Kestrel

juv

note tail and
face patterns,
upperwing
contrast

and the species has been annual on the Azores in recent years. There are single winter records for Bermuda, Martinique (Pinchon & Vaurie 1961), and Trinidad (Kenefick & Hayes 2006), and 2 records from ne. Brazil (Santana & Pinheiro 2010), all of which suggest significant overwater capabilities, although like other falcons this species rests readily on ships.

This distribution of N American records, a moderately robust world population, and the fact that the species is a long-distance if diurnal migrant, suggest there should be a steady trickle of records in e. N America. The NS/NB record, and a Dec 1946 specimen from s. BC, indicate the species can winter fairly well n. on both coasts.

Interestingly there are no records from the cen. or e. Aleutians or from the Pribilofs, yet 2 records in the se. Bering Sea. The W Coast birds presumably entered N America via AK (or perhaps were ship-assisted to farther s.) and migrated down the 'wrong' side of the Pacific.

Field Identification: Old World counterpart to American Kestrel, but appreciably larger with looser, floppier flight.

Similar Species: Male distinctive, but female could be passed over. Female *American Kestrel* appreciably smaller and more petite, with distinct dark cheek bar. Eurasian has more contrasting blackish upperwing hand without whitish subterminal spots on primaries, rusty-brown tail (not contrastingly rufous) with broader dark subterminal band. See Forsman (1999) for further information, including separation from very similar *Lesser Kestrel F. naumanni*, unrecorded in N America but a long-distance migrant from S Europe to Africa.

Age/Sex/Season: Ages and sexes differ, with adult appearance attained in 2nd summer–fall; no seasonal variation. *Adult male*: Tail blue-gray with broad black subterminal band; blue-gray head contrasts with mostly rufous back. *Adult female*: Tail rufous-brown to brownish gray with numerous dark bars and broader dark subterminal band; head and upperparts rufous-brown, rump and tail sometimes contrastingly grayer; underparts streaked and spotted dark brown. *1st-year*: Juv resembles adult female but has whitish tips to remiges and pale tips to upperparts, which by winter abrade or are lost through molt; underparts more distinctly streaked, less spotted, than adult female. Juv female upperparts have coarser and denser dark barring than male, and overall appear darker above. Variable but often extensive preformative molt of head and body feathers

(and occasionally central rectrices) in fall–winter makes differences between sexes more distinct, as some males attain adult-like back feathers. 1st-spring female often difficult to distinguish from adult but worn remiges contrast with fresher back feathers. Attains adult plumage by complete 2nd-prebasic molt, Jun–Oct.

Habitat and Behavior: Much like American Kestrel. Most common call a series of sharp notes *ki-ki-ki-ki* … , suggesting Merlin but slower-paced.

RED-FOOTED FALCON *Falco vespertinus*
28–34 cm (11–13.3"); WS 65–76 cm (25.5–30")

Summary: *Massachusetts*: 1 fall record (2004).
Taxonomy: Monotypic.
Distribution and Status:
World: Breeds mid-latitude Eurasia, from E Europe e. to around 120°E; winters S Africa.

North America: *Massachusetts*: Martha's Vineyard, 8–24 Aug 2004.

Comments: There were 4 spring–summer records of Red-footed Falcon from Iceland through 2000 (none from Greenland) and there have been 4 records since 1990 in the Azores (3 in May, 1 in Sep). In W Europe (e.g., Britain), the species is known mainly as an erratic, overshooting spring-summer drift vagrant (mainly in May–Jun), with mini-invasions in some years; 2004 was not a significant invasion year. As yet, there are no records of Red-footed Falcon from the se. Caribbean, but the species seems likely to be recorded there sooner or later. There is no pattern visible to us that casts light on the origin of the MA bird, but of course ships may have played a role.

Britain's first Amur Falcon, a 1st-summer individual, was initially identified as a Red-footed Falcon until images were viewed and the incoming underwing coverts were seen to be white, not dark. Any future N American records should be examined with this species in mind; there are no records of Amur Falcon from Iceland but a recent Nov report from the Azores.

Field Identification: Handsome small falcon, looking distinct from any N American species. Complex age/sex variation.

Similar Species: Nothing similar in N America, but cf. other possible vagrants.

Eurasian Hobby juv similar to juv Red-footed Falcon but has slightly more pointed wings, slightly shorter tail, and more dashing behavior. Hobby lacks distinct dark barring above,

adult ♀

adult ♂

1st-summer ♂

adult ♂

adult ♀

adult ♂

1st-summer ♀

1st-summer ♂

1st-summer ♂

adult ♀

dark
trailing
edge

1st-summer ♀

Red-footed Falcon

especially on upperside of tail; has longer black moustache; white of nape does not form complete white collar and head darker overall; underwing has less distinct dark trailing edge.

Amur Falcon, a long-distance migrant breeding in E Asia and wintering in SE Africa (unrecorded N America), similar in plumages to Red-footed and should be considered; all ages differ in underwing coverts, which are solidly white, not dark (adult male), or have a white, not buff, ground color (female and 1st-year; but can be very difficult to appreciate in the field). See Corso & W. S. Clark (1998) and Corso & Catley (2003) for further information.

Age/Sex/Season: Ages and sexes differ, with adult appearance attained in 2nd winter; no seasonal variation. **Adult male:** Slaty gray overall with rufous thighs, dark underwings, silvery-gray remiges above. **Adult female:** Underparts and crown cinnamon; upperparts blue-gray, barred dark. **1st-year:** Juv underparts buff to whitish, streaked dark brown; upperparts resemble adult female but browner overall, with buff tips. Variable but usually extensive preformative molt of head and body feathers (and often some to all rectrices) in 1st winter makes differences

between sexes distinct. 1st-summer male variable, usually with head and body mostly gray, often with a cinnamon chest patch; underwings barred. 1st-summer female has crown and underparts creamy to cinnamon, often with dark streaking on underparts; some are difficult to distinguish from adult female but on 1st-summer note worn remiges, barred underwing coverts. Attains adult plumage by complete 2nd-prebasic molt, in summer–early winter, with wing molt often interrupted for fall migration.

Habitat and Behavior: Similar to American Kestrel. Often hovers and alights on ground. Vagrants likely to be silent.

EURASIAN HOBBY *Falco subbuteo*
29–35 cm (11.5–13.8"); WS 70–84 cm (27.5–33")

Summary: *Alaska*: Very rare in spring and fall on w. Aleutians; exceptional in spring–summer on Bering Sea islands and w. mainland. *Pacific States and Provinces*: Single fall records from WA (2001) and BC (2006). *Northeast*: Single spring records from NL (2004) and MA (2011).

Taxonomy: 2 ssp, not known to be separable in the field. Also known as Northern Hobby.

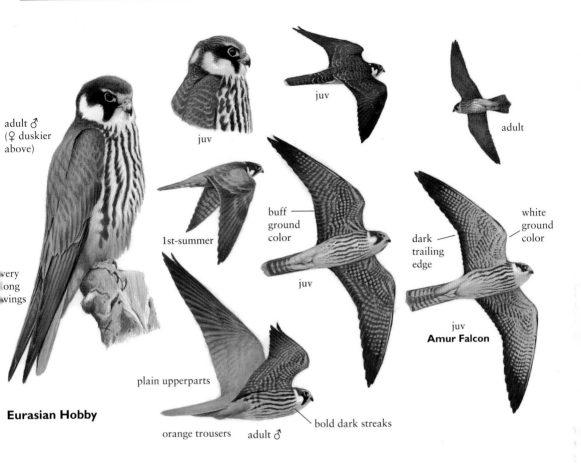

adult ♂
(♀ duskier
above)

juv

juv

adult

very
long
wings

1st-summer

buff
ground
color

juv

dark
trailing
edge

white
ground
color

juv
Amur Falcon

plain upperparts

Eurasian Hobby

orange trousers   adult ♂

bold dark streaks

Distribution and Status:

World: Breeds s. temperate and mid-latitude Eurasia, from W Europe e. to ne. Russia (around 170°E, including Kamchatka); winters primarily in S Africa and the Indian subcontinent.

North America: *Alaska*: On w. Aleutians, very rare to rare in spring–early summer (mid-May to early Jul) and fall (mid-Sep to mid-Oct; exceptionally reported early Aug, *NAB* 62:131; 5 fall birds aged as juvs, 2 as adults). Elsewhere in AK, 3 summer records from Pribilofs (late Jun to mid-Aug), and 1 from w. mainland (8 Jun 2003). *Pacific States and Provinces*: King Co., WA, 21 Oct 2001 (adult); s. Vancouver Island, BC, 29 Sep 2006 (juv). *Northeast*: Ferryland Co., NL, 21 May 2004; Plymouth Co., MA, 18 May 2011 (adult; *NAB* 65:413).

Comments: There is a record near Newfoundland, a 1st-summer that appeared 9 May 1989 on a ship about 500 km e. of St John's and stayed for 6 days (*AB* 43:398, 445), and Iceland had 17 records through 2006 (mostly mid-Apr to Jul), so further E Coast records seem possible via the

northern route, especially in spring. However, the Azores recorded its first Hobby in 2008, and there are no records from the se. Caribbean or Bermuda, so there may be little reason to expect records via the southern route.

Whether or how Amur Falcon was ruled out for all w. Aleutian fall records is uncertain; juv Amur is rather similar to Eurasian Hobby. Breeding as close as ne. China and being a long-distance, overwater migrant, Amur Falcon is certainly a candidate for vagrancy to the w. Aleutians and perhaps elsewhere in w. N America.

Field Identification: Medium-sized, striking and streamlined falcon with very long wings.

Similar Species: Among regularly occurring N American species, beware male **Merlin** (which often seizes dragonflies in flight, as does hobby) and adult and juv male **Peregrine**, if not seen well. Also cf. **Red-footed Falcon**.

Amur Falcon (unrecorded in N America) juv similar to juv Hobby but has slightly blunter wings, slightly longer tail, and less dashing behavior. Best character is conspicuous dark trailing edge to underwing versus darker overall and less contrasting underwing on hobby; also note shorter dark mustache and nearly complete white hindcollar on Amur, and more distinct dark barring on upperparts, especially tail.

Age/Sex/Season: Ages differ, with adult appearance attained in 2nd winter; sexes similar but females average larger, and adult females slightly browner above than adult males; no seasonal differences. *Adult*: Upperparts fairly plain, dark slaty gray; thighs and undertail coverts pale rufous. *1st-year*: Juv upperparts have neat buff to cinnamon fringes, thighs and undertail coverts pale cinnamon. Variable but often extensive preformative molt of head and body feathers (and occasionally central rectrices) in 1st winter produces mostly adult-like appearance to head and body by 1st spring; best aged in spring–summer by contrast of retained juv flight feathers, and by some to all rectrices with distinct buff bars visible on underside (paler bars duller and diffuse on adult). Attains adult plumage by complete 2nd-prebasic molt, fall–winter, usually renewing a few inner primaries before interrupting wing molt for fall migration.

Habitat and Behavior: A dashing aerialist, capturing birds and large dragonflies on the wing. Sits on exposed perches. Most common call a complaining *kew-kew-kew* … , with more of a mewing quality than calls of American Kestrel.

ORIENTAL SCOPS OWL *Otus sunia*
19–21 cm (7.5–8.3")

Summary: *Alaska*: 2 late-spring records from w. and cen. Aleutians (1977, 1979).

Taxonomy: 7 ssp, not known to be separable in the field, but migratory n. ssp average larger and paler overall. N American specimens are referred to ssp *japonicus*.

Distribution and Status:

World: Breeds E Asia, ne. to s. Sakhalin, s. to peninsular Malaysia. N. populations migratory, wintering in s. parts of breeding range and s. to Indonesia.

North America: *Alaska*: Buldir, 5 Jun 1977 (salvaged wing); Amchitka, 20 Jun 1979 (male); both rufous morphs (ABA 2008).

rufous morph

gray morph

Oriental Scops Owl

Comments: Phenology of the salvaged wing not determined, but 1979 bird caught alive and presumably had arrived that spring, likely as a drift vagrant.

Field Identification: Very small 'eared' owl, occurring in both rufous and gray morphs, the rufous morph considered 'very frequent' in ssp *japonicus* (König & Weick 2008:233).

Similar Species: Much smaller than N American screech-owls; differs from Flammulated Owl in plainer plumage, yellow eyes. Highly migratory *Eurasian Scops Owl Otus scops*, with which Oriental Scops Owl has at times been lumped, breeds from SW Europe e. to Cen Asia, winters in sub-Saharan Africa. Although the voices of the 2 species are different, silent birds may not be identifiable with certainty.

Age/Sex/Season: All post-juvenile plumages similar. In Eurasian Scops Owl, some spring adults distinguishable by mixed generations of secondaries (vs. uniform juv remiges on 1st-years), whereas fall adults interrupt wing molt for migration and show contrasts within primaries and secondaries;

not known if Oriental Scops is similar (study needed).

Habitat and Behavior: Typical small, nocturnal owl; prefers to roost in trees. Song, given by spring migrants, a low-pitched, resonant, incessantly repeated, metronomic 2- or 3-noted *pu pwoo pwoook*, each note longer than the last (P. Holt, pers. comm.).

NORTHERN BOOBOOK (Brown Hawk Owl) *Ninox [scutulata] japonica*
27–33 cm (10.7–13")

Summary: *Alaska*: Single fall records from Bering Sea islands (2007) and w. Aleutians (2008).
Taxonomy: 3 ssp provisionally recognized, not known to be separable in field except perhaps by voice, with northernmost ssp *japonica* the longest-distance migrant and perhaps the most likely to reach N America; several resident or largely resident taxa to the s. sometimes considered conspecific (combined species often known

alert

all plumages similar

accipiter-like in flight

Northern Boobook

as Brown Hawk Owl) but vocally distinct and better treated as separate species, as done by IOC (following B. King 2002).

Distribution and Status:

World: Breeds from cen. China e. to se. Russia (around 45°N) and n. Japan; ne. populations migratory, wintering s. to Indonesia.

North America: *Alaska*: Pribilofs, 27 Aug–3 Sep 2007 (Yerger & Mohlmann 2008); Kiska, 1 Aug 2008 (carcass found; A. L. Bond & Jones 2010).

Comments: The ne. populations of Northern Boobook are highly migratory, with long overwater legs. N American records seem likely to involve misoriented or drift vagrants, perhaps ship-assisted, as suggested for the Kiska individual (A. L. Bond & Jones 2010).

Field Identification: Medium-sized, upright-perching owl lacking facial disks.

Similar Species: None in N America.

Age/Sex/Season: All post-juvenile plumages similar. Molts apparently unstudied.

Habitat and Behavior: Nocturnal and likely to be roosting by day, for which it prefers trees. Perches and flies like an accipter. Song of *japonica* a slightly gruff, ringing hoot, often doubled in see-saw rhythm and repeated fairly rapidly and steadily, *hoó-kwoo* … (XC79309).

New World Raptors and Owls

None of the 6 New World species is considered a traditional migrant, but all engage in post-breeding dispersal or simply wandering, which on occasion can bring individuals n. into the s. US. All records are from TX and virtually all during fall–winter, which is also when birders are most active in s. TX. Five species (Double-toothed Kite, Crane Hawk, Collared Forest-Falcon, Mottled and Stygian Owls) are represented by only 1–2 records each, whereas Roadside Hawk shows a pattern of irregular winter dispersal.

Other New World raptors that seem possible in s. TX, based on distributions comparable to species that have occurred, include Lesser Yellow-headed Vulture *Cathartes burrovianus*, Plumbeous Kite *Ictinia plumbea*, Great Black Hawk *Buteogallus urubitinga*, Laughing Falcon *Herpetotheres cachinnans*, and Bat Falcon *Falco albigularis*; while Cuban Black Hawk *Buteogallus gundlachii* seems a candidate for vagrancy to s. FL (see Appendix B).

DOUBLE-TOOTHED KITE *Harpagus bidentatus* 32–35.5 cm (12.5–14");WS 63–74 cm (25–29")

Summary: *Texas*: 1 spring record from Upper Texas Coast (2011).

Taxonomy: 2 ssp, differing slightly in adult plumage. TX record presumably of n. ssp *fasciatus* (Mexico to n. S America), which differs from nominate *bidentatus* of S America in distinctly barred (vs. more solidly rufous) underparts of adults.

Distribution and Status:

World: Tropical Mexico (n. to s. Nayarit and s. Veracruz) to tropical S America.

North America: *Texas*: Galveston Co., 4 May 2011 (1st-year; *NAB* 65:480, 564).

Comments: This tropical species was not on anyone's radar as a vagrant to N America. Double-toothed Kite may be spreading northward in w. Mexico, with the first records from Nayarit in 2007 (Howell, pers. obs.), but we know of no evidence for a northward spread in e. Mexico; however, this is a relatively inconspicuous species that can be overlooked fairly easily. Double-toothed Kite has been found a few times in spring on Ambergris Caye, Belize (*NAB* 65:564) and thus is prone to some local wandering.

The TX record is one of numerous recent extralimital and northerly occurrences of tropical and subtropical raptors, many of which appear to be spreading northward; cf. steadily increasing records of Crested Caracara from coast to coast in the US, Common Black Hawk in the West, Short-tailed Hawk in the Southwest (Williams et al. 2007); cf. also with records from Michigan in Nov 2005 (*NAB* 60:173), the Baja California Peninsula, Mexico in Nov 2010 (Mlodinow 2011), and Black Hawk-Eagle in nw. Mexico (where first recorded in Nayarit in 2006; *NAB* 60:290).

Field Identification: Rather small, accipiter-like kite with pale greenish orbital ring, lores, and cere, pale amber eyes. In flight note puffy white undertail coverts, and bowed wings when gliding and soaring.

Similar Species: None if seen well, but cf. accipiters, especially Cooper's Hawk, and perhaps Broad-winged Hawk.

Age/Sex/Season: Ages differ, with adult appearance attained in 1 year; sexes differ slightly; no seasonal variation. Molts not well known.

Adult: Head and upperparts slaty gray; underparts broadly barred rufous, with more solid

adult

molting
1st-year

tail usually
held closed

adult

white
undertail
coverts often
flared

adult

juv

juv

Double-toothed Kite

rufous on chest of female; tail has 3 whitish bars on upperside, 2–3 whitish to pale gray bands on underside; eyes amber. **1st-year**: Head and upperparts dark brown; whitish underparts streaked dark brownish on chest, barred on flanks (rarely almost unmarked below); tail has 3–4 whitish bars, narrower than adult; eyes can be paler, yellowish into 1st winter. Attains adult plumage by protracted molt over 1st year; much of head and body plumage can be adult-like by spring.

Habitat and Behavior: Woodland and forest, rarely in adjacent semi-open areas. Often quite tame and confiding, perching mainly at upper to mid-levels in trees and on wires. Soars and glides on distinctively bowed wings, tail often held closed on displaying adults but more often spread slightly on imms. High-pitched whistles given mainly in flight display; vagrants likely to be silent.

CRANE HAWK *Geranospiza caerulescens*
46–54 cm (18–21"); WS 92–105 cm (36–41")

Summary: *Texas*: 1 winter record from Lower Rio Grande Valley (1987/1988).

Taxonomy: In need of revision, with up to 6 ssp recognized; n. ssp *nigra* (presumably recorded in TX) dark slaty gray overall, with adults from se. Mexico and Belize southward being appreciably paler, slaty blue-gray overall.

Distribution and Status:

World: Tropical Mexico (n. to s. Sonora and cen. Tamaulipas) to tropical S America.

North America: *Texas*: Hidalgo Co., 20 Dec 1987–9 Apr 1988 (adult).

Comments: Crane Hawks in Mexico are largely resident, and although local wandering can be expected this species would not be high on a list of potential vagrants to the US. The TX bird's wings and tail were notably disheveled, and although it has been stated that the ragged tail tips 'represent a condition that may be fairly common in Crane Hawks' (*AB* 42:194), none of numerous wild Crane Hawks seen by Howell has been this unkempt; in many other birds, such feather condition would be a red flag for captive origin. The species has been documented in FL as a free-flying exotic (Pranty 2004), and the possibility of a released or escaped captive cannot be ruled out for the TX bird.

adult

adults

juv

juv

Crane Hawk

Field Identification: Fairly large but lanky hawk with relatively small, pigeon-like head, broad rounded wings, long tail (with 2 white bands), and very long orange to reddish legs.

Similar Species: None, if seen well. Cf. very differently proportioned adult Common Black Hawk.

Age/Sex/Season: Ages differ, with adult appearance attained in 1 year; sexes similar but female averages larger; no seasonal variation. Molts not well known. *Adult*: Eyes deep red, underparts with little or no whitish barring, mainly on belly and undertail coverts, legs orange-red to pinkish red. *1st-year*: Eyes amber to reddish orange, face grizzled whitish, underparts with variable whitish barring and flecking (especially underwing coverts), legs orange to orange-red.

Habitat and Behavior: Woodland, forest, mangroves, and semi-open areas, often near water. Clambers among branches and vegetation, reaching for prey in bromeliads and crevices with its double-jointed legs, often flapping its wings for balance. Flight usually low and not prolonged, loose floppy wingbeats interspersed with glides on fairly level wings, the tail held closed or slightly spread. Can be quite confiding.

In Mexico, call is a fairly loud, clear, plaintive whistled *wheeéoo*, given infrequently.

ROADSIDE HAWK *Buteo magnirostris*
33–41 cm (13–16"); WS 68–79 cm (27–31")

Summary: *Texas*: Very rare in Lower Rio Grande Valley, mainly in winter.
Taxonomy: 12 ssp, some of which may merit species status; n. ssp *griseocauda*, occurring from ne. Mexico to Costa Rica (and presumably in TX), relatively small with relatively brownish upperparts.
Distribution and Status:
    World: Tropical Mexico (n. to Jalisco and cen. Tamaulipas) s. to tropical S America.
    North America: *Texas*: 8 winter records (Oct–Mar) in the period covered here, from Lower Rio Grande Valley, all since 1979; 7 birds first found between mid-Dec and early Feb, a few remaining for prolonged periods. Only other N American record is a specimen from s. TX, 2 Apr 1901.
Comments: Roadside Hawks are common in tropical e. Mexico. They are considered largely resident, but a pattern of occasional wandering n. to TX in fall and winter is developing. The

bright cere
and staring
eye

plain
breast

fairly even banding

rufous

adult

1st-year
variation

ult

adult

juv

**Roadside
Hawk**

species is reported almost every year in TX but there are few substantiated records, and Roadside Hawks appear to be genuinely rare in the US. Adults and 1st-year birds have been recorded in about equal numbers.

The 2004/2005 winter was exceptional for the number and diversity of Mexican vagrants recorded in s. TX; the 3 Roadside Hawks there in Jan–Mar 2005 may have been part of that event or could have been part of the snowball effect of having many birders in s. TX at that season.

Field Identification: Small buteo with fairly short, rounded wings, medium-long tail, and fairly long yellow legs; at rest, wing-tips reach about halfway down tail.

Similar Species: Fairly distinctive if seen well, but should be distinguished with care from other small butoes (Broad-winged, 1st-year Gray, and 1st-year Red-shouldered) and from 1st-year Cooper's Hawk. Note fairly even-width tail

bands (recalling an accipiter), contrast between plain (adult) or streaked (imm) chest and barred belly and sides, rufous primary panel on adult. See Howell & Webb (1995) for further information.

Age/Sex/Season: Ages differ, with adult appearance attained in 1 year; sexes similar but female averages larger; no seasonal variation. Molts not well known. **Adult:** Eyes yellowish white; cere and legs bright orange-yellow; chest fairly plain gray brown; tail has 3-4 gray bands on upperside, 3–5 narrow dark bars from below; rufous patch in primaries distinct. **1st-year:** eyes brown to pale yellowish; cere and legs duller yellow; chest streaked dark brown and whitish; tail has 4-5 grayish bands on upperside, 4-6 narrow dark bars from below; rufous patch in primaries indistinct or lacking.

Habitat and Behavior: Woodland and edge, semi-open areas, farmland with fences and scattered trees. Hunts mainly from perches, and in

Mexico often seen on roadside wires or posts, where can be confiding. Flight usually fairly low with hurried wingbeats and short glides, recalling an accipiter or w. Red-shouldered Hawk. Soars only occasionally (except in noisy courtship flight, not recorded in US), with wings held fairly level or slightly arched. Often waggles its tail briefly upon landing. Most frequent call a complaining scream, *meeéahh*.

COLLARED FOREST FALCON *Micrastur semitorquatus* 53–63 cm (21–25"); WS 76–94 cm (30–37")

Summary: *Texas*: 1 winter record from Lower Rio Grande Valley (1994).
Taxonomy: 2 ssp, not known to be distinguishable in the field. TX bird presumably of n. subspecies *naso*.
Distribution and Status:
   World: Tropical Mexico (n. to s. Sinaloa and cen. Tamaulipas) s. to tropical S America.
   North America: *Texas*: Hidalgo Co., 22 Jan–24 Feb 1994 (light-morph adult).

Comments: Collared Forest Falcons are fairly common in Mexico where they are generally considered resident. The species was not high on any list of potential vagrants to the US but it also seems an unlikely candidate for captivity, and the TX bird appears to represent an individual that wandered beyond the edge of its range. Given how inconspicuous this species usually is, it might even have wandered north as a juv and only been detected after it matured and started calling.
Field Identification: Fairly large and lanky raptor with broad rounded wings, very long, strongly graduated tail, long yellow legs and toes, and greenish-yellow lores and orbital ring.
   Similar Species: None if seen well, but some plumages of imm ***Hook-billed Kite*** can suggest light-morph forest falcon. Kites lack dark 'sideburns' and are very differently proportioned, with a heavy hooked bill, short legs, and a shorter, squared tail.
   Laughing Falcon (unrecorded in N America, but fairly common in tropical Mexico and seemingly at least as likely to reach the US) looks very

adult
light morph

adult
light morph

juv
light
morph

adult

juv
dark morph

Collared Forest Falcon

different but has far-carrying calls that suggest forest falcon. Calls of Laughing Falcon tend to be faster-paced and less aggrieved-sounding, *wah wah wah* … , and variations.

Age/Sex/Season: Ages differ, with adult appearance attained in 1 year; sexes similar but female averages larger; no seasonal variation. Molts not well known. ***Adult light morph***: Face, hindcollar, and underparts white to buff with dark crown and dark 'sideburns.' Upperparts blackish with 3 narrow white tail bars. ***1st-year light morph***: Face pattern less sharply defined, dark brown upperparts spotted pale brown, underparts barred dusky, tail with 3–4 narrow white bars. Rare ***dark morph*** has head and body blackish overall, tail as in light morph.

Habitat and Behavior: Woodland, forest, and edges. Retiring and rarely seen, forages low to high among trees and even on the ground. Does not soar and any flights are usually low and short, through or just over the canopy, infrequently across large clearings. Usually detected by voice, and heard far more often than seen; calls from high in the canopy but not often on an exposed branch. Territorial call a far-carrying, hollow *cowh*, often repeated steadily but not hurriedly, rarely faster than 1 call per 2 secs, and at times breaking into laughing series.

MOTTLED OWL *Strix (Ciccaba) virgata*
33–38 cm (13–15")

Summary: *Texas*: 2 records from Lower Rio Grande Valley (1983, 2006).

Taxonomy: 7 ssp, with at least n. ssp not known to be distinguishable in the field; US records presumably *tamaulipensis* of ne. Mexico.

Distribution and Status:

World: Tropical and subtropical Mexico (n. to cen. Nuevo Leon) s. to S America.

North America: *Texas*: Hidalgo Co., 23 Feb 1983 (roadkill) and 5–11 Jul 2006.

Comments: Although Mottled Owl is usually considered resident throughout its range, the US records suggest it wanders on occasion, and it occurs within 100 km of the US border. The roadkill record is open to question, in that it may have fallen off a vehicle that originated in Mexico. Still, given this species' nocturnal habits, it may be of more frequent occurrence in the US than presently recognized.

Field Identification: Medium-sized, arboreal, and dark-eyed nocturnal owl, much smaller than Barred and Spotted owls; lacks ear tufts.

Similar Species: Nothing really similar in N America. ***Barred Owl*** much larger, with dark scalloped barring across chest, pale grayish facial disks; ***Spotted Owl*** larger with coarse

darker bird

Mottled Owl

spotting on underparts, plainer and softer face with gray-brown facial disks.

Age/Sex/Season: Ages differ, with adult appearance attained in 1st fall; sexes similar but female averages larger; no seasonal variation but individuals in a population vary from paler and grayer to darker and browner. Molts not well known. *1st-year* perhaps distinguishable from adult by uniform generation juv flight feathers, as in other *Strix* owls (Pyle 1997b); juv (unlikely in US) is downy, buff overall with buff to whitish facial disks.

Habitat and Behavior: Forest and woodland, gardens with trees; hunts at night in adjacent open and semi-open areas from low to mid-level perches such as fence posts and open branches. Typically roosts well concealed at upper to mid-levels in trees, and rarely detected in an area unless heard. Common territorial call a series of 3–10 resonant barking hoots with the series becoming stronger and slightly faster-paced, before fading quickly with the last 1–2 hoots; also a fairly rapid, slightly bouncing-ball series of about 20 hoots, and a wailing scream.

STYGIAN OWL *Asio stygius* 38–43 cm (15–17")

Summary: *Texas*: 2 winter records from Lower Rio Grande Valley (1994, 1996).
Taxonomy: 6 ssp, perhaps not distinguishable in the field; ssp involved in US records unknown.

Distribution and Status:

World: Mexico s. locally to n. Argentina; also Cuba and Hispaniola.

North America: *Texas*: Hidalgo Co., 9 Dec 1994 and 26 Dec 1996 (both found at daytime roosts in Bentsen-Rio Grande Valley State Park).

Comments: This widespread neotropical owl is rather poorly known. Although locally fairly common in the mountains of w. Mexico it was not known from ne. Mexico until 2005, when a pair with young was discovered in Tamaulipas (*NAB* 59:659–661). The TX records suggest occasional winter wandering into the lowlands, as occurs with many other species in ne. Mexico. It is conceivable that both records refer to the same

all plumages similar

Stygian Owl

individual residing for a long period, but under-standably overlooked.

Field Identification: Fairly large, overall dark 'eared' owl; larger and bulkier than Long-eared Owl.

Similar Species: Distinctive if seen well. ***Great Horned Owl*** larger and more massive with wide-spaced ear tufts, barred underparts, lacks white forehead blaze. ***Long-eared Owl*** slightly smaller and slimmer, with tawny facial disks, variable buff to rufous plumage tones, and black vertical stripe through eyes.

Age/Sex/Season: Ages differ, with adult appearance attained in 1st fall; sexes similar but female averages larger; no seasonal variation. Molts not well known. ***1st-year*** might be distinguishable from adult by uniform generation juv flight feathers (study needed). Juv (unlikely in US) is downy, pale buff overall with dark barring and blackish facial disks merging into a mask.

Habitat and Behavior: Forest and woodland; hunts at night in adjacent open and semi-open areas, probably both in flight and from perch. Often roosts in fairly open but shady situations, usually at upper to mid-levels, and can be quite confiding in the daytime. Territorial call a single, deep, emphatic *wuupf*, repeated about every 4–10 secs.

LARGER LANDBIRDS

These include a diversity of species, most of them often grouped under the title 'near-passerines' for their traditional placement preceding passerines in many checklists, but here also including corvids (Howell et al. 2009). In N America we consider 15 such species as rare birds, 9 with Old World origins and 6 with New World origins. The Old World species are 1 nightjar, 2 doves, 2 cuckoos, 1 hoopoe, 2 woodpeckers, and 1 corvid; the New World species comprise 3 doves, 1 cuckoo, 1 quetzal, and 1 kingfisher.

Larger Old World Landbirds

These 9 species include 6 from E Asia that have reached nw. N America (mainly AK), 2 species from Europe that have reached the E Coast, and 1 species (Common Cuckoo) recorded on both coasts. Of the AK vagrants, 3 have occurred in both spring–summer and fall (Oriental Turtle Dove, both cuckoos) and 2 only in fall (Eurasian Hoopoe, Eurasian Wryneck), whereas Great Spotted Woodpecker is an irruptive vagrant. European Turtle Dove and Eurasian Jackdaw reached e. N America from W Europe or W Africa, with the latter, at least, likely being ship-assisted.

GRAY NIGHTJAR *Caprimulgus jotoka*
30–32 cm (11.8–12.7")

Summary: *Alaska*: 1 record from w. Aleutians (1977).

Taxonomy: 2 ssp, not known to be separable in the field. N American specimen referred to migratory ne. ssp *jotaka*. Here considered specifically distinct from Jungle Nightjar *C. indicus*, following Rasmussen & Anderton (2005), and Cleere (2010).

Distribution and Status:

World: Breeds from Indian subcontinent e. to n. Japan and se. Russia (n. to around 55°N); ne. populations migratory, wintering from s. China to the Philippines and w. Indonesia.

North America: *Alaska*: Buldir, May 1977 (mummified remains of female; Day et al. 1979).

Comments: No determination was made as to how long the Gray Nightjar remains had been in place. Curiously, 1977 was also the year when Oriental Scops Owl remains were found on Buldir.

Field Identification: May suggest a large whip-poor-will in overall appearance, but has more pointed wings in flight, with overall colder plumage tones and short white (male) to cinnamon (female) bar on primaries.

Similar Species: Distinguished from all N American nightjars by combination of size (larger than Common Nighthawk), tail extending to or just beyond wing-tips when at rest; and white to buff medial spots on outer primaries (often visible at rest). Male has white terminal spots on all but central rectrices. Also cf. European Nightjar *C. europaeus*, which has distribution and migration routes similar to other species that have reached AK as fall vagrants.

Age/Sex/Season: Ages differ, with adult appearance probably attained in 2nd fall–winter; sexes differ slightly; no seasonal variation. Molts not well known. ***Adult male*** has white medial band on outer 3 primaries, white subterminal band on inner webs of outer rectrices. ***Adult female*** has large cinnamon medial spots on outer webs of outer 2–3 primaries, forming broken wing band; lacks white in tail. ***1st-year***: Juv quickly attains adult-like plumage, before migration, but retains juv wings and tail at least into 1st winter (and perhaps through 1st summer; needs

adult ♂

adult ♂

Gray Nightjar

study); juv/1st-year male has buffy-white spots on inner webs of outer primaries and small white subterminal band on inner webs of outer rectrices, thus suggesting poorly marked adult male.

Habitat and Behavior: Typical nightjar. Song a resonant *chaunk* or *chonk*, repeated too rapidly to count; flushed birds usually silent (P. Holt, pers. comm.).

EUROPEAN TURTLE DOVE *Streptopelia turtur* 27–29 cm (10.7–11.4")

Summary: *Atlantic States and Provinces:* 3 records in spring–summer.
Taxonomy: 4 ssp, not certainly separable in the field but nominate *turtur* of Eurasia averages larger and darker overall than 3 African ssp. MA specimen appears to be *turtur* (Veit 2006).
Distribution and Status:
    World: Breeds in warmer mid-latitudes from W Europe e. to around 100°E in Asia, and in N Africa; winters in sub-Saharan N Africa.
    North America: *Atlantic States and Provinces:* Monroe Co., FL, 9–11 Apr 1990; SPM, 15–20 May 2001; Nantucket Co., MA, 19 Jul 2001 (salvaged roadkill).
Comments: It seems likely that European Turtle Doves reaching N America followed the n. route, and in some cases may have been ship-assisted. Although there are no records for Greenland, there were 207 records for Iceland through 2006, mainly Sep–Oct but with a minor peak in early Jun (and with records spanning all summer months). There are no records from the se. Caribbean or Bermuda, and there were only 8 from the Azores through 2011 (mainly in fall). It's also possible that N American records represent birds that reached our shores the previous fall and successfully overwintered; in this regard, the FL bird is especially suggestive.

At odds with the recent appearances in N America, turtle doves have declined markedly in parts of W Europe since the 1980s (e.g., Browne & Aebischer 2005), although records from Iceland do not reflect this decline.
Field Identification: Streamlined, medium-sized dove unlike any regularly occurring N American species. See illustration on p. 239.
    Similar Species: Cf. *Oriental Turtle Dove*, a vagrant to w. N America and very unlikely in the East.
    Age/Sex/Season: Ages differ, with adult appearance attained in 1st year; sexes similar; no seasonal variation. Complete prebasic molts and complete (to incomplete) preformative molts occur mainly on wintering grounds, but can start on summer grounds and be interrupted for migration. *Juv* duller overall than adult, with whitish-edged scapulars, duller and browner primaries distinctly edged pale buff; lacks black-and-white striped neck patch. Attains adult-like appearance by early to mid-winter, but sometimes 1–2 juv outer primaries and a few middle secondaries retained in 1st summer.
    Habitat and Behavior: Feeds on the ground, but otherwise shy and hard to see. Flight quick and direct, with flitting wingbeats. Vagrants unlikely to call.

ORIENTAL TURTLE DOVE *Streptopelia orientalis* 33–35 cm (13–13.8")

Summary: *Alaska and Yukon Territory:* Exceptional in spring–summer on Aleutians and in Bering Sea; 1 summer record from YT (2008), 1 fall record from Bering Sea islands (2011). *Pacific States and Provinces:* Exceptional in fall–winter.
Taxonomy: 6 ssp, but 4 sedentary and not considered here. Of the 2 migratory n. ssp,

adult

adult

European Turtle Dove

adult

adult

1st-year (fall–winter)

adult

adult

adult

Oriental Turtle Dove
nominate *orientalis*

1st-year (fall–winter)

e. *orientalis*, which has occurred in N America, averages larger and darker, with pale gray tail tips; w. ssp *meena* averages smaller and paler, with whiter underparts and white tail tips.

Distribution and Status:

World: Breeds Cen and E Asia, n. to about 60°N on w. side of Sea of Okhotsk and e. to s. Kuril Islands; n. populations migratory, wintering in S and SE Asia.

North America: *Alaska and Yukon Territory*: Exceptional in late spring–summer (mid-May to mid-Jul), 6 records: Pribilofs, 23 Jun–18 Jul 1984, 20–26 Jul 1986 (offshore on board a ship); Attu, 20 May–12 Jun 1989, 21 May–3 Jun 1996; Unalaska, 10 Jun–3 Jul 1995; s. YT, 30 Jun 2008. 1 fall record: St. Lawrence, 7–22 Oct 2011 (*NAB* 66:149, 194). *Pacific Provinces and States*: Exceptional in fall–winter (mid-Aug to mid-Feb), 4 records: Vancouver Island, BC, 14–25 Aug 1992; Inyo Co., CA, 29 Oct 1988; Marin Co., CA, 9–31 Dec 2002 (1st-winter); Westminster Co., BC, 18 Feb 2010 (1st-winter; *NAB* 64:486).

Comments: That there are as many records from the Pribilofs as from the w. Aleutians may simply reflect that the Pribilofs have biologists in place through the summer, and Oriental Turtle Doves are large and conspicuous. The spring–early summer records may represent overshoots, in some cases ship-assisted; 1 bird spent at least 6 days in late Jul on a ship near the Pribilofs. Given the size of Unalaska's fishing fleet, that bird may have arrived on a boat as well, and the Jun–Aug birds in nw. Canada might also have been helped in part by hitching rides on ships; birds that are largely vegetarian, such as doves, almost certainly survive better on boats than insectivores and species needing animal protein (falcons excepted).

At least 2 of the 3 late fall–winter records from BC and CA involve 1st-year birds, which may represent misoriented (reverse?) migrants. The species is a relatively late fall migrant (Sep–Oct in e. China), and in AK misoriented 1st-years may occur later in the fall than most observers are active at island outposts, hinted at by the fall 2011 record from St. Lawrence.

Field Identification: Fairly heavyset, medium-sized dove, unlike any regularly occurring N American species; cf. European Turtle Dove, a vagrant to the East and very unlikely to occur in the West.

Similar Species: Appreciably larger and bulkier than **European Turtle Dove** (may suggest Eurasian Collared Dove in bulk and heavy flight, whereas European more similar in bulk and fast flight to Mourning Dove, although still chunkier and slower than that species), and darker overall, with blue-gray versus brownish-gray rump. Outer greater and median coverts dark centered and pale tipped, often forming faint pale wing-bars (this area uniformly gray on European); tail tipped gray (*orientalis*); w. ssp *meena*, unrecorded in N America, has bold white tail tips similar to European Turtle Dove.

Age/Sex/Season: Ages differ, with adult appearance attained in 1st year; sexes similar; no seasonal variation. Complete prebasic molts and complete (to incomplete) preformative molts occur mainly on wintering grounds, but can start on summer grounds and be interrupted for migration. *Juv* duller overall than adult, with whitish-edged scapulars, duller and browner primaries distinctly edged pale buff; lacks black-and-white striped neck patch. Attains adult-like appearance by early to mid-winter, but sometimes 1–4 juv outer primaries, a few middle secondaries, and

occasionally even rectrices retained in 1st summer.

Habitat and Behavior: Flight action heavier and less 'flitting' than European Turtle Dove, and also often less wary. Much more likely to perch in the open, on trees or even on utility wires; some birds have appeared in gardens. Vagrants unlikely to call.

COMMON CUCKOO *Cuculus canorus*
32–36 cm (12.7–14.2")

Summary: *Alaska*: In spring–summer, rare and intermittent on w. Aleutians, very rare on cen. Aleutians and Bering Sea islands, exceptional on e. Aleutians, in sw. AK, and on s-coastal mainland. 1 fall record from n. AK (2008). *California*: 1 fall record (2012). *Massachusetts*: 1 spring record (1981).

Taxonomy: 4 ssp, not certainly separable in the field. N American specimens are referred to widespread Eurasian ssp *canorus*; within nominate *canorus*, e. birds (sometimes separated as ssp *telephonus*) average narrower and sparser dark bars below than birds in W Eurasia. 3 ssp breeding in s. of range average smaller and differ slightly from nominate *canorus* in color tones and average width of barring on underparts.

Distribution and Status:

World: Breeds in mid-latitude, temperate, and boreal zones from NW Africa and W Europe e. across Eurasia to China, Japan, and ne. Russia (sw. Chukotka). Most winter in sub-Saharan Africa except E Asian breeders, which winter in SE Asia and the Philippines.

North America: *Alaska*: Rare and intermittent on w. Aleutians in spring–early summer (late May–early Jul); max. 8+ on Attu, 8–10 Jun 1988. Very rare in same period on cen. Aleutians and during Jun to mid-Jul on Bering Sea islands, exceptionally in numbers; for example, 7 on St. Paul, 3–18 Jun 1999 (*NAB* 53:421). Exceptional in mid–late Jun on e. Aleutians, in sw. AK, and on s-coastal mainland, with easternmost records being a pair seen and heard in apparent courtship on Popof Island, near w. end of AK Peninsula, 21 Jun 1995 (*FN* 49:964), and a singing bird in Anchorage, 17 Jun 1999 (*NAB* 53:421). 1 fall record, 9–11 Sep 2008 in n. AK (juv, not rufous morph as reported; *NAB* 63:140). *California*: Santa Cruz Co., 27 Sep–2 Oct 2012 (juv rufous morph). *Massachusetts*: Martha's Vineyard, 3–4 May 1981.

Comments: The AK records of Common Cuckoo fit the pattern of drift vagrants, with some notable arrivals of multiple birds in early to mid-Jun. A number of AK records of nonvocalizing birds should perhaps be considered as *Cuculus* sp., given that plumage distinctions between Common and Oriental Cuckoos are poorly defined; the specimen record for Alaskan *Cuculus* is 18 Common versus 6 Oriental, which is notably different from the ratio of sight records. See Oriental Cuckoo account for discussion of fall *Cuculus* sp.

Through 2011, Common Cuckoo was the only species with so many records from AK that had not also occurred at least once elsewhere in w. N America; that changed as this book went to press, with a bird found in CA. AK specimens collected in mid-summer were often thin, and moribund birds have been found. This recalls the situation with vagrant Yellow-billed Cuckoos in W Europe, which are often weak or moribund, and suggests cuckoos may be able to undertake very long flights but then are unable to travel far upon arrival in areas lacking suitable food. However, the juv in Santa Cruz Co., CA, fed actively on local caterpillars, and thus seemed more likely to survive than birds reaching AK. The CA bird was found following the passage of a very strong storm system across the N Pacific, with winds blowing from Kamchatka to the W Coast (see p. 5).

The MA record cannot be convincingly explained on such an early date and could conceivably have arrived via either the northern or southern route (see pp. 8–9). There were 45 records from Iceland through 2006, several in late Apr but most from mid-May onward. There were only 3 post-1980 records (Mar, Jun, Jul) from the Azores through 2011, suggesting that northbound migrants are not routinely drifted offshore. There is also a Nov 1958 record from Barbados, and the species has the capacity for a 2500–3000 km nonstop spring migration flight (the maximum distance in spring across the Sahel, the Sahara, and the Mediterranean). A nonstop flight from the se. Caribbean to coastal MA seems just possible, given favorable winds, and ship assistance is always a possibility.

Field Identification: Unlike any regularly occurring N American species, but notoriously similar to Oriental Cuckoo. See illustration on p. 242.

Similar Species: ***Oriental Cuckoo*** extremely similar and silent birds rarely separable from Common Cuckoo, at least gray morphs and typical juveniles; rufous-morph adult (occurs only in female) and rufous-morph juv often separable. Male cuckoos in spring often call in AK (i.e., Commons at least, which may be more at home in open habitats than the forest-loving Oriental), making identification of such birds straightforward. On nonvocalizing *Cuculus* cuckoos, careful attention to several features may allow (provisional) specific identification, preferably with photos of underwing pattern. See Parkes (1990), Kennerley & Leader (1991), Vasamies (1998), and Lehman (2000b) for further information.

Adult gray-morph Oriental averages darker overall, especially on upperparts, and dark bars on underparts average wider but sparser than on Common, especially relative to E Asian populations of the latter. Undertail coverts of adult Oriental are buff to ochre -buff, often with sparse but coarse dark bars boldest in center; undertail coverts whitish (very rarely pale buff) on Common, with dark barring narrower and more evenly distributed; note that undertail coverts are often unbarred on both species.

Rufous-morph adult female Oriental has heavily barred rump (often unbarred on Common, but some can be faintly barred) and dark tail bars average broader than Common (usually broader than rufous bands on Oriental vs. narrower than rufous on Common).

Juvs notoriously similar in both species, but coarseness of barring below (especially at sides of breast) and tone and pattern of undertail coverts mirror adults. Rufous-morph juv Common often has barred rump, but dark barring duller and weaker than Oriental, which apparently always has strong dark rump barring.

There is a subtle difference in overall underwing pattern, which appears to apply to all ages/sexes, with the underwing being more contrastingly patterned on Oriental: the secondaries and median coverts bordering the white median stripe are darker overall on Oriental but less extensively barred than on Common; moreover, the lesser underwing coverts near the leading edge of the wing tend to be unbarred creamy buff on Oriental versus whitish with fine dark barring on Common.

Although length of the white median underwing stripe has been suggested as helpful, even diagnostic (e.g., Vasamies 1998), we found broad overlap in this feature, even with small samples (BM and MCZ specimens). On the underwing of Oriental, the stripe extended out to p5–p8 (n = 11;

adult ♀
gray morph

upperparts
slightly paler
than Oriental

narrow
dark
bars

rump
typically
unbarred

underwing
subtly different
from Oriental

white,
faintly
barred

adult ♂

adult ♀
rufous morph

narrow
dark
bands

adult ♂

white ground color;
narrow dark bars fairly
evenly distributed
(can be unmarked)

juv

juv can be rufous (similar to
rufous adult ♀) or grayish;
aged by white tips to scapulars
and upperwing coverts. Common
generally less coarsely marked than Oriental

Common Cuckoo

adult ♀
gray morph

upperparts
slightly darker
than Common

coarse
dark
bars

heavily
barred
rump

broader
dark
bands

more contrasting
underwing than
Common

unmarked
pale buff

adult ♂

adult ♂

buff ground color;
dark marks boldest
in center (can be
unmarked)

juv

juv can be rufous (similar to rufous
adult ♀) or grayish; aged by white tips to
scapulars and upperwing coverts.
Oriental coarsely barred below,
usually with buff undertail coverts

Oriental Cuckoo

reaching p8 on only 1 bird) versus to p5–p7 on Common (n = 10; reaching p7 on 4 birds); it averaged longer on adults than on juveniles, but with overlap in all age/sex classes, making it unlikely to be a helpful character on any individual bird.

Age/Sex/Season: Ages and sexes differ, with adult appearance attained in 1st winter; no seasonal variation but female dimorphic; eye color variable, averaging brighter pale yellow in adult male, duller and browner in juv, but probably not reliable for aging. Typically complete prebasic and preformative molts occur mostly or wholly on wintering grounds. **Adult male:** Head, chest, and upperparts plain gray. **Adult female:** Gray morph resembles adult male but chest has some dark bars, and sides of neck and chest have variable pale cinnamon wash. Rufous (or hepatic) morph has upperparts rufous with extensive blackish barring and no white feather tips; rump can be only lightly barred or even apparently unbarred. **1st-year:** Juv upperparts rufous to dark brownish gray with white nape patch, whitish tips to fresh feathers (especially scapulars and wing coverts). Following complete or near-complete preformative molt in 1st winter, resembles adult but some 1st-summers retain a few juv middle secondaries and exceptionally 1–2 middle primaries (mainly p3 or p6).

Habitat and Behavior: Favors fairly open country with adjacent woodland, hedges, and bushes. In flight, wingbeats steady and relaxed, mostly below the body centerline; can appear rather falcon-like. Song often heard from spring vagrants, a far-carrying, rhythmic, mellow *cúkoo*, repeated; female has an explosive harsh bubbling song. Male song posture typically with head slightly raised and tail raised above plane of wings and fanned (cf. Oriental Cuckoo).

ORIENTAL CUCKOO *Cuculus optatus*
30–34 cm (11.8–13.3")

Summary: *Alaska*: Exceptional in spring and fall on w. Aleutians and Bering Sea islands.
Taxonomy: Monotypic. Formerly *C. saturatus horsfieldi*, but the *saturatus* group was split in 2006 by AOU into 3 species including monotypic *optatus* (*Auk* 123:926–936).
Distribution and Status:
    World: Breeds boreal zone of Russia, from about 50°E e. to sw. Chukotka, s. to Japan and e. China; winters mainly from Indonesia and the Philippines s. to ne. Australia.

North America: *Alaska*: On w. Aleutians, exceptional in spring (mid-May to early Jun; 4 records); 1 fall record, 27 Aug–4 Sep 1999 (juv). On Bering Sea islands, 2 late spring–summer records (23 Jun 2005, 10–11 Jul 1989) and 3 fall records (late Aug–early Oct; 1 adult female gray morph; 1 juv; 1 rufous morph, age unknown).

Also 5 older AK specimen records (1890–1946), from cen. Aleutians (late Jun), w. mainland (late Jun), and Bering Sea islands (3, early to mid-Jul).

Comments: Vagrancy patterns mirror those of Common Cuckoo, but Oriental is much less numerous in spring. More data are needed to determine whether Oriental occurs more frequently in fall or whether this bias is simply an artifact of small samples to date.

There are also 4 fall records from AK of unidentified *Cuculus*: gray morph (age unknown) on Nunivak Island, 21 Aug 1991 (*AB* 46:138), and 3 birds in mid-Sep (2 juvs, 1 age unknown) from Adak, 2004 (2) and 2009.

Field Identification: Unlike any regularly occurring N American species, but notoriously similar to Common Cuckoo. See illustration on p. 242.

Similar Species: See Common Cuckoo.

Age/Sex/Season: Ages and sexes differ as in Common Cuckoo (see account for that species), with adult appearance attained in 1st winter; no seasonal variation. Adult female has gray and rufous morphs, as in Common. Molts as in Common Cuckoo but 1st-summer Oriental Cuckoo may more often retain juv secondaries and primaries than does Common.

Habitat and Behavior: Much as Common Cuckoo but in normal range prefers wooded rather than more open areas. Typical song a steady repetition of paired notes, with series often starting with a faster-paced series of notes, *pupupuppupuu pu-pu pu-pu pu-pu …* ; female has an explosive bubble much like Common Cuckoo. Male song posture typically slightly hunched, with head slightly lowered, throat swollen, and tail held in same plane as wings or slightly lowered (cf. Common Cuckoo).

EURASIAN HOOPOE *Upupa epops*
26–30 cm (10.2–11.8")

Summary: *Alaska*: 1 fall record from w. mainland (1975).
Taxonomy: 9 ssp, some perhaps representing separate species. Only the two n. migratory

all plumages
similar

Eurasian Hoopoe

crest often raised
on landing

ssp considered here, which average paler than tropical and s. populations: nominate *epops* in w. Eurasia, and slighter grayer *saturata* in E Asia. The AK specimen is referred to *saturata*.

Distribution and Status:

World: Breeds in warmer areas of mid-latitude Eurasia from SW Europe e. to se. Russia (n. to around 50°N), and s. to Africa and S Asia; n. populations migratory, wintering mainly in sub-Saharan Africa and S Asia.

North America: *Alaska*: Yukon-Kuskokwim Delta, w. AK, 2–3 Sep 1975 (male; Dau & Paniyak 1977).

Comments: One of the few Asian strays whose only N American record is from a continental as opposed to island location. This bird might have been in the area since late spring, but a misoriented (reverse?) fall migrant seems a more likely explanation, as with Eurasian Wryneck (see below).

Field Identification: Striking and unmistakable.

Similar Species: None.

Age/Sex/Season: Ages/sexes similar; no seasonal variation. Male averages brighter than female, and 1st-year averages duller than adult. Complete prebasic and partial to incomplete preformative molts occur mostly on wintering grounds, but can start on breeding grounds with head and body feathers, and sometimes (adults) with inner primaries before interruption for fall migration. Juv remiges, and sometimes some to

all rectrices, retained through 1st summer, appearing relatively worn and faded in comparison to adult.

Habitat and Behavior: Favors open country with scattered trees and bushes. Feeds on the ground but perches readily in trees; flight fast and fairly direct with rather deep, quick wingbeats. Usually quiet on migration.

EURASIAN WRYNECK *Jynx torquilla*
16–17 cm (6.3–6.7")

Summary: *Alaska*: 1 fall record from Bering Sea islands (2003).

Taxonomy: 4 ssp, all similar in the field; nominate *torquilla* breeds across Eurasia and presumably has occurred in AK. A 1945 specimen from AK (A. M. Bailey 1947) was referred to *harterti*, which is now synonymized with *torquilla*.

Distribution and Status:

World: Breeds mid-latitude and s. temperate Eurasia from SW Europe e. to Japan and ne. Russia (to around 65°N on n. side of Sea of Okhotsk); also farther s. in mountains of e. China and in NW Africa; winters in sub-Saharan Africa, the Indian subcontinent, and SE Asia.

North America: *Alaska*: St. Lawrence, 2–5 Sep 2003.

Comments: There is an early Sep 1945 specimen (male) from Cape Prince of Wales, w. AK, just prior to the coverage period for this book

dark stripe
obvious from behind

profile changes
dramatically
when relaxed

all plumages similar

Eurasian Wryneck

(A. M. Bailey 1947). This and the recent record likely represent misoriented (reverse?) migrants.

In Feb 2000, a desiccated Wryneck was found in s. IN on a military base; it was thought to have been entombed in a container brought from overseas (Dunning et al. 2002).

Field Identification: Small, cryptically patterned woodpecker, about the size of a White-crowned Sparrow.

Similar Species: None, if well seen. In flight suggests a sleek, rather large female House Sparrow, but grayer overall.

Age/Sex/Season: Ages and sexes similar; no seasonal variation. Prebasic and complete preformative molts occur mostly in late summer, before migration, but some secondaries of both adult and 1st-year may be retained until reaching winter grounds.

Habitat and Behavior: Favors open country with scattered trees, and mixed open woodland. Often forages on the ground, also in bushes and trees where it hops with deliberate but nervous, jerky motions, often twitching its tail and turning its head. Flight fairly direct and only slightly undulating. Usually quiet on migration.

GREAT SPOTTED WOODPECKER
Dendrocopos major 20–24 cm (7.8–9.5")

Distribution Summary: *Alaska*: Exceptional on w. Aleutians in spring and fall. 1 spring record from Pribilofs (2001), 1 fall–winter record from s. interior (2001/2002).

Taxonomy: 14 ssp, varying in extent and intensity of red on underparts and amount of white dorsally, but confusion unlikely at the species level. The 2 N American specimens are referred to *kamtschaticus*, a relatively large ssp with extensive white on upperparts, broad white bars on wings, and mostly or wholly white outer rectrices.

Distribution and Status:

World: Resident across mid-latitude Eurasia from W Europe to e. Russia (Kamchatka) and Japan. Irrupts periodically.

North America: *Alaska*: Exceptional in spring (late Apr to mid-May; 4 records) and fall (Sep–Oct; 4 records) on w. Aleutians, although fall 1985 and spring 1986 records from Attu may have involved a single bird. 1 spring record from Pribilofs, 6 May 2001, and 1 fall–winter record from s. interior, Sep 2001–22 Feb 2002.

Comments: Great Spotted Woodpecker is a common breeder in Kamchatka and, like most northern woodpeckers, given to periodic irruptions. Whether N American records correspond to documented irruptions is not known to us, but we suspect an irruption occurred in fall 2000, when 3 birds appeared in the w. Aleutians; it's also possible that the spring 2001 Pribilofs bird and even the fall 2001 mainland bird were linked to this event.

Having the same number of spring records as fall records is surprising, as typically fewer individuals return from an irruption than leave.

**Great
Spotted
Woodpecker**

ssp *kamtschaticus*

♀

♀

juv

♂

Given that there are 2 sets of records of birds seen in fall one year and spring of the next year, successful overwintering seems possible.

Field Identification: Unmistakable if seen well—combination of white cheeks, black back, white scapulars, and reddish lower belly and undertail coverts is found in no N American woodpecker.

Similar Species: None in N America.

Age/Sex/Season: Ages/sexes differ in head pattern; no seasonal variation. Complete prebasic and incomplete preformative molts occur summer–fall, with wing molt slowed or (in 1st-year) even suspended during irruptions. *1st-year*: Juv has red crown but molts quickly into adult-like plumage in summer–fall, retaining juv primary coverts and secondaries into 1st summer. Post-juvenile male has red nape patch, female has nape black.

Habitat and Behavior: A typical woodpecker, inhabiting both coniferous and deciduous forest. Forages mainly on trunks and larger outer branches. Commonest call a sharp *piic!* This is more muted and less of a shouted shriek than call of Hairy Woodpecker.

EURASIAN JACKDAW *Corvus monedula*
30–34 cm (11.8–13.3")

Summary: *East*: Complex (see below). About 15 records, birds first detected mainly in Mar–Apr, Jun–Jul, and Nov–Dec, with some remaining for prolonged periods and even breeding. Most records from the Northeast.

Taxonomy: 4 ssp recognized, differing mostly in color saturation and prominence of whitish band at rear of nape. N American records presumed to be nw. ssp *monedula* or w. ssp *spermologus*, adults of which lack the well-marked narrow white band at rear of gray nape shown by e. ssp *soemmerringii*.

Distribution and Status:

World: Mid-latitude W and Cen Eurasia, e. to around 100°E; n. populations withdraw mostly s. and w. in winter, with occasional irruptions.

North America: *East*: Complex. About 15 records (detailed below), birds mainly first detected Mar–Apr, Jun–Jul, and Nov–Dec, with some remaining for prolonged periods and even for breeding. Records through 1984 summarized and discussed by Smith (1985).

American
Crow

adult

Eurasian Jackdaw

1, 2. Nantucket, MA, 28 Nov 1982–4 Apr 1983; presumed same bird 31 Dec 1983, joined by 2nd bird, 9 Jul 1984; at least 1 remaining until 8 Dec 1986;

3. Block Island, RI, Mar or Apr 1984 (probably 1st-year);

4, 5. SPM, 23 Mar–26 Apr 1984 (3), 18 Jul to mid-Oct 1984 (4, at a kittiwake colony, presumed to include original 3), 28 Dec 1984, 23 Jan 1985, spring–summer 1985 (up to 3 again at kittiwake colony, breeding suspected, only 1 bird seen by late Jul–early Aug), 18 Apr 1986 (2 in same area) (Etcheberry 1998);

6. NS, May 1984, 1–2 birds (*AB* 38:886);

7. Sept-Rivières Co., QC, Nov 1984–Mar 1985 (52, most of which were shot or poisoned by provincial authorities who viewed the birds as unwanted; *AB* 39:149);

8. Whitby, ON, 13 Apr 1985 (*AB* 39:294);

9. Union Co., PA, May 1985–Jun 1991 (2), with breeding in 1987, 1988, 1990, successfully at least once;

10. Matinicus Rock, ME, 11 Jun 1985 (*AB* 39:888);

11. Toronto, ON, 20 Oct 1985 (Coady 1988);

12. New Haven Co., CT, 16 Feb–16 Mar 1988 (2);

13. SPM, 25 Jun–28 Sep 1991 (Etcheberry 1998);

14. Ferryland Co., NL, 2 Dec 1994–Apr 1999 (mainly in winters);

15. Halifax Co., NS, 19 Apr 2003 (perhaps present for some time previously; *NAB* 57:318).

Comments: Jackdaw illustrates both how hard it can be to determine just how a bird arrived on our shores and how many records are involved—the number of N American arrival events is clouded by the potential for longevity and wandering of birds that might be overlooked simply as 'just' crows. Thus it seems possible the 1985 ON, PA, and ME records and perhaps even the 1988 CT record were linked to arrivals in 1983–1984. (CT record rejected by state committee on grounds of origin.)

The early 1984 influx came at a time of strong Atlantic-spanning easterlies that brought numerous Greater Golden Plovers to Atlantic Canada, and Jackdaws perhaps could have made the crossing unassisted. However, the late Nov 1984 flock was seen leaving a ship in Port Cartier, QC, and was said to have boarded the vessel just off the British coast (*AB* 41:63).

Arrivals in Mar–Apr and Nov–Dec correspond to periods of migration and cold-weather movements in W Europe. Birds first detected in N America in summer likely arrived earlier in the New World but could well have been overlooked until they found and joined other jackdaws or engaged in possible breeding activities in habitats where crows would not typically nest (seabird cliffs, large stone buildings).

Why no Rooks *Corvus frugilegus* have occurred in N America is intriguing; through

2006, 634 Rooks versus 258 jackdaws had been recorded in Iceland. Both move in flocks, and both fly to the w. coasts of Britain and Ireland during European cold spells. It seems likely that the smaller, more maneuverable Jackdaw, with its penchant for human structures, takes more readily to ships, and perhaps its cute personality and staring pale eyes make it more likely to be fed. Also cf. Hooded Crow (Appendix B).

Field Identification: Small social corvid, dark gray overall rather than black, with noticeably paler gray nape and staring pale eyes.

Similar Species: None, if seen well. An old report of Jackdaw from FL referred to a leucistic Common Grackle (Stevenson & Anderson 1994:677); also beware of leucistic crows.

Age/Sex/Season: Ages differ slightly; sexes similar; no seasonal variation. Complete prebasic and partial preformative molts in fall; no prealternate molt but gray nape wears and fades paler by spring–summer. *Adult* has uniformly fresh plumage in fall–winter, uniformly worn in spring, with relatively blunt-tipped rectrices, contrasting paler gray hindneck, and staring whitish eyes. *1st-year*: Juv duller sooty blackish overall than adult, with poorly contrasting hindneck, grayish eyes. Attains adult-like plumage by partial preformative molt in fall but with relatively tapered juv rectrices; faded remiges and tail often apparent by 1st summer; eyes can take a year or longer to become staringly pale.

Habitat and Behavior: Favors cliffs, quarries, buildings, chimneys; some of the SPM birds frequented a kittiwake colony (Etcheberry 1998). Walks fairly quickly, with an upright stance. Flies with fairly fast deep wing strokes, slightly quicker and looser than American Crow. Rather aerobatic, readily sails and soars on updrafts, and then may suggest Lewis' Woodpecker. Calls distinct from American Crow; mainly a relatively high, nasal, and clipped *chaah!* or *chow!* and a nasal *kyaa*, at times in loose series.

Larger New World Landbirds

Of these 6 species, Eared Quetzal and Amazon Kingfisher have wandered n. from Mexico into border states, Dark-billed Cuckoo is an austral migrant from S America, and Zenaida Dove and both quail-doves are wanderers to FL from the Caribbean, with Ruddy Quail-Dove also recorded in s. TX (likely originating in Mexico).

Among other possibilities that might reach the s. US, Northern Potoo *Nyctibius jamaicensis* and

Tawny-collared Nightjar *Antrostomus salvini* could well be overlooked by virtue of their nocturnal habits, while a recent record of Greater Ani from FL (see Appendix B) suggests that other possibilities may defy 'logical' prediction.

ZENAIDA DOVE *Zenaida aurita* 25–28 cm (10–11")

Summary: *Florida*: Exceptional on the Keys, mainly fall–spring.

Taxonomy: 3 ssp, probably distinguishable in the field. Nominate *aurita* of Lesser Antilles is palest, with white tips to outer rectrices; *zenaida* of Greater Antilles and Bahamas (presumably the ssp occurring in N America) is darkest, with bluish-gray tips to outer rectrices; *salvadorii* of Yucatan Peninsula is dark with whitish tips to outer rectrices.

Distribution and Status:

World: Widespread in the Caribbean, n. to Cuba and the Bahamas; also n. coast of Yucatan Peninsula, Mexico.

North America: *Florida*: Exceptional on the Keys, 8 records in the period covered here: 5 during late Sep–early Mar, 1 in May, and 2 in Jun; most recently 3–6 May 2002 (*NAB* 56:270, 299–300) and 4–5 Jun 2009 (*NAB* 63:586–587).

Comments: This species may have bred locally in the FL Keys in the early 1800s but in recent years it has been an extremely rare visitor, with a sparse pattern of fall through spring records. It is a strong flier that could cross water easily. Like many doves, it can be overlooked and may be commoner than the few recent records suggest. A sighting from coastal GA in early Oct 2005 was considered to likely be this species (*NAB* 60:56).

Field Identification: Fairly chunky terrestrial dove of open country. Note distinct white trailing edge to secondaries, slightly rounded tail with pale gray corners.

Similar Species: Overall appearance suggests dark, richly colored *Mourning Dove*, which is smaller bodied and more lightly built with long tapered tail. White trailing edge to secondaries of Zenaida Dove can be hidden at rest but obvious in flight; also note slightly rounded tail with pale gray corners.

Age/Sex/Season: Ages differ, sexes differ slightly, with adult appearance attained in 1st year; no seasonal variation. Molt presumably follows complex basic strategy (see p. 35), with timing

obvious white trailing
edge to secondaries

♂

♂

**Zenaida
Dove**

variable depending on breeding season. *Male* brighter and pinker overall with richer brown upperparts. *Female* averages duller overall with grayer brown upperparts, iridescent neck patch smaller. *1st-year*: Juv resembles female but lacks iridescent neck patch, back and upperwing coverts edged cinnamon. Resembles adult after complete to incomplete preformative molt in first few months, but some may be distinguishable by retained and contrastingly faded (juv) outer primaries.

Habitat and Behavior: Favors coastal dunes, open scrub with grassy clearings, open pine woods, wooded residential areas. Mainly terrestrial, where easily overlooked until flushed; rarely perches and feeds in bushes or low trees. Usually found singly, but 2 birds together in FL on one occasion. Flight fast and strong, recalling Mourning Dove; tends to fly some distance when flushed and can be difficult to see well.

KEY WEST QUAIL-DOVE *Geotrygon chrysia* 27–30 cm (10.5–11.7")

Summary: *Florida*: Very rare or exceptional in the s. in spring–fall.
Taxonomy: Monotypic.
Distribution and Status:
    World: Bahamas and Greater Antilles.
    North America: *Florida*: Very rare or exceptional in the s., with about 12 records of single birds in the period. Most records involve

birds found in Apr–Jul, and some have stayed for periods up to 6 months; 2 records in mid-Oct.
Comments: Key West Quail-Doves appear to have been fairly common breeding summer residents in the Florida Keys in the early to mid-1800s, with withdrawal (presumably to Cuba) reported in mid-Oct (Stevenson & Anderson 1994). Their disappearance seems to have predated the mass 'development' that blights southern FL, although it is possible that humans and habitat alteration were involved in this species' disappearance, along with that of several other former presumed breeding species of s. FL (such as American Flamingo and Zenaida Dove).

The present-day pattern of summer occurrence mirrors the species' former status, and occasional breeding in FL does not seem inconceivable; indeed, rumors of nesting circulated in 1977–1979 but were unconfirmed. The 2 relatively recent mid-Oct records (1964, 1991) fit the migration window reported in the early 1800s.
Field Identification: Chunky terrestrial dove of dense undergrowth.
    Similar Species: Chunky shape, bold white cheek stripe, and bright rufous wings are distinctive among regularly occurring N American species. *Ruddy Quail-Dove* smaller with dingy pale cheek stripe, whitish to buff vertical bar at chest sides; male bright ruddy above, female cold rich

Key West Quail-Dove

brown, both lacking violet and green glossiness of Key West Quail-Dove.

Ages/Sex/Season: Ages and sexes differ, with adult appearance attained in 1st year; no seasonal variation. Molt presumably follows complex basic strategy with complete or incomplete preformative molt (see p. 35); timing variable, depending on breeding season. *Male* has glossy bright violet crown, hindneck, and back with green sheen on neck; bright rufous-chestnut wings and tail; broad white cheek stripe; pinkish foreneck and chest. *Female* duller overall; back and upperwing coverts mostly rich olive-brown with iridescent copper-violet edgings strongest at bend of wing; foreneck and chest washed dusky. *1st-year*: Juv face pattern duller; head, neck, and upperparts rich dark brown without purple gloss; upperwing coverts and tertials tipped buff; chest washed cinnamon-rufous. Quickly molts into adult-like plumage, but some 1st-year birds might be distinguishable by retained and contrastingly faded (juv) outer primaries.

Habitat and Behavior: Scrub and woodland, drier mangroves, rarely venturing into adjacent open areas such as quiet roads for dust-bathing. Mostly terrestrial, this handsome dove can be confiding and overlooked easily. Song is a moan on one pitch, gradually increasing in volume and fading rapidly (Rafaelle et al. 1998), unlike any regularly occurring FL species.

RUDDY QUAIL-DOVE *Geotrygon montana*
23–26 cm (9–10.2")

Summary: *Florida*: Exceptional in winter in the s. *Texas*: 1 late winter record from Lower Rio Grande Valley (1996).
Taxonomy: 2 ssp, not likely distinguishable in the field, with US records presumably of widespread nominate *montana*.
Distribution and Status:
    World: Tropical Mexico (n. to s. Tamaulipas) to S America, also widely in Caribbean.
    North America: *Florida*: 4 records in the period covered here: Monroe Co., 13 Feb 1952 and 15 Dec 1977; Broward Co., 11–12 Jan 2002; plus desiccated remains found on Dry Tortugas, 3 May 1962. *Texas*: Hidalgo Co., 2–6 Mar 1996 (female).
Comments: Although Ruddy Quail-Dove is usually considered resident throughout its range, the US records indicate it wanders on occasion. There are also 2 earlier s. FL records, from Dec 1888 and May 1923. Given how easy this species is to overlook in areas where it is fairly common, it may be of more frequent occurrence in the US than recognized; in contrast to the 'mainland' records of Key West Quail-Dove, 2 of the 3 most recent records of Ruddy have come from the Dry Tortugas where skulking species are relatively easy to detect. The limited records suggest a winter to early spring pattern of occurrence.

Ruddy Quail-Dove

Field Identification: Chunky terrestrial dove of forest understory, smaller and more compact than White-tipped Dove.

Similar Species: Male very distinctive, with chunky shape, ruddy upperparts, striped face, and white bar (sometimes concealed) at chest sides. Female distinctive but plainer; lacks white tail corners of larger and longer-tailed **White-tipped Dove**, which has paler upperparts, flushes less explosively.

Ages/Sex/Season: Ages and sexes differ, with adult appearance attained in 1st year; no seasonal variation. Molt presumably follows complex basic strategy with complete or incomplete preformative molt (see p. 35); timing variable depending on breeding season. **Male** has bright rufous upperparts, pinkish head and chest. **Female** has dark rich olive-brown upperparts, duller and browner face pattern than male. **1st-year:** Juv resembles female but darker, chest and upperparts extensively edged cinnamon. Quickly molts into adult-like plumage, but some 1st-years might be distinguishable by retained and contrastingly faded (juv) outer primaries.

Habitat and Behavior: Forest and woodland understory, rarely venturing into adjacent open areas. Mostly terrestrial and shy; can sometimes be watched as it walks along with an odd, bobbing gait, but usually only detected when it flushes from close range with a strong wing whirr and disappears off into the forest.

DARK-BILLED CUCKOO *Coccyzus melacoryphus* 25.5–28 cm (10–11")

Summary: *Texas*: 1 winter record from Lower Rio Grande Valley (1986).
Taxonomy: Monotypic.
Distribution and Status:
  World: Tropical S America.
  North America: *Texas*: Hidalgo Co., 10 Feb 1986 (died in care; Lockwood & Freeman 2004). Considered of unknown provenance and not accepted by ABA (2008).
Comments: This species is a long-distance austral migrant e. of the Andes in S America, present in its s. breeding areas during at least Sep–Dec (and likely later), and in its n. non-breeding areas mainly during Mar/Apr–Sep/Oct (Hilty & Brown 1986; Ridgely & Greenfield 2001; Schulenberg et al. 2007). The TX record fits into a pattern of scattered vagrant occurrences, which include Clipperton Atoll, off the Pacific coast of Mexico (mid-Aug 1958) and Panama (late Jan 1980). Records during Jan–Feb may represent overshooting 'fall' migrants, whereas the Aug record could be of a misoriented 'spring' migrant, as with Fork-tailed Flycatcher and other species.

Dark-billed Cuckoo

adult   juv

dark   yellow

Dark-billed

Mangrove Cuckoo

note subtle differences in undertail patterns and distribution of buff on underparts

Field Identification: Small *Coccyzus* cuckoo, resembling Yellow-billed Cuckoo in shape.

Similar Species: ***Mangrove Cuckoo*** appreciably larger with bigger bill, yellow base to lower mandible, and larger white tail spots; lacks contrast between cinnamon throat and pearly gray neck sides.

Ages/Sex/Season: Ages differ, with adult appearance attained in 1st year; sexes similar; no seasonal variation. Molt presumably follows complex basic strategy with incomplete preformative molt (see p. 35); timing variable depending on breeding season. *1st-year* typically retains some juv rectrices, which are narrower and more tapered than on adult, with larger but less contrastingly defined pale buffy (fading to buffy-white) tips; also note cinnamon-tipped primary coverts and relatively faded juvenile remiges. 2nd (and subsequent) prebasic molts not always complete, with some remiges retained; thus some 2nd-year birds can be distinguished by retained juv remiges, and birds with two generations of adult remiges are older than 2 years.

Habitat and Behavior: Occurs in wide variety of wooded habitats, adjacent semi-open areas, weedy and shrubby fields, hedgerows, etc. Generally silent and retiring in nonbreeding season.

EARED QUETZAL *Euptilotis neoxenus*
33–36 cm (13–14.2")

Summary: *Southwest*: Very rare in AZ, mainly spring–early winter; 1 summer record from NM (1979).

Taxonomy: Monotypic.

Distribution and Status:

World: Endemic to nw. Mexico (n. to ne. Sonora and nw. Chihuahua).

North America: *Southwest*: Very rare in se. AZ, with about 25 records (year-round, but mainly May–Jun and Aug–Dec) since the first US record there in 1977; exceptionally n. to cen. AZ. Most records involved singles, but up to 3 birds on occasion; several long-staying birds or pairs, and at least 1 nesting attempt (fall 1991; *NAB* 46:132). Also 1 record from NM: Animas Mountains, Hidalgo Co, 13 Jun 1979 (S. O. Williams III, pers. comm.).

Comments: In Mexico this is a poorly known species, but at least some of the population appears to be migratory, returning to the northwest in May–Jun to breed (egg dates are Jun–Oct). The timing of US records is concordant with some spring overshoots and also with post-breeding and winter dispersal.

adult ♂

adult ♀

juv

♀

♂

Eared Quetzal

This is often a quiet and easily overlooked species that is probably declining throughout its range. That records are scattered n. to cen. Arizona, some in rarely visited canyons, suggests that documented records represent but a fraction of actual occurrences.

Field Identification: Large and striking trogon with relatively small head, broad tail with convex sides.

Similar Species: A distinctive species, although incautious or hopeful observers might be misled by *Elegant Trogon*, a fairly common species in the mountain canyons of se. AZ. Elegant is smaller and more slender with a larger, blockier head, a straight-sided and squared tail, and a stouter yellow bill; male has pale-gray upperwing-covert panel, female has gray-brown upperparts. Voices of the 2 species very different.

Ages/Sex/Season: Ages and sexes differ, with adult appearance attained in 1 year; no seasonal variation. Molt presumably follows complex basic strategy, with partial preformative molt (see p. 35); most molting likely in fall–early winter. *Male*: Head and upper chest deep blue-green, extensive red on belly. *Female*: Gray head and chest, reduced red on belly. *1st-year*: Juv has buff spots and notching on upperwing coverts, scapulars, and tertials; belly has little or no red; rectrices narrower and more tapered than adult with more extensive black on bases of outer rectrices and narrow white tips to inner rectrices. Resembles adult after partial preformative molt within a few months of fledging, but retains diagnostic juv tail and can retain some juv upperwing coverts and tertials.

Habitat and Behavior: Pine-oak and mixed forest in mountains, especially in quiet canyons. Often fairly wary, moving and perching at upper to mid-levels and readily flying long distances. Like other trogons, feeds in hovering flight by plucking fruit from ends of twigs; probably also eats small lizards and other small critters. Nests in tree cavities and has pale blue eggs (white in trogons). Main calls are an upslurred squeal ending with an abrupt cluck (cluck may not be audible at a distance, and squeal may suggest Great-tailed Grackle); a hard clucking cackle usually given when disturbed and in flight. Song a fairly prolonged, intensifying series of 2- or 3-syllable quavering whistles that carries well.

AMAZON KINGFISHER *Chloroceryle amazona* 28–29 cm (11–11.5")

Summary: *Texas*: 1 winter record from Lower Rio Grande Valley (2010).

Taxonomy: 2 ssp, not separable in the field. TX record presumably refers to n. ssp *mexicana* of Mexico and Cen America, which averages larger than nominate *amazona* of S America.

Distribution and Status:

World: Tropical Mexico (n. to cen. Sinaloa, cen. Tamaulipas) s. to tropical S America.

North America: *Texas*: Webb County, 24 Jan–3 Feb 2010 (female; Wormington & Epstein 2010).

Comments: Amazon Kingfisher is a fairly common species in the lowlands of e. Mexico, only about 300 km (180 miles) s. of the US border. There are no data to evaluate any seasonal movements, but post-breeding and winter wandering presumably occurs, as with many tropical species. Being dependent on clean water may also make the species susceptible to local dispersal—the TX bird disappeared when the creek it frequented turned muddy and turbulent with heavy rain (Wormington & Epstein 2010).

Field Identification: Rather large, striking kingfisher, about the size of Belted Kingfisher but with a more massive bill and dark, metallic green upperparts.

Similar Species: None, if seen well. ***Green Kingfisher*** much smaller with bold white spotting on upperwings, lacks tufted crest of Amazon.

Ages/Sex/Season: Ages and sexes differ, with adult appearance attained in 1 year; no seasonal variation. Molts not well known. *Male*: Breast solidly rufous. *Female*: Underparts white with broad, broken dark green breast band; upperparts lack fine white flecking. ***1st-year***: Juv resembles female but upperparts and breast band have pale buff to whitish flecks (lost through wear and molt); upper breast may be washed cinnamon in juv male. 1st-year molts not well known. Probably has partial preformative molt in 1st fall–winter, after which may resemble adult (needs study). Attains full adult plumage by complete 2nd-prebasic molt in 2nd fall.

Habitat and Behavior: Freshwater streams, rivers, ponds, and lakes, typically with bordering trees and other vegetation for perches. Feeds mainly by diving from perch, occasionally from hovering fairly high over the water like Belted Kingfisher. Flight usually low over the water. Calls include a low, slightly rasping *krrrik* and a hard buzzy *zzzrt*, both mainly in flight and slightly

♀

♂

♀

Amazon Kingfisher

juv

suggesting much quieter flight calls of Green Kingfisher; less often, calls are run into shrill, rattling chatters.

AERIAL LANDBIRDS

We consider aerial landbirds as comprising hummingbirds, swifts, and swallows. In the period under review, 8 hummingbirds, 5 swifts, and 4 swallows have occurred as rare birds in N America, 4 of Old World origin and 13 of New World origin. Another 4 species were recorded before the review period: in 1896, Bumblebee Hummingbird occurred in se. AZ and, remarkably, the 1880s to 1890s saw US records (all specimens) of Southern Martin *P. elegans*, Gray-breasted Martin *P. chalybea*, and Cuban Martin *P. cryptoleuca*. Finding and documenting

further records of these martins are worthy challenges for today's field observers.

Old World Aerial Landbirds

Of the 4 species recorded to date, White-throated Needletail, Common Swift, and Pacific Swift have occurred very rarely in AK in spring–early summer, with Pacific Swift also recorded in fall. Common Swift has also occurred exceptionally in the East, probably as a transatlantic vagrant. Common House Martin has occurred in spring–summer in both AK and the Northeast.

Additional Old World species to consider include Alpine Swift *Apus melba*, of N African origin, which has occurred in the Caribbean in summer–fall (Buckley et al. 2009), and Asian House Martin *D. dasypus*, which seems a possible vagrant to AK.

WHITE-THROATED NEEDLETAIL
Hirundapus caudacutus 19–20 cm (7.5–8")

Summary: *Alaska*: Exceptional in spring on w. Aleutians.

Taxonomy: 2 ssp. AK specimen is of ne. and highly migratory ssp *caudacutus*, which differs

from resident Himalayan *nudipes* in having white (not black) forehead and lores, and more distinct whitish back patch.

Distribution and Status:
World: Breeds mid-latitude E Asia, e. to Sakhalin and s. Kuril Islands; winters New Guinea to e. Australia; disjunct resident in Himalayas.

all plumages similar

White-throated Needletail

North America: *Alaska*: Exceptional in spring (late May) on w. Aleutians: Shemya, 21 May 1974; Attu, 24 May 1978; Attu, 24–25 May 1984 (2); Shemya, 25–26 May 1985.

Comments: White-throated Needletails have long overwater legs on their spring migration to n. Japan and Sakhalin, and are at risk for displacement by strong weather systems. The tight date range is notable (all records in a 6-day span) and recalls the tight date ranges shown by Common Swift in N America (7-day span) and that of n. records of White-collared Swift in N America.

Field Identification: Large, powerfully built swift, unlike any N American species.

Similar Species: Nothing in N America. Distinguished from other needletails (*Hirundapus* spp.) by combination of sharply demarcated white throat, white-edged tertials, and whitish back.

Age/Sex/Season: Ages differ slightly; sexes similar; no seasonal variation. *Adult* has contrasting white lores and forehead, large white throat patch, large and contrasting whitish back patch, and strong green gloss to upperwings and tail (duller and blackish when worn, in fall). *1st-year*: Juv has forehead and lores dusky, white throat patch often smaller (with smoky-gray wash to chin and lower cheeks), and back patch duller, less contrasting; wings and tail have little green gloss. Undergoes partial preformative molt in

1st winter, after which overall resembles adult but some retain dusky lores. 1st-summer can show molt contrasts in body feathers and upperwing coverts, and contrast between fresher head and body feathers and relatively faded flight feathers, which become notably worn by 2nd fall. 2nd-prebasic and subsequent (complete) prebasic molts occur mostly on wintering grounds; on some birds, primary molt starts near breeding grounds, presumably interrupted for fall migration.

Habitat and Behavior: A powerful and very fast flier. Largely silent, but wing whoosh often audible at closer ranges.

COMMON SWIFT *Apus apus* 17–18 cm (6.7–7.2")

Summary: *Alaska*: 2 summer records from Bering Sea islands (1950, 1986). *St. Pierre et Miquelon*: 1 summer record (1986).

Taxonomy: 2 ssp, not separable in the field except perhaps for extremes: E Asian ssp *pekinensis* is variable, and while some can look much like nominate *apus* of W Eurasia, most show some degree of contrast in their plumage, with a darker back, paler greater coverts, and slightly paler rump. AK specimen referred to *pekinensis* (Kenyon & Phillips 1965).

ssp *pekinensis* averages darker saddle contrast

all plumages similar

Common Swift

Distribution and Status:

World: Breeds mid-latitude and s. temperate Eurasia from W Europe e. to around 120°E; winters in sub-Saharan Africa, primarily s. of the Equator.

North America: *Alaska*: Pribilofs, 28 Jun 1950, and 28–29 Jun 1986 (*NAB* 40:1243). *St. Pierre et Miquelon*: 23 Jun 1986.

Note: There are 4 records from the East of large swifts not identified to species but considered to be of the genus *Apus*, and almost certainly Common Swift: Montgomery Co., PA, 10 May 1996 (*FN* 50:260); Martha's Vineyard, 14 Jul 1996 (*FN* 50:930); Cape Cod, MA, 28 May 2005 (*NAB* 59:406); and SPM, 2 Jun 2006 (*NAB* 60:501). A report from MA in Jul 1995 (ABA 2008) presumably reflects confusion with the Jul 1996 record.

Comments: The AK records are notably late in the framework of Asian spring vagrants, which mostly occur from mid-May to mid-Jun. The late dates, and Bering Sea locations, may reflect spring overshoots (weather-assisted?) from the interior of E Asia, in contrast to species that migrate coastally and occur mostly in the Aleutians, and mainly earlier in the season. Common Swift is a common breeder as near as Beijing, China, and has been reported from Japan and Korea (Brazil 2009), although in ne. China migrants largely shun the coast (P. Holt, pers. comm.).

The confirmed (and presumed) Common Swifts that have occurred in e. N America seem unlikely to have been ship-assisted, given the species' behavior, size, flight speed, and ability to fly nonstop across major barriers. The 3 late May–Jun records fit the pattern of vagrants to Iceland, where there were 336 accepted records through 2006 (mainly May–Sep, with a peak in mid-May to Jul), but a more direct route, and one that seems quite possible, is from the coast of W Africa. There were about 20 records of Common Swift from the Azores through 2011 (mainly late Apr–Jun, including records of multiples), close to the midway point on a heading from W Africa to the Northeast, and birds departing Africa would be expected to carry maximum fuel loads. The early May record from PA is both relatively early and relatively far from the more 'expected' coastal locations of other e. records, and one has to wonder about the possibility of a northward-moving bird that wintered in the New World after a fall Atlantic crossing to the se. Caribbean or ne. S America. The mid-Jul record is difficult to interpret, and

may reflect a bird that had been wandering for some time before being seen.

Fall records in N America seem possible as well; there is a late fall record from Bermuda, 16 Nov 1986.

Field Identification: Large, all-dark swift with long, deeply forked tail.

Similar Species: None in N America if seen well. *Black Swift* slightly smaller with a heavier body, narrower wings, dark throat but whitish forehead frosting, and a notched or squared tail. Male of nominate Caribbean ssp *niger* has distinctly forked tail (much more pronounced than w. N American ssp *borealis*) but still much shallower than fork of Common Swift.

Also cf. *Pallid Swift Apus pallidus*, breeding in S Europe and wintering in sub-Saharan Africa. Pallid is a relatively short-distance migrant, a very rare vagrant to Britain, unrecorded in Iceland, and with but 1 report from the Azores. Nonetheless, it should be considered when dealing with an *Apus* swift in e. N America; extensive photographic or specimen evidence would be essential. Pallid is overall slightly paler than Common Swift, with slightly blunter wing-tips.

Age/Sex/Season: Ages differ slightly; sexes similar; no seasonal variation beyond wear. Adult is fresh in spring, worn in fall, whereas juv is fresh in fall, with fine whitish tipping to head and body feathers rarely visible in the field. *1st-year*: Juv undergoes partial preformative molt in 1st winter, and 1st-summer can show molt contrasts in body feathers and upperwing coverts, and contrast between fresher head and body feathers and relatively faded flight feathers, which become notably worn by 2nd fall. 2nd-prebasic and subsequent (complete) prebasic molts occur mostly or wholly on wintering grounds; exceptionally incomplete, with p10 retained.

Habitat and Behavior: Typical large swift. Call a penetrating shrill scream, rarely given by single birds.

PACIFIC (Fork-tailed) SWIFT *Apus pacificus* 17–18 cm (6.7–7.2")

Summary: *Alaska*: Very rare in fall and exceptional in spring–summer on w. Aleutians; exceptional in summer–fall on cen. Aleutians, Bering Sea islands, Gulf of Alaska and se. AK. *Yukon*: 1 fall record (2010).

Taxonomy: 4 ssp, differing slightly in plumage tones and size. N American specimens (age and sex unknown to us) are referred to highly

glossy black saddle

white rump

scaly underparts

all plumages similar

pale-tipped coverts

Pacific Swift

migratory, nominate *pacificus* breeding in NE Asia and averaging larger and paler than 3 ssp of S Asia.

Distribution and Status:

World: Breeds mid-latitude and s. temperate E Asia, e. to Kamchatka; winters mainly from SE Asia to Australia; disjunct population in Himalayas.

North America: *Alaska*: On w. Aleutians, very rare in fall (Sep–early Oct) and exceptional in spring–early summer (mid-May to Jun); 1 fall record from Adak, cen. Aleutians, 16 Sep 2004. 4 summer–fall records from Pribilofs: 25–30 Aug 1999, 26–31 Aug 2003, 12 Jul 2010 (*NAB* 64:634), 21 Jun 2011 (*NAB* 65:674); and single fall records from St. Lawrence, 15 Sep 1993; Middleton Island, Gulf of Alaska, 24 Sep 1989; and Prince of Wales Island, se. AK, 13 Oct 2010 (*NAB* 65:144). All records involved 1–3 birds except for flocks of 20–30 birds on Adak, 16 Sep 2004, and 40 on Attu, 18 Sep 2004. *Yukon*: s. YT, 28 Sep 2010 (*NAB* 65:107).

Comments: This species is remarkable in several respects. The mid-Sep 2004 influx demonstrates what can happen when a movement of birds gets enmeshed in a major weather system, and especially illustrates the effect of a bird's size, strength, and fuel load on the outcome. There have been significant fallouts of Siberian

landbirds on Attu and other islands in the w. Aleutians, but in no other species has there been one of such size as far e. as Adak. It is also true that no other obligate insectivore from E Asia has moved certainly to N America beyond the Aleutians and Bering Sea islands; the Fork-tailed Swift records from Middleton Island, Prince of Wales Island, and s. YT are notable in this regard.

Most Asian landbirds and shorebirds that occur in AK in both spring and fall tend to be commoner in spring in the Aleutians, but commoner in fall in the Bering Sea. The spring records of Fork-tailed Swift fit the pattern of drift displacement, and early fall records in the Pribilofs may reflect drift or misorientation from the relatively early fall migration of Pacific Swift. The later fall records from the Aleutians and elsewhere lie outside the classic pattern outlined above. We suspect that fall migrants far out to sea were driven north by storm systems, which in fall track north into AK and clockwise around into w. N America. Smaller and less aerially adept migrants might perish in such storms, but swifts may be able to outride them and also tend to be more conspicuous when they do get off course, compared to skulking landbirds. This pattern is analogous to that of some storm-blown seabirds such as frigatebirds and Sooty Terns.

Field Identification: Large, white-rumped swift with long, deeply forked tail.

Similar Species: None, if seen well; cf. Common Swift.

Age/Sex/Season: Ages differ slightly; sexes similar; no seasonal variation beyond wear. Adult is fresh in spring, worn in fall, whereas juv is fresh in fall. *1st-year*: Juv undergoes partial preformative molt in 1st winter, and 1st-summer can show molt contrasts in body feathers and upperwing coverts, and contrast between fresher head and body feathers and relatively faded flight feathers, which become notably worn by 2nd fall. 2nd-prebasic and subsequent (complete) prebasic molts occur mostly or wholly on wintering grounds.

Habitat and Behavior: Typical large swift. Long and deeply forked tail occasionally held closed in a point.

COMMON HOUSE MARTIN *Delichon urbicum* 13–15 cm (5.2–6")

Summary: *Alaska*: Exceptional in spring on w. mainland and in late summer–fall on Bering Sea islands. *St. Pierre et Miquelon*: 1 spring record (1989).

Taxonomy: 2 ssp (following Cramp 1988–92, vol. 5), distinct enough to represent separate species: E Asian ssp *lagopodum* (length 13–14 cm) has shorter tail, shallower tail fork, and very extensive white rump patch (lower back to uppertail coverts wholly white) relative to white rump band on nominate *urbicum* of W Eurasia (length 14–15 cm; lower back and distal uppertail coverts blue-black, tail long and deeply forked). AK specimen referred to *lagopodum* (Hall & Cardiff 1978), and photos of 2008 and 2011 birds also clearly *lagopodum*; photos of SPM bird (Etcheberry 1998; note, one photo printed upside-down) show an apparently deep tail fork and white rump band consistent with nominate *urbicum*.

Distribution and Status:

World: Breeds from NW Africa and W Europe e. across n. and mid-latitude interior Eurasia to around 170°E. Winters mainly in sub-Saharan Africa and SE Asia.

North America: *Alaska*: Nome, 6–7 Jun 1974 (male); Pribilofs, 23 Jul 2008 (St. Paul Island

shorter tail, shallower fork

lagopodum

adult

juv

adult

E Asian ssp *lagopodum* has very extensive white rump patch

white rump band

longer tail, deeper fork

European ssp *urbicum*

adult

dusky

dark

adult

juv

Common House Martin

Asian House Martin

Tour); 4–13 Aug 2011 (*NAB* 66:150). ***St. Pierre et Miquelon***: 26 May–1 Jun 1989.

Note: There have been 8 other AK reports (6 in early to mid-Jun, 2 in Aug) of unidentified house martin species: Pribilofs, 12 Jun 1974 (thought to be Common; Hall & Cardiff 1978); Thetis Island, n. AK, 11 Jun 1983; St. Matthew Island, 10 Aug 1983; Buldir, 13 Jun 1990; Pribilofs, 9 Jun 1994, 28–30 Aug 2001; St. Lawrence, 2–6 Jun 2004; and Pribilofs, 14 Jun 2009. In no case was Asian House Martin specifically excluded; this is a migratory species breeding as close to AK as the Kuril Islands, and perhaps more likely than Common House Martin in the w. Aleutians. See Similar Species, below.

Comments: As noted by ABA (2008), of the AK records several may not be referred unequivocally to Common House Martin as opposed to Asian House Martin, despite the 2 species looking quite distinct (see Similar Species, below). Indeed, on geographic grounds the spring record from Buldir seems more likely to have been Asian, whereas Bering Sea and n. AK records may more likely involve Common.

The route taken by the SPM bird is unclear. It might have arrived via either the northern or southern route (see pp. 8–10), or even possibly direct from W Africa, as noted under Common Swift. There were about 860 records of Common House Martin for Iceland through 2006, mostly May-Jun, and Greenland has 2 spring-early summer records. The species has been annual in recent years in the Azores (mainly late Apr-May), there is an early Aug specimen from Bermuda (male; Wingate 1958), and 3 records from Barbados (2 in Oct-Nov - 1 a flock of 8 birds! - and 1 in Jun), all indicating significant overwater capabilities and suggesting that additional e. N American records are likely.

Field Identification: Small, white-rumped swallow, distinct from any N American species but cf. Asian House Martin.

Similar Species: ***Asian House Martin*** (unrecorded in N America) slightly smaller (12–12.5 cm) with narrow white rump band (similar to nominate *urbicum* but quite distinct from *lagopodum*); underwing coverts darker, gray-brown (paler, dusky whitish on Common); tail less strongly forked (even than *lagopodum*, but juv Common has shallower tail fork than adult); underparts (especially female breast) washed dusky and less uniform, the undertail coverts often with distinct dark centers; and blackish cap extends slightly lower and narrowly below the bill. Calls

of Asian similar to Common, but perhaps slightly lower and harsher (P. Holt, pers. comm.).

Age/Sex/Season: Ages differ, with adult appearance attained by complete preformative molt in 1st fall and winter; sexes differ slightly; no seasonal variation. ***Adult***: Steely blue upperparts, clean white rump and underparts; male has clean white underparts, whereas female throat and breast tinged buffy gray, at least in fresh plumage (fading to white by late summer). ***Juv***: Upperparts sooty gray brown with little blue sheen and white-tipped tertials; underparts sullied dusky on throat, chest, and flanks. Attains adult appearance by complete preformative molt over 1st winter. Complete prebasic molt mainly on wintering grounds, but can include inner primaries before migration.

Habitat and Behavior: Typical small swallow. Flight (at least of nominate *urbicum*) can suggest Barn Swallow but a little quicker and snappier. Calls (of nominate *urbicum*) include a slightly rolled chirping, *chrri* and *ch-chrri*, not as liquid as Tree Swallow; alarm a harder, slightly buzzier version, *drrih* and *drri-di*.

New World Aerial Landbirds

In the period under review, 8 species of hummingbirds, 2 swifts, and 3 swallows have occurred as rare birds in N America. Of the hummingbirds, 6 come from Mexico and 2 from the Caribbean. From w. Mexico, Cinnamon Hummingbird, Berylline Hummingbird, Xantus's Hummingbird, and Plain-capped Starthroat have ranged n. into the West, mainly in late summer–winter to AZ. Green Violetear occurs widely in N America (mainly summer–fall in the East) and Green-breasted Mango has occurred very rarely in the East; occurrences of both species may largely involve misoriented (reverse?) post-breeding migrants. Cuban Emerald and Bahama Woodstar have occurred exceptionally in s. FL, mainly in summer–fall.

White-collared Swift has occurred mainly in winter–spring (likely from Mexico, and perhaps from Cen or even S America) and once in fall (from the Caribbean), whereas Antillean Palm Swift is known from a single late summer record in s. FL. Brown-chested Martin has occurred widely but only very rarely, mainly in summer–fall as a misoriented austral migrant; Bahama Swallow wanders very rarely in spring–fall from the Bahamas to s. FL; and Mangrove Swallow has occurred once, in s. FL.

Among candidates for future vagrancy, White-naped Swift *Streptoprocne semicollaris*, Chestnut-collared Swift *S. rutila*, and Sinaloa Martin *Progne sinaloae* are partly to wholly migratory, wide ranging, and breed in Mexico not too far s. of the US border, and Blue-and-white Swallow *Pygochelidon cyanoleuca patagonica* is an austral migrant that reaches s. Cen America and could overshoot or misorient to the US.

GREEN VIOLETEAR *Colibri thalassinus*
L 11–11.5 cm (4.2–4.5")

Summary: *East*: Rare in TX, mainly May–Aug; very rare or exceptional elsewhere, mainly Jul–Nov and since 1990. *West*: Exceptional, mainly Jul–Nov and since 1993.
Taxonomy: 4 ssp usually recognized, differing to varying degrees in size and plumage. N American records refer to partly migratory *thalassinus*, found from Mexico to nw. Nicaragua. Populations from Costa Rica to S America lack violet-blue on chest and lores and perhaps best treated as a separate species, Lesser Violetear *Colibri cyanotus*, with *thalassinus* called Mexican Violetear.
Distribution and Status:
World: Cen. Mexico to Andes of Bolivia (but see Taxonomy, above).

North America: *East*: Rare in spring–fall (mainly May–Aug, with a few records from Apr and into Sep–Oct) in TX, since the first N American record there in 1961; most records are from e. edge of Edwards Plateau, Lower Rio Grande Valley, and along the coast. Elsewhere in e. N America, very rare in spring–fall (mainly Jul–Oct, with a few from May and into early Nov; most records since 1990) from as far afield as QC, the Great Lakes region, New England, and the mountains of NC. *West*: Exceptional (late Jul to mid-Nov), 5 records: Kern Co., CA, 30 Jul–1 Aug 1977; Santa Fe Co., NM, 16–18 Nov 2004 (Williams 2007); La Plata Co., CO, 26–27 Jul 1998 (Lisowsky 2000); Jefferson Co., CO, 12 Sep–4 Oct 2003 (D. Faulkner, pers. comm.); and sw. AB, 13 Aug–18 Sep 1993 (J. Hudon, pers. comm.).
Comments: Populations of this species in the mountains of cen. Mexico are partly migratory, with many birds moving out (and presumably s.) during spring–summer after the winter breeding season (R. G. Wilson & Ceballos-L. 1993; Howell & Webb 1995). This exodus corresponds to the period of occurrence in N America, and we suspect that most N American records involve misoriented (reverse?) migrants. Both 1st-years and adults have been reported, but insufficient data are published to evaluate the age/sex breakdown of records. For example, are there more adults in TX than elsewhere, and are the

adult ♂

1st-year

dark band

♂

Green Violetear

with Ruby-throated Hummingbird

farthest flung records mainly 1st-years? The earlier peak in Texas (May–Aug) compared to elsewhere (Jul–Oct) suggests that birds continue to head n. and e. (and exceptionally w.) but are not detected on their return s.—assuming they do return. Alternatively, might the Oct–Nov records from Colorado and New Mexico represent surviving southbound migrants making a loop? If so, Oct–Nov might be the time to seek violetears in AZ, although by this time 'hummingbird fever' there has all but waned and observers are few. Given the established occurrence of returning 'vagrant' hummingbirds to wintering sites in the Southeast, some N American records of violetears might represent returning birds, but arguing against this possibility is that most violetears are present at a site for no more than a week.

Although it may be tempting to draw parallels between the explosion in records of this species and those of many other hummingbirds in e. N America, the latter are mainly a winter phenomenon whereas violetears are mainly a summer phenomenon. Common links may lie with improved observer awareness and a great increase in the number of hummingbird feeders over the past 30 years. It may thus be that violetears were always occurring in N America but were not being detected.

Some years may see 5 or more records, followed by a year or two with none, but the overall trend is one of increasing detection. The species' predilection for highlands is reflected by the large number of records from the Edwards Plateau of TX, and by other records such as 3 from the mountains of NC. By contrast, records of this species are relatively few from lowland coastal localities often associated with vagrants, and records from the Southeast are exceptional. The paucity of records from w. N America (for example, none from the intensively birded hummingbird mecca of se. AZ) is noteworthy, and indicates that the northward misorientation is not random in its direction.

Field Identification: Fairly large, overall dark green hummingbird with medium-length black bill. For more information see Howell (2002), and Williamson (2001).

Similar Species: None in N America, but any vagrants should be studied carefully to confirm identification. Some records were first thought to be of male *Magnificent Hummingbird*, which has appreciably longer bill, bold white postocular spot, and very different colors when seen in the right light.

Slightly larger **Sparkling Violetear** *Colibri coruscans*, native to S America, may be kept in captivity in N American aviaries, and escapes likely would be passed off as Green Violetear. Sparkling Violetear has violet from its auriculars extending forward in a band under its eyes to the chin, unlike the simple auricular patch of Green Violetear.

Southern taxa of Green Violetear might also be kept in captivity; these are told from Mexican ssp by lacking bluish violet on lores and having little or no blue on chest (similar to some Mexican females and 1st-years) and by broader buffy edges to undertail coverts (again, similar to Mexican 1st-years).

Age/Sex/Season: Ages and sexes differ; no seasonal variation. Molts not well known; likely attains adult appearance within 1 year. **Adult female:** Slightly smaller and shorter tailed than male. Plumage duller overall than male, auricular tufts smaller and less expansive, chest patch bluer (less purplish) and less extensive, sometimes reduced to a few bluish and poorly contrasting spots. **1st-year** (sexes similar): Upperparts bronzy green with fine cinnamon tips most distinct on head; purple reduced to absent in lores and averaging less on auriculars. Throat and chest dull bluish green with scattered iridescent feathers and a trace of blue on chest; undertail coverts dusky pale cinnamon-buff with variable darker centers. May attain varying degrees of adult coloration over 1st year.

Habitat and Behavior: In Mexico, favors humid to semi-arid pine-oak, oak, and evergreen forest and adjacent clearings with flowers. In N America has occurred in a wide variety of habitats, with most birds found at feeders. Often fairly wary at feeders, preferring to remain in shady vegetation rather than perch in the open. Feeding birds periodically give a hard rattled *trrrr* or *trrr*, also a single hard chip, *tk*, which can be repeated and run into rattles, *tk, tk, tk, trrrr*. Song (perhaps unlikely from vagrants) a mostly disyllabic metallic chipping, given with slightly jerky rhythm and often repeated tirelessly from perch on exposed twig; 1st-year males can give prolonged series of rough, wheezy buzzes and rattles interspersed with sharp chips.

GREEN-BREASTED MANGO
Anthracothorax prevostii L 11.5–12 cm (4.5–4.8")

Summary: *East*: Very rare in s. TX, mainly Jul–Jan in Lower Rio Grande Valley. Also single fall–winter records from NC (2000), WI (2007), GA (2007/2008), and LA (2009).

Taxonomy: 5 ssp. Birds in Mexico and n. Cen America are nominate *prevostii*, the ssp most likely to occur in N America. Other (more southern) populations average slightly shorter and more slender bills, but ssp identification requires a bird in the hand.

Distribution and Status:

World: Tropical lowlands from e. Mexico (n. to s. Tamaulipas) to n. S America.

North America: *East*: Very rare but perhaps increasing in s. TX, with about 20 records (since first recorded 1988) from Lower Rio Grande Valley n. to Nueces Co.; almost all records are mid-Jun to Feb, with singles in late May and late Apr. Exceptional farther n. and e. in fall–winter, with 4 records (all 1st-years): Cabarrus Co., NC, 2 Nov–4 Dec 2000; Rock Co., WI, mid-Sep to early Nov 2007 (when taken into care); Laurens Co., GA, 25 Oct 2007–4 Apr 2008; and Caddo Parish, LA, 20 Aug 2009 (*NAB* 64:99, 185).

Comments: Green-breasted Mangos in e. Mexico are migratory, being present there mainly Feb–Aug. N American records may reflect birds that misoriented n. at the end of the breeding season, perhaps as occurs with Green Violetear (which, however, breeds at a different season). The far-flung 1st-years traveled in only 2 basic directions, one route seemingly not correcting for the course change expected in normal migration, but the other mirroring the normal route (Fig. 16, p. 14).

Most N American records have been of 1st-years, but at least 4 adults have occurred (late Aug to mid-Feb) in s. TX, at least one of which may have returned in subsequent winters. In-hand examination of a TX bird in Jan 1992 confirmed its identity as Green-breasted, and all TX records are assumed to be of this species until such time as any other species of mango is documented in or near TX (Lockwood & Freeman 2004).

Field Identification: Large powerfully built hummingbird with thick, arched black bill.

Similar Species: None in N America, but closely related and similar taxa occur to the south. Other mango species seem unlikely to occur naturally in N America, but might be kept in captivity and could occur as escapes. Thus, any vagrant mango should be checked carefully. See Howell (2002) for details to distinguish Green-breasted from Veraguan Mango

adult ♂
(some ♀
similar)

1st-year

Green-breasted Mango

adult ♀

adult

1st-year

A. veraguensis, Black-throated Mango *A. nigricollis*, and Antillean Mango *A. dominicus*.

Age/Sex/Season: Complex plumage variation not well understood (see Howell 2002 for details); no seasonal variation. Molts not well known; likely attains adult appearance within 1 year. ***Adult male (and some females)***: Median throat velvet-black, bordered laterally by broad, iridescent turquoise-green stripes; chest blue-green. Tail coppery purple to violet overall with dark bronzy-green central rectrices; some adult females may be distinguishable from males by narrow whitish tips to outer rectrics. ***Most adult females*** have throat and central underparts white with a broad dark median stripe. Tail mostly violet-purple with bronzy-green edgings to bases of outer webs, a variable blue-black subterminal band, and distinct white tips to outer rectrices. ***1st-year***: Resembles female overall but chin and upper throat white, blackish median stripe on underparts often consists of two oily greenish-black patches on lower throat and lower chest, and malar and sides of white median stripe on underparts have distinct rusty spotting and edging.

Habitat and Behavior: Favors semi-open country with scattered tall trees, such as hedges in farmland, gardens with tall trees, and residential areas. Feeds mainly at upper to mid-levels, and often perches conspicuously on high bare branches and twigs. Most N American records have been of birds at feeders. Mangos are not especially vocal, although feeding and perched birds at times give fairly hard ticking chips that can be repeated steadily, *chik chik chik* … . Also a high, sharp *sip* or *sik*, mainly in flight, and high, shrill, slightly tinny twitters in interactions.

CUBAN EMERALD *Chlorostilbon ricordii*
L 9.5–10.5 cm (3.7–4.2")

Summary: *Florida*: Very rare, mainly in the s. during Jun–Oct, none very recent.
Taxonomy: 2 ssp, *ricordii* of Cuba and the Isle of Pines, and *aeneoviridis* of the Bahamas. Latter has slightly shorter and less deeply forked tail, but ssp may not be separable in the field.
Distribution and Status:
   World: Resident on Cuba, Isle of Pines, and nw. Bahamas (primarily Grand Bahama, Abaco, Andros).
   North America: *Florida*: From 1943 to 1991, 14 sight records from s. and cen. FL, almost all from the e. coast. Reports from all months except

adult ♂

note face pattern

adult ♀

adult ♂

adult ♀

Cuban Emerald

Feb and Dec, with two-thirds in Jun–Oct (Stevenson & Anderson 1994).

Comments: Because none of the FL reports is substantiated by a specimen or photo, this species is not accepted as occurring in N America by ABA (2008). While some of the reports may be erroneous, others are from competent observers, and Cruickshank (1964) convincingly described a male Cuban Emerald (at Cocoa Beach in Oct 1963) to the exclusion of other species (e.g., the 'deeply-lobed tail' and 'white triangle under tail,' in combination with other points of the description, eliminate other *Chlorostilbon*).

The e. coast bias to records suggests that birds are coming from the Bahamas rather than Cuba. Given that Cuban Emeralds are common on the Bahama islands nearest FL, whereas Bahama Woodstars are uncommon or rare on these islands (White 1998), it is surprising that FL records of emeralds are not more frequent. The lack of recent records is also surprising, given a general increase in both hummingbird awareness and in records of vagrant hummingbirds from the Southeast; further records seem possible at any time. Perhaps like Bumblebee Hummingbird, the small size of Cuban Emerald might lead to it being chased off from feeders by dominant larger species. Observers seeking this species should not neglect 'wild flowers,' and they would also benefit from knowing its distinctive calls.

Field Identification: About the size of Ruby-throated Hummingbird, with medium-length straightish bill and long, deeply forked tail with broad rectrices.

Similar Species: None in N America if seen well. Other emeralds in this genus occur in Mexico and the Caribbean, and any vagrant should be studied carefully to establish its identification (see Howell 2002 for details); also beware the possibility of escapes and hybrids.

Male **Ruby-throated Hummingbird** facing away often looks solidly emerald green and has a distinctly forked tail. However, Ruby-throated's tail is much shorter, and its rectrices more tapered, than male Cuban Emerald. Sounds and habits of these two species are quite distinct. Female Cuban Emerald suggests Broad-billed Hummingbird but is smaller with longer, more deeply forked tail, different voice.

Age/Sex/Season: Ages and sexes differ; no seasonal variation. Molts not well known; likely attains adult appearance within 1 year. *Adult male:* Intense glittering emerald-green overall

with a white postocular spot; white undertail coverts. *Adult female:* Face and underparts pale gray with a dark auricular mask and whitish postocular stripe. *1st-year:* Juv not well known, apparently resembles female but outer rectrices tipped pale gray to whitish. 1st-year male may show patches of emerald-green on underparts.

Habitat and Behavior: In the Bahamas, occurs in understory of open pine woods, at edges and clearings of coppice woodland, in second growth, and in gardens. Feeds mainly at low to mid-levels and regularly visits feeders (no larger dominant species are present in the Bahamas). Feeds and hovers with active wagging of slightly spread and fanned tail; male's wings make a fairly loud buzz that often draws attention, while female has an unremarkable, quiet wing hum.

Male call in flight is an abrupt, cicada-like or 'electric' buzz, *dzzzih* or *bizzz*, usually singly or doubled; from a perch male gives more prolonged and often slightly quieter series, *zzi zzi zzi-zzi zzih* or *zzi zzi zzi-zzi zzi zzi zzi-zzi zzi-zzi zzi*. Female call usually slightly quieter, a buzzy *zzzir*, often doubled or trebled, e.g., *zzi-zzih* and *chi-di-dit* or *zhi-zhi-zhit*, and longer series in flight and from perch, overall with a more rattled, less buzzy quality than calls of male.

XANTUS'S HUMMINGBIRD *Basilinna xantusii* L 8–9 cm (3.3–3.8 in)

Summary: *Pacific States and Provinces*: Exceptional in early to mid-winter.
Taxonomy: Monotypic. Sometimes placed in genus *Hylocharis*.
Distribution and Status:
World: Endemic to cen. and s. Baja California Peninsula, Mexico.
North America: *Pacific States and Provinces*: 3 records: San Diego Co., CA, 27 Dec 1986 (male); Ventura Co., CA, 30 Jan–27 Mar 1988 (female); sw. BC, 16 Nov 1997–21 Sep 1998 (female).
Comments: Xantus's Hummingbirds in N America have been found at a season when the species' range expands northward in the Baja California Peninsula, presumably to take advantage of fall rains that provide food for breeding in more northerly regions (R. A. Erickson et al. 2001). Even so, the species' normal range lies 400 km or more (about 250 miles) s. of the US border, and what might cause extreme northward pushes is unknown. In accord with the fall and winter nesting season of Xantus's Hummingbird, the 1988 record from CA involved a female

adult ♂

adult ♂

adult ♀

**Xantus's
Hummingbird**

that twice attempted to nest (the eggs failed to hatch); the specific identity of her potential mate is unknown (Hainebach 1992).

Field Identification: Medium-sized, fairly stocky hummingbird; all plumages have thick white postocular stripe contrasting strongly with broad blackish mask; cinnamon belly; and mostly rufous tail.

Similar Species: None in N America.

Age/Sex/Season: Ages and sexes differ; no seasonal variation. Molts not well known; likely attains adult appearance within 1 year. *Adult male:* Forehead and chin black, iridescent green throat often looks blackish; bill bright red with black tip. *Adult female*: Throat and underparts pale cinnamon; tail has broken black and bronzy-green subterminal band on outer rectrices. Bill blackish above, pinkish red below with dark tip. *1st-year male*: Resembles adult female but usually with some reddish at maxilla base; auriculars blacker; crown blackish green with rufous-cinnamon edging when fresh; rectrices average narrower and less truncate; subterminal tail band broader; lower throat often has some iridescent blue-green spots. *1st-year female*: Resembles adult female but crown broadly tipped cinnamon when fresh; rump and uppertail coverts more

broadly edged cinnamon; rectrices average narrower and less truncate; subterminal tail band broader.

Habitat and Behavior: Breeds mainly in arid subtropical scrub, oak, and pine-oak woodland, ranging widely to sea level in desert scrub and gardens. Common call a low, fairly fast-paced, dry to slightly wet rattle, *trrrrr* or *trrrt*, often given in short series by feeding birds (e.g., *turrrr, turrrr, turrrr turrrt*, etc.), faster-paced and lower than Ruby-crowned Kinglet-like chatter of Broad-billed Hummingbird. Song from perch apparently a quiet, rough, gurgling warble, at times interspersed with rattles and high, squeaky notes.

BERYLLINE HUMMINGBIRD
Saucerottia beryllina L 9.5–10 cm (3.7–4 in)

Summary: *Southwest*: In spring–fall, rare (uncommon in recent years) in AZ (has bred); very rare in w. TX; exceptional in spring–summer in NM. Increasing, and no longer qualifies as a rare bird.

Taxonomy: 5 ssp in Berylline Hummingbird complex, with species limits uncertain. N American records refer (presumably) to nw. ssp *viola*, not known to be reliably distinguishable in field

molting
1st-year

adult ♂

adult ♀

brownish
rump

Berylline Hummingbird

presumed hybrid
**Berylline x Magnificent
Hummingbird**

from nominate *beryllina* of cen. Mexico. Populations from s. and e. of the Isthmus of Tehuantepec (*devillei, lichtensteini, sumichrasti*) have solidly green underparts, reduced rufous in the wings, purplish tails, and appear different enough to be considered specifically distinct, as Deville's Hummingbird *S. devillei*. Has been placed in genus *Amazilia* (but see Schuchmann 1999).

Distribution and Status:

World: Mexico (n. to n. Sonora) to Honduras (but see Taxonomy, above).

North America: *Southwest*: Rare to uncommon, and increasing, in spring–fall (late Apr to mid-Oct, mainly Jun–Aug) in mountain canyons of se. AZ, with 1st N American record there in 1967; has nested (mainly Jul–Aug) on a few occasions since mid-1970s. Exceptional in spring–summer (May to mid-Jul) in sw. NM and w. TX; very rare in fall (Aug–early Sep) in w. TX. No confirmed winter records, but occasionally reported in AZ at that season.

Comments: Adjacent to AZ in Sonora, Mexico, Berylline Hummingbird is largely a summer resident, present mid-Mar to mid-Sep, with the main arrival probably in May. Most N American records are a little later in the season, when both flowers and observer coverage peak in the 'hummingbird canyons' of se. AZ, suggesting a second northward wave may occur in late summer. There are also a few spring records from AZ, however, including individuals in lowland riparian habitat, and the NM records may represent spring overshoots. Fall records from w. TX may represent post-breeding wandering. In recent years, records in AZ have exceeded our criterion of 5 per year, and this species no longer qualifies as a rare bird in the US.

Field Identification: Medium-sized hummingbird, all plumages have distinct rufous wing patch (often striking in flight); note distinctive buzzy call.

Similar Species: None in normal US range, but as always identify birds with caution and check for hybrids. In particular, a number of presumed

Berylline Hummingbird × ***Magnificent Hummingbird* hybrids** were seen regularly in se. AZ from the late 1990s through at least 2007, and often were misidentified as Beryllines. Hybrids larger and longer-billed than Berylline, with less extensive rufous in wings and golden-toned rump and tail; some show an intense blue crown and gorget unlike Berylline (see Heindel & Howell 2000; Howell 2002).

Buff-bellied Hummingbird (of s. TX, wintering to FL) superficially similar but slightly larger and longer billed. It lacks rufous wing patch, tail more strongly cleft, bill wider based (with obvious red on maxilla of adult), uppertail coverts mostly green, rufous rectrices broadly edged and tipped green, and call different.

Age/Sex/Season: Ages and sexes differ; no seasonal variation. Molts not well known; likely attains adult appearance within 1 year. ***Adult male***: Throat and chest solidly iridescent emerald-green, contrasting with dusky vinaceous to dusky buffy-gray belly. Head and back emerald-green to golden green, brightest on crown. ***Adult female***: Resembles adult male but throat and chest less intense and less solidly iridescent green, with throat mottled pale gray to whitish; crown duller, bronzy green. ***1st-year*** (sexes similar): Resembles female overall but throat and chest dingy pale vinaceous buff, mottled emerald-green at sides and often with some glittering turquoise-green down center of throat and chest; rump and uppertail coverts tipped cinnamon.

Habitat and Behavior: In Mexico favors oak-dominated and subtropical woodlands, mainly in foothills, but also ranges to temperate highlands and locally to tropical lowlands. Birds in the US have been found mainly in mountain canyons, often visiting feeders. Common call in flight and from perch a distinctive, fairly hard, buzzy *dzirr* or *dzzrit*; warning call a slightly higher, more trilled or drawn-out, buzzy *siirrr* or *dzzzir* usually given one to a few times. Flight chase call a rapid, fairly hard ticking chatter, *ji-ji ji-ji-ji*, and *ti ti-ti-ti-ti-ti* and *chi ti-ti ti-ti-ti*, etc. Song from perch varies from a short, varied, jerky to squeaky phrase, repeated (e.g., *ssi kirr-i-rr kirr-i-rr*, or *ssir, ki-tik ki-dik*, etc.), to a more prolonged squeaky warbling and chippering.

CINNAMON HUMMINGBIRD *Amazilia rutila* L 10–11.5 cm (4–4.5")

Summary: ***Southwest***: 2 fall records (1992, 1993).

Taxonomy: 4 ssp, extremes perhaps separable in the field. N American records likely refer to *diluta*, of nw. Mexico, which averages paler underparts than ssp to the s.

Distribution and Status:

World: Mexico (n. to cen. Sinaloa) to Costa Rica.

North America: ***Southwest***: Presumed adults in Santa Cruz Co., se. AZ, 21–23 Jul 1992, and Doña Ana Co., sw. NM, 18–21 Sep 1993.

adult

1st-year

adult

1st-year

Cinnamon Hummingbird

Comments: The normal range of this species lies about 800 km (almost 500 miles) s. of the US border, and there are no data from its Mexican range that might shed light on possible seasonal movements. The breeding season of Cinnamon Hummingbird in nw. Mexico may be mainly in fall, as with Berylline Hummingbird, and the extralimital nature of the 2 US records may thus mirror the pattern shown by Xantus's Hummingbird of birds overshooting n. in the breeding season. This pattern is in contrast to that shown by Green Violetears and Green-breasted Mangos in N America, which occur northward in the nonbreeding season. We still have much to learn about the hows and whys of hummingbird movements.

Field Identification: Distinctive, medium-large hummingbird similar in size and shape to Violet-crowned Hummingbird. Wholly cinnamon underparts diagnostic.

Similar Species: None in N America.

Age/Sex/Season: Ages differ slightly; sexes similar; no seasonal variation. Molts not well known; likely attains adult appearance within 1 year. *1st-year*: Upperparts duller than adult with cinnamon tips to rump, more extensive rufous on uppertail coverts, narrow cinnamon tips to secondaries. Rectrices average narrower, with broader bronzy-green edgings and cinnamon tips. Bill mostly to all-black above, with reddish at base developing over 1st year.

Habitat and Behavior: In nw. Mexico favors tropical deciduous forest and edge, ranging into semi-open areas and gardens, and wandering upslope into humid semi-evergreen forest. Has turned up at feeders in N America. Commonest calls when foraging are hard ticks with a buzzy or rattled quality, *tzk* or *dzk*, and which can run into buzzy rattles. Perched birds give a hard rattled *trrrt* or *dirrr* that may be repeated steadily. In interactions, high squeaks run into an excited chatter, and in flight chases gives a fairly hard chipping *chi chi-chi-chi-chi-chi*.

PLAIN-CAPPED STARTHROAT
Heliomaster constantii L 12–13 cm (4.7–5")

Summary: *Southwest*: Very rare in spring–fall, mainly in se. AZ.

Taxonomy: 3 ssp, probably not separable in the field. N American records presumably pertain to nw. ssp *pinicola*, which averages paler, especially below, than ssp to the s.

Distribution and Status:
World: W. Mexico (n. to s. Sonora) to nw. Costa Rica.

North America: *Southwest*: Very rare in spring–fall (mid-May to mid-Oct, mainly Jun–Sep) in se. AZ, since the first N American record there in 1969; exceptional n. to Maricopa Co., AZ, 17 Oct–28 Nov 1978. Exceptional in fall (mid–late Aug) in Animas Mountains, sw. NM, whence 3 records: 13 Aug 1989, 25 Aug 1993, and 21 Aug 2011 (*NAB* 66:135).

Comments: In Sonora, Mexico, Plain-capped Starthroat is present in some areas mid-Mar to Aug, with some birds year-round in the s. of the state. Although it may be tempting to view N American records of starthroats as representing spring overshoots and post-breeding dispersal, the breeding season of this species is not well-known in nw. Mexico (fledged young have been reported from s. Sonora in mid-May). Wing molt of adult starthroats in nw. Mexico occurs during Apr–Oct (Howell 2002), and several AZ birds have been in obvious wing molt, including a banded individual that returned in 2 successive seasons to the Huachuca Mountains (Jul–Sep 2002 and Jun–Sep 2003). Wing molt and breeding don't usually overlap in Mexican hummingbirds. Thus, the northward movements of this species into the Southwest may represent birds tracking summer and fall flowering to fuel their wing molt as part of a regular molt migration.

Field Identification: Large hummingbird with very long straight bill. All plumages have dark throat bordered by thick white moustache, white rump patch, and white flank tufts (often concealed).

Similar Species: None in N America if seen well, but confusion possible with female *Magnificent Hummingbird*, which is larger-bodied and proportionately shorter-billed (but still distinctly long billed), with a white postocular spot or short stripe; Magnificent lacks starthroat's distinctive throat pattern and white back patches, and only has white tips to outer 3 (not 4) rectrices.

Age/Sex/Season: Ages differ slightly; sexes similar; no seasonal variation. Molts not well known; likely attains adult appearance within 1 year. *Adult*: Dark sooty throat patch has variable iridescent pinkish-red to orangish-red mottling at lower edge. *1st-year*: Head and upperparts tipped buff; throat patch sooty gray with little or no iridescent red; pale moustache and postocular stripe may be washed buff. Tail like adult but central rectrices can lack black

adult

Plain-capped
Starthroat

US birds often
in wing molt

little or
no red

1st-year

tip, subterminal black band averages narrower, and white tips to outer rectrices
average bolder.

Habitat and Behavior: Favors arid to semi-arid
forest edge (from tropical lowlands up into lower
pine-oak zone), riparian woodland, semi-open
areas with scattered trees and hedges, especially
near water. Feeds low to high, often perching
high on exposed twigs or wires, whence makes
prolonged flycatching sallies with jerky, aerobatic movements. Flight generally quick and less
heavy-bodied than Magnificent Hummingbird,
and visits feeders irregularly. Common call, given
mainly in direct flight and also while hovering, a
sharp, fairly loud *peek* or *peek!* that may suggest
Black Phoebe; also a quieter *sik* or *siik*.

BAHAMA WOODSTAR *Calothorax*
evelynae L 8.5–9.5 cm (3.4–3.7")

Summary: *Florida*: 4 records in the s., with no
seasonal pattern.

Taxonomy: 2 distinct taxa usually subsumed
into this species: *evelynae*, widespread in the
Bahamas, and *lyrura* of Inagua, which is probably
different enough to be treated as a separate species, Inagua Woodstar (or Sheartail), as done by
Ridgway (1911). On geographic grounds, *evelynae*
is most likely to occur in FL, and the single
N American specimen (now lost) was of this
taxon. Often treated in the genus *Calliphlox* but
here merged into *Calothorax*, following Howell
(2002), who also suggested naming this species
Bahama Sheartail.

Distribution and Status:
    World: Endemic to the Bahamas (see Tax-
onomy, above), but uncommon to rare on islands
nearest Florida.
    North America: *Florida*: 4 records in the s.:
Miami-Dade Co., 31 Jan 1961 (mummified carcass);
Palm Beach Co., 26 Aug–13 Oct 1971; Miami-Dade
Co., 7 Apr–29 Jun 1974 and 17 Jul–24 Aug 1981 (2).
Comments: This species is appreciably less
common in the Bahamas on islands nearest to FL

adult ♂
tail

duller ♀

dult ♂

adult ♂

1st-year ♂
(variable)

adult ♀

**Bahama
Woodstar**

than is Cuban Emerald (White 1998), but its presence has been confirmed more frequently in N America. Most records of both species in FL have been during summer and fall, suggesting this may be a period of reduced flowering in the Bahamas, causing birds to wander more widely. Like Cuban Emerald, the lack of recent records for Bahama Woodstar in FL is intriguing, given how records of most other hummingbird species in the US have increased greatly in the past 20 or so years. We are aware of no data to show that Caribbean hummingbirds (at least on the Bahamas) are declining, or that N American and Mexican species are increasing. Populations of hummingbirds on some islands can crash, however, following the passage of hurricanes, which strip the landscape of flowers. In the fall of 1999, Cuban Emeralds, which are normally very common and conspicuous on Abaco, were rare and hard to find for months after the passage of Hurricane Floyd (W. Bracey, pers. comm.; Howell, pers. obs.).

Although Cuban Emerald and Bahama Woodstar regularly visit feeders in the Bahamas, there are no other hummingbirds there to compete with them. If competition does occur with Ruby-throated Hummingbirds at feeders in FL, this might influence the detection of Bahamian vagrants. When all is said and done, however, the patterns of occurrence of Bahamian hummingbirds in FL remain something of a mystery, and it seems plausible that another Bahama Woodstar—or Cuban Emerald—could show up at any time, but perhaps mainly during Jun–Oct.

Field Identification: Very small hummingbird. Bill medium-long and slightly arched, tail long and deeply forked (male) to double-rounded (female), usually held closed in a long, rounded point that projects well beyond wing-tips at rest.

Similar Species: None in N America if seen well, but female suggests *Selasphorus* hummingbirds in calls and overall plumage; told by slightly arched bill, plainer throat, and long, deeply double-rounded tail with cinnamon-tipped outer rectrices.

Age/Sex/Season: Ages and sexes differ; no seasonal variation described. Molts not well known; likely attains adult appearance within 1 year. ***Adult male***: Solid magenta-rose gorget offset by bold white forecollar; underparts dusky cinnamon, mottled green on sides. Tail long and deeply forked, outer rectrices black and cinnamon-rufous. *Adult female*: Throat dingy whitish to pale gray, above contrasting white forecollar; sides dusky cinnamon-rufous, sparsely mottled green. Tail long and deeply double-rounded, outer rectrices with cinnamon-rufous bases separated from broad black median band by a narrow green band, and with bold cinnamon tips. *1st-year male*: Resembles adult female but upperparts have narrow pale buffy tips when fresh, throat dingy pale gray to dusky cinnamon with lines of dusky flecks and typically one to several iridescent magenta-rose spots. Tail more deeply forked and outer rectrices slightly longer and narrower, mostly blackish with reduced cinnamon at base, smaller cinnamon tips. *1st-year female*: Resembles adult female but in fresh plumage upperparts have narrow pale buffy to gray tips, and throat tinged buff; sides and flanks paler cinnamon, without green spotting. Tail resembles adult female but with paler cinnamon.

Habitat and Behavior: On the Bahamas occurs widely, in understory of open pine woods, at edges and clearings of coppice woodland, in beach scrub, second growth, and gardens. Feeds mainly at low to mid-levels and regularly visits feeders. Perches with tail held closed or only slightly spread to reveal a notched tip. Flight quick and darting, not slow and bee-like as in Middle American woodstars. Tail of feeding and hovering birds usually closed to slightly spread, and wagged noticeably but not deeply. Calls include a high, fairly sharp chipping *tih* or *chi*, given in flight and often repeated persistently from perch with doubled notes thrown in; and high, thin, buzzier twitters in interactions.

WHITE-COLLARED SWIFT *Streptoprocne zonaris* L 20–21.5 cm (8–8.5"); WS 48–53 cm (19–21")

Summary: *North America*: Very rare in widely scattered locales, mainly winter and spring, with records from TX, FL, Great Lakes region, and CA.
Taxonomy: 9 ssp (perhaps including cryptic species), not known to be consistently distinguishable in the field, although Caribbean ssp *pallidifrons* averages a more extensive pale face than mainland ssp. A Mar specimen from TX appears to be n. ssp *mexicana* (Lasley 1984) whereas a Sep specimen from FL is *pallidifrons* (Hardy & Clench 1982).
Distribution and Status:
World: Mexico (n. to Jalisco and s. Tamaulipas) s. to Brazil; also Greater Antilles and locally in Lesser Antilles.

adult

spread tail tip
can be squared
or rounded

juv

paddle-shaped wing
bulge when soaring

White-collared Swift

adult
mexicana

adult
pallidifrons

averages paler face

North America: 9 records involving 10 birds: 5 birds in winter–early spring (Dec–early Mar) from coastal TX to nw. FL; 4 widely scattered singles in late spring (mid-May to early Jun): Del Norte Co., n. CA, 21 May 1982; Iosco Co., MI, 19 May 1996; Cameron Co., s. TX, 18 May 1997; and s. ON, 10 Jun 2002; 1 fall record from Broward Co., s. FL, 15 Sep 1994.

Comments: The Dec–Mar records suggest a pattern of irregular northward winter wandering from Mexico, perhaps facilitated by favorable winds, and anecdotal reports suggest that small groups may occur on occasion. The Sep record from s. FL was of an exhausted bird of the Caribbean ssp, and thus a vagrant from the Greater Antilles.

The occurrence of the other 4 widely spaced records within a 4-week span (and 3 in the 4-day span of 18–21 May) is remarkable. The timing may indicate austral dispersal from S American populations, although the CA bird was suspected to be a 1st-cycle *mexicana*; the TX bird was apparently also an imm. In-hand examination will likely be required to resolve the question of geographic origin.

Field Identification: Large spectacular swift, much larger than Black Swift. Note very large size, forked tail, and broad white collar.

Similar Species: Nothing in N America.

White-naped Swift of nw. Mexico could wander to the US. White-naped is slightly larger than White-collared, with a squared tail (notched when closed, rounded when spread) and broad white nape band, but no white across foreneck or chest; plumage overall sootier, less blackish than White-collared (perhaps appreciable in good light).

Age/Sex/Season: Ages differ with adult appearance attained in about 1 year; sexes similar; no seasonal variation. Molts not well known; likely attains adult appearance in 2nd year. **Adult:** Blackish overall with a complete white neck collar widest across the upper chest. **1st-year:** White usually restricted to a broad hindcollar; foreneck and upper chest blackish with variable white scalloping (can be hard to see).

Habitat and Behavior: Aerial and wide-ranging, this large swift could be found anywhere. In sunny weather usually forages fairly high but drops lower in cold and rain, sometimes sweeping down within a meter or so of the ground. Flight strong, with relatively slow deep wingbeats and glides on slightly bowed wings; sometimes

soars (especially in groups), when wings have a paddle-like bulge in primaries and a pinched-in trailing edge to secondaries, and tail appears squared or only slightly notched. Calls, mainly heard from groups, are loud shrieky chatters and screams that may recall parakeets.

ANTILLEAN PALM-SWIFT *Tachornis phoenicobia* L 10.5–11.5 cm (4–4.5"); WS 23.5–25 cm (9.2–10")

Summary: *Florida*: 1 late-summer record (1972).

Taxonomy: 2 distinct ssp, perhaps best treated as species and likely separable in the field given good views or photos: *iradii* of Cuba is larger with deeper tail fork (12–17 mm); nominate *phoenicobia* of Hispaniola and Jamaica is smaller with shallower tail fork (6–11 mm) and blacker upperparts.

Distribution and Status:

World: Cuba, Jamaica, and Hispaniola.

North America: *Florida*: Monroe Co., 7 Jul–13 Aug 1972 (2).

Comments: Photos of the FL birds (*AB* 26:848, 851) do not permit identification to ssp, but Cuban origin seems likely on geographic grounds. The presence of these birds in FL may have been linked to the recent passage of Hurricane Agnes, and there is some suggestion they were a prospecting pair (Stevenson & Anderson 1994). Although generally considered resident, the species has occurred as a vagrant to Puerto Rico, in mid-Jul 1969 (Rafaelle 1989). Summer may thus be the best time to watch for this species to appear again in FL.

Field Identification: Very small and slim, distinctively patterned swift; bulk about half that of Chimney Swift. Wings long and narrow with somewhat rounded tips, tail long and forked.

Similar Species: Nothing in N America.

Age/Sex/Season: Ages differ slightly with adult appearance attained in about 1 year; sexes similar; no seasonal variation. Molts not well known. *Juv* pattern on underparts slightly less contrasting overall than adult.

Habitat and Behavior: Aerial, ranging over woodland, open areas, and towns; roosts and nests in palms. Flies mainly at and slightly above tree-top level, where it may associate with Chimney Swifts and swallows. Flight very rapid with hurried wingbeats and short glides. Call a faint, high-pitched twitter (Rafaelle et al. 1998).

Nominate *phoenicobia* of Hispaniola
and Jamaica smaller, darker above

Cuban ssp *iradii* larger
with deeper tail fork

Antillean Palm Swift

BROWN-CHESTED MARTIN *Progne tapera* L 16–18 cm (6.3–7")

Summary: *East*: Very rare in summer–fall. ***Southwest*:** 1 winter record (2006).

Taxonomy: 2 well-marked taxa, perhaps better treated as species. Structure and flight manner differ from typical *Progne*, and sometimes placed in genus *Phaeoprogne*. Most or all N American records are of migratory *fusca*.

P. *[t.] tapera* ('Brown-chested Martin') resident in n. and n-cen. S America (wing molt mainly Jul–Nov), has dingy whitish throat poorly contrasting with dusky brown chest and flanks.

P. *[t.] fusca* ('Brown-banded Martin') breeds in s-cen. S America, migrates n. in austral winter (Apr–Sep) to Panama (wing molt mainly May–Sep). Well-demarcated white throat patch wraps up behind auriculars, broad dark-brown chest band and dark droplets down median chest to upper belly.

Distribution and Status:

World: Breeds cen. S America, migrates n. to s. Cen America (see Taxonomy, above).

North America: *East*: 8 widely scattered records (mid-Jun to early Jul, early Sep, late Oct–early Nov; FL and IL records not accepted

by state committees): Cape Cod, MA, 12 Jun 1983; Palm Beach Co., FL, 24 Oct 1991 (Langridge & Hunter 1993); Cape May Co., NJ, 6–15 Nov 1997; New London Co., CT, 1 Jul 2006; Grundy Co., IL, 30 Jun 2007 (*NAB* 61:586–587); Cameron Parish, LA, 6 Sep 2009 (*NAB* 64:98, 100); Plymouth Co., MA, 12–14 Oct 2009 (*NAB* 64:42); and Northampton Co., VA, 28 Aug 2011 (*NAB* 66:54). ***Southwest*:** Santa Cruz Co., se. AZ, 3 Feb 2006.

Comments: Brown-chested Martin (taxon *fusca*) is a long-distance austral migrant that 'winters' n. regularly to Panama during Apr–Sep, and very rarely to Costa Rica. The N American records in Jun–Jul may be of drift-overshooting (1st-year?) birds on northbound migration. For example, the first MA bird appeared after a late-May weather system that swept in numbers of migrants that winter in S America, such as Yellow-billed Cuckoos (Petersen et al. 1986), and absence of wing molt in Jun suggests a 1st-year bird; the recent VA bird appeared during the passage of a hurricane. The LA bird was a 1st-year male completing wing and tail molt on 6 Sep (*NAB* 64:100). The Oct–Nov records may be of birds that misoriented n. rather than s. in the austral spring, as with Fork-tailed Flycatcher (see that species account for further discussion of this

with juv
Tree Swallow

juv   adult

Brown-chested Martin

phenomenon). The anomalous AZ record is not readily explained, but it may have been wandering for some time before being found.

Nominate *tapera* has been suggested for the CT record, but a published field sketch (*NAB* 60:507) shows a strongly defined chest band atypical of that taxon; given that dark spots on the median underparts are variable in prominence and can be difficult to see in field, this record was likely *fusca*. The MA, NJ, IL, VA, and LA records have been identified as *fusca*, the 'expected' taxon.

Brown-chested Martins could occur more frequently in N America than records suggest, and the apparent recent surge in records of this relatively distinctive species may reflect observer awareness rather than any trend in occurrence. Other martin species, which are notoriously difficult to identify in the field, are surely going undetected now that the era of collecting has passed.

Field Identification: Plumage suggests a giant Bank Swallow, with brown upperparts and distinct brown chest band; variable dark droplets below center of chest band. Tail fairly long and cleft.

Similar Species: None if seen well, although could be overlooked easily among flocks of Purple Martins. Large size and powerful flight should identify this distinctive species as a martin, and plumage suggests Bank Swallow. Dark spots on median underparts variable in extent, sometimes hard to see.

Age/Sex/Season: Ages differ slightly; sexes similar; no seasonal variation. Presumed to follow complex basic strategy, with complete preformative molt (see p. 35). *1st-year*: Juv *fusca* fresh in Mar–Jun when older ages worn and molting. Juv has narrow buff edgings to tertials; attains adult appearance by complete preformative molt (mainly May–Sep in *fusca*), after which may not be distinguishable from adult.

Habitat and Behavior: Similar to other martins but flight of *fusca* often appears quicker and snappier than Purple Martin, with stiffer wingbeats, and glides on distinctly stiff, bowed wings. Associates readily with swallows and other martins both while feeding and at rest.

MANGROVE SWALLOW *Tachycineta albilinea* L 11–12 cm (4.3–4.7")

Summary: *Florida*: 1 late fall record (2002).
Taxonomy: Monotypic.
Distribution and Status:

World: Tropical Mexico (n. coastally to n. Sonora and s. Tamaulipas) to Panama.

North America: *Florida*: Brevard Co., 18–25 Nov 2002.

Comments: In Mexico, Mangrove Swallows undergo poorly known seasonal movements in some areas, including along the n. coast of the

white sometimes meets over bill

adult

adult

rounded when spread

white tertial fringes reduced with wear

wings past tail tip

adult

juv

Mangrove Swallow

sometimes spotted dusky

Yucatan Peninsula (Howell, pers. obs.), which is the nearest source area for a vagrant to FL. However, given the relative proximity of Mangrove Swallow populations to AZ and TX, few would have predicted FL as the location for the 1st N American record. The FL bird may have been present for some time before being found, although it has been suggested that prevailing weather systems earlier in Nov could have contributed to its vagrancy (Sykes et al. 2004). **Field Identification:** Slightly smaller than Violet-green Swallow and appreciably smaller than Tree Swallow, with bold white rump.

Similar Species: None in N America if seen well.

Some ***Violet-green Swallows*** (perhaps mainly birds in Baja California, Mexico) can appear to have solidly white rumps, especially at a distance in bright light, but they are slightly larger and longer-tailed than Mangrove, with a deeper tail notch and duskier underwing coverts. At any reasonable range, face pattern of adults should be apparent.

Other white-rumped swallows should always be considered when confronted with a vagrant. Congeneric Chilean Swallow *T. leucopyga* and White-rumped Swallow *T. leucorrhoa* of

S America are larger, bulkier, and longer tailed than Mangrove, similar in size to Tree Swallow. Their white rump patches are relatively narrower, with a longer tail projection behind, and their metallic blue upperparts are similar to Tree Swallow; Chilean lacks a white forehead chevron, whereas White-rumped has one.

Old World house martins (genus *Delichon*) also have a white rump patch but differ from Mangrove Swallow in larger size, appreciably longer and more deeply forked tail, bluish upperparts lacking a white forehead chevron, snappier flight manner, and distinct calls.

Age/Sex/Season: Ages differ slightly; sexes similar; no seasonal variation. Presumed to follow complex basic strategy, with complete preformative molt (see p. 35). ***Adult:*** Upperparts metallic blue-green to bluish, underparts white with fine dusky shaft streaks; some birds have dusky spots in white rump. ***1st-year:*** Juv upperparts sooty gray-brown with subdued green highlights; underparts whitish with faint dusky wash on chest, lacking fine dusky shaft streaks. Attains adult appearance by complete preformative molt in fall and early winter, after which not known to be distinguishable from adult.

Habitat and Behavior: Not confined to mangroves and occurs widely in open areas of lowlands, usually near water. Associates readily with other swallows. 'Twinkling' wingbeats recall Violet-green Swallow, and flight distinctly less powerful and sweeping than Tree Swallow, typically with brief and infrequent gliding. Chirping calls not as liquid as Tree Swallow, but slightly twangier than drier chipping of Violet-green Swallow.

BAHAMA SWALLOW *Tachycineta cyanoviridis* L 13.5–15 cm (5.3–6")

Summary: *Florida*: Very rare in the s., spring–fall.
Taxonomy: Monotypic.
Distribution and Status:
World: Bahamas, where partly migratory or dispersive, ranging to e. Cuba and s. Florida.

North America: *Florida*: Very rare visitor, with 9 well-documented records (8 in the period under review) involving 6 adults in Mar to mid-Jul, and 6 juvs in late Jun–Aug (Smith & Smith 1989, 1990); all US records but 1 (an 1890 specimen) were during 1974–1992.

Comments: The FL records appear to represent postfledging dispersal by juvs in late Jun–Aug, and spring–summer wandering, perhaps by 1st-year birds that wintered in the s. Bahamas or e. Cuba. One individual associated with a Cave Swallow colony for 5 consecutive springs, 1988–1992, and, in 1974, it is possible that nesting occurred on Sugarloaf Key. Although this species appears to be uncommon and perhaps declining, due to logging of potential nest-cavity trees, it could occur again in FL and might even be almost regular but overlooked in late summer, at a season when few birders are active (Smith & Smith 1989, 1990).
Field Identification: Distinctive, with deeply forked tail; contrast on underwing between white coverts and dark remiges recalls miniature Swallow-tailed Kite.

Similar Species: None in N America. Note deeply forked tail and snowy-white underparts, including contrastingly white underwing coverts.

Age/Sex/Season: Ages and sexes differ slightly; no seasonal variation. *Male* upperparts deep metallic green, becoming blue on rump, tail, and upperwings; tail more deeply forked (25–33mm; BM, USNM specimens). *Female* upperparts average duller and greener, with

adult

adult

juv

juv

Bahama Swallow

less distinct bluish tones; tail less deeply forked (20–27mm; BM, UNSM specimens). *1st-year*: Juv upperparts dark sooty brown with subdued green highlights, perhaps stronger on males; underwing coverts washed dusky but still contrasting with dark remiges; tail less deeply forked than adult (11–21mm; BM, UNSM). Presumably attains adult appearance by complete preformative molt in fall–early winter, after which may not be distinguishable from adult.

Habitat and Behavior: Much as other swallows, with which it associates readily. Calls include a high, fairly sharp chipping *chi* and *chirt*, suggesting Violet-green Swallow, and short gurgles that may recall Tree Swallow.

SONGBIRDS

Some 98 species of songbirds, or passerines, have occurred as rare birds in N America (54 of Old World origin, 44 of New World origin). These make up over a third of all species we treat, and their patterns of occurrence are varied. Most of the Old World species are fairly long-distance migrants whereas the majority of New World species are relatively sedentary. Old World groups that are well represented, and prefaced with short summaries, include flycatchers, chats and thrushes, warblers, wagtails and pipits, buntings, and finches. New World groups similarly treated include tyrant-flycatchers and allies, thrushes, and wood-warblers.

Old World Songbirds

In N America, we consider some 54 species of Old World songbirds as rare birds, comprising 7 flycatchers, 1 shrike, 1 accentor, 6 chats, 6 thrushes, 12 warblers, 2 wagtails, 3 pipits, 1 lark, 9 Old World buntings, and 6 finches. The great majority of these originate in E Asia (all except 4 thrushes and 1 finch), in part a reflection of the prevailing west-to-east weather patterns and in part a reflection of the proximity of w. Alaska to the E Asian flyway.

Common patterns that repeat in these different groups include spring drift and perhaps overshooting to the Aleutians, and to a lesser degree to the Bering Sea islands; and fall misorientation and drift to the Alaskan islands, especially those in the Bering Sea, but with relatively fewer records from the Aleutians than in spring. Smaller numbers of several (mainly reverse-migrating?) species also fan out in fall–winter through North America s. of Alaska, with records from the West (especially California) of the following: Taiga Flycatcher, Brown Shrike, Siberian Accentor, Red-flanked Bluetail, Siberian Stonechat, Dusky Thrush, Lanceolated Warbler, Dusky Warbler, Gray Wagtail, Olive-backed Pipit, Eurasian Skylark, Little Bunting, Rustic Bunting, Common Rosefinch, and Oriental Greenfinch. As one might expect, longer-distance migrants are recorded in fall whereas winter records involve hardier and shorter-distance migrants such as Siberian Accentor and Dusky Thrush. There are also spring records of Siberian Blue Robin, Blue Rock Thrush, Eyebrowed Thrush, and Olive-backed Pipit, which likely involved birds that wintered in the New World.

As with several species of shorebirds, a few passerine species presumed to have originated in E Asia have also been found in the East, from the Great Lakes and Maritime provinces south to the Gulf Coast, namely Brown Shrike, Siberian Rubythroat, Siberian Stonechat, Yellow-browed Warbler, and Citrine Wagtail, in addition to Black-backed [White] Wagtail and Brambling (see Fig. 19 on p. 17). And remarkably, there is a record of Dark-sided Flycatcher from Bermuda!

Although most of the more likely Old World songbird vagrants have been found in N America, there are still numerous other possibilities (especially in fall) among the many migratory species breeding in Eurasia. Most of these are likely to be found in Alaska, but a few might turn up elsewhere in N America. Given their breeding and wintering distributions, the following species of flycatchers, chats, and thrushes seem possible future vagrants to N America, especially to Alaska in fall: Blue-and-white Flycatcher *Cyanoptila cyanomelana*, Yellow-rumped Flycatcher *Ficedula zanthopygia*, Siberian Thrush *Zoothera sibirica*, White's Thrush *Z. dauma*, Gray-backed Thrush *Turdus hortulorum*, Pale Thrush *T. pallidus*, and White-throated Rock Thrush *Monticola gularis*.

Among myriad warbler possibilities, some candidates that could reach Alaska include Pallas's Grasshopper Warbler *Locustella certhiola*, Gray's Grasshopper Warbler *L. fasciolata*, Black-browed Reed Warbler *Acrocephalus bistrigiceps*, Radde's Warbler *Phylloscopus schwarzi*, Pale-legged Leaf Warbler *P. tenellipes*, Two-barred Greenish Warbler *P. [trochiloides] plumbeitarsus*, Eastern Crowned Warbler *P. coronatus*, and Common Whitethroat *Sylvia communis*.

Other pipit possibilities that might reach Alaska in fall from E Asia include Richard's Pipit *Anthus richardi* and perhaps Blyth's Pipit *A. godlewskii*, while Meadow Pipit *A. pratensis* from Europe seems a candidate in the Northeast. These are all pipits of open grassy areas, however, which are habitats that are abundant and rarely birded. Moreover, the calls of Meadow Pipit could be passed off easily as an American Pipit; the calls of Blyth's, and especially Richard's, should draw attention.

Bunting candidates for fall vagrancy to the AK islands include Black-faced *Emberiza spodocephala*, Chestnut *E. rutila*, and Chestnut-eared *E. fucata*, while finch candidates include Pallas's Rosefinch *Carpodacus roseus*.

OLD WORLD FLYCATCHERS

Small arboreal songbirds that perch fairly upright and sally for insects. Given the choice, *Ficedula* prefer wooded habitats and often forage at upper to mid-levels in leafy canopy; *Muscicapa* often favor more open habitats, clearings, and forest edge, where they sally from fairly open perches. Vagrants, of course, can be in any habitat, such as sheltered gullies and cliff faces, but usually they are found near bushes or, if present, trees. Helpful identification points are face pattern, underparts pattern, and primary projection. Juv plumages (unknown in N America) are held briefly in most species, but Dark-sided and Gray-streaked can retain much juv head and body plumage through fall migration (Leader 2010).

In N America, all species have been recorded only from the West, and almost exclusively the Alaskan islands. Spring occurrences (mainly late May to mid-Jun) are far more frequent (6 species, all recorded only or mostly in spring) presumably via drift and perhaps overshooting, whereas most of the rare fall occurrences (4 species, only 1 known solely in fall) are more likely due to misorientation, although drift displacement (as with Gray-streaked Flycatcher) also occurs.

ASIAN BROWN FLYCATCHER
Muscicapa dauurica 12.5–14 cm (5–5.5")

Summary: *Alaska*: Exceptional in late spring on w. Aleutians and Bering Sea islands.
Taxonomy: 5 ssp, with only nominate and highly migratory *dauurica* (breeding temperate E Asia, wintering SE Asia) considered here; also 4 resident or short-distance migrant ssp in S Asia.

Distribution and Status:
World: Breeds E and SE Asia, n. to Sakhalin; n. populations migratory, wintering SE Asia to w. Indonesia.

1st-year

adult

1st-year
(fall–winter)

adult

1st-summer

Asian Brown Flycatcher

1st-year
(fall–winter)

North America: *Alaska*: Exceptional in spring (late May–early Jun), 3 records: Attu, 25 May 1985; St. Lawrence, 9 Jun 1994; Buldir, 29 May 2005.

Comments: AK spring records fit the classic pattern of drift vagrancy.

Field Identification: Small *Muscicapa* fly-catcher with pale lores helping to create a 'gentle' expression; dingy unstreaked chest; relatively short primary projection; and relatively large and broad bill for a small *Muscicapa*, with basal half pinkish below.

Similar Species: Fairly distinctive, if rather plain; cf. Spotted, Dark-sided, Gray-streaked, and female and imm Taiga Flycatchers. See Alström & Hirschfeld (1991) and Leader (2010) for further information on identification.

Age/Sex/Season: Ages differ slightly; sexes similar; no seasonal variation. Prebasic and par-tial preformative molts occur before fall migra-tion. Partial to incomplete prealternate molt (can include tail in 1st-years) occurs on nonbreeding grounds. *Adult*: Plain gray-brown upperparts with relatively narrow, dull paler tips to greater coverts and tertials. *1st-year*: Distinct whitish tips to greater coverts and tertials in fall, worn and faded by spring; can show molt contrast in greater coverts.

Habitat and Behavior: Typical small *Mus-cicapa* flycatcher, often sallying from fairly exposed perches. Calls include a quiet hard *trrr* followed by *dit tit it* notes or some *chuck* notes (Brazil 2009).

DARK-SIDED FLYCATCHER *Muscicapa sibirica* 13–14 cm (5.2–5.5")

Summary: *Alaska:* On w. Aleutians, very rare in spring, exceptional in fall. Exceptional in spring on cen. Aleutians and in spring and fall on Bering Sea islands.

Taxonomy: 4 ssp, with only nominate and highly migratory *sibirica* (breeding E Asia, wintering SE Asia) considered here; also 3 short-distance migrant ssp in S Asia. N American specimens are referred to nominate *sibirica*. For-merly named Siberian Flycatcher, and in Europe sometimes known as Sooty Flycatcher.

Distribution and Status:

World: Breeds E Asia n. to Kamchatka, and disjunctly in S Asia; winters SE Asia to w. Indonesia.

North America: In spring, very rare on w. Aleutians (mid-May to Jun), exceptional on

Pribilofs and cen. Aleutians (early–late Jun); mainly singles, but max. up to 8 on Attu, 1–5 Jun 1999. 2 fall records: Shemya, 13 Sep 1977 (1st-year); Pribilofs, 23 Aug 2011 (*NAB* 66:150).

Comments: AK spring records fit the classic pattern of drift vagrancy; the fall birds were likely reverse-migrants, perhaps drift-enhanced.

There is a late Sep 1980 specimen from Bermuda, attributed to nominate *sibirica*, likely a reverse-migrant that continued e. over the N American continent, as with fall records of Brown Shrike and Siberian Stonechat from Atlantic Canada. This remarkable record suggests some birds may leave their breeding range with substantial fat reserves in order to make long overwater flights direct to their wintering grounds.

Field Identification: Small, overall fairly dark flycatcher with dark sides, dark blurry streaking below, long primary projection, and narrow whitish eye-ring usually most distinct behind eye.

Similar Species: Usually distinctive if seen well, but some well-marked birds can appear similar to Gray-streaked; also cf. Asian Brown Flycatcher, which has pale lores, bigger bill, and shorter primary projection. See Alström & Hirschfeld (1991) and Leader (2010) for further information on identification.

Gray-streaked Flycatcher averages slightly slimmer with slightly longer wings reaching nearer tail tip. It has whiter underparts with more distinct dark streaking, versus dusky sides and diffuse streaking of Dark-sided; clean white undertail coverts (vs. dark centers on Dark-sided, but latter not always apparent in field); brighter and more contrasting face pattern, versus darker head (especially lores) of Dark-sided; 1st-winter Gray-streaked has white tips to greater coverts (buff on Dark-sided).

Age/Sex/Season: Ages differ slightly; sexes similar; no seasonal variation. Prebasic molt occurs wholly or mostly on nonbreeding grounds (Alström & Hirschfeld 1991); preformative molt may start on breeding grounds but often sus-pended for migration, when birds with much juv plumage can be seen (Leader 2010). Details of any prealternate molt unknown (?). *Adult*: Relatively narrow paler tips to greater coverts and tertials. *1st-year*: Distinct buff tips to greater co-verts and tertials in fall, worn and faded to whit-ish by spring; can show molt contrast in greater coverts and some fall birds have whitish-spotted juv feathers on head and upperparts.

1st-year

adult

Dark-sided Flycatcher

1st-year
(fall–winter)

1st-year

adult

underpart
variation

1st-year
(fall–winter)

1st-year

adult

Gray-streaked
Flycatcher

1st-year
(fall–winter)

1st-year
(fall–winter)

underpart
variation

Habitat and Behavior: Typical small *Muscicapa* flycatcher, often sallying from fairly exposed perches. Calls include a thin *tsuii* or *chii* and downslurred *feeeer* (Brazil 2009).

GRAY-STREAKED FLYCATCHER
Muscicapa griseisticta 12.5–14 cm (5–5.5")

Summary: *Alaska*: On w. Aleutians, rare and intermittent in spring, very rare in fall. Very rare in spring and fall on cen. Aleutians and Bering Sea islands.

Taxonomy: Monotypic.
Distribution and Status:
World: Breeds E Asia, from ne. China to s. Kamchatka; winters Philippines to Indonesia.
North America: *Alaska*: In spring, rare and intermittent on w. Aleutians (mid-May to Jun), usually singles, but max. 27 on Attu, 2 Jun 1999; very rare (late May to mid-Jun) on cen. Aleutians and Bering Sea islands, max. 6 on Pribilofs, 19–22 Jun 2005. 1 summer record: Pribilofs, 6 Jul 2003. In fall, very rare (mid-Sep to early Oct) on w. and cen. Aleutians and Pribilofs, max. up to

9 on Pribilofs, 23 Sep–7 Oct 2007, up to 10 on Shemya, 24–30 Sep 2007.

Comments: Gray-streaked Flycatcher is a classic spring drift vagrant to the Aleutians, with records sometimes occurring in clusters. It is a long-distance migrant with migrations including long overwater segments. Some of the groups entrained must have been sizeable given the virtually simultaneous multi-island, multi-bird arrivals, as on Attu and Shemya, beginning 1 Jun 1999.

While some fall records likely fit the pattern of reverse-migrants, the arrival on occasion of groups suggests birds were displaced and drifted n. by weather systems, as with numbers on Shemya and the Pribilofs, beginning 23–24 Sep 2007; we do not have any information on the age of these birds.

Field Identification: Small, long-winged flycatcher with narrow dark streaking on whitish underparts, narrow whitish eye-ring. See illustration on p. 281.

Similar Species: Distinctive if seen well, but cf. Dark-sided Flycatcher and Spotted Flycatcher (see below). See Alström & Hirschfeld (1991) and Leader (2010) for further information on identification.

Age/Sex/Season: Ages differ slightly; sexes similar; no seasonal variation. Prebasic molt

occurs before fall migration (Alström & Hirschfeld 1991); partial (?) preformative molt may start on breeding grounds but often suspended for migration, when birds with much juv plumage can be seen (Leader 2010). Details of any prealternate molt unknown (?). **Adult**: Relatively narrow paler tips to greater coverts and tertials. **1st-year**: Distinct white tips to greater coverts and tertials in fall, worn and faded by spring; can show molt contrast in greater coverts and some fall birds have whitish-spotted juv feathers on head and upperparts.

Habitat and Behavior: Typical small *Muscicapa* flycatcher, often sallying from fairly exposed perches. Calls include a whispery, thin *heest*, slightly rising, and a thin *tsuii* (Brazil 2009).

SPOTTED FLYCATCHER *Muscicapa striata* 13.5–14.5 cm (5.3–5.7")

Summary: *Alaska*: 1 fall record from Bering Sea islands (2002).

Taxonomy: 7 ssp, differing slightly in size and plumage; none certainly separable in the field.

Distribution and Status:
World: Breeds from NW Europe and NW Africa e. to cen. Russia (around 115°E); winters sub-Saharan Africa.

adult

adult

adult

1st-year
(fall–winter)

Spotted Flycatcher

North America: **Alaska**: St. Lawrence, 14 Sep 2002.

Comments: Likely a reverse-migrant from the e. edge of the species' breeding range. Vagrants have also reached Japan (Brazil 2009).

There were 112 records from Iceland through 2006 (mainly mid-Sep to mid-Oct), but only 2 recent fall records (both Oct) from the Azores; this latter likely due to the normal migration route not favoring offshore drift to the Mid-Atlantic.

Field Identification: Relatively large, long-tailed (and poorly named!) *Muscicapa* flycatcher, with dull paler eye-ring, finely streaked crown and chest, but no obvious spotting.

Similar Species: None, if seen well; in size and shape might suggest a streaky pewee. *Gray-streaked Flycatcher* slightly smaller but with longer primary projection, darker upper-parts, duller crown streaking, contrasting whitish eye-ring, and much more distinct and extensive dark streaking below.

Age/Sex/Season: Ages differ slightly; sexes similar; no seasonal variation. Prebasic and complete preformative molts interrupted, starting with head and body before fall migration (some adults may start wing molt), completing with wings and tail on nonbreeding grounds. Partial prealternate molt on nonbreeding grounds.

Adult: Plumage typically worn in fall, whitish tips to greater coverts often worn away. **1st-year**: Plumage in fall fresh, with distinct pale buff tips to greater coverts. Following complete wing molt in 1st winter, not known to be separable from adult.

Habitat and Behavior: Typical *Muscicapa* flycatcher, perching upright in exposed locations and sallying for insects. Calls include a high, slightly shrill *zee*, in alarm followed by 1–2 dry ticks, *zee tk-tk*.

NARCISSUS FLYCATCHER *Ficedula narcissina* 13–13.5 cm (5.2–5.4")

Summary: **Alaska**: 2 spring records from w. Aleutians (1989, 1994).

Taxonomy: 3 ssp often recognized but considered monotypic by Brazil (2009), with *elissae* (breeds interior e. China) and *owstoni* (resident s. Japan) differing from nominate *narcissina* in olive-green back of adult males and in female plumage, and treated as separate species (see Brazil 2009 for further information). N American records referred to (nominate) *narcissina*.

Distribution and Status:

World: Breeds Sakhalin and s. Kuril Islands s. to Japan; winters primarily Borneo and the Philippines.

1st-year (fall–winter)

adult ♂

rusty

Narcissus Flycatcher

1st-year (fall–winter)

mottled

1st-year (fall–winter)

♀

1st-summer ♂

North America: *Alaska*: Attu, 20–21 May 1989; 21 May 1994.

Comments: Both records involved 1st-summer males, presumably drift overshoots.

Field Identification: Male handsome and striking; female and imm resemble several other Old World flycatchers but note mottled breast, brown (vs. grayish) upperparts with rusty uppertail coverts.

Similar Species: Distinctive, but cf. Mugimaki and other Old World flycatchers.

Age/Sex/Season: Ages/sexes differ; no seasonal variation. Prebasic and partial preformative molts presumably occur before fall migration (study needed); partial prealternate molts presumably occur on nonbreeding grounds. *Adult male*: Blackish upperparts with orange-yellow eyebrow, white wing panel, and orange-yellow rump. *Adult female*: Gray-brown upperparts with greater coverts evenly edged paler, throat and chest faintly mottled brownish. *1st-year male*: In fall resembles female but buff-tipped juv greater coverts retained; in 1st spring resembles adult male but averages duller overall, with brownish retained juv flight feathers. *1st-year female*: Resembles adult female but with relatively faded retained juv remiges, fresh buff-tipped greater coverts in fall.

Habitat and Behavior: Typical small *Ficedula* flycatcher. Calls include a series of plaintive upslurred whistles, *puee puee puee*, or series of downslurred *piu* notes interspersed with quite deep *chuck* notes (Brazil 2009).

MUGIMAKI FLYCATCHER *Ficedula mugimaki* 12.5–13.5 cm (5–5.3")

Summary: *Alaska:* 1 spring record from w. Aleutians (1985).

Taxonomy: Monotypic.

Status and Distribution:

World: Breeds E Asia, e. to Sakhalin; winters SE Asia to Philippines and w. Indonesia.

North America: *Alaska*: Shemya, 24 May 1985 (1st-year male). Accepted by ABA and AOU committees, but not by AK authorities, who judge the photos of insufficient quality; we consider the photos (examined Aug 2012) to support the record.

Comments: Presumably a drift-overshoot vagrant, but rare in Japan (Brazil 2009) and likely to remain very rare in N America.

Field Identification: Handsome *Ficedula* flycatcher, all post-juvenile plumages with variable orange wash on chest.

adult ♂

1st-year ♂ (fall–winter)

1st-year ♀

♀

1st-summer ♂

Mugimaki Flycatcher

Similar Species: Distinctive but cf. *Narcissus Flycatcher*.

Age/Sex/Season: Ages/sexes differ; no seasonal variation. Prebasic and partial preformative molts occur before fall migration. Extent of any prealternate molt not known to us. *Adult male*: Blackish upperparts with white postocular patch, wing panel, and bases of outer rectrices. *Adult female*: Gray-brown upperparts with greater coverts evenly edged paler, no white at base of tail; throat and chest washed orange. *1st-year male*: Grayer above than female, often with retained juv wing coverts tipped whitish; throat and chest orange; white at base of outer rectrices; in 1st spring can have whitish postocular patch. *1st-year female*: resembles adult female but often with retained greater coverts tipped whitish.

Habitat and Behavior: Typical small *Ficedula* flycatcher. Calls include a rattling *turrt* and low *chuck* (Brazil 2009).

TAIGA FLYCATCHER *Ficedula albicilla*
11–12 cm (4.3–4.7")

Summary: *Alaska*: Rare and intermittent in spring on w. Aleutians; exceptional in spring and fall on Bering Sea islands. *California*: 1 fall record (2006).

Taxonomy: Monotypic. Recently split from Red-breasted Flycatcher *F. parva*, whose breeding range lies mostly w. of Taiga Flycatcher but overlaps in w. Russia (see Comments and Similar Species, below). Sometimes known as Red-throated Flycatcher.

Distribution and Status:

World: Breeds n. mid-latitude and taiga zone of Asia from about 50°E e. to Kamchatka and sw. Chukotka; winters Indian subcontinent to SE Asia.

North America: *Alaska*: On w. Aleutians, rare and intermittent in spring (late May–early Jun); several records of multiple birds, max. 14 on Attu, 4–6 Jun 1987. On Bering Sea islands, 3 spring records (late May–early Jun) and 4 fall records (late Aug–Sep). *California*: Solano Co./Yolo Co., 25 Oct 2006 (1st-year).

Comments: AK spring records fit the classic pattern of drift vagrancy, typical of species that winter in SE Asia, migrate n. coastally or over-water, and breed in Kamchatka; the fall AK and CA records more likely represent misoriented (reverse?) migrants. The timing of the CA record corresponds with that for records of Red-flanked Bluetail and Dusky Warbler in CA, and also falls in the mid-Oct to early Nov window when many White Wagtails (ssp *ocularis*) are first found in CA. It would be interesting to know the route all

1st-year

1st-summer ♂

1st-year

adult ♂ breeding

1st-year (fall–winter, sexes similar)

♀ (nonbreeding ♂ similar)

Taiga Flycatcher

these birds took, and where (and for how long) they might have staged.

There were 25 fall records (all Oct–Nov) of Red-breasted Flycatcher from Iceland through 2006, and 1 from the Azores through 2011. In the unlikely event of an e. N American record of Taiga/Red-breasted Flycatcher, it is unclear which species would be more likely.

Field Identification: Small active flycatcher; note white base to tail excluding central rectrices (inverted dark 'T' pattern).

Similar Species: Distinctive but cf. Asian Brown Flycatcher, female and imm Mugimaki and Narcissus flycatchers.

Red-breasted Flycatcher (unrecorded in N America) very similar to Taiga Flycatcher but much of lower mandible usually pinkish (mostly black on Taiga) and distal uppertail coverts typically blackish brown (black on Taiga); orange throat patch of adult male more extensive, lacking gray band at lower border; breast of female and 1st-year usually washed buff, with orange throat of male not attained until 2nd-prebasic molt.

Age/Sex/Season: Ages/sexes differ; seasonal variation in males. Prebasic and partial preformative molts occur before fall migration. Partial to incomplete prealternate molts (can include tail) occur on nonbreeding grounds. *Adult male breeding*: Plain gray-brown upperparts, orange throat. *Adult female (adult male nonbreeding similar)*: Gray-brown upperparts with greater coverts evenly edged paler, throat dirty whitish. *1st-year male*: In fall resembles adult female but with pale buff to whitish tips to retained juv greater coverts and tertials; in 1st spring attains orange throat and resembles adult male breeding but with retained juv remiges, sometimes a molt contrast in greater coverts (see p. 36). *1st-year female*: In fall resembles 1st-fall male; in spring resembles adult female but with retained juv remiges, sometimes a molt contrast in greater coverts.

Habitat and Behavior: Small, active *Ficedula* flycatcher; often cocks and dips tail. Calls include a hard dry trilling or clicking *trrrt* or *trrrrr* (Brazil 2009).

BROWN SHRIKE *Lanius cristatus*
17–20 cm (6.7–7.8")

Summary: *Alaska*: On w. Aleutians and Bering Sea islands, exceptional or very rare in spring

and fall. Exceptional in fall in s-coastal and se. AK. *California*: Exceptional in fall–winter. *Nova Scotia*: 1 late fall record (1997).

Taxonomy: 4 ssp, often separable in adult (especially male) plumage. AK specimen referred to nominate *cristatus*, as presumed for 2nd and 3rd CA records.

Nominate *cristatus*, breeds NE Asia and is longest-distance migrant (most likely ssp to occur in N America), is an 'average' warm brown above; *confusus* breeding to s., intergrading with *cristatus*, averages paler and grayer upperparts; *superciliosus* breeds mainly Japan, has brighter rufous upperparts, blacker mask with broader white border above; *lucionensis* breeds e. China, has gray crown, gray-brown back.

Distribution and Status:

World: Breeds Cen and E Asia, ne. to Chukotka; winters from Indian subcontinent and SE Asia to Indonesia.

North America: *Alaska*: On w. Aleutians, 2 records in early Jun, 1 in early Oct (1st-year). On Bering Sea islands, 1 in early Jun, 3 in late Aug–early Sep (1 adult, 2 1st-year). Also singles in s-coastal AK, 28 Sep 1983 (1st-year), and se. AK, 26–29 Nov 1999 (age unknown). *California*: 4 fall–winter records: SE Farallon Island, 20–22 Sep 1984 (1st-year) and 24–25 Sep 2009 (adult; *NAB* 64:189); Marin Co., 28 Nov 1986–26 Apr 1987 (1st-year); Humboldt Co., 21 Nov 2010–18 May 2011 (1st-year). *Nova Scotia*: Halifax Co., 22 Nov–1 Dec 1997 (adult, ssp uncertain; *FN* 52:5, 23).

Comments: This species is largely a continental rather than coastal or overwater migrant (Brazil 2009), which helps explain the paucity of spring records. The fall bias in AK records toward Bering Sea islands (as opposed to the Aleutians) is typical of several species. The 3 fall adults, however (from AK, CA, and NS), stand out from the typical pattern of misoriented vagrants being almost exclusively 1st-years. Also of note is the apparent late Nov 'arrival' pattern suggested by records in se. AK, CA, and NS, in contrast to an earlier window of late Aug–late Sep records. Might the Nov birds have misoriented from a different population or perhaps from staging grounds in Asia? Or might they have staged or been overlooked in N America? Given the late dates of the AK and NS birds it seems possible they might have attempted to winter (as did the CA birds, successfully) but failed due to unsuitable conditions.

1st-year
(fall–winter)

♂ breeding

1st-year (fall–winter)

♀ nonbreeding
(♂ nonbreeding similar)

Brown Shrike

The NS record of Brown Shrike fits into a sparse pattern of misoriented E Asian landbirds crossing n. N America in fall, as with Dark-sided Flycatcher (see that species account) and Siberian Stonechat. There are no records of Brown Shrike from Iceland and the species is exceptional in Britain, suggesting arrivals from across the Atlantic are unlikely.

Two other ssp, *supercilliosus* and *lucionensis*, have distributions that make them possible vagrants to N America. Males of both are separable in spring–summer, after their prealternate molt completed on the wintering grounds: *supercilliosus* is much rustier above, *lucionensis* much grayer.

Field Identification: Fairly small, overall brown shrike, less thickset than Loggerhead Shrike. Distinguished from all plumages of N American shrikes by warm brown tail.

Similar Species: Unlike any N American species, although beware browner 1st-year plumages of Northern Shrike.

Red-backed Shrike L. *collurio* and **Isabelline** Shrike L. *isabellinus*, both unrecorded in N America, are long-distance migrants from regions that have contributed species to the N American list. Adults of both are uncomplicated, but juv/1st-winters can be similar to juv/1st-winter Brown Shrike. Compared to Brown, both are subtly longer winged (with longer primary projection) and smaller billed, with tail less graduated (longer outermost rectrix falls 7–14 mm short of tail tip, vs. 14–27 mm on Brown).

Isabelline normally much paler above than Brown, with contrasting rusty uppertail coverts and tail, but some dark extremes are potentially confusing; note wing and tail structure. Red-backed can be rather similar to Brown but less uniform brown above, normally showing grayish tones on rump and contrasting whitish outer web to outermost rectrix (vs. brownish or pale buff outermost web, not usually contrasting on Brown Shrike). See Worfolk (2000) for further information.

Age/Sex/Season: Ages differ, with adult appearance attained in 1 year; sexes differ slightly, with some seasonal variation. Only nominate *cristatus* considered here. Prebasic and partial to complete preformative molts often start on breeding grounds and interrupt for fall migration; notable is that prebasic wing molt starts among middle primaries (at p4 or p5); prealternate molt occurs on nonbreeding grounds but extent unclear, likely partial. **Adult male**: Averages brighter above than female, with solid black mask, plain upperparts; breeding plumage unbarred below, but nonbreeding plumage can have dusky barring at sides of breast. Bill typically black overall, often with variable pale pinkish or brownish base below in winter; legs blackish to dark gray. *Adult female*: Averages duller than male (but some indistinguishable), black mask sometimes less solid (especially in winter, when can be mostly limited to auriculars), sides of neck and chest often with dusky barring (more extensive in nonbreeding plumage). *1st-year*: In fall resembles nonbreeding adult female with reduced dark mask (lores not dark), but with variable dark barring above and more extensive dusky barring below. Bill pale pinkish gray with dark tip, legs average paler than adult, grayish. By spring resembles adult, but birds wintering in CA retain juv flight feathers (Howell, pers. obs.). Birds wintering in normal range (and tropical latitudes) usually replace all flight feathers in 1st winter, and difficult to separate in spring from adult.

Habitat and Behavior: A typical shrike, perhaps more given to perching in inconspicuous places than N American shrikes. Most common call a harsh chattering *che che che che che* (P. Holt, pers. comm.).

SIBERIAN ACCENTOR *Prunella montanella* 13.5–14.5 cm (5.3–5.7")

Summary: *Alaska*: Very rare in fall on Bering Sea islands; exceptional in fall on w. Aleutians and in late fall–early spring on mainland. *Northwest*: Very rare or exceptional in late fall–early spring.

Taxonomy: 2 ssp differing slightly in size and plumage, not certainly separable in the field. N American specimens are referred to ne. ssp *badia*.

Distribution and Status:

World: Breeds mainly in taiga zone across n. Russia, e. to Chukotka; winters ne. China to Korea, rarely Japan.

North America: *Alaska*: Very rare in fall (late Aug–early Nov; mainly Sep–early Oct), mostly from Bering Sea islands, especially St. Lawrence, but with 2 mid–late Sep records from w. Aleutians, and single fall records from n. and se. AK. 1 winter record from s-coastal AK, 21 Dec 1997–5 Apr 1998, and 1 spring record from cen. AK, 17 Apr 1984. *Northwest*: 7 records in fall–spring (late Oct–early Apr): singles overwintered in MT (Nov–Mar) and ID (Dec–Apr); also BC (2 records, 1 of 2 birds; winter and early spring), WA (2, late fall and winter), and AB (early spring).

Comments: Siberian Accentor does not typically migrate coastally or overwater in NE Asia, and thus is not prone to spring drift vagrancy in N America. Fall records presumably reflect misoriented migrants, most likely 1st-years (age data are not available, and the species is not straightforward to age in the field). The scattered winter records reflect the species' hardy nature and northerly wintering range. Spring records (in late Mar–Apr) presumably represent birds that wintered undetected somewhere in the vastness of nw. N America, where observers are few. Most winter and spring birds were at feeders.

Field Identification: Thin-billed, short-legged ground dweller with striking head pattern.

Similar Species: None in N America.

all plumages similar

Siberian Accentor

Age/Sex/Season: Ages similar; sexes similar but male averages brighter; no seasonal variation. Prebasic and partial preformative molts occur in fall, before migration; no prealternate molt. *1st-year* retains juv flight feathers, which average more worn in summer than adult, and some show molt contrast in greater coverts (see p. 36).

Habitat and Behavior: Creeps around on the ground, usually near cover and often near streams. Most common call a thin, rattling, slightly metallic *ti-ti-ti.*

CHATS AND THRUSHES
(12 species)
Chats are fairly small, arboreal and terrestrial songbirds, the arboreal species often perching fairly upright and dropping to the ground for insects. Thrushes are often larger and forage both on the ground and in fruiting trees. Some chats are relatively conspicuous but most, like thrushes, are often skulking and elusive. Thrushes in particular are strong fliers and can cover large distances when disturbed. Helpful identification points are face pattern, underparts pattern, and wing and tail coloration, contrast, and pattern. Juv plumages held briefly in most species and unknown in N America.

All 6 chats and 2 of the 6 thrushes recorded in N America originate in E Asia. Not surprisingly, most records are from AK, mainly the islands. Spring occurrences (mainly mid-May to mid-Jun) are more frequent for all species, primarily via drift and to a lesser degree through overshooting. Most fall occurrences are likely through misorientation, although drift displacement also occurs.

Of these E Asian species, 6 have also been recorded s. into w. Canada and the w. US, mainly in mid–late fall (Red-flanked Bluetail, Siberian Stonechat) and late fall–winter (Dusky Thrush), but with single spring records of Siberian Blue Robin, Eyebrowed Thrush, and Blue Rock Thrush (all 3 of which may have arrived the previous fall and wintered in the New World). Remarkably, there are also single fall–early winter records of Siberian Rubythroat and Siberian Stonechat from e. Canada.

The remaining 4 thrushes mostly originate in N Europe (and possibly Greenland, for Fieldfare), although Redwing has appeared twice in the West, perhaps from populations in E Asia. Almost all N American records for this group are from the Northeast and QC, where Redwing and Fieldfare occur mainly in late fall–spring, with single late fall records of Song Thrush and Eurasian Blackbird. Most records appear to reflect displaced and drifted late fall migrants, and transatlantic drift associated with cold-weather winter exoduses from Europe.

RUFOUS-TAILED ROBIN *Luscinia sibilans*
13–14 cm (5.2–5.5")

Summary: *Alaska*: Exceptional in spring on w. Aleutians and Bering Sea Islands; 1 fall record (2012).
Taxonomy: Monotypic.
Status and Distribution:
World: Breeds boreal forest of Cen and E Asia, e. to Kamchatka; winters SE Asia.
North America: *Alaska*: 3 recent spring records (DeCicco et al. 2009): Attu on 4 Jun 2000

1st-year

Rufous-tailed Robin

1st-year

and 4 Jun 2008 (1st-year); Pribilofs, 8 Jun 2008 (1st-year). 1 fall record: Pribilofs, 6–7 Sep 2012 (St. Paul Island Tour).

Comments: The recent spring records presumably reflect drift vagrants, whereas the fall record may be a drift or misoriented vagrant. It may simply be coincidence that this species was unrecorded in N America prior to the 2000s; however, this 'coincidence' is mirrored by vagrants to Europe, where Rufous-tailed Robin was first recorded in Oct 2004, with several others since, and all in fall–winter (Hudson & Rarities Committee 2012). Taken together, this pattern suggests the possibility of a recent range expansion or change in migratory behavior. It will be interesting to see if the trend continues.

Field Identification: Suggests a small, relatively short-legged *Catharus* thrush with scalloped rather than spotted underparts.

Similar Species: None, if seen well, but cf. female Siberian Blue Robin. Siberian Blue Robin lacks rufous tail, averages longer and heavier bill (often looks 'snouty' vs. smaller and often darker bill of Rufous-tailed), has less contrasting whitish eye-ring, and back usually grayer, versus warmer brown of Rufous-tailed.

Age/Sex/Season: Ages similar; sexes similar; no seasonal variation (extent and darkness of scalloping on underparts somewhat variable). Complete prebasic and partial preformative molts occur before fall migration; no prealternate molt (?). *1st-year*: Some may be aged by retained, buff-tipped greater coverts.

Habitat and Behavior: Ground dwelling and, if given the choice, reclusive; cocks and dips tail in manner recalling Hermit Thrush, and also quivers tail briefly when pausing or after alighting. Call a low *tuc-tuc* (Brazil 2009).

SIBERIAN RUBYTHROAT *Luscinia calliope* 14.5–16 cm (5.7–6.3")

Summary: *Alaska*: On w. Aleutians, uncommon in spring, very rare or rare in fall. On cen. Aleutians and Bering Sea islands, very rare in spring, exceptional in fall. Exceptional on nw. mainland in spring–early summer. *Ontario*: 1 winter record (1983).

Taxonomy: Monotypic.

Distribution and Status:

World: Breeds temperate and boreal forests of Cen and E Asia, e. to Kamchatka; winters SE Asia and Philippines.

North America: *Alaska*: On w. Aleutians, uncommon to rare and intermittent in spring (mid-May to mid-Jun), mainly singles or small

1st-year ♀

adult ♂

1st-year ♂

adult ♀

Siberian Rubythroat

numbers, max. 27 on Attu, 1 Jun 1992, and rare in fall (Sep to mid-Oct), max. 7 on Attu, 21 Sep 1979. Very rare in spring on cen. Aleutians (late May to mid-Jun) and Bering Sea islands (late May–Jun, stragglers to mid-Jul; *NAB* 55:471), and exceptional or very rare in fall on Bering Sea islands (mid-Sep to early Oct). Exceptional in spring–early summer (late May–early Jul) on n. and w. mainland. *Ontario*: Hornby, se. ON, near w. end of Lake Ontario, 26 Dec 1983 (male).

Comments: Siberian Rubythroat is a regular spring drift migrant through the w. Aleutians, becoming a vagrant on the Bering Sea islands. Given the frequency of spring records, the relative paucity of fall records from the Bering Sea islands seems surprising. It may be that birds leave the breeding grounds with high fat loads, and misoriented birds would easily overfly the Bering Sea unless grounded by adverse weather.

The remarkable ON record, of a male found dead (*AB* 38:313), may represent a misoriented (reverse?) migrant that was attempting to winter, having traveled about the correct distance from its breeding grounds, but in the wrong direction. It joins a small but growing list of fall–winter Asian passerine vagrants found from the Great Lakes region e. to the E Coast, including Oct–Nov records of Yellow-browed Warbler in WI and Brown Shrike and Siberian Stonechat in the Maritimes, and Dec–Jan records of Black-backed [White] Wagtails from SPM (*NAB* 56:150) and NY (*AB* 47:245).

Field Identification: Suggests a small *Catharus* thrush, but note distinctive face pattern; male has glowing ruby-red throat.

Similar Species: Distinctive, if seen well. *Bluethroat* can appear similar when viewed from behind but slightly smaller with rufous base to blackish tail; throat cleaner white.

Age/Sex/Season: Ages differ slightly; sexes differ; no seasonal variation. Complete prebasic and partial preformative molts occur before fall migration; no prealternate molt. *Adult male*: Strong face pattern, ruby-red throat, plain greater coverts. *Adult female*: Throat dingy whitish, occasionally with a reddish blush, greater coverts plain. *1st-year*: Like adult of respective sex but often retains some to all buff-tipped juv greater coverts, and female lacks red blush on throat.

Habitat and Behavior: Ground dwelling and, if given the choice, reclusive, but sings from prominent perches. Most common calls are an indrawn, nervous whistle, *ee-yu*, and a gruff *chack* (P. Holt, pers. comm.), the latter vaguely suggesting Hermit Thrush. Song is a slightly scratchy, fairly pleasant warble, varying from shorter songs, repeated after short pauses, to more prolonged and rambling series.

SIBERIAN BLUE ROBIN *Luscinia cyane*
13–14 cm (5.2–5.5")

Summary: *Alaska*: Single records in spring from w. Aleutians (1985) and in fall from Bering Sea islands (2012). *Yukon*: 1 spring record (2002).

Taxonomy: 2 ssp, not certainly separable in the field. N American specimen inferred to be of e. ssp *bochaiensis*, which averages darker above than w. nominate *cyane*.

Distribution and Status:

World: Breeds taiga and temperate forest of E Asia, e. to nw. side of Sea of Okhotsk; winters SE Asia to w. Indonesia.

North America: *Alaska*: Attu, 21 May 1985 (1st-year female); St. Lawrence, 2–4 Oct 2012 (1st-year female; D. Pavlik pers. comm., photos). *Yukon*: Dawson City, 9 Jun 2002 (male; Scheer & Eckert 2002).

Comments: The AK spring record was presumably a spring drift overshoot, and is unusual in involving a female. The Yukon male was farther e. than most overshoots, and may represent a northbound migrant that wintered in the Americas, as with spring records of Eye-browed Thrush in CA and Siberian Accentor in AB.

Field Identification: Attractive, small and skulking thrush with very pale legs; spring male unmistakable; on female, note shape and usually a bluish cast to rump and tail.

Similar Species: *Rufous-tailed Robin* can appear similar to female Siberian Blue Robin if diagnostic rufous tail of former is not seen, but most are warmer brown above and more heavily scalloped on underparts, often with a dark lateral throat stripe; Rufous-tailed also averages a smaller, less 'snouty' bill, a more contrasting white eye-ring, and tends to stand more erect.

Age/Sex/Season: Ages differ, with adult appearance attained in 1 year; sexes differ; no seasonal variation. Complete prebasic and partial preformative molts occur before fall migration; partial prealternate molt on nonbreeding grounds. *Adult male*: Upperparts blue overall, with blue edgings to flight feathers. *Adult female*: Upperparts without contrasting pale tips to greater coverts and tertials; rump often washed bluish and tail usually with some bluish edging.

1st-summer ♂

adult ♂

1st-year ♂
(fall–winter)

1st-year ♀

Siberian Blue Robin

♀

1st-year male: In fall suggests female overall but upperparts washed bluish, greater coverts tipped buff; in spring resembles adult male but with contrasting brownish remiges. *1st-year female*: Resembles adult but retains buff-tipped juv greater coverts and remiges; rump and tail can be brownish, without blue edging.

Habitat and Behavior: Typically skulks on or near ground in cover, where moves with low-slung, horizontal stance and often quivers tail. Most common call a soft *tuk*, easily overlooked (P. Holt, pers. comm.).

RED-FLANKED BLUETAIL *Tarsiger cyanurus* 13–14 cm (5.2–5.5")

Summary: *Alaska*: Very rare in spring and exceptional in fall on w. Aleutians; very rare in fall and exceptional in spring on Bering Sea islands; exceptional in spring on w. mainland (1992). *California*: 2 fall records (1989, 2011).

Taxonomy: 2 ssp, distinct in adult male plumage, with slightly larger and darker *rufilatus* of Himalayas and cen. China perhaps a separate species. NAmerican specimens referred to nominate *cyanurus*.

Distribution and Status:
World: Breeds in taiga and temperate forest from NE Europe across Eurasia to ne. Russia (Kamchatka), s. to China and n. Japan; winters SE Asia n. to s. Japan.

North America: *Alaska*: On w. Aleutians, very rare in spring (mid-May to early Jun; no adult males), mainly singles but up to 4 on Attu, 22 May–6 Jun 1988; 2 fall records, 5–6 Oct 1993, 29 Sep 2007 (*NAB* 61:133). On Bering Sea islands, exceptional in fall (mid-Sep to early Oct; 5 records, mainly Pribilofs); 1 spring record from Pribilofs, 10 Jun 1987. 1 spring record from w. mainland: Hooper Bay, 22 May 1992. *California*: SE Farallon Island, 1 Nov 1989 (1st-year); San Clemente Island, 6 Dec 2011 (1st-year; SDNHM specimen 53312).

Comments: Red-flanked Bluetail exhibits a pattern shown by several Asian landbirds in AK: spring records largely involve drift vagrants (mainly on the w. Aleutians), whereas fall records likely involve misoriented (reverse?) migrants (mainly on Bering Sea islands). The two California records are relatively late in the year and perhaps staged farther n. in the West before continuing s. on their misoriented headings.

adult ♂ worn
(spring–summer)

adult ♀

1st-year
(fall–winter)

1st-summer ♂

Red-flanked Bluetail

The Hooper Bay, AK, record is at the early end of spring occurrences, and also e. of all other spring records; the possibility exists that it represents a bird returning n. after having wintered in the New World (cf. Eye-browed Thrush in CA, Siberian Blue Robin in YT, Dusky Thrush in se. AK), but it also may simply have been an early drift-overshoot from Asia.

Field Identification: Attractive and distinctive-looking small chat; all plumages have rufous sides and blue-tinged tail.

Similar Species: Nothing in N America.

Age/Sex/Season: Ages/sexes differ; striking seasonal variation through plumage wear. Complete prebasic and partial preformative molts occur before fall migration; no prealternate molt. *Adult male*: Blue head and upperparts (extensively veiled gray-brown in fresh fall plumage); wings with variable blue edging. *Adult female*: Gray-brown head and upperparts with blue uppertail coverts and tail; wings lack blue edging. *1st-year*: In fall resembles female, but male with veiled brighter blue on head and upperparts, especially on lesser coverts; some show molt contrast in greater coverts.

Habitat and Behavior: Typically skulking. Forages mostly on or near ground in open woodland, where perches fairly upright and often quivers tail. Most common call a guttural, nervous *guk* or *gak*, often repeated (P. Holt, pers. comm.).

SIBERIAN STONECHAT *Saxicola [torquatus] maurus* 12–13 cm (4.7–5.2")

Summary: *Alaska*: Very rare in spring and fall on St. Lawrence Island. Single records on mainland and (fall) in s-coastal AK. *Elsewhere*: Single fall records from CA (1995) and NB (1983).

Taxonomy: Siberian Stonechat here considered specifically distinct from European Stonechat *S. rubicola* and African Stonechat *S. torquatus* (e.g., Brazil 2009; Sangster et al. 2011).

6 ssp provisionally recognized (Sangster et al. 2011), the 2 highly migratory n. ssp (w. *maurus* and e. *stejnegeri*) not readily separable in the field. All N American records of stonechat appear to be of Siberian Stonechat, and AK specimens are referred to *stejnegeri*, which has been considered specifically distinct by IOC as Stejneger's Stonechat *S. stejnegeri*.

Distribution and Status:

World: Breeds from SE Europe across Eurasia to ne. Russia (sw. Chukotka), wintering from Indian subcontinent to SE Asia.

1st-year ♂
(fall–winter)

adult ♂ fresh
(fall–winter)

adult ♂ worn
(spring–summer)

adult ♀ worn
(spring–summer)

pale buff rump

**Siberian
Stonechat**

1st-year ♀
(fall–winter;
adult ♀ similar)

North America: ***Alaska***: On St. Lawrence, very rare in spring (late May–early Jun; 7 records) and fall (early Sep; 3 records). Single records from w-cen. AK (19 Apr 1986; 1st-year, desiccated and probably died the preceding fall) and Middleton Island (28 Sep 1990; male). ***Elsewhere***: Grand Manan Island, NB, 1 Oct 1983; San Clemente Island, CA, 20–21 Oct 1995.

Comments: The spring records from St. Lawrence Island, mainly males, suggest overshoots; the species' relatively inland breeding range and continental (vs. coastal or overwater) spring migration route help explain the lack of records from the w. Aleutians. Fall records, including those from NB and CA, fit the pattern of misoriented (reverse?) migrants.

Although it might be tempting to view the NB birds as having come across the Atlantic, we suspect it represents a vagrant from E Asia, as with Dark-sided Flycatcher (see account, above) in Bermuda and Brown Shrike in NS. That the NB record was of a Siberian Stonechat supports

this conjecture, although Siberian Stonechats do occur as rare (mainly late fall) vagrants in W Europe. However, stonechats are rare vagrants to Iceland, with only 5 records since 1980, all but one in late Feb–early Apr, which corresponds to spring migration of European Stonechats into the W European breeding range. There is only 1 stonechat record from the Azores (in Sep) and none from the se. Caribbean, making it unlikely that the NB bird came even indirectly from W Europe or Africa.

Field Identification: Small, conspicuously perching chat of open scrubby habitats. See Hellström & Waern (2011) for information on ssp and molt.

Similar Species: Nothing in N America.

Age/Sex/Season: Ages/sexes differ; striking seasonal variation through plumage wear. Complete prebasic and partial preformative molts occur before fall migration; partial prealternate molt may occur, at least in 1st-year males (Hellström & Waern 2011). ***Adult male***: Blackish head and upperparts with white neck sides all extensively veiled gray-brown in fresh fall plumage, when difficult to age). **Adult female**: Gray-brown head and upperparts with darker streaking; darker overall in summer, when worn. **1st-year**: In fall resembles adult female, but some males have concealed blackish feather bases, and by spring resemble adult male or with variable pale veiling of black hood. Some 1st-years show molt contrast in greater or median coverts, and juv remiges retained through 1st summer and relatively more worn than adult remiges.

Habitat and Behavior: Open country with scattered bushes, scrubby heathland. Tends to perch conspicuously atop bushes, less often on the ground, where often flicks its wings. Most common call a coarse, clicking *track-track*, often repeated (P. Holt, pers. comm.).

BLUE ROCK THRUSH *Monticola solitarius*
21–23 cm (8.3–9")

Summary: *British Columbia*: 1 late spring record (1997).
Taxonomy: 5 ssp, 4 differ slightly in size and plumage tones, but male of NE Asian ssp *philippensis* (breeding E Asia, wintering se. China to Indonesia) distinct, with chestnut belly (males of other ssp dark bluish overall).
Distribution and Status:
World: Breeds from SW Europe and NW Africa e. across Eurasia to e. Russia (s. Sakhalin and s. Kuril Islands); n. populations migratory, wintering s. to N Africa, the Indian subcontinent, and Indonesia.

North America: **British Columbia**: S. interior (Gold Pan Provincial Park), 6 Jun 1997 (male *philippensis*; McDonald 1997). Not accepted by ABA committee on grounds of uncertain provenance (Robbins & ABA Checklist Committee 2003).
Comments: The migratory e. ssp of Blue Rock Thrush has breeding and wintering ranges similar to other species accepted as occurring naturally in N America. However, unlike many Asian vagrants, rock thrushes would not seek the well-vegetated areas that birders focus on in the Aleutians and thus might not be readily detected. The BC bird was in suitable habitat and far from human population centers. No records were located of captive birds that might account for the record (*FN* 51:1042), which was accepted by the provincial committee (Davidson 1999). In the absence of contrary evidence, we consider its occurrence in N America as a wild vagrant to be plausible, and thus include it here.

The location and date of the BC record suggest a northbound migrant rather than a spring vagrant direct from Asia, although the latter scenario is possible, perhaps with ship assistance. We suspect, though, that the bird reached N America the previous fall and wintered somewhere in the West, as with 'surprise' spring records of several other Asian passerines,

♂ worn
(spring–summer)

♀

♂ fresh
(fall–winter)

Blue Rock Thrush

such as Eyebrowed Thrush in CA, Olive-backed Pipit in NV, and Siberian Blue Robin in YT.
Field Identification: Attractive and distinctive-looking thrush; all plumages distinct from regularly occurring N American species.

Similar Species: Nothing in N America.

Age/Sex/Season: Ages/sexes differ; striking seasonal variation in males through plumage wear. Complete prebasic and partial preformative molts occur before fall migration; no prealternate molt. *Adult male*: Head, chest, and upperparts deep blue (extensively veiled grayish in fresh fall plumage); belly and undertail coverts chestnut. *Adult female*: Head and upperparts dark gray-brown; throat and underparts dull buff with heavy dark scalloping. *1st-year*: In fall resembles adult of respective sex but some show molt contrast in greater coverts and tertials. 1st-winter male averages broader pale grayish veiling than adult.

Habitat and Behavior: Favors open rocky and craggy areas, with *philippensis* in particular also occurring around buildings and in towns

(P. Morris, pers. comm.). Feeds mainly on ground but usually wary and flies well and swiftly; males at times perch conspicuously. Calls include a harsh *tak-tak* and *ka-tchuc-tchuc* (Brazil 2009). Song (at least of W European *solitarius*) a varied, rich, slightly burry warble, some variations of which may recall House Finch.

EYEBROWED THRUSH *Turdus obscurus*
21–23 cm (8.3–9")

Summary: *Alaska*: On w. Aleutians, uncommon to rare in spring, very rare in fall. On cen. Aleutians and Bering Sea islands, very rare in spring, exceptional or very rare in fall. Two spring records on nw. mainland. *California*: 1 spring record (2001).
Taxonomy: Monotypic.
Distribution and Status:
   World: Breeds boreal forest and taiga of cen. and e. Russia, e. to Kamchatka; winters SE Asia to Philippines.

adult ♀

adult ♂

♀

Eyebrowed Thrush

1st-year ♂

1st-year ♀

North America: *Alaska*: On w. Aleutians, uncommon to rare and intermittent in spring (mid-May to mid-Jun), mainly singles or small numbers, exceptionally 180 on Attu, 17 May 1998, and very rare in fall (late Sep to mid-Oct), exceptionally 20 on Shemya, 24 Sep 2007 (*NAB* 62:133). Very rare in spring on cen. Aleutians (mid-May to mid-Jun) and Bering Sea islands (mid-May to early Jul), max. 13 on Pribilofs, 28 May 1998; very rare in fall on Pribilofs (late Sep to mid-Oct; max. 7 on 24 Sep 2007) and exceptional on St. Lawrence (late Sep–early Oct). Single mid-Jun records from n. and w. mainland. *California*: Kern Co., 28 May 2001 (male).

Comments: Most AK spring birds are adult males, suggesting drift migrants. Fall records also involve presumed drift vagrants (cf. numbers in Sep 2007) and perhaps also misoriented (reverse?) vagrants. Like many Asian thrushes, this species can be very furtive and is easily overlooked in areas with any appreciable cover. The CA bird was found at a desert oasis with limited cover, and presumably was returning north after wintering in Mexico or points south.

Field Identification: Slightly smaller and sleeker than American Robin, with unbroken white eyebrow extending well behind eye; brownish upperparts; cinnamon-rufous sides; pale pinkish legs.

Similar Species: Distinctive, but optimistic observers can be fooled by American Robins with well-marked face patterns.

Age/Sex/Season: Ages differ, with adult appearance attained in 1 year; sexes differ; no seasonal variation. Complete prebasic and partial preformative molts occur before fall migration; no prealternate molt. *Adult male*: Blue-gray head and neck with white chinstrap, plain brownish wings. *Adult female*: Brownish crown and nape, grayish cheeks, whitish malar, plain brownish wings. *1st-year male*: Resembles adult female but with whitish tips to retained juv greater coverts. *1st-year female*: Similar to 1st-year male but averages duller overall, with brownish cheeks.

Habitat and Behavior: Typical *Turdus* thrush; normally shy. Most common call a fine, high-pitched *tssssst*, similar to Redwing.

DUSKY THRUSH *Turdus eunomus* 23–25 cm (9–9.8″)

Summary: *Alaska*: On w. Aleutians, very rare in spring, exceptional in fall. On Bering Sea islands, cen. Aleutians, and mainland, very rare or exceptional in fall–spring. *Northwest*: Exceptional in late fall–winter and summer.

Taxonomy: Monotypic. Sometimes considered conspecific with Naumann's Thrush *T. naumanni* (e.g., AOU 1998), which breeds to s. and w. of Dusky Thrush and is a shorter-distance migrant. The 2 species hybridize in their narrow overlap zone.

In N America, 3 birds showing characters of Naumann's Thrush have been seen: 2 on the Aleutians (1 in spring, 1 in fall; Gibson & Byrd 2007) and 1 on the Pribilofs (25–26 May 2003; *NAB* 57:391); at least the 2 spring birds were likely hybrids (original descriptions examined).

Distribution and Status:

World: Breeds taiga and wooded steppes of cen. and e. Russia, e. to Chukotka; winters mainly s. Japan and China.

North America: *Alaska*: In spring, very rare on w. Aleutians (mid-May to mid-Jun), mainly singles but max. 3 on Attu, 20–22 May 1983; exceptional or very rare on Bering Sea islands (late May–early Jun) and on n. and w. mainland (late May to mid-Jun; 3 records). In fall, exceptional (late Sep–early Nov) on w. and cen. Aleutians, and 1 record from St. Lawrence, 3–4 Oct 2011 (*NAB* 66:150). Also single records in winter from s-cen. AK, 12 Dec 2011–17 Mar 2012 (T. Tobish, pers. comm.) and in late fall and spring from se. Alaska: 12–17 Nov 1989, 12 May 1990. *Northwest*: 3 late fall–early spring records (late Nov–early Apr) from YT and BC, and 1 summer record from nw. YT, 28 Jun–1 Jul 2003 (Eckert & Mactavish 2003, *NAB* 57:535). Also an unseasonal report from Skagit Co., WA, 27 Jun 2002.

Comments: AK records show the common pattern of drift and overshoot migrants in spring, with fewer fall records. The YT summer record (of a singing bird) may represent a spring overshoot from Asia (cf. 2 records in Jun from the n. slope of AK) or it may represent a bird that wintered in the Americas, as we suspect is the case for the mid-May record from se. AK.

The few late fall–winter records from AK and the Northwest (including 3 in mid–late Nov) suggest that Dusky Thrushes misorient in fall. We suspect the virtual absence of fall records from Bering Sea islands may reflect the species' relatively late migration timing, when observers there are few or absent (cf. Bullfinch and Hawfinch).

Field Identification: Slightly smaller and less rangy than American Robin, with complex and attractive plumage.

pale rufous underwing

Naumann's Thrush

1st-year ♂

hybrid
**Dusky ×
Naumann's**

adult ♂

adult ♂

Dusky Thrush

1st-year ♂

1st-year ♀

Similar Species: None in N America, but beware hybrids with Naumann's Thrush, which show variably intermediate characters. Hybrids commonly have rufous spotting below and an extensively rufous tail (much like Naumann's) combined with a whitish eyebrow and malar framing relatively dark cheeks (much like Dusky).

Adult male Naumann's has eyebrow, throat, and chest rufous, underparts with extensive rufous mottling. Adult female has eyebrow buffy, throat whitish, rufous markings below less extensive. 1st-year resembles adult female but often has molt contrast in greater coverts.

Age/Sex/Season: Ages/sexes differ, with adult appearance attained in 1 year; no seasonal variation. Complete prebasic and partial preformative molts occur before fall migration; no prealternate molt. *Adult male*: Bright rufous wing edgings, bold blackish face markings. *Adult female*: Duller than male, with duller rufous wing edgings. *1st-year male*: Resembles adult female but often has molt limit in greater coverts. *1st-year female*:

Averages duller than adult female, often with molt limit in greater coverts.

Habitat and Behavior: Typical *Turdus* thrush; normally shy. Common calls include a hard *grrrrt* and other chacking notes. Song a fairly short, slightly hesitant, tinny and fluty *Turdus* warble, repeated; sometimes interspersed with clucks (Zöckler 2007).

FIELDFARE *Turdus pilaris* 24–28 cm (9.4–11")

Summary: *East*: Very rare, late fall–spring, mainly in Atlantic Canada. *West*: Exceptional in late spring in n. and w. AK; 1 winter record from BC (2003).

Taxonomy: Monotypic, but e. breeding populations average larger and paler.

Distribution and Status:

World: Breeds temperate and boreal forest zone from Iceland e. across Eurasia to e. Russia (around 135°E), and since late 1970s in sw. Greenland; winters Europe to Middle East.

adult

1st-year ♀
(winter)

Fieldfare

North America: *East*: Very rare in late fall–winter (mainly Nov–Mar) in Atlantic Canada and Great Lakes provinces, exceptionally w. to MN (Nov 1991) and s. to DE (Mar–Apr 1969). Some wintering birds have lingered to early May, and 5 other late records (mid-Apr to late May) come from ON, QC, SPM, and MA. ***West***: 4 late spring records (early to mid-Jun) from n. AK and St. Lawrence; 1 winter record from Westminster Co., BC, 28 Dec 2003. Records through the mid-1990s were discussed by Green (1998).

Comments: Fieldfares are notably nomadic and mobile thrushes of northern regions. They are regular winter visitors to Iceland, and it is assumed that records from e. N America reflect birds leaving n. Europe and bypassing Iceland, or being forced by cold weather to move sw. from Iceland; a few may come from the small, fluctuating population on Greenland (Green 1998). Most N American Fieldfares appear in Atlantic Canada in late Dec–Feb and are seen only for a day or a few days, although some have remained until Mar–May; these records fit the pattern of nomadic cold-weather winter movements. While some QC records and the NY record also fit this pattern, of note is that most records peripheral to the core of mid–late winter records from Atlantic Canada are either earlier (3 early Nov to mid-Dec records from MN and QC) or later (7 mid-Mar to late May records from ON, QC, MA, and DE, plus a late Apr record from Sable Island, NS, and an early May record from SPM).

It is possible that these spring records represent displaced birds that continued to wander s. and w., and some may have been returning n. after having wintered undetected to the s. The Nov–Dec birds may have been 'overshoots' that originated in Greenland, whence a sw. heading would take them inland of Atlantic Canada. Fieldfares do not appear to be frequent in captivity, but QC is a notorious epicenter for the cage-bird trade and there is at least an outside possibility that some early or late records might involve captive origin (see accounts of Eurasian Blackbird and Common Chaffinch for further discussion of this problem).

The source of western birds is uncertain; distances to the nearest known breeding populations, east and west, are about the same. We see nothing in the data to lend support to one route over the other, although prevailing east winds at high latitudes may favor an origin in Greenland or points east.

Field Identification: Averages larger and rangier than American Robin, with strikingly different and handsome plumage.

Similar Species: None, if well seen.

Age/Sex/Season: Ages/sexes similar but female averages duller; slight seasonal variation in bill (mostly yellow with dark tip in summer, extensively dark above in winter). Complete prebasic and partial preformative molts occur before fall migration; no prealternate molt. ***1st-year*** averages duller than adult, with whitish tips to retained juv greater coverts (vs. grayish tips on adult).

Habitat and Behavior: Similar to American Robin, with which vagrants can be found, and at times visits feeders. Feeds on ground (such as on rotting apples) as well as in trees, and favors fairly open habitats versus closed woodland. Direct flight relatively leisurely and undulating, bursts of wingbeats interspersed with brief, sweeping glides. Most common ground and low-level flight calls are a querulous, rising *qwee*, and a loud *chak-chak-chak*; in high flight, a thin *ghee*. Song a varied and prolonged gruff 'caroling' with frequently repeated phrases suggesting a mockingbird.

REDWING *Turdus iliacus* 20–24 cm (7.8–9.4")

Summary: *Newfoundland*: Very rare in late fall–spring; 1 summer record (1980). *Elsewhere in East*: Very rare in late fall–spring, mainly Maritime Provinces but s. to PA. *West*: Single late fall–winter records from WA (2004/2005) and AK (2011).
Taxonomy: 2 ssp, not safely distinguishable in the field, although *coburni* of Iceland averages larger and darker than nominate *iliacus* of mainland Eurasia.
Distribution and Status:
 World: Breeds mainly in boreal forest and taiga zones from Iceland e. across Eurasia to e. Russia (around 165°E); winters Europe, NW Africa, and Middle East.
 North America: *Newfoundland*: Very rare in late fall–spring (late Nov–Apr, with most in Jan–Feb), mainly in the se. 1 summer record from the far n., White Bay Co., 25 Jun–11 Jul 1980 (singing male; Montevecchi et al. 1981). *Elsewhere in East*: About 10 late fall–spring records (late Nov–early Apr), mainly from the Maritime Provinces w. to QC, but also single Feb records s. to RI, NY, and PA. *West*: Single records from Thurston Co., WA (21 Dec 2004–14 Mar 2005) and s-coastal AK (15–26 Nov 2011; *NAB* 66:150, 194).
Comments: Ground-feeding birds that require unfrozen ground (such as Northern Lapwing and thrushes, although the latter also feed on berries) are famously prone to cold-weather escape flights when atypical freezing conditions occur in their usual wintering grounds.
 Records of Redwing from e. N America fit well with winter movements away from W Europe, likely often linked to cold weather. In some cases birds may have come via (or directly from) Iceland and Greenland (where the species is regular during Oct–May and has bred). In other cases, birds perhaps arrived direct from the British Isles, via wind-assisted escape flights across the N Atlantic (Brinkley 2011). The one lingering summer bird suggests the possibility of occasional breeding, as occurs in Greenland.
 The AK and WA records may represent misoriented (reverse?) fall migrants from the E Asian breeding grounds, perhaps also linked to cold weather patterns. Such movements with Redwing may occur late enough (in late Oct–Nov) that they have not been detected on AK island outposts, cf. Bullfinch.
Field Identification: Slightly smaller and more compact than American Robin with distinctive plumage.
 Similar Species: None, if well seen.

all plumages similar

Redwing

Age/Sex/Season: Ages/sexes similar; no seasonal variation. Complete prebasic and partial preformative molts occur before fall migration; no prealternate molt. ***1st-year*** aged by whitish tips to retained juv greater coverts and tertials (vs. grayish tips on adult).

Habitat and Behavior: Typical *Turdus* thrush; associates readily with American Robins, foraging on the ground in fields as well as in berry-bearing trees and shrubs. Most common flight call a thin, slightly descending *gsssss*; other calls include a high, slightly trilled *ssirr*, and in alarm varied chacking notes, harder than clucks of American Robin. Song is a variable warbling, faster-paced and burrier than American Robin, repeated rather than prolonged.

SONG THRUSH *Turdus philomelos* 20–23 cm (7.8–9")

Summary: *Quebec*: 1 late fall record (2006).
Taxonomy: 4 ssp, none certainly separable in the field, with Cen Asian birds averaging paler than W European populations.
Distribution and Status:
   World: Breeds from W Europe e. to Cen Asia (around 110°E); n. and interior populations migratory, wintering s. to N Africa and Middle East.
   North America: *Quebec*: Saguenay-Lac Saint Jean region, 11–17 Nov 2006 (1st-year).
Comments: The QC bird occurred in a fall that saw unusually high numbers of Song Thrushes

reaching Iceland, where the species is an annual vagrant, mainly in Oct–Nov. It may have been wandering in ne. Canada for some weeks before working its way s. and achieving detection. Unlike Eurasian Blackbird, Song Thrush is not commonly kept in captivity, at least legally, but in QC some are held in private collections, mostly in large urban centers (Auchu et al. 2007).

Given the pattern of Iceland records, Song Thrush seems likely to occur again in N America.

Field Identification: Slightly smaller and more compact than American Robin, with plumage pattern suggesting a Swainson's Thrush with extensively spotted underparts.

Similar Species: None, if seen well. *Catharus* thrushes are considerably smaller with smaller spots limited to upper breast; different face patterns. Underwing of Song Thrush dusky overall with cinnamon-washed coverts.

Age/Sex/Season: Ages/sexes similar; no seasonal variation. Complete prebasic and partial preformative molts occur before fall migration; no prealternate molt. ***1st-year*** difficult to age in field but often has molt contrast in greater coverts, and retained juv coverts have a pale buff shaft streak in addition to buff tips (adult also has buff-tipped greater coverts).

Habitat and Behavior: Typical *Turdus* thrush. Often shy. Most common flight call a high, hard, rather unthrush-like *tsit*, which might suggest a N American sparrow flight call.

all plumages similar

Song Thrush

EURASIAN BLACKBIRD *Turdus merula*
24–27 cm (9.4–10.7")

Summary: *Newfoundland*: 1 late fall record (1994). *Elsewhere*: Status uncertain (see Comments).

Taxonomy: 9 ssp, 2 restricted to islands. Mainland populations average paler and grayer eastward, with isolated Chinese (and other Asian) populations perhaps best treated as separate species. N American specimen referred to nominate *merula*.

Status and Distribution:

World: Breeds from W Europe and NW Africa e. across mid-latitude Eurasia to the Indian subcontinent and e. China; n. and interior European populations migratory, wintering to W Europe and the Middle East.

North America: *Newfoundland*: Bonavista, se. NL, 16 Nov 1994 (adult male found dead; *FN* 49:15). *Elsewhere*: Records from Montréal, QC (23 Nov 1970) and Kent Co., ON (12 Apr 1981) are now questioned with respect to wild origin (ABA 2008; see Comments, below).

Comments: Eurasian Blackbird is a regular breeding bird (mainly since the early 2000s) and uncommon vagrant to Iceland, particularly in fall but also in early spring. In Greenland it is a rare vagrant, mainly Nov–Dec/Jan, a pattern into which the NL record fits nicely.

While the QC and ON records may have been of naturally occurring birds, they come from a region notorious for a cage bird trade that features many European species, among them commonly the Eurasian Blackbird (Ryan 1990; and see Comments in Common Chaffinch account). The QC bird was an adult male in good condition, and occurred following a 'strong windstorm blowing from the northeast' (McNeil & Cyr 1971).

Field Identification: Similar size to American Robin, but plumage dark overall; also note dark legs.

Similar Species: None, if well seen.

Age/Sex/Season: Ages differ, with adult appearance attained in 1 year; sexes differ; no seasonal variation. Complete prebasic and partial preformative molts occur before fall migration; no prealternate molt. *Adult male*: Plumage all-black, bill bright yellow (duller in winter). *Adult female*: Dark brown overall with paler throat and chest variably streaked dark brown; bill yellowish, at least below. *1st-year male*: Duller than adult male, sooty blackish to brownish black, with browner wings; bill dark in fall, becoming yellow by summer. *1st-year female*: Resembles

♀

adult ♂

1st-year ♂
(fall–winter;
bill bright
in summer)

adult ♀

Eurasian Blackbird

adult female, but some separable by molt contrast in greater coverts.

Habitat and Behavior: Feeding behavior much like American Robin but spends more time in cover. Flight when flushed often does not appear strong and streamlined but somewhat halting and jerky. Common calls include a low, fairly hard *tchok*, often in clucking series, lower and harder, or more wooden, than clucks of American Robin; when more disturbed emits a low shriek, *chrieh*, at times in an excited, accelerating or bubbling series. Most common flight call a high, trilled *dsssst.*

OLD WORLD WARBLERS (12 species)

A large, diverse, and taxonomically vexed assemblage of small insectivores (recently split into at least 5 families), analogous to the New World wood-warblers. Many species are notoriously skulking, which compounds the complex identification challenges for which the family is famous. Genera recorded to date in North America are *Locustella* (2 species; very skulking and mouselike, broad graduated tails with long undertail coverts; plumage streaked or unstreaked), *Acrocephalus* (2 species; similar to *Locustella* but less skulking, hopping and climbing easily; streaked or unstreaked), *Sylvia* (1 species; fairly skulking; fairly slender and squared tails; relatively simple and bold patterns, no streaking); *Phylloscopus* (8 species, including Arctic Warbler, which breeds in N America; vary from active and arboreal to fairly skulking; relatively small with fairly short and squared tails; unstreaked, with plumage patterns suggestive of fall Tennessee Warbler but coloration varying from brownish to greenish; some have pale wing-bars). Molt strategies vary; some species migrate in juv plumage.

Many species of Old World warblers are long-distance migrants, and the family includes numerous other species that seem possible as vagrants to N America, mainly as misoriented (reverse?) fall migrants from Asia to the Alaskan islands. To date, 12 species (including Common Chiffchaff, Appendix A) have been recorded as rare birds in fall, largely as misoriented (reverse?) migrants, 4 of which have also been recorded in spring as drift vagrants and overshoots. Almost all records come from the Alaskan islands, but in fall 2 species (plus Arctic Warbler) have reached California and 1 other has even reached the Great Lakes region! 3 species have also been recorded in w. Mexico, just south of our region.

LANCEOLATED WARBLER *Locustella lanceolata* 11–12 cm (4.3–4.7")

Summary: *Alaska*: Exceptional in spring–summer on w. Aleutians (has bred once).*California*: 1 fall record (1995).

Taxonomy: 2 ssp, not certainly separable in the field, with ssp *hendersonii*, breeding in Sakhalin to n. Japan, averaging larger and with less distinct streaking than nominate *lanceolata* of mainland Asia.

Distribution and Status:

World: Breeds temperate forest to taiga zones of Cen and E Eurasia, e. to ne. Russia (Kamchatka and w. Chukotka); winters SE Asia to w. Indonesia and Philippines.

North America: *Alaska*: Exceptional in spring–summer (Jun to mid-Aug) on w. Aleutians, 3 records: Attu, 4 Jun–15 Jul 1984 (up to 25 birds, several singing and territorial), and 2–6 Jun 2000 (2); Buldir, 8 Jun–18 Aug 2007 (5 in Jun, with up to 4 singing males; breeding confirmed in Aug; Andersen et al. 2008). *California*: SE Farallon Island, 11–12 Sep 1995 (1st-year).

Comments: A classic drift vagrant, probably making appreciable overwater flights in both spring and fall migration. That all Aleutian records involved multiple individuals suggests that groups of migrants were captured by weather and drifted to the ne; in at least one case birds remained through the summer and bred successfully (and cf. Middendorff's Grasshopper Warbler).

The fall CA record may represent a misoriented (mirror-image?) migrant, and we suspect that much of its migration may have been overwater rather than following the N American coast (see Comments in Olive-backed Pipit and Dusky Warbler accounts). Lanceolated Warblers are notoriously skulking in fall and winter, and perhaps only on the relatively barren and intensively birded Farallon Islands might such a bird be detected.

Field Identification: Small, compact, gray-brown *Locustella*, streaked above and below, and with short, graduated, gray-brown tail.

Similar Species: None in N America, but some Old World species similar.

Pallas's Grasshopper Warbler (a potential vagrant from E Asia) appreciably larger (13–14 cm) and bulkier, told readily from Lanceolated by bright cinnamon-rufous rump and narrow whitish tips to dark tail corners; dark streaks on breast only on 1st-year in fall. See Kennerley & Pearson (2010) for further information.

1st-year
(fall–winter)

dull adult

spring-summer
variation

spring (ages similar)

Lanceolated Warbler

1st-year
(fall–winter)

Age/Sex/Season: Ages differ slightly, with adult appearance attained in 1st winter; sexes similar; no seasonal variation. Complete prebasic and complete preformative molts often start on breeding grounds, with wing molt mainly in winter on nonbreeding grounds; may have partial prealternate molt on nonbreeding grounds. Some 1st-years migrate while still in juv plumage. *Adult*: Flight feathers relatively worn in fall (sometimes with interrupted molt); underparts with variable but sharply defined dark streaking (as on some 1st-years). *Juv/1st-year*: Flight feathers fresh in fall, breast and sides with relatively diffuse and reduced dark streaking on juv; resembles adult by spring.

Habitat and Behavior: Prefers damp grassy areas. Normally very skulking, creeping through grasses like a mouse and often difficult to reflush after an initial encounter. Most common call a sharp *chick*; song a high, prolonged rapid trill, easily passed off as an insect such as some kind of cricket.

MIDDENDORFF'S GRASSHOPPER
WARBLER *Locustella ochotensis* 13.5–14.5 cm (5.3–5.7")

Summary: *Alaska*: On w. Aleutians, exceptional in late spring–fall. On Bering Sea islands, very rare in fall, exceptional in summer.

Taxonomy: Usually considered monotypic, but ne. breeders (including Kamchatka) average duller than sw. breeders, with former separated as ssp *subcerthiola* by Kennerley & Pearson (2010). Also known simply as Middendorff's Warbler (e.g., Brazil 2009). Nominate *ochotensis* hybridizes locally with Pallas's Grasshopper Warbler on sw. side of Sea of Okhotsk (see Kennerley & Pearson 2010 for further information).

Distribution and Status:
World: Breeds NE Asia in s. Kamchatka and areas bordering Sea of Okhotsk; winters Philippines to n. Borneo.

North America: *Alaska*: On w. Aleutians, exceptional in spring–summer (Jun–early Aug; 4 records, including singing birds); 1 fall record, Attu, 18–25 Sep 1979 (6+). On Bering Sea islands, exceptional in summer (early to mid-Jul; 2 records) and fall (late Aug–early Sep; 3 records from St. Lawrence).

Comments: This poorly known species is a late spring migrant, arriving early to mid-Jun in Kamchatka, with drift vagrants reaching the Commander Islands and w. Aleutians, and less often reaching Bering Sea islands. Territorial singing birds occasionally remain into summer and breeding seems a possibility (cf. Lanceolated Warbler). Fall records from the Bering Sea suggest the commonly seen pattern of misoriented (reverse?) migrants, whereas the relatively large

1st-year
(fall–winter)

adult

spring (ages similar)

1st-year

Middendorff's Grasshopper Warbler

numbers on Attu in Sep 1979 suggest migrants displaced by a weather system, or perhaps the remnant of a summer breeding population.

Field Identification: Large plain *Locustella* with fairly stout bill. Note obscure darker mottling above, warmer brown rump and uppertail co-verts, moderate pale eyebrow. Tail full and gradu-ated with whitish tips to all but the central pair.

Similar Species: None in N America, but other species of *Locustella* should always be considered. See Kennerley & Pearson (2010) for further information, and identification of Mid-dendorff's relative to Styan's (Pleske's) Grasshop-per Warbler *L. pleskei* and Pallas's Grass-hopper Warbler.

Gray's Grasshopper Warbler (a potential vagrant from E Asia) is appreciably larger (16.5–18 cm) and bigger-billed than Middendorff's, and entirely unstreaked; tail lacks white tips; face and upper chest grayer.

Age/Sex/Season: Ages differ slightly; sexes similar; slight seasonal variation through wear. Molts not well known. Complete prebasic and complete preformative molts occur mostly or wholly on nonbreeding grounds, but some adults start molt before fall migration; 1st-years migrate in juv plumage (Kennerley & Pearson 2010). *Adult*: Flight feathers relatively worn in fall (sometimes with interrupted molt); overall averages colder and grayer than 1st-year (but fresh plumage buffer, worn spring plumage

often duller and grayer overall). *Juv/1st-year*: Flight feathers fresh in fall, averages warmer in fall than adult, with yellowish-buff underparts often diffusely streaked dusky on breast; juv has variable dark brown streaks on throat and breast; resembles adult by spring.

Habitat and Behavior: Prefers dense cover, such as wetlands, damp grassland, and damp understory of taiga woodland; usually skulking. Calls include a variety of churrs and short tacks (P. Holt, pers. comm.); song striking and fairly loud, starts with a few hesitant, metallic ticks and runs into an accelerating, rich, and at times buzzy chortling warble, repeated (Ueda 1999).

SEDGE WARBLER *Acrocephalus schoenobaenus* 12–13 cm (4.7–5.2")

Summary: *Alaska*: 1 fall record from Bering Sea islands (2007).

Taxonomy: Monotypic.

Distribution and Status:

World: Breeds from N Europe e. across n. and mid-latitudes to cen. Russia (around 90°E); winters sub-Saharan Africa.

North America: *Alaska*: St. Lawrence, 30 Sep 2007 (1st-year).

Comments: A classic example of a presumed reverse-migrant (see Fig. 14 on p. 12). Some European birds attain great amounts of fat prior to migration and are thought to reach the

adult

1st-year
(fall–winter)

adult
fall

Sedge Warbler

nonbreeding grounds in a single flight (Cramp 1988–92, 6:145). Projected 'backward' from its Cen Asian breeding grounds, this scenario suggests that a Sedge Warbler could potentially reach AK easily without refueling, but we have no data on staging areas or premigration fattening of e. populations.

There are 10 records from Iceland, mainly mid-Sep to mid-Oct and a recent Oct record from the Azores, suggesting an E Coast record is faintly possible, although if Iceland records represent reverse-migrants then a projection of their continued headings would take them far to the n. of the E Coast (see p. 22).

Field Identification: Small brown-and-buff *Acrocephalus* with bold eyebrow, streaked upperparts, cinnamon rump.

Similar Species: None in N America. ***Black-browed Reed Warbler*** (a potential vagrant from E Asia) has similar face pattern to Sedge Warbler but lacks streaking on crown and back, and has shorter primary projection.

Age/Sex/Season: Ages differ, with adult appearance attained in 1st winter; sexes similar; no seasonal variation. Complete prebasic and complete preformative molts occur mostly or wholly on nonbreeding grounds; some adults start head and body molt prior to migration; some adults may have partial prealternate molt on nonbreeding grounds. ***Adult***: Flight feathers worn in

fall and plumage relatively dull and cold-toned with unstreaked breast. ***Juv/1st-year***: Fresh in fall (migrates in juv plumage), with bright olive-buff tones and necklace of faint dusky streaking across breast. Not separable from adult by spring.

Habitat and Behavior: Dense grassy vegetation, reed beds; fairly skulking, but less so than many Old World 'marsh' warblers, and, at least in Europe, often responds to pishing. Most common calls are a sharp *tsek* and a dry churr (P. Holt, pers. comm.).

BLYTH'S REED WARBLER *Acrocephalus dumetorum* 12.5–13.5 cm (4.8–5.3")

Summary: *Alaska*: 1 fall record from Bering Sea islands (2010).
Taxonomy: Monotypic.
Distribution and Status:
World: Breeds scrub and temperate forest zones from E Europe e. across mid-latitude Eurasia (to around 110°E); winters Indian subcontinent e. to Myanmar.
North America: *Alaska*: St. Lawrence, 9 Sep 2010 (1st-year; Lehman & Ake 2011).
Comments: Another classic example of a misoriented (reverse) migrant. Placed by AK committee on the unsubstantiated state list, but we consider the identification reasonable. Expert

paler 1st-year

adult worn
(fall)

1st-year
(fall–winter)

Blyth's Reed Warbler

review considered the bird typical of Blyth's Reed Warbler although some reviewers felt that Large-billed Reed Warbler *A. orinus* could not be certainly ruled out from the photos. That enigmatic species breeds in S-Cen Asia and winters in SE Asia (Svensson et al. 2010); based on its known breeding and wintering ranges, and apparent rarity, we consider it an unlikely vagrant to N America.

Field Identification: Small brown-and-buff *Acrocephalus* with plain, rather uniform upperparts, short pale eyebrow, dark pinkish legs, relatively short primary projection.

Similar Species: None in N America, but several in Old World, and field identification to species can be very difficult; see Kennerley & Pearson (2010) and Lehman & Ake (2011) for details. Observers lucky enough to be confronted with an *Acrocephalus* warbler in N America should focus on overall color tones and contrast (several species have rufous tones above, especially on the rump, and show relatively dark tertial centers), face pattern (extent and prominence of pale eyebrow), length of primary projection (and, if possible, primary spacing), and leg/foot color.

Age/Sex/Season: Ages/sexes similar; no seasonal variation. Complete prebasic and complete preformative molts start with head and body feathers on breeding grounds in late summer, interrupt for migration, and complete with flight feathers on nonbreeding grounds; partial prealternate molt on nonbreeding grounds. *Adult*:

Flight feathers worn in fall and plumage averages duller than 1st-year. *Juv/1st-year*: Flight feathers fresh in fall and plumage averages brighter than adult. Not separable from adult by spring.

Habitat and Behavior: Scrub and overgrown clearings, dense grassy vegetation; typically skulking, but at least in Europe, will respond to pishing. Calls include a clicking *zeck*, often repeated 2–3 times, and a rolling *zrrrrt* (Svensson et al. 2010).

LESSER WHITETHROAT *Sylvia curruca*
12–13.5 cm (4.7–5.5″)

Summary: *Alaska*: 1 fall record from Bering Sea islands (2002).

Taxonomy: 2 ssp, not certainly separable in the field, with *halimodendri* of s. mid-latitude Asia averaging paler and browner above than widespread nominate *curruca*. 3 other ssp, including *blythi* in ne. of breeding range, have been recognized but subsumed here into nominate. Small (or Desert) Whitethroat *S. minula* and Hume's Whitethroat *S. altahaea*, both breeding S Cen Asia and wintering from Arabia to Indian subcontinent, have been considered conspecific with Lesser Whitethroat.

Distribution and Status:

World: Breeds from W Europe e. across n. and mid-latitude Eurasia (to around 130°E); winters from sub-Saharan Africa e. through Arabia to the Indian subcontinent.

adult

Lesser Whitethroat

1st-year
(fall–winter)

North America: *Alaska*: St. Lawrence, 8–9 Sep 2002.

Comments: Although not anticipated as a vagrant to AK, in hindsight this species' occurrence there in fall fits well within the pattern of (reverse) misoriented vagrants that we are coming to recognize, based on accumulating fall records of diverse Eurasian passerine species from the Bering Sea islands (see Fig. 14 on p. 12). There are at least 3 fall–winter vagrant records from Japan and Korea (see Lehman 2003), which may represent mirror-image misorientation, analogous to e. N American wood-warblers occurring on the US West Coast.

With 182 records from Iceland through 2005, virtually all Sep–early Nov and most in recent years, this species seems a possible candidate for E Coast vagrancy, given just the right weather conditions, but see p. 22. There were no records from the Azores through 2011.

Field Identification: Small *Sylvia*, gray-brown above with grayer crown, darker ear coverts, white tail sides, dark bill and legs.

Similar Species: None in N America. ***Common Whitethroat*** (a potential vagrant, breeding in W and Cen Eurasia, wintering in sub-Saharan Africa) is slightly larger than Lesser and often appears peak-crowned, lacks contrasting darker ear coverts, and has broad rusty wing-margins, pale pinkish legs.

Age/Sex/Season: Ages/sexes similar; no seasonal variation. Complete prebasic and partial preformative molts occur before fall migration; partial prealternate molt on nonbreeding grounds. *1st-year*: Eye relatively pale grayish (through fall–winter) versus darker and browner

on adult. Some show molt contrast in greater coverts, and may be aged in-hand by retained juv flight feathers.

Habitat and Behavior: Favors dense bushes and short trees; fairly skulking. Most common call a hard *tak*.

DUSKY WARBLER *Phylloscopus fuscatus*
11–12 cm (4.3–4.7")

Summary: *Alaska*: On w. Aleutians, exceptional or very rare in fall. On Bering Sea islands, exceptional in spring, rare in fall. 1 fall record from s-coastal AK (1997). *California*: Very rare in fall.

Taxonomy: 3 ssp, differing slightly in plumage tones and none certainly separable in the field. N American specimens are referred to ne. ssp *fuscatus*.

Status and Distribution:

World: Breeds taiga and temperate zone forests of E Asia, ne. to s. Chukotka; winters SE Asia.

North America: *Alaska*: In spring, exceptional in Bering Sea (late May to mid-Jun; 4 records). In fall, exceptional on w. Aleutians (early–late Sep) and rare on Bering Sea islands (late Aug–Sep; almost annual in recent years on St. Lawrence). 1 fall record from Middleton Island, s-coastal AK, 26–27 Sep 1997. *California*: Very rare in fall (late Sep–early Nov), most records since 1990.

Comments: Dusky Warbler shows the classic pattern of fall (reverse?) misorientation associated with species breeding 'inland' in e. Russia (see Fig. 12, p. 11). The continental (vs. coastal)

adult
(spring)

1st-year
variation

1st-year
(fall-winter)

Dusky Warbler

spring migration route helps explain the lack of spring records from the w. Aleutians, and the very few spring records (all from the Bering Sea) may represent spring overshoots, as with Siberian Stonechat. The 3 fall records from the w. Aleutians might represent random misorientation but also, depending on point of origin, could also reflect mirror-image or reverse vagrants.

The remarkable number of CA records (13 through fall 2011, plus 2 mid–late Oct records from Baja California, Mexico) is partly due simply to this species' abundance, in combination with it being a relatively long-distance migrant; the frequent and at times persistent calling of fall vagrants also draws attention to them. Given the number of records from cen. and s. CA, it seems surprising there are none from WA or OR, or for that matter from n. CA. However, the route taken by misoriented and perhaps drift-assisted Dusky Warblers may simply bypass these areas (see Fig. 12, p. 11), as has been suggested for Red-throated Pipit and other species (see Sullivan 2004; and Comments under Olive-backed Pipit).

Field Identification: Fairly small *Phylloscopus*, brownish above and dingy below with well-defined pale eyebrow, no wing-bars.

Similar Species: ***Radde's Warbler*** (potential vagrant from E Asia) has slightly thicker, blunter bill; eyebrow buff forward of eye and paler behind; and thicker legs often strikingly pale;

fall birds often washed yellow below, with rich ochre-buff undertail coverts. Most common call a soft, nasal *thick* or *chet*.

Age/Sex/Season: Ages/sexes similar; no seasonal variation. Complete prebasic and partial preformative molts occur before fall migration; partial prealternate molt on nonbreeding grounds. ***1st-year***: Averages buffier below than adult and can show molt contrast in median and possibly greater coverts; in-hand, extremes might be aged by shape of rectrices (see p. 40).

Habitat and Behavior: Damp weedy and grassy areas. Skulking, usually on or near the ground in cover. Even vagrant individuals call frequently, a hard, clicking *teck* that may suggest Lincoln's Sparrow.

WILLOW WARBLER *Phylloscopus trochilus*
11–12 cm (4.3–4.7")

Summary: *Alaska*: Very rare in fall on Bering Sea islands.

Taxonomy: 3 ssp, with extremes perhaps separable in the field. Nominate *trochilus* (breeding Europe) averages more greenish and yellowish (especially in fall), while *yakutensis* (breeding E Asia) averages colder and grayer overall; *acredula* of Cen Asia spans the intermediate gamut.

Willow Warbler

plumage tones vary with age and
population; E Asian birds shown here;
European populations often brighter
yellowish overall

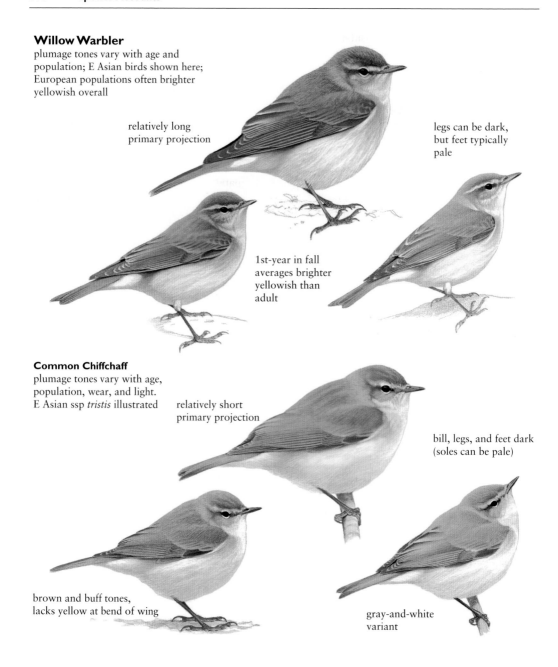

relatively long
primary projection

legs can be dark,
but feet typically
pale

1st-year in fall
averages brighter
yellowish than
adult

Common Chiffchaff

plumage tones vary with age,
population, wear, and light.
E Asian ssp *tristis* illustrated

relatively short
primary projection

bill, legs, and feet dark
(soles can be pale)

brown and buff tones,
lacks yellow at bend of wing

gray-and-white
variant

Distribution and Status:

World: Breeds boreal and temperate forests
from N Europe e. across Eurasia to ne. Russia
(cen. Chukotka); winters sub-Saharan Africa.

North America: ***Alaska***: Very rare in fall (late
Aug to mid-Sep) on St. Lawrence, with about 10
birds found there since 2002; also 1 on Pribilofs,
29 Sep 2011 (*NAB* 66:150).

Comments:

Comments: In the N American context,
Willow Warbler is a classic example of a misoriented (reverse?) migrant; its interior spring
migration route is not conducive to drift vagrancy to the Aleutians, although spring overshoots to the Bering Sea seem possible, as
have occurred with Siberian Stonechat and
Dusky Warbler.

Records from Japan, where considered rare but probably annual during Sep–Nov (Brazil 2009), may reflect mirror-image vagrancy akin to 'eastern' N American wood-warblers occurring on the US West Coast.

There were 540 Willow Warblers recorded in Iceland through 2003 (mainly Sep–Oct), and there are about 30 recent records (mainly Oct) from the Azores and a mid-Sep record from Greenland. Thus, an occurrence in e. N America seems quite possible, but see p. 22.

Field Identification: Small *Phylloscopus* with fairly long primary projection; greenish gray to grayish above with no pale wing-bars; variable pale yellowish wash on throat and chest; legs pale to dark, but soles of feet pale.

Similar Species: None in N America but several in Eurasia, although lack of pale wing-bars and yellowish plumage tones limit the possibilities.

Most similar species is **Common Chiffchaff** (see Appendix A). Chiffchaff is subtly plumper, with shorter primary projection (thus appears longer tailed), dark legs and feet (soles can be pale on E Asian birds), finer and darker bill, and subtly different facial expression: pale eyebrow averages less distinct, but whitish subocular crescent more distinct than Willow. Plumage tones of both species vary greatly with population, age, and plumage wear. In-hand or with good photos, note that chiffchaff has 4 emarginated primaries (p5–p8) versus 3 on Willow

Warbler (p6–p8); note that p10 is very short on both species, such that p9 appears to be outer primary. Call of E Asian birds ('Siberian Chiffchaff') is a mournful, high-pitched *heet* (Brazil 2009), distinct from happier sounding, monosyllabic *hweet* of W European birds (call of Willow Warbler typically a disyllabic *hu'eet*). Also cf. *Wood Warbler*.

Age/Sex/Season: Ages/sexes similar; slight seasonal variation. Complete prebasic and partial preformative molts occur before fall migration; complete prealternate molt on wintering grounds (can be partial on some 1st-years). *1st-year:* In fall averages more extensively yellow below than adult (at least in nominate *trochilus*) and can show molt contrasts in median and greater coverts; in-hand, extremes might be aged by shape of rectrices (see p. 40). Fresh fall plumage averages yellower below than spring plumage, at least in *trochilus*.

Habitat and Behavior: Favors bushes and trees, when available. Typical small, active *Phylloscopus*, occasionally dipping its tail. Common call a slightly plaintive, disyllabic *hu'eet*.

WOOD WARBLER *Phylloscopus sibilatrix*
11.5–12.5 cm (4.5–4.8")

Summary: *Alaska:* Exceptional in fall on w. Aleutians and Bering Sea islands.
Taxonomy: Monotypic.

duller individual

1st-year (fall–winter)

Wood Warbler

Distribution and Status:

World: Breeds temperate forests from W Europe e. to cen. Russia (around 90°E); winters in equatorial Africa.

North America: *Alaska*: Shemya, 9 Oct 1978 and 8 Oct 2010 (*NAB* 65:144), and Pribilofs, 7 Oct 2004.

Comments: The nearest known breeding range of Wood Warbler is about 4500 km (over 2500 miles) to the w. of even the westernmost Aleutians. Coupled with the scarcity of records in NE Asia, this suggests that AK records represent classic misoriented (reverse?) migrants (see Fig. 14, p. 12). Given that Wood Warblers have a long trans-Saharan segment to their migration, made even longer in fall when they appear to fly over the Mediterranean and N Africa as well, they clearly can carry adequate fuel loads for extended flights. Migrants from the e. edge of the breeding range also may need to put on fat to cross the large, inhospitable desert regions of Cen Asia, but we have no data to support this conjecture. Vagrants have also occurred (in late Sep–early Oct) e. to Japan (Brazil 2009) and e. China (P. Holt, pers. comm.); the tight date grouping of vagrant records in AK and E Asia is notable.

Field Identification: Long-winged *Phylloscopus* with bright greenish back, long yellow eyebrow, and yellow throat and chest contrasting with white underparts. Appears relatively short tailed.

Similar Species: None regular in N America, but cf. ***Willow Warbler***.

Age/Sex/Season: Ages/sexes similar; no seasonal variation. Complete prebasic and complete preformative molts start before fall migration with head and body feathers, finish with flight feathers on nonbreeding grounds; partial prealternate molt on nonbreeding grounds. *1st-year* has fresh flight feathers in fall, versus worn on adult; resembles adult by spring.

Habitat and Behavior: Prefers tall trees where available, foraging in upper to mid-canopy. Migrants usually silent, but most common call a sharp *zip*.

YELLOW-BROWED WARBLER
Phylloscopus inornatus 10–11 cm (3.8–4.3")

Summary: *Alaska*: Very rare in fall on Bering Sea islands; 1 fall record from w. Aleutians (2002). *Wisconsin*: 1 fall record (2006).

Taxonomy: Monotypic.

Distribution and Status:

World: Breeds temperate forests of N Asia, e. to ne. Russia (sw. Chukotka); winters mainly in SE Asia.

North America: *Alaska*: Very rare in fall (late Aug–early Oct) on Bering Sea islands (3 records from St. Lawrence, 3 from Pribilofs; all since 1999). 1 fall record from w. Aleutians: Attu, 21 Sep 2006. *Wisconsin*: Milwaukee Co., 21 Oct 2006 (*NAB* 61:74; Frank 2007).

Comments: As with numerous Asian landbirds that are being found with increasing regularity in fall on the AK islands, Yellow-browed Warbler appears to be a classic misoriented (reverse?) fall

1st-year
(fall–winter)

Yellow-browed Warbler

duller
individual

vagrant. Its continental (vs. coastal) spring migration and relatively 'inland' breeding range help explain the lack of spring records.

This species is among the most regular Siberian vagrants to reach W Europe in fall, where it appears to be increasing, and there were about 100 records from Iceland through 2006 (mainly mid-Sep to early Nov, most since 1980) and a recent Dec record from the Azores, but we are aware of no records from Greenland. Should one make landfall in the Northeast, it would be difficult to determine an east versus west origin.

The remarkable WI record, a bird carefully observed and described, may represent the tip of the iceberg in terms of Asian vagrants that pass east into the vastness of continental N America every fall but are undetected without geographical features to concentrate them, as occurs on the Pacific coast or, if they make it that far, on the Atlantic seaboard (cf. Siberian Stonechat and Brown Shrike in the Maritimes). Of interest is that the fall of 2006 also produced 2 records of Yellow-browed Warbler from AK, and a bird that presumably overwintered in the Americas: 1 was found in Baja California Sur, Mexico, 25 Mar–7 Apr 2007, likely in the area where it wintered (Mlodinow & Radamaker 2007).

Field Identification: Small, brightly marked *Phylloscopus* with two well-marked pale wing-bars, distinct pale eyebrow, faint pale central crown stripe, and contrasting pale tertial edges.

Similar Species: None regular in N America. Cf. **Pallas's Leaf Warbler**, and discussion by Lehman (2000a) of potentially similar species, especially **Hume's Leaf Warbler** *P. humei*.

Age/Sex/Season: Ages/sexes similar; no seasonal variation. Complete prebasic and partial preformative molts occur before fall migration;

partial prealternate molt on nonbreeding grounds. **1st-year** may average brighter yellowish eyebrow and more distinct pale median crown stripe than adult; in-hand, extremes might be aged by shape of rectrices (see p. 40); in summer, remiges more heavily worn than adult.

Habitat and Behavior: Prefers broad-leaved deciduous woods where moves restlessly, often twitching its wings, but AK vagrants usually have to make do with low herbaceous vegetation. Most common call a loud *swe-eet* with rising inflection; suggests call of Pacific-slope/Cordilleran Flycatcher.

PALLAS'S LEAF WARBLER *Phylloscopus proregulus* 9–10 cm (3.6–4")

Summary: *Alaska*: 1 fall record from Bering Sea islands (2006).

Taxonomy: Monotypic. Also known simply as Pallas's Warbler.

Distribution and Status:

World: Breeds taiga forest zone of E Asia, e. to nw. side of Sea of Okhotsk; winters se. China.

North America: *Alaska*: St. Lawrence, 25–26 Sep 2006.

Comments: The recent AK record of Pallas's Leaf Warbler fits the pattern of reverse migration from the breeding grounds, and the species would have been high on anyone's recent list of predictions, especially given that it is a common species and also a regular and increasing vagrant in W Europe.

Field Identification: Active, kinglet-sized *Phylloscopus* with conspicuous yellowish head stripes, 2 wing-bars, and pale yellow rump best seen when birds hover.

1st-year
(fall–winter)

Pallas's Leaf Warbler

Similar Species: ***Yellow-browed Warbler*** can appear similar if seen from below but is larger with more 'normal' *Phylloscopus* shape, narrower dark eyestripe; yellow rump of Pallas's usually hidden when wings closed. Yellow-browed has at most an indistinct pale central crown stripe.

Age/Sex/Season: Ages/sexes similar; no seasonal variation. Complete prebasic and partial preformative molts occur before fall migration; partial prealternate molt on nonbreeding grounds. ***1st-year***: Wing-bars may average broader and buffier, less yellow, than adult; in-hand, extremes might be aged by shape of rectrices (see p. 40); in summer, remiges more heavily worn than adult.

Habitat and Behavior: Arboreal, but AK vagrants usually have to make do with low herbaceous vegetation. Tiny and active, recalls a kinglet and feeds by hover-gleaning. Most common call a soft nasal *djuee* (P. Holt, pers. comm.).

KAMCHATKA LEAF WARBLER
Phylloscopus examinandus 12–13 cm (4.7–5.2")

Summary: *Alaska*: Rare and intermittent in spring on w. Aleutians; very rare in fall on w. and w-cen. Aleutians. See Taxonomy and Comments, below.

Taxonomy: Monotypic. Traditionally considered a ssp of Arctic Warbler (and often subsumed into the taxon *xanthodryas*), but differs in voice, morphology, and genetics. Herein, Kamchatka Leaf Warbler *P. examinandus* and Japanese Leaf Warbler *P. xanthodryas* (breeding in cen. and s. Japan) are considered specifically distinct from Arctic Warbler *P. borealis*, following Alström et al. (2011).

Distribution and Status:

World: Breeds s. Kamchatka, Sakhalin, Kuril Islands, and n. Japan; wintering grounds not well known, but recorded in Indonesia (Alström et al. 2011).

North America: ***Alaska***: Status unclear, due to confusion with Arctic Warbler (see Taxonomy, above), but 'xanthodryas Arctic Warbler' (including *examinandus*) considered by Gibson & Byrd (2007) to be rare and intermittent in spring (early to mid-Jun) on w. Aleutians, usually in 1s and 2s but with max. 19+ on Attu, 3 Jun 1999. In fall, very rare on w. Aleutians (mid-Sep to mid-Oct) and on w-cen. Aleutians, e. to Amchitka (mid–late Oct).

Comments: Vexed taxonomy and varying identifications of specimens have clouded the status of this cryptic species in Alaska (see Taxonomy, above). Within the traditional species of Arctic Warbler, recent authors have usually merged *examinandus* into *xanthodryas* (e.g., Gibson & Byrd 2007). Specimens from Shemya and Attu, once identified as nominate *borealis* Arctic Warbler (Gibson 1981, following Yamashima 1974,

1st-year
(fall–winter)

spring
(ages similar)

adult fall
(worn)

Kamchatka Leaf Warbler

who merged *examinandus* into *borealis*) have since been re-identified as '*xanthodryas*' (Phillips 1991); we suspect that most or all of these specimens will prove to be *examinandus*, although genetic analysis may be required to establish their identity. Kenyon (1961) was perceptive enough to ascribe his fall specimens from Amchitka to *examinandus*.

We consider Japanese Leaf Warbler (true *xanthodryas*) far less likely to occur in AK than Kamchatka Leaf Warbler (*examinandus*), and provisionally consider all AK records of '*xanthodryas*' to pertain to Kamchatka Leaf Warbler, until proven otherwise.

Spring records in the Aleutians, and perhaps fall records, fit the common pattern of drift vagrancy. Some fall records may also reflect (reverse?) misorientation, and in this respect all vagrant records of 'Arctic Warbler' in the West should be reviewed, to determine whether any might refer to Kamchatka Leaf Warbler versus Arctic Warbler. These records comprise a 1st-year in Baja California Sur, Mexico, 12 Oct 1991 (Pyle & Howell 1993) and 7 fall records (Sep–early Oct, all since 1995) from cen. and s. CA. Without specimens available for genetic analysis, however, specific identity of earlier records may not be possible. Observers finding any future vagrant 'Arctic Warblers' would do well to record any calls, which should enable specific identification. Sadly, however, migrant 'Arctic Warblers' are often silent and many birds seen in the field may not be identifiable given current understanding.

Field Identification: Very similar to Arctic Warbler, and formerly considered conspecific with it (best told by voice).

Similar Species: For recordings of calls and songs see: http://www.slu.se/sv/centrumbildningar-och-projekt/artdatabanken/kontakt1/personal-a-o/per-alstrom/per-alstroms-forskning/arctic-warblers-vocalizations/. *Arctic Warbler* very similar and perhaps not safely separated in the field except by voice, but bill of Arctic averages smaller, less broad-based, and p10 averages shorter than tips of primary coverts, versus averaging longer in Kamchatka (Saitoh et al. 2008). Typical call of Arctic a high, clipped, metallic *tziit*, and song a fairly even-paced, buzzy ringing trill, both quite different from Kamchatka. *Japanese Leaf Warbler* also best distinguished by voice, but averages a brighter yellow wash to face and underparts, which might draw attention. Call distinctly lower-pitched than Kamchatka, a

slightly buzzy *dzzrt*, vaguely suggesting call of Canyon Wren; song of paired, ringing notes slower-paced than Kamchatka.

Age/Sex/Season: Ages/sexes similar; no seasonal variation. Molts not well known but presumed similar to Arctic Warbler, although details of that species' molt remain to be elucidated (Howell 2010a). In fall, before migration, adult molts body feathers, sometimes some tertials and rectrices; on wintering grounds, both adult and 1st-year appear to undergo a complete molt. *1st-year*: In fall, averages brighter overall than adult and in fresher plumage; in spring-summer, 1st-year not known to be separable from adult.

Habitat and Behavior: Much as Arctic Warbler, foraging in bushes and trees when available. Call a harsh, gravelly, slightly metallic *chrrt* or *chrrit*, distinctly longer, lower, and more rolled than Arctic Warbler call, vaguely suggesting a metallic Common Yellowthroat call. Song, possible with spring migrants, is a fairly rapid-paced, rhythmic, ringing series of slightly buzzy, disyllabic notes, *ch'tih ch'tih … .*

WAGTAILS AND PIPITS (5 species)

A largely Old World family of mostly open country species, with numerous taxonomic and identification issues. In the New World we consider 2 wagtails and 3 pipits as rare birds. We do not treat Eastern Yellow Wagtail and White Wagtail (including Black-backed Wagtail), which breed in w. AK but are decidedly rare birds in N America away from AK. Gray Wagtail and the 3 pipits occur mainly in AK, with drift vagrants in spring and misoriented (reverse?) migrants in fall, whose occurrence is perhaps compounded by drift. Gray Wagtail and Olive-backed Pipit have also occurred along the W Coast in fall, s. to CA, and the spring Olive-backed Pipit in NV seems likely to have wintered in the New World. The 2 records of Citrine Wagtail presumably represent misoriented and perhaps drift-assisted fall–winter vagrants from E Asia.

CITRINE WAGTAIL *Motacilla citreola* 16–17 cm (6.3–6.7")

Summary: *Mississippi*: 1 winter record (1992). *British Columbia*: 1 late fall–winter record (2012/2013).
Taxonomy: 2 ssp, separable in male breeding plumage (Alström & Mild 2003): nominate *citreola*

1st-summer ♂

pale
surround

1st-summer ♀

dark

adult ♂ breeding,
variation

1st-year variation
(fall–winter)

bold
wing-bars

dark lores

pinkish base

adult ♀
(adult ♂ nonbreeding similar)

Eastern Yellow Wagtail

1st-year
(fall–winter)

Citrine Wagtail

(breeding N and W Asia) has grayish back with black band across nape, *calcarata* (breeding S Asia) has blackish back and nape.

Distribution and Status:

World: Breeds taiga, tundra, and steppes of Cen and E Asia, e. to around 125°E; winters mainly from Indian subcontinent e. to s. China.

North America: ***Mississippi***: Oktibbeha Co., 31 Jan–1 Feb 1992 (age uncertain). ***British Columbia***: Vancouver Island, 14 Nov 2012–25 Mar 2013 (1st-year; http://bcbirdalert.blogspot.com).

Comments: Of all the Asian passerine records in N America, the MS record perhaps gives the fewest clues as to origin and route (but see below). Photos of the bird show a strongly yellow face, suggesting it may have been an adult, which is even more remarkable. However, given that Citrine Wagtail and yellow wagtails hybridize (Alström & Mild 2003:315), and that photos of the MS bird (*Birding* 27:367–368,) show an apparently

whiter throat, faint dusky necklace, and duskier underparts (all features more typical of yellow wagtails than of Citrine), we are uncertain that a hybrid can be eliminated. The short mid-winter stay also seems surprising, but the bird may have been otherwise overlooked wintering near to where it happened to be seen for 2 days.

Only 10 fall records (Sep–Nov) of Citrine Wagtail from Iceland through 2006, and 1 from the Azores (Sep 2009), suggest a transatlantic origin is unlikely. The species is rare in Japan and unrecorded in w. Alaska, which might argue against an E Asian origin. However, prevailing N Hemisphere weather patterns make it considerably easier for birds to move w. to e., and there is ample evidence that birds from E Asia can travel well to the e. and s. across N America. Moreover, a Citrine Wagtail in w. N America could be easily overlooked as the much more expected Eastern Yellow Wagtail, and not surprisingly the MS bird was initially identified as a yellow wagtail (*AB* 46:278).

As this book went to press, a Citrine Wagtail was found on Vancouver Island, BC, which lends support to the idea of an E Asian origin for the MS bird. The BC wagtail, along with a Little Bunting on SE Farallon Island, CA, 14 Nov 2012 (J. Tietz, pers. comm.), were found following strong storm systems spanning the N Pacific. The wagtail and bunting are both interior breeders that would need to misorient considerably before they could be drift-assisted across the N Pacific. Might lingering, misoriented migrants in E Asia head offshore and be swept direct across the N Pacific, as with Nov–Dec records of Red-flanked Bluetails in CA? Alternatively, perhaps some such birds arrived earlier in the fall in N America and lingered undetected until bad weather forced them s. into areas with more birders.

Field Identification: Small wagtail, similar in size and proportions to Eastern Yellow Wagtail (and to Western Yellow Wagtail *M. flava*, unrecorded but possible in N America). It should be distinguished from both with care.

Similar Species: Breeding adults distinctive (with gray backs), but other plumages can be very similar to yellow wagtails; and hybrid Citrine × yellow in nonbreeding plumage not always safely told from Citrine.

1st-winter ***Eastern (and Western) Yellow Wagtail*** browner above with dark lores, more solidly dark cheeks lacking pale surround at rear, distinct pale base to lower mandible, narrower wing-bars.

1st-winter ***White Wagtail*** slightly larger and bulkier, with variable black bib, distinctly different calls.

Age/Sex/Season: Ages/sexes differ; seasonal variation pronounced in males. Only nominate *citreola* considered here. Complete prebasic and partial preformative molts occur before fall migration; partial to incomplete prealternate molt (can include tail on 1st-years) on wintering grounds. ***Adult male***: Solid yellow head with blackish nape band in spring–summer (some have solid white wing panel); molts to female-like pattern in winter (when sexes rarely separable, although male averages brighter and more extensive yellow on face). ***Adult female***: Face and throat yellow with grayish crown and cheeks. ***1st-year***: In fall–early winter, both sexes resemble nonbreeding female but lack yellow on face and chest; all juv coverts often retained, hence no

molt contrast in fall. 1st-summer resembles adult of respective sex, although males can have some dark on face, suggesting adult female but usually with some blackish on nape and less neatly defined cheek patch. Some 1st-summers can be aged if very worn juv wing coverts are retained, but all ages can have 2 generations of greater coverts in spring.

Habitat and Behavior: Much like yellow wagtails. Common flight call a buzzy, descending *dzeep*, perhaps not safely separable from call of Eastern Yellow Wagtail but often a little longer with a buzzier ending.

GRAY WAGTAIL *Motacilla cinerea* 18–20 cm (7–7.8")

Summary: *Alaska*: On w. Aleutians, rare and intermittent in spring, exceptional in fall. On cen. Aleutians and Bering Sea islands, exceptional in spring and fall. *Northwest Territories*: 1 fall record (2009). *Pacific States and Provinces*: 2 fall records from BC (1991, 2004); 1 fall record from CA (1988).

Taxonomy: 6 ssp, 3 restricted to islands; none certainly identifiable in the field. N American specimens are referred to ne. ssp *robusta*, which averages shorter-tailed and darker above than nominate *cinerea* of W Europe.

Distribution and Status:

World: Breeds extensively in Old World from E Atlantic Islands across temperate and mid-latitude Eurasia to ne. Russia (Kamchatka); winters from Europe and E Africa to the Indian subcontinent, SE Asia, and Indonesia.

North America: *Alaska*: In spring, rare and intermittent (mid-May to mid-Jun) on w. Aleutians, mainly singles and usually males, max. 4 birds on Shemya, 16–17 May 2001; exceptional (late May to mid-Jun; 4 records) on cen. Aleutians and Bering Sea islands. In fall (late Sep to mid-Oct) single records from w. and cen. Aleutians and Pribilofs. *Northwest Territories*: At sea, about 78°N 136°W, 370 km nw. of Prince Patrick Island, 4–5 Sep 2009 (C. Eckert, pers. comm.). *Pacific Provinces and States*: Monterey Co., CA, 9–10 Oct 1988; Westminster Co., BC, 8 Nov 1991; sw. Vancouver Island, 26 Oct 2004.

Comments: Gray Wagtail shows the spring drift vagrancy pattern typical of migrants moving n. up the Kuril Island chain. The paucity of fall records is not easily explained, although a similar pattern is seen in other species that are much commoner in spring, such as Eyebrowed

♂ breeding

1st-year
(fall–winter)

pinkish legs
and feet

white
underwing
stripe

♀

Gray Wagtail

Thrush and Siberian Rubythroat. It may be that in fall these species are better at gauging weather conditions for departure, and thus less prone to drift displacement, or perhaps their fall migration route is less coastal; but we have no data to support either of these conjectures.

The remarkable NWT record, of a bird photographed on a ship well north of the Arctic Circle, might conceivably refer to a bird coming from either east or west; its location does not lie far off a reverse-migration track from the British Isles continued through Iceland and over northern Greenland.

Given 36 records from Iceland through 2006, mostly late Sep–Nov, an occurrence on the E Coast seems a slim possibility. A resident ssp on the Azores masks the movement of migrants there, and there are no Barbados records.

Field Identification: Elegant, long-tailed wagtail with yellow-green rump and bright yellow undertail coverts.

Similar Species: None, if seen well. Overhead in flight note longer tail than White Wagtail, distinct whitish underwing stripe; yellow undertail coverts apparent given a reasonable view.

Age/Sex/Season: Ages/sexes differ; seasonal variation most pronounced in males. Complete prebasic and partial preformative molts occur before fall migration; partial prealternate molt on wintering grounds. *Adult male*: Solid black throat in spring–summer, molting to buffy white in winter; underparts extensively bright yellow. *Adult female*: Throat mottled black and white in spring–summer, molting to buffy white in winter; underparts in winter average less extensively

yellow than male. *1st-year*: Both sexes resemble nonbreeding female but average buffier below; some 1st-fall birds can be aged by molt contrast in greater coverts and tertials (see p. 36). 1st-summer male resembles adult male or has some whitish in throat, and thus difficult to separate from adult female.

Habitat and Behavior: Favors moving water, and wags entire rear end as it walks. Flight strong and undulating, similar to White Wagtail. Common flight calls are a sharp *tik* or *tchik!* and a disyllabic *t'sik* or *ch'sik!* Calls higher and sharper than (usually disyllabic) flight calls of most taxa in the White Wagtail complex (including *alba*, *ocularis*, and *lugens*, the only ssp of White Wagtails recorded in N America), but very similar to, and perhaps not distinguishable from, *M. [alba] leucopsis* of E Asia.

TREE PIPIT *Anthus trivialis* 14–15.5 cm (5.5–6.2")

Summary: *Alaska*: Exceptional in spring and fall on Bering Sea islands; 1 spring record from w. mainland (1972).

Taxonomy: 2 ssp, not separable in the field (Alström & Mild 2003).

Distribution and Status:

World: Breeds in temperate and boreal zones from W Europe e. across Eurasia to around 140°E; winters mainly in sub-Saharan Africa and the Indian subcontinent.

North America: *Alaska*: Cape Prince of Wales, 23 Jun 1972; St. Lawrence, 6 Jun 1995 and 21–27 Sep 2002.

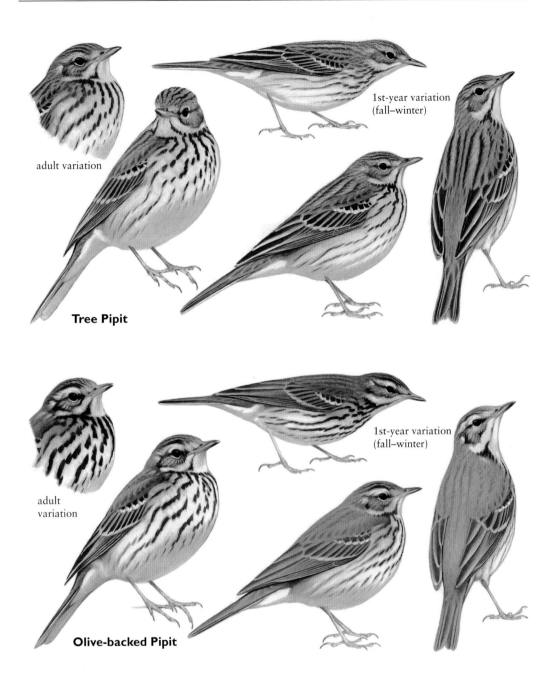

1st-year variation
(fall–winter)

adult variation

Tree Pipit

1st-year variation
(fall–winter)

adult
variation

Olive-backed Pipit

Comments: The inland and relatively westerly breeding range of Tree Pipit would appear to predispose it more to fall (reverse) misorientation than to spring occurrence in N America, but as yet there is only 1 fall record in contrast to 2 late spring records, the latter presumably overshoots from the interior of ne. Russia. We suspect fall birds could be overlooked, perhaps compounded by flight calls that might lead to them being passed off as Olive-backed Pipits. Moreover, if fall migrants put on substantial fat for long migration legs (cf. Olive-backed Pipit) then misoriented migrants might have sufficient reserves to easily over-fly the Bering Sea. Brazil (1991) listed 3 records from Japan with date, 1 in early Feb (presumably wintering) and 2 in late April.

There were only 21 records from Iceland through 2006, scattered between May and early Nov, and a single fall Azores record through 2011, suggesting an E Coast record is unlikely.

Field Identification: Small, streaky, tree-loving pipit with a short, curved hind claw. See illustration on p. 319.

Similar Species: Cf. *Olive-backed Pipit*.

Meadow Pipit (unrecorded in N America; breeding N Europe, Iceland, and e. Greenland, wintering N Africa and Middle East) very similar in plumage to Tree Pipit but favors open rough grassland and has very different call, a repeated high, slightly squeaky *tsit* and *tsi-sit* or *pi-pit* (strongly recalling American Pipit but perhaps a bit squeakier). Also note bolder flank streaks and long hind claw (difficult to see in field) of Meadow Pipit. Meadow has weaker, less sweeping flight than Tree Pipit and overhead tends to look relatively short winged and long tailed.

Age/Sex/Season: Ages/sexes similar; no seasonal variation. Complete prebasic and partial preformative molts occur before fall migration; partial prealternate molts occur on wintering grounds. Some **1st-fall** birds may be aged by molt contrasts in greater or median coverts (see p. 319), but in spring both adults and 1st-years can show molt contrasts.

Habitat and Behavior: Prefers open grassy areas adjacent to trees or within open woodland; generally skulking when on the ground. Flies into trees or bushes when flushed, where it walks readily along branches. Most common call a buzzy *tzzz*, given mainly in flight; very similar to call of Olive-backed Pipit but averages shorter, less hoarse.

OLIVE-BACKED PIPIT *Anthus hodgsoni*
14.5–16 cm (5.7–6.3")

Summary: *Alaska*: On w. Aleutians, uncommon but intermittent in spring, very rare in fall. On Bering Sea islands, very rare in spring and fall. Single 1998 records in spring on cen. Aleutians and in summer on sw. mainland. *Nevada and California*: 1 spring record in NV (1967); 1 fall record in CA (1998).

Taxonomy: 2 ssp, not certainly separable in the field. N American specimens are referred to n. ssp *yunnanensis*, which differs from nominate *hodgsoni* of S-Cen Asia in averaging less distinct dark streaking above.

Distribution and Status:

World: Breeds boreal and temperate forests of Cen and E Asia, e. to Kamchatka and w. Chukotka; winters Indian subcontinent e. to SE Asia and Philippines.

North America: On w. Aleutians, intermittent in spring (mid-May to mid-Jun), very rare in fall (mid-Sep to early Oct); usually singles or small groups, but some larger counts, exceptionally 225 on Attu, 17 May 1998. Probably nested in 1998 on Attu following unprecedented spring numbers, with 5 young in active preformative molt collected in late Aug. On cen. Aleutians, only 1 spring record, 19 May 1998. On Bering Sea islands, very rare in spring (mid-May to mid-Jun) and fall (early–late Sep). 1 summer record from sw. mainland, 27 Jul 1998. *Nevada and California*: Washoe Co., NV, 16 May 1967 (male); SE Farallon Island, CA, 26–29 Sep 1998 (1st-year).

Comments: Olive-backed Pipit is a classic spring drift migrant to the w. Aleutians, given its migration n. up the Kuril chain; yet on the cen. Aleutians there is but a single record, and it is a very rare drift-overshoot in spring to the Bering Sea islands.

The relatively paucity of fall records from Bering Sea islands is notable, in contrast, say, to Pechora Pipit. This may reflect a stronger southward fall orientation by Olive-backed Pipit relative to 'regular' reverse-migrants to the Bering Sea, perhaps in combination with the first leg of its fall migration being long and nonstop, such that most misoriented birds would have the fat reserves to overfly the Bering Sea easily. Olive-backed Pipit records from the nw. Hawaiian islands indicate significant overwater capabilities, and it has been suggested that fall records from CA and Baja California, Mexico, of strong-flying species such as Olive-backed Pipit, Red-throated Pipit, White Wagtail, and Arctic Warbler could have involved weather-assisted, misoriented, or drifted birds 'cutting across' the N Pacific rather than following the N American mainland coast all the way around (R. A. Erickson et al. 2001; Sullivan 2004; and see p. 11).

The spring record from NV was presumably of a bird that wintered in the Americas, and its inland location is in accord with an 'interior' route being more typical than a coastal route for migrants moving n. in spring out of Mexico (R. A. Erickson et al. 2001).

Field Identification: Slim, tree-loving pipit with faintly streaked back, rather distinctive face pattern, and relatively short, strongly curved hind claw. See illustration on p. 319.

Similar Species: Should be distinguished with care from other small pipits, most of which differ in longer hind claw (difficult to see in the field), prominently streaked back and/or face pattern.

Tree Pipit has more strongly streaked back and less pronounced face pattern; tertials have more distinct, pale buff edgings (vs. duller olive), and greater coverts edged whitish (vs. buff); dark flank streaking typically finer. Calls similar, but Tree Pipit call averages a little hoarser and more drawn-out.

Age/Sex/Season: Ages/sexes similar; no seasonal variation. Complete prebasic and partial preformative molts occur before fall migration; partial prealternate molts occur on wintering grounds. Some ***1st-fall*** birds may be aged by molt contrasts in greater or median coverts (see p. 36), but in spring both adults and 1st-years can show molt contrasts.

Habitat and Behavior: Typical tree pipit, favoring open woodland if available, perhaps especially conifers; when flushed, flies into trees and shrubs if available and walks readily along branches. Common flight call a high buzzy *tzzz*;

may suggest flight call of Red-throated Pipit but shorter and buzzier; lacks slightly explosive start and fading out of Red-throated.

PECHORA PIPIT *Anthus gustavi* 14–15 cm (5.5–5.8″)

Summary: *Alaska*: On w. Aleutians, very rare in spring. On Bering Sea islands, exceptional in spring, rare in fall.

Taxonomy: 2 ssp, not separable in the field by sight, but vocalizations suggest they may be specifically distinct (Alström & Mild 2003). N American specimens are of widespread nominate *gustavi* (including *stejnegeri*), which averages slightly paler and more rufescent above than *menzbieri* of ne. China and se. Russia.

Distribution and Status:

World: Breeds in taiga and shrubby tundra across n. Russia, e. to Bering Strait and Commander Islands; with disjunct population in ne. China and se. Russia; winters in Philippines and n. Indonesia.

North America: *Alaska*: On w. Aleutians, very rare in spring (mid-May to early Jun), mainly singles but max. 9 on Attu, 18 May 1998; no fall

Red-throated Pipit

no projection

primary projection

1st-year (fall–winter)

all plumages similar

Pechora Pipit

1st-year (fall–winter)

records. On Bering Sea islands, exceptional in spring (early to mid-Jun; 2 records, both from St. Lawrence but none since 1970s) and rare in fall (late Aug–Sep, mainly from St. Lawrence).

Comments: Pechora Pipit is one of several species that show a distinct dichotomy between spring drift vagrants to the w. Aleutians (with fewer reaching Bering Sea islands) versus misoriented (reverse?) fall migrants recorded only from the Bering Sea islands.

Field Identification: Small, well-marked, and notoriously skulking pipit.

Similar Species: Main concern is separation from **Red-throated Pipit**, which shares streaked rump but is slightly larger and less skulking, with no primary projection.

1st-year Red-throated has wing tips covered by tertials when at rest; finer bill; less prominent whitish 'braces'; less prominent white wing-bars; and underparts lacking the contrast between buffy breast and whitish belly often shown by Pechora. Call of Red-throated very different: a high, thin, explosive *tseeee* that tails off. Flushed Red-throated often flies some distance, and high, whereas Pechora tends to make lower and shorter flights.

Age/Sex/Season: Ages/sexes similar; no seasonal variation. Complete prebasic and partial preformative molts occur before fall migration; partial prealternate molts occur on wintering grounds. Some **1st-fall** birds may be aged by molt contrasts in greater coverts (see p. 36), but in spring both adults and 1st-years may show molt contrasts.

Habitat and Behavior: A skulking pipit, favoring wet grassy areas. Often silent when flushed, but most common flight call a distinctive, sharp, slightly buzzy chip, *dzep* or *dzip!*

EURASIAN SKYLARK *Alauda arvensis*
17–19 cm (6.7–7.5")

Summary: *Alaska*: Rare and intermittent in spring (especially) and fall on w. Aleutians; very rare in both seasons on cen. Aleutians and Bering Sea Islands; very rare in spring on e. Aleutians. Some remain into summer, and has bred on Pribilofs, probably also on w. Aleutians. ***British Columbia***: 1 late fall record (1991). ***California***: 1 (multi-year) winter record.

Taxonomy: 13 ssp, varying slightly in size and plumage tones but not safely separable in the field (cf. Lees & Ball 2011). AK specimens are referred to relatively large and dark ne. ssp

pekinensis and the CA bird was also considered to show characters of one of the ne. ssp. Introduced birds on Vancouver Island, BC, are from westernmost ssp *arvensis*, which averages paler above than *pekinensis*, but ssp differences confounded by considerable individual variation and plumage wear. It has been suggested that Eurasian Skylark comprises e. and w. clades that might best be treated as 2 species (Zink et al. 2008). Sometimes known simply as Sky Lark.

Distribution and Status:

World: Breeds from W Europe and NW Africa e. across temperate and mid-latitude Eurasia e. to ne. Russia (Kamchatka). Winters from w. and s. edges of breeding range, s. to Middle East, n. India, and s. China. Introduced to Vancouver Island, BC (whence spread to breed on San Juan Island, WA, 1960–1998), and elsewhere in the world.

North America: ***Alaska***: On w. Aleutians, rare and intermittent in spring (late Apr–May; some staying into summer and breeding suspected), and fall (mid-Sep to mid-Oct). On cen. Aleutians and Bering Sea islands, very rare in spring (May to early Jun; some staying into summer, with breeding confirmed once on Pribilofs; Baicich et al. 1996) and fall (mid-Sep to early Oct). On e. Aleutians, 2 late May–early Jun records in 2002 of up to 5 singing males. AK records involve singles and small groups, max. 10 on Attu, 17 May 1999. ***British Columbia***: Queen Charlotte Islands, 20–21 Nov 1991 (*AB* 46:141). ***California***: Marin Co., 16 Dec 1978–19 Feb 1979, and for 6 winters thereafter (late Oct–Feb).

Comments: N American records comprise classic spring drift vagrants (unlike may obligate insectivores, skylarks are relatively early spring migrants) and presumably misoriented fall birds, with the returning CA bird being of particular note. (Where did it spend the summers?) The AK islands offer abundant suitable nesting habitat for skylarks, which is not the case for many spring overshoots, and on occasion birds have occurred east through the chain to almost within sight of the Alaska Peninsula.

On Vancouver Island, BC, there are several records away from known breeding areas, which may represent vagrant *pekinensis* or wandering *arvensis*; 2 birds on the Olympic Peninsula, WA, 23 Dec 1998–1 Jan 1999, may also have been vagrant *pekinensis* (Wahl et al. 2005). We suspect, however, that such records more likely involve *arvensis*, although there is so much

variation

fresh

worn

Eurasian Skylark

habitat for this inconspicuous (in fall and winter) species in coastal parts of Pacific Northwest that it may be more regular than the record indicates. A late Nov 1991 skylark on the Queen Charlotte Islands, in company with American and Red-throated pipits, seems likely to have been a wild bird, and might represent the tip of the vagrancy iceberg in w. N America.

Much as with the larger and much more conspicuous Northern Lapwing, skylarks are well-known for their 'escape flights' from cold weather in Europe and might on occasion reach NL or other areas in the Northeast. There were 107 records of skylarks from Iceland through 2006, and 50 or so from the Azores through 2011 (many of multiples), mostly mid-Oct to mid-Nov in Iceland and late fall–winter in the Azores. There's even a record from Bermuda (admittedly in 1850, and in mid-Jun). Eurasian Skylarks are clearly capable of significant overwater movements but they favor habitats that are abundant, and also are likely to show up at times when observer numbers are low.

Field Identification: Overall brownish, streaky, terrestrial songbird with erectile crest and fairly slender bill; note narrow white trailing edge to wings.

Similar Species: Nothing very similar in N America, although CA bird initially confused with Smith's Longspur, reflecting how little was known in those days about the identification of birds from distant geographic regions.

Age/Sex/Season: Ages differ; sexes similar; no seasonal variation. Prebasic and complete preformative molts occur in late summer–fall, prior to migration; no prealternate molt. *Juv* lacks distinct crest, has whitish-tipped scaling to mottled upperparts, and dark-spotted (vs. streaked) breast. Attains adult appearance by complete preformative molt in 1st fall.

Habitat and Behavior: Typical lark, creeping and running well on the ground. Flushed birds often fly a short distance, calling, and drop to the ground with tail slightly spread. Direct flight strong and slightly undulating; commonly a diurnal migrant. Common flight calls are variations on a dryly musical, rolling *dreeet*. Famous song is given high overhead in hovering flight, a prolonged series of bubbling, whistled, and warbling notes. Numerous spring records from w. Aleutians and Pribilofs have involved singing and apparently territorial males, and other spring vagrants may give brief song flights.

OLD WORLD BUNTINGS (9 species)
The Old World equivalent of New World Sparrows, with similar behavior but on average more skulking and elusive than typical N American species. Most buntings have white tail sides, often striking in flight, which would draw attention. Identification points include overall size, bill size and pattern, head pattern, and general plumage patterns. Like North American sparrows, prebasic and preformative

molts of most species occur mainly in late summer and fall, prior to fall migration but a few species (mainly of drier breeding habitats) molt at staging grounds and on the wintering grounds.

In N America, all 9 species have been recorded only from the West, almost exclusively from the Alaskan islands. Spring records (mid-May to Jun) mainly reflect drift and overshooting, whereas most fall records (late Aug to mid-Nov) likely reflect misorientation, at times compounded by drift. In spring, 7 species have been recorded, 5 of them only or mainly in spring; in fall, 7 species have also been recorded, 3 of them only or mainly in fall; 2 species (Little and Rustic) have also occurred s. to CA in fall and winter. Of the longer-distance migrants, 2 other species may be candidates for fall records in w. N America, namely Pallas's and Yellow-breasted, although both are rare in AK. There are in fact 2 (unaccepted) records of Yellow-breasted Bunting from CA, in late winter and fall, both of which are plausible as vagrants in both time and space.

PINE BUNTING *Emberiza leucocephalos*
16–17.5 cm (6.3–6.8")

Summary: *Alaska*: Exceptional in late fall on w. Aleutians and Bering Sea islands.

Taxonomy: 2 ssp, not known to be separable in the field. N American specimen referred to widespread nominate *leucocephalos*, males of which average narrower black head stripes than *fronto* of cen. China. Hybridizes with Yellowhammer *E. citrinella* in cen. Russia.

Distribution and Status:

World: Breeds boreal and temperate forest zones of Cen and E Asia, e. to around 150°E; winters mainly sw. China, w. locally to Middle East.

♂ worn
(spring–summer)

♂ fresh (fall)

♀

dull 1st-year ♀
(fall–winter)

Pine Bunting

North America: *Alaska*: Attu, 18–19 Nov 1985, 6 Oct 1993; Pribilofs, 2–4 Oct 2012 (St. Paul Island Tour, photos).

Comments: The relative scarcity of Pine Bunting in w. AK is not surprising given that it's both a relatively short-distance and late season migrant, at a time when few observers are present on the AK islands. All records have been of males, and the Nov bird may well have arrived some time before being found, perhaps in Oct (Wagner 1990).

Field Identification: Fairly large, long tailed bunting with rufous rump, white tail sides, and, in all plumages except 1st-winter female, chestnut streaking below.

Similar Species: Confusion possible in fall with 1st-year female **Rustic Bunting**, which is smaller and shorter-tailed, with crown almost always peaked at rear; also note Rustic's brownish to rusty (not gray) nape, small whitish spot on hind cheeks, finer dark streaking below, different call.

Age/Sex/Season: Ages similar, sexes differ; distinct seasonal variation through plumage wear. Complete prebasic and partial preformative molts occur before fall migration. *Male*: Bold black and chestnut head and throat pattern (extensively veiled grayish in fresh fall plumage).

Female: Duller head pattern, throat whitish overall. *1st-year*: Resembles adult of respective sex but retains juv flight feathers, which are more tapered than on adult, and in spring–summer relatively more worn than on adult. 1st-winter female can have dark brownish streaking below.

Habitat and Behavior: Ground feeding, near trees and shrubs if available; usually flies into trees when flushed. Calls include a slightly wet, clicking chirp, often in short series, and a nasal, slightly buzzy *chieh* in flight.

YELLOW-BROWED BUNTING *Emberiza chrysophrys* 14–15 cm (5.5–5.8")

Summary: *Alaska*: 1 fall record from Bering Sea islands (2007).

Taxonomy: Monotypic.

Distribution and Status:

World: Breeds taiga zone of e. Russia, e. to around 130°E; winters se. China.

North America: *Alaska*: St. Lawrence, 15 Sep 2007 (possibly 1st-year male).

Comments: As with numerous fall records of Asian passerines on the Bering Sea islands, the Yellow-browed Bunting record is consistent with a misoriented (reverse?) migrant.

1st-year
(fall–winter)

♂ breeding

♀
(♂ nonbreeding
similar)

Yellow-browed Bunting

1st-year (fall–winter)

Field Identification: Handsome, fairly small bunting with boldly marked head pattern, yellowish eyebrow, fine dark streaking below, white tail sides.

Similar Species: None in N America, but cf. White-throated Sparrow from behind.

Age/Sex/Season: Ages differ slightly; sexes differ; slight seasonal variation through plumage wear. Complete prebasic and partial preformative molts occur before fall migration; limited prealternate molt on winter grounds. *Male*: Cheeks and crown sides black (veiled brownish in fresh fall plumage, and thus resembling female), central crown stripe white. *Female*: Cheeks gray-brown with blackish frame, crown sides blackish brown, central crown stripe buffy white. *1st-year*: Resembles adult female but retains juv flight feathers, which are more tapered than on adult, and in spring–summer relatively more worn than on adult. 1st-year female averages duller and browner head markings than adult; 1st-year male averages blacker head markings than female, with whitish central crown stripe.

Habitat and Behavior: Favors woodland edges and grassy thickets. Typical *Emberiza* bunting but keeps more to cover. Most common call a piercing *zick*, recalling Little Bunting.

LITTLE BUNTING *Emberiza pusilla* 12–13 cm (4.7–5.2″)

Summary: *Alaska*: In fall, rare on Bering Sea islands, exceptional on w. Aleutians. 1 spring record from Bering Sea islands (2008). *California*: 2 fall records (1991, 2002).

Taxonomy: Monotypic.

Distribution and Status:

World: Breeds shrubby tundra and taiga zones from NE Europe across Eurasia to ne. Russia (cen. Chukotka); winters mainly SE Asia n. to e. China.

North America: *Alaska*: In fall, rare on Bering Sea islands (late Aug–early Oct; almost annual on St. Lawrence in recent years) and exceptional on w. Aleutians (early–late Sep; 3 records); also 1 fall record from a ship in Chukchi Sea, 6 Sep 1970 (1st-year). 1 spring record: St. Lawrence, 2–4 Jun 2008. *California*: 2 fall records: San Diego Co., 21–24 Oct 1991 (1st-year), SE Farallon Island, 27–28 Sep 2002.

Comments: Little Bunting breeds only a few hundred km to the w. of the Bering Sea, and one would think spring migrants might overshoot more than the single record suggests. However, the species is a rare migrant in Japan and presumably most northward movement is w. of the Sea of Okhotsk; hence, no drift vagrancy to the w. Aleutians. The large number of fall records fit with the theory of misoriented (reverse?) migration, aided by the species' being generally common. In addition to the 2 records from CA there is 1 from Mexico's Baja California Peninsula, 8 Oct 2008 (1st-year, likely female; Radamaker & Powell 2010).

There were only 7 records of Little Bunting from Iceland through 2003 (all but one in

(♂ nonbreeding similar)

♀

1st-year (fall–winter)

♂ breeding

Little Bunting

Oct–Nov), suggesting an E Coast record from that direction would be unlikely. Given its relatively long-distance migration, however, it is tempting to suggest this species might be the next 'least unlikely' candidate for an occurrence in the Northeast, following on the heels of Brown Shrike and Siberian Stonechat.

Field Identification: Small bunting with small, rather pointed bill, rufous face, and prominent, narrow whitish eye-ring.

Similar Species: None if well seen, but always beware other possibilities, such as Chestnut-eared Bunting, which can resemble Little if views are poor.

Age/Sex/Season: Ages/sexes similar; little seasonal variation through plumage wear. Complete prebasic and partial preformative molts occur before fall migration; limited prealternate molt reported in late winter. **Male**: Averages brighter than female, with center of crown and cheeks deep chestnut to rufous, lateral crown stripes solidly black, chin rufous; head pattern veiled with buff and grayish fringes in fresh fall plumage. **Female**: Averages duller than male,

lateral crown stripes blackish to blackish brown, chin often whitish. **1st-year**: Resembles adult of respective sex (with male brighter than female in 1st fall) but retains juv flight feathers, which are more tapered than on adult, and in spring–summer relatively more worn than on adult; some have molt limits in greater coverts and tertials.

Habitat and Behavior: Favors shrubby woodland, adjacent brushy areas. Feeds on the ground and in trees; often flushes into trees or shrubs. Common flight call a sharp *tsit*, very similar to flight call of Rustic Bunting.

RUSTIC BUNTING *Emberiza rustica*
13–14.5 cm (5.2–5.7")

Summary: *Alaska*: On w. Aleutians, uncommon and intermittent in spring, very rare in fall. On cen. Aleutians and Bering Sea Islands, very rare in spring and fall. On AK mainland, exceptional or very rare in fall–winter. *Pacific Provinces and States*: Very rare, late fall–spring.
Taxonomy: 2 ssp, not separable in the field. N American specimens are referred to e. ssp

♀ breeding

♂ breeding

♀ breeding

♂ fresh (fall)

1st-year
(fall–winter)

1st-year
(fall–winter)

Rustic Bunting

latifascia, males of which differ from widespread Eurasian *rustica* in averaging blacker head markings and broader rufous chest band.

Status and Distribution:

World: Breeds boreal forest zone from NE Europe, e. across Eurasia to ne. Russia (Kamchatka and cen. Chukotka); winters mainly Japan to e. China.

North America: *Alaska*: On w. Aleutians, uncommon and intermittent in spring (late Apr to mid-Jun, mainly mid-May to early Jun), usually singles or groups up to 8 birds, but exceptionally 193 on Attu, 17 May 1998; very rare in fall (mid-Sep to mid-Oct). On cen. Aleutians and Bering Sea islands, very rare in spring (mid-May to mid-Jun) and fall (mid-Sep to late Oct). Elsewhere in AK, very rare in the se. in late fall (late Oct–Nov, 1 remaining to early May) and single winter records (Dec–Mar) from cen. and sw. AK. *Pacific Provinces and States*: About 15 records s. to n. CA, all single birds during late Oct–late Apr, with most during late Nov–late Feb. *Saskatchewan*: 1 winter record, Dec 2009–Feb 2010 (*NAB* 64:284).

Comments: Rustic Bunting is a common breeder on Kamchatka and a regular spring drift migrant to the w. Aleutians, with smaller numbers being carried by weather systems to the Bering Sea Islands and cen. Aleutians.

Unlike most bunting species recorded on the Bering Sea islands, Rustic appears much rarer there in fall than spring, with only single Pribilofs and St. Lawrence records (both mid–late Sep). But this may be an artifact of its late migration, cf. relatively numerous fall and winter records s. to CA, indicating that fall misorientation occurs regularly.

Winter records have included 2 possible returning birds, in WA (1986/1987 and 1988/1989) and se. AK (2009 and 2010). The record from SK is the only record east of the Cascades/Sierras but others seem quite possible, cf. Siberian Accentor and Brambling (Fig. 19 on p. 17). The winter 1990/1991 season, when 2 wintering Rustic Buntings were found (in AK and BC) was exceptional in the Northwest for Bramblings (which were found as far s. as cen. CA), suggesting a possible link in late fall movements between these 2 species, at least in that year.

Field Identification: Handsome bunting with peaked nape, rusty streaking below, whitish wing-bars, extensively pinkish base to bill, and white tail sides.

Similar Species: Distinctive, but especially with fall birds cf. Yellow-browed Bunting, Reed Bunting, Pine Bunting, Little Bunting.

Age/Sex/Season: Ages differ slightly; sexes differ; distinct seasonal variation through plumage wear. Complete prebasic and partial preformative molts occur before fall migration; possibly a limited prealternate molt. *Male*: Bold black-and-white head pattern and chestnut neck sides (extensively veiled brownish and buff in fresh fall plumage). *Female*: Head pattern duller, crown gray-brown, and cheeks streaked blackish. *1st-year*: Resembles adult of respective sex but retains juv flight feathers, which are more tapered than on adult, and in spring–summer relatively more worn than on adult. 1st-winter female can have dark reddish-brown streaking below.

Habitat and Behavior: Favors damp brush, open woodland understory and edge; winter vagrants have associated with *Zonotrichia* and other N American sparrows. Typical *Emberiza* bunting. Feeds on the ground; flushes to trees and shrubs if available. Common flight call a sharp *tsit*.

YELLOW-THROATED BUNTING
Emberiza elegans 15–16 cm (5.8–6.3")

Summary: *Alaska*: 1 spring record from w. Aleutians (1998).

Taxonomy: 2 ssp, not known to be separable in the field but nominate *elegans* in ne. of breeding range (most likely to occur in N America) averages paler, less heavily marked than *elegantula* of cen. China. Sometimes known as Elegant Bunting (Brazil 2009).

Distribution and Status:

World: Breeds temperate zone from China to se. Russia (n. to about 50°N); winters Japan to se. China.

North America: *Alaska*: Attu, 25 May 1998 (male; age unknown).

Comments: The wintering and breeding ranges of Yellow-throated Bunting do not appear conducive to N American vagrancy, and it seems possible that the single spring individual was a misoriented (overshooting?) 1st-year bird, assisted by intense weather conditions that caused an unprecedented fallout of Asian landbirds in May 1998 on the w. Aleutians.

Field Identification: Handsome Old World bunting with a strongly peaked crest, boldly marked face, and gray rump.

Similar Species: None, if seen well.

♀

♂ fresh (fall)

1st-year
(fall–winter)

♂ breeding

♀

Yellow-throated Bunting

Age/Sex/Season: Ages differ slightly; sexes differ; slight seasonal variation through plumage wear. Complete prebasic and partial preformative molts occur before fall migration; possibly a limited prealternate molt in spring. *Male*: Bold black-and-yellow head and chest pattern (extensively veiled grayish in fresh fall plumage) with black extending narrowly under chin. *Female*: Duller head pattern, throat whitish to buff overall with little or no yellow, no blackish on chin. *1st-year*: Resembles adult of respective sex but retains juv flight feathers, which are more tapered than on adult, and in spring–summer relatively more worn than on adult.

Habitat and Behavior: Favors open woodland, grassy edges. Typical *Emberiza*. Feeds on the ground; flushes into trees and shrubs when available. Calls include a clear, slightly wet *tsi* and *tsi-ti sip* (Brazil 2009).

YELLOW-BREASTED BUNTING
Emberiza aureola 14–15.5 cm (5.5–6.2")

Summary: *Alaska*: Exceptional in spring on w. Aleutians. Single spring (1978) and fall (2009) records from Bering Sea islands.

Taxonomy: 2 ssp, not certainly separable in the field. N American specimen referred to *ornata* of ne. Russia, which averages darker and more heavily marked than widespread nominate *aureola*; *ornata* typically completes fall molt near breeding grounds, whereas *aureola* molts at migration staging sites in China.

Status and Distribution:

World: Breeds boreal forest and n. temperate zones from Finland e. to ne. Russia (Kamchatka and cen. Chukotka); winters SE Asia. Declining in much of range (e.g., Brazil 2009; Birdlife International 2012).

North America: *Alaska*: Exceptional in spring (late May to mid-Jun; 4 records) on w. Aleutians. Single late spring (26–27 Jun 1978) and fall (2 Sep 2009; *NAB* 64:136, 184) records from St. Lawrence, both females. *California*: See Comments.

Comments: The AK spring records fit the typical drift vagrancy pattern, whereas the fall record is consistent with a misoriented (reverse?) migrant. 2 records from CA (Los Angeles Co., 5–6 Mar 2000; Southeast Farallon Island, 10 Oct 2009, *NAB* 64:151) were insufficiently documented for acceptance. At least the latter record is likely valid, however, and coincidentally occurred in the same year as the AK fall record.

1st-summer ♂

adult ♂ fresh (fall)

Juv

adult ♂ breeding

♀

Juv

Yellow-breasted Bunting

Field Identification: Handsome Old World bunting with yellow underparts, white tail sides.

Similar Species: Distinctive if seen well, but cf. 1st-winter Smith's Longspur and nonbreeding Bobolink. On dull 1st-years note narrow white wing-bars, pale median crown stripe, buffy-yellow underparts.

1st-fall *Chestnut Bunting* (unrecorded N America but breeds E Asia, winters SE Asia, and seems a possible fall vagrant) is slightly smaller with unstreaked chestnut rump, yellowish undertail coverts, and grayish-white throat (opposite of Yellow-breasted), all-dark tail, and plainer head, lacking darker frame to cheeks.

Age/Sex/Season: Ages/sexes differ; distinct seasonal variation in males. Complete prebasic molt (and likely also partial preformative molt) occurs before fall migration in *ornata*, but mainly on Chinese staging grounds in *aureola*; partial prealternate molt occurs in spring. *Male*: Black face and throat in spring–summer (throat yellow in fall–winter), dark breast band; solid white shoulder (tinged buff in fall). *Female*: Typical bunting face pattern, narrow buffy-white

wing-bars. *1st-year*: Juv of both sexes resembles female but often paler below, with more extensive dark streaking; this plumage often worn through fall migration in w. ssp, which is unrecorded in N America. Following molt in late summer (*ornata*) or mid–late fall (*aureola*), resembles adult but retains juv flight feathers, which are more tapered and relatively more worn than adult; male has distinct black centers to median coverts, duller head pattern than adult (especially in spring–summer), and bolder black back streaking.

Habitat and Behavior: Favors marshy and grassy areas with bushes. Typical *Emberiza* bunting. Feeds on the ground; flushes to trees and shrubs when available. Common flight call a sharp *tsick*, 'fuller' than Little, and especially Rustic, Bunting.

GRAY BUNTING *Emberiza variabilis*
15–17 cm (5.8–6.7")

Summary: *Alaska*: Exceptional in spring on w. Aleutians.

adult ♂ worn
(spring–summer)

1st-year ♂
(fall–winter)

adult ♀

Gray Bunting

1st-year ♀
(fall–winter)

Taxonomy: Monotypic.
Distribution and Status:
   World: Breeds s. Kamchatka to n. Japan;
winters Japan.
   North America: *Alaska*: 3 spring records from
w. Aleutians: Shemya, 18 May 1977; Attu, 29 May
1980; Shemya, 27 May 2005.
Comments: Although a relatively short-distance migrant, the spring migration includes an
overwater segment, rendering the species prone
to drift. All records involve males: 2 adults and
a 1st-year. Misoriented, reverse-migrants seem a
possibility in fall, but perhaps the relatively short
migration may mitigate against anything other
than very rare occurrences.
Field Identification: Fairly large, stocky bunting with bicolored bill, no white in tail.
   Similar Species: Female similar to a few other
Emberiza females such as Black-faced Bunting
(unrecorded in N America), but larger and chunkier, with shorter tail lacking any white.
   Age/Sex/Season: Ages differ slightly; sexes differ; distinct seasonal variation through plumage

wear. Complete prebasic and partial preformative molts occur before fall migration. *Male*: Slaty
gray overall with dark-streaked back (overall
veiled brownish in fresh fall plumage). *Female*:
Brownish overall with dark streaking below. *1st-year* in fall resembles adult female but with less
distinct streaking below; male has grayer face
and breast (wearing away to resemble adult male
by spring–summer); female averages duller and
less distinctly streaked below than adult. Retains
juv flight feathers, which are more tapered than
on adult, and in spring–summer relatively more
worn than on adult. 1st-summer male averages
browner above than adult.
   Habitat and Behavior: Prefers thick undergrowth. Most common call a fine thin *tsi*
(Brazil 2009).

PALLAS'S BUNTING *Emberiza pallasi*
12.5–13.5 cm (4.8–5.3")

Distribution Summary: *Alaska*: Very rare in
fall on Bering Sea islands; exceptional in spring

♂ fresh (fall–winter)

♂ breeding

♂ breeding

♀ breeding

♀ fresh (fall–winter)

juv

Pallas's Bunting

on w. Aleutians, Bering Sea islands, and n. mainland.

Taxonomy: 3 ssp, not known to be separable in the field. Often known in Old World as Pallas's Reed Bunting.

Status and Distribution:

World: Breeds shrubby tundra and steppe zone of cen. and e. Russia (n. Kamchatka and Chukotka); winters e. China to South Korea.

North America: *Alaska*: Very rare in fall (early–late Sep; 4 records since 2006) on St. Lawrence; single spring records (late May to mid-Jun) from w. Aleutians, St. Lawrence, and n. mainland.

Comments: N American records are consistent with spring drift-overshooting and fall misorientation. The paucity of spring records from the w. Aleutians may reflect the relatively interior spring migration route, which does not routinely take birds offshore or up the Kuril Island chain.

Field Identification: Small, fairly long-tailed bunting with small bill (pinkish below) and nearly straight culmen, white tail sides.

Similar Species: Distinctive in N America if seen well, but confusion possible with larger and bulkier *Reed Bunting*, which has larger bill that is

grayish below and usually has slightly decurved culmen. Most plumages of Reed rustier overall, with diagnostic rufous lesser coverts (gray to dull gray-brown on Pallas's); common call a thin, downslurred *tseu*. Spring male Reed has darker, gray rump; female and 1st-year Reed have median crown slightly paler than sides, and rump darker, gray or brown.

Age/Sex/Season: Ages differ slightly; sexes differ; distinct seasonal variation through plumage wear. Complete prebasic molt before fall migration; partial preformative molt often interrupted for fall migration, and some birds migrate in juv plumage; limited prealternate molt in late winter. *Male*: Black-and-white head pattern (extensively veiled brownish and buff in fresh fall plumage). *Female*: Typical female bunting face pattern; limited, diffuse dark streaking on sides of breast and flanks; plumage buffier in fall, colder and grayer-toned in spring–summer. *1st-year*: Juv resembles female but with distinct dark streaking below. By early to mid-winter resembles adult of respective sex but retains juv flight feathers, which are more tapered than on adult, and in spring–summer relatively more worn than on adult; some have molt limit in greater coverts.

♂ breeding

♂ breeding

♀ breeding

♂ fresh
(fall–winter)

Reed Bunting
ssp *pyrrhulina*

♀ fresh (fall–winter)

1st-summer male often has pale buff mottling on face and throat.

Habitat and Behavior: An open-country bunting favoring moist brushy and weedy lands. Common call a ripping House Sparrow-like *tssurp*.

REED BUNTING *Emberiza schoeniclus*
13.5–15.5 cm (5.3–6")

Summary: *Alaska*: Very rare in spring on w. Aleutians; 1 fall record from Bering Sea islands (2002).

Taxonomy: 2 ssp groups, separable mainly in-hand by bill dimensions: largely migratory and relatively small-billed *schoeniclus* group of 7 ssp breeding across N Eurasia; and largely resident and relatively large-billed *pyrrhulina* group of 11 ssp breeding from S Europe e. to China. Plumages in both groups clinal, with e. populations averaging paler and less heavily streaked. N American specimens referred to *pyrrhulina*, the easternmost ssp of *schoeniclus* group, breeding ne. Russia.

Distribution and Status:

World: Breeds from Europe e. across temperate Asia to e. Russia (s. Kamchatka) and n. Japan;

winters W Europe and e. locally across S Asia to s. Japan and e. China.

North America: *Alaska*: On w. Aleutians, very rare in spring (late May–early Jun), usually singles but 3 on Attu, 25 May–1 Jun 1989, 4 (including 3 females) on Buldir, 29 May–9 Jun 2005. 1 fall record: St. Lawrence, 28–30 Aug 2002.

Comments: The pattern of Common Reed Bunting records suggests spring drift-overshoots. Most records are of males (at least 4 adults and a 1st-year), typical of spring overshoots, and the 3 females on Buldir in 2005 may represent drift vagrants. The single fall record presumably represents a misoriented (reverse?) migrant.

There were 22 records of Reed Bunting from Iceland through 2006 (mainly late Apr–early June, but all from the east coast) suggesting that transatlantic records are unlikely.

Field Identification: Medium-sized bunting with grayish bill, white tail sides; spring male striking.

Similar Species: Distinctive in N America, if seen well, but cf. Pallas's Bunting, dull 1st-year Rustic Bunting. See Garner (2002) for discussion of migratory Reed Bunting ssp.

Japanese Reed Bunting E. *yessoensis* (unrecorded in N America but a relatively short-distance migrant, wintering in e. China) resembles Reed Bunting, but all plumages have distinctive cinnamon rump, and bill paler overall on nonbreeding birds; spring male has solid black head and rich ochre nape.

Age/Sex/Season: Ages differ slightly; sexes differ; distinct seasonal variation through plumage wear. Complete prebasic and partial to incomplete preformative molts (can include tail) occur before fall migration; limited prealternate molt in late winter. *Male*: Black-and-white head pattern (extensively veiled brownish and buff in fresh fall plumage); rump grayish. *Female*: Typical female bunting face pattern; variable dark streaking on sides of breast and flanks; rump brownish. *1st-year*: Resembles adult of respective sex but retains juv flight feathers, which are more tapered than on adult, and in spring–summer relatively more worn than on adult; some have molt limit in greater coverts and tertials. 1st-winter male often has female-like face pattern, but note grayer rump; 1st-summer male averages less extensive black bib than adult and white hindcollar often with dusky flecks (clean white on adult).

Habitat and Behavior: Prefers moist areas with reeds and rank grass. Typical *Emberiza* bunting. Common flight calls are a loud *dzu* and a thin, downslurred *tseu*.

OLD WORLD FINCHES (6 species)

Finches are often relatively hardy, seed-eating birds that exhibit irruptive and nomadic behavior in response to food availability. Most species are fairly short-distance migrants. Identification problems are slight among species that have occurred as vagrants, but several are popular as cage birds, and frequent escapes or even intentional releases can confuse patterns of vagrancy. Of the 6 species recorded as rare birds in N America, 5 originate in E Asia and are known mainly or wholly from Alaska, and 1 (Common Chaffinch) is known from the Northeast in late winter–spring (but with records confounded by possible escapes). Alaska records of vagrant finches are mainly (Common Rosefinch, Oriental Greenfinch, Eurasian Bullfinch, Hawfinch) or wholly (Eurasian Siskin) in spring and from the islands, with fewer summer–fall records; and, in the case of bullfinch and Hawfinch, some mid-winter records from mainland Alaska. There are also single fall–winter records of Common Rosefinch and Oriental

Greenfinch from California. See Appendix A for a recent record of Asian Rosy Finch in Alaska.

COMMON CHAFFINCH *Fringilla coelebs*
14–16 cm (5.5–6.3")

Summary: *Atlantic Canada*: Probably exceptional in late fall–spring, but confounded by possible escapes (see Comments, below). *Elsewhere*: Status uncertain (see Comments).

Taxonomy: 14 ssp in 3 groups (perhaps best treated as 3 species), with 7 confined to islands. Males of some ssp very distinctive, but most ssp not certainly identifiable in the field. N American records are of *coelebs* group (7 ssp breeding from W Europe e. to cen. Russia, wintering mainly from Europe to Middle East); males of this group are relatively dark overall and extensively pinkish rufous below. Males of *spodiogenys* and *canariensis* groups of N Africa and Macaronesian islands are paler overall, with variably whitish lower underparts.

Status and Distribution:

World: Breeds W Europe, N Africa, and Macronesian islands e. to cen. Russia, with n. and interior populations withdrawing w. and s. in winter to Europe and the Middle East.

North America: *Atlantic Canada*: Dates and circumstances of at least 3 late fall–spring records suggestive of wild origin: Halifax Co., NS, 27 Nov 2001–13 Jan 2002 (male; *NAB* 56:24, 151), and se. NL, 21 May 1994 (female; *FN* 48:271) and 28 Jan–22 Feb 2011 (male; *NAB* 65:217). *Elsewhere*: Reports from CA and WY, as well as most if not all other records from the East (especially the Midwest, Great Lakes region, and QC), are considered to most likely represent escaped cage birds. See Comments, below.

ABA (2008) considered 2 other records as likely pertaining to wild birds: Plymouth Co., MA 3–5 Apr 1997 (accepted by state committee) and se. QC, 18 Nov 2000 (male; not admitted to official provincial list). Feathers taken for isotope analysis from a chaffinch in Middlesex Co., MA (1 Dec 2009–Mar 2010; *NAB* 64:232-233) have yet to be analyzed (M. Iliff, pers. comm.).

Comments: This species epitomizes the difficulty of distinguishing between wild vagrants and escapes from the cage-bird trade. Chaffinches are certainly potential vagrants to the Northeast, especially to Atlantic Canada, but they are also commonly kept as cage birds. In Iceland, Common Chaffinches are scarce but regular migrants, mainly in spring and fall following

♂ worn
(spring–summer)

♂ fresh
(fall–winter)

Common Chaffinch

♀

se. winds that drift migrants off course, and there are single spring and fall records from Greenland. Interestingly, there are more records of Common Chaffinch than of Brambling in the Northeast, even though the latter is more than three times as numerous in Iceland. Moreover, most Bramblings in the East likely come from E Asia rather than Europe (see Fig 19, p. 17).

Ryan (1990) hinted at the magnitude of the cage-bird problem and noted evidence to suggest that many cage birds in the Northeast, especially European species (such as Eurasian Blackbird, Common Chaffinch, European Greenfinch, Eurasian Siskin, and European Goldfinch *Carduelis carduelis*) came through Montreal. Perhaps not coincidentally, QC and the adjacent Great Lakes region are the epicenter for field reports of species such as Common Chaffinch and European Goldfinch, with most reports being in spring, primarily May (e.g., *NAB* 60:381; *NAB* 63:390; *NAB* 64:391); the main spring migration in W Europe is during Mar–Apr (with fall migration mainly Sep–Nov). It is even possible that occasional breeding in the wild occurs in the East, at least for Common Chaffinch and European Goldfinch. The movements of these sparse, fluctuating populations of 'jail-breakers' can only be guessed at, although southward movements in winter and return northward movements in spring (paralleling the period when naturally occurring vagrants might be expected) seem the

most likely overall pattern. Thus, any records of chaffinches in N America are haunted by the possibility of captive origin.

Rather than throw out the baby with the bathwater, however, it seems reasonable to consider that some N American records of Common Chaffinch could be candidates for wild vagrancy. But which ones? The Jan–Feb 2011 record from NL coincided with an invasion to Atlantic Canada of several European species fleeing freezing conditions in their homeland, and thus seems like a good bet for natural occurrence. Likewise, the May 1994 bird in se. NL coincided with an impressive influx of European species, including Fieldfare and several shore-birds (*FN* 48:271). The Nov 2001–Jan 2002 occurrence in se. NS also seems like a reason-able bet, but could it simply have been a bird moving to the coast from summering grounds in QC? Beyond these 3 records, Pandora's Box is flung open, and we hope that future records will shed light both on patterns of vagrancy and on patterns of potentially burgeoning free-flying populations derived from escaped or released cage birds.

Field Identification: Distinctive and attractive finch with white wing-bars and obvious white tail sides (best seen in flight).

Similar Species: None in N America.

Age/Sex/Season: Ages similar; sexes differ; slight seasonal variation in males through plumage wear. Complete prebasic and partial preformative molts occur before fall migration; no prealternate molt. **Male**: Bright pinkish-rufous cheeks and underparts; duller overall when veiled dusky in fresh fall plumage. **Female**: Pale grayish to pinkish-gray cheeks and underparts. **1st-year**: Resembles adult of respective sex but retains juv flight feathers, which are more tapered than on adult, and in spring–summer relatively more worn than on adult; some have molt limit in greater coverts and tertials.

Habitat and Behavior: Prefers open woodland, parks, and gardens. Often forages on the ground and visits bird feeders. Common call while perched a sharp *pink*, and in flight a soft *yupp*.

COMMON ROSEFINCH *Carpodacus erythrinus* 13.5–15 cm (5.3–6")

Summary: *Alaska*: In spring, rare and intermittent on w. Aleutians and Bering Sea islands; exceptional on cen. Aleutians and w. and sw. mainland. In fall, very rare on Bering Sea islands and w. Aleutians. *California*: 1 fall record (2007). **Taxonomy**: 5 ssp in 2 groups, differing in extent of red on adult males: *erythrinus* group (2 ssp

breeding across N Eurasia) with red mainly on head and breast; *roseatus* group (3 ssp breeding in mountains of S Eurasia) with darker and more extensive pinkish red on underparts. N American specimens are referred to *grebnitskii* of NE Eurasia, which averages darker than nominate *erythrinus* of Cen and W Eurasia.

Status and Distribution:

World: Breeds from N Europe e. across temperate Eurasia to ne. Russia (Kamchatka and cen. Chukotka); winters from Indian subcontinent to se. China.

North America: *Alaska*: In spring, rare and intermittent (late May–Jun) on w. Aleutians and Bering Sea islands, usually singles and small groups, exceptionally 18 on St. Lawrence, 6 Jun 1977; very rare (early to mid-Jun) on cen. Aleutians. 3 summer records: Pribilofs, 7–8 Jul 2009 (2; *NAB* 63:642); w. mainland, 11–14 Jul 1997 (1st-summer male; *NAB* 51:1039); and sw. mainland, 5 Jul 1989 (male; *NAB* 43:1357). In fall, very rare (late Aug–Sep) on w. Aleutians and St. Lawrence. *California*: SE Farallon Island, 23 Sep 2007 (1st-year).

Comments: Spring records are typical of drift-overshoots, and the Jul records suggest that

1st-summer ♂
(variable)

House Finch
♀/1st-year ♂

adult ♂

shorter
projection

extensive
dark
streaking

adult ♂

adult ♀

Common Rosefinch

juv

some individuals continue east, perhaps a sign of pioneering colonists (the species is expanding its range westward in N Europe). Most spring records are of brown-plumaged birds, but red males are also noted, including at least 6 in Jun 1977 on St. Lawrence. Fall records, including that in CA, fit with the theory of misoriented (reverse?) migrants.

There were 82 records from Iceland through 2006 (mainly Sep–Oct), and Greenland's first record was 10 Sep 2010 at 78°N and about 202 km e. of land (*NAB* 65:107), suggesting the slim possibility of an E Coast record in fall.

Field Identification: Old World finch suggesting a combination between House Finch (in plumage pattern) and Purple Finch (in shape).

Similar Species: ***House Finch*** less chunky overall, with longer tail lacking strong fork, shorter primary projection, more extensive dusky streaking on underparts, and different calls. ***Purple*** and ***Cassin's Finches*** have patterned faces in both sexes and essentially straight culmens. 1st-year ***Lazuli Bunting*** can retain streaking below through fall migration; Lazuli has slightly longer, more conical bill, shorter primary projection, plainer head and back, and typically has buff wash on breast; also has different call and often twitches and dips tail.

Pallas's Rosefinch (unrecorded in N America) has distribution characteristics that make its occurrence possible, at least in fall. About 15% larger (16–17.5 cm) and proportionately longer tailed than Common Rosefinch, with stout bill and slightly decurved culmen. Adult males unmistakable; pinkish red overall with white frosting on forehead and throat, dark-streaked back, and bold white wing-bars and tertial fringes. Female and 1st-year male more similar to Common but have burnt orange-pink suffusion to finely streaked breast (least obvious in 1st-year female), pinkish rump.

Age/Sex/Season: Ages/sexes differ, with adult appearance attained in 1st winter (female) or 1st–2nd year (male); no seasonal variation. Complete prebasic molt and partial to incomplete preformative molt (often including tail, sometimes remiges in eccentric pattern; see. p. 39) occur on wintering grounds after fall migration; no prealternate molt. ***Adult male***: Head and chest reddish overall, upperparts (including wing-bars) suffused reddish, rump red. ***Adult female***: Plumage lacks red, wing-bars whitish; plumage worn in fall. ***1st-year***: Juv resembles female but fresh in fall, with broader pale buff (fading to whitish)

wing-bars, more extensive and diffuse dusky streaking below. Following preformative molt in 1st winter, resembles adult female but some distinguished by retained juv remiges and molt contrasts. Some 1st-year males attain red on face and throat, and a few resemble adult male but have narrow and worn whitish wing-bars.

Habitat and Behavior: Much like Purple Finch. Most common flight call an upslurred whisted *vieh*, not dissimilar to some calls of House Finch; song a short, measured series of bright, slightly slurred whistles, quite unlike N American finches and more likely to suggest a short, slow-paced *Passerina* bunting song.

EURASIAN SISKIN *Spinus spinus* 11–12.5 cm (4.3–5")

Summary: *Alaska*: 2 spring records from w. Aleutians (1978, 1993). *Northeast*: A scattering of records, clouded by concerns over origin (see Comments, below).
Taxonomy: Monotypic.
Status and Distribution:

World: Breeds from W Europe e. across temperate Eurasia to e. Russia (nw. side of Sea of Okhotsk, locally in Kamchatka) and n. Japan; winters mainly in Europe, and Japan to se. China.

North America: *Alaska*: Exceptional in spring (late May–early Jun) on w. Aleutians, 2 records: Attu, 4 Jun 1978, and 21–23 May 1993 (2). *Northeast*: Uncertain; see Comments, below. Records listed by McLaren et al. (1989) and ABA (2008) from NL, SPM, NB, ON, ME, MA, and NJ are considered of questionable origin.

Comments: Like several finches, Eurasian Siskins are somewhat nomadic and unpredictable in their movements, which may predispose them to at least short-range vagrancy. The AK records (all 3 involving males) presumably reflect overshoots or wandering birds (the species is considered a possible breeder in Kamchatka; Brazil 2009), and are generally considered to represent wild birds.

There have been a number of records of male Eurasian Siskins from the Northeast (e.g., see McLaren et al. 1989; ABA 2008); the lack of confirmed records of females suggests they may be overlooked. However, eastern records of Eurasian Siskin are tainted by problems associated with a flourishing and mostly legal cage-bird trade in which European finches, including Eurasian Siskin, feature prominently (see McLaren et al. 1989, Ryan 1990, and Comments in the Common Chaffinch account).

averages more yellow in wings and tail than Eurasian

finer bill

yellowish

less-defined streaking

Eurasian Siskin   ♂

Pine Siskin
'green morph'

While a wild N American record from across the N Atlantic seems plausible, none of the e. N American records seems certain to be a natural vagrant based on the lack of correlation with major influxes into W Europe and Iceland (where Eurasian Siskin is an almost annual vagrant, with arrivals mainly mid-Sep to Nov, and in May), and the absence of records from Greenland. Of note is that none were reported from the Northeast in fall 2007 or spring 2008, when record-breaking influxes occurred in Iceland: through 2006 some 248 individuals had been recorded in Iceland, but this was eclipsed in fall 2007 (at least 871 birds recorded) and spring 2008, and the species has bred there almost annually since 2007 (Y. Kolbeinsson, pers. comm.).

Field Identification: Eurasian counterpart to Pine Siskin, but overall stockier and male much more colorful.

Similar Species: Male distinctive, but female can be confused with **Pine Siskin**, especially the poorly known green morph of Pine Siskin, occurring in < 1% of the population. See McLaren et al. (1989) and Lethaby (1998) for further information on identification.

Eurasian averages smaller and stockier than Pine with a relatively deeper bill base, which might be apparent in direct comparison. Relative to typical Pine Siskins, green-morph Pines have reduced and less defined dark streaking and a variable yellow suffusion to upperparts (which appear greenish with a yellow rump) and underparts (typically including undertail coverts). Relative to green-morph Pine, Eurasian female has a yellow face and chest contrasting with a whitish belly and undertail coverts, and sharply defined dark streaking below, especially on flanks.

Escapes of other European finches should also be considered, perhaps especially **European Serin** *Serinus serinus*, which might suggest female Eurasian Siskin but differs in having a stubby bill, narrow dull wing-bars, and an all-dark tail.

Age/Sex/Season: Ages similar; sexes differ; slight seasonal variation in males through plumage wear. Complete prebasic and partial preformative molts occur before fall migration; no prealternate molt. **Male**: Cap and chin black, slightly duller when veiled grayish in fresh fall plumage; face and breast yellow. **Female**: Crown olive, streaked blackish; chin and throat whitish; face paler yellow than male. **1st-year**: Resembles adult of respective sex but retains juv flight feathers, which are more tapered than on adult, and in spring–summer relatively more worn than on adult; some have molt limit in greater coverts. Juv (unrecorded, and unlikely, in N America) resembles female but duller and browner, streakier overall with fine dark streaking on whitish underparts.

Habitat and Behavior: Similar to Pine Siskin, with which vagrants could be found. Both Pine and Eurasian Siskins have notably varied vocalizations, but most common flight call of Eurasian is a high, descending, whistled *teer* or *tliu*, suggesting a common call of Lesser Goldfinch and distinct from the ascending nasal *zheeeu* of Pine Siskin.

ORIENTAL GREENFINCH *Chloris sinica*
13–14 cm (5.2–5.5")

Summary: *Alaska*: On w. Aleutians, very rare in spring, exceptional in summer and fall. Exceptional on Bering Sea islands in spring, on cen. Aleutians in fall. *California*: 1 wintering (1986/1987).

Taxonomy: 6 ssp, mainly resident. N American specimens are referred to n. ssp *kawarahiba*, the only one that migrates (breeding Kamchatka s. to n. Japan, wintering Japan to se. China), which averages larger and browner than other ssp.

Distribution and Status:

World: Breeds E Asia, ne. to Kamchatka; n. populations migratory, wintering s. to se. China.

North America: *Alaska*: On w. Aleutians, very rare in spring (mid-May to mid-Jun), exceptional in mid-summer (late Jun–Jul) and fall (mid-Aug to Sep). Also 2 records from cen. Aleutians (Sep 2007) and 1 from Pribilofs (mid-Jun 1996).

All records of singles or small groups, max. 6 on Attu, 22 May 1976. Fall records include a (family?) group of 2 adults and 2 juvs on Shemya in Sep 1977. *California*: Humboldt Co., 4 Dec 1986–3 Apr 1987 (age and sex unknown).

Comments: In AK, spring records fit the pattern of drift vagrancy. While fall records may involve misoriented migrants, some may also reflect nomadic post-breeding dispersal, as with juvs accompanying molting adults on Shemya (adult in tail molt and growing outer primaries; D. D. Gibson, pers. comm.), and at least 1 bird in wing and tail molt on Adak, Sep 2007. Although finches in juv plumage can move some distance after fledging, an apparent family group suggests the possibility of local breeding, despite the absence of trees. Alternatively, post-breeding families of Oriental Greenfinches may disperse more than do most boreal finches.

A bird in Humboldt Co., CA, 4 Dec 1986–3 Apr 1987, was determined to be *kawarahiba* but was not accepted by the state committee. In our view this record most likely represents a wild bird, given fall records from the Aleutians, the wintering pattern mirrored by other Asian vagrants in the West (e.g., Brown Shrike, Siberian Accentor, Eurasian Skylark, Rustic Bunting, Brambling), and that *kawarahiba* winters largely to the n. of the most intense E Asian cage bird trade.

Oriental Greenfinch

Field Identification: Medium-sized finch with fairly large, pale pinkish bill; striking wing pattern apparent mainly in flight.

Similar species: None in N America. Other Asian greenfinches with extensive yellow bases to flight feathers are sedentary.

European Greenfinch *Chloris chloris* (unrecorded in N America as a wild vagrant and limited to W Eurasia; 3 records from Iceland) is greener overall (especially below) with less contrasting wing pattern and yellow limited to bases of outer primaries.

Age/Sex/Season: Ages differ, with adult appearance attained in 1st fall; sexes differ. Complete prebasic and partial preformative molts occur before winter, at times when wandering in fall. *Male*: Unstreaked. Brighter overall with greenish face, contrasting dark lores, more extensive yellow at base of tail. *Female*: Duller overall with grayish head, dusky lores, less extensive yellow at base of tail; back can show faint streaking. *1st-year*: Juv paler above than female, with dark back streaking; whitish below with fine dark streaking. Following preformative molt, resembles adult of respective sex but retains juv flight feathers, which are more tapered than on adult, and in spring–summer relatively more worn than on adult; some likely have molt limit in greater coverts.

Habits and Behavior: Favors open woodland and edge, open weedy areas with hedges and bushes. Often feeds on ground, also in weeds and trees, and visits feeders in winter. Wide range of vocalizations include a variety of forced, nasal notes such as a rising *chuwee*, *dzwee*, or *chwee*, which are repeated by perched and flying birds and have a Redpoll-like quality. Slowly delivered song could be heard from vagrants, an unmusical *tripp-tipp-tipp-tipp-tipp* often introduced by a lengthy wheeze (P. Holt, pers. comm.).

EURASIAN BULLFINCH *Pyrrhula pyrrhula* 16–17.5 cm (6.2–7")

Summary: *Alaska*: On w. Aleutians and Bering Sea islands, very rare in spring, exceptional in fall. Very rare on the mainland in late fall–spring.
Taxonomy: 9 ssp, differing slightly in size and male plumage. Among migratory and dispersive n. breeding ssp, *cassinii* of ne. Russia (to which all N American specimens are referred) is relatively large and pale with extensive pinkish red below in males; W European ssp average smaller overall and deeper pink below.

Distribution and Status:

World: Breeds from W Europe across temperate Eurasia to ne. Russia (Kamchatka). Most populations resident but some n. populations migratory or irruptive, moving s. in Europe to Mediterranean region and N Africa, and in E Asia moving s. to Korea and s. Japan.

North America: *Alaska*: In spring, very rare on w. Aleutians (mid-May to mid-Jun) and exceptional on St. Lawrence (late May to mid-Jun), mainly singles and usually males, with max. of 6 birds (5 males, 1 female) on St. Lawrence, 29 May 1992. In fall, single records (late Sep–early Oct) from w. Aleutians (1st-year) and St. Lawrence, and 4 from Pribilofs (late Sep to mid-Oct). Records farther e. in AK have been mainly in fall–winter, with 10 records in the period: 4 in Oct–Nov (3 in 1991) from w. to cen. and s-coastal AK; 2 in Dec–Jan from w. AK; and 4 in Feb to mid-May from cen. to s-coastal and se. AK (*NAB* 65:503).

Comments: Eurasian Bullfinch is the only Asian vagrant with so many mainland AK records yet none in provinces or states farther south. As a hardy, short-distance migrant, its migratory impulses may recede too soon to leave any other jurisdictions in range. The relatively high number of winter records may reflect the striking plumage of this species and its tendency to visit feeders in a winter landscape with relatively few other birds.

Spring birds in the w. Aleutians fit the pattern of spring drift vagrancy. However, given the species' breeding distribution, it's unusual for there to be so many records from St. Lawrence, especially given no spring records from the Pribilofs; we have no explanation for this apparent anomaly but multi-individual records more likely reflect drift than a collective misorientation exercise. We suspect the paucity of fall records is largely an artifact of coverage—this species is a relatively late migrant, when observers are few on the AK islands. The 5 recent fall records from Bering Sea islands (in 2007, 2010, and 2011) correspond to later fall coverage, and we expect more such records if observers continue to remain into October.

Through 2006 there were 150 records from Iceland (including many from the sw. coast), more or less evenly scattered through late Oct–Mar, with a peak in mid-Feb thought to be the discovery of late fall birds rather than new arrivals. This suggests an E Coast record is possible given the right weather conditions.

Eurasian Bullfinch

Field Identification: Hardy and ostensibly unmistakable Old World finch with black cap and white rump.

Similar species: None in N America.

Age/Sex/Season: Ages similar; sexes differ; no seasonal variation. Complete prebasic and partial preformative molts occur before fall migration; no prealternate molt. *Male*: Bright pinkish face and underparts. *Female*: Dingy pale pinkish or grayish-pink underparts. *1st-year*: Resembles adult of respective sex but retains juv flight feathers, which in spring–summer are relatively more worn than on adult; some have molt limit in greater coverts.

Habitat and Behavior: Prefers mixed woods and gardens, where usually in pairs and small groups feeding on berries; often rather sluggish and overlooked easily. Vagrants, especially in late fall–winter, can appear at bird feeders. Usually fairly quiet, with normal call a soft, plaintive, whisted *whew* or *piu*.

HAWFINCH *Coccothraustes coccothraustes*
16.5–18 cm (6.5–7.2")

Summary: *Alaska*: In spring, rare and intermittent on w. Aleutians, very rare on cen. Aleutians and Bering Sea islands, exceptional on w. mainland. Exceptional in mid-summer on w. Aleutians and Pribilofs. 1 fall record from Pribilofs (2011). 1 winter record from w. mainland (2003/2004).

Taxonomy: 6 ssp, but none of 3 migratory n. breeding ssp separable in the field. N American specimens are referred to ne. ssp *japonicus*.

Distribution and Status:

World: Breeds from W Europe and NW Africa e. across temperate Eurasia to ne. Russia (s. Kamchatka) and n. Japan; E Asian populations migratory, wintering s. Japan to e. China.

North America: *Alaska*: In spring, rare to very rare on w. and cen. Aleutians (May to mid-June, once to late Jul); very rare on Pribilofs (late May to mid-Jun, once late Jul) and St. Lawrence (late May–early Jun). Mainly singles or small groups, exceptionally 18 on Attu, 17 May 1998. Exceptional or very rare in spring (late May to mid-Jun) on e. Aleutians and w. mainland. Single records in fall from Pribilofs (3–5 Oct 2011; *NAB* 66:152), and in winter from w. mainland (27 Dec 2003–23 Jan 2004).

Comments: This species is a classic spring drift vagrant to the w. Aleutians, with some birds being carried on to the Bering Sea islands. The virtual absence of fall records may be because the species moves later in fall than observers are present on AK islands, cf. Eurasian Bullfinch.

♂ (spring–summer)

bill color varies with season

Hawfinch

♀ (fall–winter)

There is also an early Nov record of Hawfinch from the Pribilofs, in 1911, and the wintering record supports the idea that fall misorientation to AK occurs but is rarely detected.

Field Identification: Very handsome, ostensibly unmistakable finch with very stout bill, broad white tail tip, and bold white wing patches striking in flight.

Similar Species: None in N America.

Age/Sex/Season: Ages similar; sexes differ slightly; seasonal variation in bill color (blue-gray in spring–summer, dirty pinkish in winter). Complete prebasic and partial preformative molts occur before fall migration; no prealternate molt. *Male*: Averages brighter and more deeply colored, secondaries edged with bluish-purple gloss. *Female*: Averages duller, less richly colored; secondaries edged ashy gray. *1st-year*: Resembles adult of respective sex but retains juv flight feathers, which in spring–summer are relatively more worn than on adult.

Habitat and Behavior: Favors deciduous and mixed woodland, feeding in trees and on the ground, but has come to feeders in AK; often rather shy. Most common call, and usually the only one heard in flight, is a hard, sharp *pic* (P. Holt, pers. comm.).

New World Songbirds

In N America, we consider some 44 species of New World songbirds as rare birds, comprising 14 tyrant-flycatchers and allies, 2 vireos, 1 wren, 7 thrushes, 2 mockingbirds, 1 silky, 6 wood-warblers, 3 'tanagers,' 4 New World buntings and grosbeaks, 2 grassquits, and 2 orioles. Other than a handful of tyrant-flycatchers, none of the New World songbird vagrants could be considered as long-distance migrants, and relatively few species are even known to be regular short-distance migrants. Thus, mechanisms and patterns of vagrancy are rather different from those shown by Old World songbirds. But because details of local movement and seasonal distribution are poorly known for many tropical songbirds, it is difficult sometimes to divine vectors of vagrancy. About two-thirds of the New World songbird vagrant species originate in Mexico (see Table 6, p. 25), 10 in the Caribbean (wholly or mainly the Bahamas and Cuba; see Table 8, p. 28), at least 4 in S America, and 1 has uncertain origin (Red-legged Honeycreeper, from Mexico or Cuba).

Vagrants from Mexico mainly derive from overshooting spring migrants, misoriented (reverse?) migration, winter (often elevational?) dispersal, and post-breeding dispersal.

Overshooting migrants are typical of spring–summer (as with Orange-billed and Black-headed Nightingale-Thrushes, Crescent-chested and Fan-tailed Warblers, Slate-throated Whitestart, Flame-colored Tanager, Mexican Yellow Grosbeak), whereas misorientation may play a greater role in fall vagrancy (as with Piratic Flycatcher, Streak-backed Oriole, Mexican Yellow Grosbeak). Reverse migration may also be responsible for northerly spring records of species such as Aztec Thrush, Golden-crowned Warbler, and Crimson-collared Grosbeak, which could have headed north rather than south after wintering in ne. Mexico or s. TX.

Records in the West of Mexican Tufted Flycatcher, Nutting's Flycatcher, Rufous-backed Thrush, and Blue Mockingbird mainly fit a pattern of fall–winter dispersal that may have an elevational component. Poorly understood winter dispersal in northeastern Mexico is known on occasion to bring a variety of species into s. TX, such as White-throated Thrush, Golden-crowned Warbler, Crimson-collared Grosbeak, and Eastern Blue Bunting, along with exceptional records of species such as Masked Tityra and Social Flycatcher. Records of some other species along the border may be linked to post-breeding dispersal, perhaps in conjunction with northward range expansion linked to warming climate, as with Sinaloa Wren, Blue Mockingbird (in TX), Gray-crowned Yellowthroat, and Rufous-capped Warbler.

Records of Caribbean songbird vagrants are almost all from s. FL and most frequent in spring and fall. This suggests several species may undergo seasonal (inter-island?) movements that are not well understood, or not as readily detected when members of the same species occur on different islands; this bias may also reflect seasonal observer coverage in FL, however, where birders are commoner in spring than at other seasons. Species recorded only or most frequently in spring are Loggerhead Kingbird, Red-legged Thrush, Bahama Mockingbird, and Yellow-faced Grassquit; with Cuban Pewee, Thick-billed Vireo, and Black-faced Grassquit found about as often in spring as fall. Another 3 species occur mainly from fall or winter through spring: La Sagra's Flycatcher, Bananaquit, and Western Spindalis.

At least 4 species of austral migrants from S America (all flycatchers) have occurred as vagrants in N America, either by overshooting or through reverse migration and drift: Chilean Elaenia, Variegated Flycatcher, Crowned Slaty Flycatcher, and Fork-tailed Flycatcher. Some Piratic Flycatchers may also have originated in S America but the one N American specimen is of the n. Middle American subspecies.

Given the vast area from which vagrants might come, and how little we know of local movements in most Neotropical species, it is difficult to predict what other species might occur next. That said, a few of the seemingly more likely candidates among the flycatchers include Yellow-bellied Elaenia *Elaenia flavogaster*, Small-billed Elaenia (see Appendix B), White-throated Flycatcher *Empidonax gularis*, and Streaked Flycatcher *Myiodynastes maculatus*. Making predictions among other myriad possible species is a little like throwing darts at a target while blindfold. For example, in 2011 we compiled the following list of candidates for future occurrence in border states: Russet Nightingale-Thrush *Catharus occidentalis*, Golden Vireo *Vireo hypochryseus*, Altamira Yellowthroat *Geothlypis flavovelata*, Blue-gray Tanager *Thraupis episcopus*, Rusty Sparrow *Aimophila rufescens*, Godman's [Scrub] Euphonia *E. [affinis] godmani*, Elegant [Blue-hooded] Euphonia *Euphonia elegantissima*, Black-headed Siskin (records of presumed escapes exist for TX; Appendix B), and Hooded Grosbeak *Coccothraustes abeillei*. Yet this list does not include Tropical Mockingbird, which appeared in TX in spring 2011 (Appendix B).

Future possibilities from the Caribbean region are also varied, and these include Bahama Yellowthroat *Geothlypis rostrata* (unaccepted report from FL; Stevenson & Anderson 1994), the recently split Bahama Warbler *Setophaga flavescens*, Greater Antillean Bullfinch *Loxigilla violacea*, and Cuban Bullfinch (records of presumed escapes exist for FL; see Appendix B).

TYRANT-FLYCATCHERS AND ALLIES
(14 species)

A huge and widespread New World assemblage that includes both striking species, such as Fork-tailed Flycatcher, and many notoriously similar species, such as elaenias and *Myiarchus* flycatchers. Of the vagrants to N America, 6–7 species originate in Mexico and Cen America, 3 in the Caribbean, and 4–5 in S America. Other than drift-overshooting and misorientation for the few longer-distance migrants, it appears that different types of dispersal and perhaps unrecognized local migrations are responsible for the appearance in N America of a mixed bag of tyrant-flycatchers and allies.

GREENISH ELAENIA *Myiopagis viridicata*
14.5–15.5 cm (5–5.7")

Summary: *Texas*: 1 spring record from Upper Gulf Coast (1984).

Taxonomy: 10 ssp usually recognized in the Greenish Elaenia complex, but species limits vexed and in need of study; multiple cryptic species may be involved, including the *minima* group of w. Mexico and the *placens* group of e. Mexico and Cen America. Most taxa not known to be distinguishable in the field except by voice, and ssp of US record unknown.

Distribution and Status:

World: Mexico (n. to s. Sinaloa and s. Tamaulipas) s. to n. Argentina.

North America: *Texas*: Galveston Co., 20–23 May 1984.

Comments: Although the TX bird was found following a front that deposited numerous migrants, its fat deposits suggested it may not have made a long-distance flight recently (Morgan & Feltner 1985). The field identification of *Myiopagis* flycatchers is fraught with challenges, compounded by the possibility of cryptic species. In Mexico, Greenish Elaenia is a frugivore that is prone to wander, having been recorded in winter on Cozumel Island and the Honduras Bay Islands (Howell, pers. obs.), where not known to breed. While a Mexican origin may be most likely for the TX bird, Greenish Elaenia is also a short-distance austral migrant in S America (Hayes et al. 1994; Chesser 1997) and thus a more southerly origin, although seemingly unlikely, should also be considered.

The coincidence that another elaenia (genus *Elaenia*) occurred in spring 1984 on the Gulf Coast (in nw. FL in late Apr) is intriguing, but the 2 records are not necessarily related. The FL bird has been considered as a Caribbean Elaenia *E. martinica* (ABA 2008), but see Appendix B.

Field Identification: About *Empidonax*-sized but slimmer and longer tailed, with a small bill. Nothing similar in N America.

Similar Species: The genus *Myiopagis* includes numerous similar-looking species, and

adults

Greenish Elaenia

probably some cryptic species (see Taxonomy, above). For any future record to be accepted, vocalizations and DNA might be helpful or even requisite. Most similar to Greenish among recognized species is Jamaican Elaenia *M. cotta*, which is about the same size and shape but has a slightly darker (sooty) crown, a dusky brownish (less greenish) cast to the upperparts, and paler underparts with an off-white throat and paler yellow belly; calls of Jamaican Elaenia include *tseeí-chip*, ending with a slightly emphatic note; and *tsee-ii-ii-ii*, ending in a quick trill (R. Hoyer, recordings), both distinct from calls of Greenish Elaenia in Mexico.

Age/Sex/Season: Ages differ slightly, attaining adult appearance in 1st year; sexes similar; no seasonal variation beyond fading. Molts not well known; likely follows complex basic strategy (see p. 35), with partial preformative molt of n. populations in fall. ***1st-year*** resembles adult but rectrices more tapered, greater coverts more worn in spring, with slightly paler and buffier (vs. duller olive-tinged) edging. Juv (plumage held briefly, unlikely in US) head and upperparts washed brownish with less distinct face pattern than adult, no concealed yellow in crown, buffier wing edgings.

Habitat and Behavior: In Mexico, occurs in a wide range of tropical and subtropical wooded habitats, from rain forest edge to pine-oak woodland and hedgerows with tall trees. Generally quiet and unobtrusive, perching fairly upright and slowly looking around. Commonly eats

small berries, and can be found low to high at fruiting shrubs and trees. Also hover-gleans and makes occasional short sallies for insects at upper to mid-levels in foliage. Call in e. Mexico is a high, thin, slurred *tsee-eu* or *cheeé-eu*, given year-round.

CHILEAN ELAENIA *Elaenia chilensis*
14.5–15.5 cm (5.86.2")

Summary: *Texas*: 1 winter record from Lower Gulf Coast (2008).

Taxonomy: 6 ssp usually recognized in White-crested Elaenia *E. albiceps* complex, including *E. [a.] chilensis*, but species limits vexed. Striking vocal, morphological, and ecological differences (such as among *chilensis*, *modesta*, and *albiceps*) indicate that at least 3 species are involved (Ridgely & Tudor 1994; Howell, pers. obs.). Consequently, *chilensis* is here considered as a monotypic species, Chilean Elaenia, a conclusion supported by genetic data (Rheindt et al. 2009). The other 5 taxa are ostensibly resident from s. Colombia to n. Chile and thus not considered in the context of N American vagrancy.

Distribution and Status:

World: Breeds (Sep–Mar) in cen. and s. Chile and Argentina, winters (mainly Mar–Sep) n. to Amazonia, but exact nonbreeding range not well known.

North America: *Texas*: Cameron Co., 9–10 Feb 2008 (Reid & Jones 2009).

distinct whitish eye-ring

adult

Chilean Elaenia

bushy white-based crest

lacks white crown patch

adult

juv

beware similar species possible as vagrants, call distinctive

Comments: This species breeds as far as s. Tierra del Fuego, and birds withdraw n. from these s. latitudes mainly in Jan–Feb (Howell, pers. obs.), with the nonbreeding range lying in n-cen. S America and scattered records (vagrants?) n. to Colombia (Reid & Jones 2009; Ridgely & Tudor 1994). At least some 1st-year birds migrate n. in juv plumage (which they can retain into at least Mar–Apr), and adults are often relatively unworn in Feb (MCZ specimens). The TX bird appears to have been an overshooting fall migrant adult in slightly worn plumage (cf. outer primaries in fig. 12 of Reid & Jones 2009).

The field identification of *Elaenia* flycatchers is fraught with challenges, compounded by the possibility of cryptic species. Adult-plumaged Chilean Elaenia, however, is relatively distinct among the longer-distance austral migrant *Elaenia* species, and the identity of the 2008 record seems solid, unlike an earlier US record of *Elaenia* in spring 1984 on the Gulf Coast of nw. Florida (see Appendix B).

Field Identification: About the size of a large *Empidonax* flycatcher, with a bushy, white-centered crest and relatively small bill. Nothing similar in N America.

Similar Species: In terms of identification challenges, the genus *Elaenia* is a tropical equivalent to the northern genus *Empidonax*, with numerous similar-looking species that cannot be covered here in sufficient detail (see Reid & Jones 2009 for identification notes). In-hand, or with good photos, Chilean can be separated from most other *Elaenia* species (including other taxa within the White-crested complex) by a more pointed wing-tip, on which p10 is almost always longer than p5 (J. T. Zimmer 1941); some vocalizations are also diagnostic, although vagrants can be frustratingly silent. Future N American records involving this genus should be documented carefully, including vocalizations when possible.

Age/Sex/Season: Ages differ slightly, attaining adult appearance in 1st year; sexes similar; no seasonal variation beyond fading. ***1st-year:*** Juv has shorter crest than adult (head often looks simply peaked) and lacks white crown patch; wing-bars pale buffy, upperparts with browner cast than adult. Complete prebasic and incomplete (to complete?) preformative molts occur wholly or mainly on nonbreeding grounds during Apr–Sep, likely averaging later on 1st-years; some 1st-years retain inner primaries and outer secondaries, and all ages may renew 1–3 tertials in a presumed prealternate molt (P. Pyle, unpubl. data).

Habitat and Behavior: Occurs in a wide variety of wooded and forested habitats. Ranges low to high in trees and bushes, although mainly at upper to mid-levels where hover-gleans for insects and plucks berries. Common calls a slightly explosive, plaintive whistled *whéu!* or *peéoo*, grading to a burry *breeuh* and *reeu*; a plaintive whistled *beeu* or *peeu*, which may be repeated steadily; and a strongly disyllabic *whí-beuh!* with the second part slightly explosive.

MEXICAN TUFTED FLYCATCHER
Mitrephanes phaeocercus 12–13.5 cm (4.7–5.2")

Summary: *Southwest*: Very rare or exceptional in winter–spring; 1 summer record (2011).

Taxonomy: 4 ssp in Tufted Flycatcher complex, differing slightly in size but distinctly in voice and plumage, and best treated as at least 2 species (Howell, pers. obs.): *phaeocercus* group (*tenuirostris* and nominate *phaeocercus*) of Mexico and n. Cen America (Mexican Tufted Flycatcher, averaging larger and longer-winged, without a contrasting yellowish belly), and *aurantiiventris* group (*aurantiiventris* and *berlepschi*) of s. Cen America and nw. S America (averaging smaller, typically with contrasting yellowish belly). US records refer to *phaeocercus* group.

Distribution and Status:

World: Highlands and foothills of Mexico (n. to cen. Sonora and s. Tamaulipas), s. to n. Cen America (see Taxonomy, above).

North America: *Southwest*: 5 winter–spring records (Nov to mid-May) from w. TX and AZ: Brewster Co., TX, 3 Nov 1991–17 Jan 1992 and 21 Nov 2010–4 Jan 2011 (*NAB* 65:308); Pecos Co., TX, 2–6 Apr 1993; Mojave Co., AZ, 24 Feb 2005; Cochise Co., AZ, 5–30 May 2008 (*NAB* 62:459; Rosenberg et al. 2011). 1 summer record: Pinal Co., AZ, 6 Jul 2011 (*NAB* 65:669).

Comments: In Mexico this species is a noted elevational migrant in winter (especially Nov–Apr), descending at times to near sea level. These movements are somewhat facultative, with birds often moving back upslope as soon as cold conditions have passed and flying insects are once again active (Howell, pers. obs.). This pattern thus differs somewhat from the food-driven movements of frugivores, which can have a longer-term basis for their exodus from fruitless regions. The first US record, in w. TX, coincided with a spell of atypically cold weather (B. Zimmer & Bryan 1993), and the Feb and Apr records were both well n. of the border,

Tufted Flycatcher

1st-year
(worn)

adult

suggesting this species has good potential for dispersal. The Apr–May records may reflect misoriented winter migrants heading n. rather than back s., as discussed for some TX records of Rufous-backed Thrush, Aztec Thrush, and Crimson-collared Grosbeak. The recent Jul record from AZ is not easily explained.

Field Identification: Slightly smaller and more lightly built than *Empidonax* flycatchers, with an obvious crest, pewee-like behavior, and cinnamon underparts.

    Similar Species: None in N America.

    Age/Sex/Season: Ages differ slightly, attaining adult appearance in 1st year; sexes similar; no seasonal variation beyond fading. Molts not well known; probably follows complex basic strategy (see p. 35), with partial preformative molt of n. populations in fall. *1st-year* resembles adult but rectrices more tapered (retaining fine pale tips at least into early winter), wing-bars fade to pale buff or whitish by spring and average narrower and more worn than adult. Juv (plumage held briefly, unrecorded in US) head, upperparts, and rectrices tipped pale cinnamon, wing-bars average broader and often more extensive along

outer web, tertials edged cinnamon (fading to buffy whitish by winter).

    Habitat and Behavior: In Mexico, a bird of humid pine-oak and subtropical forest in highlands and foothills. Favors fairly open areas at edge of forest or in open woodland, often along streams or near water, especially in winter, when may wander out into brushy and weedy fields. Generally conspicuous and perky, with pewee-like habits: perches on open twigs, wires, or fences, and sallies out actively for insects; often returns to the same perch and quivers its tail upon landing. Bright, slightly burry whistled *tch'wee-tch'wee* or *turree-turree* call is given year round, as well as a quiet *piik*, suggesting call of Hammond's Flycatcher.

CUBAN PEWEE *Contopus caribaeus*
13.5–14.5 cm (5.2–5.7")

Summary: *Florida*: Exceptional in fall–spring in the s.

Taxonomy: 4 ssp, not known to be separable in the field although *bahamensis* of Bahamas averages paler overall than the 3 Cuban ssp;

obvious white postocular crescent

short primary projection

Cuban Pewee

plain face

long primary projection

Eastern Wood-Pewee

origin of N American records unknown. Formerly considered conspecific with Jamaican Pewee *C. pallidus* and Hispaniolan Pewee *C. hispaniolensis*, with the combined species known as Greater Antillean Pewee *C. caribaeus*.

Distribution and Status:

World: N. Bahamas and Cuba.

North America: *Florida*: 4 records: Palm Beach Co., 11 Mar–4 Apr 1995 and 29 Oct–2 Nov 1999; Monroe Co., 16 Feb 2001; Miami-Dade Co., 5–26 Sep 2010 (*NAB* 65:62–63).

Comments: Cuban Pewee is generally common in its range and not known to undergo any appreciable seasonal movements, although the US records suggest that some early spring and late fall dispersal occurs. Rafaelle et al. (1998) note that the species is 'found in pine forests from February to July, where it apparently breeds,' implying it may move seasonally between habitats. This species may have been overlooked in the past, and may still be to some extent, due to poor treatment in earlier field guides. An Oct 1984

record from Florida is not accepted (Stevenson & Anderson 1994).

Field Identification: Slightly smaller and more compact than Eastern Pewee, with shorter primary projection, distinct white postocular crescent.

Similar Species: A fairly distinctive flycatcher by virtue of its obvious whitish eye crescent, fairly dusky plumage, and pewee habits. Jamaican and Hispaniolan pewees similar overall but lack the white eye crescent. Eastern Pewee has much longer primary projection, lacks distinct whitish eye crescent.

Age/Sex/Season: Ages differ slightly, attaining adult appearance in 1st year; sexes similar; no seasonal variation beyond fading. Molts not well known; probably follows complex basic strategy (see p. 35), with partial preformative molt of n. populations in fall. ***1st-year*** resembles adult but can have molt contrast in greater coverts (Pyle et al. 2004), rectrices more tapered than adult (and more heavily worn in spring and summer). Juv (plumage held briefly, unrecorded in US) has distinct buffy wing-bars.

Habitat and Behavior: On the Bahamas found in pine woods, thicket woodland edges, and adjacent clearings. Perches low to high, where can be confiding, and feeds by sallying, often returning to the same perch. Vocalizations mainly involve variations of high, thin, slightly piercing whistles, at times repeated steadily, such as *psii̯-dii* or *wh'psii̯*.

NUTTING'S FLYCATCHER *Myiarchus nuttingi* 18–19 cm (7–7.5")

Summary: *Arizona and California*: Exceptional or very rare in fall–winter. *Texas*: 1 winter record (2011/2012).

Taxonomy: 2 ssp recognized here, not safely separable in the field. N American records presumably pertain to n. ssp *inquietus*. Vocally distinct taxon *flavidior* of Cen America best treated as a separate species, Ridgway's Flycatcher *Myiarchus flavidior* (Howell 2012b).

Distribution and Status:
World: W Mexico (n. to n. Sonora) to Cen America.

North America: *Arizona and California*: 5 records: Gila Co., se. AZ, 8 Jan 1952 (specimen); Santa Cruz Co., se. AZ, 14 Dec 1997–21 Mar 1998; Orange Co., sw. CA, 11 Nov 2000–26 Mar 2001; La Paz Co., AZ, 24 Sep 2008 (Rosenberg et al. 2011); La Paz Co., 18 Dec 2011–26 Mar 2012 (M. Stevenson, pers. comm.). *Texas*: Brewster Co., 31 Dec 2011–11 Jan 2012 (M. Lockwood, pers. comm.).

Comments: Nutting's Flycatcher is considered resident in its w. Mexican range, where it occurs to within about 75 km (45 miles) of the AZ border (Flesch 2008). The N American records suggest, however, that some fall–winter dispersal occurs, as with a few other species breeding in w. Mexico, such as Rufous-backed Thrush, Blue Mockingbird, and Streak-backed Oriole, and with N American records scattered from s. CA e. to w. TX. Dispersal in Nutting's Flycatcher may be more frequent than is recognized, given that the

secondary fringes blend from pale lemon to pale rufous

brownish cheek

grayish cheek

white-fringed secondaries contrast with rufous primaries (beware 1st-years with retained juv secondaries)

paler yellow belly

Ash-throated Flycatcher

Nutting's Flycatcher

dark shaft streak ends bluntly

dark shaft streak hooks around feather tip

care should be taken judging undertail pattern; angle can give false impression

rufous extends to tail tip

species can be unobtrusive and is easily overlooked as Ash-throated Flycatcher.

All 5 winter birds may have arrived before being detected, although the CA bird was found at a fairly well-watched locale and its arrival there in Nov would have allowed time to undergo molt before dispersing. The late Mar disappearance of 3 birds suggests a pattern, and Nov–Mar may be the best time to seek this species in the US, although some may wander n. earlier in fall (to molt?), as with the Sep record.

Field Identification: Very similar to Ash-throated Flycatcher but slightly smaller and less rangy overall with subtle plumage differences; best distinguished by voice.

Similar Species: Ash-throated Flycatcher differs in a number of subtle structural and plumage features, but is best separated by voice (see Habitat and Behavior, below). Relative to Ash-throated, Nutting's is slightly smaller and often appears less rangy, with a bushier, less peaked nape and a slightly smaller bill. Secondary edgings of Nutting's are pale lemon to pale rufous, blending with rufous primary edgings, and rufous on inner web of outer rectrices (as seen from below) extends to tail tip; beware that these last two features can be matched by juv and 1st-winter Ash-throated that retain juv secondaries and rectrices. Nutting's averages browner above, with brown of crown extending down to cheeks (Ash-throated usually looks gray-faced), and often has brighter yellow on belly. Although these two species occur alongside one another in Mexico, Nutting's favors thorn forest and denser habitats, rarely venturing into open situations such as brushy fields, where Ash-throated is often seen.

Age/Sex/Season: Ages differ, attaining adult appearance in 1st year; sexes similar; no seasonal variation beyond fading. Molts not well known but probably much like other N American species in the genus, with complete prebasic molt in fall and near-complete preformative molt in fall–winter. *1st-year* might be distinguishable by relatively worn and faded primary coverts (retained juv feathers), as in other *Myiarchus*. Juv (unrecorded in US) has extensive cinnamon-rufous edgings to flight feathers.

Habitat and Behavior: Brushy woodland and edges; often at fruiting trees in winter but rarely ranges into open situations. Habits much as other *Myiarchus* flycatchers, spending much time perched quietly and overlooked easily when not

calling. Emphatic *wheeek!* call distinctive, and given year-round. Chattering and bickering calls (usually given in interactions, and thus perhaps unlikely in U.S.) also differ in quality and cadence from Ash-throated, in particular a slightly liquid rolled *kwidik kwidik*, which can run into bickering chatters.

LA SAGRA'S FLYCATCHER *Myiarchus sagrae* 17–19 cm (6.7–7.5")

Summary: *Florida*: Very rare to rare in the s., fall–spring. *Alabama*: 1 fall record (1963).

Taxonomy: 2 ssp, both occurring in the US: *lucaysiensis* of Bahamas and *sagrae* of Cuba, Isle of Pines, and Grand Cayman Island. Cuban birds average smaller (17–18 cm vs. 18–19 cm) with a more contrasting dark crown, less rufous in the outer rectrices. FL records presumed to be of Bahamian origin, whereas AL specimen was Cuban ssp *sagrae* (Miles 1967).

Formerly known as Stolid Flycatcher when considered conspecific with Stolid Flycatcher *M. stolidus* of Jamaica, Puerto Rican Flycatcher *M. antillarum* of Puerto Rico, and Lesser Antillean Flycatcher *M. oberi* of Lesser Antilles.

Distribution and Status:

World: Bahamas, Cuba, Isle of Pines, and Grand Cayman.

North America: *Florida*: Rare in the s. in fall–spring (Sep–May, mainly Apr–May), since the first record there in 1982. *Alabama*: Dallas Co., 14 Sep 1963 (1st N American record).

Comments: The peak in FL records during Apr–May may indicate spring wandering but could also reflect wintering birds becoming more vocal in a season when more birders are in the field. The seemingly recent 'arrival' of this species in N America may be more likely due to observer awareness, combined with accurate illustrations in some field guides, than to any increasing trend in occurrence, although a year or two may still pass with no documented records.

Field Identification: Rather small, dull, and often dopey-looking *Myiarchus*, appreciably smaller than Great Crested Flycatcher and similar in size to Dusky-capped Flycatcher or even Eastern Phoebe.

Similar Species: Identification of *Myiarchus* flycatchers is notoriously difficult, and any vagrant individuals should be studied carefully. That said, La Sagra's is a fairly distinctive species and recalls *Eastern Phoebe* as much as any

lucaysiensis
(Bahamas)

browner than
sagrae

grayer overall
than *lucaysiensis*
with darker crown

faint
yellow

sagrae
(Cuba)

little or no
rufous in tail

distinct
rufous in tail

La Sagra's Flycatcher

other *Myiarchus*. Eastern Phoebe has small bill, dull wing-bars, tail-dipping habit, different voice.

Confusion possible with ***Ash-throated Flycatcher***, which also occurs rarely in FL in winter (mainly Oct–Apr). Ash-throated favors more open situations and is slightly larger and longer-tailed, more obviously crested, and heavier-billed than La Sagra's. Ash-throated has paler and grayer upperparts, slightly brighter underparts, much more obvious rufous in the tail, especially the outer rectrices (best seen from below), and whiter secondary edgings (beware 1st-winter Ash-throated with retained juv secondaries). In winter, common call of Ash-throated is a quiet *pip* or *puip*, distinct from the whistle of La Sagra's.

Age/Sex/Season: Ages differ, attaining adult appearance in 1st year; sexes similar; no seasonal variation beyond wear. ***1st-year*** might be distinguishable from adult by relatively worn and faded (retained juv) primary coverts. Juv (unrecorded in US) has pale cinnamon wing-

bars and secondary edgings, more extensive cinnamon-rufous in tail. Juv plumage replaced by near-complete preformative molt in late summer–fall into adult-like plumage (primary coverts retained, as in other member of the genus; Pyle et al. 2004).

Habitat and Behavior: FL birds have been found mostly near the coast, in or near dense second-growth hardwood hammocks, or coppice woodland (Smith & Evered 1992). Generally unobtrusive and easily overlooked, this species tends to perch quietly at low to mid-levels inside woodland rather than in the open. Can be confiding and unconcerned, leaning slightly forward to peer around, making short sallies within the foliage, and hovering to pluck berries. Often best detected by call, but still can be difficult to locate. Common call a slightly slurred whistled *zweenk* or rising *wink*, which can be given singly but is often repeated twice or more in a series, and sometimes given persistently. Also gives a variety of bright clipped chips and rolled whistles.

SOCIAL FLYCATCHER *Myiozetetes*
[similis] texensis 17–18.5 cm (6.7–7.2")

Summary: *Texas*: 2 winter–spring records from Lower Rio Grande Valley (1990, 2005).

Taxonomy: In need of study. 7 ssp, differing slightly in size and plumage but distinctly in voice, indicating at least 2 species involved: *texensis* group from Mexico to w. Ecuador (Northern Social Flycatcher), and *similis* group e. of the Andes in S America. US specimen is of northernmost ssp, *texensis*.

Distribution and Status:

World: Tropical Mexico (n. to s. Sonora and s. Tamaulipas) s. to tropical S America.

North America: *Texas*: Hidalgo Co., 17 Mar–5 Apr 1990 and 7–14 Jan 2005 (Arvin & Lockwood 2006). Also a specimen from Cameron Co., 15 Feb 1885 (BM specimen #98.17.12.88).

Comments: Social Flycatcher is a common but ostensibly nonmigratory species in the tropical lowlands of Mexico. Like many flycatchers it eats a lot of fruit, which could predispose it to periodic wandering, especially in the nonbreeding season. The first record of Social Flycatcher from the state of Nuevo Leon, Mexico, involved a breeding pair in Jun 2006 (*NAB* 60:584, 587), which may be an indication that the species is moving slowly northward; that record, at about 25°N, was only a little over 160 km (100 miles) from the TX border.

Field Identification: Like a miniature, small-billed and small-headed Great Kiskadee.

Similar Species: Unless size is badly misjudged, this striking species is unlikely to be confused, and its head and bill are much smaller than those of a kiskadee. Befitting its smaller size, Social tends to be a little quicker in its movements than Great Kiskadee. The kiskadee-like plumage pattern is shared by a number of tropical flycatchers, which may be a case of Batesian (or Mullerian?) mimicry, for these noisy and conspicuous birds are generally avoided by hawks.

Age/Sex/Season: Ages differ, attaining adult appearance in 1st year; sexes similar; no seasonal variation beyond wear. Molts not well known; probably follows complex basic strategy (see p. 35), with partial preformative molt of n. populations in fall. ***1st-year*** can be distinguished in winter from adult by relatively narrow and tapered rectrices, slightly stronger cinnamon wing edgings than adult. Juv (unrecorded in US) resembles adult but lacks orange crown patch, flight feathers (except tertials) fringed cinnamon (often wearing away on tail).

adults

Social Flycatcher

Habitat and Behavior: Occurs widely in wooded and semi-open areas, often near water, and commonly found alongside kiskadees. Perches conspicuously on wires and bare branches and often bobs its head and turns its neck to look around; also can be somewhat retiring and sluggish, particularly after having gorged itself on fruit. Flight across open areas fairly direct but slightly hesitant, or jerky, and wings can produce a dry rattling in flight, audible at closer range. Common call a piercing whistled *seeá* or *see-yh!* Also has varied twittering and bickering calls, mainly in interactions and perhaps not likely to be given by single birds, including an excitable *chiir t-chiír t-chiír*, or *teeya tortéeya tortéeya tortéeya*.

PIRATIC FLYCATCHER *Legatus leucophaius* 14.5–16.5 cm (6–6.7")

Summary: *Texas and New Mexico*: Exceptional to very rare, spring and fall. *Florida*: 1 early spring record (1991).
Taxonomy: 2 ssp, perhaps distinguishable in the field. A Sep specimen from TX has been identified as a juv *variegatus* (M. Lockwood, pers. comm.).

L. l. variegatus of Mexico and n. Cen America averages larger and heavier billed; averages brighter yellow belly; wing molt mainly Oct–Jan.

L. l. leucophaius of s. Cen America to n. Argentina averages smaller, and smaller billed; s. populations probably undergo wing molt Apr–Aug.

Distribution and Status:

World: Breeds e. Mexico (n. to se. San Luis Potosi, around 24°N), s. to n. Argentina. Both n. and s. populations migratory, wintering in n. and cen. S America.

North America: *Texas and New Mexico*: Exceptional in spring in TX (mid-Mar to early May; 3 records) and very rare in fall in TX and e. NM (Sep–Oct; 5 records through 2012, 3 from NM). *Florida*: Monroe Co., 15 Mar 1991.

Comments: This widespread and distinctive neotropical flycatcher is named for its habit of aggressively pirating nests from larger birds such as becards and even oropendolas. Its breeding season is thus tied to those of locally breeding species, but in the nonbreeding season both s-breeding and n-breeding populations are strongly migratory. Middle American birds withdraw s. to S America during Oct–Jan,

whereas birds breeding in s-cen. S America migrate north during Apr–Aug.

Since the 1st US record, from s. FL in Mar 1991 (originally identified and published as a Variegated Flycatcher), all other records have been from TX and e. NM, and all since 1996. The tight seasonal groupings of US records, and the remarkable 'concentration' of 3 Sep records in e. NM, are typical of the patterns shown by long-distance migrants with well-defined routes and migration windows.

The origin of US records is uncertain. One possibility, supported by the TX specimen and perhaps by the 3 NM birds (all juvs in Sep), is that at least some fall records involve misoriented young from n. Middle American breeding populations, which withdraw s. from Middle America in Aug–Sep; northern spring records may involve overshooting spring migrants from these same populations. Remarkably, all TX and NM records lie roughly on a line drawn from e. NM to the heart of the breeding grounds of the n. ssp, *variegatus* (see Fig. 13 on p. 12), and their timing fits with what would be expected from spring overshooting and fall misorientation of *variegatus*.

It is also possible that some Piratic Flycatchers recorded in N America originate from austral breeding populations, perhaps with overshooting 'fall' migrants in Mar–Apr (such as the FL bird?) and reverse-migrating 'spring' birds in Sep–Oct, as discussed more fully under Fork-tailed Flycatcher. Paying attention to age, plumage wear, and molt could help address these speculations.

Field Identification: About the size of an Eastern Phoebe, with short stout bill, bold head pattern, and blurry streaking below. See illustration on p. 355.

Similar Species: Nothing similar occurs regularly in N America. Variegated Flycatcher, another austral vagrant, is appreciably larger with longer bill (pinkish below at base), flattish crown slightly peaked at the nape (versus more rounded head of Piratic), slightly flared whitish eyebrow, bolder rufous edgings to uppertail coverts and tail, and paler underparts without bright yellow wash; often perches lower and in less open situations than Piratic.

Age/Sex/Season: Ages differ, attaining adult appearance in 1st year; sexes similar; no seasonal variation beyond wear. Molts poorly known, but mainly or wholly in nonbreeding season. *Juv* (plumage apparently held through migration) has crown feathers edged dull cinnamon, with little or no yellow patch, broader wing-bars washed cinnamon, narrower and more tapered rectrices with wider cinnamon edging. 1st-year molt (presumably on nonbreeding grounds) produces adult-like plumage; 1st-year may be distinguishable from adult by retained juv flight feathers and perhaps by molt contrast in greater coverts; study needed of molt timing and extent.

Habitat and Behavior: Favors forest edge and canopy, clearings with tall trees, but vagrants could occur in any habitat (1 was on an offshore oil platform). Often perches fairly high and conspicuously, like a kingbird, and mostly eats fruit. Vagrants likely to be silent.

VARIEGATED FLYCATCHER
Empidonomus varius 17.5–19 cm (6.8–7.5")

Summary: *North America*: Exceptional in spring and fall at scattered locales in mid-latitude N America.

Taxonomy: 2 ssp, with some well-marked individuals perhaps distinguishable in the field. No N American records certainly attributed to ssp, but migrant *varius* most likely to occur.

E. v. rufinus breeds n. S America. Averages smaller, with relatively diffuse dark streaking below; molt timing undescribed, some adults start wing molt Dec (MCZ specimens)

E. v. varius breeds s-cen. S America. Averages larger and brighter, with more distinct dark streaking below; wing molt mainly May–Aug (MCZ specimens).

Distribution and Status:

World: Breeds n. and cen. S America, s. populations (nominate *varius*) migrating n. in nonbreeding season (Mar/Apr–Aug/Sep).

North America: Exceptional (mid-May, Sep to mid-Nov) at scattered locales in mid-latitude N America, with 4 records, all since 1977: York Co., ME, 5–11 Nov 1977; Obion Co., TN, 13–15 May 1984; Toronto, ON, 7 Oct–6 Nov 1993; Franklin Co., WA, 6–7 Sep 2008 (Mlodinow & Irons 2009).

Comments: The fall bias in records, as with Fork-tailed Flycatcher (and perhaps Piratic Flycatcher), likely reflects post-wintering reverse migration, which may be more frequent in young birds (discussed more fully under Fork-tailed Flycatcher). The WA bird was a 1st-year, but age for the other records is unknown to us.

The n. bias to records relative to Piratic Flycatcher mirrors Variegated's longer-distance

movements and more southerly breeding latitudes. As with numerous species of vagrants in N America, increasing observer awareness combined with today's globe-trotting birders leads to more records of vagrants in general than, say, 20–30 years ago.

Field Identification: Slightly larger and longer-tailed than Eastern Phoebe with fairly slender pointed bill, bold face pattern, and streaky underparts.

Similar Species: See smaller *Piratic Flycatcher*. Variegated Flycatcher can also suggest *Sulphur-bellied Flycatcher*, which is appreciably larger (kingbird-sized) and bulkier with a much stouter bill. Sulphur-bellied also has a less contrasting face pattern, with dark streaking in the gray-brown crown and in the whitish eyebrow; it often has a thicker black lateral throat stripe, and a more extensively rufous tail.

Anther possibility to consider, as yet unrecorded in US, is austral migrant *Streaked Flycatcher Myiodynastes maculatus*. Streaked is clearly larger (20.5–23 cm) and bulkier, slightly larger even than Sulphur-bellied, from which it differs in its stouter bill with obvious pink at the base, narrower dark lateral throat stripe, and finer dusky streaking below (1st-year Sulphurbellied more like Streaked in these regards than is adult shown in most field guides).

Age/Sex/Season: Ages differ, attaining adult appearance in 1st year; sexes differ slightly; no seasonal variation beyond wear. Molts poorly known; study needed of timing and extent. Adult male has distinctly attenuated outer primaries (weakly attenuated on female). *1st-year*: Juv (plumage may be held through migration?) lacks concealed yellow crown patch, head and upperpart feathers fringed cinnamon-rufous, wing edgings cinnamon-rufous, fading to pale lemon on tertials and some inner coverts, rectrices narrower and more tapered with broader cinnamon-rufous edging; outer primaries lack attenuation, and middle primaries fringed cinnamon. Underparts of migratory s. ssp *varius* often have blurrier dark streaking below than adult, thus resembling adult *rufinus*. 1st-year molt (on nonbreeding grounds?) may include rectrices (Mlodinow & Irons 2009) and at least sometimes middle and outer primaries (MCZ #175545, *rufinus*).

Habitat and Behavior: Favors open woodland, forest edge and clearings, semi-open areas with hedges. Often inconspicuous, foraging mainly at low to mid-levels where sallies for insects; also

upperparts darker and
duller overall than Variegated

juv

small
dark bill

rufous fringes to
uppertail coverts
and tail

yellow wash
usually distinct

adult
Piratic Flycatcher

bill longer than Piratic, pinkish
base not always obvious

some show
faint yellow
wash

rufous-fringed uppertail
coverts and tail

Variegated Flycatcher

eats fruit. Vagrants likely to be silent; occasionally gives a quiet, high, thin whistled *pseee*.

CROWNED SLATY FLYCATCHER
Griseotyrannus aurantioatrocristatus 16.5–18 cm
(6.5–7")

Summary: *Louisiana*: 1 late spring record (2008).

Taxonomy: 2 ssp, not known to be separable in the field; US specimen matches migratory nominate ssp (Conover & Myers 2009).

Distribution and Status:

World: Breeds n. and cen. S America, s. populations (nominate *aurantioatrocristatus*) migrating n. in nonbreeding season (mainly Mar–Sep) to w. Amazonia.

North America: *Louisiana*: Cameron Parish, 3 Jun 2008 (Conover & Myers 2009).

adult

juv

Crowned Slaty Flycatcher

Comments: The LA bird was an adult male in worn plumage, with no molt apparent, and thus presumably an overshooting 'fall' migrant from S America. The northernmost records prior to the LA bird were from n-coastal Venezuela, early Feb 1950, and an apparent 1st-year bird in cen. Panama, early Dec 2007 (Robb et al. 2009). The Feb record likely represents an overshooting 'fall' migrant, whereas the Dec bird may have been a misoriented 'spring' migrant (see Fork-tailed Flycatcher account).

Field Identification: Distinctive flycatcher, slightly larger than Eastern Phoebe.

Similar Species: Juv plumage of Crowned Slaty not often treated in field guides and, seen only from behind, might suggest *Variegated Flycatcher*. Relative to Variegated, juv Crowned Slaty slightly smaller with slightly smaller bill (with at most only a small pinkish area at the base), plainer upperparts, and overall plain underparts (pale grayish on chest, pale lemon on belly).

Age/Sex/Season: Ages differ, attaining adult appearance in 1st year; sexes differ slightly; no seasonal variation beyond wear. Molts poorly known; study needed of timing and extent. *Adult:* Notches on outer primaries (9–13 mm on p10 of 5 males, 3–5 mm on 2 females; MCZ specimens), lacking in juv. *1st-year:* Juv (can migrate in this plumage) has dark brownish crown with no concealed yellow patch, bolder pale eyebrow than adult, rufous and pale lemon edgings to wings. Attains adult-like plumage by preformative molt;

1st-year perhaps distinguishable from adult by molt contrast in greater coverts (see p. 36), retained juv flight feathers.

Habitat and Behavior: Breeds in open woodland, forest edges and clearings, semi-open areas with hedges; also winters in rain forest canopy. Often perches conspicuously, low to high, and sallies for insects; also eats fruit. Vagrants likely to be silent; occasionally utters a weak whistled *pseek* (Ridgely & Tudor 1994).

LOGGERHEAD KINGBIRD *Tyrannus caudifasciatus* 22–23 cm (8.7–9")

Summary: *Florida:* Exceptional in spring on the Keys, all records recent.

Taxonomy: Genus and species-level taxonomy in need of revision, and perhaps not a *Tyrannus*. Formerly treated in monotypic genus *Tolmarchus* (see Smith et al. 2000). Following Garrido et al. (2009), populations from Hispaniola (*T. gabbi*) and Puerto Rico (*T. taylori*) are here considered specifically distinct from widespread *T. caudifasciatus*, although the remaining 4 taxa within *caudifasciatus* may also comprise multiple species.

Of the 2 nearest source populations, Bahamian *bahamensis* has a dark ashy cap (and concealed orange crown patch) contrasting with an olive gray-brown back, and a yellow-washed belly; nominate *caudifasciatus* of Cuba has blacker cap (with concealed yellow crown patch)

caudifasciatus
(Cuba)

Loggerhead Kingbird

bahamensis
(Bahamas)

and grayer back, lacking brown tones, and clean white underparts; both have considerable whitish wing and tail edgings. Farther afield, Jamaican *jamaicensis* and Grand Cayman *caymanensis* fall between the Bahamian and Cuban extremes.

Distribution and Status:

World: N. Bahamas, Cuba, Jamaica, and Cayman Islands.

North America: *Florida*: 3 recent spring records (Mar–Apr): Monroe Co., 8–27 Mar 2007 (*NAB* 61:376, 432, 666), 14–22 Mar 2008 (*NAB* 62:396–397), and 12–23 Apr 2009 (*NAB* 63:415, 532).

Comments: This species is a common resident in the n. Bahamas and on Cuba, and like many West Indian species it evidently wanders on occasion. The 2007 and 2009 birds showed characters of nominate *caudifasciatus* from Cuba whereas the 2008 bird appeared to have a duller crown and duller wing-bars, perhaps suggesting *bahamensis*.

Further observations are needed to determine whether the recent records represent a flash in the pan or reflect a (previously overlooked?) pattern of late winter dispersal. Several older reports from FL are considered uncertain, and earlier claims include photos of an apparent Giant Kingbird (not evaluated by the ABA Committee; Appendix B) and of an Eastern Kingbird, reflecting the poor treatment afforded this species in older field guides (Smith et al. 2000).

Field Identification: Distinctive large flycatcher, resembling a *Myiarchus*-type flycatcher as much as a conventional kingbird in habits and structure. Combination of long black bill, slightly crested black head, and short primary projection distinctive.

Similar Species: None, if seen well. Note black head with peaked nape, fairly long but not overly heavy bill, neat whitish wing and tail edgings, and relatively short primary projection. Eastern Kingbird has smaller bill, long primary projection, and bold white tail tip, usually lacks such a distinct crested look. Also cf. Gray Kingbird.

Age/Sex/Season: Ages differ, attaining adult appearance in 1st year; sexes similar (lacks primary notching typical of *Tyrannus*); no seasonal variation beyond wear. Molts not well known.

1st-year resembles adult but rectrices more tapered, with duller tips, wing-covert edgings retain cinnamon tinge at least into winter. Juv (plumage perhaps held only briefly, but no data) lacks concealed yellow to orange crown patch, wing-covert edgings (notably broader on primary coverts) and tail tip washed cinnamon.

Habitat and Behavior: Favors wooded habitats where perches low in bushes, on fence posts, less often high on wires like typical kingbirds. Tends to be more retiring and inconspicuous than other kingbirds, behaving more like a *Myiarchus* flycatcher, but also inquisitive and can respond to pishing. Hover-gleans for insects and fruit, but typically does not make conspicuous aerial sallies like other kingbirds. Calls include a rolling and loud, sharp, slightly buzzy *tireet* or rolling *brreeep*, often repeated.

FORK-TAILED FLYCATCHER *Tyrannus savana* 19–42 cm (7.5–16.5")

Summary: *East*: Rare to very rare, mainly spring and mid–late fall. *West*: Exceptional in summer–fall.

Taxonomy: 4 ssp (perhaps involving more than 1 species, given that differences between *monachus* and nominate *savana* are of a magnitude comparable to other recognized species in genus *Tyrannus*). The 2 migratory or dispersive taxa sometimes separable in the field.

The spp *monachus* breeds Mexico to n. S America (some southward withdrawal Oct–Mar). Averages smaller and shorter-tailed (19–40.5 cm), paler backed, and darker winged; wing molt mainly Jun–Sep (Howell, unpubl. data; MCZ specimens). Adult male has less deeply notched tips to outer primaries (especially p8, which lacks strong notch).

The spp *savana* breeds cen. S America, migrating n. to n. S America in nonbreeding season (Mar–Sep). Averages larger and longer-tailed (23–42 cm), duskier backed, and browner winged; (wing molt mainly May–Aug). Adult male has more deeply notched tips to outer primaries (p8 strongly notched).

Distribution and Status:

World: S. Mexico to s-cen. Argentina.

North America: *East*: Rare to very rare, with records year-round but mainly late Aug–early Dec, with a lesser peak during mid-Apr to mid-Jul and fewest records in Feb–Mar. Of about 180 records in the period, most are from fall and along the Atlantic coast from New England n. to Canada, with others scattered w. to the Great Lakes region, and s. to FL and TX. Along the E Coast and in the Northeast, about two-thirds

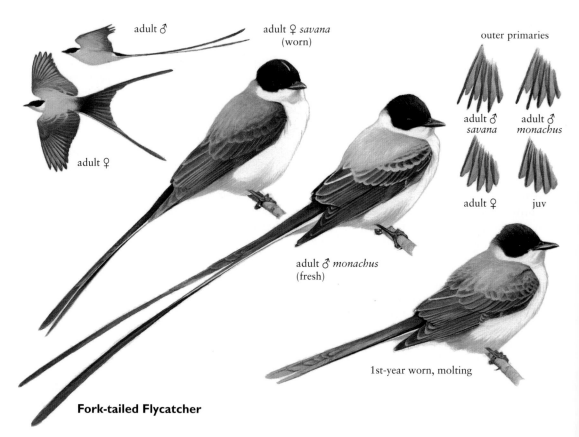

adult ♂

adult ♀ *savana* (worn)

outer primaries

adult ♀

adult ♂ *savana*   adult ♂ *monachus*

adult ♀   juv

adult ♂ *monachus* (fresh)

1st-year worn, molting

Fork-tailed Flycatcher

of the records are in Aug–Nov and only about a quarter in May–Jun, whereas on the Gulf Coast there are fewer records overall but with more than half in mid-Apr to mid-Jul and only about a third in mid-Sep to mid-Nov (Lockwood 1999). **West**: Exceptional in early summer (early Jun; 2 records) and fall (late Aug–Sep; 4 records), with records from AB, ID, WA, NV (*NAB* 64:631) and CA (2), all since 1988.

Comments: The occurrence of this striking species in N America may involve 2 different populations. Most records relate to long-distance migrant nominate *savana* from S America, but some may involve nomadic or short-distance migrant *monachus* (McCaskie & Patten 1994; Lockwood 1999).

Most N American records appear to be of misoriented *savana* heading n. rather than s. after 'wintering' in n. S America (see Fig 15, p. 13). Thus, the concentration of mid-Aug to late Nov records from the Northeast reflects mirror reversal of the species' narrow migration corridor south from Trinidad back to the breeding grounds (H. T. Erickson 1982; McCaskie & Patten 1994). Most of these birds may be 1st-years, but critical data are lacking to evaluate this specula-tion. Some birds clearly wander much farther, such as a 1st-year *savana* in CA in Sep, and the species could occur seemingly almost any-where in N America. Indeed, this species holds the distinction of being the only Neotropical passerine to have occurred as a vagrant in Europe, a bird presumably swept across the Atlantic: 19 Oct. 2002, in s. Spain (Dies et al. 2007).

Spring and summer records from the East and Northeast (mainly in Apr–Jul) presumably are of northbound 'fall' overshoots, some perhaps caught up in weather systems that swept them well to the n. of their normal nonbreeding range; many are in obviously worn plumage, often with broken tail feathers. As noted above, proportion-ately more birds occur on the Gulf Coast in spring than fall, which is consistent with shorter-distance overshooting at this season, rather than longer-distance reverse migration to the Northeast in fall; however, some spring–summer records are remarkably far north, such as 53°N in Nunavut, 22 May 2003 (Abraham 2003).

Most birds have been present only 1–3 days, suggesting they quickly reorient or at least move on, but some of the 'wintering' birds have been molting in Jun–Aug, as they would normally do on their nonbreeding grounds (McCaskie &

Patten 1994). In some instances, molt of vagrants (at least 1st-year *savana*) may be delayed relative to their normal schedule (see fig. 4 of Lockwood 1999).

A secondary pattern of occurrence may involve *monachus*, which breeds as close as se. Mexico, about 700 km (420 miles) from the TX border, although as yet there appears to be no unequivocal record of *monachus* in the US. At least 2 records from coastal s. TX during mid-Dec to mid-Jan, of birds in relatively bright and fresh plumage, are believed to involve *monachus* (McCaskie & Patten 1994), which may prove to be an irregular winter wanderer to the US. An early Feb specimen from TX, however, has been identified as *savana*, and the subspecific identity of a fresh-looking Feb 1st-year in LA is debated (*NAB* 62:258-259).

Field Identification: Striking and conspicuous large flycatcher with long and deeply forked tail (shorter on 1st-years), black head.

Similar Species: Nothing really similar in N America, but cf. Eastern Kingbird versus short-tailed Fork-tailed. Also beware the possibility of a poorly seen male Pin-tailed Wydah *Vidua macroura* in breeding plumage. This striking African bird can occur as an escape and has a black cap and very long forked black tail, but note its stout red bill and black back with white wing edgings.

Age/Sex/Season: Ages differ, attaining adult appearance in 1st year; sexes differ slightly; no seasonal variation beyond wear. Molts not well known. Male averages longer tail than female, and adult male has more distinct notching on outer primaries than adult female. **1st-year**: Juv has brownish crown (fading to cinnamon on some birds), cinnamon to buff edgings on up-pertail coverts and wing coverts, shorter tail than adult (but juv male tail overlaps adult female's in length); primaries lack distinct notches. Juv plumage appears to be held through migration in *savana*, followed by partial (to incomplete?) molt in 'winter' (mainly Jun–Aug for s.-breeding populations). Following preformative molt, 1st-year resembles adult but with worn buffy edgings to uppertail coverts and wings; outer primaries may lack distinct notches if juv feathers retained; study needed on timing and extent of 1st-cycle molts in all populations.

Habitat and Behavior: Favors open country with fences and scattered bushes. Often perches on low fences, also on low shrubs or glass clumps, less often on overhead wires. Flight strong and direct, with long tail flowing, or 'rippling' behind; partly spread tail tips tend to bow inward, like a lyre, rather than splaying outward as on Scissor-tailed Flycatcher. Vagrants likely to be silent but may utter quiet, clipped *plik* or *sik* calls on occasion.

GRAY-COLLARED BECARD
Pachyramphus major 14–15.5 cm (5.5–6.2")

Summary: *Arizona*: 1 summer record (2009).
Taxonomy: 5 ssp, differing slightly in plumage tones except for distinctive female and 1st-year male *uropygialis* of w. Mexico, which have rufous crown and blackish postocular stripe versus blackish to blackish-brown crown of other ssp. AZ record pertains to *uropygialis*.
Distribution and Status:
   World: Mexico (n. to around 29°N on Pacific slope, 25°N on Atlantic slope) to Nicaragua, mainly in subtropical highlands.
   North America: *Arizona*: Cochise Co., 5 Jun 2009 (1st-year male; J. A. Johnson et al. 2010; Rosenberg et al. 2011).
Comments: At least in Mexico, Gray-collared Becard is a noted elevational migrant that wanders widely in fall–winter in response to cycles of fruiting trees; its appearance in the US

seemed only a matter of time, with perhaps even or greater odds on the 1st record coming from s. Texas in winter. The nearest records from adjacent Sonora have been about 300 km s. of the AZ border. The AZ record presumably represented a wandering, nonbreeding individual, and given the species' unobtrusive nature it's unsurprising the bird was not seen subsequently.
Field Identification: Slightly smaller than Rose-throated Becard, with graduated tail and distinctive pale wing edgings.
   Similar Species: None in N America.
   Age/Sex/Season: Ages/sexes differ, no seasonal variation. Molts not well known; presumed complex alternate strategy (see p. 35) with complete prebasic and partial preformative molts in fall, partial prealternate molt in spring (some 1st-year males at least). *Adult male*: Plumage pale gray, black, and white, with solid black cap. *Female*: Upperparts cinnamon brown with dark wings and tail, cinnamon wing edgings and tail tips. Crown blackish brown in e. Mexico and Cen America, cinnamon-rufous with black postocular stripe in w. Mexico. *1st-year*: Juv (plumage held briefly, unrecorded in US) resembles female but plumage lax, male may have blackish-tipped central rectrices (study needed). *1st-year male*: Following preformative molt in late summer–fall,

W Mexican ssp
uropygialis

adult ♂

♀

♀

♂

1st-year ♂

**Gray-collared
Becard**

appears variably intermediate between adult male and female, differing from female in pale buffy-lemon (fading to whitish) wing edgings and tips to outer rectrices; differing from male in varying amounts of brown on back and rump, female-like head pattern.

Habitat and Behavior: Varied woodland and forest habitats, edges, and any fairly open areas with suitable fruiting trees. Like other becards, often quiet and overlooked easily, mainly at upper to mid-levels, where best found at fruiting trees; in w. Mexico, often joins mixed-species feeding flocks in fall and winter. Usually quiet in the nonbreeding season. Song of mellow whistled phrases usually given 4–6 times before pausing, *huu'whi-dit, huu'whi-dit, huu'whi-dit … .* Other plaintive to mellow whistled *peeu* and *beeh* calls given on occasion, often in series.

MASKED TITYRA *Tityra semifasciata*
21.5–24 cm (8.5–9.5")

Summary: *Texas*: 1 winter record from Lower Rio Grande Valley (1990).

Taxonomy: 9 ssp, differing slightly in size and plumage, especially among females. Males of the 2 n. ssp similar, but female *griseiceps* of w. Mexico has gray head and back, female *personata* of e. Mexico has dark brownish head and back. N American record most likely pertains to *personata*.

Distribution and Status:

World: Tropical Mexico (n. to around 27°N on Pacific slope, 24°N on Atlantic slope) s. to Amazonia.

North America: *Texas*: Hidalgo Co., 17 Feb– 10 Mar 1990 (male).

Comments: This handsome frugivore of tropical lowlands is ostensibly resident in the tropical lowlands and foothills of Mexico, to within about 300 km (180 miles) of TX. However, like other 'resident' tropical frugivores, such as Social Flycatcher, tityras wander on occasion, as with one that appeared on a ship 70 km out in the Pacific off Costa Rica, 4 Apr 2008 (*NAB* 62:490).

Field Identification: Distinctive, chunky, and boldly patterned bird unlike any regularly occurring species in N America.

adult ♀

1st-year ♂

adult ♂

adult ♂

♂ can be clouded dusky below

Masked Tityra

Similar Species: None in N America; this striking species should draw attention if it ever ranges north again.

Age/Sex/Season: Ages and sexes differ with adult appearance attained in 1 year; no seasonal variation. Molts not well known. *Adult male*: Pale gray head and back with bold black mask setting off pink orbital ring. *Adult female*: Dark gray-brown head and brownish back, no black mask. *1st-year*: Juv (plumage held briefly, unlikely in US) resembles female but whitish tail tip narrower. Following partial preformative molt in late summer–fall, male still resembles female but has slightly paler and grayer upperparts, and some birds develop traces of black mask in spring.

Habitat and Behavior: Woodland, forest and edge, adjacent semi-open areas with hedgerows and fruiting trees. Usually at upper to mid-levels in fruiting trees, where may remain quietly for long periods, hopping about sluggishly and occasionally hovering to pluck berries. In flight, slightly undulating progression and compact shape may suggest a woodpecker. Calls distinctive, including low wet quacks, often in short series, *rruk rruk* or *zzr zzrt* and *rr-rr-rrk*.

BAHAMA MOCKINGBIRD *Mimus gundlachii* 25–28 cm (9.8–10")

Summary: *Florida*: Very rare in the s., mainly in spring.

Taxonomy: 2 ssp, but differences unlikely to be apparent on single birds in the field. Nominate *gundlachii* of Bahamas and islands off Cuba presumably occurs in FL; ssp *hilli*, endemic to s. Jamaica, averages larger, with more distinct dark streaking, especially on upperparts.

Distribution and Status:

World: Bahamas, islands off the n. coast of Cuba, and s. Jamaica.

North America: *Florida*: Very rare in the s., mainly on the e. coast. Almost all records have been in spring (Apr–May, mainly late Apr to mid-May), since the 1st N American record there in 1973. Occasional records through summer and into early Sep have included attempted nesting, as well as hybridization with Northern Mockingbird in 1991–1994 and probably on other occasions.

Comments: Although some spring records might refer to birds that skulked undetected through the winter (see Blue Mockingbird) and were detected in spring when they became more conspicuous (such as when singing), the pattern of spring vagrancy appears real, with occasional birds summering. Bahama Mockingbird is generally considered resident in its range but may be commoner on Abaco in spring–summer than at other seasons (White 1998), suggesting that the FL records could be part of a wider pattern of spring dispersal. The relatively recent spate of records, with the first N American records in

adult

adult

Bahama Mockingbird

the mid-1970s, may be due to increased observer awareness but also may indicate that the species is occurring in FL with more frequency than in historical times.

Any aseasonal report of this species (such as in fall–winter) should be examined carefully; a wintering bird in 2005–2006 appeared to be a hybrid Northern Mockingbird × Bahama Mockingbird (*NAB* 60:368, 469).

Field Identification: Slightly larger and appreciably bulkier than Northern Mockingbird, lacking white wing patches and tail sides.

Similar Species: Adult fairly distinctive, but problems may arise with hybrids. One such hybrid resembled a brownish-toned Northern Mockingbird with a slightly heavier bill, no white wing patches, reduced white in the tail, and distinct dusky flank streaking. Molting juv Northern Mockingbird might suggest Bahama but smaller and slimmer, with obvious white tail sides and bold white primary patches.

Age/Sex/Season: Ages differ; sexes similar; no seasonal variation. Molts not well known; presumed complex basic strategy (see p. 35) with complete prebasic and partial preformative molts in fall. *1st-year*: Juv (plumage briefly held, unrecorded in US) has extensive dark-brown spotting on underparts, tending to short streaks on flanks; wing edgings buffy. Soon molts into adult-like plumage with retained juv rectrices narrower and more tapered than adult, and more heavily worn in spring.

Habitat and Behavior: On the Bahamas this species favors dry scrubby habitats, scrubby thickets, and woodland; feeds on the ground like a thrasher, as well as in fruiting trees and bushes. Fairly skulking unless singing, and less often in open and urban areas than Northern Mockingbird. Song (Hardy et al. 1987) can suggest Northern Mockingbird but often more rambling and continuous; some phrases are repeated within the continuous stream but typically the song is not so broken up by distinct series of repetitions like Northern; apparently does not imitate other species (J. Bond 1985); call a slurred raspy *shehhrr*.

BLUE MOCKINGBIRD *Melanotis caerulescens* 24–26.5 cm (9.5–10.5")

Summary: *Border States*: Very rare, mainly in winter or long-staying.

Taxonomy: 2 ssp, not known to be distinguishable in the field; US records presumably of widespread nominate ssp.

Distribution and Status:

World: Foothills and highlands of Mexico, n. to cen. Sonora and s. Tamaulipas.

North America: *Border States*: very rare, mainly in winter or long-staying; all 7 records since 1991. 3 records from se. AZ: Santa Cruz Co., 21 Dec–6 Mar 1992; Cochise Co., 4 Jan–4 Apr 1995; Cochise Co., 4 Feb–2 May 2009 (*NAB* 63:480). In s. TX, 2 records from Hidalgo Co.,

adults

Blue Mockingbird

Lower Rio Grande Valley: 9 May 1999–27 Feb 2002, 28 Sep 2002–26 Mar 2005. Also Los Angeles Co., CA, 5 Dec 1999–12 Mar 2000, and Doña Ana Co., NM, 7–8 Aug 1995; last 2 records not accepted by state committees.

Comments: In Mexico this species breeds mainly in the highlands and is a regular elevational migrant to the lowlands in some regions, such as in nw. Mexico (Russell & Monson 1998). For example, in some lowland sites (such as around San Blas, Nayarit), birds can be numerous in some years, virtually absent in others (Howell, pers. obs.), perhaps a reflection of food supply in the mountains. No data are available on the age composition of these elevational migrants, although apparent adults are involved. Given this elevational migration and winter wandering, the occurrence of occasional birds in border states is not surprising.

Concerns have been raised about the possibility of some N American records being of escaped cage birds. However, despite this species' striking voice and attractive plumage, it does not appear to be a popular cage bird in Mexico (Howell, pers. obs.). By contrast, Brown-backed Solitaire is a very common (and vocally conspicuous) cage bird yet it is hardly ever reported in N America, where it should be more easily detected. One concern raised about the CA bird was the presence of a leucistic outer primary; however, presumed wild individuals in Mexico can have occasional white feathers, and white feathers are quite frequent in some populations of other tropical mimids, such as Black Catbird (Howell, pers. obs.); we consider the CA bird a plausible wild vagrant. The NM bird has also been considered suspect on the grounds of origin, but could represent a bird dispersing n. in fall.

Blue Mockingbirds are notoriously skulking, at least in the nonbreeding season, and 'arrival' dates in the US may often reflect when somebody was lucky enough to find the bird, rather than when it appeared. Nonetheless, a difference between w. and e. records is apparent. CA and AZ records involved birds that spent only one winter, and fit with the pattern of lowland wintering in nw. Mexico. Their relatively late 'arrival' dates may reflect increased birding coverage at the Christmas Bird Count (CBC) season rather than the actual dates that they arrived. The TX birds, by contrast, remained for several years, and one reportedly arrived as an imm. Rather than being elevational winter

migrants, the TX birds may represent examples of post-breeding dispersal, followed by long-term residence in the newly found location, as with Sinaloa Wren in AZ. These records may be analogous to some northerly N American records of ostensibly resident species such as Curve-billed Thrasher, which appear on occasion well n. of their normal range and then remain for long periods; for example, a Curve-billed Thrasher was recorded in NE from Oct 2002 to at least winter 2007/2008 (*NAB* 62:267). Both of the long-staying TX Blue Mockingbirds appeared to be absent for long periods, primarily during summer, but tracking the movements of such a skulking species is problematic; whether these individuals just moved a few blocks or went much farther is unknown, or perhaps they became even more reclusive during prebasic molt (cf. Black-headed Nightingale-Thrush).

Field Identification: This skulking mimid might be better named Blue Catbird: it is quite distinct from a typical mockingbird (genus *Mimus*) in structure, behavior, and color, and is more likely to bring to mind a giant catbird.

Similar Species: Should be unmistakable; some calls suggest clucks of thrushes or mewing of catbird.

Age/Sex/Season: Ages differ; sexes similar; no seasonal variation. Molts not well known; presumed complex basic strategy (see p. 35). **1st-year**: Juv (plumage briefly held, unrecorded in US) has loosely textured head and body plumage dull slaty gray overall, eyes dull reddish. Following partial preformative molt in fall, resembles adult but duller overall, averaging less striking pale streaking on throat and chest, rectrices narrower and more tapered, and wings often appear contrastingly faded and slightly brownish in 1st summer.

Habitat and Behavior: Favors shady understory, dense brush, and thickets, often near water. Notably skulking, but sometimes in more open situations such as singing from an exposed perch (often sings from cover) or feeding in fairly open fruiting trees. Most often detected by voice or by following up on loud rustling in the leaf litter. Voice extremely varied, and is an accomplished mimic. Most common calls include a mellow whistled *choo* or *cheeoo*, a low clucking *chruk* or *chuk*, a nasal mewing *mejhr* or *meéah*, and a loud rich *whee-cheep* and *wheep*. Songs involve varied combinations of loud rich whistles, warbles, mews, and clucks with frequent mimicry of other species; can recall Curve-billed Thrasher, and not likely to be confused with Northern Mockingbird (Blue Mockingbird usually lacks multiple repetitions of short phrases that typify Northern Mockingbird songs).

THRUSHES (7 species)

Other than Red-legged Thrush in s. Florida, all vagrant New World thrushes are of Mexican origin, with most records not surprisingly coming from border states. Frugivores such as thrushes are prone to wander in search of fruit, but it is unknown whether variation in fruiting phenology in Mexico is behind the irregular N American incursions of species such as Aztec Thrush and White-throated Thrush. Records of both nightingale-thrushes appear to represent spring overshoots. Some Aztec Thrushes in Arizona may represent spring–summer overshooting, although others likely are post-breeding wanderers, and Texas records also suggest winter dispersal, as do records of Rufous-backed Thrush in the border states. White-throated Thrush is a winter vagrant to s. Texas, and Brown-backed Solitaire is known from 2 summer–fall records in se. Arizona.

BROWN-BACKED SOLITAIRE
Myadestes occidentalis 20.5–21.5 cm (8–8.5")

Summary: *Arizona*: 2 summer–fall records (1996, 2009).

Taxonomy: 4 ssp (Phillips 1991), not known to be separable in the field. N American record presumably refers to *occidentalis* of nw. Mexico, which averages duller and paler than ssp to the s. Also known as *M. obscurus* (Phillips 1991).

Distribution and Status:

World: Mountain forests from Mexico (n. to cen. Sonora and cen. Nuevo Leon) to Honduras.

North America: *Arizona*: Pima Co., 4–7 Oct 1996; Cochise Co., 18 Jul–1 Aug 2009 (1st-year male; Van Doren 2010; Rosenberg et al. 2011).

Comments: Brown-backed Solitaire occurs commonly in the pine-oak highlands and subtropical foothills of Mexico, breeding n. to around 28°N, a little over 300 km s. of the AZ border. There are also reports of singing birds n. to within 130 km of the border (Van Doren 2010). In western Mexico the species is an elevational migrant in fall and winter, with birds absent from n. breeding areas between Aug and Mar (Phillips

adult

some birds grayer overall on upperparts

1st-year

adult

Brown-backed Solitaire

1991; Howell & Webb 1995; Russell & Monson 1998). Birds reaching AZ may represent wandering 1st-year males as well as post-breeding dispersal of all ages and sexes (age unknown for 1st AZ record). However, because of their striking song, Brown-backed Solitaires are common cage birds, and any US record is tainted by the specter of prior captivity. In addition to the 2 accepted records there are 3 reports of Brown-backed Solitaires heard in the mountains of se. AZ, 24 Jun 1987 and 20 Sep 1991 (Van Doren 2010) and 18 May 2011 (*NAB* 65:497).

Field Identification: Similar in size and shape to Townsend's Solitaire but with brown back and wings; broken eye-ring; striking voice.

Similar Species: None in N America.

Age/Sex/Season: Ages differ slightly; sexes similar; no seasonal variation. Presumed complex basic strategy (see p. 35) with complete prebasic and partial preformative molts in fall. *1st-year*: Juv (plumage briefly held, unrecorded in US**)** has head and back pale buff with dark brown scalloping. Soon molts into adult-like plumage with retained juv rectrices narrower and more tapered than adult, and more heavily worn in spring–summer; underparts can be streaked whitish, less smoothly gray than adult.

Habitat and Behavior: Favors pine-oak and other montane forests. Quiet and overlooked easily when not singing, mainly at upper to mid-levels where most readily found at fruiting trees; also feeds on occasion in low fruiting shrubs.

Metallic jumbled crescendo song (given year-round, at times in high, ascending song flight) and squeaky-gate *yieh* call often reveal a solitaire's presence.

BLACK-HEADED NIGHTINGALE-THRUSH *Catharus mexicanus* 15–16.5 cm (6–6.5")

Summary: *Texas*: 1 spring–fall record from Lower Rio Grande Valley (2004).
Taxonomy: At least 5 ssp (Phillips 1991), not known to be distinguishable in the field; US record presumably of northernmost ssp, *smithi*.
Distribution and Status:
    World: Subtropical humid montane forest from e. Mexico (n. to s. Tamaulipas) to w. Panama.
    North America: *Texas*: Hidalgo Co., 28 May–29 Oct 2004 (male; Lockwood & Bates 2005).
Comments: In Mexico, this species breeds only about 250 km (150 miles) s. of the US border, where it is an elevational migrant that may withdraw in winter from the n. parts of its range (Phillips 1991; Howell & Webb 1995; Arvin 2001). Most birds return to ne. Mexico in mid–late Apr, a month or so earlier than the TX bird was found. However, 1st-year birds may return later and are perhaps more prone to overshoot (cf. Orange-billed Nightingale-Thrush); the TX bird also may have been present some time before being found. This species breeds in cloud forest and

Black-headed Nightingale-Thrush

subtropical humid montane forest; thus the Texas elevation and habitat were atypical, which may further suggest a 1st-year bird was involved. Remarkably, the Black-headed Nightingale-Thrush's date of discovery (28 May 2004) was the same as that of the 2nd N American record of Orange-billed Nightingale-Thrush, also found in s. TX.

The TX Black-headed Nightingale-Thrush sang during May–early Aug, and again in late Oct, before vanishing. This fall 'disappearance' and subsequent bout of song suggest a bird becoming secretive during its prebasic molt, rather than departing and returning.

Field Identification: Similar size and shape to Hermit Thrush but with distinctive plumage, orange bill, and orbital ring.

Similar Species: A fairly distinctive species, although in low light, such as late in the day or in dark understory, a dull female Black-headed Nightingale-Thrush might be mistaken for an Orange-billed; note Black-headed's dark cap, offsetting its orange orbital ring.

Age/Sex/Season: Ages differ; sexes differ slightly; no seasonal variation. Molts not well known; presumed complex basic strategy (see p. 35) with complete prebasic and partial preformative molts in fall. *Male* brighter overall with blackish cap and grayish chest. *Female* duller overall with blackish-brown cap, brown-washed chest. *1st-year* resembles adult but flight feathers are juv, and thus rectrices more tapered (although not as distinctly different from adult as on North American breeding *Catharus*). Juv (plumage held briefly and unrecorded in US) upperparts flecked cinnamon-buff; throat and underparts whitish; mottled brown and buff on chest and flanks.

Habitat and Behavior: Much like other *Catharus* thrushes, being terrestrial and reclusive unless singing. Song is a slightly tinny, jumbled warble, pleasant-sounding though slightly scratchy, and at times run into a warbled trill. Common call a buzzy, fairly harsh complaining mew, *rreahr* or *meahh*.

ORANGE-BILLED NIGHTINGALE-THRUSH *Catharus aurantiirostris* 15.5–17 cm (6–6.8")

Summary: *Texas*: 2 spring records from Lower Rio Grande Valley (1996, 2004). *South Dakota*: 1 summer record (2010).

Taxonomy: 11 ssp, varying mainly in color tones. Northern ssp not known to be separable in the field, but on geographic grounds, TX records likely of ssp *clarus*.

Distribution and Status:

World: Foothills and highlands from Mexico (n. to s. Sonora and s. Tamaulipas) to n. S America.

North America: *Texas*: Cameron Co., 8 Apr 1986 (1st-year); Hidalgo Co. (window-kill), 28 May

can have dark culmen

adult

Orange-billed Nightingale-Thrush

2004. **South Dakota**: Lawrence Co., 10 Jul–19 Aug 2010 (NAB 64:615).

Comments: In Mexico, this species breeds only about 300 km (180 miles) s. of the US border and is an elevational migrant that may withdraw in winter from the n. parts of its range (Phillips 1991; Howell & Webb 1995). The Apr bird was grounded along the coast by a front and aged as a 1st-summer (Papish et al. 1997); the second TX bird was identified as a specimen (age unknown). The SD record, of a singing bird that likely arrived there earlier than the date it was detected, may also represent an overshoot from ne. Mexico (about 2300 km, or 1400 miles, from its nearest range), although the breeding range in nw. Mexico is slightly closer (about 2000 km, or 1200 miles). An earlier (unaccepted) report of this species from AZ, in about mid-April 1974 (Phillips 1991:105) also fits the pattern of spring migrants overshooting.

Field Identification: Similar size and shape to Hermit Thrush, but with plain underparts, orange bill, and orbital ring.

Similar Species: Two similar nightingale-thrushes occur in Mexico, and vagrants should be identified with care. **Russet Nightingale-Thrush** C. occidentalis has dark bill with pinkish base to lower mandible, lacks an appreciable orbital ring, and has somewhat more mottled underparts. **Ruddy-capped Nightingale-Thrush** C. frantzii is darker overall with blackish upper mandible, orange lower mandible, no appreciable orbital ring, and plain, dusky grayish underwings. Orange-billed and Russet, like Hermit Thrush and Swainson's Thrush, have a broad buff band across the bases of the remiges, visible on underwing and often showing in flight. Also note that in low light, such as late in the day or in dark understory, a dull female **Black-headed Nightingale-Thrush** might be mistaken for an Orange-billed; note Black-capped's dark cap, which offsets its orange orbital ring.

Age/Sex/Season: Ages differ; sexes similar; no seasonal variation. Molts not well known; presumed complex basic strategy (see p. 35) with complete prebasic and partial preformative molts of n. populations in fall. **1st-year** resembles adult but flight feathers are juv, and thus rectrices more tapered (although not as distinctly different from adult as on N American Catharus). Juv (plumage held briefly and unrecorded in US) has upperparts spotted pale cinnamon, throat and underparts whitish, heavily mottled dark brown on chest and flanks.

Habitat and Behavior: Much like other Catharus thrushes, being terrestrial and reclusive unless singing. Unlike other Catharus thrushes in Mexico, Orange-billed sings in winter as well as in spring–summer: song a short, varied, slightly scratchy warble that is jerkier and tinnier, less fluty, than the songs of N American Catharus. Common call a complaining mew, meeeahr, somewhat catbird-like.

RUFOUS-BACKED THRUSH (Robin)
Turdus rufopalliatus 21.5–24 cm (8.5–9.5")

Summary: **Southwest**: Rare in late fall–winter, exceptional in spring–summer. **Elsewhere**: Exceptional or very rare in winter, w. to coastal s. CA, n. to UT, and e. to s. TX.

Taxonomy: 3 ssp in mainland Mexico, all rather variable and not distinguishable in the field; appreciably paler taxon graysoni of Tres Marias Islands may represent a separate species, Grayson's Thrush (Phillips 1991), which is unlikely to occur in the US.

Distribution and Status:

World: Lowlands and foothills of w. Mexico, n. to cen. Sonora.

North America: **Southwest**: Rare in late fall–winter (Oct to mid-Apr, mainly Nov–Dec) to Mexican border states from se. CA to w. TX, the great majority being in AZ, since the first N American record there in 1960. Very rare in spring–summer (Apr to mid-late Jul), in AZ and NM. **Elsewhere**: Exceptional in winter w. to sw. CA (Jan to mid-Apr; 2 records), n. to sw. UT (18–31 Dec 2004; NAB 59:301, 371), and very rare in s. TX (mid-Nov to early Apr).

Comments: In nw. Mexico, Rufous-backed Thrushes undergo winter wandering (Russell & Monson 1998; Howell, pers. obs.), and the N American records seem to be a well-established part of this pattern, which apparently extends on occasion into s. TX (see Fig. 18, p. 15). This pattern of northward dispersal in late fall–winter suggests that of a few other species breeding in w. Mexico, such as Ruddy Ground-Dove, Thick-billed Kingbird, and even Blue Mockingbird and Streak-backed Oriole. It mirrors the pattern found in e. Mexico (and adjacent s. TX) with species such as White-throated Thrush, Crimson-collared Grosbeak, and Eastern Blue Bunting, and reinforces the idea that dispersal and migration in tropical birds need not be southward in fall and northward in spring. Rather, such dispersals, which often have an ele-

Rufous-backed Thrush

vational component, may fan out over potentially 360° if areas to the n. have food and are not too cold. The odd spring–summer records may be of misorienting 1st-year birds, and mirror coastal TX records in spring of Aztec Thrush, Flame-colored Tanager, and Crimson-collared Grosbeak.

Rufous-backed Thrush may have been more regular in AZ in the 1970s and early 1980s than in the late 1980s and 1990s, but its occurrences may be cyclic, perhaps reflecting climate and food supply; for example, good numbers have been found since 2010, with 10 birds in AZ in late Oct–Nov 2011 alone (*NAB* 66:141); this species is thus a borderline candidate to be considered a rare bird in N America. The Nov peak in records at widely scattered localities likely reflects the main period of dispersal, following which birds find and settle in wintering areas with better cover and more food, where they may be overlooked. No data are available on age composition of birds found in the US, and it would be interesting to know to what degree adults and 1st-cycle birds are represented.

Field Identification: Size and shape recall American Robin but plumage distinctive; note grayish head, rufous back.

Similar Species: A distinctive species that should not be confused, given a reasonable view.

Age/Sex/Season: Ages differ; sexes similar but males average brighter, with brighter bill and orbital ring; no seasonal variation. Molts not well known; presumed complex basic strategy (see

p. 35) with complete prebasic and partial preformative molts in fall. **1st-year:** Resembles adult but may average duller; flight feathers are juv, and rectrices thus more tapered (difficult to judge). Juv (plumage held for a few weeks, unrecorded in US): Duller and paler overall, with buff-streaked upperparts, whitish to cinnamon underparts spotted dark brown.

Habitat and Behavior: Occurs widely in deciduous and semi-deciduous forest and woodland, riparian areas, parks and gardens; sometimes ranges up into pine-oak woodland; typically near fruiting trees. Habits much like those of American Robin but less often in open situations and can be quite shy. Vagrants often quiet, but varied calls include a fairly loud, drawn-out, mellow whistled *cheeoo* or *teeeuu* that would likely draw attention; a fairly hard clucking *chuk* or *chok*, often given in series; and a high thin *ssi* or *ssit*, often given in flight.

WHITE-THROATED THRUSH *Turdus assimilis* 23–25.5 cm (9–10″)

Summary: *Texas*: Very rare in winter in Lower Rio Grande Valley.

Taxonomy: About 14 ssp. Among the relatively dull n. populations, *suttoni* of ne. Mexico is darker and browner, less grayish, than w. Mexican populations, and US records likely pertain to this ssp, which was described as recently as 1991 (Phillips 1991). White-throated Thrush is

posture can
obscure
white collar

1st-year

adult

White-throated Thrush

sometimes merged with White-necked Thrush *T. albicollis* of S America.

Distribution and Status:

World: Subtropical and temperate montane forests from Mexico (n. to s. Sonora and s. Tamaulipas) to w. Ecuador.

North America: **Texas**: Very rare in winter (late Dec to mid-Apr) in Lower Rio Grande Valley, where first recorded Feb 1990 and since found in 4 different winters; almost half the records were during an influx in late Dec 2004–late Mar 2005.

Comments: This is another Mexican species that occasionally disperses n. (and downslope) in winter, with some individuals reaching s. TX. Whether the late-winter detections (most birds have been found in late Jan–Feb) reflect true seasonal occurrence or increased observer coverage in late winter is unclear, and this pattern contrasts with the Nov peak of Rufous-backed Thrushes in w. regions of the US.

Field Identification: Size and shape recall American Robin, but plumage much duller overall; note dark head with contrasting white forecollar (can be hard to see).

Similar Species: Distinctive if seen reasonably well. Clay-colored Thrush warmer brown and more uniform overall, lacks distinct yellow orbital ring, and undertail coverts buff (whitish on White-throated).

Age/Sex/Season: Ages differ; sexes similar; no seasonal variation. Molts not well known; presumed complex basic strategy (see p. 35) with complete prebasic and partial preformative molts of n. populations in fall. **1st-year** resembles adult but flight feathers are juv, and rectrices thus more tapered than adult (difficult to judge). Juv (plumage held for a few weeks in summer–fall, unrecorded in US): Upperparts streaked pale cinnamon, underparts whitish to pale buff, spotted and mottled dark brown.

Habitat and Behavior: In Mexico favors subtropical and temperate forest in foothills and mountains, but winter wanderers likely to occur in any wooded habitats (including suburban gardens) with fruiting trees. Habits much like those of American Robin but more arboreal and less often in open situations; can be quite shy. Varied calls include a fairly loud, slightly nasal *rreeuh* or *rreuh*, often doubled; a clucking *ch'uhk*; and a high thin *ssi* or *ssee*, often given in flight.

RED-LEGGED THRUSH *Turdus plumbeus*
25–27 cm (9.8–10.7")

Summary: *Florida*: 1 spring record (2010).
Taxonomy: 6 ssp in 2 groups, perhaps representing 2 species: *plumbeus* group (Western Red-legged Thrush, 4 ssp of Bahamas, Cuba,

adult

Red-legged Thrush

Caymans) and *ardosiaceus* group (Eastern Red-legged Thrush; 2 ssp of Hispaniola and Dominica). Western group has black throat, white chin patch; bill black to red-based. Eastern group has white throat streaked blackish; bill bright red to yellow.

The recent N American record refers to nominate *plumbeus* of the Bahamas, which has a black bill and small white chin patch. Other Western ssp have a mostly or wholly red bill and larger white chin patch.

Distribution and Status:

World: Bahamas, Cuba, Caymans, Hispaniola, and Dominica.

North America: *Florida*: Brevard Co., 31 May 2010 (Anderson & Ponce 2010).

Comments: Until this recent record, Red-legged Thrush stood out as the only frugivorous passerine common in the Bahamas but unrecorded in the US—thus it could be considered an overdue vagrant. A sighting of Red-legged Thrush from Miami in late Mar 1960 was dismissed as a presumed escape (Stevenson & Anderson 1994), but the species is not known as a cage bird (Anderson & Ponce 2010) and there seems no reason the Miami individual could not have been a wild vagrant. Although Red-legged Thrushes have almost no history of vagrancy within the Caribbean, some presumably wander on occasion and spring may be the best season to hope for further records of this handsome species in FL.

Field Identification: About the size of American Robin, with striking plumage and bright red legs.

Similar Species: None in N America.

Age/Sex/Season: Ages differ; sexes similar; no seasonal variation. Molts not well known; presumed complex basic strategy (see p. 35) with complete prebasic and partial preformative molts in fall. *1st-year*: Juv (plumage briefly held, unrecorded in US) has dusky mottling on upperparts, buff tips to wing coverts, and pale buff and dark sooty spots and short bars on underparts. Soon molts into adult-like plumage with retained juv rectrices averaging narrower and more tapered than adult, and more heavily worn in spring.

Habitat and Behavior: On the Bahamas this species favors woodland, parks, and gardens. Habits much like American Robin but perhaps more skulking and forest-based. Clucking and slightly mewing 'thrush' calls have a nasal or semi-metallic quality that would likely draw attention.

AZTEC THRUSH *Ridgwayia pinicola*
21.5–24 cm (8.5–9.5")

Summary: *Southwest*: Very rare and sporadic in spring–fall, mainly in mountains of se. AZ, exceptional in winter. *Elsewhere*: Exceptional in winter–spring in s. TX.

Aztec Thrush

1st-year ♂

molt contrast

striking underwing

adult has frosted tips to primary coverts, whitish tips to inner primaries

adult ♂

1st-year ♀

adult ♀

juv

Taxonomy: 2 ssp (Phillips 1991) not distinguishable in the field. Sometimes placed in the genus *Zoothera*.

Distribution and Status:

World: Temperate montane forests of Mexico, n. to cen. Sonora and Coahuila.

North America: ***Southwest***: First recorded in US, 21–25 Aug 1977 (juv in Brewster Co., w. TX), this sought-after species has occurred irregularly since. Most records have been in spring–fall (mid-May to late Oct, mainly late Jul–Sep) from mountains of se. AZ, where exceptional in winter (Nov–Feb). Years may pass with no records, while in some years small invasions occur, as in Aug–Sep 1986 (15–20 birds) and Jul–Sep 2006 (10+ birds). The 2 records from NM (15 Jul 2006, 27 Apr 2007) coincided with and followed an invasion in AZ. ***Elsewhere***: In s. TX, singles in Hidalgo Co., Lower Rio Grande Valley, 16–17 Feb

2010, and Nueces Co., Lower Gulf Coast, 30 Jan 1979 and 16–20 May 1996. Records through 1991 were discussed by Zimmerman (1991).

Comments: The movements in Mexico of this handsome but easily overlooked species are poorly known. There appears to be some winter withdrawal from the nw., when flocks of hundreds gather on the Volcanes de Colima, in Jalisco (Howell, pers. obs.), and most records from ne. Mexico are in winter (Phillips 1991; Howell & Webb 1995). Thus the Jan–May records from s. TX (and perhaps the Apr record from NM) may reflect winter wandering and post-wintering misorientation.

Records of Aztec Thrushes from Sonora, to the s. of AZ, include adults with fledglings in early to mid-Sep (e.g., Radamaker 2009). If late summer breeding is typical, the late summer–fall incursions into AZ may involve birds wandering in search of breeding areas, as well as possible post-breeding movements. Records later than Sep from the mountains of se. AZ are exceptional, but on occasion birds linger into winter (perhaps even into spring?) but may be overlooked easily given low observer coverage combined with the reclusive nature of this species.

Field Identification: Stocky shape and relatively short tail suggest Varied Thrush, and distinct from slimmer and longer-tailed *Turdus* thrushes. Striking plumage renders this handsome species all but unmistakable.

Similar Species: Unmistakable if seen well, although inexperienced observers have at times mistaken juv Spotted Towhee for Aztec Thrush.

Age/Sex/Season: Ages/sexes differ; no seasonal variation. Molts not well known; presumed complex basic strategy (see p. 35) with complete prebasic and partial preformative molts in fall. *Male*: Head, back, and chest blackish, with paler streaking, *Female*: Head, back, and chest gray-brown with paler streaking. *Adult*: Inner and middle primaries with large white tips, forming solid panel on closed wing; outer rectrices blunt-tipped, with broad white tips. *1st-year*: Resembles adult of respective sex but flight feathers are juv, and thus aged readily by primary pattern. Juv (plumage held a few weeks, but has been recorded in US): Upperparts gray-brown, crown and back with bold buff streaks, greater coverts edged buff, throat and underparts buffy with dark scalloping. Inner and middle primaries with narrow white tips, outer rectrices relatively tapered, with narrower white tips than adult.

Habitat and Behavior: Favors pine-oak woodland where feeds in fruiting trees, less often on the ground. Associates at fruiting trees with other species, but also occurs apart from other birds, alone or in groups. Sits quietly for long periods in trees and bushes, mainly at upper to mid-levels, and is easily overlooked. Can be located by its calls, which tend to be given infrequently: variations on a quavering whistled *wheeeirr* can carry quite well; also has a softer, slightly nasal whistled *whein* or *whieh*, which may recall Hepatic Tanager, and a high thin *ssii* or *ssiip*.

GRAY SILKY (Silky-flycatcher)

Ptiliogonys cinereus 18.5–21 cm (7.3–8.3")

Summary: *Texas*: 2 fall–winter records (1985, 1995). *California*: Uncertain (see Comments, below).

Taxonomy: Up to 4 ssp recognized (Phillips 1986); 3 Mexican ssp not known to be distinguishable in the field but *P. c. molybdophanes* of Guatemala and adjacent Mexico is notably darker. Ssp involved in US records unknown.

Distribution and Status:

World: Highlands and subtropical foothills of Mexico (n. to s. Sonora and s. Coahuila) to Guatemala.

North America: *Texas*: Cameron Co., Lower Rio Grande Valley, 31 Oct–11 Nov 1985 (male), and El Paso Co., w. TX, 12 Jan–5 Mar 1995 (male). *California*: 5 records from the s. are considered of questionable origin (Hamilton et al. 2007), although a male in the mountains of Orange Co., 29 Jan–19 Feb 1999, was at a location and season plausible for a vagrant.

Comments: The poorly understood seasonal movements of this species in Mexico, perhaps related to the tracking of food resources, suggest that it is a candidate for vagrancy to US border states. In Sonora, nw. Mexico, silkies are not well known but apparently are unpredictable in their occurrence (Russell & Monson 1998). Elsewhere in n. Mexico there is some winter movement of silkies to lower elevations, and perhaps also southward withdrawal from some n. areas (Howell & Webb 1995; Phillips 1986).

Because this species is kept in cages in Mexico, any records n. of the border are inevitably tainted with the specter of possibly being escapes. Neither of the (accepted) TX records seems any more plausible to us than a wintering bird (not accepted) in the mountains of s. CA. Perhaps surprisingly, there are no substantiated records of this generally conspicuous species from se. AZ. If winter vagrancy is the norm, this may reflect relatively low observer coverage in the AZ mountains at that season. Or perhaps it reflects less intensive cage-bird traffic in the AZ border areas than occurs in CA and TX? For now, the true status of Gray Silky in N America remains unresolved.

Field Identification: Distinctive, slender crested bird; not a flycatcher (despite a common English name) but actually in the same family as Phainopepla.

Similar Species: Nothing in N America.

Age/Sex/Season: Ages/sexes differ; no seasonal variation. Molts not well known; presumed complex basic strategy (see p. 35). *Male*: Blue-gray head, chest, and upperparts with ochre-yellow flanks, yellow undertail coverts. *Female*: Buffy gray head and body, yellow restricted to

Gray Silky

undertail coverts. *1st-year*: Juv (plumage briefly held, unrecorded in US) resembles female but belly washed yellow, and male has glossier and blacker flight feathers (including tertials). Following preformative molt, not readily distinguishable from adult although primary coverts average duller and browner.

Habitat and Behavior: Favors pine-oak woodland, adjacent open areas with bushes and trees; mainly eats berries. Often perches prominently atop tall trees, flies high with loosely undulating flight. In Mexico, often in flocks and associates readily at fruiting trees with thrushes and other birds. Calls are varied, often slightly nasal or bickering in quality, including a clipped nasal *k'lik* or *ch'pik*, a fairly dry *chi-che-rup che-chep*, and a clearer, fairly sharp *chureet* or *chu-leep*.

SINALOA WREN *Thryothorus sinaloa*
12.5–14 cm (5–5.5")

Summary: *Arizona*: 2 records in the se., 1 long-staying (2008–2010).
Taxonomy: 3 ssp, not known to be separable in the field; US records presumably of n. ssp *cinereus*.

Distribution and Status:
World: Lowlands and foothills of w. Mexico, n. to around 31°N in Sonora.
North America: *Arizona*: Santa Cruz Co., 25 Aug 2008–30 Nov 2009, and reported again 15 Aug 2010 (Brown & Baxter 2009; *NAB* 64:127, *NAB* 65:135); Cochise Co., 14–18 Apr 2009 (*NAB* 63:479).
Comments: This species is presumed to breed only about 60 km (35 miles) s. of the US border in Sonora, Mexico, where its range may be expanding northward (Flesch 2008). Although not migratory, post-breeding dispersal can be expected, apparently to the extent that birds reach the US on occasion. The Aug 2008 bird was thought to have arrived recently (Brown & Baxter 2009), and its subsequent long residence is typical of many Mexican species that are thought to reach the s. US in fall via post-breeding dispersal. The Apr 2009 bird may have arrived the previous fall–winter and been overlooked until more vocal in spring.
Field Identification: Size and shape somewhat similar to Carolina Wren; note striped neck sides, dingy underparts.

Sinaloa Wren   all plumages similar

Similar Species: Fairly distinctive but rather skulking; thus, plumage features can be difficult to see well. Voice often striking.

Age/Sex/Season: All plumages similar. Molts not well known; presumed complex basic strategy (see p. 35) with complete prebasic and partial preformative molts in fall. Juv (plumage held briefly, unrecorded in US) has looser-textured plumage and less contrasting face pattern than post-juvenile plumages.

Habitat and Behavior: Woodland and thorn forest with ground cover, adjacent thickets. Much like other woodland wrens, usually staying low and in cover, although at times responds to pishing and climbs into open situations. Song of varied, sometimes powerful, rich whistled phrases is unlike any North American bird, although overall pattern of typical songs might bring to mind a Song Sparrow. Common calls include a rough buzzy *dzzzshrr* or *rreihrr*, a rough scolding *rreh-rreh-rreh* … , and a hard dry chatter.

THICK-BILLED VIREO *Vireo crassirostris*
12–13 cm (4.7–5.2")

Summary: *Florida*: Very rare in spring and fall in the s.

Taxonomy: 5 ssp differ slightly in average plumage tones and size, but not known to be distinguishable in the field. FL birds presumed to be nominate *crassirostris* from the Bahamas.

Thick-billed Vireo is one of a group of vireos in the Caribbean and Middle American region whose relationships remain vexing. Disjunct population of vireos on Isla Providencia (taxon *approximans*) sometimes viewed as an isolated ssp of Thick-billed Vireo (AOU 1998) but better considered as a ssp of Mangrove Vireo *V. pallens* complex (Phillips 1991), or as a distinct species, Providencia Vireo (Gill & Wright 2006).

Distribution and Status:

World: Bahamas, and on scattered other islands in the Caribbean: Cayman Islands, islands off northern Cuba, and Isla Tortue off Haiti.

North America: *Florida*: At least 13 birds in the s. since 1989, in spring (Mar to mid-May; 5 birds) and fall (Aug to mid-Nov; 8 birds). Earlier reports from winter are considered uncertain (Smith et al. 1990).

Comments: This is a very common species in the Bahamas, including small islands only 85–100 km (55–60 miles) e. of FL. It has been suggested that occurrences in FL may be linked to prevailing easterly winds (Smith et al. 1990), although the spring and fall pattern of records suggests that the species may undergo regular seasonal movements among islands, which could further predispose it to drift vagrancy.

Some fall birds in FL have been molting body and tail feathers (molt of remiges was not mentioned specifically by Smith et al. 1990), and are suspected to have been 1st-year birds. Thus, some fall birds may simply represent post-fledging dispersal, as with Bahama Swallow. Spring records of Thick-billed Vireos in FL might be returning migrants, or perhaps birds that skulked undetected somewhere through the winter before becoming conspicuous in spring.

Uncertainty over some records prior to 1990 reflects inadequate or misleading treatment in earlier field guides.

stocky, large-headed appearance

broad dark eye-ring break

White-eyed Vireo

yellow spectacles

1st-year (fall–winter)

adult fresh

Thick-billed Vireo

adult worn

1st-year (fall–winter)

Field Identification: Resembles White-eyed Vireo in size but slightly bulkier and bigger headed with a slightly thicker bill that appears paler overall (due to its greater depth).

Similar Species: This subtly distinctive species can be confused with *White-eyed Vireo*. Given considerable variation in plumage tones, the face pattern and overall structure are key features. As well as a typically brighter and more contrasting appearance, note the distinct face pattern of White-eyed, with its yellow spectacles; adults have white eyes but these are dusky on 1st-year.

Separation of Thick-billed Vireo from other vireos of the Caribbean region (none yet recorded in US) should also be considered, and any vagrants documented carefully.

Cuban Vireo V. gundlachii lacks dark loral stripe and thus has somewhat wide-eyed facial expression, with large yellowish supraloral patch and yellowish postocular crescent; often somewhat paler and dingier overall, with narrower whitish wing-bars. *Mangrove Vireo* of Mexico's Yucatan Peninsula slightly smaller and more lightly built than Thick-billed, with a less stout bill; lacks dark loral stripe, so face pattern

suggests Cuban Vireo but with a smaller postocular spot.

Age/Sex/Season: All plumages similar. Molts not well-known. *1st year* might show molt limits in greater coverts (and perhaps remiges if preformative molt eccentric; see p. 39); if retained, juv rectrices more tapered and worn than those of adult. Juv (plumage weak and lax, held briefly and not certainly recorded in US); face pattern less sharply defined than adult, with paler supraloral.

Habitat and Behavior: Much like White-eyed Vireo, foraging in thickets and woodland where can be sluggish and hard to see, but often responds strongly to pishing and can be quite confiding. Calls include a drawn out harsh scold, repeated with a cadence that may resemble a 'series of low, protracted pishes' (Smith et al. 1990), distinct from the faster-paced and often insistent scolding of White-eyed. Song (has been heard from spring birds, and given at least through late fall in Bahamas) a short jerky warble, suggesting White-eyed Vireo but slower paced, more slurred, and burrier, lacking the bright emphatic quality of White-eyed (Barlow 1981).

YUCATAN VIREO *Vireo magister* 14.5–15.5 cm (5.7–6.2")

Summary: *Texas*: 1 spring record on Upper Gulf Coast (1984).

Taxonomy: 2 ssp, not known to be separable in the field. On geographic grounds, TX bird most likely nominate *magister* of Yucatan Peninsula rather than *caymanensis* of Grand Cayman Island.

Distribution and Status:

World: Resident locally in e. Yucatan Peninsula, islands off n. Honduras, and on Grand Cayman.

North America: *Texas*: Galveston Co., 28 Apr–27 May 1984 (Morgan et al. 1985).

Comments: Little is known of any seasonal movements this species might undertake in the Yucatan Peninsula, but as a frugivore it appears prone to some seasonal wandering, as does Black Catbird (Howell, pers. obs.), for which there is an old US record, from s. Texas in June 1892. The Yucatan Vireo in TX was found after a period of strong se. winds that could have facilitated its Gulf crossing, and it remained in the area for at least a month. The spring of 1984 also saw the occurrence on the Gulf coast of a Greenish Elaenia and an *Elaenia* sp. The coincidence of three vagrant frugivores being found in one spring may reflect food shortages in these species' normal ranges.

While the TX bird's facial expression and bill shape matched a Yucatan Vireo, its brown and rufous plumage tones were atypical of the species and caused some to question its identity (Phillips 1991). Assuming it was a Yucatan Vireo, it was a small, 1st-summer female with oddly colored plumage.

Field Identification: Large plain-winged vireo with big bill, contrasting creamy eyebrow set off by black eyestripe.

Similar Species: A distinctive species, although the small and atypically colored Texas bird was originally identified and banded as a Warbling Vireo. Attention to face pattern and bill size should preclude such confusion. Some birds have a diffuse dark whisker and could suggest Black-whiskered Vireo, but Yucatan is overall grayer and colder-toned, lacking contrast between the gray crown and olive back, and typically is dingier below.

Age/Sex/Season: All plumages similar, but male averages larger and larger billed than female. Molts not well known. As in related vireos, ages probably differ in shape of outer rectrices, and 1st-year birds in spring and summer (as in a photo of the TX bird in Lockwood & Freeman 2004) likely have more heavily worn flight feathers than adults.

Habitat and Behavior: Much as other large vireos, such as Red-eyed. Favors semi-deciduous thicket woodland, gardens. Forages sluggishly at upper to mid-levels and eats fruit. Calls include a soft dry chatter that may suggest Yellow-green Vireo, and a distinctive nasal *beenk* or *peek*.

WOOD-WARBLERS (6 species)

Records of vagrant wood-warblers in N America are all of Mexican species. Most records of Crescent-chested Warbler, Fan-tailed Warbler, and Slate-throated Whitestart reflect spring–summer overshoots, presumably from migrant

short primary projection adult fresh

browner individual

adult

Yucatan Vireo

populations that withdraw in winter from northern Mexico. Records of Gray-crowned Yellowthroat and Rufous-capped Warbler, on the other hand, appear to represent post-breeding dispersal and perhaps northward range expansion. Golden-crowned Warbler is an irregular winter visitor to s. Texas, although the species is not known to be a conventional migrant.

CRESCENT-CHESTED WARBLER
Oreothlypis (Vermivora) superciliosa 11–12 cm (4.3–4.7")

Summary: *Southwest*: Very rare in AZ, mainly spring–summer; 1 summer record in w. TX (1993).

Taxonomy: 5 ssp, with AZ records presumably of northernmost ssp *sodalis*, which averages larger and paler than populations to s.

Distribution and Status:

   World: Subtropical and temperate highlands and foothills from Mexico (n. to cen. Sonora and e. Nuevo Leon) to w. Nicaragua.

   North America: *Southwest*: Very rare in se. AZ, all records since 1983. About half of the records are from spring (Apr–early Jun; including a pair in late Apr to mid-May 1984), with fewer records in summer–fall (late Jun to mid-Sep; including an adult feeding a recently fledged juv in 2007), and fewest in fall–winter (mid-Sep to late

Mar; including a bird presumed to have returned in successive winters, 1992/1993 and 1993/1994). 1 record from w. TX: Brewster Co., singing bird on 2 Jun 1993.

Comments: In adjacent Sonora, Mexico, this species may be mainly a summer resident (present mid-Mar to mid-Sep), with wintering birds occasionally found in riparian areas (Terrill 1985). The AZ records appear to reflect occasional spring overshoots, irregular breeding, and northward fall and winter dispersal, all traits common to a number of Mexican species that wander n. to the s. US. The TX bird may have originated from the migratory nw. Mexican population, or from the ne. Mexican population (ssp *mexicana*), which is usually considered resident.

Field Identification: This 'parula with a paint job' is a bird of montane oak woodlands in Mexico. Eponymous chestnut chest crescent small but usually apparent.

   Similar Species: Nothing really similar in N America. Note bold white eyebrow, plain blue-gray wings, bright yellow bib with a chestnut spot on mid-chest, and pointed bill.

   Age/Sex/Season: Ages/sexes differ slightly and extremes may be distinguished; no seasonal variation. Molts not well known; likely complex basic strategy (see p. 35). ***Adult female***: Averages duller and paler than adult male, with narrower and paler chestnut chest patch (rarely

1st-year

adult ♂

adult ♀

adult ♂

Crescent-chested Warbler

almost absent). *1st-year*: Juv (lax plumage held briefly) head and upperparts duller than adult, with pale cinnamon wing-bars; throat and underparts dirty buff, becoming whitish on belly. Following partial preformative molt, resembles adult of respective sex but retained juv flight feathers are more strongly worn in spring–summer and tend to be browner overall, with reduced blue-gray edgings; rectrices slightly more tapered; chest crescent of female often reduced to a faint rufous smudge or even absent.

Habitat and Behavior: Oak and pine-oak woodland in n. Mexico, also ranging rarely in winter to deciduous or semi-deciduous lowland riparian habitats. Forages mainly at upper to mid-levels in trees, usually in outer foliage clumps where often probes dead-leaf clusters, hangs upside down like a chickadee, and hover-gleans. Song distinctive, a fairly level dry buzz of up to about 1 sec. duration, may suggest an anemic Pacific-slope Spotted Towhee; call a high sharp *tsik* or *sik*, suggesting Orange-crowned Warbler.

GRAY-CROWNED YELLOWTHROAT
Geothlypis poliocephala 13.5–14.5 cm (5.3–5.7")

Summary: *Texas*: Very rare in the s., mainly spring–summer, some long-staying; formerly bred.
Taxonomy: 5 ssp recognized, differing slightly in size and plumage tones. Mexican populations have distinct white eye-arcs whereas Cen American populations have eye-arcs reduced or lacking. Nominate *poliocephala* (overall the dullest and palest ssp) has occurred in s. TX. Populations in ne. Mexico (and formerly TX) sometimes separated as ssp *ralphi*, although Ridgway himself, who described *ralphi*, later found it not distinguishable from *poliocephala* (Ridgway 1902).
Distribution and Status:
World: Lowlands and foothills of tropical Mexico (n. to cen. Sinaloa and cen. Tamaulipas) to w. Panama.

North America: *Texas*: Several recent records (year-round, mainly late Mar to early Jul) from the s., all since 1988 (most recent prior record 1927). Following 4 records in 1988–1989 (mid-Feb to early Jul), and 2 in 1999–2000 (late Mar to late Jun), there were ongoing reports during Feb 2004–Jun 2006 of at least 1–2 birds from Cameron Co., where nesting was reported in 2005 (Lorenz et al. 2006); however, at least one of these birds appears to have been a hybrid (see Comments, below).

Comments: Why this species disappeared from s. TX around the turn of the 20th century is not known, although habitat alteration may have been involved. The status of Gray-crowned Yellowthroat in adjacent Tamaulipas, Mexico, is poorly known and thus sheds no light on the matter. Gray-crowned Yellowthroats are not conventional migrants, but being somewhat tied

dark lores
white eye-arcs

hybrid with **Common Yellowthroat** intermediate features note extent of black mask

often has bushy crest

adult

Gray-crowned Yellowthroat

1st-year

to grasslands, which are cyclic successional habitats, they must have inherent dispersal abilities. The slow 'return' of this species to s. TX, starting in the late 1980s, corresponds with appearances in the US of a number of tropical Mexican species whose ranges appear to have started extending n. in about the 1980s.

Recent US records of this species are clouded by potential hybridization with Common Yellowthroat (see Similar Species, below), a situation recalling that of Flame-colored Tanager in se. AZ. One male in 1995–1996 was considered a hybrid, and one male from 2004 (Howell, pers. obs.) to 2006 (M. O'Brien, photo) was banded, and also appears to have been a hybrid, although accepted as pure by state committee.

Field Identification: Distinctive but typically skulking warbler of drier grassy habitats. Larger and bulkier than Common Yellowthroat, with longer, more expressive tail; relatively stout bicolored bill has decurved culmen. Beware hybrids with Common Yellowthroat, as well as perhaps presumed hybrid Common Yellowthroat × MacGillivray's Warbler, which can superficially resemble Gray-crowned Yellowthroat (see *NAB* 64:668).

Similar Species: A distinctive species, but identification in the US confounded by hybridization with **Common Yellowthroat**. 1st-winter male Common, with limited black mask, can superficially resemble Gray-crowned, but latter is bulkier with a stout bill that has a decurved culmen and is bicolored year-round (bill of breeding male Common usually all-dark), a longer and more expressive tail, and distinct voice. Note, though, songs of young birds are presumably learned, which means that a dispersing 1st-year male Gray-crowned might learn Common Yellowthroat song. But this might not explain why the singing of one 'Gray-crowned' (at Sabal Palm Sanctuary) reportedly shifted from being like Gray-crowned in winter to like Common in spring (*NAB* 58:564).

Birds that appear to be hybrid Gray-crowned Yellowthroat × Common Yellowthroat have been found in TX. 2 presumed hybrids (1995–1996 and 2004–2006) looked rather similar to one another, and both more closely resembled Gray-crowned than Common. As well as giving atypical vocalizations, these birds were structurally intermediate, with bicolored bills that recalled Gray-crowned in pattern but were slightly slimmer, with no strong decurvature to the culmen; 1 bird (1995–1996) had a relatively

short tail. The forehead and cheeks were extensively blue-gray with a black loral mask similar to Gray-crowned but extending quite broadly over the bill base; 1 bird (1995–1996) had only a white subocular arc, similar to 1st-year male Common, while the other bird had white eye-arcs.

Age/Sex/Season: Ages/sexes differ slightly and extremes may be distinguished; no seasonal variation. Molts not well known; perhaps complex basic strategy (see p. 35). **Adult female**: Averages duller and paler than male, with dark slaty (not black) lores, the dark not extending across base of bill (as sometimes on male); crown more extensively washed olive-brown, with little gray apparent. **1st-year:** Juv (lax plumage held briefly) brownish olive overall, slightly brighter below, with narrow buffy wing-bars. Following partial preformative molt, resembles adult of respective sex but in fall–early winter averages browner overall, with lores duller blackish and eye-arcs sometimes tinged lemon; flight feathers are juv, which in spring–summer are more strongly worn and tend to be browner overall, with narrower and duller olive-green edgings; rectrices average more tapered.

Habitat and Behavior: Tall dense grassland and savanna, usually with scattered low bushes or palms; also ranges into pastures and cane fields; not usually in wet marshes like Common Yellowthroat. Generally skulking, but sings openly from a low bush, grass stem, or fence. Often responds well to pishing, perching fairly upright and calling, with crest raised and tail twitched from side to side. Calls include a slightly nasal *cheédle* or *cheedl-eet*, rarely a single *chee* (does not have a gruff *chek* call like Common Yellowthroat), usually given by a bird perched up in sight, and a series of rich but slightly plaintive whistles, rising then falling, and vaguely reminiscent of Canyon Wren, *whiu whiu whiu* … . Song is a rich to slightly scratchy warble, recalling *Passerina* buntings, and sometimes given in flight.

FAN-TAILED WARBLER *Basileuterus lachrymosus* 14.5–16 cm (5.7–6.3")

Summary: *Southwest*: Very rare, mainly late spring and in AZ; exceptional e. to NM and TX.

Taxonomy: Monotypic, although birds in n. of range average paler overall. Sometimes placed in monotypic genus *Euthlypis*.

1st-year

adult

Fan-tailed Warbler

Distribution and Status:

World: Mexico (n. to s. Sonora and s. Tamaulipas) to w. Nicaragua.

North America: **Southwest**: Very rare in spring–fall (mid-May to early Sep, mainly mid-May to early Jun) in se. AZ, since the 1st US record there in 1961. Also Roosevelt Co., e. NM, 18–19 May 2009 (*NAB* 63:476), and Brewster Co., w. TX, 13 Aug–27 Sep 2007.

Comments: In nw. Mexico this species is partly migratory, with the main arrival in Sonora during May; there are no data on southward withdrawal. The AZ birds, and the recent NM individual, appear to be spring overshoots, with most present no more than a week, and some singing strongly. The early Sep record may reflect a misoriented fall migrant, indicating that southward withdrawal from Sonora could occur in Aug–Sep. This conjecture may be supported by the TX record, apparently an adult undergoing prebasic molt (although reported as a juv; *NAB* 62:192), which also raises the question of whether Fan-tailed Warblers in nw. Mexico might undertake a degree of molt migration.

The only other extralimital records of this handsome species are from northernmost Sonora, close to the AZ border, in late May, and from Baja California, Mexico, in Dec, perhaps a bird that arrived there in fall.

Field Identification: Fairly large and distinctive warbler, often fairly skulking and mostly terrestrial.

Similar Species: Nothing really similar in N America. Note Fan-tailed's eponymous lachrymose face pattern and long, floppy, white-tipped tail.

Age/Sex/Season: Ages differ; sexes similar; no seasonal variation. Molts not well known; likely complex basic strategy (see p. 35). *1st-year*: Juv (plumage held briefly, unknown in US) with fluffy plumage, dark sooty gray overall with narrow whitish wing-bars, pale yellow vent and undertail coverts. Following partial preformative molt, resembles adult but averages duller; flight feathers are juv, which in spring–summer are more strongly worn and tend to be duller and browner overall, with less distinct blue-gray edgings; rectrices average more tapered.

Habitat and Behavior: Deciduous forest and woodland, usually with open rocky understory and often near water. Forages mostly on or near the ground, around logs, rocks, and vine tangles; also at low to mid-levels on branches. Singing birds can range to upper levels in bushes and trees. Song a fairly short, pleasant, rich warbled series, typically upslurred at the end. Calls include a high, thin, slightly tinny *tseein*.

RUFOUS-CAPPED WARBLER
Basileuterus rufifrons 12–13.5 cm (4.7–5.3")

Summary: *Southwest*: Very rare but increasing in AZ and TX, some staying prolonged periods and breeding; exceptional in NM.

Taxonomy: 5 ssp, differing to varying degrees in plumage tones. N. populations, including *caudatus* of nw. Mexico (and AZ) and *jouyi* of ne. Mexico (and probably in s. TX), have grayer upperparts and restricted yellow bib; populations from cen. Mexico to n. Cen America have greener upperparts and more extensive yellow below. Chestnut-capped Warbler *B. delattrii* of Cen America sometimes considered conspecific (AOU 1998; but see Howell & Webb 1995).

Distribution and Status:
World: Mexico (n. to n. Sonora and cen. Nuevo Leon) to Guatemala.

North America: *Southwest*: Rare but overall increasing, with records split almost equally between TX (where 1st found in 1973) and se. AZ (1st in 1977). Marked increase in records since mid-1990s; first NM record was Jan–Feb 2009 (*NAB* 63:302). Records are year-round (mainly Mar–Aug; see Comments, below) and in some areas birds have remained for long periods, with pairs confirmed nesting in several years from se. AZ, and a suspected small population in w. TX (Val Verde Co.) in 1997–2001 (breeding unconfirmed).

Comments: In AZ, there are at least 6 fall–early winter records (Sep–Dec) from canyons and riparian areas away from breeding sites, and 4 records from s. TX (where birds are not seen in summer) are also in fall–winter (late Oct–Mar). Birders tend to be more active in winter in s. TX than in the Edwards Plateau and w. Texas, whence come most records. Thus, although most AZ and TX records are during Mar–Aug, this pattern may reflect seasonal observer coverage combined with birds becoming more conspicuous in spring; there also may be some local seasonal movement of long-staying birds, such that they may not be found in winter around the nesting sites.

This species is largely resident and appears to remain paired year-round in much of Mexico; it is not known to be a seasonal migrant in the n. of its range unlike Crescent-chested Warbler and Fan-tailed Warbler. Given its life history traits, combined with the pattern of US records, we suspect that most Rufous-capped Warblers arrive in fall and winter; some find suitable habitat and may remain to breed, staying for years at a site until the immigration event peters out.

often cocks tail

juv

adult

adult

Rufous-capped Warbler

In both AZ and TX the first records were in the mid-1970s, with only 3 records in the 1980s (from TX), followed by a marked upsurge in the 1990s that continued into the 2000s, especially in AZ.

Field Identification: Perky, attractive warbler with striking head pattern, long cocked tail.

Similar Species: Nothing in N America. Note bold white eyebrow, rufous cap, bright yellow bib, long cocked tail, and excited chipping calls.

Age/Sex/Season: Ages differ; sexes similar; no seasonal variation. Molts not well known; likely complex basic strategy (see p. 35). **1st-year:** Juv (lax plumage held briefly) brownish overall, becoming buff on belly, with pale cinnamon wing-bars, traces of adult head pattern. Following partial preformative molt, resembles adult but averages duller; flight feathers are juv, which in spring–summer are more strongly worn and tend to be duller and browner overall; rectrices average more tapered.

Habitat and Behavior: Brushy scrub, semi-open areas with scattered bushes and weedy patches, woodland edge with brushy and weedy growth; in fairly dry areas as well, as along watered canyons. Forages mainly at low to mid-levels, sometimes on the ground, clambering and gleaning on weed stalks and other foliage, occasionally sallying. Can be somewhat retiring and easily overlooked if not calling, but also curious, often responding to pishing by chipping loudly and perching up with tail cocked, crown slightly raised. Common call a sharp chipping *chik* or *tik*, often run into excited chippering series; also a quieter high *tsi* or *tik*. Song a varied, rapid, often accelerating series of chips and trills, the overall effect sometimes suggesting a goldfinch or siskin.

GOLDEN-CROWNED WARBLER
Basileuterus culicivorus 12–13.5 cm (4.7–5.3")

Summary: *Texas*: Very rare, mainly in winter and in Lower Rio Grande Valley. *Elsewhere*: 1 spring record from New Mexico (2004).

Taxonomy: 13 ssp (perhaps comprising 3 species). Middle American birds comprise the *culicivorus* ssp group ('Stripe-crowned Warbler'), 4 ssp that differ slightly in plumage tones. In general, n. populations of *culicivorus* group average slightly duller overall with grayer upperparts and yellower (less orangy) crown stripe; northernmost ssp *brasherii* occurs in ne. Mexico and, presumably, TX.

Distribution and Status:

World: Lowlands and foothills of tropical Mexico (n. to s. Nayarit and cen. Nuevo Leon) s. to n. Argentina.

North America: *Texas*: Very rare in late fall–winter (late Oct–Mar; also single records in late Apr, mid-Aug) in Lower Rio Grande Valley, exceptional n. to Nueces Co., 24–29 Apr 2001. All records in the period covered here have been since 1979, but also 2 records from 1890s. *Elsewhere*: Roosevelt Co., NM, 8–10 May 2004.

Comments: TX records largely conform to a pattern of winter dispersal from ne. Mexico, where this species is common. The 'extralimital' late Apr–early May records may represent birds that misoriented after wintering in the

fresh plumage

crown stripe variation

Golden-crowned Warbler

lowlands of s. TX or ne. Mexico, or perhaps were overshooting migrants (although the species is not considered migratory). The single mid-Aug record (a mist-netted 'adult') does not fit any obvious pattern. The rate of records has remained fairly steady since the 1980s.

Field Identification: Quite plainly patterned warbler of woodland understory; note face pattern but beware that 'golden crown' is often not apparent and can be veiled grayish in fresh plumage.

Similar Species: Grayish upperparts, head pattern, and voice are distinctive, although face pattern and general coloration might suggest Orange-crowned Warbler.

Age/Sex/Season: Ages differ; sexes similar; no seasonal variation. Molts not well known; likely complex basic strategy (see p. 35). *1st-year*: Juv (plumage held briefly, unknown in US) with fluffy plumage brownish overall, becoming buff on belly, with pale cinnamon wing-bars. Following partial preformative molt, resembles adult but flight feathers are juv, which in spring–summer are more strongly worn and tend to be browner overall; rectrices average more tapered.

Habitat and Behavior: Semi-deciduous and evergreen forest and woodland. Mainly forages at low to mid-levels in forest understory, gleaning amid foliage and sometimes sallying for insects; often holds tail slightly cocked and sometimes twitches wings. Regularly associates with mixed-species feeding flocks, in TX with Black-crested

Titmice and other passerines. Calls include a fairly quiet, hard smacking *tk* or *stk*, sometimes doubled or run into a chatter, and vaguely reminiscent of Western Winter Wren (Pacific Wren). Song (rarely heard in US) a pleasant warbled series, upslurred at the end.

SLATE-THROATED WHITESTART
Myioborus miniatus 13–14 cm (5–5.5")

Summary: *Southwest*: Very rare, spring–fall. *Elsewhere*: Exceptional in spring in s. TX (2002, 2003).

Taxonomy: 12 ssp, differing mainly in plumage features such as belly color and the amount of white in the tail. Mexican populations are red-bellied, whereas populations from Costa Rica southward are yellow-bellied. Northernmost ssp is nominate *miniatus*, the only ssp recorded (or likely) in the US. Often known in N America as Slate-throated Redstart.

Distribution and Status:

World: Highlands and foothills of Mexico (n. to cen. Sonora and s. Nuevo Leon) s. to Bolivia.

North America: *Southwest*: Very rare or exceptional in spring (late Mar–early Jun) in se. AZ (7 records) and w. TX (4 records); 2 summer–early fall records (late Jun–early Aug) from w. TX. Also Lea Co., se. NM, 16 Apr 1962 (1st US record). *Elsewhere*: 2 spring records from s. TX: Nueces Co., 10 Apr 2002 (2); Hidalgo Co., 12–13 Mar 2003.

adult

duller 1st-year

brighter adult

Slate-throated Whitestart

Comments: Northernmost breeding populations of this species in Mexico are migratory, and mostly present during Mar–Aug; they withdraw south and sometimes into the lowlands during winter. The US records mostly reflect a pattern of overshooting spring migrants, some of which were males that sang vigorously in potentially suitable habitat for a while but then disappeared. Some have turned up in unsuitable breeding habitat, such as coastal TX, and the NM bird was at a migrant trap of willows amid mesquite desert grassland (Harris 1964). Data on the ages of birds would be of interest—for example, do 1st-years overshoot more, or, farther, in spring?

The Jun–Aug records from w. TX were from areas not covered intensively, and may represent summering birds that were detected late in the season. Given the increasing tempo of records (1 in the 1960s, 2 in the 1970s, 0 in 1980s, 4 in the 1990s, 9 in the 2000s), it would not be surprising to find Slate-throated Whitestarts breeding in the US before too long.

Field Identification: Distinctive arboreal warbler with expressive, white-tipped tail.

Similar Species: Nothing really similar in N America. Seen from below, Painted Whitestart has brighter but more restricted red on underbody, contrasting more sharply with black upper chest and black flanks, more extensive white in tail (outer rectrices white to base, vs. broadly tipped white on Slate-throated), different call.

Age/Sex/Season: Ages/sexes differ slightly and extremes may be distinguished; no seasonal variation. Molts not well known; likely complex basic strategy (see p. 35). **Adult female**: Slaty blackish face and throat average less contrasting than male, crown patch averages smaller and duller. **1st-year**: Juv (plumage held briefly, unknown in US) with fluffy plumage sooty blackish overall, washed pinkish on underparts. Following partial preformative molt, resembles adult of respective sex but averages duller; flight feathers are juv, which in spring–summer are more strongly worn and tend to be browner overall; rectrices average more tapered.

Habitat and Behavior: Breeds in montane forest, especially canyons and valleys with brushy understory; migrants and nonbreeding birds wander to brushy woodland and semi-open areas with hedges and thickets. Forages low to high, even on the ground, but mainly at low to mid-levels in trees, bushes, and weedy flower banks, where it can be retiring. Generally active, moving with tail slightly fanned and swung from side to side, and often making short flycatching sallies. Song a variable series of high chips, often changing in pitch partway through and ending fairly abruptly or with an upslurred note; may suggest song of American Redstart, but more spirited. Call a high sharp *tsi* or *tsit*, often fairly quiet, may suggest call of Chipping Sparrow.

YELLOW-FACED GRASSQUIT *Tiaris olivacea* 10–11 cm (4–4.3")

Summary: *Florida*: Very rare in the s., mainly spring. *Texas*: Very rare in the s.

Taxonomy: 5 ssp, the northernmost being *pusilla* of e. Mexico and *olivacea* of Cuba, Jamaica, and Cayman Islands. Relative to *olivacea*, male *pusilla* has larger black chest shield and more black in the face, female averages stronger face pattern. Male *intermedia* of Cozumel Island, off Mexico's Yucatan Peninsula, is intermediate in terms of black on the underparts; 2 other resident ssp (of Puerto Rico and Panama) not considered here. TX records refer to *pusilla*, FL records to *olivacea*.

Distribution and Status:

World: Lowlands and subtropical foothills and highlands from e. Mexico (n. to cen. Nuevo Leon) to nw. S America; also Greater Antilles.

North America: *Florida*: 6 records from the s. (late Jan to mid-Jul), with 3 from Dry Tortugas in late Apr–early May. *Texas*: 3 records from Lower Rio Grande Valley (22–24 Jan 1990, 8–29 Jun 2002, 29 Sep 2003), 1 from Aransas Co., 30 Jan–20 Mar 2011 (*NAB* 65:310, 385, 483). All US records have been since 1990.

Comments: As with many other species commonly sold in the cage-bird trade, the question of escapes hangs over US records of Yellow-faced Grassquit. This is not a popular cage bird, however, and most of the birds imported into the US have apparently been *pusilla*, although *olivacea* may also be smuggled into FL (Restall & White 2003). 2 birds in Miami, late Sep 1992, were considered to have been hurricane-related escapes.

Yellow-faced Grassquit is usually considered resident, although recent records from Nuevo Leon, Mexico (in the 1990s), suggest it may be expanding northward (Behrstock & Eubanks 1997). The 2002 TX record was of a male singing and building a nest, and several of the FL records have been of singing males, including 2 birds on the Dry Tortugas, a well-known vagrant trap. Although some accepted US records may be of

♀ *pusilla*

1st-year ♂
olivacea (fall)

♀ *olivacea*

adult ♂ *olivacea*

adult ♂ *pusilla*

Yellow-faced Grassquit

escapes, overall they seem to reflect an ongoing northward expansion that mirrors that of other neotropical species, such as Black-capped Gnatcatcher and Rufous-capped Warbler. The pattern of US records for Yellow-faced Grassquit is in striking contrast to that of Black-faced Grassquit, of which there are also 9 records in the period here, but with most prior to 1990.

Field Identification: Very small, mostly olive, finch-like bird with relatively stubby conical bill, distinctive face pattern.

Similar Species: Male handsome and distinctive; note extent of black chest shield with respect to possibility of escaped *pusilla* in s. FL. Female and juv unremarkable, told from Black-faced Grassquit by distinct face and throat pattern.

Cuban Grassquit T. *canorus* occurs in s. FL as a presumed escape; both sexes have striking yellow eyebrow and neck patch surrounding black (male) to chestnut (female) face and throat.

Age/Sex/Season: Ages/sexes differ; no seasonal variation. Molts not well known; may follow complex basic strategy (see p. 35). *Male*: Bright yellow eyebrow and throat patch boldly bordered black. *Female*: Pale yellow eyebrow and throat patch without distinct black border. *1st-year*: Juv

resembles female but dingier overall, with only vestiges of face and throat pattern; soon attains adult-like plumage by preformative molt, which can include central rectrices and tertials, but 1st-year male has less black than adult on throat and chest, and veiled grayish in fall–winter. Whether pale pinkish base to mandible in winter indicates 1st-year or seasonal variation remains to be elucidated.

Habitat and Behavior: Open and semi-open areas, forest and woodland edges, gardens. Feeds mainly on the ground, also among seeding grasses, and may associate loosely with other weed-eating birds. Males usually sing from a low perch, such as a fence post or wire. Song (in Mexico) a very high-pitched, slightly stuttering trill, usually of about 1–2 secs' duration, which can be passed off as an insect. Calls include a high thin *sik* or *tsi*.

BLACK-FACED GRASSQUIT *Tiaris bicolor* 10.5–11.5 cm (4.2–4.7")

Summary: *Florida*: Exceptional or very rare in the s., mainly spring and fall.

Taxonomy: 8 ssp, distinguished mainly by extent and contrast of black on head and

1st-year ♂
(winter–spring)

1st-year ♂
(fall–winter)

♀

adult ♂

Black-faced Grassquit
ssp *bicolor*

underparts of males. Critical review of ssp differences could help with evaluating US records. Of geographically closest ssp, male *bicolor* of Bahamas has face and underparts extensively black, *marchii* of Hispaniola has black restricted to a fairly well-defined face and chest shield, with some blurry dusky streaking at the lower edge where its meets the dusky-lemon belly. Male *omissa* of Jamaica and Puerto Rico similar to *bicolor*, but upperparts average brighter olive, such that black face may contrast more strongly with greenish-olive crown.

Distribution and Status:

World: Widespread in the Caribbean, n. to the Bahamas; absent from Cuba, where replaced by Cuban Grassquit.

North America: *Florida*: 9 records from the s., with 4 during late Mar to mid-May, 2 in Sep–Oct, singles in late Jul and Dec, and 1 found mummified in mid-Dec. Also, 2 specimens from late 1800s (mid-Jan, mid-Apr). No US records since 2004.

Comments: Birds recorded in the US are presumed to be nominate *bicolor*, originating in the Bahamas. Almost half of the records have been in spring, which may be the best time to find this species, although birds have been found in all seasons.

Like many small passerines, the question of escaped cage birds hangs over US records, although this underwhelming species is rare in

captivity (Restall & White 2003), and thus most FL records likely involve wild vagrants. Observers should try to document the ssp of any (male) Black-faced Grassquits they are lucky enough to find.

Field Identification: Very small, mostly olive, finch-like bird with relatively stubby conical bill.

Similar Species: Rather dull but distinctive. Female and juv unremarkable, told from Yellow-faced Grassquit by lack of yellowish face and throat pattern, pinkish base to lower mandible.

Age/Sex/Season: Ages/sexes differ; no seasonal variation. Molts not well known; may follow complex basic strategy (see p. 35). **Adult male**: Face and underparts black. **Female**: Olive overall, paler and grayer below, especially on belly. **1st-year**: Juv (plumage held briefly, unrecorded in US) resembles female but plumage lax. Soon attains adult-like plumage by preformative molt (extent of which needs study) but 1st-year male has less black than adult, with variable black mottling on throat and chest.

Habitat and Behavior: Much like Yellow-faced Grassquit, and easily overlooked unless singing. Song on Bahamas is 1–2 introductory *sk* or *peep* notes followed by a short, rapid, jumbled metallic gurgle or garbled trill, with a gravelly quality that may recall Savannah Sparrow; calls include a short high *seip*, recalling Savannah Sparrow (B. Sullivan, pers. comm.).

BANANAQUIT *Coereba flaveola* 9.5–10.5 cm (3.7–4.2")

Summary: *Florida*: Very rare, mainly winter–spring.

Taxonomy: About 40 ssp (likely comprising multiple species), differing mainly in size and throat color. Of populations nearest the US, *bahamensis* of the Bahamas (which occurs in FL) has dirty whitish underparts with a bright yellow chest patch; slightly larger *caboti* of Cozumel Island, Mexico, has a white throat and upper chest; *portoricensis* of Puerto Rico and *bananivora* of Hispaniola have sooty gray throats; and *mexicana* of mainland s. Mexico and Cen America has a dusky gray throat.

Distribution and Status:

World: Tropical se. Mexico and the Caribbean (n. to the Bahamas but absent in Cuba) to tropical S America.

North America: *Florida*: Very rare in fall–spring (mid-Sep to mid-May, with most records Jan–Mar) in s. FL; exceptionally n. to the cen. peninsula.

Comments: The pattern of FL records suggests occasional fall and winter dispersal from the Bahamas, and some birds have arrived in juv plumage. There are also a few older FL records, dating back to the 1920s, and the species shows no obvious trend of increasing or decreasing frequency in the US. Some birds have sung persistently and built nests, and breeding in FL might occur given

an influx with enough birds; note, though, that Bananaquits build nests for roosting as well as for breeding. Bananaquits are not known to be kept in captivity (B. Pranty, pers. comm.).

The only record from the FL Gulf coast was a 'white-throated' bird in Pinellas Co., 19–23 Oct 2002 (*NAB* 57:48); photos show a bird that resembles the Bahamian ssp rather than the white-throated *caboti* from Mexico's Yucatan Peninsula.

Field Identification: Very small, active, warbler-like bird with decurved black bill, pink gape patch, attractive plumage.

Similar Species: None in N America.

Age/Sex/Season: Ages differ; sexes similar; no seasonal variation. Molts not well known; likely complex basic strategy (see p. 35). *Adult*: Black upperparts with white eyebrow; underparts whitish to pale gray with bright yellow chest patch; tail tipped white, broadly on r6–r4 (mostly on inner webs), narrower on r3–r1. *1st-year*: Juv duller overall than adult. Upperparts dark dusky grayish, eyebrow washed dusky and sometimes interrupted above eye; yellow on chest duller and less extensive, with pale-yellow suffusion extending up into throat; white on tail reduced, mainly on r5–r6. Soon attains adult-like plumage by preformative molt, which may include tertials and rectrices (study of molt needed).

Habitat and Behavior: Woodland and forest edges, gardens, and other semi-open areas with flowers. Forages low to high in trees and bushes,

adult

juv

adult

Bananaquit

mainly taking nectar from a variety of flowers. Song of *bahamensis* comprises bursts of rapid-paced metallic ticking and gurgling, sometimes preceded by up to 3 ticks; call a tinny *chik* or *tchiu* with slightly liquid, warbler-like quality, unlike calls of *caboti* from Cozumel or *mexicana* from mainland Mexico.

RED-LEGGED HONEYCREEPER
Cyanerpes cyaneus 11–12 cm (4.3–4.7")

Summary: *Florida*: Exceptional in the s., mainly in spring.

Taxonomy: 11 ssp, differing slightly in size and plumage tones, not known to be separable in the field. N American records presumed to be *carneipes*, of Mexico s. to Colombia; 10 other ssp in S America not considered here.

Distribution and Status:

World: Tropical se. Mexico to Brazil.

North America: *Florida*: At least 6 single males in the Keys and far s., all since 2003: 4 during late Mar–early May, plus singles in mid-Jan and late Feb (*NAB* 57:339; *NAB* 58:219, 360; *NAB* 59:248).

Comments: Red-legged Honeycreepers are kept in captivity, and thus recent FL records are not accepted by the state committee (Pranty 2004). However, the species reportedly has been imported into FL at present levels since the late 1960s (Anderson 2004); yet records have only been recent, with most in fairly remote

locations such as the outer Keys, to which escaped cage birds are not known to fly (Pranty 2004). Some recent imports reportedly have been from Suriname (Anderson 2004), where the ssp is nominate *cyaneus* (differing from *carneipes* in slightly larger pale blue crown patch, but unlikely distinguishable in the field). The breeding season in Mexico and Cuba is mostly Mar–Aug, and Mexican males attain breeding plumage mainly in Feb–Mar. Thus, all-blue males in winter (say, Sep–Jan) would be suspect and might represent escapes from recent imports, although cage birds surviving more than a year might adjust their molt to a northern/Mexican schedule.

Red-legged Honeycreepers are somewhat migratory, at least in e. Mexico, and are capable of crossing water as evidenced by fall and winter records from Cozumel Island, where the species does not breed. Red-legged Honeycreepers also occur in Cuba, where they are locally common (Garrido & Kirkconnel 2000). Although it has been suggested that honeycreepers were introduced into Cuba from Mexico (Garrido 2001), there are no data to support this conjecture; it is also possible that the species colonized Cuba from Mexico. Most birds withdraw s. in fall from the Atlantic slope of e. Mexico (mainly to the warmer Pacific slope of n. Middle America); whether small numbers of this species wintering in the e. Yucatan Peninsula, including Cozumel Island, derive from Mexican or Cuban populations is unknown. Mexican migrants start to

sulphur-yellow underwing on both sexes

♀

♂ breeding (Feb–Aug)

molting ♂ (Feb–Mar)

♀

Red-legged Honeycreeper

return n. in late Feb–Mar, and might on occasion overshoot to FL. At least one of the recent records, from Key West on 21–22 Apr 2005, arrived with a wave of migrants from the s. (C. Goodrich, pers. comm.), and we consider it plausible that at least some of the US records refer to wild birds, either from Cuba or Mexico. We encourage observers to document further records of this species such that patterns may be elucidated.

Field Identification: Small, somewhat warbler-like songbird with distinctly decurved bill, red or reddish legs.

Similar Species: None in N America, but beware the possibility of escaped cage birds of other exotic species. Note bright sulphur-yellow in wings, striking in flight.

Age/Sex/Season: Ages/sexes differ; seasonal variation in males. In n. populations, complete prebasic and preformative molts occur late summer–fall, usually before migration; partial prealternate molts in late winter–spring, before or during migration. *Male breeding* (mainly Feb/Mar–Aug in Mexico): Blue head and underparts, iridescent turquoise crown, and black back; patchy molting males often seen in Feb–Mar and Aug. *Male nonbreeding* (mainly Aug–Feb in Mexico): Head, back, and underparts greenish, contrasting with black wings and tail. *Female*: Green overall year-round, without contrasting black wings and tail of male, legs duller. *1st-year*: Juv (plumage held briefly, unknown in US) resembles female but legs duller, more pinkish; soon attains adult-like plumage (male has complete preformative molt into nonbreeding plumage), probably before migration (study needed).

Habitat and Behavior: Occurs in wooded habitats, gardens, forest edges, etc., feeding mainly at upper to mid-levels, especially at flowers where it probes for nectar. Associates loosely with other species, mainly at flowering or fruiting trees, and in Mexico often occurs in flocks, especially during migration and winter. Calls include a rough mewing *meeahr*, that may recall a soft catbird, and usually in flight, a high thin *ssit*, often doubled.

WESTERN SPINDALIS *Spindalis zena*
14.5–16 cm (5.7–6.3")

Summary: *Florida*: Rare in the s., mainly winter–spring (has bred).

Taxonomy: 5 ssp, distinguishable mainly in adult male plumage; also note female tail

patterns. 2 extralimital ssp not considered here: *salvini* on Grand Cayman and *benedicti* on Cozumel Island, Mexico; see Garrido et al. (1997) for details. Most FL records refer to nominate *zena* from the Bahamas, but also single well-documented records of a male *pretrei* in Nov 2004–Apr 2005, and of a green-acked male thought to be *townsendi*, Jan–Apr 2007.

S. z. zena breeds cen. and s. Bahamas. Adult male has black back, chestnut hindcollar tipped yellow-ochre, and chestnut lower rump; r6 has a broad white median patch, r5–r4 have large white tail spots on inner webs; female has reduced whitish distal patches on inner webs of r5–r6. 1st-year male has back feathers edged greenish, cf. *townsendi*.

S. z. townsendi breeds n. Bahamas (Grand Bahama and Abaco). Adult male similar to *zena* but back olive or mottled with black; female lacks distinct whitish tail spots.

S. z. pretrei breeds Cuba. Adult male has golden-olive back, golden-ochre hindcollar and rump (ochre replaces chestnut of other subspecies); white in tail mainly on r5–r6; female usually has diffuse whitish distal spots on r5–r6.

Distribution and Status:

World: Bahamas, Cuba, Grand Cayman, and Cozumel Island, Mexico.

North America: *Florida*: Rare in the s., with all records since 1957 (see Pranty & Smith 2001). Records virtually year-round but with almost none in summer, and most during mid-Mar to May and in Dec, with several wintering records from Nov–Dec to Mar–Apr. Most records involve singles, but groups of 3–7 birds have been seen. Breeding was confirmed in 2009 on Long Pine Cay: a black-backed male was found singing in late Jul, 2 females were present, a nest built, and 3 young fledged on 1 Sep (*NAB* 63:587).

Comments: The appearances of this species in FL (cf. Pranty & Smith 2001) at first suggest a bimodal pattern of winter and spring vagrancy. The Dec peak, however, may simply reflect increased observer coverage related to Christmas Bird Counts, with several of these birds perhaps having arrived in fall. The spring peak may reflect spring dispersal from the Bahamas, but might also reflect greater observer coverage combined with birds becoming more conspicuous during their migration back to the Bahamas after having wintered undetected in FL.

From 8 to 23 individuals were reported in each 10-year period during 1960–1999 (Pranty & Smith 2001), with a 'lull' in the 1980s and the

adult ♂
zena

1st-year ♂ zena

adult ♂
pretrei

♀ zena (worn)

adult ♂
townsendi

♀ zena (fresh)

Western Spindalis

peak in the 1990s; up to 4 years passed with no records. Like numerous tropical and subtropical frugivores, Western Spindalis may be somewhat nomadic in response to fruiting cycles, which may drive its dispersal to FL.

Field Identification: Formerly known as Stripe-headed Tanager, this distinctive bird is appreciably smaller than Summer Tanager but larger than goldfinches.

Similar Species: Handsome male striking, and like no other N American bird. Drab female might be puzzling but also doesn't look much like any other species; note size and shape with gray bill, pale edgings to greater coverts and tertials, whitish patch at base of primaries.

Age/Sex/Season: Ages/sexes differ; no seasonal variation. *Male*: Bold black-and-white head and wing patterns. *Female*: Dingy grayish olive overall. *1st-year*: Juv (plumage held briefly) resembles female but with lax plumage tinged buffier below and browner above. Following partial preformative molt, resembles adult of respective sex but distinguished by retained juv flight feathers (tertials and central rectrices

can be replaced), which can appear worn and faded in spring–summer; smaller white patch at primary bases on males. 1st-year male *zena* has back feathers edged greenish.

Habitat and Behavior: Woodland and forest, edges, gardens, adjacent semi-open areas with fruiting trees. Forages low to high in trees and bushes, mainly taking fruit. Typical calls are high thin notes, often difficult to locate. Song on Bahamas is a short, high, thin, slightly jerky warble, usually introduced with a separate, slurred thin *tssi*.

FLAME-COLORED TANAGER *Piranga bidentata* 18–19 cm (8–8.5")

Summary: *Southwest*: In spring–fall, rare and perhaps increasing in AZ (has bred), very rare in w. TX. *Elsewhere*: Exceptional in winter–spring in s. TX (2002, 2005).

Taxonomy: 5 ssp, differing mainly in color of male plumages. Male *bidentata* of nw. Mexico is flame-orange overall, versus deep orange-red in other mainland Mexican ssp, including *sanguinolenta* of ne. Mexico. Records from Southwest are

brighter adult ♀

adult ♂

white tail corners

1st-year ♂ worn (summer)

adult ♀

both sexes of E. Mexican ssp. brighter

adult ♂

adult ♀

adult ♂

juv

hybrid with **Western Tanager** variable intermediate features (see text)

Flame-colored Tanager

of *bidentata*, but a male *sanguinolenta* was found in s. Texas, 3 Mar. 2011 (Arnold et al. 2011).

Distribution and Status:

World: Foothills and highlands from Mexico (n. to cen. Sonora and cen. Nuevo Leon) to w. Panama.

North America: ***Southwest***: Rare in spring–fall (late Mar–Aug) in se. AZ, since the 1st N American record there in 1985. Nesting pairs have been found on several occasions since 1985, and mixed Flame-colored and Western Tanager pairs have also nested (at least in 1998 and 2006).

Most arrivals appear mid-Apr (rarely from late Mar), with fledging in Jul and a few records into Aug. Returning birds have been assumed, in some cases for 8 successive years (*NAB* 64:476). At least 2 presumed hybrid Flame-colored × Western Tanagers have been photographed, in mid-May 2000 (M. M. Stevenson, pers. comm.) and May 2006 (G. H. Rosenberg, pers. comm.). In w. TX, very rare in spring–summer (mid-Apr to Jul; all records since 1996); also 1–5 Oct 2001. *Elsewhere*: Exceptional in late winter–spring (late Feb to mid-Apr) in s. TX (3 records, all since 2002).

Comments: This is another species that has started to show up (or at least be found) in N America since the 1980s, with the steady accumulation of records suggesting a genuine northward range expansion. The AZ records have a well-defined pattern, although the apparent increase in records since the mid-1980s may partly reflect increasing observer awareness. The virtual absence of records after Jul is probably a combination of difficulty in detecting birds that have fledged, stopped singing, or become reclusive during molt, combined with presumed southward withdrawal in Aug–Sep.

The TX records are, not surprisingly, concentrated in the w. The s. TX coastal bird in Apr 2002 may have been a misoriented bird that headed the wrong way after wintering somewhere in ne. Mexico or s. TX, or perhaps was an overshooting spring migrant.

Field Identification: This s. counterpart of Western Tanager resembles its n. relative in voice and behavior, and the 2 species have hybridized in AZ.

Similar Species: Flame-colored Tanagers are distinctive, although female plumage is similar to much larger and massive-billed female *Mexican Yellow Grosbeak*, which has narrower wing-bars, small white flash on primary bases, and white, not yellow, undertail coverts.

Problems arise mainly with the possibility of *hybrid Flame-colored × Western tanagers*. Some hybrid adult males resemble Flame-colored but may differ in their yellower overall coloration with a more solidly black back, brighter and more contrasting rump and uppertail coverts, and a strong yellow suffusion to the upper wing-bar, which may include a row of lesser coverts (only broad tips to median coverts on Flame-colored). Other presumed male hybrids resemble Western Tanager but have slightly larger

and grayish bill, less extensive and paler, orangy red on face and throat, and ghosting of large whitish tail patches. Female hybrids appear to be undescribed. Beware of age, as 1st-summer Flame-colored males may exhibit supposed 'hybrid' characters.

Age/Sex/Season: Ages/sexes differ; no seasonal variation. Molts not well known, likely similar to Western Tanager but may lack prealternate molt. *Adult male*: Bright flame-orange head and underparts, palest on belly; uniform generation wing coverts and remiges with white wing-bars (upper wing-bar sometimes suffused orange) and tertial tips; wing-bars and tertial tips can be worn away by mid-summer. *Adult female*: Head and underparts yellow overall; some (older?) birds have scattered orange patches on head and underparts. *1st-year*: Juv (plumage held briefly) resembles female but plumage soft and weak, underparts streaked dark brown. Following partial preformative molt in late summer–fall, both sexes resemble adult female but are distinguished by retained juv flight feathers, which are browner overall and often heavily worn in 1st summer, with narrower and abraded white wing-bars, tertial tips, and tail corners. 1st-summer male often has head and underparts variably mottled orange (as may some old females).

Habitat and Behavior: Oak and pine-oak woodland, adjacent riparian groves, especially with fruiting trees. Forages mainly at upper to mid-levels in trees and overlooked easily if not vocal. Song of 3–5 slightly jerky phrases perhaps not distinguishable from song of Western Tanager, but may average burrier and lower pitched; calls of the two species also very similar, although Flame-colored's *pi-tuk* or *pi-t-ruk* call slightly drier, more even pitched.

CRIMSON-COLLARED GROSBEAK
Rhodothraupis celaeno 21–22 cm (8.3–8.7")

Summary: *Texas*: Very rare, mainly Lower Rio Grande Valley in late fall–spring; exceptional in late winter–spring on Gulf Coast.

Taxonomy: Usually considered monotypic, but appreciable geographic variation undescribed. In general, s. lowland males (e.g., in n. Veracruz) have heavy black markings on underparts, and females can be dusky backed, whereas n. interior males (in w. Tamaulipas) are paler pinkish red below with reduced blackish mottling, and females have plain olive backs.

adult ♂

adult ♀

1st-summer ♂

adult ♂

Crimson-collared
Grosbeak

1st-year ♀
(fall–winter)

pale tips to retained
juv wing coverts

Distribution and Status:

World: Lowlands and foothills of ne. Mexico, n. to cen. Nuevo Leon.

North America: *Texas*: Very rare, mainly in late fall–spring (Nov–Apr; exceptional singles in late May 2006, late Jun–early Jul 1974) in Lower Rio Grande Valley, exceptionally nw. to Webb Co. In some years mini-invasions occur, as with 5 birds in 1987–1988 winter and at least 14 in 2004–2005 winter. Exceptional on cen. and upper Gulf Coast: Aransas Co., 3 Feb–9 Apr 1988 (female/1st-year) and 18 Apr 2005 (male); Galveston Co., 6–9 May 2005 (female).

Comments: The sporadic winter invasions of Crimson-collared Grosbeak into s. TX are presumably linked to conditions (such as fruiting cycles) in ne. Mexico, although the species may be more regular in the US than recognized. Given its fairly skulking habits, it could easily go undetected until large numbers draw attention and observers start to seek others. The 2 coastal records in spring 2005 may represent examples of post-winter misorientation, with birds heading n. rather than s; both occurred after a banner wintering season for the species in s. TX. Like almost all Mexican songbirds this species may be kept in cages, which might explain the anomalous mid-summer bird in 1974, which was the first record for the US.

Field Identification: A distinctive bird (placed in its own genus), slightly slimmer than Northern Cardinal, with a rather rounded head, long tail, and fairly stubby bill.

Similar Species: None in N America.

Age/Sex/Season: Ages/sexes differ; no seasonal variation. Molts not well known; may follow complex alternate strategy (see p. 35). **Adult male**: Pinkish-red collar and underparts contrast with black hood and dark upperparts. **Adult female**: Head and chest black, underparts yellow-olive, upperparts olive with no distinct pale tips to upperwing coverts. **1st-year**: Juv plumage apparently undescribed, and unrecorded in US. **1st-year male**: In winter resembles adult female but black hood averages less extensive, often has retained juv greater and median coverts with distinct pale lemon to whitish tips; 1st-summer has black hood much like adult male, often one or more blackish tertials and central rectrices, and sometimes scattered patches of black and pinkish red on body. **1st-year female**: In winter resembles adult female but black hood more limited, mainly on face and throat. 1st-summer has black hood much like adult but may be distinguished by retained juv greater and median coverts with pale lemon to whitish tips, and by worn, relatively tapered remiges.

Habitat and Behavior: Brushy woodland and edge where forages low to high. Usually seen most readily at fruiting trees, perhaps especially potato tree and hackberry, where it eats leaves as well as fruit; at other times skulks in dense bushes and on the ground, foraging in leaf litter. Calls include a high, penetrating slurred whistle that rises then falls, *psseeuu*, a piercing double-whistled *seeip seeeiyu*, and a lower, slightly nasal *wheyh* in flight. Song a varied, rich to burry short warble, often ending with an upslurred whistle.

MEXICAN YELLOW GROSBEAK
Pheucticus chrysopeplus 21.5–24 cm (8.5–9.5")

Summary: *Southwest*: In AZ and NM, very rare in spring–summer and fall, exceptional in winter.
Taxonomy: 4 ssp, differing mainly in intensity of yellow plumage on adult male: head and underparts of males in nw. Mexico lemon-yellow (*dilutus*, which presumably occurs in US), becoming yellow-orange in s. Mexico and Guatemala. Sometimes known simply as Yellow Grosbeak.
Distribution and Status:
World: Subtropical foothills and lowlands from w. Mexico (n. to cen. Sonora) to Guatemala.
North America: *Southwest*: In se. AZ, very rare in spring–fall (May to mid-Aug, mainly Jun–Jul), since 1st US record there in 1971; 1 fall record, Pima Co., 27 Oct 1987 (1st-year male). Exceptional or very rare in NM, with 6 records, all males: 3 in May to mid-Jul, 2 in early–late Oct (adult, 1st-year), and 1 in Dec–early May; see Comments, below.
Comments: Mexican Yellow Grosbeaks are common summer residents of tropical deciduous forest in s. Sonora, occurring n. to around 28°N, or within about 160 km (100 miles) of the US border. The main arrival there is in mid-May, and southward withdrawal mainly in Sep (Russell & Monson 1998). The majority of AZ records conform to a well-defined pattern of occasional spring–summer overshoots, with males more numerous than females (of spring–summer records where sex has been noted, at least 12 involve males and only 4 females).

Because yellow grosbeaks are kept in captivity (Hamilton 2001), extralimital records in both time and space are open to question. A 1st-year male in Tucson, AZ, late Oct 1987, was considered suspect in terms of origin (and not accepted by the state committee), but note the NM 1st-year male (elsewhere reported as a female; *NAB* 57:144; ABA 2008) in mid–late Oct 2002, with both of these birds occurring at a time when misoriented fall migrants might be expected. The wintering male in NM was found in early Dec but could have arrived in fall and been overlooked. Thus there may be an emerging pattern of fall–winter occurrences in addition to the accepted spring–summer pattern.

2 records from NM (15–18 Jul 1989, 4 Oct 1999) were not accepted by the state committee (Williams 2007), although the Jul record falls within the main window of occurrence in AZ, and the Oct record fits what may be an emerging pattern (discussed above); we provisionally treat both records as being of wild birds.

Additional single records from IA (1st-year male, Nov 1990–Jan 1991; Kent & Dinsmore 1996), CA (male, Jul–Aug 2006), and FL (male, Sep 2007) are also treated as presumed escapes (ABA 2008); the aberrant bill and plumage of the CA bird support this view. Interestingly, the IA and NM winter records mirror the pattern of winter vagrancy shown by Streak-backed Oriole, a species whose breeding range and migration are similar to those of Mexican Yellow Grosbeak. Observers should not assume that extralimital records of this species are escaped cage birds, and all such occurrences should be carefully documented.

Field Identification: Appreciably larger and bulkier than Black-headed Grosbeak, with a massive bill, yellow underparts.

Similar Species: None likely to occur wild in US. ***Southern Yellow (Golden-bellied) Grosbeak*** *P. chrysogaster* (of S America, at times considered conspecific with Mexican Yellow) might occur as an escape. Differs from Mexican Yellow in slightly smaller size and less massive bill. Male has more solidly black back, often with black spots on uppertail coverts, smaller white tertial tips, and smaller white tail spots (length of white spot of r6 along shaft usually <30 mm on Southern Yellow, vs. >30 mm on Mexican Yellow). Female Southern Yellow has stronger and blacker streaking on crown, nape, and upperparts.

Age/Sex/Season: Ages/sexes differ; no seasonal variation. Molts not well known, likely similar to Black-headed Grosbeak. ***Adult male*:** Head and underparts bright yellow; wings

adult ♂

adult ♂

1st-year ♀

adult ♀

1st-year ♂

Yellow Grosbeak

black with bold white wing-bars, tertial spots, and patch at primary bases; mandible mostly steely gray. *Adult female*: Head and underparts yellow with olive wash and dusky streaking on crown, nape, and cheeks. Wings dark slaty with white wing-bars, tertial spots, and small patch at primary bases; mandible mostly grayish. *1st-year*: Juv (plumage held briefly, unrecorded in US) resembles female but plumage lax, underparts pale yellow. Following partial preformative molt in late summer–fall, both sexes resemble adult female but distinguishable by retained juv flight feathers, which are browner overall and often heavily worn in 1st summer, with narrower and abraded white wing-bars and tertial tips; mandible mostly pale pinkish, at least into winter. *1st-year male* also averages brighter than adult female with

reduced olive wash on crown, nape, and cheeks, bolder black centers to upperparts, larger white patch at primary bases.

Habitat and Behavior: Deciduous to semi-deciduous forest and woodland, riparian groves and adjacent thorn forest. Forages mainly at upper to mid-levels in trees where generally sluggish, and overlooked easily if not vocal. Most readily seen when singing or visiting feeders, which is how several N American birds have been found. Commonest call, given while perched, a high squeaky *iehk* or *plihk*, more similar to call of Rose-breasted than Black-headed Grosbeak; also a mellow *whoi* or *huoi* (perched and in flight); female at least also has a slightly piercing whistled *psieu* or *pseeu* given when foraging. Song a variable, short rich warble, sweeter and more slurred than choppier song of Black-headed Grosbeak.

EASTERN BLUE BUNTING

Cyanocompsa parellina 13–14 cm (5–5.5")

Summary: *Texas*: Very rare and sporadic, late fall–spring, mainly in Lower Rio Grande Valley. ***Louisiana*:** 1 winter record (1979).

Taxonomy: 4 ssp of Blue Bunting usually recognized, although *indigotica* of w. Mexico best treated as a separate species, Western Blue Bunting, which is paler overall and has a high *ssip* call. Eastern Blue Buntings are darker overall and have a metallic *chink* call, with n. birds averaging paler overall than s. birds. Recent genetic work also supports this split (Maldonado et al. 2012). As far as is known, all birds recorded in the US have been Eastern Blue Buntings, presumably of n. ssp *beneplacita*. Sometimes known simply as Blue Bunting.

Distribution and Status:

World: Lowlands and lower foothills from e. Mexico (n. to cen. Nuevo Leon) to w. Nicaragua.

North America: ***Texas*:** Very rare and sporadic in late fall–spring (mid-Oct to early Apr, mainly mid-Nov to mid-Mar); almost all records from s. TX, especially Lower Rio Grande Valley, since first records there in 1979/1980 winter. Also 2 winter records (mid-Dec 1987 to mid-Feb 1988) from Brazoria Co., Upper Texas Coast. ***Elsewhere*:** Cameron Parish, LA, 16 Dec 1979 (specimen, 1st US record).

Comments: This species' occurrence in s. TX is sporadic, with occasional invasions in some years perhaps reflecting food shortages in ne. Mexico. The biggest invasions of Blue Bunting, in the winters of 1987/1988 (10+ birds) and 2004/2005 (7+ birds), corresponded to those of Crimson-collared Grosbeak, although the

♂

1st-year ♀

♂ fresh
(fall–winter)

adult ♂ worn
(late winter–summer)

stout
bill

smaller bill
than Blue Bunting

adult ♀

lacks blue
edgings on tail

Blue Bunting

often has blue
edgings on wings
and tail

Varied Bunting ♀

bunting mainly eats seeds (with some fruit) whereas the grosbeak mainly eats fruit and leaves. Studies are still needed to identify the climatic and food-related variables that trigger the winter wanderings of a diverse suite of species that inhabit ne. Mexico.

Field Identification: Slightly larger and bulkier than Indigo Bunting, with stouter bill and slightly decurved culmen.

Similar Species: Male distinctive, but beware mottled or molting adult male Indigo Buntings in winter, which may be unfamiliar to most US observers. Female and 1st-year Blue Bunting can suggest fresh-plumaged female Indigo Bunting or Varied Bunting but Blue is larger and chunkier with a stouter bill; cutting edge on upper mandible of Blue has a slight 'tooth', least distinct in 1st-years, lending it a faint 'sneer' unlike the 'softer' look of Varied and Indigo. Blue also lacks distinctly paler wing-bars and blue edgings to remiges and tail, and is not streaked below, as brown-plumaged Indigo Buntings usually are in winter.

Age/Sex/Season: 1st-year molts and plumages need study. Ages/sexes differ; no seasonal variation other than wear and fading. **Adult male**: Blue-black overall with blue crown, lores, shoulders, and rump; variable (usually fine) brownish to cinnamon edgings on fresh head and body plumage usually abrade by spring. Bill black, often with pale base to mandible in fall and winter. **Adult female**: Rich cocoa brown overall, some birds with bluish edgings to lesser coverts. **1st-year**: Juv (plumage held briefly, unknown in US) resembles adult female but paler overall, with lax plumage, tapered rectrices. 1st-year male: Some (especially Western?) resemble adult female but with darker tail, occasional blue spots on body in 1st summer; bill becomes black by 1st summer. Others (Eastern only?) apparently resemble adult male but with brown-tinged wings, broader cinnamon edgings to body feathers, sometimes with molt contrast in greater coverts; bill more extensively pale below. 1st-year female resembles adult but lacks blue edgings to lesser coverts; juv rectrices relatively tapered but, like male, may replace tail in preformative molt and show molt contrast in greater coverts.

Habitat and Behavior: Brushy woodland understory and edge. Feeds low to high, from canopy of fruiting or flowering trees to low in seeding grasses and on the ground; mainly at low to mid-levels, and often fairly retiring and easy to overlook. Usually occurs singly but occasionally in pairs or small groups. Call a metallic *chik* or *chink*, recalling Hooded Warbler. Song a short, slightly sad, sweet warble of about 2 secs' duration.

BLACK-VENTED ORIOLE *Icterus wagleri*
20.5–23 cm (8–9")

Summary: *Southwest*: Exceptional in spring–fall. *Elsewhere*: Exceptional in s. Texas (records year-round).

Taxonomy: 2 ssp described but not safely distinguished in the field: *castaneopectus* in nw. Mexico, and *wagleri* from ne. and cen. Mexico southward; former averages a stronger chestnut blush, or band, below the black chest bib, latter averages reduced chestnut (rarely absent). However, both types occur throughout the species' range (Miller et al. 1957), suggesting the species might best be considered monotypic.

Distribution and Status:

World: Mexico (n. to cen. Sonora and s. Nuevo Leon) to Nicaragua.

North America: *Southwest*: Exceptional in spring–fall (mid-Apr to early Oct) with 3 records, all of single adults: 2 from Brewster Co., TX, returning in successive summers, mid-late Apr to late Sep–early Oct, 1968–1970, and 6 Oct 2006; 1 from Santa Cruz Co., se. AZ, 18 Apr 1991. *Elsewhere*: Exceptional (year-round) in s. TX, with 4 records, all single adults: Kleberg Co., 17 Jun–4 Oct 1989; Cameron Co., 10–11 Apr 2010 (*NAB* 64:462); Hidalgo Co., 13 Dec 2010–20 Mar 2011, and returning 13 Oct 2011 (*NAB* 65:226, 310, 483; *NAB* 66:126); Cameron Co., 28 Apr–6 May 2011 (*NAB* 65:483).

Comments: In w. Mexico at least, this species is partly migratory or nomadic, but details of its movements are poorly known. In general, birds move to the Pacific coastal lowlands in winter (often to palm plantations where they feed on the flowering coconuts), and return to breed in the interior mountains in spring–summer. US records largely suggest a pattern of spring migrant overshoots arriving in mid–late April and sometimes staying through fall (the 1989 and 2006 Texas birds may have arrived before mid-Jun and early Oct, respectively); alternatively, the Oct 2006 bird may reflect misoriented fall dispersal, and there is one recent record of wintering.

The returning TX summer bird was identified as nominate *wagleri* (A. R. Phillips, in Wauer 1970), which might suggest it came from ne.

no white
wing-bars

adult
(sexes similar)

1st-year
variable

Black-vented Oriole

Mexico, although individual plumage variation in this species may render moot any ssp determination (see Taxonomy, above).

Field Identification: Fairly large oriole with long, relatively slender bill, the culmen straight or only slightly decurved, and long, strongly graduated tail. All plumages lack white wing-bars.

Similar Species: Adults striking and unlikely to be mistaken for any regularly occurring N American species; note solidly black back, wings, and tail, with black tail coverts. Imms can be puzzling, but do not closely resemble any N American oriole species: note long bill, strongly graduated tail, yellow underparts, and fairly plain wings (no white wing-bars).

Scott's Oriole 1st-summer in worn plumage, with white wing-bars reduced or missing, has lemon-yellow rather than ochre-yellow tones to underparts, tail slightly shorter and less strongly graduated, with yellowish on base of outer rectrices, *Audubon's Oriole* 1st-year has more extensive black on head, fresh wings have a narrow whitish wing-bar on greater coverts.

Age/Sex/Season: Ages differ; sexes similar; no seasonal variation. Molts not well known; may follow complex basic strategy (see p. 35). *Adult* has solidly black head, back, wings, and tail, with black tail coverts. *1st-year*: Juv (plumage held briefly, unrecorded in US) plumage lax, lacking black on throat, underparts pale yellow, greater upperwing coverts dark brown, edged olive-yellow. Soon molts into variable 1st-year plumage via partial preformative molt. Crown and back grayish olive to dull yellowish, often with some dark mottling; underparts ochre-yellow with variable black mask and bib; some birds attain one or more black tertials and rectrices, sometimes greater coverts.

Habitat and Behavior: Open and semi-open areas with flowering trees (favors coral bean flowers), from desert scrub to flowering hedgerows, gardens, and coconut plantations; may also visit feeders with fruit. In Mexico, associates readily with other orioles at flowering trees. Common call a nasal, slightly gruff *nyeh* or *yahn*, sometimes repeated a few times.

STREAK-BACKED ORIOLE *Icterus*
pustulatus 19–21 cm (7.5–8.3")

Summary: *Southwest*: Very rare, mainly in fall–spring; has bred. *Elsewhere*: Exceptional in coastal CA, e. OR, CO, WI, and e. to TX coast.

Taxonomy: 8 ssp, with complex geographic and individual variation in s. Mexico and n. Cen America (see Howell & Webb 1995 for summary). N American records are of migratory northernmost ssp *microstictus*, which breeds in nw. Mexico. A presumed escape of one of the s. ssp has occurred in AZ (late Dec 2007; *NAB* 62:285).

Distribution and Status:

World: Lowlands and foothills from w. Mexico (n. to cen. Sonora) to nw. Costa Rica.

North America: *Southwest*: Very rare year-round (mainly in fall–winter) in se. AZ, with at least 3 nesting records, 1993–2002 (Corman & Monson 1995), exceptionally n. to cen. AZ and sw. AZ. Exceptional in fall–winter (Oct–early Jan) in se. CA (4 records) and cen. and s. NM

(4 records); 1 fall record from El Paso, Co., w. TX, 16 Sep 2005. *Elsewhere*: Exceptional in coastal s. and cen. CA (4 records, late Sep–late Mar; plus an earlier record from San Diego Co., on the anomalous date of 1 May 1931); also single fall–winter birds in Harney Co., e. OR, 28 Sep–1 Oct 1993; Iron Co., WI, early to 15 Jan 1998; Fort Bend Co., TX, 12 Dec 2004–8 Apr 2005; Larimer Co., CO, 8 Dec 2007–2 Jan 2008; and El Paso Co., CO, 25 Nov 2011 (*NAB* 66:131).

Comments: In Mexico this species is partially migratory. In nw. Mexico, birds move s. from Sonora in Sep–Oct and return in Mar–Apr, with nesting during May–Aug; migrants winter to at least as far s. as Guerrero in sw. Mexico, about 1500 km (900 miles) from the n. breeding grounds—about the same distance as from e. OR to nw. Mexico, but in the reverse direction.

Away from potential nesting areas in se. AZ (whence most summer records are in Jun–Aug), almost all N American records have been mid-Sep to early Apr. Most birds have been found in Nov–Dec, which may reflect increased

adult ♂

adult ♂

adult ♂

adult ♀

1st-year ♂ fresh
(fall–winter)

1st-year ♀

Streak-backed
Oriole

CBC-related birding at that season rather than actual arrival dates.

The potential for escaped cage birds should always be considered with extralimital records. For example, a Streak-backed Oriole photographed in QC, 23–26 Oct 2011, was considered to be from a nonmigratory population and thus an escape (*NAB* 66:36).

Field Identification: Medium-sized, fairly stocky oriole with relatively stout bill, straight culmen, and medium-length, slightly graduated tail. All ages have dark-tipped lower mandible and white wing edgings that do not form discrete wing-bars.

Similar Species: Adult male Streak-backed Oriole distinctive, but female and 1st-year can be confused with Bullock's and Hooded orioles. Note Streak-backed's fairly stocky shape, relatively stout bill with straight culmen, medium-length tail, and white wing edgings.

Bullock's Oriole slighter overall with slightly shorter tail, longer primary projection, and slightly slimmer bill that typically has an all-pale lower mandible (dark-tipped on Streak-backed). 1st-year male Bullock's can have distinct narrow dark back streaks but belly usually pale gray (rarely solidly orange-yellow below), white wing-bars often better defined, and black eyeline narrower than black loral 'mask' of Streak-backed.

Hooded Oriole smaller and slimmer than Streak-backed, with long tail, slimmer bill with decurved culmen, and 2 distinct white wing-bars; adult male has black mask extending back to rear of eye, female lacks black on face and throat. Note that fresh-plumaged adult male Hooded has mostly pale back with black marks (concealed feather bases) tending to be scallops, not streaks.

Age/Sex/Season: Ages differ; sexes similar; no seasonal variation. Molts not well known; may follow complex basic strategy (see p. 35). **Adult male**: Bright flame-orange head and chest, orange back with distinct blackish streaks, extensive white on wings; tail blackish with narrow white tips to truncate outer rectrices. **Adult female**: Duller overall, head and underparts orange, nape and back washed olive with less distinct dark streaks; tail dark brownish olive with truncate rectrices. *1st-year*: Juv (Jul–Sep) has upperparts dull grayish olive with indistinct duskier streaks (can look plain overall), lacks black lores and bib (attained by molt after migration), underparts pale yellowish; lower mandible pale pinkish with dusky tip. Molts into variable 1st-year plumage via partial preformative molt. *1st-year male*: Overall appears variably intermediate between adult male and female, usually with some flame-orange tones on head; note browner remiges (wing-tips very worn in summer), olive tail with tapered rectrices (sometimes with one or more darker formative rectrices). *1st-year female*: Duller than adult female (face and chest yellow to dull orange-yellow) with paler head and underparts, indistinct dusky lores and bib, and relatively indistinct dusky back streaks; note retained juv flight feathers, as male.

Habitat and Behaviorn: Riparian woodland and thorn forest, ranging to gardens and semi-open areas with flowering trees; vagrants could occur in a variety of wooded habitats, usually near edges or in adjacent clearings. Common calls are a rough nasal *yehr* or *yehnk*, a hard rattled chatter recalling Bullock's Oriole but more of a rattle than a slurred chatter, and a whistled *wheet* or *whieh* (not distinctly ascending as is typical *wienk?* of Hooded Oriole). Varied songs tend to be slower-paced and with more repetition of notes relative to the hurried warble of Hooded Oriole.

Appendix A: Species New to North America, Fall 2011–Summer 2012

Any work such as this will be out of date before it is published, although we suspect that most if not all newly recorded species will fit into the patterns of vagrancy we have described. As well as the 3 species included here, see Hooded Crane, Tropical Mockingbird, and Small-billed Elaenia, all discussed in Appendix B.

EURASIAN BITTERN *Botaurus stellaris*
69–81 cm (27–32")

Alaska: Buldir, w. Aleutians, 14–25 Jun 2012 (http://blog.aba.org/2012/06/abarare-eurasian-bittern-alaska.html); not reviewed by state committee as of Sep 2012.

Eurasian Bittern breeds widely across mid-latitude Eurasia and was on our informal list of likely future vagrants to AK. Its distribution and migration patterns are typical of other E Asian herons recorded in spring–summer on the Aleutians and presumably it was a drift vagrant. The report we have seen, supported by poor photos, sounds convincing but whether documentation is sufficient for the state committee remains to be seen.

COMMON CHIFFCHAFF *Phylloscopus collybita*
11–12 cm (4.3–4.7")

Alaska: St. Lawrence Island, n. Bering Sea, 30 Sep–3 Oct 2011 (P. Scully, pers. comm., photos); not reviewed by state committee as of Sep 2012.

Common Chiffchaff breeds from W Europe e. across N and mid-latitude Eurasia to around 150°E. It winters from SW Europe to sub-Saharan Africa and in S Asia, e. to the Indian subcontinent. E populations are sometimes treated as a separate species, Siberian Chiffchaff *P. tristis* (e.g., Brazil 2009), which is a rare vagrant to W Europe (see Dean et al. 2010). The occurrence of chiffchaff in w. AK seemed only a matter of time, and the recent fall record (a bird showing characters of Siberian Chiffchaff) fits the pattern of misoriented (reverse?) migrants that occur in fall in AK, especially on the Bering Sea islands. Remarkably, a *Phylloscopus* warbler seen 6–7 Jun 2012 on St. Lawrence Island also appears to have been a chiffchaff, but its identity is still being debated (P. Lehman, pers. comm.; Davis 2012).

Habits much like Willow Warbler, but frequently dips tail downward (tail twitched, but not strongly dipped by Willow). Should be separated with care from Willow Warbler (see identification discussion and plate on pp. 310–311).

ASIAN ROSY FINCH *Leucosticte arctoa*
16 cm (6.3")

Alaska: Adak, cen. Aleutians, 30 Dec 2011 (*NAB* 66:332, 370); accepted by state committee.

Asian Rosy Finch breeds in E Asia (including Kamchatka) and winters mainly in e. China and n. Japan, with migration perhaps linked to local weather conditions; migrants arrive in Japan mainly from late Nov onward (Brazil 1991). The AK record may represent a misoriented or storm-drifted post-breeding migrant, but we do not know when it arrived versus when it was found.

Habits much like N American rosy finches. Overall rather dark and dull, differs from dullest Gray-crowned Rosy-Finch in blackish face and chest, contrasting in e. ssp *brunneonucha* (to which N American record pertains) with warm brown nape sides.

Appendix B: Species of Hypothetical Occurrence

Sundry records that might qualify species for inclusion as rare birds in North America are floating around in the literature and elsewhere, but most are not generally accepted on the basis of questions about origin or identification. Here we include some of the more notable and recent candidates. We acknowledge that drawing a line between some of these species and others that we include in the main accounts is arbitrary. Future records may help place some of these records in context and prompt their reevaluation.

Little Shearwater *Puffinus assimilis*. A bird photographed in Monterey Co., CA, 29 Oct 2003, was accepted as the first N Hemisphere record of this species (Hamilton et al. 2007). Careful review of the record, however, indicated the bird was a Manx Shearwater and the record is no longer accepted (Heindel & Garrett 2008, Howell 2012a). Although Little Shearwater is maintained on the AK unsubstantiated list, we consider these reports unlikely to pertain to Little Shearwater (Howell 2012a). N Atlantic records of 'Little Shearwater' have been modified through taxonomic revision and are considered as Barolo Shearwater.

Humboldt Penguin *Sphensicus humboldti*. An adult was caught in a fishing net off se. AK on 18 Jul 2002 (*NAB* 56:402, 471), and is preceded by 4 other records of penguins from the Pacific Coast between BC and WA (1944, 1975, 1978, 1985), as summarized by Van Buren & Boersma (2007). While vagrancy among penguins is frequent (and may span 10,000 km or more), it is typically a longitudinal phenomenon, with birds remaining in water masses of similar temperature and being aided by ocean currents that encircle southern latitudes of the globe. A record of a distressed 1st-year Magellanic Penguin *S. magellanicus* from El Salvador, in Jun 2007 (*NAB* 61:649), might conceivably represent a natural vagrant that reached the limit of its northward dispersal before succumbing to the heat.

Even though penguins can survive days without food (and weeks when molting on shore), a swimming journey to waters off the West Coast seems improbable if not physiologically impossible, given the intervening areas of warm water that would need to be crossed. The most likely

scenario for penguins recorded in N American waters is that birds were transported aboard ships and then released or escaped (Van Buren & Boersma 2007).

Brown Skua *Catharacta antarctica*. Several large skuas seen in the w. N Atlantic have shown characters of Brown Skua (McLaren & Lucas 2004), as is true of at least one bird seen in CA (Howell 2005). Given that hybrids of Brown Skua × South Polar Skua may not be separable in the field from Brown Skua, and that a pure Brown Skua has not been certainly recorded n. of the equator in the Atlantic or Pacific, we consider N American records possible but unproven.

Gray Gull *Larus modestus*. A dark-plumaged gull photographed in Cameron Parish, LA, 19 Dec 1987 (*AB* 42:277), was initially thought to be this S American species. Review of the photos suggests the bird may have been a discolored or melanistic Laughing Gull, and the record is not accepted by the state committee (Dittmann & Cardiff 2003); thus it is unlikely to be reviewed by the ABA committee (Pranty & ABA Checklist Committee 2011).

Little Tern *Sternula albifrons*. A bird on Buldir, w. Aleutians, AK, 4–6 Jul 2005, was likely this species but could have been a Least Tern (Gibson & Byrd 2007). The bird was photographed only at rest and no attention was paid to rump color or voice, hence it cannot be identified to species.

Kentish Plover *Chardrius alexandrinus*. A 1st-year small plover seen in w. AK, 23–24 May 1991, was considered a Snowy Plover, prior to the split of Old World populations as Kentish Plover (Gibson & Kessel 1992; Pranty & ABA Checklist Committee 2011). Photos (examined by us) do not help resolve the identification, and even suggest a leucistic Semipalmated Plover may have been involved.

Hooded Crane *Grus monacha*. An adult in Hall Co., NE, 25 Mar–11 Apr 2011, was mooted to have been a bird that escaped in 2006 from an aviary in Idaho (*NAB* 65:476, 569) and may have been the same individual as seen 13 Dec 2011–30 Jan 2012 in Meigs Co., TN (*NAB* 66:230, 291), and 8–12 Feb 2012 in Greene Co., IN (NAB 66:278–279). At the time of going to press, these records were still being researched to determine if provenance could be established. As with Common

Crane and Demoiselle Crane, a vagrant Hooded Crane is plausible, its breeding range being nearer to N America than that of Demoiselle, farther than that of Common.

Baillon's Crake *Porzana pusilla*. A small crake observed on Attu, w. Aleutians, AK, 20–21 Sep 2000 (*AB* 55:89; Gibson & Byrd 2007) was probably this species (descriptions examined). However, views were brief and only in flight, and the species is placed on the state's unsubstantiated list.

Scarlet Ibis *Eudocimus ruber*. The status in N America of this popular captive species is unclear. ABA (2002) stated, "no unequivocal documentation of a natural occurrence exists," but with no additional evidence, ABA (2008) changed this to "apparently casual or accidental in Florida." A few specimens and reports from s. FL in the late 1800s (Stevenson & Anderson 1994; ABA 2008) might refer to wild occurrence, but there have been no reports in over 100 years that we consider likely to represent natural occurrence.

Chinese Sparrowhawk (Gray Frog Hawk) *Accipiter soloensis*. A red-breasted *Accipter* seen 8–9 Jun 1995 on Nizki, w. Aleutians, was thought to be this species (*FN* 49:292); color photos taken are not definitive (Gibson & Byrd 2007; examined by us, July 2012) and the species is placed on the AK unsubstantiated list. Eurasian Sparrowhawk *A. nisus* and Japanese Sparrowhawk *A. gularis* occur closer to N America, and males of both are red-breasted (although not such regular migrants over water, and any species could be ship-assisted). Eurasian breeds in Kamchatka, where Japanese is a straggler; Chinese Sparrowhawk is unrecorded in Kamchatka.

European Honey Buzzard *Pernis apivorus*. A large hawk seen in flight on 11 Aug 1997 in Kent Co., DE, was probably this species; later reports from nearby areas, 27 and 31 Aug 1997, are unconvincing and at odds with the first description (all descriptions examined by us). The 11 Aug description does not eliminate the similar (but seemingly very unlikely) Crested Honey Buzzard *P. ptilorhynchus*, and the species is not accepted by the state committee.

Eastern Buzzard *Buteo japonicus*. Included (as Common Buzzard *B. buteo*) on the AK unsubstantiated list on the basis of a sight report from Nizki, w. Aleutians, 26 May 1983 (*AB* 37:902; Gibson & Byrd 2007); we find the description unconvincing, although a buzzard may have been seen.

Cuban Black Hawk *Buteogallus gundlachii*. An adult photographed in Harris Co., GA, 10 Apr 2009, was rejected by state committee on grounds of provenance, and thus was not reviewed by the ABA committee (Pranty & ABA Checklist Committee 2011). We have not reviewed the record. Some reports of *Buteogallus* hawks from s. FL during 1972–1991 may have involved wild vagrants of Cuban Black Hawk, but the specific identity of such birds has remained uncertain (W. B. Robertson Jr. & Woolfenden 1992, Stevenson & Anderson 1994). Cuban Black Hawk was split by AOU in 2007 from Common Black Hawk (*Auk* 124:1109–1115) and seems a plausible vagrant to the FL Keys.

Variable (Red-backed) Hawk *Buteo polyosoma*. An adult female in Gunnison Co., CO, Aug–Oct 1987 (*AB* 42:112) apparently returned in subsequent years and paired with a Swainson's Hawk (Nelson 1991; AOU 1998). The species is a partial migrant within S America, and some birds (mainly 1st-years) withdraw n. in the austral fall up to about 3000 km (1800 miles), as from s. to nw. Argentina (Juhant 2011). Whether one could associate with Swainson's Hawks and continue on to N America is anyone's guess. In the absence of any other vagrant n. records, the species was not accepted by the state committee, based in part on the misconception that the species is highly sedentary (Allen 1988; Nelson 1991).

Hooded Crow *Corvus cornix*. A 1st-year found at Staten Island, NY, 20 Jun–8 Jul 2011, reappeared in Ocean Co., NJ, on at least 17 Jul 2011 (*NAB* 65:603). Given 88 accepted records through 2006 from Iceland (with peaks in Mar–May and Oct–Nov), and 2 old Mar–May records from se. Greenland (1897, 1907), the possibility of natural occurrence in N America seems plausible, although first landfall might be expected in Atlantic Canada. If not an escape, the NY bird was almost certainly ship-assisted, although whether it traveled without restraint or direct assistance we will likely never know. Some might argue this record deserves as much a place on the North American list as other possibly or certainly ship-assisted species such as Red-footed Falcon and Eurasian Jackdaw, but for now we place it on the hypothetical list.

House Crow *Corvus splendens*. In recent years, breeding groups of House Crows have been documented twice on the Gulf coast of FL, presumably ship-assisted immigrants, perhaps coming from Port of Tampa: first, in Sarasota Co.

(Nokomis Beach), 2001–2008, up to 4 birds; then in Manatee Co. (Palmetto), 2009–2010, up to 6 birds in an apparent family group (*Florida Field Naturalist* 31:69, 88; 33:64; 35:35; 36:18; 38:84; 39:66; photos in Pranty 2004). Neither group is still extant (B. Pranty & J. Greenlaw, pers. comm.). Recent records of single House Crows also exist from LA (2008; *NAB* 62:427) and VA (2008; *NAB* 63:58), and the species might next appear anywhere around a major port along the East Coast or Gulf Coast.

Whereas intentional, non-native introductions are required to become established for a certain number of generations before admittance to the N American list, no such rule applies to species arriving on their own. Thus, this species represents a unique case in N America, of an ostensibly non-migratory human commensal arriving (apparently) of its own volition via ship and establishing a breeding population, albeit short-lived for now. By means of hitching rides on ships (see Cheke 2008), House Crows have reached scattered sites around the world; for example, self-introduced breeding populations occur locally from Israel s. to South Africa, where the species is considered a pest in some areas. A small population of house crows in the Netherlands is treated as 'wild' and countable, because ships are considered an integral part of this species' ecology. Conversely, 2 records from Ireland, of long-staying singles first found in Nov 1974 and Sep 2010, are relegated to an appendix of species that arrived with human assistance (K. Mullarney, pers. comm.). As with Hooded Crow, it could be argued that House Crow deserves a place on the N American list, although for now the FL committee has not passed judgment on the matter (J. Greenlaw, pers. comm.).

Greater Ani *Crotophaga major*. A 1st-year bird was photographed in Miami-Dade Co., FL, 16 Dec 2010 (*NAB* 65:260, 381). The state committee could not agree on provenance, and the record remains in review (Pranty & ABA Checklist Committee 2011). Although seemingly an unlikely vagrant, this largely S American species also seems an unlikely candidate for captivity, and anis as a whole have demonstrated a penchant for vagrancy.

Japanese Tit (Eastern Great Tit) *Parus minor*. One was seen 2 Sep 1988, on Little Diomede Island, AK, in the Bering Strait (*AB* 43:153; descriptions examined), and the species is placed on the state's unsubstantiated list.

Northern populations of Great Tit *P. major* are irruptive, at least in W Eurasia, where birds often disperse sw. in fall, with banding recoveries exceptionally indicating movements of up to 1880 km (Cramp & Perrins 1993–94, vol. 7). If similar irruptions occur with Japanese Tits, a record from AK seems feasible, but we have no data from ne. Russia that might help place the AK record in context.

Barred Antshrike *Thamnophilus doliatus*. A bizarre record from s. TX (of a bird recorded singing at night) is accepted by the state committee but not by the ABA committee (Pranty & ABA Checklist Committee 2007); we also consider the record remarkable enough to not accept it here.

Caribbean Elaenia *Elaenia martinica*. An *Elaenia* flycatcher photographed in Escambia Co., nw. FL, 28 Apr 1984, was accepted as this species (*ABA* 2008), although to our eyes the photos do not eliminate other species in this notoriously problematic genus. The record has since been downgraded to *Elaenia* sp. by the state and ABA committees (Kratter 2010; Pranty & ABA Checklist Committee 2009).

Small-billed Elaenia *Elaenia parvirostris*. This austral migrant from S America may have occurred twice to date in N America. A bird photographed in Washington Co., RI, 10 Nov 2008 (N. Conway, unpubl. photos), appears to have been an elaenia, likely this species, but the record has not been formally submitted to the state committee (S. Mitra, pers. comm.). Another elaenia, studied at length in Cook Co., IL, 17–22 Apr 2012, appeared to be a worn 1st-year, making specific identification more problematic than usual within this genus; as of Sep 2012, its identity had not been resolved but most observers felt it likely to have been Small-billed (D. Stotz, pers. comm.).

Giant Kingbird *Tyrannus cubensis*. A kingbird in Monroe Co., FL, 29 Dec 1971–late Jan 1972 may have been this poorly known Cuban endemic; reportedly it returned the following winter, 1972/1973 (Stevenson & Anderson 1994; Smith et al. 2000). A photo taken 31 Dec 1971 was considered by James Bond, the leading authority on Caribbean birds at the time, to pertain to Giant Kingbird (Stevenson & Anderson 1994; Smith et al. 2000). Given our lack of familiarity with this species in life we are uncertain of the identification based on a single published photo (Smith et al. 2000:236), although we see no reason to doubt Bond's assessment. However, given dissenting opinions from some Cuban observers familiar with Giant

Kingbird (J. Dunn, pers. comm.), it seems the record may rest in limbo indefinitely, without being formally submitted to any committee.

The FL record fits with a pattern of winter wandering by this apparently declining species, which has also been found in winter (all records from late 1800s) in the southern Bahamas and on Mexico's Yucatan Peninsula. This last occurrence was considered hypothetical by Howell & Webb (1995) but is here considered likely valid, following Smith (2001). The species' present day rarity may mitigate against future occurrence in N America, but further records seem possible, perhaps especially on the Florida Keys in winter.

Tropical Mockingbird *Mimus gilvus.* One found 18 Apr 2012 in Jefferson Co., TX, on the Upper Gulf Coast, stayed through at least summer 2012 and bred with a Northern Mockingbird, producing 2 young (M. Lockwood, pers. comm.; Davis 2012). While this may represent natural dispersal, perhaps ship-assisted across the Gulf of Mexico, it also may relate to an escaped cage bird (although why anyone who lives in an area full of Northern Mockingbirds would want a caged mockingbird is not entirely clear). The state committee had not voted on the record as of Sep 2012 (M. Lockwood, pers. comm.).

Cinnamon-rumped Seedeater *Sporophila torqueola.* West Mexican populations of the White-collared Seedeater complex differ in plumage and voice from e. Mexican populations (*S. [t.] morelleti*) and are best considered a separate species. Like Ruddy Ground-Dove, Cinnamon-rumped Seedeater is expanding northward in nw. Mexico, and has been found since at least 2009 in s. Sonora (*NAB* 65:171). It has also established breeding populations (of unknown provenance) since at least 2007 in s. Baja California Sur, Mexico, where first recorded 2002 (R. Erickson, pers. comm.), with a fall vagrant recorded n. to the Vizcaino Peninsula in 2010 (*NAB* 65:169). Small numbers have been found on several occasions in San Diego Co., CA (Unitt 2004), presumably derived from the cage bird trade in adjacent Tijuana, Mexico. In AZ, a male was in Santa Cruz Co., 25 Jun–24 Aug 2007

(Rosenberg et al. 2011) and another in Maricopa Co., on at least 3–7 Oct 2008 (M. Stevenson, pers. comm.). Given that this species is a fairly popular cage bird, US records are considered of uncertain provenance, but natural vagrancy to AZ seems plausible and future occurrences should be carefully documented.

Rufous-collared Sparrow *Zonotrichia capensis.* A singing bird was in Clear Creek Co., CO, from 8 May 2011 into at least the fall (*NAB* 65:488; *NAB* 66:131). The nearest populations to the US of this abundant species are in Cen America and adjacent s. Mexico, and these are not known to be migratory. Although the CO bird was far from where one might expect an escape, and the species is not commonly held in captivity, the sedentary nature of the closest populations argues against natural vagrancy—but it also reinforces how little we know of the lives of so-called resident tropical birds.

Cuban Bullfinch *Melopyrrha nigra.* A male in Miami-Dade Co., FL, 24–25 Oct 2011 (*NAB* 66:65, 67) showed signs of cage wear and is considered of uncertain provenance by the state committee (J. Greenlaw, pers. comm.). A few earlier FL records, including a singing male in Miami-Dade Co., 26 Aug–5 Sep 1960, are also usually treated as probably involving escaped cage birds, although it has been noted that the species is a plausible natural vagrant (W. B. Robertson Jr. & Woolfenden 1992).

Black-headed Siskin *Spinus atratus.* An adult of this Mexican species was photographed in Cameron Co., TX, 4 Mar 2009 (*NAB* 63:468, 536). The species is common in the highlands of Mexico, and at least in the nw. of its range, in Sonora, birds appear migratory and withdraw s. in Aug–Feb (Russell & Monson 1998). The TX bird appeared to be in unworn plumage, and the species is certainly a plausible vagrant to border states. However, siskins are also reported to be popular cage birds in ne. Mexico, and the record was not accepted by the state committee (Lockwood 2010). Future records should be documented to determine whether any patterns emerge to indicate potentially wild occurrence.

Appendix C: Birds New to North America, 1950–2011

Records are listed by year (and by group within year, rather than chronologically) and by state or province of first record. Italics indicate species known in North America from only single records (through 2011).

1950	Common Swift, AK
1951	*Auckland Shy Albatross, WA*
1952	Tundra Bean Goose, AK
	Nutting's Flycatcher, AZ
1953	Pink-footed Goose, DE
1954	Black-tailed Gull, CA
	Little Egret, NL
1955	Spotted Redshank, RI
1956	Gray-streaked Flycatcher, AK
	Eyebrowed Thrush, AK
1957	Garganey, NC
	Common Crane, AB
	Kamchatka Leaf Warbler, AK
	Western Spindalis, FL
1959	Redwing, NY
1960	Smew, AK
	Black Noddy, FL
	Lesser Frigatebird, ME
	Rufous-backed Thrush, AZ
1961	European Golden Plover, NL
	Little Stint, AK
	Eastern Curlew, AK
	Double-striped Thick-knee, TX
	Green Violetear, TX
	Bahama Woodstar, FL
	Gray Wagtail, AK
	Fan-tailed Warbler, AZ
1962	Common Greenshank, AK
	Olive-backed Pipit, AK
	Slate-throated Whitestart, NM
1963	Red-footed Booby, FL
	La Sagra's Flycatcher, AL
1965	Temminck's Stint, AK
1966	Common Sandpiper, AK
1967	*Gibson's Albatross, CA*
	Berylline Hummingbird, AZ
	Dusky Thrush, AK
	Eurasian Skylark, AK
1968	Belcher's Gull, FL
	Pallas's Bunting, AK
	Black-vented Oriole, TX
1969	Wedge-rumped Storm-Petrel, CA
	Plain-capped Starthroat, AZ

1970	Eastern Spot-billed Duck, AK
	European Storm-Petrel, NS
	Little Bunting, AK
1971	Jabiru, TX
	Common Cuckoo, AK
	Mexican Yellow Grosbeak, AZ
1972	Terek Sandpiper, MB
	Paint-billed Crake, TX
	Antillean Palm Swift, FL
	Common Rosefinch, AK
	Tree Pipit, AK
1973	Black-browed Albatross, MA
	Yellow-legged Gull, QC
	Bahama Mockingbird, FL
	Rufous-capped Warbler, TX
1974	Little Ringed Plover, AK
	Marsh Sandpiper, AK
	Chinese Egret, AK
	White-throated Needletail, AK
	Common House Martin, AK
	White-collared Swift, TX
	Crimson-collared Grosbeak, TX
1975	Great Frigatebird, OK
	Streaked Shearwater, CA
	Eurasian Hoopoe, AK
	Reed Bunting, AK
1976	Eurasian Curlew, MA
	Spotted Rail, PA
	Oriental Greenfinch, AK
1977	Broad-billed Sandpiper, AK
	Gray Nightjar, AK
	Oriental Scops Owl, AK
	Eared Quetzal, AZ
	Taiga Flycatcher, AK
	Brown Shrike, AK
	Dusky Warbler, AK
	Dark-sided Flycatcher, AK
	Gray Bunting, AK
	Variegated Flycatcher, ME
	Aztec Thrush, TX
1978	Green Sandpiper, AK
	Siberian Stonechat, AK
	Wood Warbler, AK
	Yellow-breasted Bunting, AK
	Eurasian Siskin, AK
1979	Red-tailed Tropicbird, CA
	Stejneger's Petrel, CA
	Eastern Blue Bunting, LA
1982	Eurasian Hobby, AK

	Eurasian Jackdaw, MA		*Eurasian Blackbird, NL*
	Red-flanked Bluetail, AK		Common Chaffinch, NL
1983	Solander's Petrel, WA	1995	*Zino's Petrel, NC*
	Black-winged Stilt, AK		Common Redshank, NL
	Western Reef Heron, MA		Cuban Pewee, FL
	Mottled Owl, TX	1996	Gray-faced Petrel, CA
	Brown-chested Martin, MA		Gray Heron, NL
	Great Spotted Woodpecker, AK		Chinese Pond Heron, AK
	Crescent-chested Warbler, AZ		Brown-backed Solitaire, AZ
1984	Bulwer's Petrel, FL		Orange-billed Nightingale-Thrush, TX
	Little Curlew, CA	1997	*Blue Rock Thrush, BC*
	Oriental Turtle Dove, AK	1998	White-faced Whistling-Duck, FL
	Lanceolated Warbler, AK		Gray-hooded Gull, FL
	Greenish Elaenia, TX		*Yellow-throated Bunting, AK*
	Yucatan Vireo, TX	1999	*Tasmanian Shy Albatross, CA*
1985	Swallow-tailed Gull, CA		*Hen Harrier, AK*
	Oriental Pratincole, AK		Yellow-browed Warbler, AK
	Asian Brown Flycatcher, AK	2000	*Chatham Albatross, CA*
	Mugimaki Flycatcher, AK		Rufous-tailed Robin, AK
	Pine Bunting, AK	2001	*Nazca Booby, CA*
	Siberian Blue Robin, AK		Greater Sand Plover, CA
	Flame-colored Tanager, AZ		*Demoiselle Crane, CA*
	Gray Silky, TX	2002	*Mangrove Swallow, FL*
1986	White-chinned Petrel, TX		Willow Warbler, AK
	Azure Gallinule, NY		*Lesser Whitethroat, AK*
	Xantus's Hummingbird, CA		*Spotted Flycatcher, AK*
	Dark-billed Cuckoo, TX	2003	*West Indian Whistling-Duck, VA*
1987	*Crane Hawk, TX*		*Ruddy Shelduck, NU*
1988	Green-breasted Mango, TX		*Salvin's Albatross, AK*
1989	Kelp Gull, LA		Red-legged Honeycreeper, FL
	Yellow Bittern, AK	2004	Black-bellied Storm-Petrel, NC
	Narcissus Flycatcher, AK		Cape Verde Shearwater, NC
	Thick-billed Vireo, FL		*Red-footed Falcon, MA*
1990	European Turtle Dove, FL		*Black-headed Nightingale-*
	Yellow-faced Grassquit, TX		*Thrush, TX*
	Masked Tityra, TX	2005	Greylag Goose, NL
	White-throated Thrush, TX		*Hornby's Storm-Petrel, CA*
1991	Pintail Snipe, AK		*Parkinson's Petrel, CA*
	Mexican Tufted Flycatcher, TX	2006	Tristram's Storm-Petrel, CA
	Piratic Flycatcher, FL		Southern Lapwing, FL
1992	Hawaiian Petrel, CA		Intermediate Egret, AK
	Collared Plover, TX		*Song Thrush, QC*
	Cinnamon Hummingbird, AZ		*Pallas's Leaf Warbler, AK*
	Citrine Wagtail, MS	2007	*Newell's Shearwater, CA*
	Blue Mockingbird, AZ		Northern Boobook, AK
1993	Whiskered Tern, NJ		*Yellow-browed Bunting, AK*
	Bermuda Petrel, NC		*Sedge Warbler, AK*
	Swinhoe's Storm-Petrel, NC		Loggerhead Kingbird, FL
1994	*Lesser White-fronted Goose, AK*	2008	*Sungrebe, NM*
	Light-mantled Sooty Albatross, CA		*Antipodes Albatross, OR*
	Eurasian Oystercatcher, NL		Solitary Snipe, AK
	Western Marsh Harrier, VA		*Crowned Slaty Flycatcher, LA*
	Collared Forest-Falcon, TX		*Chilean Elaenia, TX*
	Stygian Owl, TX		Sinaloa Wren, AZ

2009	Common Shelduck, NL		Blyth's Reed Warbler, AK
	Bare-throated Tiger Heron, TX		*Red-legged Thrush, FL*
	Gray-collared Becard, AZ	2011	*Double-toothed Kite, TX*
2010	*Common Moorhen, AK*		*Common Chiffchaff, AK*
	Amazon Kingfisher, TX		*Asian Rosy Finch, AK*

Literature Cited

Abbreviations

AB: *American Birds*
ABA: American Birding Association
AMNH: American Museum of Natural History
AOU: American Ornithologists' Union
BOC: British Ornithologists' Club
BOU: British Ornithologists' Union
NAB: *North American Birds*

Publications with 7 or more authors are cumbersome to cite and indicated simply as, for example, 'Yew, F., & 6 coauthors.'

ABA. 2002. *ABA Checklist: Birds of the Continental United States and Canada*, 6th ed. ABA: Colorado Springs, CO.

———. 2008. *ABA Checklist: Birds of the Continental United States and Canada*, 7th ed. ABA: Colorado Springs, CO.

Abbott, S., S.N.G. Howell, & P. Pyle. 2001. First North American record of Greater Sandplover. *NAB* 55:252–257.

Abraham, K. 2003. First record of Fork-tailed Flycatcher for Nunavut. *Birders Journal* 12:160–162.

Alford, C. E. 1928. "Assisted passage" of Greenfinches across Atlantic. *British Birds* 21:282.

Allard, K., K. McKay, & L. McKinnon. 2001. Sighting of Ruddy Shelducks at East Bay, Southampton Island, Nunavut. *Birders Journal* 10:86–89.

Allen, S. 1988. Some thoughts on the identification of Gunnison's Red-backed Hawk (*Buteo polyosoma*) and why it's not a natural vagrant. *Colorado Field Ornithologists' Journal* 22(1):9–14.

Alström, P., & E. Hirschfeld. 1991. Field identification of Brown, Siberian, and Grey-streaked Flycatchers. *Birding World* 4:271–278.

Alström, P., & K. Mild. 2003. *Pipits and Wagtails*. Princeton Univ Press: Princeton, NJ.

Alström, P., & U. Olsson. 1989. The identification of juvenile Red-necked and Long-toed Stints. *British Birds* 82:360–372.

Alström, P., & 8 coauthors. 2011. Arctic Warbler *Phylloscopus borealis*—three anciently separated cryptic species revealed. *Ibis* 153:395–410.

Amos, J. R. 1991. *The Birds of Bermuda*. Corncrake: Warwick, Bermuda.

Andersen, E. M., C. Schlawe, & S. Lorenz. 2008. First record of the Lanceolated Warbler breeding in North America. *Western Birds* 39:2–7.

Anderson, B. H. 2004. Florida region. *NAB* 58:217–219.

Anderson, B. H., & M. S. Ponce. 2010. First record of Red-legged Thrush (*Turdus plumbeus*) for Florida and the North American mainland. *NAB* 64:364–367.

Anon. 1998. First record of a Western Marsh Harrier (*Circus aeruginosus*) in Virginia. *Raven* 69:56.

Anon. 2004. Field Observations. *Florida Field Naturalist* 32:34–41.

Anon. 2009. Wandering Albatross in Oregon. *NAB* 63:182.

Anon. 2012. Western Palearctic news. *Birding World* 25:320–325.

Antas, P.T.Z. 1991. Status and conservation of seabirds breeding in Brazilian waters, pp. 141–158 in *Seabird Status and Conservation: A Supplement*, J. P. Croxall (ed.). ICBP Technical Publication no. 11.

AOU. 1957. *Checklist of North American Birds*, 5th ed. AOU: Washington, DC.

———. 1998. *Checklist of North American Birds*, 7th ed. AOU: Washington, DC.

Arnold, K. A. 1978. First United States record of Paint-billed Crake (*Neocrex erythrops*). *Auk* 95:745–746.

Arnold, K. A., B. D. Marks, & M. Gustafson. 2011. First specimen of Flame-colored Tanager (*Piranga bidentata*) for the United States. *Bulletin of Texas Ornithological Society* 44:97–99.

Arvin, J. C. 2001. *Birds of the Gomez Farias Region, Southwestern Tamaulipas, Mexico: An Annotated Checklist*. Texas Parks and Wildlife Department: Austin, TX.

Arvin, J. C., & M. W. Lockwood. 2006. First photographically documented record of Social Flycatcher (*Myiozetetes similis*) for the United States. *NAB* 60:180–181.

Auchu, C., C. Giraud, & G. Savard. 2007. First record of Song Thrush (*Turdus philomelas*) in North America. *NAB* 61:166–168.

Austin, J. J. 1996. Molecular phylogenetics of *Puffinus* shearwaters: Preliminary evidence from mitochondrial Cytochrome b gene sequences. *Molecular Phylogenetics and Evolution* 6:77–88.

Austin, J. J., V. Bretagnolle, & E. Pasquet. 2004. A global molecular phylogeny of the small *Puffinus* shearwaters and implications for systematics of the Little-Audubon's Shearwater complex. *Auk* 121:847–864.

Austin, O. L. 1929. Labrador records of European birds. *Auk* 46:207–213.

Bagg, A. M. 1967. Factors affecting the occurrence of the Eurasian Lapwing in eastern North America. *Living Bird* 6:87–121.

Baicich, P. J., S. C. Heinl, & M. Toochin. 1996. First documented breeding of the Eurasian Skylark in Alaska. *Western Birds* 27:86–88.

Bailey, A. M. 1947. Wryneck from Cape Prince of Wales, Alaska. *Auk* 64:456.

Bailey, S. F., P. Pyle, and L. B. Spear. 1989. Dark *Pterodroma* petrels in the North Pacific: Identification, status, and North American occurrence. *AB* 43:400–415.

Bain, M. 2002. Cross-Canada round-up, April and May 2002. *Birders Journal* 11:74–94.

Banks, A., M. Collier, G. Austin, R. Hearn, & A. Musgrove. 2006. *Waterbirds in the UK 2004/05*. The Wetland Bird Survey, BTO/WWT/RSPB/JNCC: Thetford, UK.

Barlow, J. C. 1981. Songs of the vireos and their allies. Ara Records, Gainesville, FL.

Behrstock, R. A., & T. L. Eubanks. 1997. Additions to the avifauna of Nuevo Leon, Mexico, with notes on new breeding records and infrequently seen species. *Cotinga* 7:27–30.

Benter, R. B., H. M. Renner, & M. Renner. 2005. First record of a Shy Albatross in Alaska. *Western Birds* 36:135–137.

Bieber, G., & S. Schuette. 2009. First record of Solitary Snipe (*Gallinago solitaria*) for North America on Saint Paul Island, Alaska. *NAB* 63:178–181.

BirdLife International. 2012. Species factsheet: *Emberiza aureola*. Accessed 5 April 2012, http://www.birdlife .org.

Blake, E. R. 1977. *Manual of Neotropical Birds*, vol. 1. Univ. Chicago Press: Chicago, IL.

Bland, B. 1998. The Wilson's Snipe on the Isles of Scilly. *Birding World* 11:382–385.

Blem, C. R. 1980. A Paint-billed Crake in Virginia. *Wilson Bulletin* 92:393–394.

Boertmann, D. 1994. Meddelelser om Gronland: An annotated checklist to the birds of Greenland. *Bioscience* 38:1–63.

Bond, A. L., & I. L. Jones. 2010. A Brown Hawk-Owl (*Ninox scutulata*) from Kiska Island, Aleutian Islands, Mexico. *Western Birds* 41:107–110.

Bond, J. 1985. *Birds of the West Indies*, 5th ed. Houghton Mifflin: Boston, MA.

Bowman, R. 2000. Thirteenth report of the Florida Ornithological Society Records Committee: 1996–2000. *Florida Field Naturalist* 28:138–160.

Brazil, M. 2003. *The Whooper Swan*. Poyser: London.

———. 2009. *Birds of East Asia*. Princeton Univ. Press: Princeton, NJ.

Brazil, M. A. 1991. *The Birds of Japan*. Smithsonian Institution Press: Washington, DC.

Brinkley, E. S. 2003. The changing seasons: Displacements. *NAB* 57:307–315.

———. 2007. Bulwer's Petrel (*Bulweria bulwerii*) new to Virginia. *Raven* 78:15–19.

———. 2010a. The changing seasons: Provenance. *NAB* 64:20–31.

———. 2010b. A White-winged Tern (*Chlidonias leucopterus*) at Chincoteague National Wildlife Refuge in 2002, with comments on identification and ageing of the species and a review of regional records. *Raven* 81:3–10.

———. 2011. The changing seasons: Escapes. *NAB* 65:216–233.

British Columbia Rare Bird Alert. July 2011. Accessed May 2012, http://bcbirdalert.blogspot.com/2011_07 _01_archive.html.

Brown, M. C., & R. A. Baxter. 2009. First United States record of Sinaloa Wren (*Thryothorus sinaloa*). *NAB* 63:196–201.

Browne, S., & N. Aebischer. 2005. Studies of West Palearctic birds: Turtle Dove. *British Birds* 98:58–72.

Buckley, P. A., E. B. Massiah, M. B. Hunt, F. G. Buckley, & H. F. Hutt. 2009. The Birds of Barbados. BOU Checklist 24.

Byrd, G. V., J. L. Trapp, & D. D. Gibson. 1978. New Information on Asiatic birds in the Aleutian Islands, Alaska. *Condor* 80:309–315.

Campbell, C. 2000. White-winged Tern—possible anywhere. *Birding* 32:216–230.

Campbell, R. W., N. K. Dawe, I. McT.-Cowan, J. M. Cooper, G. W. Kaiser, & M.C.E. McNall. 1990. *The Birds of British Columbia*, vol. 2. Royal British Columbia Museum: Victoria, BC.

Cardillo, R., A. Forbes-Watson, & R. Ridgely. 1983. The Western Reef-Heron (*Egretta gularis*) at Nantucket Island, Massachusetts. *AB* 37:827–829.

Carey, G., & U. Olsson. 1995. Field identification of Common, Wilson's, Pintail, and Swinhoe's Snipe. *Birding World* 8:179–190.

Cheke, A. 2008. Seafaring behaviour in House Crows *Corvus splendens*—a precursor to ship-assisted dispersal? *Phelsuma* 16:65–68.

Chesser, R. T. 1997. Patterns of seasonal and geographical distribution of austral migrant flycatchers (Tyrannidae) in Bolivia, pp. 177–204 in *Studies in Neotropical Ornithology Honoring Ted Parker*, J. V. Remsen (ed.). Ornithological Monographs 48.

Clark, T. 1999. Autumn 1998 on the Azores. *Birding World* 12:205–212.

Clark, W. S. 2008. Hybrid Bald eagle × Steller's Sea Eagle from Vancouver Island, British Columbia. *Birding* 40(4):28–31.

Cleere, N. 2010. *Nightjars, Potoos, Frogmouths, Oilbird, and Owlet-nightjars of the World*. Princeton Univ. Press: Princeton, NJ.

Coady, G. 1988. Ontario Bird Records Committee report for 1987. *Ontario Birds* 6:42–50.

Cole, L. 2000. A first Shy Albatross, *Thalassarche cauta*, in California and a critical re-examination of northern hemisphere records of the former *Diomedea cauta* complex. *NAB* 54:124–135.

Conover, P. E., & B. M. Myers. 2009. First United States record of Crowned Slaty Flycatcher (*Empidonomus aurantioatrocristatus*). *NAB* 62:638–639.

Constantine, M., & The Sound Approach. 2006. *The Sound Approach to Birding: A Guide to Understanding Bird Sound*. Sound Approach: Poole, Dorset, UK.

Cooksey, M. 1998. A pre-1996 North American record of Stygian Owl. *Field Notes* 52:265–266.

Cooper, B., & G. Mackiernan. 2011. First record of Solander's Petrel (*Pterodroma solanderi*) for Alaska. *NAB* 65:704–708.

Correia-F. C., & H. Romano 2011. A Black-bellied Storm-petrel off Madeira—a new Western Palearctic bird. *Birding World* 24:326.

Corman, T., & G. Monson. 1995. First United States nesting records of the Streak-backed Oriole. *Western Birds* 26:49–53.

Corso, A., & G. P. Catley. 2003. Separation of transitional second calendar-year Red-footed Falcon from Amur Falcon. *Dutch Birding* 25:153–158.

Corso, A., & W. S. Clark. 1998. Identification of Amur Falcon. *Birding World* 11:261–268.

Cramp, S. (senior ed.). 1977–1994. *Handbook of the Birds of Europe, the Middle East, and North Africa: The Birds of the Western Palearctic*, 9 vols.. Oxford Univ. Press: Oxford, UK.

Cramp, S. (senior ed.). 1983. *Handbook of the Birds of Europe, the Middle East, and North Africa: The Birds of the Western Palearctic*, vol. 3. Oxford Univ. Press: Oxford, UK.

Cramp, S. (senior ed.). 1988–1992. *Handbook of the Birds of Europe, the Middle East, and North Africa: The Birds of the Western Palearctic*, vols. 5–6. Oxford Univ. Press: Oxford, UK.

Cramp, S., & C. M. Perrins (eds.). 1993–1994. *Handbook of the Birds of Europe, the Middle East, and North Africa: The Birds of the Western Palearctic*, vols. 7–8. Oxford Univ. Press: Oxford, UK.

Cramp, S., & K.E.L. Simmons (eds.). 1977. *Handbook of the Birds of Europe, the Middle East, and North Africa: The Birds of the Western Palearctic*, vol. 1. Oxford Univ. Press: Oxford, UK.

Crochet, P. A., & M. Haas. 2008. Western Palearctic list update: deletion of White-bellied Storm Petrel. *Dutch Birding* 30:17–18.

Cruickshank, H. G. 1964. A Cuban Emerald Hummingbird. *Florida Naturalist* 37:23, 32.

Dau, C. P., & J. Paniyak. 1977. Hoopoe, a first record for North America. *Auk* 94:601.

Davidson, G. S. 1999. B. C. Field Ornithologists Bird Records Committee report for 1996–1997. *British Columbia Birds* 9:15–18.

Davis, A. 2012. Sightings. *Winging It* 24(4):11–12.

Day, R. H., E. P. Knudtson, D. W. Woolington, & R. P. Schulmeister. 1979. *Caprimulgus indicus, Eurynorhynchus pygmaeus, Otus scops*, and *Limicola falcinellus* in the Aleutian Islands, Alaska. *Auk* 96:189–190.

Dean, A., C. Bradshaw, J. Martin, A. Stoddart, & G. Walbridge. 2010. The status in Britain of 'Siberian Chiffchaff.' *British Birds* 103:320–338.

DeBenedictus, P. 1971. Wood warblers and vireos in California: The nature of the accidental. *California Birds* 2:111–128.

DeCicco, L. H., S. C. Heinl, & D. W. Sonneborn. 2009. First North American records of the Rufous-tailed Robin (*Luscinia sibilans*). *Western Birds* 40:237–241.

Delaney, S., & D. Scott. 2006. *Waterfowl Population Estimates*, 4th ed. Wetlands International: Wageningen, Netherlands.

del Hoyo, J., A. Elliot, J. Sargatal, & D. Christie. (eds). 1992–2011. *Handbook of Birds of the World*. Vols. 1-16. Lynx Edicions: Barcelona.

DeSante, D. F. 1973. An analysis of the fall occurrences and nocturnal orientations of vagrant wood warblers (Parulidae) in California. PhD dissertation, Stanford Univ., Palo Alto, CA.

———. 1983a. Vagrants: When orientation or navigation goes wrong. *Point Reyes Bird Observatory Newsletter*, Spring 1983:12–16.

———. 1983b. Annual variability in the abundance of migrant landbirds on Southeast Farallon Island, California. *Auk* 100:826–852.

Dickerman, R. W., and F. Haverschmidt. 1971. Further notes on the juvenal plumage of the Spotted Rail (*Rallus maculatus*). *Wilson Bulletin* 81:207–209.

Dies, J. I., and 7 coauthors. 2007. Observaciones de aves raras en España, 2005. *Ardeola* 54:405–446.

Dinsmore, S. J., and T. M. Harms. 2011. First record of Comb Duck (*Sarkidiornis melanotos*) for Costa Rica. *NAB* 65:362–363.

Dittmann, D. L., & S. W. Cardiff. 2003. Ninth report of the Louisiana Bird Records Committee. *Journal of Louisiana Ornithology* 6:41–101.

———. 2005. Origins and identification of Kelp × Herring Gull hybrids: The "Chandeleur" [sic] gull. *Birding* 37:266–276.

———. 2009. The alternate plumage of the Ruby-throated Hummingbird. *Birding* 41(5):32–35.

Donald, P. F. 2007. Adult sex ratios in wild bird populations. *Ibis* 149:671–692.

Double, M. C., R. Gales, T. Reid, N. Bothers, & C. L. Abbott. 2003. Morphometric comparison of Australian Shy and New Zealand White-capped Albatrosses. *Emu* 103:287–294.

Driessens, G., & L. Svensson. 2005. Identification of Collared Pratincole and Oriental Pratincole— a critical review of characters. *Dutch Birding* 27:1–35.

Duffy, K. E., W. S. Clark, and J. R. Hough. 2012. Probable Hen Harrier (*Circus cyaneus cyaneus*) at Cape May, New Jersey. *NAB* 66:4–8.

Duley, P. A. 2010. A Bermuda Petrel (*Pterodroma cahow*) off Massachusetts: First photographic record for New England. *NAB* 64:528–529.

Dunn, J. L. 1999. 1998–1999 ABA Checklist Report. *Birding* 31:518–524.

Dunning, J. B. Jr., A. Beheler, M. Crowder, S. Andrews, & R. Weiss. 2002. A Eurasian Wryneck specimen from southern Indiana. *NAB* 56:265–267.

Dwight, J. Jr. 1897. A species of shearwater (*Puffinus assimilis* Gould) new to the North American fauna. *Proceedings of the Biological Society of Washington* 11:69–70.

Ebels, E. B. 2002. Transatlantic vagrancy of Palearctic species to the Caribbean. *Dutch Birding* 24:202–209.

Eckert, C. D. 2000. Bean Goose: a Yukon first at Whitehorse. *Birders Journal* 8:305–309.

Eckert, C. D., & B. Mactavish. 2003. Canada's first Bluethroat nest and other noteworthy sightings from Ivvavik National Park, Yukon. *Birders Journal* 12:250–257.

Ellis, J. C., M. C. Stoddard, & L. W. Clark. 2007. Breeding by a Lesser Black-backed Gull (*Larus fuscus*) on the Atlantic coast of North America. *NAB* 61:546–548.

Erickson, H. T. 1982. Migration of the Fork-tailed Flycatcher through southeastern Brazil. *AB* 36:136–138.

Erickson, R. A., R. A. Hamilton, & S.N.G. Howell. 2001. New information on migrant birds from the northern and central portions of the Baja California Peninsula, including species new to Mexico, pp. 112–170 in *Birds of the Baja California Peninsula: Status, Distribution, and Taxonomy*, R. A. Erickson & S.N.G. Howell (eds.), Monographs in Field Ornithology 3.

Etcheberry, R. 1998. Rare and unusual birds in Saint-Pierre et Miquelon. *Birders Journal* 7:187–200.

Faulkner, D. 2006. Reassessment of a frigatebird record for Wyoming: Lesser Frigatebird (*Fregata ariel*). *NAB* 60:328–330.

———. 2007. A Streaked Shearwater (*Calonectris leucomelas*) in Wyoming. *NAB* 60:324–326.

Fintel, W. A. 1974. First Masked Duck sighting in Tennessee. *The Migrant* 45:47–48.

Fjeldsa, J., & N. Krabbe. 1990. *Birds of the High Andes*. Zoological Museum, Univ. of Copenhagen: Denmark.

Flesch, A. D. 2008. Distribution and status of breeding landbirds in northern Sonora, Mexico, pp. 28–45 in *Birds of the U.S.-Mexico Borderlands: Distribution, Ecology, and Conservation*, J. M. Ruth, T. Brush, & D. J. Kreuper (eds.). Studies in Avian Biology 37.

Flood, R. L. 2009. "All-dark" *Oceanodroma* storm-petrels in the Atlantic and neighboring seas. *British Birds* 102:365–385.

Forsman, D. 1999. *The Raptors of Europe and the Middle East*. Poyser, London.

Frank, J. 2007. Rare bird documentation. *Passenger Pigeon* 69(3):349–358.

Franzke, C., S. B. Feldstein, & S. Lee. 2011. Synoptic analysis of the Pacific-North American teleconnection pattern. *Quarterly Journal of the Royal Meteorological Society* 137:329–346.

Fraser, P. 1997. How many rarities are we missing? Weekend bias and length of stay revisited. *British Birds* 90:94–101.

Galindo, D., S. G. Mlodinow, R. Carmona, & L. Sauma. 2004. Terek Sandpiper (*Xenus cinereus*): A first for Mexico. *NAB* 58:454–455.

Garner, M. 2002. Identification of eastern Reed Bunting. *Birding World* 15:74–86.

———. 2008a. American (Laughing) Moorhen, pp. 104–107 in *Frontiers in Birding*, M. Garner and friends. BirdGuides Ltd.: Sheffield, UK.

———. 2008b. Female-type Green-winged and Baikal Teals, pp. 138–145 in *Frontiers in Birding*, M. Garner and friends. BirdGuides Ltd: Sheffield, UK.

Garner, M., I. Lewington, & R. Slack. 2003. Mongolian and Lesser Sand Plovers: An identification review. *Birding World* 16:377–385.

Garrett, K. L., & K. C. Molina. 1998. First record of the Black-tailed Gull for Mexico. *Western Birds* 29:49–54.

Garrett, K. L., & J. C. Wilson. 2003. Report of the California Bird Records Committee: 2001 records. *Western Birds* 34:15–41.

Garrido, O. H. 2001. Was the Red-legged Honeycreeper *Cyanerpes cyaneus carneipes* in Cuba introduced from Mexico? *Cotinga* 15:58.

Garrido, O. H., & A. Kirkconnel. 2000. *Field Guide to the Birds of Cuba*. Cornell Univ. Press: Ithaca, NY.

Garrido, O. H., K. C. Parkes, G. B. Reynard, A. Kirkonnell, & R. Sutton. 1997. Taxonomy of the Stripe-headed Tanager, genus *Spindalis* (Aves: Thraupidae) of the West Indies. *Wilson Bulletin* 109:561–594.

Garrido, O. H., J. W. Wiley, & G. B. Reynard. 2009. Taxonomy of the Loggerhead Kingbird (*Tyrannus caudifasciatus*) complex (Aves: Tyrannidae). *Wilson Journal of Ornithology* 121:703–713.

Gerasimov, Y. N., Y. B. Artukhin, & E. G. Lobkov. 1999. *Checklist of the Birds of Kamchatka*. Kamchatka Institute of Ecology, Russian Academy of Science, Far Eastern Branch: Moscow. Dialogue-MSU.

Gibson, D. D. 1981. Migrant birds at Shemya Island, Aleutian Islands, Alaska. *Condor* 83:65–77.

Gibson, D. D., & G. V. Byrd. 2007. *Birds of the Aleutian Islands, Alaska*. Series in Ornithology 1. Nuttall Ornithological Club & AOU.

Gibson, D. D., S. C. Heinl, & T. G. Tobish. 2003. Report of the Alaska checklist committee, 1997–2002. *Western Birds* 34:122–132.

———. 2008. Report of the Alaska Checklist Committee, 2003–2007. *Western Birds* 39:189–201.

Gibson, D. D., & B. Kessel 1992. Seventy-four new avian taxa documented in Alaska, 1976–1991. *Condor* 94:454–467.

Gill, F., & M. Wright. 2006. *Birds of the World: Recommended English Names*. Princeton Univ. Press: Princeton, NJ.

Gill, R. E., P. Canevari, & E. H. Iversen. 1998. Eskimo Curlew (*Numenius borealis*). The Birds of North America Online (A. Poole, ed.), http://bna.birds.cornell.edu/bna/. Cornell Lab of Ornithology: Ithaca, NY.

Gill, R. E. Jr., & 9 coauthors. 2009. Extreme endurance flights by landbirds crossing the Pacific Ocean: Ecological corridor rather than barrier? *Proceedings of the Royal Society* B 276:447–457.

Gilroy, J. J., & A. C. Lees. 2003. Vagrancy theories: Are autumn vagrants really reverse migrants? *British Birds* 96:427–438.

Godfrey, W. E. 1986. *The Birds of Canada*, revised ed. National Museums of Canada: Ottawa.

Gosselin, M., N. David, & P. Laporte. 1986. Hybrid yellow-legged gull from the Madeleine Islands. *AB* 40:58–60.

Gould, P. J., W. B. King, & G. A. Sanger. 1974. Red-tailed Tropicbird (*Phaethon rubricauda*), pp. 206–217 in *Pelagic Studies of Seabirds in the Central and Eastern Pacific Ocean*, W. B. King, (ed.). Smithsonian Contributions to Zoology 158.

Green, P. 1998. Possible anywhere: Fieldfare. *Birding* 30:212–219.

Guris, P. A., M. D. Overton, M. H. Tove, & R. Wiltraut. 2004. First North American record of Black-bellied Storm-Petrel (*Fregetta tropica*). *NAB* 58:618–621.

Haas, M. 2012. *Extremely Rare Birds in the Western Palearctic*. Lynx Edicions, Barcelona.

Hainebach, K. 1992. First records of Xantus's Humming-bird in California. *Western Birds* 23:133–136.

Hall, G. E., & E. A. Cardiff. 1978. First North American records of Siberian House Martin *Delichon urbica lagopoda*. *Auk* 95:429.

Hameed, S., H. H. Norwood, M. Flanagan, S. Feldstein, & C-h. Yang. 2009. The influence of El Niño on the spring fallout of Asian bird species at Attu Island. *Earth Interactions* 13-007:1–22.

Hamilton, R. A. 2001. Records of caged birds in California, pp. 254–257 in *Birds of the Baja California Peninsula: Status, Distribution, and Taxonomy*, R.A. Erickson & S.N.G. Howell (eds.). Monographs in Field Ornithology 3.

Hamilton, R. A., Patten, M. A., & Erickson, R. A. (eds.). 2007. *Rare Birds of California*. Western Field Ornithologists: Camarillo, CA.

Haney, J. C., & S. C. Wainright. 1985. Bulwer's Petrel in the South Atlantic Bight. *AB* 39:868–870.

Haramis, G. M. 1982. Records of Redhead × Canvas-back hybrids. *Wilson Bulletin* 94:599–602.

Hardy, J. W., J. C. Barlow, & B. B. Coffey Jr. 1987. Voices of all the mockingbirds, thrashers, and their allies. Ara Records: Gainesville, Florida.

Hardy, J. W., and M. H. Clench. 1982. First United States specimen of the White-collared Swift. *American Birds* 36(2):139–141.

Harris, B. K. 1964. First United States record for the Slate-throated Redstart, and first specimens of various species for New Mexico. *Auk* 81:227–229.

Harris, M. P. 1969. The biology of storm petrels in the Galapagos Islands. *Proc. CAS* 37:95–166.

Hass, T. 1995. An additional record of Bulwer's Petrel *Bulweria bulwerii* off the southeastern United States of America. *Marine Ornithology* 23:161–162.

Haverschmidt, F. 1983. First record of the Little Egret (*Egretta garzetta*) in Suriname. *Wilson Bulletin* 95:315.

Hayes, F. E., & M. Kenefick 2002. First record of Black-tailed Godwit *Limosa limosa* for South America. *Cotinga* 17:20–22.

Hayes, F. E., P. A. Scharf, & R. S. Ridgely. 1994. Austral bird migrants in Paraguay. *Condor* 96:83–97.

Hayes, F. E., G. L. White, M. D. Frost, B. Sanaise, H. Kilpatrick, & E. B. Massiah. 2002. First records of Kelp Gull *Larus dominicanus* for Trinidad and Barbados. *Cotinga* 18:85–88.

Hazevoet, C. J. 1995. The Birds of the Cape Verde Islands. BOU Checklist No. 13.

Heindel, M. T., & K. L. Garrett. 2008. The 32nd report of the California Birds Records Committee: 2006 records. *Western Birds* 39:121–152.

Heindel, M. T., & S.N.G. Howell. 2000. A hybrid hummingbird in southeast Arizona. *Western Birds* 31:265–266.

Heller, V. J., & J. S. Barclay. 1977. Third specimen of frigatebird for Oklahoma. *Bulletin of the Oklahoma Ornithological Society* 10:9–10.

Hellström, M., & M. Waern. 2011. Field identification and ageing of Siberian Stonechats in spring and summer. *British Birds* 104:236–254.

Higgins, P. J., & S.J.J.F. Davies (eds.). 1996. *Handbook of Australian, New Zealand, and Antarctic Birds*, vol. 3. Oxford Univ. Press: Oxford, UK.

Hilty, S. L., & W. L. Brown. 1986. *A Guide to the Birds of Columbia*. Princeton Univ. Press: Princeton, NJ.

Hirshfeld, E., C. S. Roselaar, & H. Shirihai. 2000. Identi-fication, taxonomy, and distribution of Greater and Lesser Sand Plovers. *British Birds* 93:162–189.

Holling, M., & Rare Breeding Birds Panel. 2011. Rare breeding birds in the United Kingdom in 2009. *British Birds* 104:476–537.

Howell, S.N.G. 1994. Magnificent and Great Frigatebirds in the eastern Pacific: A new look at an old problem. *Birding* 26:400–415.

———. 2002. *Hummingbirds of North America: The Photographic Guide*. Academic Press: San Diego, CA.

———. 2005. Revisiting an old question: How many species of skua occur in the North Pacific? *Western Birds* 36:71–73.

———. 2006a. Immature Shy Albatrosses. *Birding* 38(3):56–59.

———. 2006b. Identification of 'black petrels,' genus *Procellaria*. *Birding* 38(6):52–64.

———. 2009. Identification of immature Salvin's, Chatham, and Buller's Albatrosses. *Neotropical Birding* 4:19–25.

———. 2010a. *Peterson Reference Guide to Molt in North American Birds*. Houghton Mifflin: Boston, MA.

———. 2010b. Identification and taxonomy of White-bellied Storm Petrels, with comments on WP report in August 1986. *Dutch Birding* 32:36–42.

———. 2010c. Moult and ageing of Black-browed Albatross. *British Birds* 103:353–356.

———. 2012a. *Petrels, Albatrosses, and Storm-Petrels of North America*. Princeton Univ. Press: Princeton, NJ.

———. 2012b. M-M-M-Maybe you just ain't seen Nutting yet? *Neotropical Birding* 10:14–17.

Howell, S.N.G., C. Corben, P. Pyle, & D. I. Rogers. 2003. The first basic problem: A review of molt and plumage homologies. *Condor* 105:635–653.

Howell, S.N.G., J. Correa S., & J. Garcia B. 1993. First records of the Kelp Gull in Mexico. *Euphonia* 2:71–80.

Howell, S.N.G., & J. L. Dunn. 2007. *Gulls of the Americas*. Houghton Mifflin: Boston, MA.

Howell, S.N.G., M. O'Brien, B. L. Sullivan, C. L. Wood, I. Lewington, & R. Crossley. 2009. The purpose of field guides: taxonomy vs. utility? *Birding* 41(6): 44–49.

Howell, S.N.G., & J. B. Patteson. 2008. Swinhoe's Petrel off North Carolina and a review of dark storm-petrel identification. *Birding World* 21:255–262.

Howell, S.N.G., J. B. Patteson, K. Sutherland, & D. T. Shoch. 2010. Occurrence and identification of the Band-rumped Storm-Petrel (*Oceanodroma castro*) complex off North Carolina. *NAB* 64:196–207.

Howell, S.N.G., L. B. Spear, & P. Pyle. 1994. Identification of Manx-type Shearwaters in the eastern Pacific. *Western Birds* 25:169–177.

Howell, S.N.G., & S. Webb. 1994. Occurrence of Snowy and Collared Plovers in the interior of Mexico. *Western Birds* 25:146–150.

Howell, S.N.G., & S. Webb. 1995. *A Guide to the Birds of Mexico and Northern Central America*. Oxford Univ. Press: Oxford, UK.

Hoyer, R. C., & S. D. Smith. 1997. Chinese Pond Heron in Alaska. *Field Notes* 51:953–956.

Hudon, J., & 6 coauthors. 2011. Tenth report of the Alberta Bird Record Committee. *Nature Alberta* 41:42–44.

Hudson, N., & Rarities Committee. 2012. Report on rare birds in Great Britain in 2011. *British Birds* 105: 556–625.

Huey, L. M. 1952. *Oceanodroma tethys tethys*, a petrel new to the North America avifauna. *Auk* 69: 460–461.

Iliff, M. J., & B. L. Sullivan. 2004. Little Stint (*Calidris minuta*) in North America and the Hawaiian Islands: A review of status and distribution. *NAB* 58:316–323.

Jackson, C. F. 1936. *Sporophila lineola* taken in New Hampshire. *Auk* 53:221.

James, D. J. 2004. Identification of Christmas Island, Great, and Lesser Frigatebirds. *Birding Asia* 1:22–38.

James, P. C. 1986. Little Shearwaters in Britain and Ireland. *British Birds* 79:28–33.

Jiguet, F., & P. Defos du Rau. 2004. A Cape Gull [= Kelp Gull] in Paris—a new European bird. *Birding World* 17:62–70.

Johnson, A. W. 1967. *The Birds of Chile*, vol. 2. Platt S. A.: Buenos Aires, Argentina.

Johnson, J., A. Pellegrini, & R. Davis. 2010. First record of Gray-collared Becard (*Pachyramphus major*) for the United States. *NAB* 64:180–182.

Johnson, T. 2012. Barolo Shearwaters in Canadian waters. *Birding World* 25:395.

Jones, H. L. 2000. First record in the Galapagos Islands of Gray-headed Gull *Larus cirrocephalus*. *Cotinga* 14:103.

Jouventin, P., 1990. Shy Albatross *Diomedea cauta salvini* breeding on Penguin Island, Crozet Archipelago, Indian Ocean. *Ibis* 132:126–127.

Kaplan, J., & G. Hanisek. 2012. Seventeenth report of the Avian Records Committee of Connecticut. *Connecticut Warbler* 32:33–50.

Juhant, M. A. 2011. Where to watch raptor migration in South America. *Neotropical Birding* 9:8–16.

Kenefick, M., & F. E Hayes. 2006. Trans-Atlantic vagrancy of Palearctic birds in Trinidad and Tobago. *Journal of Caribbean Ornithology* 19:61–72.

Kennerley, P., & D. Pearson. 2010. *Reed and Bush Warblers*. Helm: London.

Kennerley, P. R., & P. J. Leader. 1991. Separation of Cuckoo and Oriental Cuckoo. *Dutch Birding* 13: 143–145.

Kent, T. H., & J. J. Dinsmore. 1996. *Birds in Iowa*. Published by the authors: Iowa City and Ames, IA.

Kenyon, K. W. 1961. Birds of Amchitka Island, Alaska. *Auk* 78:305–326.

Kenyon, K. W., & R. E. Phillips. 1965. Birds from the Pribilof Islands and vicinity. *Auk* 82:624–635.

Kessel, B., & D. D. Gibson. 1978. *Status and Distribution of Alaska Birds*. Studies in Avian Biology, No. 1.

King, B. 2002. Species limits in the Brown Boobook *Ninox scutulata* complex. *Bulletin of BOC* 122: 250–257.

King, W. B. 1974. Wedge-tailed Shearwater (*Puffinus pacificus*), pp. 53–95 in *Pelagic Studies of Seabirds in the Central and Eastern Pacific Ocean*, W. B. King (ed.). Smithsonian Contributions to Zoology 158.

Kobaya, T., & M. Matsui. 2001. *The Songs and Calls of 420 Birds in Japan*. Shogakukan, Tokyo. (Book & 6 CDs in Japanese.)

König, C., & F. Weick. 2008. *Owls of the World*, 2nd ed. Helm: London.

Konyukhov, N. B., & A. S. Kitaysky. 1995. The Asian race of the Marbled Murrelet, pp. 23–29 in *Ecology and Conservation of the Marbled Murrelet*, C. J. Ralph et al. (eds.). Pacific Southwest Research Station: Albany, CA.

Kratter, A. W. 2010. Nineteenth report of the Florida Ornithological Society Records Committee: 2009. *Florida Field Naturalist* 38:150–174.

Kushlan, J. A., & J. W. Prosper. 2009. Little Egret (*Egretta garzetta*) nesting on Antigua: A second nesting site in the Western Hemisphere. *Journal of Caribbean Ornithology* 22:108–111.

Langridge, H. P., & G. Hunter. 1993. Probable sighting of a Brown-chested Martin in Palm Beach County, Florida. *Florida Field Naturalist* 21(1):18–19.

Lasley, G. W. 1984. First Texas specimen of the White-collared Swift. *AB* 38:370–371.

Lasley, G. W., & T. Pincelli. 1986. Gray Silky-flycatcher in Texas. *Birding* 18:34–36.

Lasley, G. W., C. W. Sexton, & D. Hillsman. 1988. First record of the Mottled Owl in the United States. *AB* 42:23–24.

Leader, P. 1999. Identification forum: Common Snipe and Wilson's Snipe. *Birding World* 12:371–374.

Leader, P. J. 2010. Brown, Siberian, and Grey-streaked Flycatchers: Identifcation and ageing. *British Birds* 103:658–671.

Leader, P. J., & G. J. Carey. 2003. Identification of Pintail Snipe and Swinhoe's Snipe. *British Birds* 96:178–198.

Lee, D. S. 1984. Petrels and storm-petrels in North Carolina's offshore waters: Including species previously unrecorded for North America. *American Birds* 38:151–163.

Lee, D. S. 1987. December records of seabirds of seabirds off North Carolina. *Wilson Bulletin* 99:116–121.

Lee, D. S. 1988. The Little Shearwater (*Puffinus assimilis*) in the western North Atlantic. *AB* 42:213–220.

Lee, D. S. 2000. Photographs of Black-bellied and White-faced whistling-ducks from North Carolina, with comments on other extralimital waterfowl. *Chat* 64:93–99.

Lees, A. C., & A. Ball. 2011. Shades of grey: 'Eastern' Skylarks and extralimital subspecies identification. *British Birds* 104:660–666.

LeGrand, H. E., Jr., P. Guris, & M. Gustafson. 1999. Bulwer's Petrel off the North Carolina coast. *NAB* 53:113–115.

Lehman, P. E. 2000a. First record of Yellow-browed Warbler (*Phylloscopus inornatus*) in North America. *Western Birds* 31:57–60.

Lehman, P. 2000b. Oriental Cuckoo versus Common Cuckoo. *Birding World* 13:321–323.

———. 2012. San Diego's hybrid wader. *Birding World* 25:346–349.

Lehman, P. E. 2003. Gambell, Alaska, autumn 2002: First North American records of Willow Warbler (*Phylloscopus trochilus*), Lesser Whitethroat (*Sylvia curruca*), and Spotted Flycatcher (*Muscicapa striata*). *NAB* 57:4–11.

———. 2005. Fall bird migration at Gambell, Saint Lawrence Island, Alaska. *Western Birds* 36:2–55.

Lehman, P. E., & R. L. Ake. 2011. Blyth's Reed Warbler (*Acrocephalus dumetorum*) at Gambell, Alaska: First record for North America. *NAB* 65:4–12.

Lemoine, V. 2005. Little Ringed Plover (*Charadrius dubius*) in Martinique: First for the West Indies. *NAB* 59:669.

Lethaby, N. 1998. Identifying Eurasian and Pine Siskins. *Birding* 30:118–123.

———. 2000. The identification of Long-billed Murrelet in alternate plumage. *Birding* 32:438–444.

Lethaby, N., & I. A. McLaren. 2002. The identification of Gray Heron. *Birding* 34:24–33.

Levesque, A., & L. Malgalaive. 2004. First documented record of Marsh Harrier for the West Indies and the New World. *NAB* 57:564–565.

Lewington, I., P. Alström, & P. Colston. 1991. *A Field Guide to the Rare Birds of Britain and Europe.* HarperCollins: London, UK.

Lisowsky, B. 2000. Report of the Colorado Bird Records Committee: 1998 records. *Journal of the Colorado Field Ornithologists* 34(3):168–184.

Lockwood, M. W. 1997. A closer look: Masked Duck. *Birding* 29:386–390.

———. 1999. Possible anywhere: Fork-tailed Flycatcher. *Birding* 31:126–139.

———. 2010. Texas Bird Records Committee report for 2009. *Bulletin of the Texas Ornithological Society* 43:53–60.

Lockwood, M. W., & R. Bates. 2005. First record of Black-headed Nightingale-Thrush (*Catharus mexicanus*) for the United States. *NAB* 59:350–351.

Lockwood, M. W., & B. Freeman. 2004. *The Texas Ornithological Society Handbook of Texas Birds.* Texas A & M Press: College Station, TX.

Lopez-V., D., & J. Sagardia. 2011. A Black-bellied Storm-petrel off the Canary Islands—the second Western Palearctic record. *Birding World* 24:384–385.

Lorenz, S., C. Butler, & J. Paz. 2006. First nesting record of the Gray-crowned Yellowthroat (*Geothlypis poliocephala*) in the United States since 1894. *Wilson Journal of Ornithology* 118:574–576.

Lorenz, S., & D. D. Gibson. 2007. Intermediate Egret (*Egretta intermedia*) in the Aleutian Islands, Alaska. *Western Birds* 38:57–59.

MacInnes, C. D., & E. B. Chamberlain. 1963. The first record of Double-striped Thick-knee in the United States. *Auk* 80:79.

MacKinnon-H., B., J. L. Deppe, & A. Celis-M. 2012. Birds of the Yucatan Peninsula in Mexico: An update on the status and distribution of selected species. *NAB* 65:538–552.

Mactavish, B. 1988. Greater Golden-Plover invasion, 1988. *Birding* 20:242–249.

———. 1996. Common Redshank in Newfoundland. *Birding* 28:302–307.

Madeiros, J. 2010. *Cahow Recovery Program: Breeding Season Report for 2010.* Department of Conservation Services: Bermuda.

Madge, S. C., & H. Burn. 1988. *Waterfowl.* Houghton Mifflin: Boston, MA.

Maldonado, E., J. Klicka, & P. Escalante. 2012. Phylogeography of the Blue Bunting, *Cyanocompsa parellina* (Aves: Cardinalidae). Abstract PS1.1 presented at North American Ornithological Conference, Vancouver, BC, Aug 2012.

Marchant, S., & P. J. Higgins (eds.). 1990. *Handbook of Australian, New Zealand, and Antarctic Birds*, vol. 1. Oxford Univ. Press: Oxford, UK.

Marín, M. 2004. *Annotated Checklist of the Birds of Chile.* Lynx Edicions: Barcelona.

Martin, J. P. 1997. The first Southern Lapwing *Vanellus chilensis* in Mexico. *Cotinga* 8:52–53.

———. 2008. 'Northern Harrier' on Scilly: New to Britain. *British Birds* 101:394–407.

———. 2009. The *Fregetta* storm-petrel in Avon—a bird new to Europe. *Birding World* 22:457–458.

Martin, J. P., & M. Garner. 2012. Moult and ageing of male Falcated Ducks in autumn. *British Birds* 105:11–22.

Massiah, E. 1997. Identification of Snowy and Little Egrets. *Birding World* 9:435–444.

McCaskie, G. 1970. The occurrences of four species of Pelecaniformes in the southwestern United States. *California Birds* 1:117–142.

McCaskie, G., & M. A. Patten. 1994. Status of the Fork-tailed Flycatcher (*Tyrannus savana*) in the United States and Canada. *Western Birds* 25:113–127.

McDonald, I. 1997. A Blue Rock-Thrush *Monticola solitarius* in British Columbia. *Birders Journal* 6:162–163.

McEneaney, T. 2004. A Whooper Swan (*Cygnus cygnus*) at Yellowstone National Park, Wyoming, with comments on North American reports of the species. *NAB* 58:301–308.

McLaren, I. 2001. A Ruddy Shelduck in Nova Scotia. *Birders Journal* 10:169.

McLaren, I. A. 2012. *All the Birds of Nova Scotia*. Gaspereau Press: Kentville, NS.

McLaren, I., & Z. Lucas. 2004. A possible Brown Skua (*Stercorarius antarcticus*) on Sable Island, Nova Scotia. *NAB* 58:622–626.

McLaren, I., B. Maybank, K. Keddy, P. D. Taylor, & T. Fitzgerald. 2000. A notable autumn arrival of reverse-migrants in southern Nova Scotia. *NAB* 54:4–10.

McLaren, I. A., J. Morlan, P. W. Smith, M. Gosselin, & S. F. Bailey. 1989. Eurasian Siskins in North America: Distinguishing females from green-morph Pine Siskins. *AB* 43:1268–1274, 1381.

McNair, D. B. 1989. The Gray-hooded Gull in North America: First documented record. *NAB* 53:337–339.

McNair, D. B., L. D. Yntema, C. D. Lombard, C. Cramer-B., & F. W. Sladen. 2005. Records of rare and uncommon birds from recent surveys on St. Croix, United States Virgin Islands. *NAB* 59:536–551.

McNeil, R., & A. Cyr. 1971. European Blackbird (*Turdus merula*) in Quebec. *Auk* 88:919–920.

McVaugh, W. 1975. The development of four North American herons, II. *Living Bird* 14:163–183.

Merkord, C. L., R. Rodríguez, & J. Faaborg. 2006. Second and third records of Western Marsh Harrier (*Circus aeruginosus*) for the Western Hemisphere in Puerto Rico. *Journal of Caribbean Ornithology* 19:42–44.

Miles, M. L. 1967. An addition to the avifauna of the United States: *Myiarchus stolidus sagrae*. *Auk* 84:279.

Miller, A. H., H. Friedmann, L. Griscom, & R. T. Moore. 1957. *Distributional Check-list of the Birds of Mexico*, part 2. Pacific Coast Avifauna no. 33.

Mlodinow, S. G. 1997. The Long-billed Murrelet (*Brachyramphus perdix*) in North America. *Birding* 29:461–475.

———. 1998. The Magnificent Frigatebird in western North America. *NAB* 52:412–419.

———. 1999a. Spotted Redshank and Common Greenshank in North America. *NAB* 53:124–130.

———. 1999b. Southern Hemisphere albatrosses in North American waters. *Birders Journal* 8:131–141.

———. 2004. Bean Goose (*Anser fabalis*) at Hoquiam, Washington: A first state record. *NAB* 58:298–300.

———. 2011. First records of the Short-tailed Hawk and Gray Hawk for the Baja California Peninsula. *Western Birds* 42:183–187.

Mlodinow, S. G., & D. S. Irons. 2009. First record of Variegated Flycatcher for western North America. *Western Birds* 40:47–49.

Mlodinow, S. G., & K. A. Radamaker. 2007. First record of Yellow-browed Warbler (*Phylloscopus inornatus*) for Mexico. *NAB* 61:358–362.

Montevecchi, W. A., B. Mactavish, & I. R. Kirkham. 1981. First North American photographic record of the Redwing (*Turdus iliacus*). *AB* 35:147.

Montevecchi, W. A., & J. Wells. 1984. Two new specimen records for insular Newfoundland: Barnacle Goose and Tricolored Heron. *AB* 38:257–258.

Morgan, J. G., & L. M. Feltner. 1985. A neotropical bird flies north; The Greenish Elaenia. *AB* 39:242–244.

Morgan, J. G., T. L. Eubanks Jr., V. Eubanks, & L. N. White. 1985. Yucatan Vireo appears in Texas. *AB* 39:245–246.

Murphy, R. C. 1936. *Oceanic Birds of South America*, 2 vols. AMNH: New York.

———. 1938. The Wandering Albatross in the Bay of Panama. *Condor* 40:126.

———. 1951. The populations of the Wedge-tailed Shearwater (*Puffinus pacificus*). *American Museum Novitates* 1512.

Nelson, D. 1991. The CFO records committee report for 1989. *Colorado Field Ornithologists' Journal* 25(4):119–125.

Newton, I. 2008. *The Migration Ecology of Birds*. Academic Press: London.

Nirschl, R., & R. Snider. 2010. First record of Barethroated Tiger-Heron (*Tigrisoma mexicanum*) for the United States. *NAB* 64:347–349.

Nunn, G. B., & S. E. Stanley. 1998. Body size effects and rates of Cytochrome b evolution in tube-nosed seabirds. *Molecular Biology and Evolution* 15:1360–1371.

Oates, J. 1997. Identification of Taiga Bean Goose and Tundra Bean Goose. *Birding World* 10:421–426.

O'Brien, M., R. Crossley, & K. Karlson. 2006. *The Shorebird Guide*. Houghton Mifflin: Boston, MA.

O'Brien, M., J. B. Patteson, G. L. Armistead, & G. B. Pearce. 1999. Swinhoe's Storm-Petrel: First North American photographic record. *NAB* 53:6–10.

Olson, C. S. 1976. Band-tailed Gull photographed in Florida. *Auk* 93:176–177.

Onley, D., & P. Scofield. 2007. *Albatrosses, Petrels, and Shearwaters of the World*. Princeton Univ. Press: Princeton, NJ.

Osgood, C. 2003. *Attu: Birding on the Edge*. ABA: Colorado Springs, CO.

OSJ (Ornithological Society of Japan). 2000. *Check-list of Japanese* Birds, 6th revised ed. OSJ: Japan.

Pagen, R., P. Pyle, & L. T. Ballance. 2008. A *Fregetta* storm-petrel off western Mexico. *Western Birds* 39:225–227.

Palliser, T. 2002. Tristram's Storm Petrel *Oceanodroma tristrami* off Sydney, New South Wales: A new bird for Australia. *Australian Bird Watcher* 19:215–218.

Papish, R., J. L. Mays, & D. Brewer. 1997. Orange-billed Nightingale-Thrush: First record for Texas and the U.S. *Birding* 29:128–130.

Parkes, K. C. 1990. Identification of Common and Oriental Cuckoos. *Birding* 22:191–193.

Parkes, K. C., D. P. Kibbe, & E. L. Roth. 1978. First records of the Spotted Rail (*Pardirallus maculatus*) for the United States, Chile, Bolivia, and western Mexico. *AB* 32:295–299.

Patten, M. A. 1993. First record of the Common Pochard in California. *Western Birds* 24:235–240.

Patteson, J. B., & G. L. Armistead. 2004. First record of Cape Verde Shearwater (*Calonectris edwardsii*) for North America. *NAB* 58:468–473.

Patteson, J. B., M. A. Patten, & E. S. Brinkley. 1999. The Black-browed Albatross in North America: First photographically documented record. *NAB* 53:228–231.

Patteson, J. B., K. Sutherland, & S.N.G. Howell. 2009. Recent records of European Storm-Petrel (*Hydrobates pelagicus*) off North Carolina. *NAB* 62:512–517.

Patteson, J. B., S.N.G. Howell, & K. Sutherland. 2009. Swinhoe's Storm-Petrel (*Ocenodroma monorhis*) off North Carolina. *NAB* 62:518–520.

Paulson, D. 1993. *Shorebirds of the Pacific Northwest.* Univ. of Washington Press: Seattle, WA.

———. 2005. *Shorebirds of North America: The* Photographic *Guide.* Princeton Univ. Press: Princeton, NJ.

Paxton, R. O. 1968. Wandering Albatross in California. *Auk* 85:502–504.

Peters, J. L. 1924. A second North American record for *Puffinus assimilis. Auk* 41:337–338.

Petersen, W. R., B. J. Nikula, & D. W. Holt. 1986. First record of Brown-chested Martin for North America. *AB* 40:192–193.

Phillips, A. R. 1986. *The Known Birds of North and Middle America*, part 1. A. R. Phillips, Denver, CO.

———. 1991. *The Known Birds of North and Middle America*, part 2. A. R. Phillips, Denver, CO.

Piersma, T., & R. E. Gill Jr. 1998. Guts don't fly: Small digestive organs in obese Bar-tailed Godwits. *Auk* 115:196–203.

Pike, J. E., & D. M. Compton. 2010. The 34th report of the California Bird Records Committee: 2008 records. *Western Birds* 41:130–159.

Pinchon, P. R., & C. Vaurie. 1961. The Kestrel (*Falco tinnunculus*) in the New World. *Auk* 78:92–93.

Pineau, O., Y. Kayser, M. Sall, A. Gueye, & H. Hafner. 2001. The Kelp Gull at Banc d'Arguin—a new Western Palearctic bird. *Birding World* 14:110–111.

Pitman, R. L., & L. T. Ballance. 2002. The changing status of marine birds breeding at San Benedicto Island, Mexico. *Wilson Bulletin* 114:11–19.

Pitman, R. L., & J. R. Jehl. 1998. Geographic variation and reassessment of species limits in the "Masked" Boobies of the eastern Pacific Ocean. *Wilson Bulletin* 110:155–170.

Poole, C. M., P. Jin-Young, & N. Moores. 1999. The identification of Chinese Egret and Pacific Reef Egret. *Oriental Bird Club Bulletin* 30:39–41.

Pranty, B. 2004. Florida's exotic avifauna: A preliminary checklist. *Birding* 36:362–372.

Pranty, B., & P. W. Smith. 2001. Status, distribution, and taxonomy of the *Spindalis* complex ("Stripe-headed Tanager") in Florida. *Florida Field Naturalist* 29: 13–25.

Pranty, B., & G. E. Woolfenden. 2000. First record of the Northern Lapwing in Florida. *Florida Field Naturalist* 28(2):53–56.

Pranty, B., E. Kwater, H. Weatherman, & H. P. Robinson. 2004. Eurasian Kestrel in Florida: First record for the southeastern United States, with a review of its status in North America. *NAB* 58:168–169.

Pranty, B., & ABA Checklist Committee. 2007. Annual report of the ABA Checklist Committee: 2007. *Birding* 39(6):24–31.

———. 2009. Annual report of the ABA Checklist Committee: 2008–2009. *Birding* 41(6):38–43.

———. 2011. 22nd annual report of the ABA Checklist Committee. *Birding* 43(6):26–33.

Prince, P. A., & S. P. Rodwell. 1994. Ageing immature Black-browed and Grey-headed Albatrosses using moult, bill, and plumage characteristics. *Emu* 94:246–254.

Prince, P. A., S. Rodwell, M. Jones, & P. Rothery. 1993. Molt in Black-browed and Grey-headed Albatrosses *Diomedea melanophris* and *D. chrysostoma. Ibis* 135:121–131.

Prince, P. A., H. Weimerskirch, N. Huin, & S. Rodwell. 1997. Molt, maturation of plumage, and ageing in the Wandering Albatross. *Condor* 99:58–72.

Pyle, P. 1997a. *Identification* Guide to North American Birds, part 1. Slate Creek Press, Bolinas, CA.

———. 1997b. *Flight-Feather Molt Patterns and Age in North American Owls.* Monographs in Field Ornithology, no. 2. American Birding Association, Colorado Springs, CO.

Pyle, P., & S.N.G. Howell. 1993. An Arctic Warbler in Baja California, Mexico. *Western Birds* 24: 53–56.

Pyle, R. L., & P. Pyle. 2009. The Birds of the Hawaiian Islands: Occurrence, History, Distribution, and Status, Version 1. B. P. Bishop Museum: Honolulu, HI. http://hbs.bishopmuseum.org/birds/rlp-monograph/. Last modified, 31 December 2009.

Pyle, P., G. Friedrichsen, T. Staudt, C. Oedekoven, & L. T. Ballance. 2006. First record of Ringed [=Hornby's] Storm-Petrel (*Oceanodroma hornbyi*) for North America. *NAB* 60:162–163.

Pyle, P., A. McAndrews, P. Veléz, R. L. Wilkerson, R. B. Siegel, & D. F. DeSante. 2004. Molt patterns and age and sex determination of selected southeastern Cuban landbirds. *Journal of Field Ornithology* 75:136–145.

Radamaker, K. A. 2009. Juvenal plumage of the Aztec Thrush. *Western Birds* 40:247–249.

Radamaker, K. A., & D. J. Powell. 2010. A Little Bunting reaches Baja California Sur. *Western Birds* 41:55–58.

Raffaele, H. A. 1989. *A Guide to the Birds of Puerto Rico and the Virgin Islands*, revised ed. Princeton Univ. Press: Princeton, NJ.

Raffaele, H., J. Wiley, O. Garrido, A. Keith, & J. Raffaele. 1998. *Birds of the West Indies*. Princeton Univ. Press: Princeton, NJ.

Rasmussen, P. C., & J. C. Anderton. 2005. *Birds of South Asia, The Ripley Guide*. Smithsonian Institution & Lynx Edicions: Washington DC and Barcelona.

Reid, M., & D. Jones. 2009. First North American record of White-crested Elaenia (*Elaenia albiceps chilensis*) at South Padre Island, Texas. *North Amercan Birds* 63:10–14.

Remsen, J. V., & T. A. Parker III. 1990. Seasonal distribution of the Azure Gallinule (*Porphyrula flavirostris*) with comments on vagrancy in rails and gallinules. *Wilson Bulletin* 102:380–399.

Renner, M., & P. D. Linegar. 2007. The first specimen record of Gray Heron (*Ardea cineria*) for North America. *Wilson Journal of Ornithology* 119:134–136.

Restall, R., & A. White. 2003. Grassquits in the United States. *Birding* 35:356–366.

Rheindt, F. E., L. Crisitidis, & J. A. Norman. 2009. Genetic introgression, incomplete lineage sorting, and faulty taxonomy create multiple cases of polyphyly in a montane clade of tyrant-flycatchers (*Elaenia*, Tyrannidae). *Zoologica Scripta* 38: 143–153.

Richards, J. M., R. Tymstra, & A. W. White. 2002. *Birds of Nunavut: A Checklist*. Birders Journal Publishing: Whitby, Ontario.

Ridgely, R. S., & P. J. Greenfield. 2001. *The Birds of Ecuador, vol. 1: Status, Distribution, and Taxonomy*. Cornell Univ. Press: Ithaca, NY.

Ridgely, R. S., & J. A. Gwynne Jr. 1989. *A Guide to the Birds of Panama*, 2nd edition. Princeton Univ. Press: Princeton, NJ.

Ridgely, R. S., & G. Tudor. 1989. *The Birds of South America*, vol. 1. Univ. of Texas Press: Austin, TX.

———. 1994. *The Birds of South America*, vol. 2. Univ. of Texas Press: Austin, TX.

Ridgway, R. 1902. *The Birds of North and Middle America*. Bulletin of the United States National Museum, no. 50, part 2. Government Printing Office: Washington, DC.

———. 1911. *The Birds of North and Middle America*. Bulletin of the United States National Museum, no. 50, part 5. Government Printing Office: Washington, DC.

Rines, M. 2005. Ninth report of the Massachusetts Avian Records Committee. *Bird Observer* 33(2):86–91.

Robb, R. R., D. Arendt, K. Larsen, & P. Sherrell. 2009. First North American record of Crowned Slaty Flycatcher. *Cotinga* 31:50–52.

Robb, M., K. Mullarney, & The Sound Approach. 2007. *Petrels Night and Day*. The Sound Approach: Poole, Dorset.

Robbins, M. B., & ABA Checklist Committee. 2003. ABA Checklist Committee 2002 annual report. *Birding* 35:138–144.

———. 2004. ABA Checklist Committee 2003 annual report. *Birding* 36:38–41.

Roberson, D. 1980. *Rare Birds of the West Coast*. Woodcock Publications: Pacific Grove, CA.

———. 1998. Sulids unmasked: Which large booby reaches California? *Field Notes* 52:276–287.

Robertson, C.J.R., J. Klavitter, & R. McCarthy. 2005. Salvin's Albatross (*Thalassarche salvini*) on Midway Atoll. *Notornis* 52:236–237.

Robertson, C.J.R., & G. B. Nunn. 1998. Towards a new taxonomy for albatrosses, pp. 13–19 in *Albatross Biology and Conservation*, G. Robertson, & R. Gales (eds.). Surrey Beatty & Sons: Chipping Norton, UK.

Robertson, C.J.R., & J. Warham. 1992. Nomenclature of the New Zealand Wandering Albatrosses *Diomedea exulans*. *Bulletin of the BOC* 112:74–81.

Roberston, W. B. Jr., & G. E. Woolfenden. 1992. Florida *Bird Species: An Annotated List*. Florida Ornithological Society special publication 6.

Rogers, D. I., C.D.T. Minton, A. N. Boyle, C. J. Hassell, & A. Silcocks. Unpublished ms. Growing up slowly by the sea-side: Age of first northwards migration of shorebirds from Australian non-breeding grounds. Chapter 6 in D. I. Rogers (2006). Hidden costs: Challenges faced by migratory shorebirds living on intertidal flats. PhD dissertation, Charles Sturt Univ.

Rogers, D. I., C. Hassell, J. Oldland, R. Clemens, A. Boyle, & K. Rogers. 2009. Monitoring Yellow Sea migrants in Australia (MYSMA): Northwestern Australian shorebird surveys and workshops, December 2008. Australian Wader Studies Group report to Department of Environment, Water and Heritage, and to Western Australia Department of Conservation and Land Management.

Rogers, M. M., & A. Jaramillo. 2002. Report of the California Bird Records Committee: 1999 records. *Western Birds* 33:1–33.

Rosenberg, G. H. 1991. Double-striped Thick-knee—the final chapter? *Birding* 23:118–119.

Rosenberg, G. H., & J. Witzeman. 1998. Arizona Bird Committee report, 1974–1996: Part 1 (nonpasserines). *Western Birds* 29:199–224.

———. 1999. Arizona Bird Committee report, 1974–1996: Part 2 (passerines). *Western Birds* 30:94–120.

Rosenberg, G. H., K. Radamaker, & M. M. Stevenson. 2011. Arizona Bird Committee report: 2005–2009 records. *Western Birds* 42:198–232.

Rottenborn. S. C., & E. S. Brinkley. 2007. *Virginia's Birdlife: an Annotated Checklist*. Virginia Avifauna no. 7. Virginia Society of Ornithology.

Rozemeijer, P. J. 2011. First record of Sungrebe *Heliornis fulica* on Bonaire, Netherlands Antilles. *Cotinga* 33:123–124.

Russell, S. M., & G. Monson. 1998. *The Birds of Sonora*. Univ. of Arizona Press: Tucson, AZ.

Ryan, R. 1976. Escapes, exotics, and accidentals. *Birding* 8:223–228.

———. 1990. Busting illegal bird traffic: Information on illegal bird trade and escaped species in eastern North America. *Birding* 22:190–191.

Saitoh, T., Y. Shigeta, & K. Ueda. 2008. Morphological differences among populations of the Arctic Warbler, with some intraspecific taxonomic notes. *Ornithological Science* 7:135–142.

Sangster, G., J. M. Collinson, A. J. Helbig, A. G. Knox, & D. T. Parkin. 2005. Taxonomic recommendations for British birds: 3rd report. *Ibis* 147:821–826.

Sangster, G., & G. J. Oreel. 1996. Progress in taxonomy of Taiga and Tundra Bean Geese. *Dutch Birding* 18:310–316.

Sangster, G., & 6 coauthors. 2011. Taxonomic recommendations for British birds: 7th report. *Ibis* 153:883–892.

Santana, W., & A. P. Pinheiro. 2010. On the occurrence of the Eurasian Kestrel *Falco tinnunculus* Linnaeus, 1758, and Little Egret *Egretta garzetta* (Linnaeus 1766) in the Archipelago of São Pedro e São Paulo, Brazil. *Revista Brasileira de Ornitologia* 18:118–120.

Scheer, A., & C. D. Eckert. 2002. Siberian Blue Robin in Dawson City: A first for Canada and mainland North America. *Birders Journal* 11:183–184.

Schuchmann, K. L. 1999. Family Trochilidae (Hummingbirds), pp. 468–680 in *Handbook of the Birds of the World*, vol. 5, J. del Hoyo, A. Elliott, & J. Sargatal (eds.). Lynx Edicions: Barcelona.

Schulenberg, T. S., D. F. Stotz, D. F. Lane, J. P. O'Neill, & T. A. Parker III. 2007. *Birds of Peru*. Princeton Univ. Press: Princeton, NJ.

Schwab, D. J., Sr., & M. Suomala. 2004. West Indian Whistling-Duck *Dendrocygna arborea* at the Great Dismal Swamp National Wildlife Refuge, Virginia. *NAB* 58:164–167.

Sealy, S. G., H. R. Carter, W. D. Shuford, K. D. Powers, & C. A. Chase III. 1991. Long-distance vagrancy of the Asiatic Marbled Murrelet in North America. *Western Birds* 22:145–155.

Shimba, T. 2007. *A Photographic Guide to the Birds of Japan and Northeast Asia*. Helm, London.

Shirihai, H. 2007. *A Complete Guide to Antarctic Wildlife*, 2nd ed. Princeton Univ. Press: Princeton, NJ.

Shirihai, H., V. Bretagnolle, & F. Zino. 2010. Identification of Fea's, Desertas, and Zino's Petrels at sea. *Birding World* 23:239–275.

Shirihai, H., D. Christie, & A. Harris. 1996. *The Macmillan Birder's Guide to European and Middle Eastern Birds*. Macmillan: London.

Sibley, F. C., & R. B. Clapp. 1967. Distribution and dispersal of central Pacific Lesser Frigatebirds *Fregata ariel*. *Ibis* 109:328–337.

Slack, R. 2009. *Rare Birds, Where and When: An Analysis of Status and Distribution in Britain and Ireland* (vol. 1: *Sandgrouse to New World Orioles*). Rare Birds Books, York, U.K.

Smith, P. W. 1985. Jackdaws reach the New World. *AB* 39:255–258.

———. 2001. Comments on George F. Gaumer and the provenance of a Giant Kingbird *Tyrannus cubensis* from Mexico. *Bulletin of the BOC* 121:249–252.

Smith, P. W., & D. S. Evered. 1992. La Sagra's Flycatcher. *Birding* 24:294–296.

Smith, P. W., & S. A. Smith. 1989. The Bahama Swallow *Tachycineta cyaneoviridis*: A summary. *Bulletin of the BOC* 109:170–180.

———. 1990. The identification and status of the Bahama Swallow in Florida. *Birding* 22:264–271.

Smith, P. W., G. E. Woolfenden, and A. Sprunt IV. 2000. The Loggerhead Kingbird in Florida: The evidence revisited. *NAB* 54:235–240.

Smith, P. W., D. S. Evered, L. R. Messick, & M. C. Wheeler. 1990. First verifiable records of the Thick-billed Vireo from the United States. *AB* 44:372–376.

Snyder, D. E. 1961. First record of the Least Frigatebird (*Fregata ariel*) in North America. *Auk* 78:265.

Spear, L. B., & D. G. Ainley. 2007. Storm-petrels of the eastern Pacific Ocean: Species assembly and diversity along marine habitat gradients. *Ornithological Monographs* no. 62.

Spear, L. B., M. J. Lewis, M. T. Myres, & R. L. Pyle. 1988. The recent occurrence of Garganey in North America and the Hawaiian Islands. *AB* 42:385–392.

Spencer, B., & W. Kolodnicki. 1988. First Azure Gallinule for North America. *AB* 42:25–27.

Stevenson, H. M., & B. H. Anderson. 1994. *The Birdlife of Florida*. Univ. Press of Florida: Gainesville, FL.

Sullivan, B. L. 2004. The changing seasons: The big picture. *NAB* 58:14–29.

Sullivan, B. L., M. J. Iliff, P. L. Ralph, C. J. Ralph, & S. T. Kelling. 2008. A Lesser Frigatebird (*Fregata ariel*) in California: A first for the state and fourth for North America. *NAB* 61:540–545.

Svensson, L., K. Mullarney, & D. Zetterstrom. 2010. *Birds of Europe*, 2nd ed. Collins: UK.

Svensson, L., R. Prys-Jones, P. C. Rasmussen, & U. Olsson. 2010. The identification and distribution of the enigmatic Large-billed Reed Warbler *Acrocephalus orinus*. *Ibis* 152:323–334.

Sykes, P. W., Jr., L. S. Atherton, M. Gardler, & J. H. Hintermister V. 2004. The first Mangrove Swallow recorded in the United States. *NAB* 58:4–11.

Taylor, B. 1998. *Rails: A Guide to the Rails, Crakes, Gallinules, and Coots of the World*. Yale Univ. Press: New Haven, CT.

Taylor, P. B. 1982. Field identification of sand plovers in East Africa. *Dutch Birding* 4:113–130.

Terrill, S. B. 1985. A sight record of the Crescent-chested Warbler from lowland Sonora. *AB* 39:11.

Thorup, K. 2004. Reverse migration as a cause of vagrancy. *Bird Study* 51(3):228–238.

Tickell, W.L.N. 2000. *Albatrosses*. Yale Univ. Press: New Haven, CT.

Tobish, T. 2000. The next new ABA-area birds: Western Alaska. *Birding* 32:498–505.

Tobish, T. G., Jr., & L. G. Balch. 1987. First North American nesting and occurrence of *Haliaeetus albicilla* on Attu Island, Alaska. *Condor* 89:433–434.

Ueda, H. 1999. 283 *Wild Bird Songs of Japan*. Yama-Kei Publishers: Japan. Compact disc.

Unitt, P. 2004. *San Diego County Bird Atlas*. Proceedings of the San Diego Society of Natural History Memoir No. 39.

Unitt, P., M. A. Faulkner, & C. Swanson. 2009. First record of Newell's Shearwater from the mainland of North America. *Western Birds* 40:21–2128.

Van den Berg, A. B., M. Constantine, & M. S. Robb. 2003. Out of the blue: Flight calls of migrants and vagrants. *Dutch Birding* 25-5, compact disk with journal issue. (CD).

Van Buren, A. N., & P. D. Boersma. 2007. Humboldt Penguins (*Sphensicus humboldti*) in the Northern Hemisphere. *Wilson Journal of Ornithology* 119: 284–288.

Van Doren, B. 2010. A Brown-backed Solitaire (*Myadestes occidentalis*) in Arizona. *NAB* 64: 176–179.

Vasamies, H. 1998. The first Oriental Cuckoos in western Europe. *Alula* 3(4):114–116.

Veit, R. R. 2000. Vagrants as the expanding fringe of a growing population. *Auk* 117:242–246.

———. 2006. First record of European Turtle-Dove (*Streptopelia turtur*) for Massachusetts. *NAB* 60: 182–183.

Veit, R. R., & L. Jonsson. 1984. Field identification of smaller sandpipers within the genus *Calidris*. *AB* 38:853–876.

Veit, R. R., & W. Petersen. 1993. *Birds of Massachusetts*. Massachusetts Audubon Society: Concord, MA.

Vinicombe, K. 2007. Vagrancy and melting ice. *Birdwatch* 177 (March 2007):42–43.

———. 2008. Category D vagrants, pp. 72–80 in *Frontiers in Birding*, M. Garner and friends. Bird-Guides Ltd.: Sheffield, UK.

Vinicombe, K., & D. L. Cottridge. 1996. *Rare Birds in Britain and Ireland: a Photographic Record*. Harper Collins: London.

Vinicombe, K. E., & A.H.J. Harrop. 1999. Ruddy Shelducks in Britain and Ireland, 1986–94. *British Birds* 92:225–255.

Wagner, G. F. 1990. Pine Bunting on Attu Island, Alaska. *AB* 44:1089–1091.

Wahl, T. R., B. Tweit, & S. G. Mlodinow (eds.). 2005. *Birds of Washington: Status and Distribution*. Oregon State Univ. Press: Corvallis, OR.

Walbridge, G., B. Small, & R. Y. McGowan. 2003. Ascension Frigatebird on Tyree—new to the Western Palearctic. *British Birds* 96:58–73.

Walsh, J., V. Elia, R. Kane, & T. Halliwell. 1999. *Birds of New Jersey*. NJ Audubon Soc.: Cape May Point, NJ.

Warzybok, P., R. Bradley, & S.N.G. Howell. 2009. First North American record of Tristram's Storm-Petrel (*Oceanodroma tristrami*). *NAB* 62:634–636.

Wauer, R. H. 1970. The occurrence of the Black-vented Oriole, *Icterus wagleri*, in the United States. *Auk* 87:811–812.

Wetmore, A. 1981. *The Birds of Panama*, part 1. Smithsonian Institution: Washington, DC.

Wheeler, B. K., & W. S. Clark. 1995. *A Photographic Guide to North American Raptors*. Academic Press: San Diego.

White, A. W. 1998. *A Birder's Guide to the Bahama Islands (including Turks and Caicos)*. ABA: Colorado Springs, CO.

White, A. W. 2004. Seabirds in the Bahamian archipelago and adjacent waters: Transient, wintering, and rare nesting species. *NAB* 57:436–451.

Wilds, C., & D. Czaplak. 1994. Yellow-legged Gulls (*Larus cachinnans*) in North America. *Wilson Bulletin* 106:344–356.

Williams, S. O. 1987. A Northern Jacana in Trans-Pecos Texas. *Western Birds* 18:123–124.

Williams,S. O., III. 2007. Fifth report of the New Mexico Bird Records Committee. *New Mexico Ornithological Society Bulletin* 35(3):61–86.

Williams, S. O., III, J. P. DeLong, & W. H. Howe. 2007. Northward range expansion by Short-tailed Hawk, with first records for New Mexico and Chihuahua. *Western Birds* 38:2–10.

Williams, S. O., III, S. A. King, S. M. Fettig, J. R. Oldenettel, & J. E. Parmeter. 2009. A Sungrebe (*Heliornis fulica*) in New Mexico: A first for the United States. *NAB* 63:4–9.

Williamson, S. L. 2001. *Hummingbirds of North America*. Houghton Mifflin: New York.

Wilson, B. 1985. Bean Goose in the Midlands. *Iowa Bird Life* 55:83–86.

Wilson, R. G., & H. Ceballos-L. 1993. *The Birds of Mexico City*, 2nd ed. BBC Printing and Graphics: Burlington, Ontario, Canada.

Wingate, D. B. 1958. House Martin (*Delichon urbica*) and Canary (*Serinus canaria*) in Bermuda. *Auk* 75:359–360.

Winker, K., & 6 coauthors. 2002. The Birds of St. Matthew Island, Bering Sea. *Wilson Bulletin* 114:491–509.

Withrow, J. J., & D. W. Sonneborn. 2011. Important recent bird records from Attu Island, Alaska. *Western Birds* 42:115–119.

Worfolk, T. 2000. Identification of Red-backed, Isabelline and Brown shrikes. *Dutch Birding* 22:323–362.

Wormington, A., & R. M. Epstein. 2010. Amazon Kingfisher (*Chloroceryle amazona*): New to Texas and to North America north of Mexico. *NAB* 64:208–210.

Wrishko, K. 2004. Common Crane near Leader, SK. *Blue Jay* 62:47.

Yamashima, Y. 1974. *Check-list of Japanese Birds*, 5th ed. Ornithological Society of Japan, Gakken: Tokyo.

Yerger, J. C., & J. Mohlmann. 2008. First North American record of Brown Hawk-Owl (*Ninox scutulata*) on St. Paul Island, Alaska. *NAB* 62:4–8.

Zimmer, B., & K. Bryan. 1993. First United States record of Tufted Flycatcher. *AB* 47:48–50.

Zimmer, J. T. 1941. Studies of Peruvian Birds, 36: The genera *Elaenia* and *Myiopagis*. *American Museum Novitates* 1108.

Zimmerman, D. A. 1991. The Aztec Thrush in the United States. *Birding* 23:318–328.

Zink, R. M., A. Pavlova, S. Drovetski, & S. Rohwer. 2008. Mitochondrial phylogeographies of five widespread Eurasian bird species. *Journal of Ornithology* 149:399–413.

Zino, F., R. Phillips, & M. Biscoito. 2011. Zino's Petrel movements at sea—a preliminary analysis of datalogger results. *Birding World* 24: 216–219.

Zöckler, C. 2007. *Birdsounds of Northern Siberia*, MP3-CD. Birdsounds.nl. Compact disc.

Index

Italics refer to plates and figures

Accentor, Siberian, 21, 22, 278, 288
Albatross, Antipodes Wandering, 100
    Auckland Shy, 95, *98*
    Black-browed, 94
    Chatham, *98*, 99
    Gibson's Wandering, 100
    Light-mantled Sooty, 102
    Salvin's, 97
    Shy. *See* Auckland Shy and Tasmanian Shy Albatrosses
    Tasmanian Shy, 95, *98*
    Wandering. *See* Antipodes Wandering and Gibson's
        Wandering Albatrosses
    Western Yellow-nosed, 92
    White-capped. *See* Auckland Shy Albatross
    Yellow-nosed. *See* Western Yellow-nosed Albatross
Ani, Greater, 406
Antshrike, Barred, 406
Austral migration, *13*, 24, 26, 29

Bananaquit, 30, 343, 388
Becard, Gray-collared, 14, 360, 410
Bittern, Eurasian, 2, 403
    Little, 194
    Yellow, 194, 409
Blackbird, Eurasian, 289, 302, 409
    Tawny-shouldered, 2
Bluetail, Red-flanked, 21, 278, 292, 409
Bluethroat, 1
Boobook, Northern, 229, 409
Booby, Blue-footed, 30, 119
    Nazca, 1, 117, 409
    Red-footed, 30, 74, 121, 408
Brambling, 1, 17, *36*, 335
Bullfinch, Cuban, 343, 407
    Eurasian, 340
    Greater Antillean, 343
Bunting, Black-faced, 279
    Blue. *See* Eastern Blue Bunting
    Chestnut, 279, 330
    Chestnut-eared, 279
    Eastern Blue, 28, 343, 397, 408
    Gray, 330, 408
    Little, 22, 278, 317, 324, 326, 408
    Pallas's, 324, 331, 408
    Pine, 324, 409
    Reed, 21, *40*, 333, 408
    Rustic, 21, 278, 327
    Yellow-breasted, 21, 324, 329, 408
    Yellow-browed, 325, 409
    Yellow-throated, 328, 409
Buzzard, Common. *See* Eastern Buzzard
    Eastern, 405
    European Honey, 217, 405

Caribbean vagrants, *10*, 28–30
Catbird, Black, 2, 377
Chaffinch, Common, 17, 303, 334, 409

Chiffchaff, Common, 2, 303, 310, 403, 410
Coot, Eurasian, 194, 209
Corncrake, 22, 194, 206
Cowbird, Shiny, 1
Crane, Common, 16, 22, 194, 205, 408
    Demoiselle, 1, 194, 203, 409
    Hooded, 404
Crake, Baillon's, 194, 405
    Corn. *See* Corncrake
    Paint-billed, 15, 27, 210, 213, 408
    Spotted, 194
Crow, Hooded, 405
    Indian House, 405
    Tamaulipas, 1, 27
Cuckoo, Common, 5, 22, 237, 240, 408
    Dark-billed, 1, 248, 251, 409
    Oriental, 22, 243
Curlew, Eastern, 141, 165, 408
    Eurasian, 142, 162, 409
    Far Eastern. *See* Eastern Curlew
    Little, 21, 141, 162, 409
    Slender-billed, 2

Disorientation, 16
Dispersal, 14
Dotterel, Eurasian, 21, 141, 150
Dove, European Turtle, 22, 237, 238, 409
    Oriental Turtle, 237, 238, 409
    Ruddy Ground, 1
    Zenaida, 248
Drift, 7, *8–10*
Duck, Eastern Spot-billed, 22, 44, 57, 408
    Falcated, 21, 44, 55
    Masked, 26, 27, 29, 30, 65, 69
    Muscovy, 1

Eagle, Booted, 217
    Steller's Sea, 22, 217, 219
    White-tailed, 22, 217
East Asian vagrants, 16–22
Egret, Chinese, 194, 199, 408
    Intermediate, 194, 198, 409
    Little, 16, 194, 200, 408
Elaenia, Caribbean, 1, 406
    Chilean, 343, 409
    Greenish, 24, 344, 409
    Small-billed, 343
    White-crested. *See* Chilean Elaenia
    Yellow-bellied, 343
Emerald, Cuban, 2, 30, 260, 264
Euphonia, Elegant, 343
    Godman's, 343
European vagrants, 16–17, 22–24

Falcon, Amur, 217, 226, *227*
    Bat, 230
    Collared Forest, 230, 234, 409

Falcon, Amur (*cont.*)
  Laughing, 230
  Red-footed, 22, 225, 409
False vagrants, 16
Fieldfare, 289, 298
Finch, Asian Rosy, 15, 403
Flamingo, American, 1
Flycatcher, Asian Brown, 279, 409
  Blue-and-white, 278
  Crowned Slaty, 343, 355, 409
  Dark-sided, 278, 279, 280, 408
  Fork-tailed, 7, 11, *13*, 14, 28, 29, 343, 358
  Gray-streaked, *5*, 279, 281, 408
  La Sagra's, 30, 343, 350, 408
  Mexican Tufted, 28, 29, 343, 346, 409
  Mugimaki, 284, 409
  Narcissus, 282, 409
  Nutting's, 15, 27, 28, 343, 349, 408
  Piratic, 12, 29, 32, 343, 353, 409
  Siberian. *See* Dark-sided Flycatcher
  Social, 28, 343, 352
  Spotted, *12*, 22, 281, 409
  Streaked, 343
  Taiga, 21, 278, 285, 408
  Tufted. *See* Mexican Tufted Flycatcher
  Variegated, 29, 343, 354, 408
  White-throated, 343
  Yellow-rumped, 278
Frigatebird, Great, 113, 408
  Lesser, *10, 114,* 116, 408
  Magnificent, *115*

Gallinule, Azure, 27, 210, 214, 409
Garganey, 10, 21, 22, 44, 57, 408
Gnatcatcher, Black-capped, 1, 27
Godwit, Black-tailed, 132, 160
Goose, Barnacle, 1, 49, 50
  Greylag, 44, 51, 409
  Lesser White-fronted, 44, 50, 409
  Pink-footed, 44, 48, 408
  Taiga Bean, 44, 47
  Tundra Bean, 44, 46, 408
Grassquit, Black-faced, 343, 386
  Yellow-faced, 26, 27, 29, 343, 385, 409
Greenfinch, European, 7, 335, 340
  Oriental, 278, 334, 339, 408
Greenshank, Common, 141, 142, 190, 408
Grosbeak, Crimson-collared, 12, 28, 29, 343, 393, 408
  Hooded, 343
  Mexican Yellow, 14, 28, 29, 343, 395, 408
  Yellow. *See* Mexican Yellow Grosbeak
Gull, Belcher's, 27, 124, 127, 408
  Black-tailed, 15, 124, 128, 408
  Gray, 124, 404
  Gray-hooded, 16, 124, 125, 409
  Heuglin's, 124
  Kelp, 27, 124, 133, 409
  Mediterranean, 124
  Swallow-tailed, 30, 74, 124, 409
  Yellow-legged, 22, 130, 408

Harrier, Hen, 2, 22, 222, 409
  Western Marsh, 1, 221, 409
Hawfinch, 334, 341
Hawk, Crane, 230, 409
  Cuban Black, 405
  Gray Frog. *See* Chinese Sparrowhawk
  Great Black, 230
  Red-backed. *See* Variable Hawk
  Roadside, 230, 232
  Variable, 405
Heron, Bare-throated Tiger, 24, 210, 410
  Chinese Pond, 194, 195, 409
  Gray, 21, 22, 194, 196, 409
  Purple, 194
  Squacco, 194
  Striated, 194
  Western Reef, 10, 16, 194, 202, 409
Hobby, Eurasian, 22, 217, 226, 408
Honeycreeper, Red-legged, 1, 24, 342, 389, 409
Hoopoe, Eurasian, 237, 243, 408
Hummingbird, Berylline, 16, 29, 260, 266, 408
  Bumblebee, 255
  Cinnamon, 260, 268, 409
  Xantus's, 260, 265, 409

Ibis, Scarlet, 405

Jabiru, 27, 210, 211, 408
Jacana, Northern, 27, 194, 210, 215
Jackdaw, Eurasian, 237, 246, 409
Jay, Brown, 1, 26

Kestrel, Eurasian, 22, 217, 224
Kingbird, Giant, 406
  Loggerhead, 356
Kingfisher, Amazon, 24, 248, 254, 410
Kite, Black, 217
  Black-eared, 217
  Double-toothed, 24, 230, 410
  Plumbeous, 230
Knot, Great, 17, 19, 141, 142, 179

Lapwing, Northern, 1, 9, 141, 142
  Southern, 1, 27, 65, 190, 191, 409
Lark, Sky. *See* Eurasian Skylark

Mango, Green-breasted, *14*, 28, 260, 262, 409
Martin, Asian House, *259*, 261
  Brown-chested, 29, 260, 274, 409
  Cuban, 2, 255
  Common House, 22, 255, 259, 408
  Gray-breasted, 2, 255
  Sinaloa, 261
  Southern, 2, 255
Mexican vagrants, 2, 15–16, 24–29
Migration, 4–6
Mirror-image migration, 10–14
Misorientation, 10–14
Mockingbird, Bahama, 362, 408
  Blue, 3, 16, 27, 28, 343, 368, 409
  Tropical, 343, 403, 407